"Got My Mind Set On Freedom"

Maryland's Story
of
Black & White Activism
1663-2000

Barbara Mills
Baltimore CORE Activist & Officer

Heritage Books, Inc.

Published 2002 by

HERITAGE BOOKS, INC.
1540E Pointer Ridge Place
Bowie, Maryland 20716

1-800-398-7709
www.heritagebooks.com

ISBN 0-7884-2268-5

A Complete Catalog Listing Hundreds of Titles
On History, Genealogy, and Americana
Available Free Upon Request

Dedicated to the many blacks and whites,
young and old,
named and unnamed in this book,
who have given selflessly of themselves
in the fight for freedom, justice and equality
for all people.

**Incident**

Once riding in Old Baltimore
Heart-filled, head-filled with glee,
I saw a Baltimorean
Keep looking straight at me.

Now I was eight and very small,
And he was no whit bigger;
And so I smiled, but he poked out his tongue,
And called me "Nigger."

I saw the whole of Baltimore
From May until December;
Of all the things that happened there,
That's all I remember.[1]

---

[1] "Incident," by Countee Cullen is found in his first collection of poems, _Color_, 1925. Cullen lived from 1903-1946; his place of birth in dispute. However, he must have spent at least some of his youth in Baltimore before he was adopted by the Cullens of Harlem in 1918. He was married to Yolanda, daughter of W.E.B. DuBois in 1928; they divorced in 1930. He was an active part of the Harlem Renaissance in the 1920s and 1930s.

CONTENTS

ILLUSTRATIONS

Author's Preface

One might have thought this writer, both of whose parents grew up in Florida (where I was born), would have become a segregationist. My limited experience of blacks after we moved to Jackson, Kentucky, a small Appalachian town of 3,000, when I was only a year old, might have made it seem even more likely.

Across the street and rising up near the front of my house was what everyone referred to as "Nigger Hill".[1] This hill was a strange, forbidding and fascinating place for us kids. Even though it offered a short-cut up to our school, our parents warned, "Don't go up there!" They never said why, but it looked sort of scary so we never did venture up, except on the rare occasions when we were overcome by curiosity or when some older boy would dare us.

Rickety, unpainted, one- and two-room shacks lined the sides of the narrow dirt road, rutted and muddy any time it rained, dusty and dirty the rest of the time. It was the only street in town that wasn't paved. We often saw raggedy-dressed black children going into their one-room school, or dressed up adults entering their little box-like church. As we left to go to our church, which was at the top of the hill that rose up *behind* our house, we often could hear the sounds of their voices raised in song floating across to us. There was one equally decrepit-looking store that seemed too small to meet all their needs, small as their community was, but I never saw a black person shopping in town, nor working as domestics, or even as janitors.

At the movies where we went regularly on Saturday afternoons, if you looked back and up you could see black folks in the tiny balcony, and it was a black man who ran the barber and shoeshine shop next to the hotel. It never occurred to me to wonder what all the others blacks on "Nigger Hill" did.

At the time I guess I was too young to wonder about such things or to ask questions that have since been of special interest—Why black kids lived on a street and in houses so inferior to those of us whites? Why they didn't go to school with us? But just recently I was intrigued to learn that in 1904 it was a legislator from "feud-ridden 'Bloody Breathitt'" [which is where I lived] who introduced and succeeded in getting passed a bill that came to be called the Day Law. Among other things, this law proclaimed that any teacher of a *mixed class* would be fined $100 a day, and their students $50 a day.

Except for listening to *Amos and Andy* (who weren't even black, I later learned), my only other "exposure" to blacks in my childhood

---

[1] I can't imagine hardly anyone daring today to label a place "Nigger Hill," but no one thought it unusual then. Some things do change—at least on the surface.

came one time when Mom and I were visiting with some of her friends. I was sitting on the floor coloring when the grown-ups began to get all excited, started waving their hands, their voices all tight and squealy. "How dare that uppity nigger buy a house in our neighborhood!" I heard one of them exclaim. "He must make too much at that damn hotel barbershop. Do you realize the house he's buying is only two blocks from mine?"

They were talking about the house recently vacated by my friend from school. She had moved to Jackson, then out again just one year later, and was ostracized by most of our classmates and made fun of because she "looked funny." Her hair was snow white except for one black streak in front, and her face and arms, and I guess her whole body, were splotchy, with big pure white patches here and there. Mom said she was an albino. But they weren't talking about Abbie Mae, but about some "uppity-nigger-barber" who was daring to move into the house where she'd lived. I didn't understand what all the fuss was about and didn't ask. Despite the fuss that day, I don't remember anyone making any actual trouble for the him after he moved. They just went out of their way to ignore him.

It was only after our move to Rhode Island (when I was twelve) and came under the influence of our very socially conscious Baptist minister that I actually met a black person. He paid my way to a Quaker-sponsored conference in New Hampshire that brought together blacks and whites, students and grown-ups, all sleeping, eating, playing, studying and talking together for two weeks. My most lasting impression from that experience came the day about fifty of us were sitting together in a circle on a grassy knoll under the branches of a big maple tree on the rolling lawns of the University of New Hampshire campus. The principal of a small black school in Mississippi, a short, squat ebony-colored man with sort of sad eyes, was describing the appalling conditions his students faced.

"In my class rooms," he was saying, "we have to use the torn and raggedy books that are discarded by the white schools. My students can't afford to buy supplies so we make do with stubby pencils and scraps of paper from the white school's trash cans. Most of our blackboards are broken, the floors are unfinished and splintery. Pot-bellied stoves heat the crowded rooms and sometimes the younger ones get bad burns when they bump into one."

He had a far away, wistful look in his eyes as he raised them upward toward the clear blue sky and fluffy white cumulous clouds floating by. He looked again at us and continued, "Many of our kids come to school barefoot, often dirty I'm sorry to say. Most live in one-room shacks, without electricity or running water, on dirt streets that are mud slicks every time it rains and dusty when it doesn't."

x

My thoughts jumped to "nigger hill." He could have been describing Jackson and I hadn't even realized.

"It's hard for them to be clean, to keep anything clean." Again, he looked far away. "In the beginning they all have such eager bright faces." He couldn't say any more. He didn't need to.

I had finished my third year at Brown University when, in 1949, I spent a summer in another Quaker-sponsored project that brought together in a still very segregated Washington, DC, 100 students from all over the country, male and female, black and white. We took over what was, in the winter, an all-black hotel; the only place that would accommodate an interracial group. We soon learned that although blacks didn't discriminate, not so whites.

We got constant complaints all summer from our neighbors down the street who lived in a "white" apartment building. They called our place a whore house, allowing boys and girls to live together, and of course, they objected to our "mixing the races," shouted "nigger lover" as we'd walk by. One Southern boy in our group said his parents and classmates at the University of Mississippi would have had a worse fit if they'd known he was living with blacks. He seemed totally comfortable with the experience but was not going to "tell all" on return.

Knowing what happened during the '60s when they tried to integrate the University of Mississippi and when SNCC and others tried to register black voters—beaten, jailed, knifed, shot at, some killed—it became crystal clear why he'd planned to keep his interracial experience to himself. I wondered if our summer together had made a difference in how he'd felt and acted during that time.

All that summer, even when blacks weren't with us, on principle, we confined our eating out to restaurants in the black community, which welcomed us all, and to those in federal buildings—the only ones in white areas that were integrated. We also went to movies only in the black areas.

And so it was that, somehow, I ended up radically pro-equality, even though it took me until the mid-60s to become an activist. By then, I was living in Baltimore, Maryland (from 1957-1970), was married to an Economics Professor at Johns Hopkins University and had two children (both attended Mt. Washington elementary school, Alan attended Roland Park Junior High). By the time I became an activist and officer in Baltimore CORE, I found it impossible to understand why it was so hard to see blacks as equals; why it was even a question; why it still haunts America.

I left Baltimore for Princeton in 1970, but after leaving my husband, returned in 1974; was a librarian in the public school system while my daughter attended Western High School. I left Baltimore once more in 1981, but in 1988 returned to Prince George County in Maryland and a job in Washington, D.C. During this final stay in Maryland that ended in 1991, I drove each Sunday to Baltimore to attend Heritage UCC; Wendel Phillips, pastor. I was the only white member.

•••

In the account of black-white relations in Baltimore and parts of Maryland that follows, "black" is most often used. My having gone through one transition, from "Negro" to "black" while an active participant in the Civil Rights Movement, I find it hard now again to change terminology. However, the terms "colored," "nigger," "Negro" and "African American" can be found at various points throughout, as appropriate to the period being discussed, or as part of quotes.

•••

I hope that this detailed account of the black-white experience in Maryland will enable the reader to feel and appreciate the many battles fought to get where we are today—and to realize how far we still have to go to achieve freedom and equality for all.

I also hope the reader will realize just how much effort went into organizing each and every law suit and each and every demonstration —and can share with the "change agents" the deep emotions they felt as they participated.

"The reward for participating in a movement for social justice is not the prospect for future victory. It is the exhilaration of standing together with other people, taking risks together, enjoying small triumphs and enduring disheartening setbacks—together."
Howard Zinn, You Can't Be Neutral On A Moving Train

Those who favor freedom and yet deprecate agitation, are men who want crops without plowing up the ground. They want rain without thunder and lightning. They want the ocean without the awful roar of its water. This struggle may be a moral one or it may be both moral and physical, but it must be a struggle. Power concedes nothing without a demand. It never did and it never will. Find out just what people will submit to and you have found out the exact amount of injustice and wrong which will be imposed upon them and these will continue until they are resisted with either words or blows or with both. The limits of tyrants are prescribed by the endurance of those whom they oppress.
Frederick Douglass, often quoted by Walter Carter,
a leader in Baltimore CORE.

<u>*Civil Liberties*</u> *are the rights which allow an individual to be DIFFERENT from everyone else. These rights are guaranteed in the Bill of Rights of the Constitution of the United States. They include all the freedoms and equalities, such as freedom of speech, religion, assembly, press, and the famous Fifth Amendment that states no one may be compelled to be a witness against himself, nor be deprived of life or liberty without due process of law.*

<u>*Civil Rights*</u> *are the rights which individuals have to be LIKE everyone else, and enjoy the SAME rights, freedoms, and privileges as others.* Fred Weisgal, a civil rights/civil liberties attorney in Baltimore, as he explained the difference when asked by a reporter.

A Liberal is an activist, unsatisfied with just recognizing poverty and racism, unable just to stand by while afflicted people try vainly to solve their problem alone. He recognizes racial injustice as "a denial of basic liberties inherent in Americanism, and until all Americans can freely exercise all liberties due them, no Americans are truly free.
Johns Hopkins Student Newspaper, 10/30/1964

Part 1
In the Beginning

"All Men are Created Equal"

- "We hold these truths to be *self-evident* that all men are created equal"; noble words by our forefathers on July 4, 1776 in the Declaration of Independence.
- Eleven years later, the Constitution started with more noble words: "We the People of the United States, in Order to form a more perfect Union, establish Justice..."— for whom? Article 1, section 2, reduced slaves to "three-fifths of a person.
- Over seventy-five years later, after three years of a bloody Civil War Abraham Lincoln, on January 1, 1863, issued the Emancipation Proclamation, freeing blacks in those states in rebellion against the union, namely, Arkansas, Texas, Louisiana (except New Orleans), Mississippi, Alabama, Georgia, South Carolina, North Carolina and Virginia.

Since the war was still raging, rendering it impossible immediately to enforce this mandate, and since the proclamation specifically excluded Kentucky, Delaware, Missouri and Maryland (for fear they'd leave the union and join the confederacy), the proclamation was primarily of psychological import. It did serve to increase the number of slaves running away to join the union army.

- Ten months after the Proclamation, on November 1, 1864, a very divided Maryland legislature voluntarily changed its constitution to free its slaves. Its new constitution was headed with a statement similar to the Declaration of Independence:

> All men are created equally free; that they are endowed by their creator with certain unalienable rights, among which are life, liberty, the enjoyment of the proceeds of their own labor, and the pursuit of happiness...

More lofty rhetoric. Blacks were now legally "free," but not free from violence, persecution, rebuke and scorn.

- It was not until after Lee's surrender to Grant on April 9, 1865, and after Lincoln's assassination less than a week later (April 14), that Congress passed the 13th Amendment to the Constitution on December 18, 1865:

> Neither slavery nor involuntary servitude, *except as a punishment for crime* whereof the party shall have been duly convicted, shall exist within the United States, or any place subject to their jurisdiction. Congress shall have power to enforce this article by appropriate legislation.

Aware of that bold exception, the freed blacks gave as much import to gaining the right to be on juries as to getting the right to vote. And well they might have been concerned about the possibility of equal justice for blacks.[1]

• Congress ratified the 14th Amendment in 1868, stating *"All* persons born or naturalized in the U.S., and subject to the jurisdiction thereof, are citizens of the United States and of the State wherein they reside. No State shall make or enforce any law which shall abridge the privileges or immunities of citizens of the U.S.; nor shall any State deprive any person of life, liberty, or property, without due process of law; nor deny to any person within its jurisdiction the equal protection of the laws."

• It took until 1870, before the 15th Amendment made black men whole persons with the right to vote: "The right of citizens of the United States to vote shall not be denied or abridged by the United States or by any State on account of race, color, or previous condition of servitude." In Maryland, free black men had had the right to vote until 1810; a state constitutional amendment that year took away that right:[2] it's unclear whether they had ever exercised that right.

• It took another fifty years, until 1920, before the 19th Amendment extended this same right to women, black or white.

Regrettably, the end of slavery did not mean the end of inequality. Soon, through a combination of legal and extra-legal actions, the white power structure deprived blacks of equal access to education, jobs and housing. This book examines this history as it played out in Maryland (focusing primarily on Baltimore and near-by areas) and demonstrates

---

[1] In 1997 in Maryland, according to the *Bureau of Justice Statistics, Correctional Population in the U.S.*, there were 17,196 blacks under some federal or state penal authority, compared to only 4,998 whites.
[2] See Gregory, pp. 35-36

that blacks did not meekly succumb to these deprivations, but continuously struggled to be included in the self-evident truth that "all men are created equal" as proclaimed in 1776.

•••

Maryland has always been a state in the middle—part southern, part northern—both in the way it has dealt with race issues, and in the way it is perceived. Many in both the north and south regard it as northern because it did not join the confederacy in the Civil War and because, historically, it has been more industrialized than other states to its south. But, in fact, Maryland is south of the Mason Dixon line, and, as conflicted as it was internally over slavery, it remained a slave state until near the end of the war. The historian, Leroy Graham, called Baltimore, the state's largest city and a center for slave traders, the "nineteenth century black capital."

The conflicted sentiments of its citizens regarding the Civil War were apparent on April 19, 1861 (exactly a year after the war began at Fort Sumter, South Carolina) when a mob assaulted Union troops as they passed through on their way south. This resulted in the city's occupation for the rest of the war to protect Washington, D.C. and to ensure that Union troops would not be cut off from the North.

In the 1960s one could look to the chameleon qualities of Spiro Agnew as a personification of the north-south tension that existed in Maryland. Where else would an opponent of integration be regarded as a "sympathetic mediator" to be called upon for help in the midst of such battles as those which were taking place at Gwynn Oaks Amusement Park in Baltimore, and in Cambridge, Maryland.[3]

Agnew was then Baltimore County Executive. Later, when he ran for Governor, it was the votes of white liberals and blacks, including this author, who elected him. His openly racist opponent was stirring up opposition to "Open Housing" with the slogan, "Your Home is Your Castle." This election and his subsequent callous treatment of black leaders at a meeting

---

[3] For more detail of Agnew's role, see sections of Part II and Housing sections: "CORE Ripped Apart" and "Inner City's Challenge" for more on these events.

in 1968 led to Nixon's choosing Agnew as his Vice President, an office he used to rail against the "hopeless, hysterical hypochondriacs of history" and "an effete corps of impudent snobs who characterize themselves as intellectuals."[4]

Given the continuing existence of this tension between the southern and northern aspects of Maryland's soul, and the impact this has had on blacks in their long struggle for equality, it's hard to understand why historians have largely ignored Maryland as a unique place to study race relations.

---

[4] Used, respectively, in an address at San Diego, 9/11/70 and in the *NY Times* on 10/20/69, denouncing a Moratorium Day protest against the Vietnam War.

Free Blacks and Slaves

Beat and cuff your slave, keep him hungry and spiritless, and he will follow the chain of his master like a dog. But feed and clothe him well, work him moderately, surround him with physical comfort, and he will dream of freedom.[5]

In October 1663, between 130 and 140 passengers that included two Jesuit priests, sons of Catholic gentry and Protestant farmers left England on the 350 ton Ark and the smaller Dove sailing vessels. Stopping first at the Canary Islands and then Virginia, they reached what would become St. Mary's, Maryland in March 1634. One of the priests, Father Andrew White, had with him a mulatto servant, Mathias de Sousa, and later added another, Francisco. It is believed these first blacks to arrive in Maryland were not slaves but serving fixed terms like the many white indentured servants who came during the 17th Century. But whatever their status, there is no doubt blacks were always regarded as inferior to whites. As early as 1638, a law distinguished between whites, including indentured servants, and black chattels as to their civil rights. A 1663 law went further and specifically recognized black servitude as perpetual. It also established punishments for white servants who ran away with blacks.[6]

In 1664, "An Act Concerning Negroes and Other Slaves" was passed that makes their future status clear. It provided that "all blacks and *other* slaves either within the colony or thereafter imported into the colony, as well as their children, shall be slaves for life." It also provided that "any freeborne (white) woman who thereafter married a slave would be required to serve the master of such slave during her husband's life, and that any children born of this union would be slaves" [the first of Maryland's miscegenation statutes].[7]

Despite these laws, Thomas Hagleton, an African and a Catholic, who had come from England as an indentured

---

[5] Douglass, *Life and Times*, p. 55

[6] See Brugger, p. 43

[7] Discussed by Alpert, Jonathan, "The Origin of Slavery in the U.S.: the Maryland Precedent," XIV, *Am.J.Legal Hist.* 189 (1969)

servant, was able in 1676 to gain his freedom when his master, Major Thomas Truman, tried to keep him beyond the four years he'd contracted for. Similar cases occurred in 1678 and 1693, one even "winning a suit of clothes and supply of corn from his former master."[8]

A 1681 statute repealed the 1664 law but passed another that included a provision that continued the status of blacks as slaves, and also a provision meant to discourage masters from contriving to have a freeborn white woman [in his service] marry a Negro or Slave to satisfy their "lascivious & Lustfull desires." A practice apparently common at the time. The law provided that if a master did so contrive, "then that servant would be absolutely discharged from her indentured service, and all her children would be born free." Both the masters who permitted such marriages, and the ministers who married them "were subject to fines of 10,000 pounds of tobacco."

The Maryland legislature soon realized that this law had the unintended consequence of encouraging white servants to marry a black as a means of terminating their service obligations. As a result, a law passed in 1692 forbade all interracial marriages and sexual relations. "White women who had a child by a black man were required to serve for seven years, and if the black were free, he was required to serve for seven years. The children of such unions were required to be servants until they were 31 years old." Bell is no doubt correct when he concludes in his study, *Race, Racism & American Law* that the legislative intent was as much to "define status" as to "discourage interracial sex and marriage."[9]

From the beginning a number of whites had come voluntarily to this country as indentured servants, but the number arriving involuntarily increased substantially after the English Parliament in 1717 passed an act "empowering courts [in England] to sentence offenders directly to transportation." It is quite likely that convicts and slaves began to arrive in Maryland on the same ship; Jonathan Forward then becoming one of the biggest transporters.

---

[8] Brugger, p. 43.
[9] Information on statutes and quotes (including those above) are from Bell, pp. 66--67

Jonathan Forward, a young London merchant with extensive contacts in Maryland, obtained a lucrative subsidy of three pounds for every Newgate [a prison] felon and five pounds for every convict taken from the provinces....Forward was experienced in the African slave trade and had recently shipped two vessels with 171 convicts to Maryland.[10]

With the arrival in Baltimore's growing harbor of more and more blacks from Africa—an estimated 4,000 between 1695 to 1708— many in a weakened condition after facing the crowding, lack of sanitation, food and water on a typical slave ship—Maryland's statute books, accordingly, began to reflect slavery as we now know it.[11]

At least initially, few of these slaves could have been destined to stay in Baltimore since as late as 1752, the census counted only thirty settlers in Baltimore Town, still "little more than a cluster of huts standing in a wilderness." However, even as Baltimore grew to a community of thirteen thousand in the next twelve years, slaves still only amounted to "just over 9% of the population; this at a time when nearly one-third of the people of Maryland were slaves."[12]

By July 1775, three months after Lexington and Concord, Baltimore had grown sufficiently to have seven companies under arms. The colonists were reluctant to recruit blacks, fearing that if they were armed they might then fight for their own freedom. But by 1780 when white enlistments began to decline, alone among the slave holding states, Maryland began to recruit both free blacks and slaves. While some did escape and join the Loyalists who promised them freedom, others served in the militia, and still others served throughout the Revolution as pilots on ships patrolling the Chesapeake Bay and Maryland's rivers.

Perhaps this participation by Maryland's slaves in the Revolution may help account for the large number of manumitted blacks (formally released from slavery) in Maryland compared to other slave states in the years between the Revolution and the start of the Civil War.

---

[10] Jordan, pp. 44 & 73-74, and Christianson, p. 23.
[11] See Brugger, p. 46
[12] Fields, pp. 40-41

By the time the Civil War started in 1861, the numbers of
free blacks and slaves were virtually equal statewide, the
number of free blacks in Baltimore far outnumbering its
slaves. (By then Baltimore's *white* population had grown from
48,055 in 1820 to 184,520 in 1860 to become the fourth
largest city in the country.) Most of the city's slaves were
domestics, families rarely having more than five, one or two
the most common.[13]

	Slaves: MD/Baltimore	Free Blacks: MD/Baltimore
1790	103,036 / 1,255	8,043 / 323
1800	105,635 / 2,843	19,587 / 2,771
1810	111,502 / 4,672 (peak)	33,927 / 5,671
1850	90,368 / 2,946	74,723 / 25,442
1860	87,189 / 2,218	83,942 / 25,680

As early as 1789, several hundred Baltimoreans came
together to form an active "Society for Promoting the Abolition
of Slavery and the Relief of Poor Negroes unlawfully held in
Bondage."[14] They helped assist runaways and free blacks, and
raised money to support their education. However, after a few
years, opposition from those opposed to manumissions
became so intense the Society was forced to disband.

Further, a 1796 law ordered those "without visible means
of support or found wandering about...to post bond, leave the
state, or be sentenced to six months' servitude."[15] As for the
slaves, unlike the practice in other slave states that reserved
their penitentiaries for confining criminals "from the master
class," in the years from 1812 to 1819, Maryland sentenced
sixty slaves to its penitentiary, as well as 466 free blacks and

---

[13] The figures found in the table on the status of Maryland's and
Baltimore's blacks are from Wright's and Fields' histories; their
numbers derived from census figures. They are of interest, even if,
as the author's note, the exact numbers are unreliable, especially
in the case of the slaves whose owners had every incentive to
undercount in order to avoid paying the taxes most places
imposed for slaves.

[14] Information on Society found in Wright, p. 347

[15] Quote from law found in Jordan, pp. 407-408

514 whites. After 1819 the law required either the hanging of convicted slaves or their selling to an entity outside its borders.[16]

In some states, free blacks were looked on more favorably and relied upon to keep the peace, but in Maryland, in addition to regarding all blacks as "thievish," and "receivers for goods stolen by slaves," slaveholders "considered free blacks a standing incitement to servile disorder and continued to seek their elimination in the years following the Revolutionary period right up to their final emancipation."[17] This attitude may be explained by the scare that pervaded Baltimore following Nat Turner's uprising in 1831, a time when a secret document came into the hands of Baltimore's mayor detailing plans for a similar uprising in his city. Eight hundred people were said to be ready in town "to help murder the damned white people." The alarm, while false, was unusual only in its precision.[18]

The generally negative view most held of blacks, free or not, no doubt explains why manumission did not necessarily improve the condition of the freed blacks. In many instances, left to support themselves in a society that discriminated against them, they were worse off than the slaves: lived in worse conditions and had less access to health care. Douglass may have thought this when he first set foot in Baltimore (also giving us a picture of the city at the time):[19]

> Once in Baltimore, with hard brick pavements under my feet, which almost raised blisters, by their very heat, for it was in the height of summer; walled in on all sides by towering brick buildings; with troops of hostile boys ready to pounce upon me at every street corner; with new and strange objects glaring upon me at every step, and with startling sounds reaching my ears from all directions, I for a time thought tjat, after all, the home plantation was a more desirable place of residence than my home on Alliciana street, in Baltimore. My country eyes and ears were confused and bewildered here; but the boys were my chief trouble. They chased me, and called me "Eastern

---

[16] Information found in Sellin, p. 144
[17] Fields, p. 4.
[18] Wade, pp. 227-228
[19] Douglass, *My Bondage*, p. 110

Shore man," till really I almost wished myself back on the Eastern Shore. I had to undergo a sort of moral acclimation, and when that was over, I did much better.

He presumably had been acclimated when he soon-after wrote:

> I had resided but a short time in Baltimore before I observed a marked difference, in the treatment of slaves, from that which I had witnessed in the country. A city slave is almost a freeman, compared with a slave on the plantation. He is much better fed and clothed, and enjoys privileges altogether unknown to the slave on the plantation....Few [slaveholders] are willing to incur the odium attaching to the reputation of being a cruel master; and above all things, they would not be known as not giving a slave enough to eat.[20]

This said, Douglass points out "painful exceptions," a neighbor of his being one.

> Directly opposite to us, on Philpot Street, lived Mr. Thomas Hamilton. He owned two slaves, Henrietta and Mary....Added to the cruel lashings to which these slaves were subjected, they were kept nearly half-starved....I have see Mary contending with the pigs for the offal thrown into the street. So much was Mary kicked and cut to pieces, that she was oftener called "pecked" than by her name.

However precarious their status, the rights free blacks enjoyed were obvious to those who poured into Baltimore and cannot easily be dismissed. Along with their large numbers, they played a decided role in their readinessto participate in politics post-civil war. Maryland's and especially Baltimore's blacks, had an experience with social and economic independence not shared by those in other slave states.

Having acknowledged the limitations to equality faced by free blacks, Wright in his history of the free Negro in Maryland, also recognizes the benefits:

> The free Negro enjoyed a wide liberty in getting a living. He had a right to engage in agriculture, in the mechanical

---

[20] Douglass, *Narrative of the Life of Frederick Douglass, An American Slave*, pp. 79-80.

trades, in business, or to hire himself to any employer whom he could serve and to collect and expend his earnings. The law barred him wholly from no legitimate calling saving politics and military service...

The free Negroes enjoyed the right to hold property by all of the common methods of possession and ownership.[21]

Arrival of Freedmen and their Families at Baltimore. An everyday scene..
©Maryland Historical Society

Free blacks could be found throughout Baltimore, even though the largest number were forced to live in shacks or "dilapidated two and three story buildings in side streets or in disease infested alleys"—only a few of the better-off managed to live in brownstone houses further from the city-center.[22] They were not, however, passive acceptors of their fate.

Early-on the better-off blacks began actively to resist discrimination. By 1781 black parishioners who attended the

[21] Wright (1921), Introduction & pp. 36-37
[22] Information found in Paul, pp. 9-10 & 14; Olson, pp. 4, 34 &120; Wright (1921), Introduction & pp. 36-37. In Baltimore there were over 25,000 *free* blacks, the largest number in any community in the country.

predominantly white Lovely Lane Methodist church on Redwood Street were tired of being forced to sit in the back. They were also tired of being denied the right to take communion with whites at the altar. This led them to form the Colored Methodist Society, and, in 1802, to build the first Sharp Street Memorial United Methodist Church (replaced by a larger building in 1898). It quickly became a center not only for worship but also provided a platform for speakers, and a place for discussing issues of concern, and for raising funds to help fleeing slaves. From 1867 to 1872, Sharp Street also housed the Centenary Bible Institute which eventually became Morgan University.[23]

As early as 1860, there were at least twelve black churches in Baltimore providing otherwise all-too-rare "opportunities for leadership development and self expression" and "a climate for the preservation of black pride and the development of black hope."[24] Free blacks also established welfare organizations, and sought out ways to educate their children, generally through the church and a few charity schools.[25]

Unsuccessful attempts were made by whites in 1827, 1840 and again in 1860 to have the legislature pass laws that would exclude blacks from holding certain jobs; other unsuccessful attempts were made by slave-holders to win expulsion [from the country] or re-enslavement of free blacks, claiming they were "economically injurious to white workers."[26] It was probably the protest activities of free blacks, determined not to stand idly by while their civil rights were diminished, that at least helped prevent these measures ever being passed.

However, there were always *some* whites, although always a minority, who supported the blacks in their efforts to gain rights and to prevent passage of more restrictive laws. One

---

[23] Fee et al, p. 63 & Paul, pp. 25-27. Free blacks were not legally barred from local public elementary and high schools but were implicitly excluded. They were explicitly excluded from private colleges, and professional and fine arts schools.

[24] Shoemaker, p. 265.

[25] More will be said of this in the Education section.

[26] Paul p. 9-10, 22 & 25; Wright, p. 332

such was William Lloyd Garrison, who, in 1824, was aged twenty-four. That year the Quaker, Benjamin Lundy, had persuaded Garrison to join him in Baltimore as junior editor of his weekly paper, called *Genius of Universal Emancipation.* Unlike Lundy who was very careful in his choice of words in his pronouncements against slavery, Garrison in heated rhetoric boldly demanded the immediate and total emancipation of all slaves and an end to any talk of deportations of blacks to Haiti and Liberia.

When in 1829 Garrison described "fellow Yankees engaged in trading Maryland slaves to New Orleans as 'highway robbers and murderers,'" he ended up in court, indicted under an old criminal libel statute that hadn't been used for a generation.[27] The indictment charged:

> "unlawfully, wickedly and maliciously...[printing and publishing]...false, scandalous, and malicious matter and libel...to the great scandal, damage, and disgrace of the said Francis Todd [a slave trader], to the evil example of all others in like manner offending, and against the peace, government, and dignity of the state."[28]

Usually truth was an acceptable defense against libel charges but in this "politically rigged" case it didn't matter that, in fact, Todd owned the ship *Francis* that had been piloted by Providence's Nicholas Brown when it transported eighty-eight slaves from Baltimore to New Orleans—the subject of Garrison's article. The defense attorney, Charles Mitchell, serving for free, had argued that "instead of having [his client's] words tortured into criminal conduct, the editors of the *Genius* deserved praise for their efforts and ought to have their freedom sustained, 'not only by the jury, but by their country.'" The prosecution asked the jurors "to consider the 'malicious intent' of the 'Black List' article and expressed confidence that they would do their duty": within fifteen minutes they returned with a guilty verdict. In sentencing Garrison to six months in jail, Judge Brice succeeded in lifting him from obscurity.

---

[27] Information and quotes about this case are from Mayer, pp. 84-94 & Brugger, p. 215
[28] Brugger, p. 215

Garrison had served forty-nine days of his sentence in Baltimore's Jail when a New York philanthropist, Arthur Tappan, paid one hundred dollars for his liberty, and another hundred to aid in re-establishing *Genius*, which had pretty much folded after Garrison's trial. Later Garrison said that during his time in jail "he had come to an understanding that would inform his entire career as a writer and agitator....[He] had learned to speak the truth, come what may, and [like many prisoners of conscience] he had turned the state's stigmata into a badge of honor." While still in jail, Garrison had written:

> It is my shame that I have done so little for the people of color. A few white victims must be sacrificed to open the eyes of this nation, and to show the tyranny of our laws. I am willing to be persecuted, imprisoned and bound for advocating African rights, and I should deserve to be a slave myself, if I shrunk from that duty or danger.

Both Lundy and Garrison soon after the latter's release left Baltimore. "Lundy declared that 'the spirit of tyranny' in Baltimore had become 'too strong and malignant.'" Garrison left for Boston where, in January 1831, he published the first issue of the *Liberator*, a paper he continued to publish until December 1865, the year the 13th Amendment to the Constitution was adopted. Garrison had become one of America's best known abolitionists; the *Liberator* their voice.

•••

Prior to the Civil War, even free blacks could not travel extensively for fear of being taken for slaves. The danger was heightened after passage of fugitive slave acts in 1793 and 1850 that empowered slave hunters to seize and accuse any black of being an escaped slave, and barred the seized black from testifying in court. This resulted in numbers of free blacks, in effect, being kidnapped and re-enslaved. Douglass provided us with a colorful description of the risks when talking about his own escape:[29]

> Keen is the scent of the slaveholder; like the fangs of the rattlesnake, his malice retains it poison long; and,

---

[29] Douglass, *My Bondage...*, p 249

although it is now nearly seventeen years since I made my escape, it is well to be careful, in dealing with the circumstances relating to it. Were I to give but a shadowy outline of the process adopted, with characteristic aptitude, the crafty and malicious among the slaveholders might, possibly, hit upon the track I pursued, and involve some one in suspicion which, in a slave state, is about as bad a positive evidence. The colored man, there, must not only shun evil, but shun the very appearance of evil, or be condemned as a criminal.

The danger of being recaptured was especially great in Maryland where the Underground Railroad had deep roots; many escaping slaves passing through the state en route north. Some escaped by boat from Annapolis or Baltimore ports; others from more obscure points on the Chesapeake Bay to the Susquehanna River and into Pennsylvania; still others followed the Appalachian route.

The most famous black conductor on the Underground Railroad was Harriet Tubman, born in Dorchester County, Maryland. Despite the constant danger, she made innumerable trips between the South and North leading slaves to safety. But whites who helped these escaping slaves were also in danger. For example, in June 1850, one white couple, James Bowers and his wife, so charged, were acquitted in court for lack of evidence, but then faced "a mob of slaveholders [who] seized the couple in their home, tarred and feathered them, and drove them out of the community."[30]

Slaves who successfully escaped from their owners were not necessarily safe; might still be caught and returned to captivity. One such was Grandison Briscoe who escaped with his mother, pregnant wife, and child to the District of Columbia right after Congress abolished slavery in the District in April 1862—only to have a slave catcher, within just a few days, drag them back into bondage (the fugitive slave act was not repealed until 1864). Two years later he signed an "affidavit describing the fate of his family." It told how his wife and mother had been taken to a barn, "their clothes raised and tied over their heads to keep their screams from disturbing the neighborhood" while they were severely

---

[30] Blockson, p. 96.

whipped. Afterwards they were taken to the Upper Marlborough jail [in Maryland] where his wife gave birth to child who died soon after it was taken from its mother. Her husband wrote:[31]

> I have sent them clothing & other articles frequently until the first or near the first of January 1864 [ten months before Maryland freed its slaves]. Since which the new jailer has refused to allow them to receive any thing from me. They have been in prison for the Crime of coming to Washington to reside, ever since about the fourth of April 1862 now a year & ten months.

• • •

Despite all the restrictions on their freedom faced by free blacks, when they saw the auction block in Baltimore and the slave trader's pens full of helpless blacks destined for southern plantations, they knew their lot could be worse. Most of Maryland's slave-trading took place in Baltimore: at least a dozen well-known "resident traders" operated there, supplemented by any number of "resident petty traders" and "visiting traders." Douglass had this to say about them:[32]

> These Negro buyers are very offensive to the genteel southern Christian public. They are looked upon, in respectable Maryland society, as necessary, but detestable characters. As a class, they are hardened ruffians, made such by nature and by occupation. ...They have grown intimate with vice and blood; they gloat over the wildest illustrations of their soul-damning and earth-polluting business, and are moral pests. Yes; they are a legitimate fruit of slavery; and it is a puzzle to make out a case of greater villainy for them, than for the slaveholders, who make such a class possible. They are mere hucksters of the surplus slave produce of Maryland and Virginia— coarse, cruel, and swaggering bullies, whose very breathing is of blasphemy and blood.

The daily newspapers regularly carried advertisements of slave auctions that circulated throughout the state. The quotes regarding one representative trader, Slatter, are more than

---

[31] Account found in Berlin & Rowland pp. 23-26
[32] Douglass, *My Bondage...*, p. 231.

sufficient to understand why blacks preferred freedom, however limited.

> Hope H. Slatter wanted from 75 to 100 Negroes from 8 to 25 years of age and "particularly to purchase several seamstresses and likely small fancy girls for nurses." ...He was buying for the "southern market" and would go, or send his agent, to any part of the State to inspect Negroes for sale....
>
> His selling-prices: "likely fellows" from 28 to 25 years old were from $500 to $650; women of the same age and quality, from $300 to $500—the best fieldhands, from $300 to $400. And he was enthusiastic about a sprightly, bright mulatto girl only seven years old, as fine a servant as he ever saw, who could intelligently run errands and market for small articles; she was for sale for $250....
>
> A few years later he had a large new jail, "fitted up with bolts and bars", on one of the principle streets. It sometimes contained 300 or 400 slaves. Antislavery callers frankly admitted that cleanliness and order were conspicuous in it [as it wasn't, apparently, in many others] and that the physical wants of the slaves were not neglected by Slatter.[33]

•••

The Regions of Maryland, 1850

NORTHERN MARYLAND
SOUTHERN MARYLAND
EASTERN SHORE

Maryland was (and for the most part still is) a state with

---

[33] See Bancroft, pp. 37-40; quote pp. 38-39

vast sectional differences that in large part account for their different attitudes towards blacks from the beginning: (1) 16% of population of the more industrial Northern Maryland (Allegany, Baltimore, Carroll, Frederick, Harford and Washington counties and Baltimore City) was black, only 5% of these slaves; (2) 54% of the more agricultural Southern Maryland (Anne Arundel, Calvert, Charles, Prince George's, Montgomery, and St. Mary's) was black, 44% slaves; and (3) 40% of the more diversified agricultural Eastern Shore (Caroline, Cecil, Dorchester, Kent, Queen Anne's, Somerset, Talbot, and Worcester) was black, 20% slaves. Baltimore forms a separate "county" in Maryland.

Not surprisingly, in those parts of Maryland where the largest numbers of slaves were concentrated, free blacks had a much more difficult time in becoming independent wage-earners than those in Baltimore. They often ended up in substantially the same position as the slaves. More often than not, in order to survive, they worked for slave landholders, even their own former owners, under agreements that paid them only nominal amounts.

•••

It was in those same regions with heavy concentrations of slaves that enlisting blacks to fight in the Civil War, whether slave or free, was most controversial. Colonel William Birney, with the Union Army, complained to the War Department's Bureau of Colored Troops in August 1863 of a scheme in Maryland "to obstruct and arrest" recruitment officers.[34] He expressed his concern that—

> it intimidated the people of color, giving them the impression that the United States was powerless to protect them against their enemies in this state. That act alone [arresting agent J.P. Creager] caused me to lose between one and two hundred recruits who were ready to come to the rendezvous at Baltimore.

Col. Birney also calls attention to John Singer,

> a free man of color, [who] was arrested, when on the point of leaving for Baltimore with the avowed intention of

---

[34] Berlin et al, pp. 339-340

joining the U.S. Colored Troops, on a pretended writ....The men who were concerned in this arrest avow their intention to prevent enlistments by issuing the writ in all similar cases [such writs not known to the law of Maryland].

Many Union soldiers, never having previously had any contact with blacks, initially looked askance at having blacks in their army, only later discovering their usefulness as scouts, and in work around the camps cleaning and cooking. However, as time passed and the soldiers encountered more and more "desperate slaves and haughty slave owners," it was not unusual for them to turn on the owners, even, on occasion, violently. Further, though none regarded themselves as fighting to free the slaves or to gain them equality, many refused to enforce the controversial fugitive slave law which required that runaway slaves be returned to their owners.[35]

Before the war ended, 8,718 black Marylanders had formed six regiments. They had not just helped out as scouts and around camp but had fought in such bloody battles as that at Fort Fisher, North Carolina and at Petersburg Crater, one of General Lee's last battles. Many died there, entombed in the tons of loose dirt that resulted from a blast placed under the Confederate line. A quote in dialect of one black soldier, published in the *Baltimore Daily Gazette* in October 1863, brings home the fact that even though most of the black soldiers were probably illiterate, they nonetheless knew exactly why they were fighting.

"King of Kings and God ob battles, help us to be able to fight wid de union sojers de battles for de Union. Help us to fight for de country—fight for our own homes and our own free children and our children's children."[36]

As a border state, the Civil War had presented real crises for Maryland, especially traumatic for its counties whose economies depended on large numbers of slaves. While the northern parts of Maryland had economies that were tied to the North, the slave-holding parts had no such economic

[35] See Berlin et al, pp. 12 & 31.
[36] Found in Brugger, pp. 304-305

cushion and only the South offered them the "institutional basis of its society." But even those counties with fewer slaves had other kinds of ties to the slave-dependent parts—family and friends living there; Baltimore lawyers who drew up deeds of sale for slavers.[37]

The fact that different Marylands evolved over the decades and would remain so divided, prevented blacks from achieving the freedom they hoped for while fighting in this and in each of the country's subsequent wars. It accounts for the rescinding of much of Maryland's 1864 constitution in 1867 after the all-white, anti-black Democratic party regained control of the state legislature, after the withdrawal of the Union troops who had occupied the state throughout the war.

THE INVASION OF MARYLAND—CITIZENS OF BALTIMORE BARRICADING THE STREETS MONDAY EVENING JUNE 29th 1863

The Invasion of Maryland during the Civil War: Citizens of Baltimore Barricading the Streets. June 29, 1863. ©Maryland Historical Society

The Democrats had promptly pushed through a constitution that opposed Lincoln's war policy [though it stated that slavery could not be revived], allowed the counting

---

[37] See Fields, p. 22.

of blacks in determining legislative apportion-ment [which increased the political power of the slave-holding counties], and did away with "progressive provisions for education."[38]

But even before the Democrats resumed political power in 1867, "armed marauders terrorized the freed people" and hundreds of former slave owners made use of pre-War apprenticeship laws to have black children bound over to them, in effect, reenslaving these blacks and breaking up families.[39]

> A federal military officer on Maryland's Eastern Shore found himself besieged by frantic parents who feared the loss of freedom's promise: a secure family....In many instances, boys of 12 and 14 years are taken from their parents, under the pretence that (the parents) are incapable of supporting them...the Orphan's Court, as yet, has never taken any testimony relative to the ability of the parents to support their children...in plain terms—the Rebels here are showing an evident determination to still hold this people in bondage, and call upon the Orphan's Court to give their proceeding the sanction of law.

The courts simply ignored witnesses who testified that the children being taken "were old enough to earn their own wages and that former owners withdrew many of them from jobs that had been arranged by their parents."

•••

By a slim margin, Maryland's legislature had freed her slaves in 1864, but clearly the fight for equality for all the people did not end there. As we begin now to focus separately on different aspects of the black struggle to achieve the equality promised by the constitution— employment, public accommodations, education and

---

[38] Based on accounts by Wagandt, pp. vii &268; Paul p. 58. Maryland had this debate regarding the counting of blacks before it emerged amongst the framers of the US constitution. We generally think of the fact that blacks were counted as only 3/5ths of a person in the Constitution as "bad," but, in fact, since blacks had no vote, it was a compromise with the South to prevent them counting their slaves as a "whole" which would have unduly increased Southern power in governance as it had in Maryland's Slave-holding counties.

[39] Information and quotes are from Berlin & Rowland, pp. 211-213 and from Berlin et al, p. 370.

housing—it is clear that although their constant struggle from the beginning has gained them significant progress since the days of chattel slavery, their fight for equality, of necessity, continues and may still take generations.

Part II
Employment

The Fight for Jobs

Blacks' always tenuous hold on jobs was exacerbated beginning in 1850 as immigrants, especially Germans and Irish fleeing political revolutions in Europe and famine in Ireland, began arriving in a more industrial-oriented Baltimore. Black men and women suddenly saw these newly arrived "white" immigrants replacing them even in jobs they'd long dominated— as warehouse laborers, coal handlers, draymen, attending forges at foundries, hod carriers, carters, domestics, washers, and ironers. At the same time, "native whites," feeling threatened by Baltimore's declining economy (the country experienced a depression in 1857), began to resent blacks in the few skilled and semi-skilled jobs they held—as ship-caulkers, tailors, blacksmiths, harness-makers, shoemakers, caterers, butchers, carpenters and seamstresses. The stage was set for an eruption of violence and riots in Baltimore, especially in the Fells Point area which, as we can see from the account given us by Frederick Douglass of his experience there about 1836, had always been a flashpoint.

Frederick Douglass, then still a slave, was hired out by his master, Hugh Auld, to William Gardiner, a ship-builder on Fells Point.[1] He intended that Douglass should learn the caulking trade, but Gardiner, then under time constraints to build two large man-of-war vessels for the Mexican government or risk financial ruin, had no time for instruction and assigned Douglass the impossible task of responding to the demands of twenty-five workmen.

Douglass calls the circumstances which led to his Master's taking him away as "a brutal outrage, committed upon me by the white apprentices of the ship-yard. The fight was a desperate one, and I came out of it most shockingly mangled." He not only had to put up with white apprentices talking "contemptuously and maliciously of 'the Nigers;' saying, that 'they ought to be killed,' but also had the impossible task of responding to orders simultaneously

---

[1] Most detailed account of his experience found in Douglass, *My Bondage...*, pp. 238-247. But writer also used account in Douglass, *Life and Times*, pp. 66-69.

given him by twenty-five workmen:[2]

> "Fred, go get a fresh can of water," "Fred, bring that
> roller here," "Fred, come help saw off the end of this
> timber," "Fred, go quick and get the crow bar," "Hurra,
> Fred, run and bring me a cold chisel," "I say, Fred, bear a
> hand, and get up a fire as quick as lightning under that
> steam-box," "Halloo, nigger! Come, turn this grindstone,"
> "Come, come! Move, move!" "I say, darkey, blast your eyes!
> Why don't you heat up some pitch?" "D--n you, if you
> move I'll knock your brains out!" Such, dear reader, is a
> glance at the first eight months of my stay at Baltimore.

He goes on to describe how his "troubles suddenly
exploded."[3]

> Until a little while before I went to Gardiner's, the white
> carpenters had been content to work side by side with the
> handful of black carpenters who were employed there.
> Some of the blacks were first rate workmen and were given
> jobs requiring the highest skill. All at once, however, the
> white carpenters stopped work, saying that they would no
> longer work on the same shipyard with negroes. They
> demanded that Mr. Gardiner discharge his few colored
> workmen.

With no whites available to replace the blacks, malice
and bitterness followed, affecting all blacks in the shipyard,
including Douglass. But Douglass, unlike others, struck
back when cursing turned to violence, whatever the
consequences, and managed pretty well as long as he kept it
one on one.

> In the fight which ended my stay at Mr. Gardiner's, I was
> attacked by four of them at once....They struck on all sides. I
> was stunned by a blow [on my head] and fell heavily on the
> ground among the timbers. Taking advantage of my fall, they
> rushed upon me and began to punch me with their fists.
> They did me little damage so far, but finally getting tired of
> that sport, I suddenly rose to my hands and knees. When
> they saw me staggering under the blows they had given me,
> my eye completely closed and my face covered with blood,

---

[2] Douglass, *My Bondage...*, pp. 238-239. Also Douglass, *Life and
Times*, pp. 66-69
[3] This and following quotes: Douglass, *Life and Times*, pp. 66-69.

they left me....No fewer than fifty white men stood by and
saw the encounter. Some cried out, "Kill him! Kill him! Kill
the d...n nigger! Knock his brains out! He struck a white
person!'

Douglass concludes his account by stating he is amazed
that he wasn't murdered. After he told his master of the
incident, he attempted to get justice for his slave in the
court, but neither Douglass's visible face and head wounds,
nor his testimony were sufficient without a white witness to
back it up, and, of course, none came forward and the case
was dropped. Douglass was then put to work at another
shipyard where his master was a foreman.

> Here I became expert in the use of calkers' tools, and in
> the course of a year I was able to command the highest
> wages paid to journeymen calkers in Baltimore.[4]

Della in an article on the problems of black labor tells
us of the violence that again erupted at Fells Point in May
1858, this time in the brickyards when a black worker was
shot[5] The police had to remain on guard for several days
before the terrorized blacks would return to work. Then, a
year later black workers at the Fells Point shipyards were
attacked and beaten.

Until 1864, when Maryland freed her slaves, it was
common practice for masters to hire their slaves out when
they themselves did not need them; often to jobs in
Baltimore, as in the case with Douglass; sometimes as
house servants to middle and lower class whites who could
not afford to own a slave. Hiring a slave gave these whites
status, but it often resulted in worse treatment for the
slaves than when serving their wealthier owners.

However, gradually, as an increasing number of
unemployed whites glutted the labor market, ownership of
slaves and their hiring-out became less and less profitable.

---

[4] Douglass notes that he escaped from slavery soon after and
migrated to New Bedford where he found, "that such was the
strength of prejudice against colored, among the white caulkers,
that they refused to work with me, and of course I could get no
employment." *Narrative...*, p. 150.

[5] See Della, pp. 14, 17 and 25-28.

Unable to find his slaves work, an owner would sell "unneeded" slaves, and if the buyer also could not find them work, he, in turn, would most often sell them to a slave trader. The final result, most often, was purchase of the slaves by a plantation owner further south.

In the decade leading up to the Civil War, the job situation clearly was deteriorating for blacks whether slave or free.

•••

Black-owned businesses provided virtually the only clerical jobs available to blacks,[6] but most of these businesses were very small and unable to counter the on-going usurping of black jobs by whites. One notable exception occurred in 1866, soon after the end of the Civil War (which lasted from 1861-1865). That year Isaac Myers, born in Baltimore in 1835 of free parents, a ship caulker since he was sixteen, spearheaded a drive to raise $10,000 to start-up the Chesapeake Marine Railway and Dry Dock Company. The fifteen blacks who invested included social, religious and political leaders. Simultaneously, Myers organized the Colored Caulkers Trade Union Society, one of the first black labor organizations in the country.[7]

For eighteen years, this virtually unprecedented black-owned and operated business gave employment to some three hundred black workers, most of whom had previously been harassed, even beaten, by white workers who had sought to terrorize them in order to eliminate them from competition for these lucrative jobs. However, as successful as the black-owned and operated company was up until 1884 (having had lucrative contracts from local merchants and the federal government), by then their finances were inadequate to upgrade their increasingly obsolete facilities, and the labor market had become so competitive that the directors were forced to close down the business. Nonetheless, their early success had resulted in the white

---

[6] In Baltimore in 1910, there were 52 out of 5,276 hired in clerical jobs; this number did not substantially change until 1940 when the number tripled.

[7] See Chappelle, pp. 166 & 168.

caulkers' union accepting blacks into their ranks[8]—but it was a hollow victory, since, by then, black dominance in Baltimore's caulking trade had ended, and the prominent positions Negro artisans formerly held in the skilled trades also were a nostalgic memory.[9] Nonetheless, Myers' career as a black leader had evolved and it held fast even after more radical blacks tried to undermine him, claiming he was too conservative.

In 1872 the first national black organization in the country, the National Colored Labor Union (NCLU), became "a political appendage of the Republican party," and the local Colored Labor Union (CLU), founded by Isaac Myers, collapsed soon after. Myers' succeeding efforts to gain membership for the black artisans in the white unions and to gain passage of a civil rights bill, on either the federal or state level, fared no better, despite his close connections with the Republican party. Not one to give up, in 1875, Myers again tried to gain black acceptance into local white unions and apprenticeship programs by founding the Colored Men's Progressive and Co-Operative Union. He hoped that through this early civil rights organization Maryland's blacks might achieve the same "rights and privileges" that all other Americans enjoyed.

Myers also organized a labor fair to display the works of black artisans. However, none of his efforts succeeded either in promoting black workers or in furthering their civil rights. Despite these failures, until his death in 1891, Myers remained loyal to the Republican party, still hoping, as an insider, to gain more leadership positions and patronage jobs for blacks.[10]

The lack of headway Myers experienced with the unions is not surprising given the existing pervasive racism, exploited by employers to keep wages low and working conditions poor. It enabled them to counter any demands for higher wages or better working conditions with the threat that there was a vast unemployed pool of black workers available, all too eager to

---

[8] See Fee, pp. 125-126 &128-129 and Chappelle, p. 168.
[9] See Paul p. 344.
[10] See Paul, pp. 5, 100-101, and Fee, p. 129

take their replace.

When the Knights of Labor started actively recruiting blacks in Baltimore in 1882, espousing solidarity regardless of color, it seemed that both skilled and semi-skilled black workers might finally have found a way to secure employment. This unusual worker solidarity had grown out of the strike that began on July 16, 1877 in West Virginia amongst railroad workers protesting a cut in wages. Before it ended on July 29, after President Hayes had called in federal troops to restore order, it had spread into Pennsylvania, Illinois and New York. This reinforced what Hayes' selection of corporate attorneys and directors to Cabinet posts had already shown: his close ties to the Republican party's "corporate bourgeoisie." Though the strike itself had not spread to Baltimore, it nonetheless fostered a unity among workers generally, that "foreshadowed the spectacular rise of the Knights of Labor in the 1880s."[11]

In 1882, the Knights succeeded in organizing both white and black grain carriers and ship caulkers in their union, and in 1886, the canmakers, brickmakers, Fells Point wagoners, Montgomery Street stevedores, longshoremen, blacksmiths, carpenters and painters. Perhaps the very success the Knights manifested in a massive Labor Day parade of some 25,000 racially mixed workers proved to be their demise. It seemed to confirm for the white power structure that the Knights, representing as they did a united labor force, spelled trouble. They did not round up members of the Knights and prosecute them for conspiracy to riot as they had in Chicago after the Haymarket riot in May, 1886, but through propaganda, they had successfully linked them to the anarchists in the public mind. Further the Knights faced a growing national labor organization, The American Federation of Labor (AFL). As a consequence, by early 1890, their union was virtually defunct.[12]

The AFL did not pose the same threats to white workers as had the Knights, even though the AFL's President, Samuel Gompers, claimed his union too did not discriminate. In the 1890s he had pressured some locals to remove "whites-only"

---

[11] Foner, pp. 583-585
[12] See Paul, pp. 352-354 & Olson, p. 234.

provisions from their constitutions, he did little to actually stop their excluding blacks from membership. By 1910, he had given up all pretense that blacks were welcome in the AFL as members.

With the end of a racially united labor movement as envisaged by the Knights of Labor, the building trades became entrenched in a caste system and employers regularly exploited ethnic rivalries in labor disputes. Fire fighters, police officers, railroad firemen, accountants, nearly all the construction crafts, and most public services were restricted to whites. The only good jobs for blacks were in their separate institutions such as schools, hospitals, funeral parlors and beauty parlors—perhaps seven hundred in all, a fifth of these barbers and hairdressers.[13] In 1888 when Myers organized the Colored Businessmen's Association, he placed the number of black businesses at only 150-200, comprised of grocery stores, confectionery stores, barbershops, saloons, dress shops, tailor shops, and catering shops— and these serving mostly whites.[14]

Despite the Association's collapse after Myers's death in 1891, and the discrimination blacks faced in lending, bonding, insurance and real estate practices, they did attempt to establish more sizeable businesses. In 1894, ten years after demise of the Chesapeake Marine Railway and Dry Dock Company which had operated from 1866 to 1884, the Northwestern Family Supply Company, capitalized at $50,000, opened offering consumers an extensive line of groceries, meats, clothing and household goods. It collapsed in just two years, despite maintaining six horse drawn wagons to make deliveries and keep it well stocked. Other attempts made between 1897 and 1907 to establish black businesses met the same fate within a few years of their opening—a bank, cooperative furniture store, cooperative shirt factory, cooperative machine shop, building and loan association, shoe shop, and department store offering a variety of dry goods. Lack of experience, inadequate capital, and, above all, lack of black patronage, combined to account for their demise.

---

[13] See Olson, pp. 275. & 327
[14] See Paul, p. 369.

With these more "respectable" black businesses having such a hard time, most of those which did flourish, pool halls, pawnshops, and an occasional restaurant and clothing store, were found in the alleys.[15]

As for the trade unions Myers put so much faith in, until 1900 Baltimore did manage to sustain a few small integrated local unions: brickmakers, ship caulkers, coachmen waiters, barbers, and, the strongest, the hod-carriers with a membership of 1,000. They "provided sick and death benefits, conducted a successful strike in 1900 to maintain a per diem wage of $2.50, and refused to affiliate with the AFL."[16]

Black craftsmen were by then virtually eliminated from the skilled trades, and the degree to which black participation along-side whites had declined was obvious in 1904 when a portion of the city was gutted by fire. The only role blacks were allowed to play in the city's reconstruction was in such menial tasks as carrying hods and wheeling away debris. After the founding of the Committee for Industrial Organization (CIO) by John Lewis in 1935, the CIO local did challenge racism in the unions, but it was 1945 before blacks again were represented in local unions in any significant number.[17]

•••

With these facts in mind, it is hard to understand what prompted the Bureau of Industrial Statistics and Information of Maryland at the beginning of the 20th Century to publish a report noting that "of a total city black population of approximately 81,381 persons, the census listed 52,405 gainfully employed in some 230 different occupations." Naming a list of occupations blacks had long engaged in, the report "noted that this occupational diversity was truly remarkable considering that immediately following the Civil

---

[15] See Paul pp. 370-372, Mayers, p. 169 & Olson, pp. 327-328
[16] Paul, p. 355-356
[17] Late in 1935 John Lewis broke with the craft-oriented AFL and founded the Committee for Industrial Organization, later called the Congress of Industrial Organization. John Lewis resigned as the union's president in 1940 when the union endorsed Roosevelt for President.

War Negroes in the city were 'only fit to fill menial positions.'"
The report concluded that this augured well for their future.
"The disheartening fact was that collectively the black
population in Baltimore was close to economic prostration."[18]

The only accurate statement in the above report was the
fact that the majority of blacks had always been engaged in
menial, low income jobs; *not* because it was "all they were fit
for," but because it was all they found open to them. As we've
seen, this was increasingly true after the depression in 1873
when jobless whites and an influx of German and Irish
immigrants began to compete for the same unskilled jobs.

Nonetheless, racism as a factor is surely revealed in the
1900 census which reported that 80% of blacks were engaged
in the occupations of "agricultural laborer, janitor, launderer,
common laborer, servant, waiter, drayman, hackman, hostler,
peddler, messenger, porter, or newsboy." And more and more
blacks were pushed into these unskilled jobs as discrimination
grew in the skilled occupations. This 80% figure contrasts with
16% of native whites and 20.5% of foreign-born in the same
jobs.

Between 1885 and 1898, white laborers, Italian
immigrants and labor "drifting in" from New York, succeeded in
displacing blacks from even such unskilled jobs as hod carriers
and domestic servants, and forced them to become street
vendors and "performers on harp and organ.[19]

•••

Domestic service that included scrubbing the marble
steps, and newly installed bathrooms and kitchens of better-
off Baltimoreans, dressmaking, seamstress, milliner, waitress,
and laundress had always been virtually the only employment
open to black women. A few men were also amongst the
estimated fifteen thousand blacks employed as house servants,
and a few of these achieved the skills and job security that
accorded them the same prestige as successful black
professionals and businessmen. They patterned their standards,
aspirations, and manners on the wealthiest members of
Baltimore society. Olson in her history of Baltimore writes:

---

[18] Paul, p. 360
[19] Olson, p. 234.

Richard Macks, for example, born a slave in Charles County, came to Baltimore when Grant was elected [President] and served four or five employers [as a butler] , each wealthier and more demanding than the last. Toward the end of the century, after being Tom Winan's and then Robert Garretts's butler for many years, he founded his own catering business.[20]

By 1900, caterers were amongst the most financially successful of the black professionals. Other successful blacks included musicians, "thirty doctors, a few lawyers, more preachers, more teachers, undertakers, an increased number of rental agents and real estate dealers, and wagon owners who did moving and hauling or who dealt in coal, ice, rags, bottles, and junk."[21]

[Caterers] served the lavish entertainments of the wealthy and suburban residents. Black middlemen also catered to the demands of other classes of society for food, sex, entertainment, and cocaine. At the Marsh market dance halls the black piano players made their reputation, among them Eubie Blake, Baltimore's great ragtime improviser....The dance halls were frequented by sailors, steamboat hands, and cattlemen. ...At Sparrows Point a thousand black men were living, recruited from Virginia without their families. Red-light districts existed in black neighborhoods... for the convenience of white patrons and traveling salesmen who would not be recognized. Readily exploited were young girls recruited from Virginia by the boatload to work as domestic servants in Baltimore. Among blacks in the city there were perhaps 117 women for each 100 men.

Few of the black women in domestic service fared so well. They began to leave these jobs early in the 20th Century, after passage of a ten-hour law excluded domestic work from coverage. They were tired of working fourteen or sixteen-hours a day for just one dollar and found cleaning offices and hotel rooms, serving lunches and minding women's children more lucrative. However, those who took factory jobs, expecting better pay, hoping to escape from the personal type

---

[20] See Olson, p. 234.
[21] Olson, pp. 273-274.

domination that existed in domestic work, too often were disappointed. Too often they found themselves stuck in the lowest-paid, dirtiest jobs in cigarette and garment factories, or stuck behind sewing machines in a shirt factory.[22]

•••

In her memoir of life in Baltimore in the 1880s and 1890s, (the cover of her book reproduced), Meredith Janvier, in brief colorful descriptions of blacks she knew, gives us

[22] See Olson, 363

both a look at some of the opportunities open to blacks at that time, and, simultaneously, reveals just how they were perceived, at least by some better-off whites, such as herself. She begins with a number of domestics she recalls from her childhood:[23]

> In Baltimore there were always a number of interesting characters and useful citizens among the Negro race. My own recollection brings to mind two remarkable cooks and old retainers in the family of the late Rev. Augustus P. Stryker, rector in all of the eighties and the first half of the nineties of St. Barnabas Protestant Episcopal Church at Biddle Street and Argyle Avenue.
>
> "Aunt" Rachel was the elder. I recall her gray hair, thin face and high cheekbones when I was a child. She was succeeded by "Aunt" Susan, whose lightbread in an oversized loaf was better than most cakes.
>
> At St. Barnabas there was for years a solitary colored member of the congregation, Myra Harris, a good and highly esteemed woman. Faith without works was not Myra's idea and at night in her off time she carried the church basket, stocked with crochet work, iron-holders and the many useful and fancy articles dear to housekeepers, to the homes of the parishioners. From her sales she realized tidy sums which were turned over to the church funds at regular intervals. Years after...when I attended an evening service at the new place of worship, ...of those who passed me I saw only one familiar face—Myra Harris, now grown old, but vigorous still, and it was a pleasure to see her kindly face among so many strange ones.

Janvier also recollects "Archie", the elevator operator in the old Herald Building before the 1904 fire— "He had a game leg, a pointed gray beard and wore a fancy skull cap. He was a fine old man, indeed." Janvier then describes a number of others she recollects:

> Possibly the most dignified and best mannered colored man I knew in those days was Grafton Gale. He was, I believe, interested in North Baltimore real estate. His dark, smooth skin and gray beard of formal cut gave him the appearance of some Moorish potentate.
>
> Nearly thirty years ago when I was having some work

---

[23] Janvier, pp. 248-249

done I engaged one Harrison Pegee, a colored carpenter. He was then about sixty years old, had mutton-chop whiskers, was energetic and a very fair workman. His young assistant showed a tendency to lean on door frames and side walls and otherwise loaf on his job. Suddenly Pegee would turn on him explosively and say, "Boy, what you doing standing still? If you can't find nothing to do jump up and down, 'cause you got to keep a-moving when you are working for me." This same Harrison Pegee was a most adaptable man, for at lunch time when asked what he would like to drink with his sandwiches his reply was: "Coffee if you got coffee; if you ain't, then I'll take some tea, and if you ain't got tea, give me a cup of hot water."

Amelia Barnes was my cook in those far-away nineties, short and slim, a mere handful of a woman; she was a veritable queen of the kitchen whose Sunday morning waffles, made no one ever did know how, literally melted in the mouth.

She also has some less kindly recollections:[24]

There was an old toothless colored man called by the children, both white and black, "Hoggie." A senseless rhyme something like this was shouted at him: "Hoggie, hoggie giselite, stole my mother's fizzletights." The old man would ignore his persecutors for a space, then turn on them fiercely, which would cause the crowd of children to disperse in all directions.

And some remarkable efforts to make a living:

Oysters then were fine and cheap. Old darkies peddled them, walking the streets all day, in each hand a two-gallon bucket, crying, :Oh-ie-oh-ie!"

In summer the same men went through the streets, especially at night, with baskets of devil crabs, and they cried "Crabbie, crabbie, crabbie. Don't you want to buy my devil crab?" The game man would bring partridges and ducks to your door, or stand on the corner with his birds. The hot waffle fellow with his corner drove his kitchen on wheels and white-aproned boys chased about the crowd delivering the sugared dainties. Scissors grinders were more common, also the "umbrellas-to-mend mechanic. These itinerants die hard and there are still a few left.

---

[24] Janvier, pp. 32-33, the following two descriptions

The last two decades of the 19th Century and the early years of the 20th did see at least some symbolic gains by blacks—schools opened named after Benjamin Banneker, Frederick Douglass, and Paul Lawrence Dunbar; Pennsylvania Avenue reveled in an Easter parade that presented an opportunity for blacks to show off their finery; "live music in the night spots created a backbone for 'soul';" and "some four hundred social and political clubs could be found in the Negro community."[25]

•••

In 1906 Harry Pratt, a disciple of Booker T. Washington, organized a local affiliate of the National Negro Business League Washington had founded in 1900. But Pratt had no more success in developing jobs for blacks than had Isaac Myers.

By 1912 there were still only about 600 black retail dealers in the city, less than one per cent of the black population—and discrimination was then on the *increase*.[26] Despite these depressing statistics, blacks did seem at least to have recovered from the loss of unskilled jobs that had occurred in the 1850s. In the years from 1910 to 1920, which include the years of World War I, blacks were employed at much the same rate as whites, giving them a certain stability even though their jobs were largely poorly paid and dead-end. However, the Great Depression of the 1930s, of which we'll hear more later, wiped all that out.

As might be expected of a Booker T. Washington disciple, and sounding as though he was unaware of past efforts to stop the decline in jobs available to blacks, Harry T. Pratt was amongst those who started calling on the black community to change its priorities; urged them to heed Washington's message and "to subordinate politics to economics, to cease civil rights protests, and to concentrate upon fostering a spirit of economic nationalism within the larger black community."[27] Like many other blacks who had

---

[25] Olson, p. 328.
[26] See Paul, p. 380.
[27] Paul, p. 366

become disgusted with politics as a remedy, Pratt, like Washington, believed strongly in "self-help" as the key to the black community's economic health. His arguments presage those heard in the 60s from the Black Muslims and the proponents of "black power."

The Right to Vote

In 1870, the year the 15th Amendment was ratified giving black men the right to vote, roughly half of Maryland's population was black and in Baltimore about 15%, making its urban black community one of the largest in the country. And despite widespread white hostility, blacks took full advantage of this new right.[28] Unfortunately, they discovered that voting in a political system based on free elections and competitive parties was not sufficient to end discriminatory practices. Even though M. L. Callcott confirms this in her assessment of black voting patterns, she makes two important additional points that should be heeded even today—

(1)   that black participation in politics does *not* depend on socioeconomic position (blacks' social standing and economic worth were worse then than now, but nonetheless they participated in as large or larger numbers than whites); and,

(2)   that participation does not depend on urban cohesiveness (rural blacks participated to an even greater extent than urban blacks).[29]

•••

Isaac Myers played a leadership role in insisting on black enfranchisement and continued to urge blacks to vote. Although he believed, like Booker T. Washington, that economic opportunity was of prime importance to blacks, he, unlike Washington, placed equal emphasis on gaining political and civil rights. Because of this, the more militant blacks who thought Myers too conservative were unable to undermine his leadership. They did, however, in 1876 go against the advice of Myers, broke with the Republicans, and, for the first time supported the Democrats' presidential candidate, Samuel Tilden. After much behind-the-scenes politicking on both sides; reminding one of the more recent, contested Bush-Gore

---

[28] As indicated previously, in Maryland, until 1810, free black men had had the right to vote; a state constitutional amendment that year took away that right: it's unclear whether blacks had ever exercised that right.

[29] See M. L. Callcott, pp. ix-x

election, Rutherford B. Hayes, the Republican, got 184
electoral votes to Tilden's 165, twenty in dispute. A "stacked"
electoral commission [*that included five Supreme Court
justices*] found in favor of Hayes, making him President.[30]

This election also marked the end of Reconstruction: the
withdrawal of the last of the federal troops from the South,
and among other things, the end of new school construction
for blacks, and the end of the election of blacks to state and
federal legislatures in the South. It's hard to know if the
election of Tilden would have been of any greater benefit to
blacks, for he, too, had campaigned on a platform to end
Reconstruction—which had not, in any case, touched
Maryland.

Despite the efforts of a number of blacks, 1877 saw
conservatism growing in the Republican party and interest in
black rights diminishing, including enforcement of the
Fourteenth and Fifteenth Amendments.

In Maryland, in 1880, a long-time black activist, Dr. H.J.
Brown, criticized the Republicans for not using their
patronage powers to provide blacks with more jobs. He
pointed out that even though a few could be found in menial
jobs in the Baltimore Customs House and the post office, none
could be found in responsible offices. He asserted that
Maryland's blacks were worse off than in any of the southern
states. Later that year, perhaps believing he could influence
the Republicans from the inside, Brown accepted the
presidency of a newly organized Colored Republican Central
Club meant to encourage black voter registration.[31]

Undeterred by the lack of party endorsement, four blacks
ran for the City Council that same year. They all lost, but so
did all the Republican candidates—and one of the blacks,
George E. Briscoe, actually received more votes than any of
the Republican candidates. The following year, 1881, when
the Republicans again refused to place any blacks on the
ticket, two blacks again ran independently; Joseph Briscoe
this time claiming he lost only because black votes were
destroyed. The militants kept up their demand for more
recognition by the Republican party, held protests at the

---

[30] See Foner, pp. 575-583, for details
[31] See Paul, pp. 190 & 197.

conventions and at rallies, and in 1881, 1885 and 1886, ran five more blacks for office. Again they all lost.

In 1883, the Supreme Court found the Civil Rights Act of 1875 unconstitutional, the majority opinion written by Joseph P. Bradley, one of the five justices who had helped make Hayes president.—"blacks must cease to be the special favorite of the laws." John Marshall Harlan, from Kentucky, was the only dissenter. He warned that the country was entering "an era of constitutional law, when the rights of freedom and American citizenship cannot receive from the nation that efficient protection which heretofore was unhesitatingly accorded to slavery."[32]

It was during this time that the militants had added a new strong voice to their numbers. Rev. Harvey Johnson, then just 29 years of age. He had come to Baltimore from Virginia in 1872 to become pastor of Baltimore's Union Baptist Church.[33] In the next five years Reverend Johnson not only managed to increase membership in his church from 276 to 1,368, and construct a new church building at a cost of approximately $20,000—the money raised almost exclusively from his own church members—but also became recognized in the community as a courageous leader in the fight for civil rights. And Reverend Johnson remained a leading civic and religious leader in the black community for fifty years (his church carrying on the tradition at least into the 1970s).

In June 1885 Rev. Harvey Johnson brought together in his home a group of local ministers and others interested in civil rights. After the meeting, Johnson, together with four other black Baptist ministers, drafted a constitution for "The Brotherhood of Liberty" that established as its purpose "to use all legal means within our power to procure and maintain our rights as citizens of our common country." [34] Johnson, quickly

---

[32] See Foner, pp. 586-587

[33] Johnson had been to a Quaker school in Philadelphia before entering Wayland Seminary in Washington, DC in 1868. His calling to Union Baptist followed his graduation from Wayland in 1872.

[34] Information and quotes on Brotherhood are from Paul, pp. 207-210. On pp. 6-7, Paul expresses his belief that the activism of black militants during this era, by successfully employing "legal rather than lethal tactics for redress, in retrospect helped to

designated as President of the new organization, expressed the hope that it would unite conservatives and fractious militants in their mutual desire for the advancement and protection of black rights, locally and nationally. Because the Niagara Movement (Johnson a founding member), and later the NAACP, were founded with similar goals, the Brotherhood has generally been recognized as the model for both.

By 1885, black activists were disgusted with the Republican party's demeaning of blacks, but in order for the Brotherhood not to be seen simply as a vehicle for chastising the party, it adopted a comprehensive approach to civil rights and invited the prestigious Frederick Douglass to give its inaugural address. But far from adhering to Harry T. Pratt's advice to concentrate on economic grievances and not challenge Jim Crow laws and efforts at disfranchisement, the Brotherhood wanted to do it all.[35]

> [They] called for legal action to repeal the discriminatory bastardy law [that prevented black women from suing the father for child support]; championed integrated trade unions and equal school facilities, including the employment of Negro teachers; and offered their brethren throughout the country financial aid and legal counsel to fight railway and steamboat discrimination and lynching. The Brotherhood pleaded not for special legislation but rather for impartial enforcement of existing laws, notably the 14th Amendment....[They] urged persistent agitation in defense of civil rights.

An outspoken and fearless Johnson "bitterly condemned the Republicans for giving the black man liberty and the franchise but little else." He accused the party of wanting their support but refusing to assure them jobs, or to protect their rights. "Johnson argued that the Negro 'cannot live on what men did for us forty years ago; we want men to stand up for the rights we have not got today.'"[36]

---

prepare the way for the Niagara Movement, the NAACP and the emergence of a man like W.E.B. DuBois." Gregory also discusses Johnson, pp. 228-236.

[35] Paul, p. 208

[36] Paul, p. 211

Perhaps it was pressure from the Brotherhood, or perhaps the fact that the City, in 1888, had annexed another twenty-three square miles of land and added 38,000 people, or perhaps the fact that for the first time blacks made up a majority of eligible voters in a City Council ward, whatever the reason, finally, in 1890, the Republicans officially endorsed the candidacy of a black for election to the Baltimore City Council. Harry Sythe Cummings, barely out of law school, won over his Democratic opponent to become the first black in Maryland to be elected to public office.

In 1889, Cummings and Charles W. Johnson had graduated with honors from the Maryland Law School—the first and last blacks to do so for many years. Cummings had been accepted at the law school after graduating from Lincoln University in Oxford, Pennsylvania, located mid-way between Philadelphia and Baltimore. Once a refuge for runaway slaves, Lincoln[37] was regarded as the black man's Princeton; the place where many of Baltimore's up-and-coming blacks went when faced with Maryland's segregated education facilities. It was quite an achievement for the son of a skilled chef and a sometimes-domestic servant, and the grandson of slaves from Baltimore County.

Cummings served in the City Council from 1891-1892 and again from 1897-1898 and 1907-1917 (until his death in 1917).[38] During his tenure, he secured the admission of the first black student, Harry T. Pratt, to the Maryland Institute of Art and Design in 1891 [*a battle that cost him the re-election in 1892 and one that had to be fought again in the 1940s*] and successfully labored to get the Council to establish a Negro manual training school in 1892. In 1906 President Theodore Roosevelt offered Cummings a consul post in Paraguay but he declined.

During the years 1895 and 1896, when Cummings had been defeated at the polls, another black, Dr. John Marcus Cargill, a friend of Cummings, won the seat on the City

---

[37] In later years, Thurgood Marshall and the noted lobbyist, Clarence Mitchell, Jr., would be amongst Lincoln's graduates—and also instrumental in once again desegregating the University of Maryland's law school.

[38] Paul, pp. 214 & 257. See also Greene, pp. 204-205.

Council. During his brief tenure, Dr. Cargill was influential in seeing the establishment of Provident Hospital to serve his people. After his tenure ended in 1896, Dr. Cargill joined the approximately dozen black physicians then practicing in Baltimore. His specialty, women's diseases, Dr. Cargill also "invented and patented several medical preparations which were approved under the Pure Food and Drug Act of 1906."[39]

•••

In 1893, Grover Cleveland, the Democrat who'd been elected President in 1885, was running again against Benjamin Harrison, the Republican who'd defeated him to become President in 1889. The choice facing blacks was a difficult one: on the one hand, they were increasingly disgusted with their treatment by the Republican party, and, on the other, the virtually all-white Democratic party was openly calling for white supremacy in the most flagrant racist rhetoric. The fact that almost one-third of registered blacks (about 5,000) voted Democratic is indicative of just how disgusted with the Republicans blacks were. After four years of losses in both local and state elections, it portended great changes for blacks (not necessarily advantageous) when the Democratic party won the Presidency (carrying Maryland for a second time). This was followed by victories for governor, in both houses of the Maryland General Assembly, and for the Baltimore Mayor. Democrats were once again in charge throughout Maryland.[40]

They immediately sought to strengthen their hold on the state by trying to disenfranchise blacks and extending segregation beyond the schools, correctional and charitable institutions where it then existed "into public transportation, residential housing, and public accommodations."[41] At the time, blacks in Baltimore numbered 79,000 out of a total population that had grown to 500,000 as former Confederate soldiers, blacks, Russian Jews and Poles arrived in the city, all

---

[39] Greene, p 205
[40] Paul, p. 270
[41] M. L. Callcott, p. ix

looking for a more prosperous life.[42]

That the Democrats should want to disenfranchise blacks who had traditionally supported their opponent's party is not surprising. Maryland's blacks always had had exceptional access to the ballot box, compared to those in other borderline and southern states. And, at least since Reconstruction in 1876, had made full use of it. However, the Democrats' unremitting assaults on the participation of blacks in the Republican party, were seen "as attacks on what had become a firmly established party system that served important interests aside from those of race," and, as a consequence, whites joined blacks in countering the attacks. M. L. Callcott concludes that "the almost mechanistic manner in which the party system reacted to preserve itself was a crucial factor in maintaining Negro suffrage in Maryland."[43]

Democrats attempted three times, in 1903, 1905 and 1908, to pass legislation that would have disenfranchised blacks. They failed only because other political groups, especially newly arrived immigrants, joined with them in opposing it. For different reasons The Colored Law and Order League, representing blacks and the Foreign Born Voters League, both strongly opposed literacy tests. Further, the leaders of both parties feared the imposition of a requirement that voters demonstrate an understanding of the constitution. They felt "an understanding" was too subjective, would give voter registrars the power to use this against a party out of power.[44]

Thus, the legislature's efforts to disenfranchise blacks failed, but the blacks' "decade long struggle to retain the right to vote seemed to spur, rather than halt, the trend toward racial segregation, and increased the ill feeling of whites toward blacks,"[45] most of whom remained in low-paying jobs, were living in run-down, crime and disease infested inner city

---

[42] See Power, *Apartheid*, pp. 290 & 308. The US Bureau of Census 1918, p. 51, puts the percentage of blacks in Maryland in 1870 at 22.5%, by 1900, 19.8% and by 1910 at 17.9%.

[43] See M. L. Callcott, pp. viii-x

[44] See Olson, p. 275.

[45] Paul, p. 286.

ghettos, and were without access to health services or a good education. Nonetheless, as the city in general was prospering in the early decades of the 20th Century, so, too, a substantial number of blacks managed to achieve middle-class status— mostly small businessmen (e.g., barbers, morticians), musicians, doctors, ministers, teachers, and lawyers.

As the city built its first skyscrapers, paved 929 miles of streets, constructed houses at a pace of 6,000 annually, and built spacious schools, playgrounds and recreational facilities (for whites only), substantial numbers of blacks moved out of the slums to housing along Eutaw Place, Druid Hill Avenue, Madison Avenue and Mosher Street, for the most part into housing purchased from German Jews who were moving, along with their synagogues, further out to the city's growing suburbs. These blacks had had to overcome white fears, and legal barriers, and often had needed the help of black lawyers who first had had to fight their own battle to practice in Maryland.

The Reverend Harvey Johnson, whom we met soon after his arrival in Baltimore in 1872, was among the growing number of black activists who encouraged another new arrival—the black lawyer, Charles S. Taylor—to fight for the right to practice in Maryland. Already a member of the Massachusetts' Bar in good standing, he quickly set up office across from the Court House, and applied for admission to practice in the federal courts. This achieved, he proceeded to challenge the section of the recently adopted State Constitution that required all persons admitted to the Maryland Bar to be a "free white male citizen of Maryland, about the age of twenty-one years."[46]

After he presented himself to the Supreme Bench of Baltimore City and was "courteously" refused, he filed a Petition with the Maryland Court of Appeals at Annapolis, arguing that the State Constitution conflicted with the 14th Amendment to the U.S. Constitution; that a State couldn't deny a citizen a right to earn a living by a profession, or trade, because of his color or racial origin. However, the Appellate Court disagreed, and on December 20, 1877

---

[46] MD Constitution, Act of 1876, Chap. 264, sec. 3.

handed down its ruling:

> The limitation of the privilege of admission is not repugnant to the 14th Amendment of the U.S. Constitution ....The power of regulating the admission of attorneys in the Courts of a State is one belonging to the State and not to the Federal government. [47]

Taylor returned to Massachusetts, but he had stirred to action a small but powerful segment of the public that included the Mayor, prominent white attorneys and journalists and the city's leading newspapers. But despite a hundred signatures on a demand submitted to the State Legislature that they change the Constitution to permit blacks to practice law, the Legislature refused.[48] A *Baltimore Sun* editorial declared:

> In all seriousness the law has no right to keep a colored man from earning his bread in any honest way he may see fit, provided that he show himself able to meet the requirements imposed on all other classes of citizens.[49]

It was not until Saturday, February 7, 1885, that those advocating a change in the constitution succeeded in persuading Charles S. Wilson to again challenge the State provision regarding lawyers. He was a school teacher who had finished a law course and been licensed in Massachusetts before moving to Maryland and becoming a teacher. The courtroom was filled on the day his petition for admission to the bar was to be heard by the State Supreme Court. The prominent attorney, Alexander Hobbs, who was sponsoring Wilson, made "an eloquent plea" as to the merits of the case, using much the same arguments that had been made in Taylor's case. On March 19, 1885 the court, in essence overruling the earlier Appeal Court's decision, unanimously ruled "that the excluding clause in the [Maryland] Constitution of 1864 violated the 14th Amendment and was therefore unconstitutional."[50]

Since Wilson did not really want to practice law, the

---

[47] Koger, p. 5, quoting 48 MD 28
[48] See Paul, p. 206
[49] *Sun*, 2/7/1884
[50] Found in Paul, p. 206

Rev. Harvey Johnson turned to Howard Law School to find a willing attorney. He succeeded in persuading a recent graduate, Everett J. Waring, to come the Baltimore and apply for admission.

On October 10, 1889 Waring became "the first Negro to practice before the Supreme Bench and the first Negro admitted to practice in any non-federal court in the history of the state" —and, incidentally, became a new member of Rev. Johnson's Union Baptist Church. In June 1892, after receiving his law degree from Howard University, W. Ashbie Hawkins, of whom we'll hear more later, became the first black admitted to the Maryland bar "on examination."[51] Within a very short time, six blacks could be found practicing law in Baltimore and in the state courts.[52]

However, as satisfying as the legal victory was for black lawyers, it helped only a tiny percentage of blacks needing employment. Nonetheless, as incremental as each battle might have been, the blacks' battles for equality never ceased, *and* they never abandoned the country that seemed all too willing to abandon them.

•••

On the eve of the U.S. entering World War I and only months before his death in 1917, Harry S. Cummings, then a member of the City Council, wrote to Maryland Governor Emerson C. Harrington urging him to call upon blacks to serve in the army. He wrote:[53]

> Among our population there are more than 225,000 people of my race, among these there are probably 50,000 available under proper circumstances for military service...
>
> Personally, I feel that I cannot lay down my life in any greater service than in the defense of my country and I know that thousands of men of my race feel the same way...Our black brothers fell at Carrizal last week—this

---

[51] From article by Hawkins in *Baltimore American-Sunday* paper, 9/16/1899, p. 20

[52] Paul, p. 206

[53] Greene, p. 213, quoting from the Cummings family papers and the *Sun*, 6/27/1916

was only a repetition of history. Attucks fell on Boston Commons in the Revolutionary War; Nick Biddle shed his blood during the Civil War. The gallant Tenth saved Roosevelt's life at San Juan Hill during the Spanish-American War, and catching the spirit of the brave men of our race, we are willing and ready to defend our State and Nation. We know but one country and one flag.

Determining just how many of Maryland's blacks served in the war has proved illusive, but references to them are scattered through [Emmett J.] *Scott's Official History of the American Negro in the World War.* He refers to the fact that, according to War Records, Maryland's black National Guard Unit, 1st Separate Company, with three officers and 154 men, was called into Federal service on July 25, 1917. Eventually it was "amalgamated" with troops from Massachusetts and Tennessee and sent overseas from Camp Stuart, Newport News, Virginia as members of the 93rd Division (Provisional) under command of Brigadier General Roy Hoffman.[54]

In another table dated December 16, 1918, Scott notes the number of blacks drafted in Maryland "during the entire war" as 9,212 (26,211 whites).[55] Still later Scott states that the black 1st Separate Company of Maryland was among those that were part of the "372nd Regiment, US Army, brigaded together with the 371st Infantry throughout the entire period of service overseas, with the 157th Division of the French Army, the famous "Red Hand" Division."[56] His book also includes a number of pictures of Maryland blacks.[57]

1. "Baltimore Saturday night dance at the WCCS Colored Club."

2. "Sgt. Rufus Pinckney, Baltimore, MD, 1st Separate Company, 372nd Inf., wears highest honors from French Government; captured fifteen Germans, saved French Officer's life, fought in Champagne, Argonne and at Verdun."

3. "Baltimore War Camp Community Circle. Some of the

---

[54] See Scott, pp. 33-34

[55] See Scott, p. 68

[56] See Scott, p. 239.

[57] These photos are in unnumbered groups of pictures that follow, in order, pp. 48, 176, 192, 400, and 417.

beds at the War Camp Community Service Colored Club which is typical of many such clubs organized throughout the entire U.S."

4. "Colored messengers of Motorcycle Corps, 372nd Headquarters who kept communication lines alive at all hours during the big drive in Champagne, Argonne and at Verdun."

5. "Sgt. Wm. Butler of Salisbury, MD., who received the Croix de Guerre from the French Government and Distinguished Service Cross and Sharpshooter's Medal from the U.S. Government."

These seemingly positive accounts of black participation in the war do not negate the fact that they faced considerable harassment and discrimination; were assigned menial work; were sent into combat ill-equipped, then accused of cowardice. DuBois on a trip to Europe corroborated much of this and accused Scott of either covering up or ignoring the pervasive racism.[58] However, whatever their role, whatever their treatments, the thousands of blacks who served in the military hoped their participation would lead to greater acceptance at home. Instead, just as after the Civil War, on their return home they faced job discrimination, financial troubles, and, if anything, a *decline* in their general status.

George Callcott in his book, *Maryland & America*, calls the 1920s the worst period for blacks since the end of slavery, and in his summing up of their position, Argersinger would seem to agree:

> Concentrated in menial and service occupations, blacks lived in the oldest and most congested areas of the city where they suffered disproportionately from unemployment, crime, disease, and infant mortality. Aside from teachers in "colored schools," blacks accounted for less than 2% of all municipal employees, and of that small number nearly 80% were classified as "common laborers."

> There were no black librarians, streetcar drivers, fire fighters, or police officers in the entire city. Moreover, even among school teachers—and in violation of state law— blacks received less pay; white teachers in elementary schools, for example, received about twice the salary of their black counterparts....over 50% of black women were

---

[58] Lewis, pp. 563-580.

in the paid work force; and among these wage-earning black women, about 87% were employed as domestics or personal servants, earning no more than $6 a week....

Finally, blacks were more likely than whites to be arrested; their arrest rate in the 1920s, for example, was about twice that for whites, and by 1934, the population of Baltimore's City Jail was nearly 50% black. [*Would these figures be the same or worse today?*] [59]

Baltimore, for its part, in 1918 tripled in size, annexing over fifty square miles that included parts of Baltimore and Anne Arundel counties. The motivation for at least part of this annexation was to acquire land needed to attract large scale factories which, until then, had been rare. The Baltimore Association of Commerce (BAC) in its brochures emphasized the industrial advantage of Baltimore's being the nation's seventh-largest city, and lauded the fact it was a "low-wage" town, "nonunion, predominantly white," and with a "'100% American' work force." They also proclaimed that the truly "'American workers, whether white or black, are rarely found among the ranks of the Communists' and added that if labor problems occurred there was also an 'ample supply' of unskilled blacks to call on for strikebreaking services." H.L. Mencken is quoted as calling BAC members "boomers, go-getters and other such ballyhoo men." [60]

Mencken disagreed with those who held that what the city needed was more industrial development. In fact, he argued that they needed fewer; factories only creating "ninth-rate towns" where "the poor half-wits they employ" are "entertained by evangelical religion and the Klan." [61]

As many of those opposed to more industrial development had feared, after the annexation Baltimore zoned the sections near the proposed new industrial sites that were occupied by whites as residential, and left the approximately 11,000 homes occupied by blacks and immigrants within the polluted industrial zone. [62] Baltimore

---

[59] Argersinger, pp. 3-4.
[60] Argersinger, pp. 1-2
[61] Power, *Unwisdom...*, p. 659, quoting *Notes of a Baltimorean, The Evening Sun*, 9/10/1923.
[62] See Power, *Unwisdom...*, p. 660.

attracted at this time 103 new plants, including Western Electric, American Sugar, McCormick Spice, and the Lever Bros. and Proctor and Gamble soap factories. Bethlehem Steel, which drew many of its workers from within the city, spent $100 million to expand its plant in nearby Sparrows Point. Its president, Charles Schwab, believed Baltimore the prime place in the country for successful industrial development.[63]

Despite the fact that Sparrows Point, and specifically Bethlehem Steel, hired more blacks than any of the other large industries, it makes a telling case study of the black struggle for equal treatment and equal access to jobs. Their story follows.

---

[63] See Argersinger, pp. 1-2

Bethlehem Steel: A Case In Point

> You work in a steel mill, with red-hot molten steel all around you. You watch for spills, listen for noises that indicate trouble...Everything is fine while the steel stays on the conveyor belt, traveling red hot at high speeds, pressed thinner and thinner by stands of rolling mills. But if it slips off, someone will likely get hurt. You remember stories of steelworkers speared by an errant rod in the wire mill, or others, in different parts of the mill, burned alive in a cauldron of steel.[64]

> Big, burly men...covered in coal dust and grime, open-hearth men. They wore long johns, denim coveralls, flame-retardant jackets....They worked in 150-degree heat. Sometimes they fainted, sometimes they caught fire. Once in a while a man slipped or fell into the ladle of molten steel, the same steel that girded the Golden Gate Bridge, Rockefeller Center, and the U.S. Supreme Court.[65]

Although generally associated with Baltimore City, Bethlehem Steel at Sparrows Point is in Baltimore County and was not part of the city's 1918 annexation. As the story unfolds of the black employees' fight to resist and overcome Bethlehem Steel's racist practices, one needs to remember that it nonetheless probably offered blacks the best-paying jobs available to them. This fact serves both to underline the extent of job-discrimination faced by blacks generally, and helps explain why fear of losing their jobs at Bethlehem Steel often impeded blacks joining the fight for better treatment.

The industry's origins can be traced back to 1857 when the Saucona Iron Company formed in South Bethlehem, Pennsylvania. By the time a steel mill and shipyard were built at Sparrows Point, it had become the Bethlehem Steel Company, producing the first Bessemer steel railroad rails and heavy forgings and armor plates for the U.S. Navy.

The site in Baltimore County was chosen in 1887 by an

---

[64] Fee (ed.), Linda Zeidman, quoting black worker, Ed Gorman, in 1940s, found on opening page of Chapter 9.

[65] Fradkin, Susan, "Lunching with Ghosts," *Baltimore City Paper*, September 13-19, 2000.

engineer named Frederick Wood, and took its name from the Sparrows family which had owned and farmed the land since before the American Revolution. By 1901, when Charles M. Schwab became President of the corporation, a company town had been built. It had its own police station, store, doctor, clergy, schools and housing— "everything from mansions for the bosses to tarpaper cabins for the immigrants and Southern blacks who worked the dirtiest, most dangerous jobs."[66]

Housing, entirely rental, was laid out to accommodate its workers along lettered streets that reflected the racial, ethnic and economic prejudices of the time. A street had only the general manager's house. Upper managers and the school superintendant lived on B and C Streets. D Street, the business district, divided them from the general employees who were housed on E and F Streets. Next came a creek that served to segregate blacks on the remaining lettered streets. Assignments of housing depended on the foremen's assessment of a worker's status. Not surprisingly, since blacks had the worst jobs, they also had the worst housing.

Because black males were deliberately denied the education and training they'd need for promotion to more skilled jobs, their families often had to take in boarders to supplement the men's pay. Education for the black females was limited almost entirely to homemaking, sewing, and laundry.[67]

By 1916, as Bethlehem Steel expanded to meet the increased demand for ships during World War I, the need for more housing for their workers also increased. As a result, in 1916 the company established Dundalk on the peninsula immediately west of the steel mill. These houses, unlike the rental units in the company town, were mostly owned, and occupied almost exclusively by whites—2,000 by 1920. With very little alternative housing available, they

---

[66] Fradkin, Susan," Lunching with Ghosts," *Baltimore City Paper*, September 13-19, 2000.

[67] See Fee (ed.), Linda Zeidman, Chapter 9, for more detail regarding houisng at Sparrows Point and education opportunities for blacks.

put up with the constant battle they faced in trying to get rid of the fine powder given off by the mills that daily covered everything—sidewalks, cars, porches et al. As the company's need for workers continued to increase, another almost exclusively white community, Highlandtown, was established. "By the 1930s, all but 2,000 of the 25,000 person workforce lived outside the company town."[68]

Clearly the fact that these two new towns were predominately white emphasized the fact that the company still was hiring few blacks despite the increased need for labor as thousands of Baltimore's men were enlisting in the military (62,000 serving in some branch during WWI). And Sparrows Point was not alone. The biggest beneficiary was not black men but women, hired in appreciable numbers for the first time.

Sparrows Point during this time created another 100 acres for its own expansion, filling in the shoreline with slag, steel's waste product. They were then producing guns, armor, armor piercing projectiles and explosive shells for the military.

●●●

It was not long after the end of World War I, on September 9, 1926, that Charlie Parrish, aged sixteen, a black sharecropper newly arrived in Baltimore from Virginia, got his first job at Bethlehem Steel. In many ways his story is that of all the blacks at Sparrow's Point, in other ways he was luckier than the vast majority. Claiming to be eighteen when asked, Charlie was assigned to the blast furnaces as part of a "colored labor gang," a rough, "surly and profane" lot "who played pranks on one another and hooted it up when a new fellow fainted from the heat."[69] They did all the heaviest hottest work on the casting platform, such as digging ditches and cleaning up slopped out slag.

Charlie was luckier than most blacks at Sparrows Point

---

[68] Fee (ed.) Chap 9, p. 183

[69] This writer does not attempt to retell the whole story of Sparrows Point as recounted by Mark Reutter in his book by that name, but does extract from it much of Charlie' story—the source of information and quotes regarding this black worker.

when a white foreman, for reasons unknown, early-on singled him out to move to the mechanical gang as a "burner helper"; he became one of a select few blacks trained to "use oxygen torches and burner equipment," and his pay was increased from 37¢ an hour to 41¢. This job, though safer than that at the blast furnace, did not prevent Charlie, soon after his "promotion," from losing a finger joint after a copper plate slipped off its rigging and smashed his hand. Accidents at the company were common; life expectancy was seven years less than for those with professional jobs. When the Great Depression of 1930 hit Bethlehem Steel, and lay-offs followed, few of its workers, like those nationally, had unemployment to help them through the hard times. In addition to those laid off, about 12,000 others were working only part-time. Charlie was no exception. By December 1931, he was working only three days a week.[70]

Charlie would have agreed with the *Iron Age* when, in its January 5, 1933 issue, it described 1931 as a "calamitous' year." He was married by then, living in the newly developed hamlet of Turner's Station (largely occupied by blacks, unlike Dundalk and Highlandtown); his wife, Alice, was pregnant, and he was making hardly enough to pay for food. Charlie supplemented his meager earnings with money from doing roofing for neighbors, even his boss's house, and he supplemented their food supply by growing his own sweet potatoes, turnips, onions, green beans and tomatoes.

By the end of 1932, the number still working at Sparrows Point had dropped from 18,000 to 3,500; Charlie's biweekly pay for his 30 work hours had dropped to $11.40. President Hoover was blamed; Franklin D. Roosevelt was elected; everyone wondered what he would do to turn things around.

Finally, near the end of 1933, after the Public Works Administration began to place orders for capital construction and ordered more railroad-related steel items, the figures in the Sparrow Point's ledgers gradually turned from red to black. And Charlie Parrish gradually saw his

---

[70] See Reutter, pp. 210-211

hours and pay checks creep back up to their 1929 level—$50 biweekly. But this still was hardly enough to live on and steel workers began to listen to union organizers who wanted to change the Chamber of Commerce's projection of Baltimore as a nonunion town to one that proclaimed it a Union Town.

Early-on a few began to meet secretly knowing full-well that Bethlehem at best harassed union sympathizers, and, more often fired them. Organizing became somewhat easier after passage of the Wagner Act in 1935 that offered at least a modicum of protection to organizers. Soon after, John Lewis of the United Mine Workers abandoned the reactionary, racist AFL, organized the militant CIO, and established the Steel Workers' Organizing Committee (SWOC). This new union was committed to non-discriminatory industrial unionism.[71]

Baltimore, however, proved an especially hard nut to crack. The CIO campaign lasted from 1936-1941; their slogan, "Organize Sparrows Point or Bust." But local businesses, including Bethlehem Steel, hired men from the notorious Pinkerton firm to expose CIO organizers as Communists and outside trouble-makers. Superintendents saw a Red behind every CIO button.[72] Those workers who dared join the union in face of all this, hid their buttons under their lapels.

Union organizing was further handicapped at Sparrows Point when Bethlehem Steel set up a company union (which soon collapsed), and by the controversy that black participation aroused. It was still fresh in the memories of both blacks and whites that black men had been lynched on the Eastern Shore in 1931 and 1933 as a result of efforts to establish an integrated union. Despite this, SWOC organizers were convinced that, with close to a third of the workers at Sparrows Point by then black [5500 out of 16,500], a larger percentage than in any of Bethlehem Steel's other plants, a union had to be integrated to succeed.

The organizers were helped considerably when they won the support of the black community: the NAACP distributed favorable literature; the Interdenominational Ministers' Alliance endorsed the CIO campaign; black ministers opened

---

[71] See Fee (ed.) p. 187
[72] See Ryon, p. 21.

their doors to CIO organizers for meetings, and informed their congregations from the pulpit about strikes, negotiations and rallies; red-baiting was counteracted by CIO organizers joining their churches, even singing in their choirs. Even the *Afro*, which was, in general, very anti-union, "carried news, times, dates, and places of rallies before they were held."[73] Thurgood Marshall, then a 28-year-old lawyer for the Baltimore NAACP, endorsed the union drive, as did John P. Davis of the National Negro Congress.

In August 1937, unable to meet on the premises of the company town, the organizers arranged the first of several rallies in "the heart of the black ghetto," where they succeeded in persuading fifty-two courageous Sparrows Point employees to sign SWOC membership cards.[74] Gradually, the numbers signing up increased to 400 and finally about 3,000, but many were afraid of the company's power, especially those who rented their houses from Bethlehem Steel and those who used the company store. In 1940, fear of management, an open shop tradition, and race remained obstacles to progress in union organizing.

The union organizer's approach to Charlie proved to be a turning point. He and his wife, Alice, together looked at the pamphlet, *What SWOC Means to You*, that he'd been given. It offered a wage increase, job security, paid vacations, and grievance procedures. The pamphlet also urged blacks to unite and actively work for their freedom.[75] Charlie thought of the street cars he rode to work, how he was relegated to the "colored only" car, how Alice couldn't try on hats at the department stores; how they were excluded from most of Baltimore's lunch counters. They also were well aware that the majority of the black workers at Bethlehem Steel were in the lowest paying jobs—furnace workers in the hot pits, janitors throughout the plants, or carriers of steel to white cutters and molders—as Ryon put it, "the white worker's domestics."[76]

Charlie knew he was better off than these workers;

---

[73] Ryon, pp. 22-23
[74] See Reutter, p. 292
[75] See Reutter, p. 193
[76] See Ryon, p. 23

nevertheless, he was tired of training newly hired white workers who were then put on as "Helper A" while he remained in the inferior status of "Helper B." Convinced of the need for this union, Charlie spearheaded a recruitment drive among the black workers at Bethlehem Steel, making use of the segregated lunch rooms, baths and locker rooms, where no white bosses ever came, to talk to them.

Of course, it wasn't just the blacks who brought the union to Bethlehem Steel, but it was they whom the SWOC district director, Nicholas Fontecchio, singled out as making the crucial difference when Bethlehem Steel, finally, after six to seven years of organization efforts, allowed an election on September 25, 1941. 10,813 of the 15,714 steelworkers voted; 6,000 of the 7,500 blacks did so, the overwhelming majority of them for the union.[77] The *Afro-American* quoted Fontecchio as saying:

> Had their [blacks'] vote been against us we would have lost the election. I want it known that we appreciate their support and we are going to work for the common good of all along the policy of the CIO which frowns on all race, color or creed discrimination.[78]

The campaign at Bethlehem Steel roused other black workers to seek CIO unions, where there were none, and encouraged blacks to make demands of unions that had previously ignored them. *People*, a small, left-leaning, bi-weekly paper that sold for 5¢ a copy, then being published by Fred Weisgal, who later became well-known in Baltimore as a civil rights lawyer, gives a clue as to how pervasive the problem was. In an article on March 27, 1944, Weisgal wrote:[79]

> The National Maritime Union, CIO, accused Fred Huber, manager of the Lyric Theatre, of anti-union bias and racial discrimination, because it refused to rent the theatre for an NMU affair, at which Paul Robeson, noted

---

[77] Figures according to Reutter, p. 298.
[78] Found in Fee (ed.) p. 190 and in Ryon, p. 25.
[79] These quotes from *People* are from the original publication, first used by the writer in her biography of Fred Weisgal: *"...And Justice for All": The Double Life of Fred Weisgal, Attorney and Musician.*

Negro actor and singer, was to appear. Said James Drury, NMU port agent at Baltimore: "Mr. Huber's refusal is dictated by anti-union hatred and Negro bias because the NMU as a union is sponsoring the affair and the great Negro, Paul Robeson, will be present." [More will be heard later of the discrimination policies of the Lyric.]

Ryon writes of more promising actions:

Claiming to represent hundreds of black porters and attendants, the United Federal Workers launched a campaign for a reduced, forty-eight hour week in 1939 for low wage employees. The United Sugar Refining Workers, organizing at the large downtown Domino plants, appealed to five or six hundred blacks in a work force of about eight hundred and ousted the white only affiliate in 1938...The amalgamated and the ILGWU [which] claimed jurisdiction over clothing workers in the city, including perhaps seven or eight hundred blacks,...became more militant and began to serve blacks.

The ILGWU sponsored the city's first sit-in;...the Amalgamated took up the banner of workers in city dry cleaning plants in 1939 [who were working] twelve to sixteen hour days in hot, unventilated steam rooms for low wages...A massive CIO effort among Baltimore marine and shipyard workers overcame years of bitter black-white resentments.[80]

•••

In 1942, a year after Bethlehem Steel was unionized, Charlie Parrish put their union's promises to the test. He filed a grievance stating he wanted more money "because I am doing the work satisfactory. I lays off material and I fit it up. I am a first class Burner, and a copper Burner and teach men that don't know the job. I am asking for repairman A." When his promotion was denied, claiming he wasn't qualified, he appealed. And he appealed again when the Superintendent called him "a very good worker" but claimed he could not read the required drawings.

The shop steward (who was black) and the white head of the grievance committee called the blueprint matter a "smokescreen," since Parrish had been doing the work for 15

---

[80] Ryon, pp. 25-26

years in his crew. Finally, on February 5, 1943, on the fourth step of the appeal the personnel director, acknowledging that the union had a winnable case, promoted Charlie.[81]

By then the U.S. had been a part of World War II for two years. When it began, only one in twelve factory workers was black, and most of those were employed in "the hot spots at Bethlehem Steel." So, perhaps appropriately on May 23, 1943, a Liberty Ship built in their shipyard was christened the *Frederick Douglass*, "the occasion celebrated with a lunch at a Negro hotel, while black laborers scraped the grease off the ways to ready them for the next launching."

But despite its practice of hiring relatively large numbers of blacks (motivated primarily, no doubt, by the resistence of whites to do the dirtiest, hottest jobs), racism was still pervasive at Bethlehem Steel.

Just two months after the launching of the *Frederick Douglass*, 125 white riveters went on strike to protest an agreement Bethlehem Steel had signed to train fifteen blacks as riveters. When the company dropped the black trainees, 600 black workers walked out. When they were reinstated, 7,000 white employees walked out. As this stand-off continued, the U.S. men were fighting and dying overseas. Finally, a compromise agreement was reached based strictly on seniority with each department. The long-term results, as Olson writes, was "a structure of hundreds of watertight compartments of personnel" which simply hardened the caste structure that seemed fluid during the war.[82]

On June 16, 1944, a near-riot took place at Bethlehem Steel. In an article that appeared in *People* on June 22nd, Fred Weisgal is especially interested in the biased coverage of this event by the *Sun*. He writes:

> Last Friday a Negro was beaten and arrested on the grounds of the Bethlehem-Fairfield Shipyards. Baltimoreans read the story of the beating in The Sun. But like many of the stories in the local press, not all the facts were printed....Using a heading: "TEAR GAS USED TO QUELL

---

[81] Quotes and information in this and the next three paragraphs from Reutter, pp. 347-352.
[82] Olson, pp. 363-364

MELEE" The Sun ran a smaller caption, "Hundreds Of Negroes Figure In Row Over Arrest."...The Facts: There were not only Negroes present but hundreds of white people, and the row was not a racial disturbance. It was a very simple matter of company violence and brutality.

The article then points to the *Sun*'s bias in ignoring the presence of union officials, and quoting only Bethlehem Steel officials. It also questions the *Sun*'s contention that tear gas was necessary when the police were unable to hold back the crowd.

Note there was no violence on the part of the crowd; no signs of force. But a "score of plant police" were unable to hold the crowd back...Doesn't it seem strange that tear gas must be used [here], while a few policemen can hold back a crowd of thousands watching a fire?...Witnesses have stated that as many as twenty and perhaps thirty [tear gas bombs] were shot into the crowd. About a hundred people had to be treated for eyeburn....

By the way, the Negro who figured in the beating was 48 years old and weighed about 115 pounds. He had been out sick because a weight had dropped on one of his arms, rendering that arm useless for work. Yet, this 115-pounder was made to appear as a terrific Joe Louis, beating up guards and police by the dozens.

•••

Meanwhile, Charlie Parrish is having his own problems at Bethlehem Steel. After he was finally promoted in 1943, he worked for five years in the "stack-and-bin gang", always hoping eventually for a promotion to millwright. It was 1948 and the War had ended by the time such a vacancy occurred and Charlie thought his long hoped for promotion to millwright was about to be fulfilled. Instead, his seniority was ignored and a white worker, Tricinelli, with nine years less seniority, was designated to fill the position. Charlie filed another grievance. But this time he lost in all the first four grievance levels, setting in motion for the first time an openly racially-based case to be undertaken at arbitration.

The back and forth arguments were heated, Charlie admitting he had ended his education at 5th grade and that he could not read blueprints. But the questions remained, *Did he need to? Why hadn't he been offered training in the technical*

"Gas School" which had never enrolled a black? Why had Tricinelli, with 14 years experience as a repairman, been offered formal training, while Charlie, with 20 years, was not? The union concluded, "Racial Discrimination."

The arbitrator disagreed and on May 25, 1949, dismissed the union's charge, saying that management was within its rights under the USWA contract to decide placement of its workers so long as their decisions were based on objective criteria. Charlie was angry, felt the arbitrator in essence gave management the right to continue its all too obvious and long-standing racist practices in training and promotions.

However, Charlie bided his time, and a year later, in 1950, when another opening for millwright occurred, he again applied. This time, after the master mechanic and foreman conferred and talked to Charlie, they reluctantly gave him a chance. If they hoped, or at least expected, Charlie to fail, he disappointed them.

Reutter does not tell us what happened to Charlie after this promotion, but it is probably safe to say that he spent the rest of his working life at Sparrows Point...probably without any additional promotions. Fourteen years later, "on April 14, 1964, at the annual meeting of Bethlehem Steel, a stockholder asked Edmund F. Martin, chairman of the board of directors, why no blacks could be found in management positions. 'We would like to employ Negroes in top jobs, but we can't get them,' was the executive's answer." Charlie could have given a more credible answer.[83]

It would probably be fair to say that as rough a time as Charlie had had, he had done well compared to most blacks employed by Bethlehem Steel, even in his experience with the union. The latter may not have discriminated, per se, but in an industry with about one sixth of its workers black, the United Steelworkers national union had few paid blacks in staff positions, and none at all on its executive board. Perhaps at least partly as a consequence, they did little to change the allocation of jobs at the plant.

Blacks in the plants were disproportionately among the unskilled laborers—comprising 28% of all unskilled

---

[83] Reutter, p. 352

steelworkers but only 6% of the skilled workers. Thus, at the huge Baltimore Sparrows Point Plant of Bethlehem Steel, most of the blacks were employed in all-black or overwhelmingly-black departments. Construction, refuse disposal, and maintenance workers ranged between 94% and 100 % blacks; employers in the unpleasant blast-furnace department were 81% black. But skilled job categories, such as lubrication, pattern shop, machine shop, and tin and strip mills, were between 99% and 100% white. [84]

•••

At Sparrows Point in the early 1960s there were about 7,300 blacks out of a work force of 22,300. Conditions at this plant were still so patently discriminatory that as late as 1967 "the U.S. government ordered the integration of locker rooms and rest rooms." [85] John Strohmeyer tells of his tour of the plant prior to that:

> I was appalled to see "white" and "colored" toilets, separate locker rooms, and even "white" and "colored" drinking fountains. The tolerance of this policy not only provided an insight into the conscience of the company but also suggested the United Steelworkers Union was a partner in discrimination. I wondered how much support a black could expect from his union if he filed a grievance.
>
> No major company dependent on federal contracts was more vulnerable than Bethlehem to the sweeping changes that engulfed the nation after passage of the Civil Rights Act [in 1964].[86]

1964 saw the coming together of a few disgruntled blacks, dissatisfied with their union, to demand more job opportunities at all levels, in the plants and in the union itself, and they made a few gains, but "it was the leverage afforded by the federal government rather than the union that resolved the seniority problem."[87] Even then, it did not come either easily or quickly but followed long and protracted court battles initiated by the NAACP, demonstrations by CORE activists, and negotiations

---

[84] Meier & Rudwick, *From Plantation...*, pp. 330-331
[85] Meier & Rudwick, *From Plantation...*, p.331
[86] Strohmeyer, p.89.
[87] Meier & Rudwick, *From Plantation...*, p. 331

that involved the U.S. Justice Department, Labor Department and the Equal Employment Opportunities Commission (EEOC) often seemingly at loggerheads with each other as to acceptable terms for a settlement with Bethlehem Steel.

This writer remembers the day in July 1966 when a worker from Bethlehem Steel came to the Baltimore CORE office[88] for a meeting with Irwin Auerbach, one of our volunteers. It was very secretive, an aura of fear transparent, both aware that management kept tabs on complainers; the powers on top denying promotions to the disloyal, withholding business contracts from outsiders. The complaint that day was by a laborer in an all-black department who had received a temporary promotion to supervisor, and then, when his contract was up, was demoted back to his former, lower paying and less responsible, rank and file position. No reason was given; he had proved well-qualified for the job. A call to the union resulted in a claim that supervisors were out of their jurisdiction.

Members of Baltimore CORE's Economics' Committee—Irwin Auerbach, John Burleigh and Larry Ageloff, all then employees at the national Social Security offices in Baltimore—then began to organize Bethlehem Steel's blacks to protest the blatant segregation they faced daily, as well as the more insidious seniority policies that kept them in the dirtiest, most dangerous and poorest paid jobs. In May, after first marching around the plant, 350 workers boarded seven buses for the trip to Washington, D.C. There they marched back and forth in front of the Labor Department demanding to see the Secretary of Labor. Finally the undersecretary came out on the steps to talk with them. TV cameras were whirring as he made all kinds of promises. But the department's investigation dragged on for so long it became sort of a myth.[89]

It was 1971 before the NAACP "secured in the federal courts modification of the separate lines of progression at

---

[88] More will be said of Baltimore CORE, its origin and activities, in later sections.

[89] Strohmeyer, p. 94 and James Dilts, "The Warning Trumpet," *Sun Magazine*, December 1, 1968. p. 48

Bethlehem Steel's Lackawanna, New York plant,"[90] and 1973 before the "government launched an all-out assault. The company became the largest industrial facility ever ordered by the Labor Department to correct discrimination against minority workers or face cancellation of all federal contracts." [91] It was 1974 before "a sweeping agreement arranged by federal agencies, the industry and the union acceded to the dismantling of the discriminatory provision of the seniority system." [92]

> The steel industry satisfied the government by agreeing to the most expensive civil rights settlement in history. The nine steel companies consented to pay $30.9 million in back wages immediately and about $25 million more in the next two years to about forty thousand minority-group workers in 255 facilities [including Bethlehem Steel at Sparrows Point]. This amounted to an average payment of $700 in compensation for the amount each minority worker was underpaid during the previous two and a half years. Further, the steel companies also agreed that one-half the future openings in skilled jobs would be filled by minorities and women until their numbers equaled their overall percentage of employment in each plant.[93]

"Although black protest leaders in and out of the union have asserted that the agreement did not go far enough toward redressing inequities and its provisions have not been fully implemented, it nevertheless marked an important precedent."[94] An industry "renowned for its arrogant protection of self-interest, provided the government with its biggest impetus ever to end such discrimination in all other industries."[95]

•••

The steel worker's hard-fought and protracted victory seemed hollow when only a year later, in 1975, lack of orders forced Sparrows Point to work at only two-thirds

---

[90] Meier & Rudick, *From Plantation...*, p. 331
[91] Strohmeyer, p. 94
[92] Meier & Rudick, *From Plantation...*, p. 331
[93] Strohmeyer, p. 96
[94] Meier & Rudick, *From Plantation...*, p. 331
[95] Strohmeyer, p. 97

capacity. As usual, it was women, youths, and blacks who suffered the most: "last hired, first fired."[96] By the 1980s with the U.S. steel industry in decline worldwide, employment at Sparrows Point declined even more rapidly, from about 16,500 production workers in 1980 to about 8,000 at the end of the decade; the union was unable to protect jobs, benefits or wages.

The last vestiges of the Point as a company town had already ended in 1975 when the company demolished its last remaining houses. Though Bethlehem Steel is still there, it is no longer "the most complete and comprehensive steel town in the East." It barely gives a hint of the power it once wielded over the lives of its workers, and over the economy of the whole City.[97]

---

[96] See Olson, p. 366
[97] Reutter, p. 439/

The Great Depression

In Maryland in 1930 blacks numbered 276,379, or 16.9% of the state's population of 1,631,526; in Baltimore the numbers were 142,106 blacks, 17.6% of the city's population of 804,874. By 1940, according to the Sixth Decennial Census, the numbers in Baltimore were 165,843 blacks, or 19.3% of the 859,100 total.[98] It had "the fourth-largest black population and contained the largest percentage of blacks of the nation's ten largest cities;...nearly 60%...born in Maryland, most of them having migrated to Baltimore from rural areas."[99] These are the years that encompass the Great Depression; a time when fifteen million Americans, black and white, were unemployed; a time when those still with jobs constantly faced the prospect that they, too, would suddenly see their source of livelihood disappear.

The impact of the 1930's depression on blacks was devastating, as has been the case in all periods of depression in this country. The pronounced job discrimination of the 1850s that had been partially overcome in the "boom times of the 1920s", again became rampant. "By 1932 the black bourgeoisie in Baltimore was as insignificant numerically as it had been in the 1890s,"[100] while the number of unemployed blacks, unable adequately to provide for their families, had markedly increased. By 1934, at least 40% of Baltimore's black population were on relief compared to only 13% of its whites. The menial jobs once held by blacks were either eliminated as "unnecessary luxuries" or given to whites desperate for work.

•••

When Franklin D. Roosevelt took office in March 1933, the city and state were ambivalent in regard to the many

---

[98] Franklin and McNeil, p. 58. These 1930 figures for Baltimore are notably different than those this writer quoted earlier for 1900, found in Paul using figures of the Bureau of Industrial Statistics and Information of Maryland. *Was there an influx of 60,725 blacks from the South during this 30 year period?*

[99] Argersinger, p. 15.

[100] Farrar, p. 90.

programs soon put in place by the new administration; programs such as the Civil Works Administration (CWA), Federal Emergency Relief Administration (FERA), National Emergency Council (NEC), National Recovery Administration (NRA), National Youth Administration (NYA), Public Housing Administration (PHA), Public Works Administration (PWA), and Works Progress Administration (WPA).

"Baltimore's Democratic Mayor, Howard Jackson, who served the city between 1923 and 1927 and from 1931 to 1943," like many in his party was "not particularly receptive either to the notion of public responsibility or to the people [the New Deal programs] would benefit....[H]e consistently maligned the government for interfering in city problems and emerged in the 1930s as one of the New Deal's harshest critics....Yet Jackson was not above using the New Deal to his political or personal advantage." [101]

One might have thought blacks would have had some influence with Mayor Jackson, despite their traditional support of the Republican party, after they were encouraged by the *Afro* to vote for him in the very contentious 1923 election. The newspaper had taken this position after the Republican mayor, William Broening, had allowed the KKK to march in Baltimore in 1922 despite Governor Albert Ritchie's having refused to grant them a permit to parade and twice denied them the use of the Baltimore armory.

To the dismay of Catholics and Jews alike, the Klan that year was actively recruiting new members, and the working-class community of Hampden was supporting an active Klan local, their clergy cooperating with Klan members. [102] Baltimore, rich in Klan enemies—Catholics, immigrants, Jews, blacks and union members—offered fertile grounds for recruitment, and it took some time before the city deprived Klan members of anonymity by passing an anti-masking ordinance. Fortunately, internal scandals led to the Klan's demise before "it became as dominant a force in Baltimore as it did in other cities, and a gradual return of prosperity resulted in a distinct decline in the limited

---

[101] Argersinger, p. 12-13 & 181-182
[102] Argersinger, p. 7 & 179

popularity that the group did enjoy."[103]

The black vote might have counted for more if the considerable number of blacks who had recently arrived in Baltimore had not been virtually deprived of their ability to vote by the law, passed in 1902, that required the potential voter to appear in court *a year in advance* to register their intent. Enforcement of the law was arbitrary, but most forceful in the case of blacks and immigrants.[104] And so the black vote changed nothing in Jackson's general ambivalence to the federal programs nor in his practiced discrimination in their implementation.

Whether it was a "relief", housing or jobs programs, Baltimore tried either to illegally exclude blacks from the benefits offered, or, at best, to offer them the least possible.[105] The *Afro-American* was one strong voice that "consistently exposed these abuses as well as supported black community groups, the unemployed, labor unions, and progressive white organizations in their efforts to ensure fair, generous, and non-racist administration of local New Deal programs."[106]

There were constant fights between the city, state and federal governments over their respective responsibilities for funding the various programs, and it inevitably was the most needy blacks, living in "congested colored" and "slum areas," who were the first to be cut from the city's relief roles when they felt they didn't have sufficient funding. Transients, often referred to as "loafers," were confined to monitored and guarded "prison-like" camps in the Aberdeen area (*bringing to mind the camps where Japanese-Americans would be confined not too many years hence*). The camps for blacks were far inferior to those for whites, consisting of outdoor shelters without walls or heat, and without toilets. Mayor Jackson simply ignored protests organized first by the city's ministers, and later by other groups.[107]

---

[103] Chapelle, p. 185

[104] Argersinger, p. 13

[105] A study by the Urban League in 1934 found that "black families typically received smaller relief sums and were removed from relief rosters before whites." Ryon, p. 19

[106] Farrar, p. 92.

[107] Argersinger, p.37 & 121

Whites especially resented blacks in the competition for jobs, and Mayor Jackson was slow in implementing available job programs, objecting to the matching funds required by the Federal Emergency Relief Administration (FERA), and to the regulation of employee hours, wages and working conditions required of employers by the National Industrial Recovery Act (NIRA). Under another program, the Civil Works Administration (CWA), blacks received only 28% of the jobs even though they made up "about 42% of the city's total relief population."[108]

The WPA which replaced the CWA in 1935, focused on work-relief, a fact the city found objectionable, and thus sought and received from the federal government permission to merge it with the PWA program that emphasized projects of "lasting benefit." Unfortunately, this resulted in fewer job opportunities in total— "thirty thousand employables remained unemployed."[109] Black women were relegated to training programs for domestics, and black men, "traditionally excluded from the building trades, suffered from the city's emphasis on major construction."[110]

Despite local officials simply ignoring the federal mandate that prohibited discrimination, the efforts of a number of activists did produce a few jobs for blacks—on the Montebello tunnel system, on short-term paving projects, and in a number of white-collar projects. But racism and fear of economic competition led whites to resent blacks in even these few jobs. They were called "gin drunk niggers," and a city magistrate charged that "darkies" were taking taxicabs to and from work.[111]

Black youth also encountered discrimination in the New Deal programs. Even when the Civilian Conservation Corps (CCC), introduced in 1935, could not fill its quota with white youth, it nonetheless denied young blacks the opportunity to participate. Even after repeated protests by the Urban League and intervention by the federal authorities finally "persuaded state officials to organize two camps for 500 black youths,"

---

[108] Argersinger, p. 64
[109] Argersinger, p. 67.
[110] Argersinger, p. 79
[111] Argersinger, p. 82

248 others from relief families, referred to officials by the League, were left without help, and a substantial number of black youths were denied even an application. Those lucky enough to become members of the CCC camp still had to face racial hostility and in 1938 several from Baltimore were "wounded by shotgun blast while at a prayer meeting in Chestertown, Maryland."[112]

Despite being discriminated in nearly every New Deal program, blacks appreciated the federal government's concern for them, and many voted Democratic for the first time in the 1936 Presidential election. As one state Democratic leader noted, "'the colored race is more in favor of our party than they have ever been,' adding that he had received many 'requests from them desiring to organize, cooperate, and have headquarters in various sections of the city.'" Roosevelt won over 68% of the Baltimoreans vote in the 1936 election; but in the two black wards it was 70% and 88%. In contrast, Mayor Jackson lost in both those wards.[113]

•••

During this period a number of those blacks who had managed to achieve middle class status despite the odds committed themselves to helping those blacks who had not been so fortunate. "Over 400 social clubs and more than 200 churches in the city's black community attempted to spread the message of the necessity for a more enlightened and equitable government."[114] Black fraternal groups did much to provide assistance in black neighborhoods when other programs did not. But the actions of two Baltimoreans, beginning in the summer of 1931, stand out. These two seemed destined from an early age to become leaders of the Civil Rights movement.

One, eighteen year old Juanita Jackson, had just graduated from the University of Pennsylvania and could not find a job. She was the daughter of Lillie Mae Carroll Jackson, a graduate of the Colored High and Normal School where she

---

[112] Argersinger, p. 86
[113] Argersinger, p. 14 & 188-189
[114] Argersinger, p. 14

received teacher training and taught second grade at the old Biddle Street School for one year before marrying and traveling with her husband around the United States. They returned to Baltimore in 1919 and she gradually became relatively well-off as a property owner. Lillian had sent her two daughters (Virginia was interested in art) to colleges in Pennsylvania after they'd been rejected by the University of Maryland; admonishing them "not to come back and separate yourselves into an intelligent few, but to give back so our people can be free." Juanita began to show her commitment to changing the status quo while still at the University, successfully leading an effort to end racial segregation in the dormitories.

The other, Clarence Mitchell, had graduated in 1931 from Lincoln University in Oxford, Pennsylvania. He'd become interested in his people's struggle for equality when, as a reporter for the *Baltimore Afro-American,* he'd witnessed the lynching of a black man on the Eastern Shore. At the time he met Juanita, he had just recently become national NAACP's chief lobbyist—a role he'd continue to play with increasing import for most of his life. His association with this office, and the fact that the local NAACP by then had become almost moribund, would explain national's interest in the soon-to-be-organized City-Wide Young People's Forum, right from its inception. The symbiotic relationship of these two organizations was responsible, in the long run, for reactivating the long-dormant local NAACP chapter.

> The Forum served as a training ground for civil rights advocacy and the conduit for information regarding recommendations or programs of the national NAACP. The emphasis of the national NAACP on using the Constitution to obtain legal recognition of civil rights both inspired the Forum members and affirmed the propriety of the Forum's activism.[115]

Clarence Mitchell and Juanita Jackson, who had been unable to find a job after her graduation and return to Baltimore, first met at a meeting held at the home of Elizabeth Coit Gilman, daughter of the first president of

---

[115] Franklin & McNeil, p. 73

Johns Hopkins University. Elizabeth, like her father, was an independent thinker who had become a prominent Socialist. She regularly opened her home in one of Baltimore's most exclusive neighborhoods to the self-help Community Workshop for the Unemployed, as well as to a well-attended Open Forum that discussed all sorts of ideas and concerns of the day. On one occasion, when none of Baltimore's hotels would allow sixteen whites and six blacks to dine together, she held the dinner in her home that celebrated the tenth anniversary of the liberal magazine *The Nation*, edited by Oswald Garrison Villard, a founding member of the NAACP.[116] All these "subversive" activities had made her persona non grata in Baltimore's elitist white society.

The meeting Mitchell and Jackson had attended at Gilman's proved to be the inspiration for them to organize the City-Wide Young People's Forum, which held its first public meeting on Friday, October 2, 1931. Soon hundreds of young blacks, ages sixteen to twenty-four, from all over the city, representing working class, middle class and upper class, were spending their Friday evenings together at the Forum—in the first year, meetings averaged five hundred. The Forum offered all Baltimore's black youth, frustrated at their inability to find jobs, something challenging to do and to think about.

In early elections, Juanita was made president and Howard Cornish, Maceo Howard, Elmer Henderson, and Clarence Mitchell were made vice presidents—all college students or graduates. But young people with less elitist backgrounds, representing as many as twenty black churches and six Protestant denominations, were appointed to other positions. And, in order to remain on good terms with the adults, one was elected as an officer and two as advisors. Juanita's mother, Lillie Carroll Jackson, assumed the role of general adviser, assisting Forum members with everything from arranging meeting places to advising on "how to maintain a progressive, 'palatable,' community-support."[117]

The Forum's undertakings were multi-faceted:

[116] See Watson, pp. 97-98
[117] Franklin & McNeil, pp. 60-61

1. They sustained for a decade, from 1931 to 1941, a weekly lecture series that included such speakers as Congressman Oscar DePriest; W.E.B. DuBois [the merits of industrial, biracial unionism was a hot topic in debates he initiated], Mary McLeod Bethune, president of Bethune Cookman College; Charles Hamilton Houston and Thurgood Marshall, leading civil rights attorneys; Walter White and Roy Wilkins, NAACP executives; James Weldon Johnson, poet-professor; and E. Franklin Frazier, social scientist.

2. They joined other groups in protesting racial injustice and denials of equal rights that they believed were in violation of the constitution.

3. They joined others in holding political candidates and incumbents accountable for their positions on issues that affected racial discrimination in Baltimore, the state and the nation. In 1934 they supported the candidacy of their own Clarence Mitchell for election to Maryland's House of Delegates.

4. They sponsored a number of programs designed to develop leadership among black youths, such as hosting the annual "Inter-Collegiate Oratorical, Vocal and Instrumental" contest; arranging a biracial "Good Will Tour" of black businesses, institutions, etc.; and organizing "Forum Frolics" that provided a chance for blacks of all socioeconomic backgrounds to interact in a recreational setting and discover mutual interests.

5. After consultation with adult advisers and community leaders, as well as some polling of the interests of the black community in general, in 1933 they initiated a number of employment projects.

With the Depression directly affecting job-opportunities for the young people and their families, early-on the Forum made employment their primary concern. And because of "the scramble for jobs, the movement developed and became a catalyst for other protest activities."[118]

One of the Forum's first objectives was to force the publicly-funded Enoch Pratt Free Library to train and hire blacks for staff positions—six thousand signatures were collected protesting this unconstitutional discrimination. Success, however, was slow in coming. Hundreds of black

---

[118] Watson, p. 90

applicants had been refused training before, in 1945, a federal judge, in *Kerr v. Enoch Pratt Free Library*,[119] finally ruled in favor of Louise Kerr, a secretary of the Forum, in her demand that the library train her for a librarianship position.

The U.S. Court of Appeals for the 4th Circuit reversed the ruling of District Court, Judge Chesnut declaring that since Baltimore and Maryland were the primary source of the library's operating funds, it was an *"instrumentality of the state"* and hence fell within the purview of the 14th Amendment of the Constitution.[120] Further, Judge Soper, in writing the appelate court's opinion, found that since the state provided no equal facility for training librarians, Pratt was in violation of the Amendment's equal protection clause in not admitting blacks to its library training classes.[121] The black attorney, W.A.C. Hughes, Jr., had been the guiding force for the young people as they fought for their rights in this case.

A second Forum objective, to increase the number of black welfare workers, undertaken in conjunction with the Baltimore Urban League, had a more immediate result. During 1933 and 1934, the Baltimore Emergency Relief Commission appointed sixteen blacks as social workers, including two forum members.

Another Forum objective was to increase the number of blacks employed in retail stores serving the black community. As early as January 1931 the *Afro-American* had noted the dominance of white ownership and white employees in the stores along Pennsylvania Avenue, the very heart of the black community. But there had been little response to their calling for black organizations to push for the hiring of more blacks until 1933. It was then that the Forum had set this as a goal and had established boycotts and picketing as an effective tool for achieving the goal—

---

[119] Kerr et al v. Enoch Pratt Free Library of Baltimore City et al, 54 F. Supp. 514 (D.C.D.Md. 1944) reversed 149 F. 212 (C.C.A. 4th, 1945) certiorari denied 66 S. Ct. 26.

[120] As we've seen previously, the equal protection afforded by the 14th Amendment had been interpreted to protect against state actions, though not against private/individual actions.

[121] See Olson p. 365; Franklin & McNeil, pp. 64-65; Levin p. 494-495

long before the 1960s Civil Rights Movement made the tactic famous.

In November 1933 the young people started their campaign by trying to persuade the manager of an A & P store in their community which served only blacks, but employed only whites, to hire blacks. When this failed utterly, they adopted the slogan "Buy Where You Can Work," and on November 18th, with strong support from the community whose trust they had earned, enthusiastically began their boycott and picketing of the store. Soon, however, the Forum members extended their campaign to include all the A & P stores in black neighborhoods. Juanita's mother, Lillie Carroll Jackson, headed the contingent of adults who supported the young people, some marching, others providing meals and a place to rest.

Within weeks the A & P's were hurting financially as a result of the almost total boycott by their usual black clientele. As a consequence, in December the A & P's adopted a new hiring policy that resulted in-eight young blacks being hired either full or part-time as clerks.

Encouraged by their success with the A & P chain of stores, the young people moved their campaign on to the stores in the 1700 block of Pennsylvania Avenue that depended on blacks for much of their retail business, but where virtually none were employed. The *Afro* ran articles exclaiming that with these merchants deriving so much of their income from black customers, they ought to return some of the money to the black community through hiring at least some blacks to work in their stores. They asked the two sides in the dispute to compromise their differences.[122]

However, compromise was far from the minds of either the stores' owners and managers or the protesters. Unlike the settlement they'd agreed on with the A &P's, or the position of the *Afro* which was not championing all-black employees, this time the picketers wanted it all. They refused an offer of 50% black employees and the day and night picketing—sometimes hundreds at a time—continued. Virtually the whole black community was outraged when

---

[122] See Farrar, pp. 90-91

the merchants sought and received a temporary injunction from the local court in December 1933.

For a year the experienced black attorneys, W.A.C. Hughes, Jr. and Warner McGuinn, fought the injunction in vain, finally losing in March 1934 when Judge Albert S.J. Owens of the Circuit Court of Baltimore granted a permanent injunction that barred picketing, labeling it a "criminal conspiracy." Though Owens didn't object to their demeanor, calling the hundreds of black picketers "respectable, well educated and essentially religious," he declared that their presence day and night clearly was disturbing the merchants' businesses. He proclaimed that however commendable their cause might be, it could not "justify their actions in this case."[123]

Clarence Mitchell, speaking for the Forum, and their attorney, Hughes, labeled his decision a step back to the "stone age of economics." Mitchell proclaimed that Judge Owens "did not administer justice in the case, but I do believe that he tried to administer the law. His knowledge of the law, however, is apparently not such as teaches him to weigh the forces of hunger, moral decay, idealism, and lack of employment opportunity when making a decision."[124]

Judge Owens' decision did not end the boycott of stores on Pennsylvania Avenue nor did the April 2, 1935 decision of the Maryland Court of Appeals which upheld the injunction against picketing. It held that this was not a labor dispute but "a racial or social question," and thus the rules of labor disputes did not apply. However, in making the injunction against picketing permanent, it permitted "publicizing the boycott in a non-coercive fashion."[125] Thus it was that the *Afro* pointed out "that the use of newspapers, handbills, meetings, and posters to publicize the consumer boycott ...was not prohibited by the court. [And using these], eventually the boycott succeeded; blacks began to obtain employment on Pennsylvania Avenue."[126] How long it took to surpass the 50% offered by the owners

[123] Watson, pp. 91-93
[124] Watson, pp. 91-93
[125] Bell, p. 451
[126] Farrar, p. 92

early-on is not stated.

Three years after this Maryland decision, the U.S. Supreme Court ruled on a Washington, D.C. case almost identical to Maryland's: *New Negro Alliance v. Sanitary Grocery Company*.[127] Like the Forum, the Negro Alliance, a black mutual improvement group, had requested stores that served blacks also to employ them and when they refused, picketed with signs reading much like the Forum's: "Do your part! Buy where you can work! No Negroes employed here!"[128]

In this case the U.S. Supreme Court reversed the lower courts, upholding of the issuance of an injunction against picketing. Unlike the Maryland Appeals Court, they held that the fact that the dispute was "racial" in nature did *not* remove it from the scope of labor disputes. Thus, "the Supreme Court found that the racial message was entitled to a special heightened protection as compared to a similar labor boycott."[129]

This ruling opened the way for "black carpenters, bricklayers, painters, plasterers, plumbers, electricians, and workers in other trades" to use picketing as a tool to obtain work.[130] It does not seem, however, that skilled black workers had made any noticeable progress by 1942-1943 when the country began its build-up to meet the demands necessitated by our entry into WW II.

•••

Franklin & McNeil in their study of the City-Wide Young People's Forum conclude that much of the group's success was due to the fact that its members were admired for their "principled conduct, militancy and activism....While serving as a catalyst for political action, employment, and civil rights activism" the Forum's young people overcame the "general despair" of the Great Depression and changed "the conditions of life for African-Americans in their city, and improve[d]

---

[127] *New Negro Alliance v. Sanitary Grocery Company*, 303 U.S. 552 (1938)

[128] Bell, p. 451

[129] Bell, p. 451.

[130] *New Negro Alliance v. Sanitary Grocery Company*, 303 U.S. 552 (1938). Also Franklin & McNeil, pp. 65-66 & Watson, p. 92

intergenerational relations in the African-American community." [131]

The authors also point to the importance of the role played by the broader community of parents, teachers, clergy and other professionals who listened to and advised the young people; the emphasis these adults placed on education while discouraging idleness; their firm rejection of theories of inferiority; and, last but not least, the financial support they extended to the young people.

They do not suggest a reason for the group's demise in 1941; for varying reasons most groups do disintegrate over time. In the Forum's case, it is quite possible that its members had simply grown older, found jobs, and, in any case, felt confident that their activism they initiated would live on under the leadership of the no-longer-dormant Baltimore chapter of the NAACP. It had revived in 1935, at least partially as a result of their activism with the Forum.

---

[131] Franklin & McNeil, pp. 72-75

The Troika in Action

The roots of the NAACP, as indicated earlier, can be traced to the Brotherhood for Liberty, organized in 1885 by Reverend Harvey Johnson, the black minister of Baltimore's Union Baptist, followed by the Niagara Movement spearheaded by W.E.B. DuBois in 1905. Both the Brotherhood and the Niagara Movement had challenged Booker T. Washington's prevailing gradualist, accommodating approach to civil rights. Whereas he advised blacks to avoid politics and civil rights protests, and instead focus on learning a useful trade, these groups sought to unite blacks who would regularly speak out against all aspects of racial discrimination and would openly agitate for their full constitutional rights.

It is not surprising to learn that Reverend Harvey Johnson was present at the founding meeting of the Niagara Movement at Fort Erie, Ontario, in 1905 and remained one of its keenest supporters. He'd already proved he had no stomach for Washington's compromises in the pursuit of civil rights, blaming "this compromise business" as the cause of the world's being "so shamy and frothy in every fibre."

Other prominent Baltimoreans active with the Movement, some as officers, were the Reverends G. R. Waller and George Bragg, Jr.; Mason Hawkins, a local school teacher; Harry Cummings, the lawyer we've already met as the first black elected to the Baltimore City Council; Ashbie Hawkins, editor of a local Niagara journal, the *Lancet*; and John H. Murphy, then-head of Baltimore's largest black newspaper, then called the *Afro-American Ledger* (in 1900 it had merged with an earlier black newspaper, the *Ledger*, but soon after dropped this from its name).

The rivalry between supporters of Booker T. Washington's philosophy of accommodation and W.E.B. Dubois' philosophy of fighting for full participation of blacks in every aspect of the nation's life led to many confrontations during the NAACP's founding meetings, and their rivalry continued until the former's death in 1915. (DuBois died in 1963.) In November 1962, the NAACP's magazine, *The Crisis*, declared these two as having become "a prototype for cleavage in the leadership image itself." It wrote:

> Leaders have been and continue to be appraised as either "militant" or "accommodating," as fighters or as "Uncle Toms," and the desire to avoid the appearance of the latter sometimes becomes a major influence in leadership decisions. The image of Booker Washington that has survived for most Negroes is [as] the preacher of doctrines of subservience, the darling of white people anxious to keep the Negro in subordinate status....[DuBois] remains for many the arch exponent of uncompromising insistence on Negro rights, and contradictions of fact are unlikely to impair his inspirational importance in the fashioning of today's militants—including many who have only the foggiest idea of what DuBois actually said and did in the day of his leadership.

It's unclear exactly when or why the Brotherhood disappeared, but the Niagara Movement, which had been composed primarily of a small nucleus of upper class Negro journalists, lawyers, teachers and clergymen, was absorbed into the National Association for the Advancement of Colored People (NAACP) soon after the latter's structure was formalized in 1910. Two years later, in April 1912, with the Reverends Johnson and Waller taking the lead, an NAACP chapter was chartered in Baltimore—a time when such an activist organization was badly needed.[132] Then, in 1914, the national NAACP held its sixth annual conference in Baltimore, "the 'farthest South' that the conference had met." [133]

The conference did not go entirely smoothly, ending on a decidedly discordant note when the delegates found themselves locked out of Johns Hopkins' McCoy Hall where their last session was scheduled to meet. Discussing the event after retreating to Bethel AME Church, some of the delegates wanted to censure the university for what they believed was an act of discrimination; others chose to believe the university officials who claimed it was simply a misunderstanding with the committee that had arranged the meeting. Board members Joel Spingarn, W. Ashbie Hawkins and Bishop John Hurst were especially doubtful of this explanation, believing the registrar the "chief culprit" responsible for a "plot hatched in

---

[132] Information from Paul, pp. 285-286.
[133] Kellogg, p. 127-128.

advance" by students who were determined that a group preaching social equality would never speak at their university.[134]

It's not difficult to believe that the university administration itself was behind the "lockout." It was the very next year, 1915, that Carl J. Murphy, a graduate of Harvard and owner of the *Afro-American* newspaper, was refused admission to the Hopkins' summer school, because, they claimed, no provision had been made for colored students. When he protested, President Frank J. Goodenow replied that it was the educational policy of Maryland to provide separate schools. Since the university received a considerable appropriation from the state, he could not depart from the official policy.[135]

Whether or not all this contentiousness was a factor in the subsequent demise of the Baltimore Chapter of the NAACP is not clear, but it had had trouble from the very beginning "attracting members, finding competent leadership, and developing a consistent strategy to fight racial oppression." Some had hoped that Carl Murphy would be its "savior," but for reasons undetermined, he never became its president.[136]

•••

The Reverend William Alexander had founded the *Afro-American* newspaper in 1892 intending to use it as a vehicle for encouraging blacks to become more militant politically. In 1896 John H. Murphy, Sr., a former slave, and his wife, Martha Murphy, took it over. Since then the paper has remained in the hands of Murphys. In 1922 after John Murphy's death, it had passed to the Harvard and Howard University educated Carl Murphy. Under his skilled direction, the *Afro-American* grew from a Baltimore weekly to a national chain.[137]

However, despite the fact that the *Afro* was regularly in the forefront in the fight for equality, it did not succeed in the early part of 20th Century in making black presence really felt in Baltimore. Since the NAACP had become dormant soon after its founding in 1912, there was no organized group to

---

[134] Kellogg, pp. 196-197
[135] Kellogg, pp. 196-197
[136] Farrar, pp. 179-180
[137] Fee et al, pp. 67-68.

counter the mandate of the white-dominated Interracial
Commission created in 1927. The Commission encouraged
black "thrift, industry, education, sobriety, and all the virtues,"
and in five years of annual reports repeatedly congratulated the
state on its "harmonious race relations."[138] Black voices might
have been lost entirely during these years except for its
"politically minded ministers," a few black leaders who had
become "toughened rather than demoralized," and Carl Murphy
at the *Afro-American*.[139]

Then, in 1935 Murphy, a member of national NAACP's
board of directors, took the lead in reactivating its local chapter.
Impressed with Lillie May Carroll Jackson's leadership of the
adults who'd supported the City-Wide Young People's Forum,
and wanting the *Afro-American* to be known as a supporter of
the struggle for civil rights, Murphy encouraged her to run for
the presidency and continued to support her after her election.
Beginning that same year and through 1958, Murphy also
regularly spelled out his goals for the movement in his paper:[140]

1.   Colored policemen, policewomen and firemen.
2.   Colored representatives on City, County and State
Boards of Education.
3.   Equal salaries for equal work for school teachers without
regard to color or sex.
4.   Colored members of boards of state institutions where
inmates are colored.
5.   The organization of labor unions among all groups of
colored workers.
6.   A university and agricultural college for colored people
supported by the state.
7.   Closer cooperation between farmers and the state and
federal farm agents.

Murphy was not interested in "overthrowing" the
"establishment", but wanted blacks to become part of it. The
series the paper ran mid-1942 entitled "Nazi of the Week"
reflected the irony, recognized by blacks, that they were
fighting a war for democracy abroad while still treated as
unequals at home. Sounding bitter, the paper called the

---

[138] Callcott, George, pp. 145.
[139] Callcott, George, pp. 145-146.
[140] Shoemaker, p. 267.

American organizations that refused blacks employment or kept them in menial jobs, "Hitler's allies," and accused them of sharing Hitler's view that whites composed the "Master Race." It went further and called the Red Cross "fascist" for keeping its donated blood segregated by race.[141]

•••

After assuming leadership of the local NAACP chapter, Lillie May Carroll Jackson quickly allied herself with Murphy and the black ministers who were part of the powerful Interdenominational Ministerial Alliance, creating a troika that proved to be an effective and strong force in Baltimore's and Maryland's fight for civil rights. To strengthen the local chapter, Lillie replaced the "polite preacher-teacher intellectual" board members "who feared she moved too fast and alienated too many" with labor leaders and longshoremen. She oversaw the addition of almost 2,000 new members in its first year under her leadership and, by 1946, the once defunct chapter had become the largest in the country.

Rev. Vernon Dobson, the Union Baptist minister who became a prominent member of the Interdenominational Ministerial Alliance, a mostly black organization, recently shared his childhood memory of Lillie Jackson, who lived across the street from his family. "She was like a grandmother to me and all the neighborhood children; always on the young people to get involved; to demonstrate." Janice Woolridge, who was a childhood friend of Lillie's daughter, Juanita Jackson, and who later became a counselor at Morgan College, said much the same thing about Lillie, adding:. "She was a fascinating woman, she could talk, you could never get a word in."[142]

After a Maryland Chapter was established in 1942, Lillie simultaneously headed that organization as well as the Baltimore Chapter, until 1962 when she relinquished the Maryland Chapter to her daughter, Juanita. In 1937 Juanita had married Clarence Mitchell, the co-founder with her of the City-Wide Young People's Forum. By the time her mother

---

[141] Shoemaker, pp. 268-269
[142] Rev. Dobson was interviewed by this writer, and both Dobson and Woolridge were interviewed by Hopkins' students.

turned over the Maryland Chapter to her, Juanita had become an attorney (one of the first blacks to graduate from the University of Maryland Law School after a 1936 NAACP-initiated law suit forced it to integrate), and had been legal counsel for the Baltimore Chapter for some time. Clarence had become an effective lobbyist for the national NAACP in Washington D.C., and would become a prime mover of the 1964 and 1968 Civil Rights Acts. Jack Greenberg, who became an attorney with the NAACP Legal Defense and Educational Fund in 1949, had this to say of Clarence and Juanita Mitchell:

> [Clarence Mitchell] was so highly regarded on Capitol Hill that at times he was referred to as the 101st Senator. He was as grave in demeanor and measured in his speech and conduct as [Juanita] was passionate and fiery. [In court] she argued with a passion that was hard to deny. Juanita raised a powerful family of sons who moved into high positions in government.[143]

After Lillie Jackson, Juanita's mother, retired in 1970, Enolia Pettigrew McMillan succeeded her as president of the Baltimore chapter of the NAACP. McMillan, along with Ruth Green, had been the first two black teachers assigned to former white junior high schools after the *Brown* decision in 1954 found segregated school systems unconstitutional.

•••

Determining how many black Baltimoreans served during World War II, and in what capacity, has proved elusive, but as in all the past wars, it's clear that despite continuing discrimination they did serve in large numbers. A brief sentence by Brugger in his history of Rhode Island suggests one facet of their involvement—the manning of the merchant ships turned out in the Glenn L. Martin plant, which came under the control of the U.S. War Shipping Administration (WSA). Brugger writes: "Captain Hugh Mulzac, a black skipper from Baltimore, commanded the Booker T. Washington in Atlantic convoy duty; his ship, with a racially mixed crew, received high ratings."[144]

---

[143] Greenberg, Jack, "In Memoriam."
[144] Brugger, p. 539

However, fighting against dictators in other countries did not free blacks of discrimination at home. Baltimore even had separate and unequal War Service Centers for its black and white servicemen on leave. The black center, called the Gold Street Club, was directed by Mrs. Lillian Jordan, honored for her more than four thousand hours of community service there. The center served meals to over 250 men daily, to as many as 350 on weekends.[145] The club sponsored dances for the soldiers and provided a variety of other entertainments.

Other black women also contributed to the war effort through knitting, sewing, home nursing and first-aid work. They took cooking classes for tips on wartime food preparation (rationing limited amounts available; fat was collected and turned in at designated stores), and volunteered at the black YWCA and YMCA to help servicemen and their families find lodging (a service provided for whites at their War Service Centers). Both black men and women served as air raid wardens, but received their training separately from whites. As reported in the *Afro*, nine black women were dismissed as wardens because they mistakenly attended a whites-only course. Indignant, they retorted they "didn't feel that discrimination was necessary since bombs aren't particular whether they fall on colored or white homes." [146]

•••

Baltimore may have resembled the North with its industrial-based economy, but in the 1940s Southern Jim Crow characteristics were still pervasive, blacks and whites living "in separate and unequal worlds." On the job front, despite the fact that overall unemployment in Baltimore dropped to under 10% during this time, and the lot of blacks somewhat improved,[147] a 1942 survey of "the ten largest firms in Baltimore showed that not a single black was employed above the unskilled level. And only a few had jobs above the janitorial level." Glenn L Martin aircraft plant, for instance,

---

[145] Though the writer has been unable to locate figures regarding the number of blacks who served during WWII, these figures suggest the number must have been considerable.
[146] Bentley, p. 432, quoting the *Afro*, April 11, 1942.
[147] Bentley, pp. 422 & 424

which in 1943 "employed more than 20,000 workers, [employed] only 175 blacks, and yet the company continued to advertise for workers as far away as New Jersey."[148] It's hard to determine whether the gradual change that would soon follow was due more to the war or to the renewed activism of the local NAACP and other civil rights' actions—or perhaps both working together.

Blacks made some advances in 1941 after President Franklin D. Roosevelt, fearing the planned black "March on Washington" would be disruptive, ordered the integration of plants holding war contracts. The March was being organized under the leadership of A. Philip Randolph, President of the Brotherhood of Sleeping Car Porters, an active member of the Fellowship of Reconciliation (founded during WWI), and the acknowledged "patriarch of the black protest movement.." Randolph expected 50,000 to 100,000 of "the black laboring classes" to participate— most of them employed either in menial jobs or not at all. The intent was to press President Roosevelt to act against job discrimination.

Though the march was never held, the threat proved sufficient to provoke Roosevelt into establishing a Fair Employment Practices Committee [FEPC].[149] Unfortunately, the FEPC lacked any enforcement provisions and soon became so wrapped in controversy, it even lost most of its persuasive powers. Despite these weaknesses, it did manage to encourage some private war industries to employ blacks, primarily as a spill-over effect from its demand that. federal agencies, and state and local governments, employ blacks. FEPC's greatest achievement may have been its establishing a precedent that suggested that fair employment should be regarded as a civil right.[150] A. Philip Randolph had been influenced in his tactics by Gandhi's non-violent direct actions in India (as were the subsequent leaders of the 1960s Civil Rights Movement) and by the 1936-1937 auto factory sit-down strikes.

In Baltimore, various federal actions helped blacks gain

[148] Callcott, George, pp. 45 & 149
[149] Meier & Rudwick (eds.) *Black Protest...*, Intro p. 4.
[150] Meier & Rudwick, *From Plantation...*, pp. 268 & 272-273

new employment opportunities. The War Manpower Commission forced Triumph Industries, Glenn L. Martin and Bethlehem Steel to increase black employment as a condition of renewing their federal contracts. The Maryland Council of Defense was forced to maintain an integrated staff, and the National Security Administration set up USOs for black workers. The forced integration caused only a few short-lived flare-ups: at Western Electric and Maryland Drydock where workers objected to sharing cafeterias and restrooms with blacks, and at the USOs in Elkton and Middle River—but on the whole the integration was accomplished without incident. More might have been accomplished if President Roosevelt had not held back for fear of losing needed southern support. Nonetheless, "black industrial employment in [Baltimore] grew from 7% of total industrial employment in 1940 to 17% in 1945, *a proportion that never declined* [writer's italics]."[151]

Bentley would seem to disagree with this latter point, stating that "as the demand for wartime materiel declined and employment needs shifted, women and blacks were among the first to be laid off—regardless of how well they had performed jobs.... Full employment had defused racial tension, but the calm did not long endure in peacetime. One could easily find racial disparities in the pattern of layoffs and firings."[152]

Meanwhile, in Baltimore during this period, black protestors against job discrimination faced considerable resistance, even violence; ten were killed by policemen at a rally in 1942. This so angered the black community that the NAACP was able to rally some 2,000 blacks, representing 125 religious, civic, and fraternal organizations, to join together in a protest at the state capital in Annapolis. On April 23, 1942 they met at the Sharp Street Methodist Church in Baltimore (where it had been holding planning meetings) where chartered buses awaited to take them to Annapolis. The demonstrators had filled both houses of the General Assembly when Governor O'Connor arrived at the State House at two o'clock to meet with them. Lillie May Carroll Jackson and Carl Murphy were the lead speakers who argued with the Governor

---

[151] Callcott, George, p. 46.
[152] Bentley, p. 438.

to do something about job discrimination. Their main achievement seems to have been the replacement of an ineffectual Interracial Commission, created in 1927 with a new Commission to Study the Problems Affecting the Colored Population. Though only educational, by deliberately making employers feel that hiring blacks was "patriotic," the commission seems to have made them more accepting of black workers.

The solidarity in the black community, demonstrated by the large turnout for the rally in Annapolis, may at least partially explain why there were no riots in Baltimore in 1942, at a time when they were occurring in Harlem and Detroit. Juanita Mitchell felt that black anger and frustration had been given an outlet in the massive planned protest that had achieved at least a modicum of success.[153]

The NAACP, not only had spear-headed this March on Annapolis, but by the end of the war had increased its membership to over twenty thousand, giving it new political clout—used early-on to force the Baltimore Police Department to begin hiring blacks, though not able to prevent their imposing restrictions on the hiring of blacks not imposed on whites—the blacks had to be college graduates, were not issued uniforms, and were not given the power to make arrests.[154]

As it had earlier, during the 1940s, the *Afro-American* continued to play an important role in the black struggle for equality. One of its most interesting campaigns, dubbed "orchids and onions," began early in 1945. The paper, long disturbed by reports of discrimination by the downtown department stores, sent reporters to canvas the stores, listing on the front page as "orchids" those found not to be discriminating and as "onions" those which were. Within three weeks this was beginning to have an effect; the black Domestic Workers Union deciding to boycott the "onions." After a month, the reporters were giving forty-four stores "orchids" and only fourteen "onions"; the onions, however, including the city's largest—Hutzler's, Hochschild's, the May Company, and O'Neill's. These would have to be tackled again

---

[153] Callcott, George, p. 149 & Shoemaker, pp. 271-172.
[154] Callcott, George, pp. 146 & 149

in the 1960s (of which we'll hear more later) before they would finally give in.[155]

•••

In most cities racial tension mounted after the war as jobs became scarce, but under the enlightened leadership of Mayor Theodore McKeldin between 1943 to 1947, Baltimore, in large part, avoided this. The Mayor was well aware of the growing number of blacks in the city and of their emphasis on voter registration in the 1940s. Blacks had poured into the city from the rural counties during this time, resulting in an increase from 50% to 75% of the black population of Maryland living in Baltimore—changing the composition of the city from 19% black in 1940 to 24% by 1950. The proportion of blacks in every other Maryland county [Baltimore being the equivalent of a county in Maryland] declined.

Further, black voters had become sophisticated, helping elect Republican McKeldin as governor in 1950 and to reelect him in 1954 despite the efforts of his opponent, Dr. H. C. Byrd, former President of the University of Maryland, to exploit McKeldin's support of civil rights legislation. At a time when the south was still all-Democrat, McKeldin became the first two-term Republican governor in Maryland's history. The extraordinary solidarity of black voting had made it a force to be reckoned with: voters in the city's three black wards changed their party allegiance five times in a span on only eighteen years.[156]

Despite this, clearly blacks had not attained the equality they'd hoped for as a result of their participation in the war at home and in the military. There's little doubt, however, that they had broken-down many of the long held stereotypes of black inferiority. And the actions of the NAACP, the *Afro* and the religious community during the 1940s set the stage for the civil rights movement that would follow some years later.

---

[155] Farrar, pp. 183-184
[156] See Callcott, George, p.148-150

Gradualism/Tokenism

Despite the economic gains blacks achieved during the war, they clearly still had a long way to go to reach even a modicum of equality with whites. Nothing could make this clearer than the booklet, *Toward Equality*, published by the Sidney Hollander Foundation.[157] It summarizes the annual awards given between 1946 and 1961 to various persons and groups for outstanding achievement in fostering equal rights and opportunities for Maryland's blacks, and includes information provided by the Baltimore Urban League, the Maryland Commission on Interracial Problems and Relations, the Housing Authority of Baltimore and the *Sun* and *Afro-American* newspapers.[158]

•••

Toward Equality notes only one change in 1949, that of the admission of Baltimore's black physicians to the Baltimore City Medical Society. They became the first such group in the south to afford full professional participation to doctors regardless of race. In a conversation with a reporter for the *Sun* on April 19, 1950, at the time the Hollander committee presented them with that year's award for their action, Dr. John M. T. Finney, Jr., president of the Society, noted that old records showed that there were three Negro members back in 1880, but because other records were destroyed by fire, they didn't know exactly when they joined, how long they were members, or why they left. As for the present award, an

---

[157] *Unless otherwise noted*, all the quotes that follow are from this booklet, and are used with the permission of Sidney Hollander, Jr. who loaned her his copy of same.

[158] The foundation was established in 1941 by Sidney Hollander's sons in honor of his 60th birthday. Delayed by the war, the first award of $250 (a significant amount at the time) was not given until 1947, for the year 1946. In addition to the booklet loaned the writer by Sidney Hollander, Jr., he assured the writer of access to his files now in the Moorland Spingarn collection in Washington, D.C.— which requires a cite for each item used from the collection. This booklet and the Foundation awards will be referred to, as appropriate to the subject in each of the sections to follow Hollander himself plays a role in the Housing section, "Blockbusting."

editorial in the *Evening Sun* on April 22, 1950 noted:

> The importance of this step [admitting blacks] may not be apparent, yet many advantages for the Negro physician, and thus for the whole community, stem from it. Unless he is a member of his local medical society, a Negro physician cannot belong to his state society or to the American Medical Association. He thereby is deprived of major benefits....
>
> Just as disease knows no racial distinction, so should a body of scientists devoted to the prevention and cure of disease know none. It is gratifying that the Baltimore Medical Society's action upon that principle has been given public recognition.[159]

The award perhaps moved Johns Hopkins Hospital to begin the professional integration of its doctors that year; its first step being the appointment of Dr. Ethel L. Nixon to its psychiatric staff. The same year Franklin Square Hospital undertook the integration of its nurses and the year following a program of psychiatric training for black nurses was established at Crownsville State Hospital. Also that year, black inspectors were used by the Health Department for the first time. The Urban League noted in its annual report that medical and lab technicians were also hired. Regrettably the Baltimore City Dental Society was not so forward-looking, and, as late as 1959, was still excluding black dentists from membership, depriving them of professional contacts and membership in the National Dental Society.

For 1951 the Hollander Foundation chose the Yellow Cab Company for its award, citing its successful integration of white and Negro taxi-cab drivers, which served to open up new employment opportunities for blacks in Baltimore. Other cab companies did follow suit, and approximately 260 black drivers were hired, their earnings, in combination, adding up to over half a million dollars. In presenting the award to Robert Freedman, President of the Yellow Cab Company, Martin Jenkins, President of Morgan State College[160], emphasized that Freedman had demonstrated "what in this

---

[159] Moorland Spingarn, Box 50-1, folder 28.

[160] A distinguished black college in Northeast Baltimore, about which more will be said in later sections.

community *ought* to be done in good conscience, in brotherhood, and in democratic America, *can* be done." Freedman's acceptance speech, quoted in part, was quite moving: [161]

> Having always had an abiding faith in the justice and fair play of my fellow men, and being convinced that men of all colors and creeds respond in the same manner when treated equally, I could see no sound reason why the people in Baltimore should be deprived of the services of many taxicabs when qualified men and women of color were available and seeking honorable and gainful employment.
>
> Believing as I do in the dignity of man I could see no reason why any white person wouldn't be satisfied to ride in a Yellow Taxicab driven by a Negro driver, when it was common knowledge that some of the best white families in this state were actively seeking Negroes to drive their personal and expensive limousines and to butle [be butlers] in their very homes.
>
> If my humble efforts have contributed to the general welfare of Negroes in Maryland and have in any measure brought about greater equality of opportunity and helped to improve understanding and human relations between the races, I am grateful indeed.
>
> As a member of a faith whose ancestors have felt the heavy hand of discrimination and segregation over the centuries, I understand fully the meaning of those words and am overjoyed that by this simple act I was able to do something to benefit other victims.

The hiring of black cab drivers was followed in 1952 by the Baltimore Transit Company's hiring of ten black transit operators, perhaps influenced by the former's peaceful integration, but also influenced by the fact they had 200 job vacancies. By 1953, 336 of the 1,900 operators were blacks. The public seemed barely to notice these new drivers, but the white operators were less sanguine. Some quit, some called in sick, and in 1952, still provoked, went on strike after being ordered to adopt a uniform dress code. The black drivers remained.

---

[161] Quote from Moorland Spingarn box 50-2, folders 48 & 49. Headline montage from an Urban League Annual Report.

Other jobs opening up to blacks in 1952 included the Enoch Pratt's hiring of a librarian for their children's room, and white-collar jobs that included "a private secretary, office manager and typists in downtown offices, clerical and field workers for a loan company, a number of additional sales representatives and market analysts, two more hospital laboratory technicians and five chemists at nearby Edgewood Arsenal."

For 1952 the Hollander award went to Governor Theodore R. McKeldin who, for the first time appointed blacks as police magistrates, as parole officers, and as members of the State Boards of Welfare, of Health, and of Education. During this time, blacks also were finally making headway on state commissions and to appointive government positions. The following year George H. Rosedom became the first black appointed as an assistant state's attorney and in 1955, John Hargrove became the first black appointed as Assistant United States Attorney.

For his part, McKeldin's actions led, in the 1954 election, to his opponent branding him "an integrationist," but his re-election to a second term despite this, as indicated earlier, a first for a Republican Governor in Maryland history, suggests that the public was becoming more receptive to the idea of integration. That same year, three blacks were elected to the General Assembly from the 4th District: Harry Cole to the State Senate; Emory Cole and Truly Hatchett to the House of Delegates.

In 1953, the Urban League felt real progress had been made when a number of blacks were hired in technical, professional, clerical and sales positions that had previously excluded them. The League concluded that employer's attitudes toward hiring blacks had changed. This trend continued, and in 1954 Bendix Radio Corporation placed a number of blacks in jobs they had never before held.

Also in 1953 the Fire Department "ended ninety-five years as an all-white municipal agency" by integrating its firehouses with an initial appointment of ten blacks. "Except for some transitional complaints of discrimination within individual fire houses," the integration was accomplished with very few objections. By the end of the second year seventy-eight black fire fighters had been hired, dispersed amongst almost all stations throughout the city. However, it took until 1956 before the "white" and "colored" signs over toilets were removed from firehouses.

In 1955, the progress blacks had made in state appointments continued: the Maryland Commissioner of Personnel eliminated separate white and black lists of applicants for state jobs; blacks were hired as toll takers at the Susquehanna River and Chesapeake Bay bridges; as engineering aides by the State Roads Commission; and as guards at the Patuxent Penal Institution (at the time an independently operated special prison for those with psychiatric problems). The Chesapeake and Potomac Telephone company began to transfer its black personnel into previously all-white units, "with all employees sharing the same facilities." However, telephone operators remained all-white until 1956.

Perhaps most revealing of the overall status of blacks at this time came with the 1955 publication of *The Baltimore Community Self-Survey of Inter-Group Relations*, a study which had taken over two years to complete. Called *An American City in Transition*, it was endorsed by the forward-looking Governor Theodore R. McKeldin and the City Council President, Thomas D'Alesandro Jr., as well as leaders in the business and religious communities. The book's preface reads, in part:

> Baltimore is a great American city. We who live here are proud of its greatness. We boast of its history and its size...its waterfront and its industry...its public buildings and its parks...its schools and its universities...its libraries and its museums. These important attributes make it a great city.

But, we must realize that there is a vast difference between a city and a community ....A community is...a spiritual entity. It has a collective personality. It possesses such human attributes as courage and compassion, responsibility and brotherliness....Its loftiest aim is to provide equal opportunities and high morale for all its inhabitants....

The ideal American community is yet to emerge. If it is a little slow in coming, it is due in large part to its very nature....one of the sorest points in our communal life is the strain and tension, the prejudice and discrimination which exist within groups of people of different origin, color, religion or nationality....

The broad purpose of the Baltimore community Self-Survey is to help make our great American city of Baltimore also an ideal American community.

Under the Chairmanship of Dr. Israel M. Goldman, rabbi of Chizuk Amuno, over sixty-eight civic, religious and fraternal organization participated in collecting material for the book, and almost 500 persons of every race, creed and social position volunteered as interviewers (of about 100,000 Baltimoreans), clerks or workers on six separate committees— Negro Family, Housing, Employment, the Public Schools, Health and Welfare Services, Religious and Civic organizations, and Public Accommodations. It is perhaps surprising—or indicative of their living with their heads in the sand— that many in Baltimore and across the country were shocked after millions exposure to the *Survey*'s findings in a TV documentary, "The Search."

Using census figures, the *Survey* noted that "in 1950 there were 519,969 persons employed in non-agricultural industries in Metropolitan Baltimore of whom 418,846 or 80.55 % were white; 100,670 or 19.36 %, Negro; and 453 or .09% other non-white persons (classed with blacks for remainder of study)."[162]

It also reported that "the average (median) income of Negroes who had an income in 1949 in Metropolitan Baltimore was 56.07 % of whites, i.e., $1,345, while the average for whites was $2,399. The corresponding yearly incomes by sex were as follows: male, white, $2,957; female, white, $1,390, Negro, $844. The median income of Negro men was 63.04% of

---

[162] U.S. Bureau of Census, Bulletin P-C 20 Table 83, p. 157.

whites; that of women, 60.72 % of whites."[163] Other findings in the *Survey* include the fact that—

> At the end of a decade of unprecedented industrial activity, in 1950 there remains a wide discrepancy between the levels of employment opportunity available to the average white and Negro worker. Racial differences in level of educational attainment do not appear sufficient to explain this discrepancy. [noting that especially at the managerial and professional level, whites represented two out of ten; blacks one out of twenty.]
>
> Approximately one-half of the firms utilized blacks labor before and during WW II while almost three-fourths of them have employed blacks at some time since the close of WW II. The occupational pattern of blacks in the plants employing them in 1954 is remarkably similar to that which prevailed prior to WW II. Negro male employees are absent from the labor force of almost one-third and Negro women from two-thirds of the business establishments of Baltimore.

Blacks found little protection in unions, and unemployment among blacks was considerably higher than among whites: 5.2 % for all males, 10% for blacks; 5% for all females, 8.3% for black females—black women employed mainly in private households. The most promising note in the study may be that the majority of employers reported no problems with "Negro-white relationships." They also reported no problems in hiring blacks, though they did report that problems increased with hirings "above the semi-skilled level." The "problems" included "not responsible," "tardiness," "objection of white workers," and "objection of customers."

The *Baltimore Sun* carried a lengthy four part account of the *Survey* report, introducing it on the front page under the title "The City We Live In." It marked a shift in the paper's attitude to blacks, which, in turn, reflected something of a shift in the community's attitude.[164]

> In the 1920s [the upper middle-class *Sunpapers*] were outspokenly hostile to blacks as a source of crime, a threat to middle-class values. By the 1930s, the anti-black stance

---

[163] U.S. Census of Population, 1950, Maryland Detailed Characteristics, Bulletin P-C 20, Table 87, p. 169.
[164] Callcott, George, p. 153.

faded, but the papers still pandered to prejudice by conspicuously identifying miscreants by race and by conspicuously ignoring black achievements.

By the 1940s this attitude in turn had evolved to a patronizing sympathy, and by the mid 1950s to full support....The papers gave sympathetic coverage to the Alabama bus boycott. Society pages began to cover black weddings, and sports-page editors launched a small crusade for the integration of athletic teams and facilities.

In 1956, the year following publication of *The Baltimore Community Self-Survey of Inter-Group Relations*, John Catlin and James Rucker, finally, after a fifteen-year fight, became the first blacks to be issued master plumber licenses. Catlin had spent from 1941 to 1949 pursuing a journeyman's license, and seven more years before he was issued the master's license. The Baltimore City Council's passing a Fair Employment Practices Ordinance in April 1956 had perhaps forced the hand of the license issuing agency. It read, in part:

> ...It is hereby declared to be public policy of this city to foster the employment of all persons in accordance with their fullest capacities, regardless of their race, color, religion, ancestry or national origin.

The ordinance led to the adoption by the State Employment Security Division of a no discrimination policy in hiring, testing, counseling, and job placement. Also that year, the Baltimore headquarters of the Department of Motor Vehicles integrated its clerks. However, the Ordinance lacked an enforcement provision, so when the Baltimore Equal Employment Opportunity Commission (EEOC), headed by Philip A. Camponeschi, began to function in 1957, its pronouncements, though making headlines, were largely ignored. Little changed even though the EEOC found the City's Bureau of Recreation discriminated against eligible Negroes in its selection of directors for its recreation centers—or after the EEOC issued an order forbidding newspapers or other media from printing or publishing discriminatory employment-related advertisements.

That same year, 1957, in a secret ballot, the previously all-white, all-male Baltimore Bar Association admitted both blacks and women for the first time—the vote had been 614 to

409 in favor of admitting women and 606 to 417 in favor of blacks. Governor McKeldin again broke precedent with three black appointments: E. Everett Lane as Associate Judge of the People's Court (the next year he was elected to a full term by a five-to-one margin), Robert B. Watts to replace Lane as Traffic Court Magistrate Judge, and George L. Russell, Jr. as Baltimore Magistrate-at-Large. Also that year, Lorenzo Campbell became the first black deputy sheriff in Maryland and the Chief Police Inspector, Fred L. Ford, ordered the police not to use racial designations in their testimony at court or grand jury hearings unless it was of specific relevance to the case. In 1961, Charles Richardson, Jr., became the first black "to hold a clerkship in a Maryland court of record."

In 1958, yet another new field was opened to blacks when the Urban Renewal and Housing Agency hired two blacks as real estate appraisers. Also that year Baltimore's Planned Parenthood clinic, which long had operated on an interracial basis, added a black gynecologist to its medical staff; and the Maryland Commission on Interracial Problems and Relations found that "the majority [of family and child-care agencies] had integrated their boards, staffs or both and were generally providing services to all races."

The ambivalence that still existed about black professionals is obvious when a hospital granted staff privileges to a black physician, but insisted its name be withheld. In 1959 five predominantly white hospitals employed black nurses, three accepted blacks for nurses' training and four extended staff privileges to black doctors, but, again, all insisted their names be withheld.

More open in their support of expanded job opportunities for blacks, in 1958 the Council of Churches made its position clear by distributing "thousands of mailing stickers for use on checks and bills to express to stores and public utilities the willingness of their patrons to be served by persons without regard to race, creed or color."

There were also some encouraging indications in 1958 that blacks were again being hired in skilled and semi-skilled jobs even though their exclusion from most trade unions still tended to relegate the majority "to inferior or segregated status." The booklet, *Toward Equality*, cited two positive examples:

The President's Committee on Government Contracts reported that nearly a tenth of eighteen thousand employees of the Martin Company were Negroes, including nine hundred in skilled jobs, fifty in clerical and stenographic positions and twelve serving in professional technical and supervisory capacities.

[Also, as we've seen] Bethlehem's Baltimore plant at Sparrows Point, was recorded as having 9,360 colored employees in a force of 29,600 with some Negroes in skilled and supervisory capacities.

The booklet also noted a few other gains blacks had made without specifying the year—black patrolmen assigned to radio cars and on motorcycles, and "several elevated to the rank of sergeant;" insurance agents employed by predominantly white companies; clerical workers found in most of the hospitals and in the Federal Bureau of Old Age and Survivors Insurance whose national headquarters are in Baltimore; two blacks licensed as electricians.

A number of additional gains are also noted in the 1961 Supplement to *Toward Equality*—the General Assembly enacted a law providing for a non-discriminatory employment clause in State contracts and replaced a previous administrative regulation with a law prohibiting employment discrimination; four banks hired blacks, as well as at least one insurance company; more blacks were hired as salespeople by department stores and other retail establishments; Westinghouse engaged a former Urban League employee, Marvin Jones, as an employment interviewer to recruit black talent both locally and in black colleges; Baltimore's Meter Maids became part of an integrated police unit; Mayor Grady named the first black, Sonja Reynolds, as a clerk in the Mayor's office; the EEOC was able to persuade the Baltimore branch of the National Association of Postal Supervisors to extend membership to eleven blacks they had previously rejected; the Maryland Bridge Association voted 156 to 34 to accept black members and the Baltimore Junior Association of Commerce admitted its first two black members.

Despite these additional incremental gains in 1961, the conclusion arrived at in 1959 by the Hollander Foundation, regrettably, still held true— that "the employment picture remains a gloomy one....the great majority of colored

Baltimoreans continue to sweep and scrub, push and haul, tote and carry in menial, unskilled occupations." They continued:

> It is still difficult for Negroes to get apprenticeships in the building trades and in industry generally, even though the public schools give colored pupils the same basic training that white pupils receive. It is still difficult for colored women to obtain sales and clerical positions, even through they, too, have had the necessary school training. The large employers of clerical help—insurance companies, banks and other financial institutions—generally maintain a white-only policy. Executive training courses offered by many firms are also closed to Negroes....Finally, Negro employment opportunities will remain inferior as long as the colored worker is denied membership in unions and professional organizations.

•••

The wording of Baltimore's Fair Employment Practices Ordinance that had passed in 1956 was laudable, but without an enforcement provision, its impact was slight at best. The City Council can perhaps be applauded for trying again in 1964 when it passed another ordinance that affected employers of fifteen or more persons. Those employers could not:

1. Discriminate in respect to hire, tenure, promotion; or terms, conditions or privileges of employment;
2. Deny or limit by a quota system;
3. Make inquiry regarding race, color, religion, national origin or ancestry prior to employment.

The provisions in the Ordinance that made it unlawful to indicate race on employment applications or to publish complaints filed with the Baltimore Community Relations Commission which administered the laws, had the perhaps unintended consequence of making it very difficult to accumulate accurate statistics regarding the extent of employment discrimination. Nevertheless, even the casual observer could see that such discrimination was still extensive; the time was ripe for the unfolding of a Civil Rights Movement that, with the help of television, would move the conscience of a nation, a movement that would involve hundreds of blacks and whites in the struggle for *equality for all.*

Where Equality?

In the late 1950s, the NAACP, with a local membership of 21,000, was still the leading organization fighting for equal rights for blacks.[165] However, at the same time its emphasis on legal and legislative actions increasingly was viewed as insufficient for achieving the sought-after black equality. In fact, each legal and legislative success served to raise expectations to such a degree that some sort of explosive revolt against the discrimination and segregation imposed on them by whites seemed inevitable.

Direct actions were beginning in Baltimore as in other parts of the South, their non-violent techniques winning successes, supported by passage of new anti-discrimination laws and decisions emanating from the Supreme Court. White public opinion seemed to be shifting away from racism, embarrassed by Communist Russia which was regularly pointing to the hypocrisy of United State's racist practices in light of its democratic pretensions. Blacks felt increasingly that the time was ripe to abolish the "humiliations of second-class citizenship" they so often encountered.

•••

Clearly equality of opportunity was far from a reality as the 1960s began. Joblessness among black males in Baltimore was 12%; of those employed, nearly two-thirds were in unskilled or semi-skilled jobs; the annual wage for blacks was $3,700 compared to $6,900 for whites; 35% earned less than $3,000 per year. But the Urban League was perhaps the only concerned black issue-oriented organization that continued in the 60s to focus almost exclusively on increasing employment opportunities, still believing that working with the white business community was the best way to effect change. Dr. Furman Templeton, head of the Baltimore Urban League, blamed this employment picture for blacks on the continuing hostility of employers toward blacks; on "the contemptuous belief," as he put it, "that the Negro is fit only for menial jobs."

---

[165] Membership numbers are from an article in the *Evening Sun*, 6/24/70.

Templeton declared, "If past practices and inadequate qualifications hold the Negro back in some occupations and keep him out of others, it is the general lack of commitment to accelerated hiring standards which keeps a group representing 40% of the city's population from making up less than 10% of the work force in some of those occupations—service, retail, manufacturing, financial—which other immigrant groups, themselves unqualified at the time, used as economic steppingstones."[166]

During the 1960s the local NAACP chapter did remain committed to voter registration and education, a fact which helped elect twenty-two year old Clarence Mitchell III as an assemblyman in the Maryland State Legislative in 1962. Son of Clarence Mitchell (national NAACP's lobbyist in D.C.) and Juanita Mitchell (newly President of the local branch), he beat an entrenched political machine in "a low-budget hectic campaign." His sixteen year old brother, Michael, had acted as his campaign manager, recruiting high school and college students to work on his behalf, and persuading Jackie Robinson to make a tape that was played on the radio and TV. On election day, they defeated machine tactics of turning away voters by claiming broken machines—quickly getting them repaired and rounding up the turned-away voters, returning them to the polls "in well-coordinated car-pools."[167]

By 1968, local NAACP membership had dropped from its 1950 high of 21,000 to 8,897 and a year later to 7,642, which included 219 lifetime memberships which did not have to be renewed annually.[168] Always ambivalent about the newer civil rights groups which were grabbing all the headlines during this period, it nonetheless was often the NAACP which provided them with bail money and lawyers when their members were arrested.

Such groups as the Congress of Racial Equality (CORE),

---

[166] From *The Catholic Review*, June 3, 1966, "Civil Rights Here: A Look at the Issues", J. Michael Arisman.

[167] The *Crisis*, a monthly publication of national NAACP, August-September 1962.

[168] Membership numbers are from an article in the *Evening Sun*, 6/24/70

Southern Christian Leadership Council (SCLC), Student NonViolent Coordinating Committee (SNCC) and Baltimore's own Civic Interest Group (CIG), had shifted the focus away from legal challenges, and for the most part, away from job discrimination to public accommodations, education, and, finally, housing. These were more amenable to direct action tactics than were employment practices. However, Baltimore CORE, at any rate, did not entirely abandon employment.[169]

•••

In the fall of 1963, soon after the famous March on Washington, Baltimore CORE, led by its then-Chairman, Ed Chance, opened a campaign that demanded an increase in employment opportunities for blacks in the city's department stores. Chance no longer is able to recall why Stewart's was selected as the focus for picketing, but he does remember well that it went on daily for about three months, albeit without much success, until the Christmas season was approaching. Every weekday he came right from work to lead the pickets, sometimes five or ten, at other times, dozens. Even though it got little press coverage, they made an impact, right in the middle of downtown Baltimore. Chance describes an encounter with the police on one occasion:

> The police decided they were going to tell us how to picket because we were stopping people from going into the stores. I told them we were not going to picket as far apart as they were demanding, but would continue as we'd been doing. The officer said, "Well, if you keep on like that, I am going to arrest you." And I stood right there with no prior intention of being arrested at all, and all of a sudden, I said, "Arrest us." You know, you just knew, that this was what you had to do. You could not give in to this doggoned police captain. After that, the *Afro* and Equal Opportunity Commission wanted to know what needed to be done for us to stop these demonstrations downtown.[170]

---

[169] We'll hear more of the origins of CIG and CORE, local and national, in the Public Accommodations section, as well as more about the March on Washington.

[170] Interview with Hopkins' students on 12/08/2000. This writer also talked to Ed Chance.

In the Spring of 1960, Stewart's, more grudgingly than the other department stores, had opened its restaurants to blacks following weeks of picketing (more later), but they still hired very few blacks, and then primarily as elevator operators (not yet automatic) and janitors. Especially as the Christmas shopping season approached, Stewart's was worried about the effect the picketing was having on people wanting to come to the store. David Glenn,[171] then head of the Baltimore Equal Employment Opportunity Commission, set up a meeting with management. The result was an agreement by Stewart's to hire forty more blacks, to promote to executive positions two of the five blacks already in their employment, and to advertise jobs in the *Afro*; an ad appearing in the paper the very next day. CORE had made a sufficient impression on other firms downtown, that they, too, began hiring blacks in order to avoid CORE picket lines; the ripple-effect producing an estimated two hundred new clerical and sales jobs for blacks.

•••

Rev. Vernon Dobson,[172] unable to remember the date, recalled the involvement of the Interdenominational Ministerial Alliance in another negotiation; this with the management of Western Electric regarding hiring more blacks, in general, and, especially, their policy regarding promotions to management positions. Claiming they knew no one qualified, Dobson said, "We gave them three names and they chose one of them to hire as the Entrance Officer for Employers. You go through him and you get a job. We just rejoiced. And so, we started sending people down to get jobs. And he'd send them all back." Dobson continued, So finally we had a conversation with him. Do you know how you got this job? He said, "No, I just got in. You should cool it, I'm going to let a few in." A man said, "Kill this sucker." I said, "Man are you crazy?"

---

[171] Glen died in June 2001. He was head of the Baltimore Equal Opportunity Commission from 1961-1963, appointed by mayor McKeldin, he headed the city's Human Relations Commission from 1967-1973, and headed the state Human Relations Commission from 1978-1987.

[172] Interviewed by Hopkins' students, and by this writer on a number of occasions.

Dobson seemed angry as he continued, "That's how a whole lot who broke ground felt. 'I'm in, so we've been affirmed.' So that's the unfortunate thing about the struggle. There are too many people who think that the struggle has been met and affirmed when they are in. And[with that attitude], once you get some of the fruits of your labor, ... [it is] hard to continue to purify the systems. *I think that is what has happened to the movement.* [writer's italics]

•••

Photo courtesy of Mike Waller, Publisher, *Baltimore Sun.*

On March 30, 1964, despite a 1½ inch snowfall, 2,000 committed civil rights supporters peaceably marched 1½ miles, heartily singing freedom songs and carrying signs, from the state office buildings to the War Memorial Plaza in front of City Hall. There they huddled together to hear Hyman

Pressman, Baltimore comptroller; Senator Javits (R., NY); the Rev. Robert Newbold, pastor of Grace Presbyterian Church; the Rt. Rev. Msgr. Austin J. Healy, representing the Catholic Archdiocese; Rabbi Morris Lieberman of the Baltimore Hebrew Congregation; baseball's great Jackie Robinson; and comedian Dick Gregory adding his special brand of "cutting social comments.

Rev. Marion Bascom, pastor of Douglas Memorial Community Church and Chairman of the labor committee of the Interdenominational Ministers Alliance, who organized the demonstration, believed thousands more would have come out if it hadn't snowed. The aim of the rally was to point up the failure of city and state government to practice fair employment and promotion policies, as well as the lack of equal housing legislation. In his speech, Thomas D'Alesandro 3rd, President of the Baltimore City Council, put it this way:

> Unless and until we in the communities not only preach but practice brotherhood...not only work for equal treatment, but guarantee equal treatment for all, the efforts of Washington cannot be wholly effective.[173]

•••

On May 28, perhaps encouraged by the earlier turnout, John Burleigh, an employee and leading CORE activist, orchestrated another demonstration at the huge Social Security complex in the Woodlawn section of Baltimore—the national center of the government's vast Social Security program.

Earlier that month, the Advisory Committee Report on Personnel Practices at Woodlawn had been released substantiating that the Social Security agency represented "twenty-seven years of racial injustice." John Burleigh, black and an employee, was determined to change that. Another involved employee, Larry Ageloff (white, who subsequently joined CORE and was instrumental in activating a CORE Employment Committee), described the situation at the complex this way:

---

[173] Quoted in *The Evening Sun*, March 30, 1964. Event also reported in the March 31st edition. Photo appeared in the *Sun*, April 5, 1964

Here was an agency that presented itself as a model employer, but most of whose black employees were doing the most menial and dulling work under the supervision of an all-white supervisory work force. Frequently whites were promoted into these jobs with absolutely no experience. They learned on the job after being trained by the black employees they supervised.

Photo courtesy of Mike Waller, Publisher, *Baltimore Sun.*

The turn-out for the demonstration was not the 2,000 that had been predicted in advance. But the two hundred or so who did assemble at Noon that Thursday included, in addition to the employees who'd dared to show up, members of CORE, the National Alliance of Postal Workers, Gloria

Richardson, a leader at Cambridge, Maryland,[174] Stanley Branch, from Chester, Pennsylvania's NAACP, Fred Weisgal, the civil right's attorney (in a rare appearance on a picket line), and Dick Gregory, a popular activist comedian who's presence assured the demonstrators the press coverage they needed. Gregory and Weisgal had just left the turmoil at Cambridge, and were heading for the Baltimore airport where Gregory was enplaning for a return to New York, but had first stopped at Woodlawn to join in the demonstration.[175]

As with the earlier demonstration, the turnout was less than expected. Burleigh, in his comments to the press, explained that the Social Security Commissioner, Robert Ball, had made a threatening-like speech to employees two days earlier. In any case, Ageloff called it a huge success because it "embarrassed the top management of the Social Security Administration, made it realize that black employees might no longer settle for the crumbs from the table, and led to the beginning of an effective affirmative action program."

Carrying placards, some reading, "The veterans died for freedom, let us die for freedom," and singing freedom songs, the demonstrators marched slowly across Security Boulevard to the administration building where officials and employees were conducting a Memorial Day service. Many employees were watching them from the office grounds, others from the windows of the building. Echoing Joshua's assault on Jericho, the demonstrators circled the huge complex six times between noon and 3:00 p.m. Dick Gregory repeatedly urged the onlookers to join the demonstration. "We are fighting for equality for all, as well as freedom now," he told them. "If there is not proper justice here, they will take their protest to Washington."

Larry Ageloff recently talked about this event; the first time he met CORE's attorney, Fred Weisgal:

---

[174] A complete account of the events in Cambridge can be found in the section, "Public Accommodations: Cambridge."

[175] This information comes from news clippings, papers unknown, but most probably the *Sun* and *Evening Sun*, plus a recent interview with Larry Ageloff, then an employee, who later became an attorney in the State Attorney General's office.

There he was, smoking his pipe, carrying a sign, and calmly talking to Dick Gregory and the ordinary working stiffs who took part. Now I think all of this was quite wonderful. Here you have a successful and commercially sought after comedian and a local, professionally successful lawyer, neither of whose careers could possibly be helped by their participation, especially Fred's, and, I believe, despite recognizing at least the possibility of adverse consequences, nevertheless were participating because they believed it was the morally and ethically correct thing to do.

•••

Both nationally and locally, CORE quickly became known for its activism, picketing and sit-in strategies, but, in many cases, its reputation alone, or the mere threat of demonstrations, proved sufficient to induce change (as demonstrated in the aftermath of the Stewart's campaign). This seemed especially true of the work of the newly activated Employment Committee which regularly followed CORE's general approach of researching potential targets before selection, and then becoming informed about the target's policies and modus operandi before attempting meetings and negotiations. Such an approach often proved successful without demonstrations.

Then again, sometimes the "target" came to them. During the summer of 1964, while John Burleigh and Irwin Auerbach were both out of town, Larry Ageloff represented CORE after it was approached by a worker at the City Department of Public Works about the incredible discrimination and humiliations they faced daily on the job. Taken on a tour of the Department's building, he "found a plantation. From Supervisor on up, it was lily white; blacks were barred from the indoor rest rooms and had to use outdoor 'Johnnie-on-the-spots,' hot in summer, cold in winter, no place to change or wash up."

During a meeting with the officials, after one of them had referred to the black workers as "boy" several times, Larry spoke up: "These are men, many old enough to be my father." The blacks broke out in applause as the manager squirmed, turned red, and mumbled something or other. After CORE had identified an eager group of men, led by Jim Plaxton, whom they felt confident would pursue the changes demanded and see that they were implemented, CORE backed out and let the group take over. This was in keeping with the usual practice of the Employment Committee, and it seemed to work here as elsewhere.

•••

Another target in 1964 proved a more difficult challenge, even if the initial situation was not so flagrantly discriminatory. The U.S. Labor Department had just published a report that named banking as one of the fastest growing white collar industries in the country, and predicted a fifty percent increase in employment for the coming decade as banks automated their operations.

Two facts made banks an excellent industry for CORE's Employment Committee to tackle: they had a high turnover rate, meaning they had a continuing need for new employees; and, the commercial banks in Baltimore employed an estimated 4,000 in their downtown and neighborhood branches—the majority in clerical positions that didn't require previous experience [only a high school diploma, a passing grade on a fairly simple arithmetic aptitude test, and a pleasing personality], but they also employed a substantial number in professional, technical, supervisory, managerial and executive positions.

In December, without any publicity or fan-fare, Larry Ageloff and Irwin Auerbach (both white), John Burleigh and William Bush (both black), members of CORE's Employment Committee, between them visited each of Maryland's major banks—the Equitable Trust, First National, Maryland National, Mercantile Trust, National City and Union Trust—to observe the number of black employees. Except for one or two black tellers in the branches in black neighborhoods, all they saw was white, white, white.

As their next step, the Committee chose the Maryland National Bank, the bank with the largest assets and the most employees (1,000) for their first meeting with officials; an effort to determine how many blacks were employed in total (to include those in behind-the-scenes positions not visible to the public). What they got was total non-cooperation, though they did eventually learn that none of the commercial banks hired blacks in a substantial number; the few tokens they did hire were primarily in beginning clerical jobs—the First National employed the highest percentage, 7.5; Maryland National only three percent; National City, none; the average was 3.5%.

After the meeting with Maryland National officials, CORE's Committee members, on January 14, 1965, met with a group of bankers at the Baltimore Clearing House, an organization representing all the commercial banks. There they expressed the need for the banks to make more and better jobs available to blacks—clerical, professional, supervisory, managerial and executive. An eleven point plan was presented to help achieve the goal they set "that 20 % of the bank positions should be filled by Negroes as of June 30, 1965." The points included advertising all job openings in the *Afro-American*, using the phrase, "An Equal Opportunity Employer," in their ads, and various other techniques to improve their recruitment and placement practices. They did not ask for, nor desire, preferential treatment.[176]

The Clearinghouse group said that each bank would have to assess CORE's demands, and that CORE should have their answer in two weeks. Almost a month later, even after a follow-up letter was sent on February 2nd, CORE had heard nothing. On February 9, 1965, members of CORE, wearing large CORE buttons, went from bank to bank downtown, performing a sort of guerrilla theater; Bill Bush, a big burly black dressed in his army fatigues, an especially intimidating figure, his arm out-stretched, his finger pointing as he counted employees, noted their race. The threat of massive demonstrations downtown that would tie up the whole city seemed "to scare the shit out of them." [177]

Not long after, CORE received a telephone call from the president of the Clearing House telling them the banks were ready to meet with CORE on an individual basis. CORE had an answer for each of the banks' "explanations" for their lack of black employees; worth repeating because they are

---

[176] The quote and other information is from a mimeographed report, "Report on Discrimination in Employment by the Commercial Banks of Metropolitan Baltimore," prepared and circulated by Baltimore CORE's Employment Committee in 1965.

[177] Larry Ageloff's words when telling this writer of their campaign.

"explanations" given by all sorts of discriminating employers, with CORE's answers equally appropriate across the board.

1.   "Lack of enough qualified Negroes": the Social Security Administration and the City of Baltimore, for example, which required similar qualifications, had discovered "that the number of qualified Negroes available was much greater than that employed by the banks"—In contrast with city and federal agencies, banks have never really welcomed Negroes and have only opened their doors but a crack in the last few years.

2.   "Those qualified prefer the higher paying government jobs": This would apply equally to whites but has not prevented the banks from finding whites to fill their positions.

3.   "Go-slow is essential in order to avoid possible negative reactions of stock holders, depositors and other employees": This implies continued discrimination despite fact that a Baltimore Ordinance in 1956 made it against the law and the federal government will do the same effective July 1965. Managers no longer have the option, in this respect, to "manage its own business." But aside from the legal and moral issues involved, "large and small firms, north and south, report that none of the predictions of dire consequences resulting from implementing a fair employment policy materialized."

4.   "Banks have already developed techniques to comply with fair employment practices": CORE is only judging by results and has offered techniques that have worked elsewhere. They have not suggested "special privileges."

5.   "The 20% goal by June 30th is unreasonable": The goal was based on the fact that qualified Negroes were available for white collar jobs in percentages well in excess of 20%, as proven by the experience of Baltimore City Civil Service, the Social Security Administration and the federal government generally in this area....If any bank can demonstrate that attaining the goal is not possible because of limited turnover or limited expansion, we will be glad to consider a goal suited to that bank's situation.

Nothing much was accomplished until Cardinal Shehan intervened and arranged a meeting that included the diocese's attorney, Francis Murnaghan, Jr. Even though they still offered more excuses, the open push by the diocese for change soon led to the adoption of most of CORE's proposed "techniques"— such as ads in the *Afro* and the inclusion of "equal opportunity employer" in *all* their ads. Also the Maryland State Employment Service agreed to make referrals of blacks to bank jobs, and the banks themselves began sending recruiting officers to the Morgan State and Howard University campuses, and to the high schools. By the time CORE issued its report on the banks in 1965, two had, for the first time, placed a black in their Branch Management Trainee Program, and college graduates were being advised to apply for such training.

Besides believing six months was adequate time for the banks to hire significantly more blacks, CORE also had other reasons for choosing June as a target date: it was the date when the employment provisions of the Civil Rights Act became operative—and the date when summer vacation began for thousands of student activists who work with CORE and other civil rights groups. If their early progress continued it would seem they might not need to demonstrate at the banks.

•••

It would have been trickier if demonstrations had been needed to try to force the Police Department to employ more blacks. They had, technically, been integrated since 1961, but few black officers could be found at any level. It was kind of amusing when they complained at one meeting that it was difficult to recruit blacks because no one could draw them for their recruitment posters and literature. CORE had the perfect solution: Tom Lewis, an artist and active member of CORE, was only too willing to solve that problem for them. This was not a trigger for change, but gradually more and more blacks could be found in the Police Department; and, eventually, at all levels.

•••

Another 1965 project by CORE's Employment Committee coincided with that of its Urban Renewal Committee.[178] This time John Burleigh, Irwin Auerbach and Larry Ageloff began to work with the Community Relations Commission seeking a ban on city contracts for construction, maintenance, and suppliers who discriminated in employment. They were demanding that all

---

[178] More on this in the section "Housing: CORE & the Poor.".

companies doing business with the city be required to submit reports on the number of blacks employed, and that authorization be given to boycott firms that failed to comply.

Though seemingly having little impact at the time, such demands by local CORE, combined with similar demands nationwide, had contributed to the issuing of federal orders and passage of civil rights laws. However, even after passage of the 1964 Civil Rights Act that forbade racial discrimination in hiring and firing, enforcement was left to the state's and cities; federal agencies primarily offering direction and financial assistance—and the campaigns initiated by CORE in 1965 clearly demonstrated that change was not going to happen easily.

•••

"Affirmative action," a topic of increasing controversy since the 1990s, started with President Lyndon Johnson's 1965 Executive Order 11246. This required that any firm expecting to do business with the government must have a specific plan with stated goals and a timetable for "enhancing the status of minority groups." This also affected organizations and local governments seeking government grants.

Now, instead of *not* asking race on job applications in order to not be accused of discrimination, they were again asking in order to prove compliance with the new federal mandate. In line with this, in 1968, the old Maryland State Commission on Interracial Problems and Relations was reorganized as the Maryland Commission on Human Relations; it began to hear about two thousand grievances a year, mostly employment connected.

•••

Meanwhile, in 1965, despite its by-then emphasis on housing issues, CORE lent at least modest support to the organizers of the new Maryland Freedom Union which sought to unionize primarily black workers in the retail and service industries, beginning with the workers in nursing homes who earned only 35¢ to 60¢ an hour. Many of these workers were on strike for weeks, daily sitting-in and picketing one selected nursing home, and in front of its owner's home. Stu Wechsler came down from national CORE to help.[179]

It was very cold in the wintry months of 1965-66 when the nursing aid workers were bravely picketing. And this writer remembers well that on several mornings she brought from home our big thirty-cup pot of freshly brewed coffee to help warm them, and then shivering along side them as they picketed. It's not clear how successful they ever were over the long haul in this campaign, nor how many were arrested, but CORE's attorney, Fred Weisgal, did appear in court on behalf of a goodly number, getting most, if not all, out on their own recognizance. The writer found no evidence to indicate that these trials ever took place.

•••

Photo by Carl X Harden; provided by David Eberhardt

That summer, on July 14, 1966, the Freedom Union

---

[179] In a recent conversation with this writer, Stu, who had later returned to Baltimore as part of Target City, said, "Organizing is tough work and doesn't usually get much press. I wish Target City had stuck with developing the Freedom Union, which, initially, was one of the things that led national later to choose Baltimore as its Target City."

again made the news when they won representation for thirty-five workers at the Tommy Tucker variety store on Baltimore's Pennsylvania Avenue (which at that time was still the black community's "main street").

But even as some workers were counting the ballots in this election, seven others who'd been regularly picketing at the store for some time, were appearing in Western Municipal Court on charges of disorderly-conduct. They were all released on their own recognizance, pending Criminal Court proceedings, after the attorneys, including Fred Weisgal, agreed to waive a preliminary hearing. Those arrested had included Jim Griffin from local CORE and two from national's Target City campaign, recently ensconced in Baltimore. The writer found no evidence to indicate that these trials ever took place either.

•••

It was during this period that the Target City crew from national CORE, and the black power movement came on the scene, and Baltimore CORE was split apart.[180] Then came the assassination of Martin Luther King in 1968, the ensuing riots that tore the whole city apart, and the period of despondency that followed.

It all seemed to mark the end of massive civil rights demonstrations. A smaller Baltimore CORE did seek job training grants, and a number of black ministers sought ways to release blacks "trapped within an economically oriented power structure," to use the words of Martin Luther King.[181]

Reverend James L. Moore, pastor of Baltimore's Sharon Baptist Church was instrumental in bringing together leaders of the black clergy, industry and government to form a chapter of the Opportunities Industrial Center (OIC) modeled after one in Philadelphia. Its Board members met at his church until they raised sufficient funds to purchase a building where they held job-training classes for the unemployed and underemployed in

---

[180] Even though much of Target City's work in inner-city Baltimore was in the area of employment, the impact of their arrival in Baltimore from New York was so tied to the issue of housing that it is discussed in that section. More also will be said of the riots in that section.

[181] The descriptive phrase from Milobsky quoting King, p. 284.

carpentry, auto repair, and secretarial skills.

Reverend Vernon Dobson, now pastor of the ever-active Union Baptist Church, was chosen as the OIC's first executive director. In addition, Dobson's church paid to construct a community center adjacent to their building on Druid Hill Avenue that provided job training, literacy classes, and child care services. Reverend Marion Bascom's Douglass Memorial Community Church purchased the entire 1300 block of Madison Avenue, employed blacks to renovate the buildings, and converted them to low-income housing. Projects like Moore's, Bascom's and Dobson's demonstrated the capability of Baltimore's black ministers to mobilize their churches for new and innovative uses, and their ability "to demolish barriers to their community's economic/social develop-ment and construct programs aimed at eliminating them."[182]

An interfaith group headed by Rev. Wendell Phillips, Rev. Vernon Dobson and Msgr. Clare O'Dwyer between 1977 and 1980 were successful in organizing BUILD which, focusing on community needs, has gotten stronger with each passing year.

To name just a few of their successes (done in co-operation with Industrial Areas Foundation (IAF) and the union, AFSCME[183]: ended payday lending which violated usury laws that were impoverishing families; won state support for "Child First" after school programs; opened Fellowship Houses for drug rehabilitation; arranged low interest mortgages for home purchases; got the city to pass the first "Living Wage Ordinance" in the country; and conducted "Get Out the Vote" campaigns that saw a 53.6% turnout for the 1998 election, a 12.49% increase over the 1994 turnout.

Although this group is one of the most active and promising in Baltimore, it nonetheless is barely able to make a dent in the needs of the black community, including their need for more and better jobs.[184] One might have hoped the

---

[182] Milobsky, pp. 285-286.

[183] IAF is a body of professional organizers founded by Saul Alinsky in the 1940s; AFSCME embodies low wage workers, including janitors, bus aides, secretaries, cooks, construction workers, maintenance and other service workers.

[184] Another promising organization that is having an impact on Baltimore is the recently established branch of ACORN (Association

Greater Baltimore Committee, composed of the area's most prominent business leaders, might have done more for Baltimore's increasingly black and poor population, but their focus on regional economic development would seem to offer only a distant hope. In a 1999 report to the city's political leaders, a GBC report states:

> Baltimore has significant strengths and economic assets—many of which are nationally recognized and celebrated. Baltimore City and the Greater Baltimore region clearly have substantial potential for global business prominence in the 21st century. For that potential to be fully realized, however, Baltimore's future leaders must squarely address three key issues—public safety, education and population decline....The correlation between the issues of public safety, education, and population growth is clear and compelling.[185]

Meanwhile, employment, which once had dominated complaints to the Maryland Commission on Human Relations, began to decline after its mandate was extended in 1978 to include discrimination based on sex, age, the handicapped, homosexuals, and the obese— issues primarily affecting whites.

This inclusiveness of issues could hardly be helpful to either black or white Baltimoreans living in a city where 59% of its 736,000 total population in 1970 was black (the 6th highest percentage in the nation's urban centers); where the city ranked 11th nationally in unemployed; where 21.9% had incomes below the poverty level, and 41% of its housing was built before 1939. In 1989, 8,621 whites (out of 287,933) had an income of less that $5,000, compared to 23,054 blacks (out of 435,619).

By the year 2000, Baltimore's blacks represented over 64% of the city's population which had declined to 651,154 (still ranked 6th highest); 23.7% were living below the poverty level; 12,634 were institutionalized; 42,481 housing units were vacant, and only 191 building permits were issued for housing units. Even though most of these figures are not broken down

---

of Community Organizations for Reform Now), a national activist organization that organizes low-income workers and the poor around issues that concern them. More will be said of their activities in Baltimore in the concluding section, "In the End."
[185] See www.gbc.org.

by race, it is not unrealistic to surmise that blacks make up a large share of the numbers.[186]

Gloomy as the outlook still looks for the majority of black Baltimoreans, there can be no denying that since passage of the laws making employment discrimination illegal, the number of black faces among employees in government offices, and even in private businesses, has gradually increased. It is only regrettable that race has "fallen off the radar screen" as a major concern of the general public, in Baltimore, and in most of America at a time when it still profoundly affects blacks' living conditions and public policies. Institutional racism clearly remains firmly entrenched.

---

[186] Figures come from *County and City Data Book*, US Dept. of Commerce 1994, and from the US Census Bureau "Quick Tables" and Baltimore City MapStats from FedStats, found on the internet.

Part III
Public Accommodations

Not Alongside Us

The years following the end of slavery in 1864 were ones of "social fluidity" for blacks in Baltimore. Well into the 1880s they had access to the city's many flourishing theaters, its libraries, public transportation, places of amusement, concert halls, hotels, and lecture rooms. They could be found alongside whites in the city parks, at political rallies and in civic parades. But as the 19th Century was ending and the 20th beginning, blacks, whatever their social or economic status, increasingly experienced daily insults and humiliations. And as the new exclusionary practices grew, Baltimoreans began to reflect more and more the same kind of intolerant racism that had permeated the South since the ending of the Reconstruction period that followed the Civil War.

> In 1905, the *Afro-American Ledger* had reported that whites and Negroes frequently ate together in public places; two year later the paper reported that most public eating places were segregated. In 1910 relations between Negroes and whites were so poor in Baltimore that the mayor, fearful of riots and bloodshed, was forced to cancel the public showing of movies of the latest triumph of Negro heavyweight champion Jack Johnson.[1]

•••

Blacks did not accept this increased discrimination passively, but despite their extensive use of the right to vote and a number of victories in the courts, they could not stop the new wave of discriminatory legislation.

One discrimination law blacks tackled in 1870 had required them to ride on the uncovered platform of streetcars. That year a visiting black from New York City filed suit in the U.S. Circuit Court against the Baltimore City Passenger Railway Company challenging the law. That April, in ruling in favor of the plaintiff, the court, while validating the "separate but equal" doctrine, had also insisted on the "equality" side of the equation by declaring that forcing blacks to ride on the streetcar's uncovered platform was not equal.[2] The victory

---

[1] Paul, p. 288; also see pp. 4 & 195
[2] See Paul, p. 101

proved something of a hollow victory since the railway company responded by providing special cars for Negro passengers. Nonetheless, blacks now had a roof over their heads, and, perhaps even more important, their victory encouraged blacks to turn to the courts both to challenge threats to their rights and to extend those rights.

The number of militant blacks willing to do just that was growing. One of the most courageous was Reverend Harvey Johnson. He became immediately active after his arrival in Baltimore in 1872 to become pastor of Baltimore's Union Baptist Church—a church that has remained active in the struggle for civil rights through the 1960s and 1970s.[3]

In January 1885 Rev. Harvey Johnson filed another transportation-related case in the U.S. District Court against the steamer *Sue* which ran between Baltimore and Virginia. Four members of Rev. Johnson's church had been forced to travel in inferior, second class cabins, even though they held first class tickets. Blacks, now admitted to the bar, argued the case. Once more the court ruled that separate but equal was constitutional, but that in this case the *Sue* passengers had not been given equal quarters. Therefore, the steamer company's discrimination violated the 14th Amendment. The four plaintiffs were awarded $100 each.[4]

In 1904, on a strict party vote, the Democrats, who then controlled the Maryland General Assembly, enacted two Jim Crow laws: one requiring railroads to furnish separate cars or compartments for blacks, and, the second, requiring steamship companies to provide separate seating, dining and sleeping facilities. Again, blacks fought back, and the first summer after the act's passage they successfully boycotted any transportation companies that invoked these segregation laws. However, the second summer, the boycott ended after black ministers refused to support it, upset that they were being deprived of "monies usually collected at outings and picnics."[5] So stymied, others again were willing to use the

---

[3] We met Johnson previously in the Employment sections: "Right to Vote" & "Troika in Action."

[4] Paul, p. 205

[5] Paul, pp. 287, 288

courts to fight off imposition of these new laws, and though not entirely successful, did manage to drive a wedge in the doctrine of separate but equal.

A year after its passage, a law professor at Howard University, William H. H. Hart, set out to test the Maryland Act as it applied to interstate railroad passengers. Hart bought a ticket from New York to Washington DC on a train of the Philadelphia, Baltimore & Washington Railroad Company that operated "cars and coaches by steam." [6] When they arrived at the Maryland border, Hart refused to move to a "Jim Crow" coach when ordered to do so. He was arrested, tried in the Circuit Court of Cecil County, convicted, and fined $5. He refused to pay the fine, small as it was, and filed an appeal with Maryland's Appelate Court, attorney Henry M. McCullough representing him.

After citing a great many related cases, the court held that the Maryland Act, "requiring carriers to provide separate coaches [of equal quality and convenience] for the transportation of white and colored passengers, and making it an offense for a passenger to refuse to occupy the car to which he is assigned by the conductor, [was] valid in so far as it affects commerce wholly within the state." However, the Court found the Maryland Act to be "invalid as to interstate passengers under the commerce clause of the federal constitution," thus reversing Hart's conviction in the lower court and making no provision for a new trial.

•••

By 1920, with blacks no longer welcome at the city's many theaters and vaudeville houses and no longer welcome at the merrymaking at the summertime park concerts where the Colored Municipal Band had regularly played, Pennsylvania Avenue emerged as the center of black culture. In the decades that followed, its own Royal Theater, and those smaller clubs near-by, attracted large crowds to hear such luminaries as Eubie Blake, Count Basie, Cab Callaway, Duke Ellington, Ella Fitzgerald, Nat 'King' Cole, Dizzy Gillespie, and Billie Holiday.

---

[6] *Hart vs. State*, 60 Atlantic Reporter, pp. 457 (MD App. 1905)

The movie houses were not so successful, only able to acquire "worn-out films from the cheapest white theaters." More promising were the colored YMCA, stores and businesses that soon lined the Avenue, catering to blacks though not generally owned by them. Also, annually, on Easter, the Avenue saw blacks parading its length, showing off their finery, not caring they were now excluded from the white Easter parade around Mt. Vernon.[7]

•••

On another front, by 1928, blacks were confined to a poorly staffed and inadequately equipped section of Druid Hill Park; black children had use of a swimming pool smaller than that for whites, a small wading pool, and a small concrete-surfaced playground. In July that year the *Afro* ran a series of articles highlighting this injustice. It reported that, including the playgrounds attached to the thirteen black elementary schools, these facilities could accommodate about 600 of the city's 25,000 black children; that only $3,000 of the city's $250,000 recreation budget was spent on blacks.

The *Afro*'s campaign to improve recreation facilities available to black children continued in 1929 when it published an editorial on October 19 asserting the damage that Baltimore's "meanness and injustice" was having on black children "who ought to have a fair chance to grow into full-fledged American boys and girls." [8]

The *Afro*'s attack continued in the 1930s, for example in a June 30, 1934 editorial it "deplored the Playground Athletic League's failure to maintain the Druid Hill Park playground properly; it also noted that because of their tax contribution blacks were entitled to more than one park playground. Then the *Afro-American* asserted that racially segregated playgrounds were 'deplorable in view of the preponderant scientific proof that children of different racial groups and economic strata can play together harmoniously.'"

---

[7] Chapelle, pp. 192 & 194; brief quote from Olson, p. 279. The demonstrations that opened job opportunities for blacks in these stores on Pennsylvania Avenue were discussed in the Employment section: "The Great Depression."

[8] *Afro* quotes found in Farrar, pp. 184-185

Despite complaints by some that too much time was spent on civil rights actions rather than on advancing job and political opportunities for blacks, the focus on public accommodations was understandable. Discrimination in this area was the source of daily insults and humiliations suffered by all blacks, whatever their social or economic status. Further, the "enemy", in many instances, was easily identifiable, and hence easier to confront than the more amorphous or hidden perpetrators of job and housing discrimination.

Watson in his autobiography of Clarence Mitchell, tells how Mitchell was asked, early in the 1930s while a young reporter for the *Afro-American* newspaper, to desegregate the double-decker bus that ran up "the very elegant Charles Street, Baltimore's version of Fifth Avenue....For some inexplicable reason," he writes, "blacks were not supposed to ride the double-deckers even though there was no ordinance prohibiting them from doing so." When the *Afro* complained that the bus driver would not stop for Mitchell, "the transit company insisted it did not have a segregation policy. Thereafter, that form of segregation ended, but on cold days drivers still slammed their bus doors shut on blacks and sped away."[9]

Blacks suffered similar discrimination on the railways, ferries and taxis, some in accord with the law, some despite the law. It was 1951 before the state legislature grudgingly scrapped a dozen pages of obsolete transportation laws that segregated passengers on intrastate trains, interurban trolleys, steamboats and ferries.[10]

Commercial establishments in downtown Baltimore were so segregated that the only blacks regularly venturing down were those who worked there.[11] A 1943 guide for city newcomers is revealing of the extent of segregation in the 1940s. It listed:

> segregated YWCAs, white and "Negro" nursery schools and day care centers, and five hospitals—four for whites and one

---

[9] Watson, p. 83
[10] The latter statement according to *Toward Equality*.
[11] Watson, p. 83

for blacks. Also listed were white and "colored" Boy Scout and Girl Scout troops and a Salvation Army Red Shield Boy's Club "open to any white boy between 6-18." African Americans sat in the balconies of downtown movie houses and theaters (if allowed in at all) and were turned away from downtown department stores, lunch counters, and most hotels. The restaurant at the train station was one of the few places allowing blacks and whites to dine together. The downtown Friendly Inn, charging thirty-five cents a night, advertised beds and a lounging room "for colored men."[12]

•••

Though affecting only an elite group of blacks, the City's public golf courses became a target for protests in the 1940s. The city maintained three quality 18-hole courses from which blacks were excluded, and one poorly maintained 9-hole course at Carroll Park that "lacked golf pros, sandtraps, bunkers, flagpoles, practice greens and other prerequisites for a professional quality golf course. It alone was open to blacks." In May 1942, following black protests, the Park Board did briefly open all the courses to blacks, but reverted to the old policy after whites protested the appearance of the *Afro's* advertising director, Arnett Murphy, at the Mount Pleasant course with his friends. After Murphy and his wife were barred in June, he filed suit in Baltimore City Court demanding that all the golf courses be open regardless of race. When they won their case, the city appealed.[13]

> The Maryland Court of Appeals directed the Park Board to either improve the Carroll Park 'colored' golf course, construct a new, better course for blacks, or eliminate racially segregated golf courses. In its appeal the local Park Board's attorneys argued that recreation was not a civil or political right; since blacks had some recreational facilities provided for them, there was no constitutional right for them to have any specific form provided, in this instance, golf.

In his opinion, Chief Judge Bond stated that "Separation of the races is normal treatment in this state." The City,

---

12 Found in Bentley, p. 122.
13 Information and quotes about the golf courses, unless otherwise noted, are from Farrar, pp. 184-187.

hence, retained its right to segregate the races on public golf courses and tennis courts.[14]

By 1943, the *Afro's* owners had become far less tolerant of "separate but equal" solutions to their demands, and in an April 24, 1943 editorial, the paper "blasted" the "out-of-court settlement by the Black Golfers Association and the Baltimore Park Board which temporarily gave blacks access to municipal golf courses until the Jim Crow Carroll Park course was renovated." Further, in questioning why the city had funds to spend on "renovating the 'colored' golf course" but could not, according to the city, afford to upgrade the swimming pools and other recreational facilities provided for blacks, the *Afro* linked its golf campaign that mainly concerned a small well-off segment of the black community with its recreation campaign that affected the whole community.

Having allowed blacks to use the "white" golf courses while renovating the Carroll Park course, once that work was complete, the Park Board again barred blacks from the other three. New court actions followed, Arnett Murphy of the *Afro* again was one of the plaintiffs. The *Afro* and the NAACP paid some of the legal costs involved; George Callcott in his book, *Maryland & America*, perhaps a bit generously, over-credits Willie Adams as being responsible for "mobiliz[ing] protesters and employ[ing] lawyers to gain the right of blacks to use the city's golf course."[15] It was a time when Willie Adams had become a millionaire via liquor (presumably after blacks were allowed to own taverns) and gambling.

Late in 1947 the case moved to federal court which rendered its ruling mid-1949: "Judge Calvin Chesnut ruled that Negro golfers were entitled to play on all municipal courses; could not be limited to the nine-hole Carroll Park course while three 18-hole courses were reserved for whites-only."[16]

Racist as ever, the Park Board then designated separate schedules for white and black use of the courses. It was July

---

[14] *Durkee v. Murphy*, 1942, 181 MD. 259, 29A.2d 253

[15] Callcott, George, p. 148.

[16] From *Toward Equality*. In a seeming contradiction, the same judge had ruled in June 1948 that the Maryland Art Institute, even though it too received government funds, could restrict enrollment to whites. Mills, *"...And Justice for All"*, p. 74.

1951 before they agreed to permit interracial play at all municipal golf courses.

•••

The tennis courts, too, had been a source of contention along with the golf courses. In July 1948 the Young Progressives of Maryland (loosely associated with the Progressive Party that was supporting Henry Wallace for President) arranged an interracial tennis match in Druid Hill Park to test the segregation policy of the Park Board. Prior to the event, the Park Board was made aware of their plans. On July 10, the day before the match, leaflets were distributed that had such slogans as "Kill Jim Crow!" "Demand Your Rights!" and "Organize to smash discrimination in recreational facilities." They all urged people to "Be present to lend your support." About 250 to 300 people showed up to watch the match.[17]

After the players refused the Park Police's demand that they leave, twenty-two people were arrested, some charged with disturbing the peace, some simply with violating a rule of the Park Board by engaging in interracial activities. After realizing their case was weak, in September, before trial, the original charge was dropped and all twenty-two were charged with riot (despite there being no disturbance at all until the arrests, and then only name-calling) and conspiracy to disturb the peace.

At the Criminal Court level seven were found guilty, but before the Supreme Bench, they were convicted only of the conspiracy charge. They were then sentenced to various term in the House of Correction (a medium security prison in Jessup), and were fined. The sentences were suspended and they were placed on probation for two years. They appealed, claiming they had a right to test the Park Board's policy and a free-speech right to distribute leaflets. "They contended that the testimony in the case showed no evidence whatever of any conspiracy on their part to do anything but to exercise their lawful rights."

The appellate court held that they had had their day in

---

[17] Information from *Winkler et al v. State*, 194 Md. 1; 69A.2d 674; 1949 Md. LEXIS 378

court, have had the evidence reviewed by the state's Supreme Court, and that, "under our established practice, continuing over a period of many years, we should not re-examine that evidence upon the grounds urged upon us." They affirmed the lower court's judgement. One judge wrote a lengthy dissent. He declared:

> There is no such thing as a "fair" method of depriving a person of constitutional rights, even if it is done "in good faith and in the exercise of an honest judgement." A conviction in violation of constitutional rights cannot stand, "whether accomplished ingeniously or ingenuously."....It is to be regretted that Maryland should add to the list of cases in various states (many of them involving racial matters) in which a prosecution has succeeded, against law and justice, by manipulation of procedural devices, in attaining conviction and escaping correction in the state courts.

In 1950 the U.S. Supreme Court refused to review the convictions. It was not until 1951, at the same time that they allowed interracial play on the golf course, that the Park Board finally allowed interracial play at several of their tennis courts.

•••

In 1949, the *Afro* ran another series on recreational segregation. It affirmed that blacks and whites were forbidden to play any games and sports together, and noted only "one swimming pool for blacks, eight out of 110 tennis courts, nine playgrounds out of forty, two parks out of twenty, and eight community centers out of twenty-three," in addition to the then still segregated golf courses.

In December that year, Judge Chesnut presided over a case, *Boyer et al. v. Garrett et al*,[18] in the U.S. District Court for the District of Maryland that did not question the "equal" aspect of segregated recreational facilities, but wished to test the constitutional legality of state segregation laws. The case was dismissed "on the authority of *Plessy v. Ferguson*[19], which had upheld separation of the races, and had become "the

---

[18] *Boyer v. Garrett*, 88 F. Supp. 353; 1949 U.S. Dist. LEXIS 1889. Also cases 183 F. 2d 582; 1950 U.S. App. LEXIS 2983 and 340 U.S. 912; 1951 U.S. LEXIS 2320.

[19] *Plessy v. Ferguson*, 163 U.S. 537, 16 S. Ct. 1138, 41 L.Ed. 256

established policy and practice in seventeen of the forty-eight state, including Maryland." The U.S. Court of Appeals 4th Circuit affirmed the lower court's decision on July 17, 1950, asserting that the Supreme Court had never overruled the Plessy decision and it was for them, "not us, to overrule its decisions or to hold them outmoded [a claim of the appellees]." On January 2, 1951, The U.S. Supreme Court refused to her the case because "the application therefor was not made within the time provided by law. (28 U.S.C. 2101 (c).

Meanwhile, the *Afro*'s drum-beat of opposition to segregated recreation facilities became even louder. The Park Police in May 1950 had again stopped a mixed tennis match; this one between a Negro tennis club and a visiting team from nearby Fort George Meade. Then, in June they broke up a baseball game in which a Negro team was host to a team of sailors from a visiting naval vessel. All this negative publicity over the Park Board's segregationist policies, did not prevent the Court's finding in the above case but may have helped provoke the decisions made in 1951 to allow interracial play at all its municipal golf courses and at some of its tennis courts (already noted), as well as at baseball diamonds, playgrounds and athletic fields. But its swimming pools and beaches remained entirely segregated.

•••

In 1951 the Board finally responded to prolonged black protests at Fort Smallwood Bathing Beach and reserved formerly whites-only facilities there for blacks for one third of each summer month. A year later, in 1952 the Park Board decided to develop separate black bathing facilities at Fort Smallwood rather than continue its separate "white" and "colored" weeks. This was far from satisfactory to the black protesters and in May 1952, a lawsuit was filed on their behalf asking that the City, the Park Board and other named defendants be "restrained from operating the bath houses and bathing facilities on a segregated basis, alleging that the facilities afforded Negroes are not equal to those afforded whites."

In an effort to prove this, the attorneys hired an expert on the subject of recreation. "He went to the beach, paddled around with flippers and a snorkel mask, and concluded that the bottom of the black beach had many pointy rocks, which made it inferior to the white beach's sandy bottom."[20]

In September 1953, after a U.S. Judge banned segregation at Sandy Point State Park until separate but equal facilities were established, the state was forced to build separate-but-equal facilities there. Meanwhile, *Brown v. Board of Education*[21] was working its way through the courts, challenging the whole concept of separate but equal. In May 1954 the Supreme Court rendered its decision that separate educational facilities were inherently unequal. It was two months later that the U.S. District Court for the District of Maryland would render its opinion in the joined segregation cases of Sandy Point State Park and Beach, Fort Smallwood Park and the Baltimore City's swimming pools.[22] The arguments in this consolidated case make obvious the lack of clarity in *Brown* as to the Court's intent—did they intend that in all areas, separate was inherently unequal, or only in the case of education?

Judge Roszel P. Thomsen, "with zero moral or legal imagination,"[23] ruled that *Brown* did not expressly overrule all of *Plessy v. Ferguson*—it did not declare that the "separate but equal" doctrine could not be applied in the field of recreation. The U.S. District Court in this case had chosen to construe the Supreme Court decision narrowly, and looked to the case of *Durkee v. Murphy* where the Maryland Court of Appeals had held that separation was valid where there was a need "to avoid any conflict which might arise from racial antipathies." This 1942 case had also held that "Separation of the races is normal treatment in this state." In essence, Thomsen found the facilities for blacks and whites "inherently" as well as physically equal, thus upholding the "separate by equal" doctrine as constitutional.

The case was appealed to the U.S. Court of Appeals, 4th Circuit and argued on January 11, 1955. It was decided on

---

[20] Greenberg, Jack, "In Memoriam."
[21] This case, *Brown v. Board of Education*, 1954, 347 U.S. 483, 74 S.Ct. 686, and its immediate impact on Baltimore's public school system is discussed in the Education section: "Poly "A" & Brown."
[22] *Lonesome v. Maxwell et al*, 123 F. Supp. 193 (Md. 1954)
[23] Greenberg, Jack, "In Memoriam."

March 14, 1955.[24] This court overturned the District Court's dismissal of the blacks' request for injunctive relief against enforcement of racial segregation in the three consolidated cases. It found that "segregation cannot be justified as a means to preserve the public peace merely because the tangible facilities furnished to one race are equal those furnished to the other....It is obvious that racial segregation in recreational activities can no longer be sustained as a proper exercise of the police power of the State..." Whether intended or not, the *Brown* decision was becoming the linchpin for ending the "separate but equal" doctrine in all cases.

Thus, it's not surprising that on November 7, 1955, the U.S. Supreme Court upheld the Appelate Court's decision that ended "separate-but-equal" publicly-owned parks, playgrounds and pools.[25]

The next summer there was a brief training period for the mixed-race lifeguards and pool staff before opening the much larger, until then whites-only swimming pool in Druid Hill Park—the much smaller, formerly all-black pool in the park had been closed. White attendance began to fall at all the integrated pools as opposition to integrated use of the pool remained strong.

In the summer of 1958, when the Y.W.C.A. wanted to use the Druid Hill Park Pool and adjacent play areas as part of an integrated girl's day camp program (Camp Y-Ho-Wa), they had to overcome strong opposition by members of the Park Board and the neighboring community, fearful that whites would be overwhelmed by large numbers of black participants. In fact, without incident, during its six-week program, the camp served 226 blacks and 242 whites, and the 1958 Hollander award went to the Y.W.C.A for "demonstrating voluntary and workable racial integration in using public supported pool and park facilities for summer camping.[26] Coming so soon after President Eisenhower had found it necessary to federalize the Arkansas National Guard to escort black students into Central

---

[24] *Dawson v. Mayor & City Council of Baltimore*, 220 F. 2d 386 (4th cir. 1955)

[25] Mayor & City Council of Baltimore v. Dawson, 350 U.S. 877 (1955)

[26] Moorland Spingarn, Box 50-4, Folder 116

High School in Little Rock, Arkansas, it is not surprising that he sent a congratulatory letter praising the Y.W.C.A. for giving life and substance to the American tradition of "respect for the God-given rights of the individual citizen."[27]

•••

Meanwhile, between 1940 and 1952 while these public accommodation fights were going on, Baltimore's NAACP succeeded in nearly doubling the number of registered black voters. With the support of the black ministers (the Reverends John Tilley, Vernon Dobson and Hiram Smith playing key roles in the registration committee) who held their congregations responsible for the geographic area surrounding their churches, the NAACP had been able to register more than nine thousand new voters.[28]

Additionally, in 1946, a new force was added to the political picture: Willie Adams's wife, Victorine, organized the Colored Democratic Women. It represented "a core of black voting power which was non geographic and separate from the Democratic clubs—and more powerful than most of them."[29]

The combination of black ministers and the NAACP that had resulted in the registration of so many new black voters proved just as effective again in 1958. The number that year topped 100,000; making a total of 22,000 new voters added just since the 1956 presidential election. "Ballots and not Bullets" had been the slogan of Lillie Jackson, head of the NAACP.

•••

Having utilized information from the Baltimore Urban League, Maryland Commission on Interracial Problems and Relations, the Housing Authority of Baltimore and the *Sun* and *Afro-American* newspapers, the Sidney Hollander Foundation's publication, *Toward Equality,* as alluded to previously, summarizes the annual awards they gave to

---

[27] Moorland Spingarn, Box 50-4, folder 118. The Little Rock event was on September 24, 1957.

[28] Figures that follow are from *Toward Equality.* Voting drive information is from Shoemaker, p. 265-266 & Milobsky, p. 278.

[29] Callcott, George, p. 148.

various persons and groups honoring their achievements in race relations. What follows is an overview of those achievements in the area of Public Accommodations between the years 1946 and 1953. They serve as an uncomfortable reminder of the times; revealing both how far blacks had come, and how far Baltimore still had to go.

In 1946 the *Sunpapers* received the first of the Hollander awards. The reasons for the selection were enumerated at the award's ceremony—the *Sun*'s editorial opposition to lynchings and the Ku-Klux Klan, and its support for repealing the state's Jim Crow laws, for Morgan College's purchase of land in Baltimore County, and for its own abandoning of "racial designations in headlines where they tend to make an unfavorable impression." Most of all, the selection committee pointed to the *Sun*'s "impartial reporting of the human activities of Negroes as a part of the total community."

In accepting the award on behalf of the paper, Hamilton Owens, editor-in-chief, stated it would be turned over to Morgan College "with the suggestion that the President of that admirable institution, Dr. Dwight O. W. Holmes, select a worthy student and provide him with one year's tuition and board." He added: "The *Sunpapers* will contribute the small additional amount necessary to round out the full cost."[30]

Speeches that evening also recognized two groups with an Honorable Mention. The first, Mr. And Mrs. Milton Wagner who had opened Friends' House, an integrated neighborhood center offering recreation, education and spiritual guidance: "prejudice dissolves when people get together." The second, the Baltimore Presbytery, which included all the city's Presbyterian churches, for electing a Negro to the high office of Moderator: "It has set an example of Christian brotherhood that is certain to extend far beyond the confines of this community."

It was also in 1946 that civic organizations protested cuts in the city's budget for recreation; then got funds restored for

---

[30] Quotes in this and subsequent paragraph, Moorland Spingarn, Box 50-1, Folder 19 and box 50-1, folder 18 (the two Honorable Mention awards appearing again in folder 101 (mistakenly filed with 1955 information according to news clippings for 1947).

the first year-round program at Cherry Hill, a black residential community.

In 1947 Morgan State College presented "Deep Are the Roots" to non-segregated audiences after the playwright refused to permit production at segregated Ford's Theater. The Council of Churches organized three faith campaigns against antiquated Jim Crow transportation laws. At a four-day city-wide Institute on Race Relations, the American Missionary Association joined in the presentation of Negro problems in housing, health, education, employment, welfare and religion. Dr. Ralph Young became the first Negro at Johns Hopkins Hospital: a part-time clinician in the Out-Patient Department. A local practitioner, he had done much to promote the Chick Webb Recreation Center for colored youth and to focus attention on the high rate of tuberculosis among Negroes. Baltimore Museum of Art conducted integrated children's art classes and held the first Negro Art Show.

In 1949, whites protested use of Clifton Park by black Dunbar High School students. On a more positive note, the Maryland Theatre became the first legitimate theatre to operate on a non-discriminatory basis.

In 1950 the Maryland Commission on Interracial Problems and Relations was created. The NAACP and others protested police brutalities, citing sixteen instances. The police department at the time was a "bastion of racism." Blacks were herded into police stations "if they happened to be walking by when there was a lineup. Hundreds were arrested on 'suspicion' and held for days without bail. It was awfully easy to get arrested for nothing. Furthermore, for the police, 'the third degree was more or less standard operating procedure.'"[31]

•••

The Y.W.C.A. had been integrated for some time when the Y.M.C.A., in 1957, moved to integrate. In 1955, on the occasion of their father's 75th birthday, members of the Hollander family had singled out the Y.M.C.A. to criticize for its self-proclaimed purpose of "extending Christian brotherhood," while it clung to "segregation as the world

---

[31] Watson, p. 84.

passed them by." The Hollanders' ended their chastisement by stating: "Some kind soul should tell them the facts of life."[32] Perhaps they were listening. It was also in 1957 that the Boy Scouts followed the Girl Scouts and integrated their troops and staff.

Returning to the year 1952, Baltimore's Friendship International Airport opened the dining and drinking facilities to Negroes who could show they had plane tickets. [Three years later, in 1955, it ended all discrimination in its restaurants.] Also in 1952, members of the Commission on Interracial Problems and Relations met with representatives of the Retail Merchants and the Parks Department. At the conclusion, despite the number of peaceful voluntary integrations that had occurred by then, they issued a statement to the effect that "the people of Maryland wished to maintain the status quo and would respond with indignation and possibly violence to any change."

The opening section of the booklet, *Toward Equality* noted that at the end of World War II, in Baltimore, white and black friends could eat together only at the railroad station facility, and that "taxicab drivers often disregarded the frantic waving of would-be riders who happened to be of the wrong color." "Department stores were in such a state of indecision as to what Negroes could or could not buy that colored shoppers never knew what to expect from week to week or from one counter to the next. Always there was the risk of soul-searing experiences, such as having a floor-walker shoo colored children away from the white Santa Claus." "Entertainment was rigidly restricted," and "Ford's, the city's principal legitimate theatre, confined colored patrons to its precipitous second balcony."

The long struggle to integrate Ford's theater[33] had started on February 17, 1947 soon after the Washington branch of the NAACP asked Baltimore's branch to join them in picketing the Mechanic's National Theater in D.C. This had followed

---

[32] Moorland Spingarn, Box 50-3, folders 86 & 88.
[33] This account based on an *Afro* clipping 2/24/1948 (especially the arrest account) and article in the *Sun*, 9/17/1993 by Robert Kaufman.

Ingrid Bergman's refusal to star there in George Bernard Shaw's *St. Joan* because it was segregated. From February 17th on, at every performance at Ford's, six nights a week and two matinees, until it capitulated in 1952, at least one picket was there carrying signs asking patrons and performers to boycott the theater. Regulars on the picket line included Ada Jenkins, a homemaker and piano teacher who later became a founding member of CORE, Don Altwood who had left a job with Social Security to head Fellowship House, Bob Kaufman, only sixteen at the time, and a number of the Mitchells—Parren, Lillie, Juanita, and Clarence, Jr.

Morgan students also often were amongst the picketers, and two managed to get arrested on February 20, 1947, a day when there were thirty picketers covered the entire sidewalk in front of the theater. They had refused to comply when told by the manager, John Little, that they were picketing so close together they were blocking the way of patrons trying to get in. After he called the police, the tavern owner next door, Benny Benjamin, joined him in the complaint, saying the picketers had spread onto the walk in front of his entrance, making potential customers believe it was he who was being picketed.

When the two students appeared before Magistrate Pairo, represented by Calvin Douglass and Ernest Perkins, NAACP attorneys, they were released with a warning to, in the future, correct the complaints cited above, and an admonition that he thought ten to twenty pickets were sufficient to serve their purpose.

At first the *Afro* gave the demonstrators their only publicity, and responses to letters written to artists were slow in coming, but eventually artists and producers, including Jose Ferrer, Richard Rodgers and Oscar Hammerstein agreed to support the boycott. Others, like Charles Boyer, agreed to make a public statement (carried on the city's largest radio station), against the segregation policy, but felt he had to honor his contract and appear, as scheduled, in the play, "Red Gloves." After Actors' Equity agreed to honor the boycott and stopped sending actors and plays, Ford was able to produce only three plays in 1952, its final year of segregation. Looking back, Bob Kaufman, one of the pickers, recalled an event that occurred soon after their victory:[34]

> Lillie Jackson, NAACP president and grande dame of
> the Mitchell clan, bought Ada Jenkins and me orchestra
> seats for Ford's first interracial play, The Merry Widow. I
> haven't been to the theater or its successor since.

Of the significance of this early and prolonged action by
so many Baltimoreans, Kaufman had this to say:

> Breaking the color line at Ford's accomplished two
> very important things. It demonstrated to the prejudiced
> white majority that fear of what might happen was
> nonsense. More important, it proved that the time was
> right for determined interracial groups to move forward.

The same year Ford's finally changed its policy, the
Hollander Foundation gave its award to Governor Theodore R.
McKeldin for initiatives he had taken in the area of
employment, but also cited the role of his Commission on
Interracial Problems and Relations in achieving the
"elimination of racial segregation at Ford's Theater."[35]

The differing policies of the Ford's and Lyric theaters
clearly demonstrates the absurdity and arbitrariness of
segregation. In the case of Ford's, it had long permitted
Negroes to appear on stage but until 1952 had restricted black
patrons to the second balcony, reached only by steep stairs
starting in the back alley. In the case of the Lyric Theater, it
had no restrictions on seating patrons but would not allow
Negroes on stage.

In November 1953 the Lyric changed that policy after the
public outcry that arose following their refusal to book Marian
Anderson.Thus it was on January 8, 1954, sponsored by the
Baltimore Interracial Fellowship, that Anderson became the
first Negro to appear on the Lyric's stage. Later in 1954, the
Howard University Glee Club also performed there without
any opposition. In 1953, the Hollander Foundation awarded
Honorable Mention to Fellowship House, the Maryland
Commission on Interracial Problems and Relations and the
Baltimore Commission on Human Relations for their part "in

---

[34] The *Baltimore Sun*, September 17, 1993.
[35] Moorland Spingarn, Box 50, folder 53.

ending racial discrimination in the selection of artists to perform at the Lyric Theatre."[36]

Also in 1953 Negro shoppers in the downtown area, for the first time, were able to take a break for lunch and eat it sitting down at at least six downtown chain variety and drug store lunch counters.[37] For this achievement the Hollander Foundation award that year went to CORE (then known as the Committee on Racial Equality). McQuay Kiah, CORE's 1954 Chairman (and a Dean of Students at Morgan) and Ben Everinghim, CORE's 1953 Chairman, received the award on the organization's behalf, selected for their efforts "to convince downtown store operators that it would not only be good democratic practice to open their eating facilities to Negroes, but also sound economy."

In accepting his award, Everinghim warned that "there are at least fifty years of solid work to be done to rid Baltimore of inequality." They were The presenter, J. Arnett Frisby stated, "Your achievements, to date, speak for your persuasive powers. Once again, it has been proven that we have nothing to fear but fear itself. Once the decision was made by these stores to follow the concepts of democracy—the transition was made without fanfare—without incident. I hope your ranks will grow—and grow—for the brotherhood it engenders."[38]

This recognition of CORE by the prestigious Sidney Hollander Foundation was only a taste of the actions—negotiations, boycotts, sit-ins and jail-ins—that soon would be undertaken in Baltimore and surrounding areas by both CORE and Morgan's Civic Interest Group.

The fifties was a decade when the activist NAACP had increasingly turned to the courts for change, and, ironically their successes there, more than any other single factor, was responsible for "the revolution in expectations." Supported by Supreme Court decisions and new anti-discrimination laws, sit-ins increased. White public opinion began to shift away

---

[36] *Toward Equality*, Appendix 2.

[37] More will be said of lunch-counter demonstrations in the sections that follow.

[38] Moorland Spingarn, Box 50-2, folder 69. Also from Sun, 11/14 &11/15, 1954

from segregation, especially as Soviet Union propaganda began to embarrass the United States; pointing to the hypocrisy of its racist practices in light of its democratic pretensions. Blacks "no longer felt they had to accept the humiliations of second-class citizenship," and their increasing impatience with segregation accounted in large part for "the rising tempo of nonviolent direct action" that culminated in the sit-ins that inaugurated what has become popularly known as the "Civil Rights Movement." Baltimore was no exception in turning away from the courts and legislation as the exclusive technique for challenging the status quo.[39]

---

[39] Quotes and information in this paragraph from Meier & Rudwick, *Black Protest in the Sixties*, Intro, pp. 7-8.

CORE & the Morgan Students

In 1990, in a conversation with James Farmer, former head of the Congress of Racial Equality (CORE), this writer asked him why he thought that Martin Luther King received so much adoration while he was all but forgotten. He answered: "I made the mistake of not being killed." In a recent conversation with the Reverend Vernon Dobson, pastor of Union Baptist Church,[40] he offered this same explanation as to why he, like most Baltimoreans, also talk about King, whose presence was virtually nil in Baltimore, and rarely, if ever, mention James Farmer, who was far more relevant to the city. To this writer that still seems an inadequate explanation for why this charismatic man who contributed as much to the cause of civil rights as did King is so neglected. But Farmer himself, in our conversation, did not sound bitter, even as he was then struggling with life as a diabetic, a condition that had left him blind, and with an amputated leg (finally, before his death, with both legs amputated).

A former national CORE staffer, Stu Wechsler, said: "I think it's actually a tribute to Farmer's integrity" that he did not receive credit for the accomplishments of his "loyal foot soldiers", as Farmer referred to them. But, Stu added, "I was honored to be present in January 1998 when Farmer was awarded the Presidential Medal of Freedom, the country's highest civilian honor." It was at least a token of recognition; nonetheless, one that stands in sharp contrast to the national holiday that annually celebrates King's achievements. The award rated only a brief mention in the side-bar of a back section the writer's hometown newspaper, *The Providence Journal*; quoting Farmer: "I'm grateful it came before I died. It's a vindication. I certainly was ignored and forgotten." His death on July 9, 1999 rated little more, the announcement found amongst many others on the obituary page. Only the *New York Times* gave his death the coverage it deserved: an article on the front page and a full page obit.

•••

---

[40] Extensive phone interview in June 2001.

James Farmer, as well as Rev. Vernon Dobson, were products of Howard University's School of Religion, and much influenced in their non-violent activism by Howard's President, Mordecai Johnson[41], and by Vernon Johns (the predecessor to King at the Dexter Avenue Church[42]). Neglected by most historians, Rev. Dobson called Johnson and Johns "the moral force behind the 1960s civil rights movement." Johnson, Dobson said, changed Howard University from "a little school" into a world class academic institution, and Johns he called "a one-man Civil Rights Movement."

Described Johns as having a chiseled face, "mean, handsome, and rugged, " Rev. Dobson delights in telling how Johns had been admitted to the previously all-white Oberlin College after he met their President's challenge to answer questions in three languages. Both Johnson and Johns were noted as brilliant speakers—Johns so much so that King, according to Dobson, in later years, feeling the inadequacies of his own preaching, sought Johns out in the hope of finding new inspiration, only to learn that the eccentric Johns never wrote out any of his sermons.

Rev. Dobson went on to tell how Johns would say things in a forum that "I wished I could say." As early as the 1940s he had begun to acquire the reputation that accompanied him throughout his life: so outspoken on behalf of equality for blacks that he regularly irritated even other black ministers.

Late in life, in 1957 Johns came to Baltimore to head the now-defunct Maryland State Baptist Center and School of Religion which had been founded in 1942, jointly, by the white Southern Baptists and the black National Baptist Convention. During his five years in Baltimore, he spoke at churches, conferences and universities not only locally, but in such diverse places as Virginia, Kentucky, North Carolina, and New

---

[41] Johnson, born in 1890, was Howard's first black President (from 1926-1960). He died in 1976.

[42] Johns, a contemporary of Johnson, was born in 1892, died in 1964. He had a tumultuous time as minister at the Dexter Avenue Church from 1948-1952. The members of this middle-class conservative church found Johns both too bohemian in his behavior (selling vegetables like a street peddler), and too radical in is preaching and pronouncements on race.

Jersey; always emphasizing his belief that "black salvation" lay with their becoming economically independent, with keeping their money in the black community, in black banks.[43]

Late in the summer of 1960 Johns' radical outspokenness so irritated the black and white ministers holding a convention at the Seventh Baptist Church in Baltimore, that he was soon-after asked to resign his position. They hadn't taken kindly to his lambasting them for emphasizing Jesus' death and forgiveness of sins, rather than his teachings while alive. After leaving Baltimore, in addition to his travels from place to place, lecturing and preaching, he edited a magazine called Second Century of Freedom that included articles representing his diverse interests, and, especially his belief in the importance of establishing strong black businesses. Some felt this emphasis put him out of touch with the civil rights movement as defined by Martin Luther King, and led to his not being invited to participate in the March on Washington that made King famous. Johns was in Washington, D.C. when he died on June 11, 1964.

For his part, Rev. Dobson, a 1953 Howard University graduate, inspired as he was by Mordecai Johnson and Vernon Johns, has carried on the activist tradition of Union Baptist Church's forbear, Harvey Johnson. Of this, Rev. Dobson made a telling remark with which many who were part of the 60s Civil Rights Movement, including this writer, agree:

> The Movement for me was a joy because, I think, I sensed the possibility of people providing empowerment for themselves like I've never experienced since.

Rev. Dobson knew Martin Luther King before he became predominant in the Civil Rights Movement. In talking to this writer, Dobson said that King, early-on, while still trying to determine how best to create a viable, nationwide civil rights movement, had come to ask him and others in Baltimore's already active Interdenominational Ministerial Alliance for advice. To student interviewers, Dobson said:

> We were a little further ahead in the work that we were

---

[43] Cooney & Powell, Chapter 27. Information that follows about Johns is from this source as well as interview.

doing in Baltimore in Civil Rights than he was. So, much of the work that he was doing was empowered by what we were doing here in Baltimore.

After naming a number of blacks and whites, Jews and Catholics who contributed to the Civil Rights Movement, Rev. Dobson gave special credit to a "great collection of preachers," Lillie Jackson, the woman who dominated the NAACP in Baltimore for years, and Carl Murphy, owner of the *Afro-American*, as responsible for Baltimore's being ahead of King in the movement. Rev. Dobson also said it was to those Baltimore preachers that King turned near the end of his life when he was conflicted by the schism in his ranks. He described his personal experience with King at this time:[44]

> About six months before King died, he got a Ford Foundation grant, took 25 of us down to Florida for two-weeks of intense, intense and rigorous dialogue about moving from the rural south to up south...further north. And I saw him naked in his pain. After those two weeks, he was a man who really was not in touch with the next steps. And so his death to me was more than the tragedy of one man dying. It was the tragedy of knowing he died not being fulfilled. At the time, he had gotten the Nobel Peace Prize and all these other things, but in his own center, he was in conflict.

As for James Farmer, after graduating from Howard's School of Religion in 1941, he disappointed his minister-father by not accepting a calling to a Methodist church, despite the fact that Howard regarded him as a fabulous preacher. Farmer explained that, in good conscience, he could not be part of a faith that discriminated. Instead, as a conscientious objector during World War II, he went to work for the Fellowship of Reconciliation, an organization founded during World War I that was committed to non-violence. Then, in June 1942, only a year after leaving Howard, he led an interracial group of students, mostly from the University of Chicago, into the Jack Spratt restaurant in Chicago, Illinois where they sat down and refused to leave until they were served. The participants immediately thereafter formed the Chicago Committee on Racial Equality. A year later, in mid-

---

[44] In a December 1999 interview with Hopkins students.

June 1943 at a weekend conference in Chicago, [45] *national* CORE, renamed Congress of Racial Equality, was formed to coordinate the activities of the growing number of local CORE groups. James Farmer was appointed its Executive Director. He had wanted to be part of a group more activist-oriented than the Fellowship of Reconciliation.

Baltimore CORE joined this growing number of local COREs sometime between 1951 and 1953, most likely in 1952.[46] Herbert Kelman, a white psychologist at the Phipps Psychiatric Clinic, apparently was the first to become interested in CORE's Ghandian nonviolent social action philosophy, but for some months was unable to find enough people to join him to start a local chapter. It took almost a year of effort before Kelman was able to bring together twenty-five to thirty interested people in the Windsor Hill's living room of Ben Everinghim, a white history teacher at Edmondson High School. Some of those present were middle class whites, others were black from an array of occupations—Robert Watts, an attorney; Ada Jenkins, a former music teacher and founder of the interracial Fellowship House;[47] a minister and his wife; Dr. Earl Jackson, a Morgan Professor and head of Morgan's NAACP branch; and trade unionists from the International Ladies Garment Workers Union (some of whom were said to have marched down Baltimore's Pennsylvania Avenue in the '30s protesting job discrimination). Kelman was especially interested in the liaison with activist Morgan students, some of whom may have been present at this organizing meeting.

•••

Robert Watts, a black attorney, represented the defendants in most all the early civil rights cases. In a

---

[45] In an interview in the *St. Louis Jewish Light,* March 7, 1973, Fred Weisgal, who became a leading civil rights litigator in Baltimore, said he was at this founding meeting of CORE in 1943.

[46] In an interview with Ben Everinghim for the *Sun,* 12/1/68, he said "1951," but he also gave January 1953 as their first action "almost immediately after" CORE's formation. In his book on CORE, Meier puts it at January 1953 (p. 57), but it is more likely that this is the date of their first action.

[47] She'd been a member of national CORE since its founding.

conversation with this writer shortly before his death, he stated that at least until May 1, 1961, he was the attorney representing the Morgan College student's organization, CIG (Civic Interest Group), CORE *and* the NAACP—a curious fact to contemplate since these named civil rights groups were competitive and often contentious with one another—a fact all, except Watts, seem to have recognized. Watts insisted that leaders of all these groups, regularly and amicably, met at his house for planning and strategy sessions.

John Roemer, who was white and an active member of CORE in the 60s, had this to say of Watts' contention: "He was such an affable guy, he could pretty-much get along with anyone." Meier agreed: "[Watts was] a lawyer whose gifts were enhanced by a personality that charmed judges and even hostile policemen...."[48]

At some point Fred Weisgal, recognized in Baltimore as a pioneer in civil rights and civil liberties litigation, became local CORE's attorney. Watts suggested it had been after May 1, 1961, when he gave up practicing as an attorney to accept an appointment as one of eleven judges to the newly established Municipal Courts. However, in 1962, after he ran for a seat on the Supreme Bench and lost, he returned to his legal practice and again assumed a prominent role in representing civil rights activists. But then, again, at the end of 1963, Watts said, "Governor Tawes appointed me, the first black, to the Supreme Bench, and I stopped practicing altogether." After that, Fred Weisgal became almost the only attorney in Baltimore who consistently was willing to undertake representing the increasing number of civil rights activists being arrested all over Maryland.

Early on Weisgal had contributed to the fight for racial equality in school segregation and housing covenant cases, but, during the sixties, civil rights cases (usually *pro bono*, for free) became a major part of his practice. Even though he rarely walked a picket line and was never present when arrests were made, he played a more prominent behind-the-scenes role than is generally played by an attorney. Rather

---

[48] Meier, *White Scholar...*, p. 24. As noted earlier, regrettably, Robert Watts died on 10/8/98 before this book was completed.

than becoming involved "after the fact," as is typical in civil liberties and criminal work, Fred regularly became involved "before the fact." Often activists and civil rights leaders met in his home, for he was a trusted advisor whom they wanted to participate in their planning and strategy sessions (just as had Thurgood Marshall, Bob Watts and others before him). He advised them on the kinds of cases that were needed to change laws, on what actions might precipitate what charges by the police, and what might happen in court. And, perhaps most important of all, he assured demonstrators they could count on him. One of the early sixties activists, John Roemer, recently expressed it well:

> Knowing you had people like Fred who would back you up in the courts gave you the kind of feeling of support you needed to continue demonstrating and getting arrested. It gave you a sense you could use the legal system to get your rights instead of being repressed by it.
>
> It was guys like Fred who made decisions like *Brown v. Board of Education* real and not just some Supreme Court decision you'd heard of.

•••

A spontaneous action early-on by Bayard Rustin, one of National CORE's first members, when on a visit to Baltimore, vividly demonstrates the organization's approach to civil rights.[49]

> He arrived in Baltimore one rainy night...and found no taxi driver at the train station would pick him up. So he walked into the middle of the taxi lane and stood for ninety minutes blocking traffic until he got a taxi.

With such members, it's not surprising that Baltimore CORE quickly became known for its direct action—sit-ins, stand-ins, lie-ins, picketing and boycotts. In its first years, with a still-small membership, it acted primarily as part of a coalition of civil rights groups that succeeded in integrating a number of establishments.

•••

In 1953, members of the recently organized local chapter

---

[49] The *Sun*, 12/1/68.

of CORE joined students at Morgan State College in an all-out effort to desegregate lunch counters throughout Baltimore. At first the Morgan students had been sort of an underground movement of eager students who saw a wrong they were determined to right, but by 1953, they had become loosely organized as the Student Government's Social Action Committee. By an informal agreement between the two organizations, CORE would concentrate its efforts downtown; the students would concentrate on desegregating the movie theater and lunch counters in the stores at the Northwood Shopping Center in Northeast Baltimore, just a few blocks from the almost all-black Morgan State College. Before the advent of fast food places like McDonald's and Burger King, store-based lunch counters were almost the only places where you could go for an inexpensive meal.

•••

More will be said of the history of Morgan College later in the Education and Housing sections, including the opposition this mostly black school encountered when it moved in 1917 from downtown to its present site. By the 1950s, the area around Morgan had become densely populated with white-owned red brick row-houses lining the streets, and a near-by segregated Northwood Shopping Center, with its movie house, stores and lunch counters, had been built to serve the areas whites. Their exclusion from the Shopping Center had become an increasing irritant to Morgan's students, mostly Christian and mostly from Baltimore's upwardly mobile black working class. Some then on campus may already have participated in picketing; an article in *Afro-American* on February 24, 1948, having noted that police arrested two Morgan students for "obstructing free passage" while picketing at the Ford's theater.

With Morgan's history of resistance to segregation, it is not surprising that by the Spring of 1952 as many as a hundred students at a time could be found protesting at Northwood's movie theater. Initially it was an unorganized group of students, encouraged "off the record" by the Dean of Students, McQuay Kiah, himself at one time Chairman of CORE. Typically, the students stood in line, books open studying, and when refused a ticket, returned to the rear of the line to repeat the process. Others sat-in at the Arundel Ice Cream store and the Hecht-May Company Roof-Top café (in the largest department store in the Shopping Center, its main store downtown), leaving only after the reading of the Maryland Trespass Law, a legal requirement in Maryland before arrests for trespassing can be made.

It would be eight years before the theater admitted blacks, and not until March 18, 1959 that Arundel Ice Cream opened its store to all. Until that Wednesday in 1959 when George Kerchner, company supervisor, told the students that they would be just as welcome as anyone, as many as 450 students had been regularly appearing at the shopping center to picket the theater and to sit-in at the Ice Cream Shop and at the Hecht-May Roof-Top café. It was a whole year later before Hecht opened its restaurant to blacks.

More will be said of the department store sit-ins later, but it should be noted that the use of picketing and sit-ins by Morgan students predated by almost a decade the more famous, nationally publicized, student sit-ins at Greensboro, North Carolina in the 1960s. Clearly the Morgan students were carrying on a local tradition started by the city's young people in the 1930s, ignored though all these actions generally have been by historians writing about the civil rights movement.[50]

•••

Following their general approach to anticipated actions, CORE started their first action in January 1953 by first testing to confirm the existence of discrimination. Letters to local managers followed in an attempt to reach an agreement, and, when appropriate, also to out-of-state owners. Next came the distribution of handbills to customers outlining CORE's position. CORE hoped these actions would exert sufficient pressure on an establishment to achieve integration without the need for boycotts, sit-ins and picketing. Ben Everinghim put it this way:

> The whole idea of CORE originally was that men's

---

[50] See account of City-Wide Young People's Forum in Employment section: "The Great Depression."

attitudes could be changed and consequently their actions. We used to have meetings before demonstrations and reiterate this principle of CORE's.[51]

Everinghim went on to describe their first demonstration at Kresge's dime store:

> One noon-time, an integrated group sat down at the lunch counter and weren't served. We made an appointment with the manager and met with him. We always tested and conferred with the manager or owner before demonstrating. [National] CORE went to Kresge's headquarters in New York and demonstrated. The home office said they'd integrate the lunch counters. [Using this letter] we got a promise from Woolworth's that they'd integrate if Kresge's would.[52]

A clipping from an unnamed newspaper, probably the *Afro*, reported the event this way:

> The sudden change in policy was wrought because of hard, behind-the-scene work of the Committee on Racial Equality, commonly dubbed CORE. This organization, inter-racial in both character and intent, worked on segregated eating facilities in the downtown area for several months before attaining any success....CORE is a non-political organization which recognizes no creed except that of complete anti-segregation. A philosophy of non-violence is strictly adhered to....
>
> [Now] at each lunch counter dishes ranging from complete meat-and-two-vegetable meals to toast and tea can be purchased. Both counters are more than a block long—running the length of each store....In no instance was there any marked puzzlement or resentment registered by white patrons [after colored were served].

However, even after McQuay Kiah gave the Morgan students a copy of the letter from the national Kresge office in Detroit, and it was shown to the Northwood store, they refused to integrate, maintaining "business reasons." An adult committee was formed to complement the student's efforts. It was headed by Morgan Professor, Eugene Stanley, and included CORE's Ben Everinghim, Mary Schollsberg, Bertha Johnson, Ada Jenkins and Lillian Watson. Finally, CORE

---

[51] James D. Dilts, *Sun*, "The Warning Trumpet", 12/1/1968
[52] James D. Dilts, *Sun*, "The Warning Trumpet", 12/1/1968

received a second letter from Kresge's Detroit office in the summer of 1953 advising them to retry their Northwood store. An interracial team, then, much to their surprise, was promptly and courteously served when they sat down at the lunch counter.

A number of the other chains then also integrated but in the fall of 1953, Grant's was still a stubborn hold-out. In New York, Bayard Rustin undertook negotiations with the company's headquarters, but they refused to overrule the local store. As Christmas approached and expecting a fall-off in support from his troops, Kelman and Everinghim, the local CORE leaders, undertook two final protests that saw thirty-eight willing to sit-in, distribute leaflets and carry signs.[53] Simultaneously, New York's local CORE prepared to demonstrate in Harlem's Grant's. The Grant's manager remained undaunted either by these actions, by the sit-ins that resumed after-Christmas, or by the meeting he'd agreed to with representatives from CORE and the Governor's Commission on Interracial Problems and Relations.

On April 27, 1954, James Peck, from national CORE, spoke to the Board of Directors at Grant's national headquarters. He must have been persuasive because a week later, in May, the directors agreed to integrate. This agreement brought the Baltimore CORE chapter to the forefront as a bona fide civil rights organization to be respected by the black community.[54]

CORE then joined the Morgan students in their on-going, so far unsuccessful, efforts to integrate the lunch counter at Read's drug store near Northwood. It was a locally owned chain with thirty-seven stores in the Baltimore area. Once a week for almost eight months, thirty or more Morgan students had been sitting-in; CORE added a nationwide write-in campaign and initiated negotiations with the management. Ironically, despite the fact that the manager had hired some black waitresses, he continued to refuse service to blacks—until January 1955 when some of the black waitresses broke down and served them.

---

[53] Horn, p. 82
[54] Meier & Rudwick, *CORE*, p. 57.

This did not, however, mean the manager had capitulated; he transferred the black waitresses elsewhere and the demonstrations continued. The occasion did seem to provoke Read's management into serious negotiations with the lawyers and representatives of the students—Joan Wertheimer, McQuay Kiah, Dean of Students at Morgan, and Ben Everinghim, co-Chair of CORE. Finally, in mid-January, the management agreed to integrate the lunch counters at all thirty-seven of its drugstores.

Horn says this of these joint CORE-Morgan student efforts:

> The two formed a good team. Yet despite the success, at the conclusion of the luncheon counter campaign the two groups parted company. There was a significant change in the leadership of CORE, which may account for the change of direction. Herbert Kelman moved to take a job in California. Ben Everinghim ceased active participation for personal reasons that are not entirely clear.[55]

After their success at Read's, the students turned once again to their earlier target, the Northwood's movie house (a campaign that encompassed eight years). CORE, on its part, turned again to its annual campaign to integrate Gwynn Oak Park (which also encompassed an eight year period). Lunch counters and restaurants were not forgotten, however, as we will see.

---

[55] Horn, p. 85

Gwynn Oak & March on Washington

Gwynn Oak,[56] opened in 1895, was a 68-acre park, just west of the Baltimore City line, owned by the brothers Arthur, James and David Price. Over the years such well-known performers as Les Brown, Glenn Miller, Doris Day and the Three Stooges had performed in its ballroom. By the mid-fifties it featured over twenty-five rides, including an old-fashioned wooden roller coaster, a Ferris wheel, bumper cars and games of chance. The Price brothers promoted it as a family-oriented place for picnics and outings—alcoholic drinks and women smoking cigarettes banned (except on "German Day"). Once a year on "Report Card Day," it opened its gates for free rides to children who had good school marks—except black children who were never allowed in.

Even at the annual "All Nations Day Festival" when other foreign embassies were asked to participate, African embassies were excluded from this "spectacle of harmony." They were never among those invited to send representatives dressed in their native attire, to bring samples of their local cuisine, and to perform native dances. This irony was not lost on CORE.

•••

CORE began demonstrating at Gwynn Oak Park in July 1955, when as many as forty CORE members turned out on "All-Nations Day" to protest the amusement park's refusal to admit blacks. Ironically, it was earlier that same year, in May, that the manager of the Dixie Ballroom, a part of the Gwynn Oak Park complex, told a committee of Hopkins students that even though they had a policy against "colored people" in the amusement park, colored would be welcome at a dance in the ballroom. The subject had come up when a black student inquired if he would be welcome at the Lord Baltimore Hotel

---

[56] Information for this account comes from an assortment of news clippings from personal collections (in most cases the name of paper not given; the date elicited from content), an account by Chester Wickwire to the *Evening Sun* July 16, 1993, from interviews with John Roemer, Francis Murnaghan and Robert Watts, since deceased, as well as from Meier's book, *CORE*....

where they had planned to hold their June Week prom. When June Week committee members went to the hotel for an answer, the management told them they would stop the dance if Negroes attended.

In addition to the Dixie Ballroom, the committee asked the Southern Hotel for its policy and were told it would admit all couples, but reminded the students of the Maryland law that required segregation in public bars. Bowley's Resort said they would admit all couples except in their swimming pool. Eventually the committee settled on the Alcazar for their senior prom, June 7; Bowley's for a bull roast, June 8; the Dixie for the Sports Dance, June 9; and the Southern for the senior Banquet and Dance, June 11.

The May 20 *Hopkins Newsletter* expressed the hope that this year's concern for the treatment of its black students would not again be overlooked as it had been "since the first colored undergraduate received his degree in the late 1940s." They praised this year's June Week Chairman, Ed Goldberg, "for his quick and decisive correcting of an honest mistake, a regrettable lack of foresight in the fall which led to the contracting of a segregated hall." Goldberg explained he "simply hadn't realized the existence of a problem."

•••

Since 1955, CORE had demonstrated annually at Gwynn Oak Park on "All Nations Day" but had not attracted substantial public notice even in 1959 when four pickets were "violently assaulted and dragged from the Park." A letter written by CORE at the time[57] names the four as Joseph Sheehan, ex-Chair of CORE, then on the Advisory board [not related to Cardinal Shehan]; Dale Drews, Juretha Joyner, and Helen Brown, Project Director with Sidney Hollander Associates, a well-respected Baltimore business. Francis Murnaghan, an attorney, tried to take their case to the Supreme Court, but *certiorari* was declined despite a sympathetic opinion by Justice Warren. (At least four justices must agree before the Supreme Court will hear a case.). It had not reached the Supreme Court until 1964, by which time a

---

[57] John Roemer, active with CORE, sent the writer a copy of this letter, written at the time, which contained this information.

state public accommodations law had passed; the court thus assuming the issue was moot, returned it to the state Court of Appeals. There, in September, their convictions were upheld. It's probable, however, that the Court of Appeals eventually changed its mind and reversed these convictions, as it did in the Hooper's case (more later).

•••

One might have thought that Gwynn Oak would have been affected by the 1962 Supreme Court case, *Griffin v. Maryland* [58] but it does not seem to have been. The *Griffin* case "arose out of the conviction of black youths entering Glen Echo, a privately owned amusement park near Washington D.C. and boarding a carousel, despite Glen Echo's policy to exclude blacks. The youths had been arrested by a private detective employed by the park, who had been deputized by the county sheriff and wore a deputy sheriff's badge when he made the arrest." From an attorney's point of view the arrests in this case were not quite as clear-cut regarding violation of the Fourteenth Amendment as some of the other arrests by state or city police. Nonetheless, it provoked disagreement amongst the Supreme Court justices and was held over until the 1963 term to be re-argued. By the time the Glen Echo case was again heard, it had opened the park to blacks, so that the court's eventual five to four decision reversing the conviction "because of the participation of a deputy sheriff in the exclusion of the demonstrators" was essentially irrelevant.

•••

In 1962, as planning was underway for that year's "All Nation's Day" at Gwynn Oak, John Roemer, white, newly-elected Vice-Chair of CORE, and Walter Carter, black, elected Chair only a year after joining CORE in 1961, decided it was time to raise the level of protest.

Robert Watts, the black attorney who was a founding member of CORE, told this writer in an interview prior to his death that it was he who brought Walter into CORE and convinced him to become its Chairman. Walter represented

---

[58] Information on *Griffin* found in Schwartz, pp. 480 & 509, which can be referred to for more detail.

what has been termed the second generation of CORE activists, eventually becoming known to many as "Baltimore's Mr. Civil Rights". Many thought he would have been mayor had he not died in 1971.

Walter was born in Monroe, North Carolina, a town of 6,000, a third of whom were black. He was the seventh of nine children; his father, a barber, was of Japanese-German descent. Walter's eyes definitely reflected his oriental heritage; his pale brown skin had a yellowish tint—but how he would have hated that description. He hated anything yellow—"yellow" was high on the scale, near white, in the Negro's color-caste-system—which he hated—a caste system that prevailed at Howard University where he earned a Master's in Social Work.

Walter explained how he'd chosen college after a couple of days picking cotton: " My back hurt like hell. That wasn't for me," he told this writer on one occasion. He also told her how, during his years at North Carolina Agricultural & Technical College, he'd been involved with Wallace's Progressive Party—like the writer, only she wasn't in danger—and how he'd helped register blacks to vote. *This had taken courage— Negroes were hanged for far less at a time when he'd watched as the Ku Klux Klan marched openly through Monroe.*

Walter also sometimes talked about Robert Williams, a former NAACP official from his home-town of Monroe, who had fled to Cuba after being charged with kidnapping a white couple. Later Williams went to China from which he issued bulletins advocating armed guerilla warfare. Walter felt Williams had become a target "for meeting the armed threat of whites in Monroe with gunfire." Walter was the most non-violent person this writer has ever encountered, yet he understood, and at least in part sympathized with those who came to feel that bloodshed was necessary for a suppressed people to become truly free.

After graduating near the top of his class, Walter had joined the Army—before President Truman issued the executive order in July of 1948 that integrated the services. "I sure as hell resented having to serve in an all-black unit," he said. "We were very limited in what we were allowed to do, but still and all, I stayed hopeful that our contributions would lead to changed attitudes in the country after the war." Walter rarely talked about the fact he had been a clerk in charge of an ammunition dump, had earned five battle stars, and had narrowly escaped death when the dump exploded from enemy bombs. He did once say to a reporter, *"You almost get killed one night and you say 'what for?' And you try to discover this democracy you were defending."*

He was clearly bitter when he said to this writer on one occasion, "I could hardly believe it when I left the army, my college degree in hand, and all the North Carolina Employment Office would offer me were 'shovel and mop' jobs." Walter had used some of his GI benefits to come to Baltimore (in 1948) and to get his real estate license. He started counseling other black veterans about pursuing decent housing through the Veterans Administration and Federal Housing Assistance programs and about the educational opportunities offered by the GI Bill. In 1953, he accepted a position as social worker with the Department of Welfare. When this writer met Walter, he was a Social Worker with the Public Schools, which meant, in fact, he was a "truant officer"—something the schools still had. As such, he went to truants' homes to find out why they were cutting school. He was great at helping families solve home problems—solutions that often resulted in totally new attitudes towards school by both children and parents.

It had not been hard to persuade Walter to accept the Chairmanship of CORE in 1962, nor is it surprising that CORE immediately became a more activist organization under his charismatic leadership. John's commitment was perhaps a bit more surprising, certainly a shock to his very conservative parents.

•••

Walter and John started their planning for CORE's 1962 protest at Gwynn Oak's "All Nation's Day" by calling the invited embassies and asking them to refuse to participate. After the Indian Embassy responded, "We don't interfere in local affairs," they decided that on Saturday, August 25, they'd put into effect phase two of their plan. John recalled it this way:

> In the past I'd been to the Park many times, without incident, to their country music shows but by the time

Walter and I went there that day, I'd already been pushed around a bit by the private security guards at the Park. We'd go there to picket and Jim Price would scream and holler and stones would be thrown. It wasn't a pretty situation. I felt Jim Price had taken a particular dislike to me; perhaps because I taught his son in 7th grade at Friends School. So before going that Saturday, I called the *Afro-American* and told them to cover CORE's next picketing at Gwynn Oak if they wanted a major story. "Send a photographer, too, because I think these guys will beat the crap out of us the next time we go over there."

As I approached the gate along with Walter, as expected, the guard asked us to leave, but I replied, "I'm not going to leave because I think everyone should be allowed to ride the roller coaster."

"What's your name?" he asked. Instead of answering, I reached into my pocket and pulled out a pad of paper.

"Tell me your name and badge number," I requested of him.

At that point he reared back and hit me smack in the nose. The *Afro-* photographer jumped out to snap the picture. Walter and I were both arrested, but we got a big story.

According to a newspaper report, they both refused to post the $103 bail and stayed in jail overnight. They also accused the security guards of brutality, Walter claiming he was clubbed on the leg, and John that he'd been pushed to the ground.[59] Rather than stopping CORE from further protests, the incident served to help their cause as they'd hoped. They again called the embassies, emphasizing the park owner's brutality and asking if they really wanted to be a part of such behavior. To the Indian Embassy, they asked how it would look for the largest democracy in world to seem to be condoning such behavior.

On All Nations Day itself, all the embassies having backed out, John, a few others from CORE, and several from New York Local 1199E of the Retail Clerks Union went to the Park to demonstrate. Barred from entering by the security guards, John decided to create a diversion by having most of the others go around to the back of the park where it was

---

[59] The charges are reported in the *Afro*, 8/28/1962

possible to enter by wading across a small stream. As John described it, "when someone suddenly yelled, 'the Niggers have got in the Park,' the guards went running off and I went in through the gate.

> I was then severely beaten by a bunch of goons who held me, smashed my glasses, stomped on me, ripped my clothes and finally threw me at the feet of a county cop, standing nearby, who arrested me for trespass. The guys from 119E were impressed that non-violence and non-retaliation could be adhered to under the circumstances; I believe they showed up at the big demonstration the next year.

This trespass case was never tried. After the trial for the August 28th arrest ended in a hung jury, the prosecution feared that the same result, or worse a finding of not guilty, in another trial would set an unwanted precedent. Fred Weisgal had represented John and Walter in that trial before a jury in Baltimore County on March 8, 1963, almost a year after the incident itself. The focus then was not on the brutality, but instead, as Fred said in talking to the *Sun* reporter covering the trial: "Mr. Carter was evicted because of his race and nothing else."

At the time, several trespass cases were pending in the higher courts and it was generally felt that soon such cases as this would become moot, but at this trial the prosecutor asked the jury, *despite this* (which he admitted), "to uphold the law *the way it is*;" and admonished the jury to "forget about the morals." Fred, on the other hand, argued it was *all about morals* and asked them to read the sign, written in capital letters, on the wall behind the Judge, beneath the Maryland Seal: "Equality and Liberty Under The Law Is The Foundation Of A Government Of Free People."

Fred further argued that the trespass act was not set up to enforce segregation "and it is up to you to strike it down...This law of trespass does not apply and when a law is wrong the jury has the right to interpret the law to make it right...I ask you to interpret it that way.... During the hour and a half the jury was out they asked to see a copy of the law. When they returned, the decision was six-six. John believes the one black woman on the jury had managed to win over five other jurors to oppose their conviction, hence the hung jury.

After the jury reported they could not reach a decision, the judge continued John's and Walter's $100 bail, but the prosecutor declined to comment as to when—or whether—the state would re-try the case. (They never did.)

On March 12, the *Afro* noted: "[This Gwynn Oak trial] marked the first time integration leaders escaped conviction at a trial on trespassing charges since anti-segregation demonstrations began in Maryland." It was also the first time a trespass case had been tried by a jury (previously they had been tried by a judge only). Of the court's decision, Fred told a reporter, "There is no doubt in my mind that the Trespass Law is on its way out. This shows that people are very upset about a law which legalizes discrimination."

The decision in this case had come only one week after the Baltimore Grand Jury had thrown out the charges against 413 college students for trespassing during the Northwood Theatre protests. It also came only a month before Baltimorean Bill Moore was killed en route to Mississippi (more later), precipitating Walter Carter's resignation as Chairman of CORE. He was disgusted that Bill should have had to "pay for his own death" as Walter put it, while CORE had to struggle just to get "a lousy dollar bill from the living to carry on the fight."

•••

Meanwhile, back in the Fall of 1962, letters were sent by CORE and the NAACP to the Ambassadors of Mexico, Greece, India, Norway, Indonesia and the Philippines urging them not to participate in the Park's 12th "All Nation's Day" scheduled for September 2; recognizing the Day's lack of inclusiveness and the Park's discrimination against blacks. After they finally agreed to withdraw, the *Afro-American* ran an article on September 1, 1962, declaring:

> Segregated Gwynn Oak Park in Baltimore County finds itself as of now, roughly in the position of a bride, dressed for a wedding, and no bridegroom in sight. The park is to play host to an "All-Nations Day" on Sunday with one variation. None of the nations invited to the fête will have anything to do with it because of the park's segregation.

An editorial on the same date declared:

> We have never understood how the All Nations Day was so named when it welcomed no black peoples and was held at an amusement center...where admittance is refused colored persons....It is a sad situation when citizens of this great democracy, in the name of brotherhood, maintain a course so at variance with democratic principles that representatives of foreign nations find it necessary to disassociate themselves from their activities.

Typical embassy responses had been "polite," but in "cool, clear language:"

> ...After receiving additional information about the festival...we do not intend to participate...because all persons are not allowed to participate. We have informed the person in charge of the exhibit.

That same September, the Morgan College student's Civic Interest Group (CIG) wrote Pope John XXIII a letter urging him to advise the Maryland Council of the Knights of Columbus, a fraternal organization of Catholic laymen, to cancel their plans for a state-wide reunion at the park. The letter suggested an—

> unwitting cooperation with and condonation of immoral and uncharitable conduct by otherwise well-meaning people. This sort of unthinking action should bot be allowed to recur. Any effort on Your Excellency's part to more clearly define the moral precepts violated by the practice of discrimination would be most welcome.

The Knights of Columbus had previously denied CIG's request that they seek another site. On September 5, CIG picketed the organization's headquarters at Cathedral and Madison, carrying signs such as one that read: "Racial Segregation is Un-Christian." There's no indication that either action by CIG had any result.

Unfortunately, none of these actions had ended Gwynn Oak's policy of excluding blacks, so again the following summer, on Thursday, May 30, 1963 eight CORE members were again demonstrating at Gwynn Oak Park. This was just after Walter Carter had resigned, in disgust, as Chairman of CORE following the death of Bill Moore. As a consequence, Ed Chance, a social worker then in the same Welfare Department as Walter, had superseded him and taken over planning the Gwynn Oak Park protests. It was a time when Cambridge was "hot" and occupied by the National Guard. Some in CORE wanted to go there and confront them, but Chance, remembering his time in the army, was against this: "I knew damn well you don't play with the United States. I'm not going down there and go up against the U.S. National Guard. Instead, Chance looked at Gwynn Oak and proclaimed: "No more symbolic stuff there. We've been pussy-footing with them long enough, let's bust it, let's do it."[60]

Ed Chance had always been interested in fighting segregation, his father had been the plaintiff in a ground-breaking transportation suit in their native North Carolina,[61] but it was only after Ed left the army, graduated from Howard's School of Social Work and moved to Baltimore that he became an activist; decided to join CORE rather than the Urban League or NAACP because their non-violent direct action approach appealed to him. But until Gwynn Oak, Ed had been happy as Walter's "second lieutenant" (as the *Sun* described it), had participated in the picketing of segregated restaurants, but had never been arrested nor gone to jail. Now, as Chairman of CORE, he was ready to do whatever it took "to bust open Gwynn Oak."[62]

This time, the eight who had been arrested on May 30, 1963 were charged with *conspiring to break the trespass law,* as well as with the usual trespassing. The press quoted Fred Weisgal, the attorney who represented them at arraignment, as saying that this was "something completely new" to racial

---

[60] Quotes from an interview of Chance by Hopkins students, 12/08/2000. This writer also interviewed Chance at length.
[61] *Chance v. Lambeth* et al 186F2d879 (1951); *Atlantic Coastline v. Chance* 198F2d 549 (1952); 73 Supreme Court 172, Petition for writ of certiorari to U.S. Ct. of Appeals for the 4th Circuit denied 11/10/52. Similar to the early state case, *Hart v. State* (1905), Ed Chance's father had contested the right of a railroad to segregate passengers in interstate travel, been arrested and fined. He eventually won his case, but only awarded $50 in damages. Judge Soper, the circuit judge in this case, was also the Judge in the Pratt Library case to be discussed later. In addition to reviewing the cases themselves as this writer did, there is a brief overview in the auto-biography of one of Chance's lawyers. See Hill, p. 143.
[62] *Sun,* August 23, 1998

demonstrations in Maryland. Fred explained that in order to be convicted of conspiracy you have to be conspiring to commit an illegal act. However, in this case, CORE was merely attempting to break down racial restrictions. [Further], conspiracy implies that a group is meeting secretly, but these people are meeting openly.

Bail was set at $103 for the trespass and $253 for the conspiracy counts. These cases, like so many of the trespass cases, most likely never came to trial; probably because the public accommodations law was passed before they were scheduled.

•••

These arrests, in any case, were only a forerunner to the plans for Thursday, July 4, 1963. CORE, together with a whole array of other groups that included students from Morgan's CIG, anticipated a very different kind of observance of our 187 years of freedom and independence than that planned by the city, which they'd dubbed, "Let Freedom Ring." As the organizers met in CORE's dingy, hot little basement office, someone asked Walter Carter what they were going to do about arrests at the demonstration. "We haven't got enough in the treasury to bail out three people," he'd replied, leaning back, typically, with his eyes half-shut, appearing almost asleep. "We'll get 400 people arrested, including a lot of clergymen. Then they'll let everybody out on his own recognizance."[63]

They knew that all the letters written by and to various organizations locally and in other states[64] promoting the demonstration, all the handbills passed out, all the meetings with church leaders and others, and all the speeches given had paid off when eight hundred people, black and white, showed up for a mid-morning rally at Frank Williams' black Metropolitan Methodist church in downtown Baltimore. Included were prominent Catholic, Protestant and Jewish

---

[63] From John Roemer's files, probably a record of his own memory.
[64] Among other out-of-state groups, the new Interfaith National Commission on Religion & Race, organized in January 1963, had undertaken the mobilization of whites to participate in this demonstration as their first project. See Meier & Rudwick, CORE, p. 223.

clergy, many participating in direct action for the first time, most prepared to be arrested for the first time. Rev. Dobson said of that meeting:

> We had an affirming yes: that it was the right thing for us to go to Gwynn Oak to challenge this racism. In religious terms, heaven came down and our souls were revived in glory and found the mercy. We went out of that place charge, charged with commitment to our struggle.[65]

Two hundred demonstrators arrived from New York in four buses, and twenty-five from Philadelphia in another bus. A *Sun* article reported:

> Caught up in the spirit of the younger demonstrators, priests, ministers and rabbis clapped and joined in the obviously unfamiliar words of "We Shall Overcome" and "I Woke up This Morning With Freedom on My Mind".

Rev. Marion Bascom, a prominent black Baltimore clergyman told the group:

> I am the one who said all along I will not go to jail, but I will help others who go. But this morning I said to myself I have nothing to lose but my chains. So if I do not preach at my pulpit Sunday morning, it might be the most eloquent sermon I ever preached.

Rev. Dr. Eugene Carson Blake, chief executive officer of the United Presbyterian Church, described by the *New York Times* as "a square-jawed six footer, who played football at Princeton University in the twenties," also spoke to the mostly white group:

> The churches in this country have for a long time been saying a great deal about discrimination. Almost all the churches have made the right statements, but we can no longer let the burden of winning freedom for the Negro or any other oppressed people be the burden only of the oppressed people themselves.

By three that afternoon, when three hundred fifty of those who'd been at the church rally left for the Park by car and bus, "about 1,500 holiday customers were on the thrill rides

---

[65] Student interview, 12/08/99

and vying to win kewpie dolls at the park." [66] The would be demonstrators arrived in waves, each joining others already there in marching up and down on the median strip of Gwynn Oak Avenue in front of the Park, carrying placards proclaiming "Equality Now," "Segregation is Un-American," "Free State Isn't Free," "Public Means Negro and White," "All Men Are Created Equal," "Give Me Justice or Give Me Jail.". Frequently the demonstrators burst into freedom songs; even "The Star-Spangled Banner" (since it was the 4th of July).

With so many of the demonstrators clergymen, Mr. Price, the Park owner, said the demonstration looked like a revival meeting. When asked to comment on their presence, he said:

> It's analogous to my shooting crap and when the police come I begin to pray and say I was arrested for praying.[67]

The Rev. Dr. Eugene Carson Blake led one group of twelve into the park which was not fenced: "the main entrance is a long concrete walk about 15 feet wide, flanked by a parking lot on one side and an administration building on the other and fringed by shrubs and flowers. The booths that sell food and amusement tickets to white only are situated well inside the entrance." Mr. Price confronted them as they approached the booths and read them the Maryland Trespass Law.

"The ferris wheel whirled in the background and the games of petty chance went on," as the county's then-new police chief, Robert Lally, a former FBI agent, warned the protestors they must leave or be arrested. When they refused to move, "the police moved in politely and put the group under arrest." The police then put the demonstrators in a patrol wagon and drove them the two miles to the Woodlawn station.[68]

Gradually, all those courting arrest—students, professors, actors, housewives and ordinary workers—broke into groups of twenty or thirty, and similarly entered the park. The press was especially taken with the fact that so many clergy were being arrested—twenty-three from Baltimore; ten

---

[66] *New York Times*, Friday, July 5, 1963.
[67] *New York Times*, Friday, July 5, 1963.
[68] *New York Times*, Friday, July 5, 1963.

from out of town. In addition to Dr. Blake, they included such prominent personages as Bishop Daniel Corrigan of the National Council of Protestant Episcopal Churches; Msgr. Austin J. Healy, Archdiocese of Baltimore; Rev. William Sloan Coffin, Chaplain of Yale University and Rabbi Morris Lieberman, of the Baltimore Hebrew Congregation.

Photo was gift of *Sun* newspaper to Mildred Atkinson, 1963

Rev. Dobson adds a special note to the participation of Rabbi Lieberman:

> His doctor told him he had a bad heart and that he shouldn't go. The Rabbi, however, determined to participate, made his doctor come with him, go to jail, and have his medicine with him. "He stayed in there a while to fulfill his obligations; it was really taking his own life into his hands. People don't know this: I mean this man was in danger of dying;. just from the pressure, this man would be.[69]

Also of note among those arrested during the "two hour assault on the racially segregated park" (as the *Afro* put it)

---

[69] Hopkins Student's interview, 12/08/99

were such as John Wilkinson, an assistant dean at Yale University, James Van Dyke, a professor of fine art at the University of Pennsylvania, and Furman Templeton, head of the Baltimore Urban League. By 6 p.m. almost three hundred demonstrators had been arrested; only thirty demonstrators remained at the Park. The *Afro* reported:

> Perspiration flowed freely as [the police] labored endlessly but gently to carry hundreds of limp demonstrators who sat in the main walkway to waiting buses nearly 25 yards away.
>
> "Don't you want to walk?" one puffing and perspiring officer asked a healthy demonstrator. "No," was the reply.
>
> "For God's sake, you are too big to carry, man," he said disgustedly as he and a partner flexed their muscles for the weighty trip to the bus.

Those talking to the press remarked about how decently they were treated by the police, compared to prior years when demonstrators had been man-handled by the Park's security force. Credit was given to Robert Lally, who had met earlier with the Gwynn Oak Park force and told them *they* would be arrested for any use of excessive force.

The crowds outside the park which numbered in the hundreds were not sympathetic with the kid-glove handling of demonstrators by the police. Some shouted, "Drop 'im on his head!" "Throw 'em in the bus!" "They shrieked with glee as each group was led or carried out under arrest;... shouted their approval when someone threw a cherry bomb into the midst of the demonstrators, injuring Miss Nora Avins, 26 years old, of 3940 Orioff Street, the Bronx."[70]

Even with two police stations called into service to book them all, it took most of the night as two hundred and fourteen of those arrested were charged with violations of Maryland's Trespass Act; another sixty-nine with both trespassing and disorderly conduct. Most were released on bail,[71] but eighty-six refused to post bail and stayed in jail

---

[70] *New York Times*, Friday, July 5, 1963.

[71] Baltimore County Executive, Spiro Agnew asked that they be released on their own recognizance, explaining "I feel that the trespass law is antiquated, but while we're waiting for a decision from the Supreme Court, these people should be released on their own

until the Magistrate Court hearing at the Woodlawn Police Station scheduled for 7:30 p.m. the next day (Friday).[72] At midnight they still had not been fed. Dr. Chester Wickwire, Chaplain of Johns Hopkins University, was one of those who remained in jail and he tells something of their experience:

> Our jailers were nasty. A diabetic was denied his regular injection of insulin for hours. As I was going down the stairs for breakfast, my crutches were snatched from me on the grounds that I might use them to attack a guard. [Dr. Wickwire was crippled by polio while a student at Yale.]
>
> When Rev. Bascom requested water, a sneering warder simply topped off his half-filled cup of coffee with water. We had to stop singing because it disturbed other prisoners. When a guard failed to provide writing paper to Rev. Harrison Bryant, he scrawled a note to his bishop on a piece of paper sack. It began, "I'm writing from prison..."[73]

Undeterred from acting just because they were incarcerated, Reverends Frank Williams and Marion Bascom organized the seven ministers who'd chosen to stay in jail,[74] along with Edward Chance, the newly-elected Chair of local CORE,[75] into an Ad Hoc Committee to Desegregate Gwynn Oak Park. And a CORE spokesperson immediately announced another mass demonstration for that Sunday—attracting three hundred or so, almost all from Baltimore. They faced a far more hostile crowd than had been encountered three days earlier. The Baltimore County Police Chief in charge, above the calls "Kill all them Niggers" and "Get those Nigger Lovers," was heard to say. "This is a vicious crowd. One little spark could set 'em off."

---

recognizance." But the judges ignored him." I have no control over them," Agnew told the press, "since they're appointed by the governor."

[72] The men refusing bail were distributed to various police station throughout the county, the women transported to the Civil Defense Fire Station in Middle River, where beds and cots were installed for them. The hearing for those out on bail was scheduled for Monday.

[73] In an interview with *Evening Sun*, July 16, 1993

[74] Besides Wickwire, Bascom and Williams were the Revs. William Mango, Vernon Dobson, David Andrews and Clinton Coleman.

[75] Walter Carter had resigned, disgusted, after the murder of Bill Moore in April.

One white woman was hit by a rock; a black woman was slugged by a gang of white youths while she was trapped in the women's rest room. There were never-ending shouts of "Nigger lover," "Go back to Africa," and "You belong in the zoo." One paper reported a counter demonstration by eight or nine Fighting American Nationalists (F.A.N.) bearing signs reading: "Integration Stinks," "Keep Gwynn Oak White, and "U.S. for Whites—Africa for Blacks." And "every once in a while they would let forth with the segregationist chant first heard in Little Rock six years previously: Two, four, six, eight, we don't want to integrate.'"[76] K-9 police dogs were called out to separate them from the other pickets.

After about two hours and another hundred arrests, the demonstration began to break up. Another thirteen clergymen were among those charged with trespassing, including Rev. James David Andrews, the white assistant chaplain at Morgan State College, dressed in a red, white and blue Uncle Sam suit, and Michael Schwerner, who less than a year later would be murdered while working for civil rights in Mississippi.[77]

Also hauled away for booking were the entire families of two Johns Hopkins faculty members: Dr. James Coleman, professor of sociology, holding his eight year old son Thomas with one hand, and his son John by the other; his wife behind them, carrying their five months old son in her arms; and William Leight, a research assistant in biophysics with his wife, an art teacher in the public schools, carrying their six month old daughter.

In 1968 Ada Jenkins, a founding member of CORE, had this to say to a reporter of these events at Gwynn Oak:

With all the demonstrating, there was a great deal of

---

[76] There is a story that on one occasion when FAN was picketing in front of Baltimore's NAACP office, Clarence Mitchell started to turn his garden hose on them until reminded by his son that they had a right to picket. He then made a sign with black shoe polish that read "FAN is made up of Human Skunks" and led a counter picket line. Watson, p. 448.

[77] On 6/21/64, Michael Schwerner, James Chaney and Andrew Goodman were released from jail in Philadelphia, Miss. They were never seen alive again. Their bodies were found on August four.

writing and contacting influential people. I went to New York
to the U.N. and to the embassies and various national groups
to ask them not to participate in All Nation's Day at Gwynn
Oak Park because no colored were allowed in. It came to a
head in August 1963. The clergy took a stand and 200 were
arrested. We picketed the Woodlawn station house where the
trial was held. Two buses came up and the clergymen
marched in—I never saw anything like that.[78]

•••

While CORE's attorney, Fred Weisgal, was on vacation
and occupied with two death penalty cases (one of which went
to the Supreme Court), Bob Watts, then between
appointments to judgeships, represented the demonstrators
as they came before the court on that Friday and Monday in
July to plead. Recently Judge Watts recalled how he'd had
Elsbeth Bothe,[79] another attorney, send the arrested
demonstrators into the courtroom, ten at a time, to ask for a
jury trial. Soon after, the Marylanders were released on their
own recognizance; those from out of state on bonds. Three
local clergy, The Reverends Bascom, Williams and Bryant,
refused to sign recognizance bonds and sought to stay in jail,
but Magistrate John Serio ordered them released in the
custody of their attorneys.[80]

Watts went on to proclaim he'd never had a conviction,
except one. "By the time they get to Circuit Court (necessary for
a jury trial), usually many months, even a year later, we've
worked out a deal to drop charges," he explained. The exception
had been Mark Lane, "a radical who disrupted my process."

He kept insisting on asking the judge to try him,
exclaiming he hadn't done anything wrong.

"Okay," I told him, "You go right ahead." And I made sure
what happened did happen. The judge told me, "I'll take care
of him."

Lane came before the judge, pled not guilty and didn't ask

[78] James D. Dilts, *Sun*, "The Warning Trumpet", 12/1/1968
[79] Watts said it was Elsbeth Bothe but I believe he mis-remembered.
Bothe remembers nothing of this, and the press makes no mention
of her. Rather it states that the NAACP black attorney, Juanita
Mitchell, was also present representing those arrested.
[80] *New York Times*, Tuesday, July 9, 1963

for a jury trial. Two police officers testified he was there, ordered to leave, refused, so they arrested him. "He's a trespasser."

Lane started sounding off about his constitutional rights and all, which we knew would never prevail in our courts in those days. The judge fined him $250 and he went by me in handcuffs. He just refused to follow our procedure.

•••

On July 10, 1963 *Baltimore Sun* reported that the day prior Senator Hubert Humphrey had charged that the massive arrests were a "'flagrant abuse' of the Constitution that proved the need for a Federal public accommodations law." It went on:

> In a long, angry speech before the Senate, Mr. Humphrey called Maryland's trespass law 'anachronistic' and said local leaders 'are not privileged to be despots' and suggested that the wrong persons had been taken into custody.

In Maryland, the Baltimore County Executive, Spiro Agnew, called the Gwynn Oak protests "irresponsible," but then promised to create a commission to arbitrate the matter if the demonstrations would cease. As a result, over the protest of many of the activists, they were halted to give the commission time to try to reach an agreement. Over the next several days, offers and counter offers were made by both sides regarding opening the Park. Meanwhile, Bob Watts and Rabbi Lieberman went on television to discuss the Gwynn Oak imbroglio. And afterwards, one of the Price brothers [the Park owners] came up to Watts and said, "You win. I plan to drop all charges and open the park."

Next day it was announced that Gwynn Oak would integrate on August 28, 1963—*ironically, the very same day that thousands surrounded D.C.'s reflecting pool at the March on Washington*. It was only four months after Baltimore's Bill Moore had been killed en route to Mississippi.

The Fighting American Nationalists (FAN), led by Charles Luthardt, Sr., were not pleased with the Park's decision to integrate and next day, on August 29, a car load arrived at the park, picketing with signs demanding that it be kept segregated. Soon after they left, Leo Burroughs, Jr. arrived with four others also intending to demonstrate, in their case for immediate integration. Rev. Joseph Connolly and Dr.

Chester Wickwire advised them against doing so; CORE removed Burroughs from his position with the organization when he refused, at least initially, to stop demonstrating; and they issued a statement disassociating CORE from any further attempts to demonstrate at the park. It expressed the feeling that they were morally bound to respect the formal agreement that had promised to cease demonstrations at once.

Some have claimed that integration led to Gwynn Oak Park's demise, but Dr. Wickwire, a long-time respected Baltimore activist, disclaims this. In an *Evening Sun* article, he said:

> Integration was not economic suicide for Gwynn Oak. Though it became badly neglected, it was open until June 22, 1972, when tropical storm Agnes destroyed most of it. The last usable building, the Dixie Ballroom, burned in 1975. Now owned by Baltimore County, the site is flood-plain parkland used for relaxation and recreation by blacks and whites.

In an article a month after the Park integrated, Price told reporters that thus far it had been an economic success, and that prospects for the next year were better than ever—groups that had stopped using the Park had returned and were booking for the next year. Threats of a boycott had never materialized, there had been no disorders, and receipts were better than for the analogous period the year before.

On the 35th anniversary of Gwynn Oak's integration, the *Sun* did a follow-up story of some of those involved. One worth noting was Ed Chance, CORE's Chairman in 1963. Since then, Ed, on behalf of his autistic son, had battled a different kind of discrimination in Maryland. After his son's behavior deteriorated and the special school in Chinquapin felt it could no longer handle him, he was placed in a special treatment center at Hopkins, and then one in Washington, D.C. He was finally transferred to Spring Grove, a hospital in Maryland for mental patients. But they, too, weren't equipped to deal with autistic children, and kept Ed's son in physical restraints day and night for over four years. Only after television's Channel 45 exposed his treatment, did the state agree to pay to send his son to an out-of-state facility qualified to deal with autistic children. Recently, Ed told this writer that his son, now grown, was in a supervised home and doing fine. They have a suit pending against the state for the treatment he had received at Spring Grove. "Who would think a state would shackle a person like that in this day and age. It goes to show you that you can't take freedom for granted."[81]

That *Sun* story also listed ninety-three participants, men and women, young and old, Baltimoreans and those from elsewhere, who had been arrested, some more than once, in the Gwynn Oak Park protests on July 4 and 7, 1963.

•••

Sharon Langley was the first black allowed to enter Gwynn Oak Park. It was on August 28, 1963, the very same day of the March on Washington, a march that had been patterned after the earlier March on Washington Movement organized by A. Philip Randolph. And initially, like it, the intent was to emphasize jobs, but at the request of SCLC its goal became the passage of the Civil Rights Bill. The NAACP and Urban League also prevailed over CORE and SNCC in vetoing the inclusion of sit-ins at the capitol as part of the day's events. Due to this moderation of tactics, some of the CORE chapters lost their enthusiasm. However, in Baltimore, CORE's Walter Carter became Maryland's March Coordinator and helped mobilize 12,000 to 15,000 who took buses to Washington for the occasion.

Rev. Dobson had this to say of the minister's role:

> All the major churches that went; had responsibilities of getting buses together. We stayed up all that night making certain we had people, worried that we had overestimated what we were going to do in Baltimore, knowing that if we didn't do a big thing, the whole movement might be in default. So we had to get out. We went to Lafayette Square that morning; buses would pull up and they would fill up, and then another would fill up. It was just amazing.
>
> And it almost just made you teary-eyed the whole day, you just couldn't help but thank God. And as fast as we

---

[81] This writer interviewed Ed Chance in the Spring 2001 and again in April 2002, at which time he was recovering from cancer treatment that had affected his vocal chords. Hopkins students interviewed him on 12/08/2000.

could load a bus up, they'd go. And then when we got on the road, the buses were bumper-to-bumper. From Memphis, Tennessee, Mississippi, buses on the road toward Washington. By the time we got to Washington, the place was overcrowded. And then the whole day, not even breathing space. As far as you could see, people. Amazing.

They had predicted there were going to be riots; and at times we felt like it. We were all revolutionaries in our souls at that time. We hadn't done enough. We needed to tear Washington up. But the place was orderly. The people picked up the trash. Not one person was locked up. So, that was a great day for me. [82]

The day had proved the inspiration for many of Baltimore's black ministers to become involved in the civil rights movement, but the man who already had inspired Baltimore CORE's leaders was not there. Even though he had helped plan the event, James Farmer on the big day was in jail in Plaquemine, Louisiana. Perhaps if he had been there to deliver the speech he'd prepared for the occasion, one very similar to the one which made Martin Luther King famous, he too would be remembered.

Few realize that Farmer, like King, was a graduate of a divinity school and used the same cadenced speech, so typical of black ministers, to stir his troops and inspire them to act, even in the face of name-calling, threats by the Klan, and physical assaults.

However, on that day, Farmer's speech was read by the far less charismatic Floyd McKissick. It began with a reference to the 232 freedom fighters jailed with him: "I cannot come out of jail," he said, "while they are still in, for their crime was the same as mine, demanding freedom now...I cannot let the heroic Negro citizens of Plaquemine down by leaving them now when they are behind bars...."

To the marchers, Farmer concluded (much as King did, but with a more down-to-earth concreteness): "We will not come off the streets until we can work at a job befitting of our skills,...until our kids have enough to eat and their minds can study...without being cramped in Jim Crow schools,...until we can eat and play with no closed doors blocking our

---

[82] Interview with Hopkins' students, 12/08/99

way,...until the heavy weight of centuries of oppression is removed from our backs and like proud men everywhere we can stand tall together again."

•••

August Meier in some of his writings on the civil rights movement suggests a difference between the leadership of James Farmer and Martin Luther King that is illustrated in the choice Farmer made to stay in jail with his "freedom fighters" rather than to appear at even such a major event as the March on Washington. Meier points out how Farmer, unlike King, always praised his loyal troops and gave them credit for the work they did without him, and down-played his own contribution after he appeared on the scene. This is offered by Meier as at least a partial explanation of why history has never accorded Farmer the same recognition for his contribution to the civil rights movement as they have King—despite the fact he became active prior to King and made just as great a contribution during the movement's heyday.[83]

---

[83] See especially Meier, *White Scholar...* This writer agrees with Meier's analysis but also suggests it has to do with King's family who've made it a mission to promote him, while Farmer's children have always avoided any discussion of their father with either the media or authors interested in writing about their father.

Morgan's Civic Interest Group (CIG) & the Northwood Theater

With Morgan's very existence, as the students knew it, having depended on its willingness to fight discrimination,[84] it is not surprising that in the spring of 1955, having finally succeeded in January in opening the lunch counters at the Read's drug stores, the students would return to demonstrating at the Northwood Movie Theater— more determined than ever to integrate the whole of the Northwood Shopping Center. Their struggle at the theater, paralleling that at Gwynn Oak Amusement Park, also lasted until 1963.

The Morgan students started their renewed attempt to integrate the theater with two letters from their Social Action Committee to the theater's manager, John Wyatt. But when he ignored them, students began to plan for renewed demonstrations; help was sought from Johns Hopkins University students; and the *Afro-American* was informed that a major demonstration was planned for Friday, April 29, 1955.

One hundred fifty students, including a small number from Hopkins, gathered in front of Holmes Hall at Morgan early that Friday evening and heard a spokesperson tell them: "Anyone here who has plans for fighting tonight might as well leave now. Take the insults. It is the discipline that will make this thing a success." The Dean, McQuay Kiah, advised them not to march down as an army would, but to arrive in waves, in smaller groups.[85] As they approached, the manager hurriedly scribbled out and posted two signs in the ticket window:

> Until the Motion Picture Theater Owners of Maryland, of which this theater is a member, and the courts of Maryland advise otherwise, this theater reserves the exclusive right to select its patronage.
>
> Please refrain from any activity that might require police action.[86]

---

[84] As previously indicated, this history will be told in the Education and Housing sections.

[85] Johns Hopkins student newsletter, May 6, 1955

[86] *Afro*, 4/30/1955

The protest began with a student from Hopkins and one from Morgan trying to purchase two tickets to the movie, "Untamed," then showing. The manager refused and warned the group they were breaking the law. A few customers seemed sympathetic, one remarked: "I don't blame them. Both sides have it rough, but it's the only way to do it." Another said: "My pastor tells me they're my equals, but I just can't believe it." Another walked away after declaring: "If they can't go in, damn if I am either!"[87] After a few other students tried unsuccessfully to purchase tickets, the group left, but again appeared at the start of the second showing. This time they found the ticket window closed and the theater's neon marquee lights off.

Concerned that the presence of so many students would scare off his regular customers, the manager agreed to a meeting that would include members of Morgan's Social Action Committee, the Maryland Commission on Interracial Problems and Relations[88] and the Baltimore City Commission on Human Relations. However, the very next day, as soon as he learned the students had called off their demonstration to await the results of the meeting, the manager reneged on his agreement to meet.

As a consequence, on Tuesday, May 3, more than 250 students, 50 from Hopkins, showed up, and proceeded to march peacefully in front of the theater. This time the manager immediately closed the ticket window and started selling tickets inside to pre-screened potential customers. The police were present but made no arrests. The police sergeant told the manager: "We can't do a thing as long as they remain quietly in line."[89]

After three weeks of picketing, the manager remained unmoved and customers began to taunt the picketers with

---

[87] Johns Hopkins student newsletter, May 6, 1955

[88] The Governor's Commission continued to try to mediate this issue with the manager but the theater's owners remained convinced they would lose business by integrating, and a white community association submitted a petition the Commission actively opposing the integration. However, in 1958, one chain of seven downtown theaters finally gave in and integrated.

[89] Johns Hopkins student newsletter, May 6, 1955

comments such as "Go to your own theaters," and "Sue us if you don't like it."[90] The police had become antagonistic and seemed particularly irritated by the presence of white students. On May 30, they arrested one such student from Hopkins, Sherman Merrill. The fact he refused to give his name and objected to the officer having put his hands on him, resulted in a charge of "disorderly conduct" and "assaulting a police officer." "Bystanders reported hearing such words as 'Communists,' and 'Nigger Lover'."[91]

The black attorney, Robert Watts, represented Merrill after this arrest and continued as the primary attorney representing students arrested here and at other sit-ins. However, there is evidence that suggests Fred Weisgal was also involved at times, probably because of his work with ACLU on civil rights cases. Fred was then Executive Board Chairman of the local ACLU chapter. In any case, the following article appeared in the ACLU newsletter in September 1955 under the title, "The Civil Rights of Pickets."

> The incident involves an attempt by a group of students to gain access for Negroes to the theatre located in the Northwood Shopping Center.
> [ACLU advised] that the issues are the right of pickets to make their views known while on private property and the right of a theatre owner to discriminate against Negroes.
> As to both questions,...there is no law specifically on point pertinent to these issues....[It also] emphasized that while there is a strong moral argument on the side of the pickets, there is no legal basis for forcing the theatre owner to accept Negro patrons. However, [it was] felt that if the owner attempted to have the Courts enforce his rights that the Courts would not do so because they would, in effect, be enforcing discrimination and violating the U.S. Constitution.

Having advised the group of the undetermined nature of the legal issues, the Maryland Branch [of] ACLU nonetheless expressed their willingness to defend them if the need should arise.

Douglas Sands, then student council president-elect (later a minister and executive director of the State Commission on

---

[90] See Horn, Master's Thesis
[91] *Afro*, May 31, 1955.

Interracial Problems and Relations), referred to the recently ended Korean War as a tool to attract more demonstrators. In a letter circulated at Morgan he noted that blacks had fought and died alongside whites for the privileges of American citizenship, yet were denied them in Baltimore. Sands nonetheless concluded on a note of optimism: "I believe that Baltimore must yield one day to the challenge of democracy and Christianity." He saw the integration of the Northwood theater as a beginning that would act to persuade others to get involved, especially young people.[92]

•••

Morgan's President, Martin Jenkins, was in an awkward position: sympathetic with the students, he refused to order them to halt their demonstrations; yet he was worried about the college's funding which depended on the state legislature, whose members were already being pressured by the theater manager to stop the demonstrations. Trying to insulate himself, Jenkins wrote a letter to the *Afro* declaring that the students were acting as "well-intentioned, independent citizens." The students, in order to give their position exactly that status, severed their connection with the school's Student Government Social Action Committee and formed the Civic Interest Group, more often referred to simply as CIG. This freed them from adult control, and, according to Clarence Logan, who was later director of CIG (from December 1960 to January 1964), the students quickly developed a reputation for putting their emphasis on action, not negotiation.[93]

•••

By the end of May 1955, with the Northwood's Theater manager as recalcitrant as ever, even refusing all efforts to hold a meeting to discuss the theater's policy, the number of demonstrators gradually began to decline. Between 1955 and 1963 the focus of the students' protests began to shift to the lunch counters and restaurants in the Shopping Center and downtown (more later) that were still segregated. The only demonstration at the theater that made the news during these

---

[92] See Horn, who had interviewed Sands (p. 92).
[93] See Horn, p. 102.

years seems to have been during the college's Easter break in 1959, when groups of ten to twenty students picketed the theater in shifts. Janice Woolridge, then a counselor at Morgan, said she didn't think the young people got the support they should have gotten from the older people. "Too many people believed the demonstrations would never work— such a generation gap, plus, I guess, they felt their security, their jobs, would be threatened."[94]

By February 1963, the Northwood Theater had become the only holdout in the shopping center that had not integrated, and so the students decided it was time, once again, to make it their target. Many, by then, had been arrested in sit-ins and they decided to include mass arrests in their tactics at the theater. The students started by recruiting Morgan athletes, members of sororities and fraternities, and even the 1963 Miss Morgan, who would be willing to participate and be arrested. They knew their involvement would attract the largest number of students, generally, to participate.

The first of this new wave of protests began on Friday, February 15, 1963 when fifty students picketed; twenty-six were arrested and charged with disorderly conduct. On Saturday, sixteen students were arrested (one for the second time) and charged with disorderly conduct. On Sunday, after a hundred more appeared at the theater, twenty-four were arrested and charged with trespassing, including Morgan's chaplain, Rev. James David Andrews, who was additionally charged with disorderly conduct.

After the theater manager, Aaron Seidler, had finished reading Rev. Andrews Maryland's Trespass Act, the Reverend read President Kennedy's message commemorating the centennial of the Emancipation Proclamation to the manager. All asked for a jury trial; the first group was released by Judge Joseph Finnerty on their own recognizance, bail was set at $100 for all the others, with the exception of the twice-arrested

---

[94] Recent interview with Hopkins' students. As a teenager, Woolridge had been one of those who'd picketed stores on Pennsylvania Avenue—presumably as part of the City-wide Young People's Forum, though she doesn't mention the group by name.

student. His was set at $150.

Fred Weisgal's partner at the time, Sidney Albert, in an interview told the writer that when these arrests started, he went down to the Northern Police District where the students were taken, because Fred couldn't be located (perhaps because so many had been arrested, CIG's attorney, Bob Watts, felt the need for additional attorneys, or perhaps Fred's office just assumed it). In any case, Albert said, "I went down with a bail bondsman so they wouldn't have to stay in jail overnight. They were just Morgan kids." He added, "Few local black lawyers, or white for that matter, would get involved with civil rights at the time."

Five hundred students attended a meeting held by CIG on Monday morning, February 18. The prominent black minister, Reverend Marion Bascom, who chaired their adult advisory committee, spoke to them about the power of non-violence and advised them that the committee had changed its position and now supported mass arrests.[95]

This was all the students needed to act. That night 150 of the estimated three hundred students who picketed the theater went to jail. The patrol wagons shuttled back and forth as the police took groups of twenty or more at a time to lock-ups—there were so many "they ran out of police vehicles, had to use trucks, vans to load them in." Sixty-four men were taken to the Northeastern Police District, including the postal clerk, William L. Moore, 35, who would be killed only two months later en route to Mississippi (more later). Eighty-six women were taken to the Eastern Police District, the women's Pine Street jail already having reached its capacity. Later, some of the women students told their Morgan counselor they'd never go to jail again in their lives. They were fearful enough, thrown in with prostitutes, that they took turns guarding so the others could sleep.

> We would just get together and talk. I was not in a position to make any judgement or evaluate; no grades involved, so that was one place they could just let loose. The girls would tell me about going down to jail, defleaing and delousing. And all that stuff. I think it helped a lot of them to

---

[95] Palumbos, p. 479

understand the other side of the world that some other
people had been living that they hadn't. How some people
lived in and out of those jails. Their lives had been a little
more protected and a little more secured, and a little more
comfortable. It was an awakening for them.

You could write a book just about their experiences there.
I was worried about one student who was epileptic and took
his medicine to him in jail. Some parents were supportive,
but others said they didn't want to be inconvenienced.
That's why I was disgusted with a lot of them. Some of the
social groups I was in I got out of because of their attitude. It
was a fascinating period. I don't know whether I will ever see
that kind of thing again or that kind of unity, but I hope to.[96]

After these arrests, Judge Finnerty set bail at $600 each,
a total of $90,000. Unable to pay such an exorbitant amount,
the students had no choice but to stay in jail, although they
were not at all prepared or pleased by this prospect. However,
most of them realized that filling the jails was an effective
addenda to mass arrests.

Rather than deterring protests, the punitive bail provoked
an even larger turn-out on Tuesday, February 19. As
hundreds "poured into the area," as the *Sun* put it, 120 more
students were arrested; at least another hundred were not
arrested, but only because the jails were too full to receive
them. For the first time Hopkins and Goucher students joined
those picketing and those arrested.

That same day, Moses Lewis, city chairman of CIG and
Clarence Logan, state chairman, sent a telegram to Mayor
Philip Goodman, who faced a contested primary election in two
weeks, asking his help. They denied that at any time any of the
demonstrators had acted in a way "to disturb the public peace."
They also complained of the exorbitant bails, as did a member
of the Commission on Interracial Problems and Relations,
disturbed by the implications of such a bail for misdemeanor
charges. The mayor said he would be willing to meet with both
sides "in the interest of having this community problem solved
without any further public embarrassment to anyone."[97]

Also that day Fred E. Weisgal and officials from Morgan

---

[96] From Hopkins' students interview
[97] *Evening Sun*, 2/19/1963.

met with William J. O'Donnell, State's attorney, about the charges. Afterwards, Weisgal indicated that an effort would be made to have the defendants released without having to post bail. However, not all the CIG students were pleased at this announcement; ten marched in front of City Hall "protesting what they called an attempt by city officials to stop the demonstration."[98] The Morgan students felt encouraged when they heard their President, Martin D. Jenkins, warn the theater's manager that if he didn't promptly integrate, as many as 2,400 students would be in jail by the end of the weekend.[99] Some students were talking about soliciting help from students nationwide; others were talking of quitting.

Janice Woolridge, a Morgan counselor at this time, recently gave a rare look at the sacrifices some of the Morgan students were making during these extended protests; as well as at the support they received from one "eccentric" professor:[100]

> Many of the students were first-generation at a college, and their parents just didn't understand what this was all about. Some of the students were threatened not to come back home, and that they [the parents] weren't going to pay for them any more. I ran into the problem of getting money for some of them. We would go around having fund raising cocktail parties, card parties, every kind of party you could think of; go down to the flea market and put up a stall and sell clothes and things like that; collecting money to pay bails. Some got grants or work study or something to keep them going.
>
> But it was rough; a rough battle between one generation and another. This went on for quite some time until it started breaking down. Some of the younger faculty you would see joining the picketers in winter when it was snowing and all that. The older ones had had a hard time getting where they were and weren't going to rock the boat.
>
> I remember the Jewish man [Augie Meier], the history professor, was the main leader of all this—an eccentric, a brilliant man; the type professor who walked in the room and the window was opened, he would throw his coat out. But he really kept the students going; he was a strategist, a

---

[98] Sun, 2/20/1963.

[99] See Meier, *A White Scholar...*, p. 142.

[100] Hopkins students' interview.

mountain, a backbone. I was surprised at the number of our professors who were not supportive, because you know, the President [Jenkins] was—he encouraged them that it was their right.

One night they had really just about run out of steam, they didn't really feel that they were getting anywhere. And their attorney, an African-American [Bob Watts] came to their   meeting that night and told them to call it off. You know, he was of that older generation too. But this professor [Meier] said, "No way." And do you know, the very next day, it broke. They won. The very next day.

As the students continued their protest for a sixth day, the *Baltimore News-Post* reported a bomb threat.[101]

The threat was telephoned to the segregated theater shortly after the vanguard of 300 pickets—the largest number so far—began its demonstration.

About 75 patrons were ordered into the lobby while police searched the theater, but no trace of a bomb was found. A fire truck also stood by for an hour as a precautionary measure.

Police arrested 74 pickets—44 women and 30 men— bringing to 415 the number of demonstrators taken into custody since the protest began Friday night.

The *Sun,* in its report the same day, added the fact that a number of the demonstrators were white, including Allan Brick, assistant professor of English at Goucher, and Madalyn Murray, an atheist who then lived in Northwood, and who would go down in history for her successful battle to end the saying of prayer in public schools. Parents of the demonstrators had organized to provide their children with coffee and donuts at a time when Baltimore was experiencing cold winter weather. The numbers of spectators, said to be 250, now matched the number of demonstrators, requiring the assignment of a dozen motorcycle police to control the crowds.[102] The *News-Post* went on to report:

A total of 268 pickets, most of them Negro students from Morgan State College, are being held in the Baltimore City Jail unable to raise $600 bonds. [The Sun put the number

---

[101] *Baltimore News-Post,* 2/21/1963.
[102] *Sun,* 2/21/63.

jailed at 343—in one article stating 105 of them women, 12 from Goucher; another putting the number at 195 women.]...

The influx of student prisoners at the jail gave it a population of 1,450. This was the second highest on record, topped only by 1,637 in 1961. Because of the overcrowding, prisoners were sleeping on cots in corridors and dormitories and four and five to a cell.[103]

Thursday morning the theater owners, finally, apparently having had enough, called the Mayor and agreed to integrate if the demonstrations ended first. The mayor so informed the student's attorney, Robert Watts, who then met with three student leaders of CIG and August Meier, a faculty member and supporter of CIG. That afternoon, February 21, Mayor Goodman appeared on the steps of city hall and announced the theater management had agreed to open its doors to Negroes the following day if the demonstrations stopped. He added:

> After two days of continuous negotiation and mediation this matter has now apparently been resolved to the satisfaction of all parties. I am gratified that this situation has been alleviated since it has been giving our city and its people a bad reputation.[104]

Following the mayor's statement, the thirty-five protesters who had been marching in front of City Hall, tore up their signs and left. They had included John White, President of the local branch of the National Alliance of Postal Employees, and Juanita Mitchell of the NAACP.

For the first time in a week there was no demonstration that night. Next day, the first black was admitted to see the Walt Disney movie then showing, "In Search of the Castaways." Twenty-three in all attended. There were no disturbances. In a television interview that evening, the theatre's manager said he was "happy to join the ranks of progressive businessmen in northeastern Baltimore."[105]

---

[103] *Baltimore News-Post*, 2/21/1963, & the *Sun*, 2/21 & 2/22/63.
[104] *Afro*, 3/2/63
[105] Meier, *A White Scholar...*, p. 143.

Clarence Logan, then head of CIG, savors their hard-fought victory,
©AfroAmerican, 3/12/1963

On Thursday, February 21, as a result of meetings regarding those jailed, Judge Anselm Sodaro of the Criminal Court vacated all the bails requirements, and the 326 demonstrators still in jail were released on their own recognizance (seventeen had already been released on bail earlier in the day). At six p.m., the demonstrators began to emerge from the jail. When Robert Watts, Rev. Bascom and Moses Lewis went to inform the women of their release, there were screams, hugs, tears and prayers of gratitude, as some jumped up and down in their exuberance. The men, when told, merely shook hands all around, one saying he was going to write a tune, "Jailbird Rock."

However, the State's attorney, surprised by this decision, said he would have to meet with the grand jury regarding the charges, and the theater operators and police would have to drop all charges before they could be dismissed and the students released. Finally, late in the afternoon, the Baltimore Supreme Bench intervened and agreed that the bail should be dropped, but delayed a decision about dropping the charges.

It was not until the grand jury met in special sessions on February 26 and 27 and heard testimony from Police Lt. Frederick Gladstone and one of the theater owners, Joseph Grant, that the announcement was made that all the cases were being dismissed— some eight hundred as a result of multiple charges and arrests of some. On hearing the news, Mayor Goodman commented that justice may wear a blindfold but is not blind.[106]

Moses Lewis, a senior at Morgan, had this to say of CIG's victory—after an eight year struggle:

> I think the city of Baltimore and the State of Maryland are just coming into the Twentieth Century. This is a victory, it's true. But by no means has the Negro come into his own in Maryland. We want full equality and full rights.[107]

Confirming that Baltimore was not the only place with a long way to go, on the same day that the *New York Times* wrote of CIG's victory, there was another article beside it stating that the all-white University of Georgia was considering admitting a West African as a foreign student, but not as a Negro.[108]

•••

As a footnote to the students' victory, an article in an unnamed paper appeared on July 8, 1963, reporting that business at the theater had declined 30% since it integrated four months earlier. Ironically, however, the general manager, Aaron Seidler, blamed the publicity that had surrounded the demonstrations rather than the fact the theater had integrated. He noted that none of the other theaters that integrated at the same time had shown such a decline in business.[109]

Janice Woolridge, the Morgan counselor, best sums up the significance of the students' actions:

---

[106] *Afro-*, 3/2/63.

[107] *Sun*, 2/22/63

[108] *NY Times*, 2/23/63

[109] According to *Toward Equality*, a few downtown movie houses had integrated, without public notice or any problems, as early as 1956. It notes further that in 1958, all the downtown movie houses integrated. This true, it's hard to understand why the Northwood theater was so determined not to integrate.

I look at many of those students who were in that movement; they learned so much from it, grew, went on to politics and other areas like that and did very well.

And I think the students set all of us free in more ways than one; an awakening out of our own submissions, oppressions, our own feeling of worth and what you could do if you tried, and not to be intimidated. It was an awakening for the whole country. And we need another awakening now.

Now, it's more a class, economic thing; the haves and have nots. And I don't think our group is any different in that; it's the economics that decides what group you are in rather than your color. The black middle class is still small, so you still got the masses to help. I think that is what a lot of the fraternal organizations are doing. I know my sorority is putting forth a lot of effort to do that with mentoring and tutoring programs.[110]

---

[110] From an interview by Hopkins students.

Hopkins, Morgan & CORE:
Sit-Ins Continue Into the 60s

Nicholas Schloeder, a Coach at Gilman School, recounted the arrival of a New Yorker in Baltimore, for the first time, the summer of 1955:

> I remember getting off the train and asking somebody where the men's room was...I went over and there were two entrances, and carved in the stone was "white" and on the other one was "colored." I mean it was not a sign that you could take down, it was not a sign you could paint over, it was chiseled into the stone. You knew they were not gonna take this thing down. So I went into the white one, and as I came out, I passed a water-fountain and I just stopped and sure enough it was one of those water fountains that was built into the wall [marked] "white only" and "colored only." Two different spigots, fountains, and I was thinking, you know, it's the same water. I mean it's coming out of the same pipe! So that was Baltimore.[111]

•••

It was about this time that Baltimore had undertaken the self-survey, published in 1955 as *An American City in Transition*. It included reports on the Negro Family, Housing, Employment, the Public Schools, Health and Welfare Services, Religious and Civic organizations and Public Accommodations.[112]

The *Survey's* findings in the area of public accommodations are what concern us now; the desegregation noted in some places almost certainly reflecting policy changes effected through demonstrations initiated by CIG and CORE.

Curiously, however, this *Survey* is never referred to even as CIG's and CORE's demonstrations continued.

---

[111] From an interview done for a research paper by Park School student, Ruth Goldstein, written in 1996 (See Education section). In the same interview Schloeder explains that in the same train station with the offensive signs, blacks and whites could eat together at "a four stool counter" —as unaccommodating as this was, it was about the only place blacks and whites could then eat together.

[112] *Baltimore Self-Survey*, pp. 9 & 10, 206-217.

CORE had been recognized by the Sidney Hollander Foundation in 1953 for successfully opening a few downtown restaurants to blacks, but most restaurants and taverns, if they served blacks at all, did so only on a take-out basis.[113]

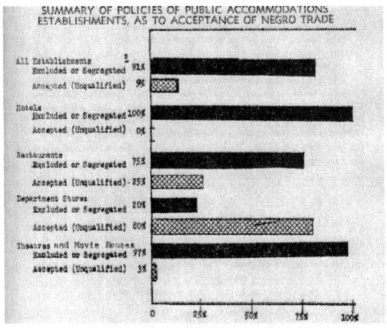

SUMMARY OF POLICIES OF PUBLIC ACCOMMODATIONS ESTABLISHMENTS, AS TO ACCEPTANCE OF NEGRO TRADE

Prepared by the Public Accommodations Committee for *American City in Transition*

In general, department stores, whose restaurants would soon become the focus of CORE and CIG demonstrations, did not allow blacks to use their food services, rest rooms or beauty parlors, and until 1952 did not even allow them to purchase clothes there; and most still denied them the right to try on clothes or return purchases. One denial that certainly rancored the head of Baltimore's NAACP, Lillie May Jackson, was the refusal of the department stores to sell her daughter, Virginia, a wedding gown. The irony is that the financially

---

[113] For more on this foundation, see footnote in Employment section: "Gradualism."

better-off blacks who would not tolerate these department stores' humiliations went to Wannamakers and the better stores in Philadelphia, and ended up better-dressed than they would have been if they had purchased them in Baltimore.

Rev. Vernon Dobson pointed out another, different kind of lesson that at least he learned from his mother in connection with department store policies: "because of who you are, you are expected to touch things that don't belong to you. When you go down, keep your hands off of thing and if there is any buying going on, I'll buy it. Do you understand?" Dobson, in an interview, continued talking about his mother and her attitude toward her six children:

> If any talking is to be done, I will do it. Not because "running your mouth can get you in trouble," but "because you're fine young men. You are beautiful children and you know how to behave; I will discipline you." In the 40s "my mother could be easily provoked in a racist society to be defensive about her children. And she would say to the police and anybody else, they are my children; they behave; if they do anything in this community, you see me, but don't say anything to them.
>
> I was able to find out later, because there were some Jewish people who grew up in our neighborhood, that they were also segregated, but because of their religion. And it's a strange thing, over the years, I've remembered with fond affection that the Jewish Mother and Black Mother are much alike in the way they model for their children's courage.

On the other hand, Rita Crooms recently told a Hopkins student interviewing her of how her aunt, who graduated from high school in 1922, circumvented segregation. When asked by Rita where she got her dress, she said at O'Neals. Since Rita knew they'd never let blacks enter, knew they'd close before allowing it, she said: "Oh, come now!" But, Aunt Mae explained: "My grandmother worked for a wealthy white lady and she went down and got the dress. If it didn't fit, she took it back and changed it until she found something that I could wear."

Regarding hotel policies, the booklet *Toward Equality* pointed out that in 1954 Baltimore had become a major league baseball city, but that the Hotel Association continued to refuse to admit Negro guests. The *Survey* indicated one hotel did establish an open policy, limiting overnight stays to "a member of a visiting team or special group"; otherwise, they limited service to blacks to "special meetings, conventions and related matters." Soon, however, they reverted to segregation since even their limited open policy was contrary to the policy of Baltimore's Hotel Association. In 1956 the Commission on Interracial Problems and Relations met with members of the Hotel Association, emphasizing that the city was losing conventions because of their discriminatory policy. But the Association was not deterred, refused to change their policy.

In 1959, one hotel, the Sheraton Belvedere, was singled out by the Hollander Foundation for its award as the first hotel in Baltimore "to open its guest and dining rooms to colored persons." However, the hotel declined the award, perhaps because they'd previously "suffered an embarrassingly large Negro influx during an earlier short-lived and widely publicized attempt at non-discrimination." Their present policy had been "accomplished quietly and without fanfare [in 1957] and they wanted to leave it that way." As a consequence, no award was made that year.[114] The Lord Baltimore and Congress hotels followed soon after the Sheraton and announced an open-to-all policy.

The *Survey* found that only fifteen of twenty-nine hospitals accepted Negroes as patients, and only four of these allowed Negroes into their training programs for the medical and dental professions. Adding to the record of discrimination, *Toward Equality* noted that in 1954, the Baltimore Dental Society voted to continue its exclusion of Negro dentists, making them ineligible as members of the American Dental Society. It also noted that in 1955, ten mentally disturbed Negro children were transferred from Crownsville State Hospital to previously all-white Rosewood Training School, and, on a lighter note, for the first time, the Maryland Division of the American Automobile Association accepted Negro members.

On May 15, 1955 Levering Hall at Johns Hopkins University hosted a free all-day conference designed to bring together student groups from all colleges in the area to discuss

---

[114] *Toward Equality*, p. 43.

the *Community Self-Survey*'s report. Rabbi Israel Goodman gave the keynote address, followed by workshops on the various components of the survey. It was an awakening for many of Hopkins' students who had been slow, on the whole, in opposing discrimination, even in recognizing its existence.

•••

Johns Hopkins had officially stopped excluding blacks in 1944, but between than and 1964 only thirty-four were admitted. Especially when contrasted with its neighboring women's college, Goucher, discrimination was not an item of great concern to Hopkins' students, staff or administration.

The actions of the Morgan students at Northwood had roused a few Hopkins' students to join them, and the stir over choice of a hotel for June week in 1955 (already discussed in the Gwynn Oak section), coming as it did on the heels of the Self-Survey's workshop, aroused the awareness of discrimination in the student body generally.

The determined Morgan demonstrators and their own hotel incident probably account for the Hopkins' chapter of Students for Democratic Action (SDA), later that year, undertaking a campaign to desegregate local hotels and restaurants. They formed a committee that sought to list all those willing to desegregate, and requested their parent group, the national Americans for Democratic Action (ADA), to solicit promises from organizations around the country that they would use those on the list for their conventions and banquets. A member of the committee pointed out "that Baltimore was the only city with major league baseball in which team members must stay at separate hotels because of racial discrimination."[115]

The SDA was also stirred to action in October that year when they learned that the Student Council had not invited Baltimore's two most prominent black high schools to be part of Hopkins' recruitment day. They pointed out the need to

---

[115] *JHU Newsletter*, 12/2/1955 and Palumbos' thesis, p. 460. He noted that members of the ADA, formed in 1941, were "mostly white liberal and labor leaders concerned with issues of fair employment, racial discrimination and anti-communism. Student groups became affiliated with ADA in the mid-1940s."

make a special effort to recruit black students. Nothing more
is said in the Hopkins' newsletter or elsewhere of either of
these campaigns, leaving one to surmise that they
accomplished little. However, many of the students involved in
the campaigns did join other SDA chapters around the
country in raising money for the Montgomery bus boycott, and
they also joined in other such activist projects.

A long letter to the editor from John Brewer appeared in
the Hopkins newsletter on April 1, 1958. It described in some
detail the refusal of service to a Negro at a restaurant "scarcely
five blocks from Homewood" (the Baltimore neighborhood
where Johns Hopkins is located). As a consequence of his
refusal, three "pure-bred Caucasians" with him left, and
subsequently a few others returned to tell the waitress that
they would no longer patronize the restaurant unless they
would serve blacks. She seemed undaunted and told them,
"This is Baltimore, and we can't do that."

The letter went on to recount how the previous summer,
"a Negro transfer student attending summer school here had
to get by with two meals a day at times because the only place
at which he could eat, outside Levering Hall Cafeteria (which
closed at 4:00), served food which could at best be described
as unpalatable." Returning to the original episode which
provoked the letter, Brewer wrote: "[The Negro who was
refused service] is well-known and equally well-liked; a
gentleman, an athlete, a scholar, and a damned nice guy; but
what can we do?" he concludes his letter this way:

> In this time and in this country, in a city that has
> received praise for its courage in simply allowing children
> with two types of skin pigmentation to attend school
> together, the fact remains that Hopkins is truly an island of
> freedom and equality in a wide, tragic sea; and that we are
> still isolated, still sealed off from the people of this city.

Shortly after this a "somewhat weak and disorganized sit-
in" was held at the Blue Jay Restaurant on St. Paul Street,
near the University, and failed.[116]

It was not until Monday, February 22, 1960 that another
effort was made to integrate this restaurant. That afternoon

---

[116] *JHU Newsletter* editorial, 11/17/61

about sixty students entered the Blue Jay and asked to be served. Fred Paxenos, the owner, didn't directly refuse but told them he had too many customers and was closing for a while. They left but within moments returned to find the restaurant open. This time he told the students to leave or face arrests.[117]

Later that evening, following a performance at the University, Duke Ellington, his manager, and two others, including his host, the Hopkins Chaplain, Dr. Chester Wickwire, went to the restaurant. They were told the place was closed. Riled, the students sat-in on each of the days following; then, on Thursday night while the group was meeting to lay out plans for extending their sit-ins to other restaurants in the area, a fire blazed up at the Blue Jay. Thirteen pieces of fire-fighting equipment were required to put it out; the place needing to be rebuilt, almost in totality, before again being useable.

Dr. Wickwire was convinced it was not an accident. In talking to this writer about it, he said the police had investigated but nothing ever came of it. The fire did, however, prompt all the other restaurants in the area to inform the *Afro* that they were considering integrating and were inviting the students to meet with them to talk about it. However, it is not clear whether any of the area's restaurants integrated before the city passed a Public Accommodations Act in 1962.

Dr. Wickwire told this writer about an incident that occurred at the Blue Jay soon after the Act's passage. This time he'd gone there with one of Baltimore's most prominent black Presbyterian ministers, the Rev. Robert Newbold—to test its willingness to serve blacks.

> We had to wait and wait, but eventually were served. Then, when I went to the counter to pay, the cashier literally threw the change at me, much of it landing on the floor. She'd said, 'You, (pointing to the black minister) are welcome any time, but you (pointing to Dr. Wickwire) get the hell out and don't come back!

He surmised that they felt that "as a white, I had betrayed them."

---

[117] This and the Ellington incident are based on *Baltimore New-Post* article, 2/23/1960, and account by Dr. Wickwire to this writer.

Now in his 80s and retired (but virtually as active as ever], Dr. Chester Wickwire came to Johns Hopkins as Chaplain in 1953, just after he'd received his doctorate in religion from Yale University and been ordained as a minister of the United Church of Christ. He was a survivor of polio, his Yale studies interrupted by a thirty-eight month hospital stay,  and another six month stay at Warm Springs, Georgia, in what he called Klan territory. He credited his admission there to the direct intervention of Eleanor Roosevelt. Wickwire was left crippled, but able to walk with crutches [only confined to a wheelchair in 2001], and it never held him back in his determination "to make a difference."

He told this writer that his encounter with polio left him with a new attitude toward life; in his words, "more honest, open, transparent," able to say, "to hell with authority." Further, he felt that since his salary was paid half by Hopkins and half by the YMCA, he was safe in making waves on campus, dared by no one else. But, he emphasized, "I always tried to be responsible."

Palumbos had this to say of Dr. Wickwire:[118]

> [He] and his staff aided in the development of student activism by providing a haven for liberals on an otherwise conservative campus. Out of Levering Hall [where he had his office], Wickwire ran various student life programs such as concerts, dances, and movie screenings while simultaneously organizing political discussions about civil rights, pacifism, the Cold War, and Vietnam. Dr. Wickwire himself had strong liberal views. He was a perennial figure in Baltimore civil rights activity who served on human relations committees, organized protests, and later helped to give protection to the

---

118 Palumbos, p. 461

Black Panthers.

In 1956 a city-wide conference on discrimination was held at Levering under the auspices of Hopkins Young Adult Council. They sent invitations to all the colleges in Baltimore and to numerous religious, political and social organizations in the area, hoping that this disconnected group could be united in purpose. It was an early step in making Levering Hall "*the* liberated spot on the silent campus."[119]

In 1959 another daring event, initiated by Dr. Wickwire, brought him together with Walter Carter for the first time. They joined forces to arrange a jazz concert at the 5th Regiment Armory in downtown Baltimore that would be open to blacks and whites alike—in a city that was still very segregated. Wickwire was a firm believer that jazz had "theological significance" and he definitely felt that the university should extend itself to the black as well as the white community. Walter, for his part, saw jazz as an expression of black freedom, an outlet for their anger and frustrations, at a time when blacks could not safely express these feelings in action.

Wickwire gave this writer his account of the event:

> The Hopkins administration was up in arms, fearing a race riot, but was unable to stop us. I did, however, agree to hiring Pinkerton guards for the evening as a precaution and to help alleviate any fears that Baltimoreans might have about attending the concert.
>
> The night of the concert, the armory was filled; Dave Brubeck, Duke Ellington and other greats performed; and there were no outbreaks of violence. The concert was a great success for all but me. In back-room hanky-panky, ticket moneys were stolen or surreptitiously pocketed, making it impossible for him to recoup the money he'd personally invested to make the concert happen. I almost lost my home which I'd mortgaged to finance the event.

Wickwire expressed his belief that, in some ways, this event marked the beginning of a sustained civil rights movement in Baltimore. It certainly marked the beginning of a long-lasting close friendship between Walter Carter and Dr.

---

[119] Palumbos attributes this quote to Tom Hayden referring to Austin's YMCA, but correctly says it applies equally to Levering Hall, p. 462

Wickwire—two people who loved jazz, and shared a vision of what might be, what should be. A mutual love of jazz might also explain their later close relationship with Fred Weisgal, who became CORE's attorney in the 1960s. He not only loved jazz, but was himself admired for his jazz piano playing, something that had enabled him to earn enough to pay his way through law school.

•••

Actually Fred was often torn between his love for jazz and his commitment to civil rights. At one point he almost abandoned law school to devote himself entirely to jazz. But friends have said that even had he done so, he would have found a way to fight for civil rights. As evidence they referred to an incident Fred liked to recall that got him in trouble with the musicians' union for playing before an integrated audience at Rehoboth Beach, Delaware in the 1940s.

> The boardwalk was strictly segregated, and so were the clubs. So I firmed up plans to rent a large barn-like hall on my night off for an interracial dance. It turned out to be the greatest evening I ever had as a performer—despite very little advance notice, more than five hundred people showed up and we had a sixteen-piece orchestra. The musicians' union, though, was so displeased that it ended up slapping a fine of $250 on me—trumping up the excuse that I had violated my contract by working seven days in one week....

•••

Soon after Dr. Wickwire and Walter Carter met, the latter became one of the most sought after speakers at Hopkins' Free University classes, started by Wickwire; he, in turn, became a valued behind-the-scenes advisor and supporter of Walter's many de-segregation campaigns. As an active member of the otherwise black Interdenominational Ministerial Alliance, Dr. Wickwire provided CORE with an entrée to the pastors of the member churches—the largest and most influential in the city. Wickwire was the only white member of this otherwise all-black group of forward-looking ministers who often took positions on issues that were in advance of the thinking of most of Baltimore's three hundred black ministers and of their congregations. His name, along with the Reverends Vernon Dobson and Marion Bascom, were most often found in reports noting ministers involved in civil rights actions.

•••

Even while CIG was focusing on integrating the Northwood's Theater and CORE on Gwynn Oak Park, they had also continued their sit-ins at still segregated lunch counters and restaurants both at Northwood and downtown. However, tensions and a competitive spirit between the various civil rights organizations had become manifest, even as their members could be observed, on many occasions, demonstrating side-by-side; and even though some would, on occasion, identify themselves as members of CIG and on another as members of CORE. All the groups resisted efforts by the local NAACP to control their methods or choice of targets, but none could afford to alienate the NAACP entirely because they needed the older, richer, organization for help with posting bonds, and sometimes for legal assistance. In general, the NAACP did not oppose these more activist organizations, but neither did it often participate with them. Instead, as indicated earlier, the NAACP now, unlike in earlier days, preferred to wage its battles for equal rights in the courts and legislatures.

•••

Morgan students still led the way in picketing and sit-ins at eating places, and on March 12, 1960 (while also still picketing at the Northwood theater) resumed their efforts to desegregate Hecht-May's Roof-Top restaurant in the Northwood Shopping Center. An editorial in the *Afro* on March 19 encouraged the students to continue their "calm and dignified manner" and to be patient. "Success cannot be expected overnight," they wrote. "The walls of segregation took years to build and will take weeks or perhaps months before they fall." In a separate article, the *Afro* described the students as "neatly dressed, orderly, and intelligent college students. Their speech is soft and their manner is one of quiet dignity. They are asking to be treated as other Americans."

On March 26, the *Afro* reported that the students had refused a request by the Governor's Committee on Interracial Relations and Problems to halt the demonstrations while negotiations took place, saying they had agreed to this previously and nothing happened. Instead, three hundred students descended on Hecht's in a final "push," and the management went to court seeking an injunction. Hecht claimed it had had a 49% drop in restaurant use and a 35% decline in its retail business. Judge Joseph Allen granted an injunction that limited the number of picketers to *two* to be stationed at the store's entrance.

Ironically, this injunction did the students a favor. It prompted them, for the first time, to take their demonstrations downtown to the city's four large department stores—Hecht-May, Hochschild Kohn, Hutzler's and Stewart's. According to Meier, Baltimore's department stores had been the most discriminatory in the nation. He states:[120]

> Beginning in the 1920s they effectively discouraged Negro trade by refusing Negroes charge accounts and refusing to permit them to try on or return articles. Certain firms, it appears, in effect rejected Negro patronage entirely. It was only during and after the Second World War that, under the pressure of various interested groups and agencies, the department stores gradually—and in piece-meal fashion—modified their discriminatory policies.

In a recent interview, Janice Woolridge told Hopkins' students of a visit paid her home by Mr. Hutzler as part of a study he was making of the spending by blacks in his store.

> I think he wanted to see who they were. I was paying over $500 a month myself shopping. So I know some people were paying more. So they had moved into the direction where you could try on clothes, but you still could not eat in the dining room. That's where the hang-up came. I told Mr. Hutzler that I didn't see that I should spend that kind of money in his store and run down the street to some place else to find some place to eat. It doesn't make sense.
>
> I was eating there anyway, but I didn't tell him that [the student didn't ask her to elaborate; presumably she was light-skinned]. When the demonstrating started, I didn't; it was a matter of principle. I was with the cause. My friends and their children, so many of my relatives, were involved in this thing. So what we did, we closed out all our accounts at all the stores.

---

[120] Meier, *White Scholar...*, p. 119

In 1960 these stores were under increasingly intense pressure to open their restaurants. Suddenly the city's newspapers began covering the demonstrations, awakening the whole city to the students' cause. Students from other colleges and adults from CORE joined CIG in their picketing and sit-ins. On one occasion, thirty ministers joined the students.[121] At the NAACP, Lillie Jackson, its President, announced they would provide bail money for any arrested students and Juanita Jackson said she was forming a "Mother's Committee" in support. Pronouncing their arrests "ideal test cases," the NAACP asked Robert Watts to head a battery of lawyers to defend arrested students, and said they expected Thurgood Marshall to be in Baltimore for the trials. Ministers throughout the city offered to pay bond money and the Baltimore Urban League and Governor's Commission began "closed-door" meetings with management.

©AfroAmerican, 3/28/1960

Palumbos describes the beginning of the downtown demonstrations this way:

---

[121] Afro, 4/16/60

On March 26, 1960, four buses brought students from
Morgan State to the city [chartered buses paid for by the
NAACP] where they divided into four teams, each one
targeting a store. Guards waiting at Hecht-May refused to
admit the students. At Stewart's department store the dining
room closed immediately upon the team's arrival. Hutzler's,
the city's leading store, allowed the students to sit down until
closing time. The Hochschild-Kohn department store was
also prepared for the demonstrators; when the students
arrived the staff received them with what the Afro-American
described as "prompt and courteous service." [122]

In a recent conversation, Mildred Atkinson laughingly
recalled how surprised they were to be served. Not expecting
it, she was almost the only one with any money on her, so had
gone from table to table, giving the students enough money to
enable them to order and pay for it.

Clarence Logan, Morgan's student leader, later quoted
Hochschild Kohn's President, Martin Kohn, as stating that he
believed "all decent people should be served," adding that "if
the community accepts it, we will continue the policy." His
decision to change the store's policy helped rally public
opinion behind the students.[123] Groups such as Fellowship
House, an integrated organization providing educational,
social and cultural events, the Catholic Interracial Council,
and the YWCA wrote letters praising Hochschild-Kohn for
opening their restaurant to all, and letters to the other stores
urging them to do the same.

Palumbos continued his account of the student actions:

> With this victory behind them and community support
> growing every day, the Civic Interest Group pressed on, using
> sit-ins whenever possible and pickets at the three remaining
> stores for the next three weeks. Students protested two or
> three days a week, and the stores began to shut down their
> restaurants at the first sign of their coming, a tactic that was

---

[122] Palumbos, p. 466. An article in the *Afro*, April 23, 1960, seems
to contradict his statement regarding the buses, stating that
throughout the downtown demonstrations, the bus company
transported the students to and from the area without charge.
[123] From letter supplied by Clarence Logan that he wrote in
October 1998, quoting *Baltimore American*, Sunday, March 27,
1960. Also see Meier, *A White Scholar...*, p. 123.

to CIG's advantage, as shown when eight students managed to close all four dining rooms at Hutzler's by themselves.[124]

After three weeks of demonstrations by hundreds of mostly-students, the stores were beginning to feel their loss of revenue—customers were canceling their accounts and refusing to enter the store. With a "reservoir of young blacks flooding the city, some whites reacted as if the sit-ins signaled the start of the revolution."[125] For their part, the other department stores' owners all seemed to be awaiting the position of Hutzler's before they would make a move to change their policy. An interesting side-light to this story is the fact that Hutzler's restaurant manager was John Roemer, Jr., the father of John Roemer III, who became an officer in CORE and one of its most active demonstrators. He did not participate in these demonstrations, but his father was appalled to learn that it was at this very time that his son had "joined the enemy."

Hutzler's President, Albert Hutzler, Jr., had been away on vacation until April 15. On April 16, he met with Robert Watts, CIG's attorney, Furman Templeton, executive director of the Urban League, David Glenn, assistant to the director, and four Morgan students, Ronald Merriwether, Melvin Scott, John Quarles and Levin West. They were informed he'd already decided to integrate his restaurants, and immediately called Stewarts and Hecht-May to tell them his decision. The *Afro* on April 19, 1960 quoted Hutzler's Vice President, E. L. Leavey, as stating:

> In keeping with our evolutionary policy, we have lifted restrictions in restaurants in all of the stores. We hope the situation has been resolved to the satisfaction of all concerned. The students have been able to do what the stores themselves haven't. They have awakened the community's attention to a situation that needed correcting. They should be congratulated for the manner in which they conducted the demonstration. We feel it's (the policy) good for the community. It was never a question of principle. It was a matter of time. And we think this is the time...

---

[124] Palumbos, p. 466. An account of these department store demonstrations can also be found in Meier, *White Scholar...*, pp. 122-125.

[125] *Evening Sun* 6/8/1982

They went on to quote Geoffery Swaebe, Vice President of Hecht-May, who made a less gracious, more self-serving comment:

> Our policy has been consistent. We were ready to act whenever the community dictated it....The students started by picketing the store in Northwood. We thought it was not a one-store matter and as soon as the other stores agreed to the new policy we were ready and did act.

For his part, Stewart's President, Raymond Greenhill, merely confirmed that his company would also open its restaurants.

All the criminal charges that had been brought by the stores against demonstrators were dropped. Officials from the less prestigious department stores, Montgomery Ward and Brager-Gutman, hastened to inform the *Afro* that they'd been serving Negroes for some time, and Sears said their lunch counter was only for employees but this included Negroes. These department stores began to change other policies at the same time—policies that had, among other things, denied blacks credit accounts, restricted them to separate rest rooms, and had not allowed them to try on wearing apparel, nor to return purchases. Despite these humiliations, many blacks had been forced to continue patronizing the stores because they were the only place they could find variety and quality goods without traveling to Philadelphia or farther north— which many could not afford to do.[126]

•••

In 1960, Morgan's Civic Interest Group (CIG) received the Sidney Hollander award "for courageous and effective use of non-violent action to abolish racial discrimination in places of public accommodation, constituting an outstanding contribution toward the achievement of equal rights and opportunities for Negroes in Maryland."[127] They had submitted

---

[126] Information is in a letter from Clarence Logan, written in October 1998. To whom is not stated, but letter's opening paragraph indicates it was to someone at the Episcopal Diocese of Maryland.

[127] The quote and the CIG listing that follows is from Moorland Spingarn, Box 50-4, folder 131

to the award selection committee a remarkable list of their
successes in opening restaurants, cafeterias and lunch-counters:
Hecht-May,   Hutzler's,   Hochschild-Kohn,   and   Stewart's
department stores; Thompson's Bickford's, and Oriole's Chain
Cafeterias; Arundel (Northwood); Kresge's; Nats's and Leon's;
Virginia Dare; Branding Iron; White Tower and Little Tavern
Chains; Saratoga Coffee Shoppe; Century Luncheonette; and
Tommy Tucker's, Hot Shoppe, Whalen Drug Store and Arundel
Ice Cream Shop in Edmondson Village.

They added a list of those which opened "prior to any
demonstrations" (presumably after negotiations or because they
desired to avoid becoming targets): Regent House, Howard
Johnson's, Brager-Gutman Department Store, Nedick's, Read's
Drug Store, Montgomery Wards, Pixie Pizza Shops, Chung King,
Arthur's Bakery Luncheonette, and Ameche's Drive-in. They
might also have mentioned that in 1957, the Lexington Market
removed their "white" and "colored" signs.

Despite these successes, knowing these policies were
subject to change at the whim of their owners, CIG also noted
its support for the passage of the Public Accommodation bills,
House Bills #33 & 27 and Walter Dixon's City Council bill (all
defeated).[128]

What is most remarkable about this submission by CIG
to the Hollander Award's Selection Committee for consideration is that no credit for any of these achievements is given to
any other group; and especially to CORE, which was very
much involved and earlier itself received a Hollander award for
related successes. It would have been gracious also to have
acknowledged the novel campaign of the Council of Churches
which, in 1958, had distributed thousands of mailing stickers
for use on checks and bills to express to stores and public
utilities the willingness of their patrons to be served by
persons without regard to race.

One further peculiarity of the list submitted by CIG is the
inclusion of the White Tower chain. That same year, on
February 16, 1960, the United States District Court for the
District of Maryland, ruled on a case brought by Sara Slack, a
black newspaper reporter, who claimed she had wrongfully

---

[128] In 1955 Walter Dixon had become the first black City
Councilman elected since 1931.

been refused service in its restaurant at Pulaski Highway and Highland Avenue in Baltimore on June 8, 1957. She *lost*.[129] Slack had claimed that at the time she was refused service, 75% of Baltimore's restaurants were segregated, but 25% were integrated, including the Howard Johnson's that was only a short distance from the restaurant where she was denied service. Additionally, she reminded the court that Maryland in 1951 had repealed a number of its Jim Crow laws, *Brown v. Board of Education* had forced school integration in 1954, and *Dawson v. Mayor et al* had integrated the city's parks and beaches in 1955. Despite this and the citing of city involvement in restaurants as a result of licensing requirements, the court decided that restaurants had a right to choose their customers—and dismissed the case.

The CIG list did not include Dickman's, Miller Brothers, the Chesapeake, and the White Coffee Pot as successes, perhaps because these restaurants had only said they were *considering* whether they would begin serving blacks, and the students believed, rightly, there was still much to be done. Arrests were still taking place and the huge sign at Miller Brothers [eventually removed] painted on one of its outside walls "advertising that it was on the site of what was once a slave auction house"[130] was especially galling. At least as late as April 10, 1962 it was still segregated. The *Afro* reported picketing by CIG as Governor Millard Tawes was inside that day celebrating his birthday.

Myles Katz, President of the White Coffee Pot chain, claimed there was a rightful distinction to be made between what he called his cafeterias, located in public buildings, where he served blacks, and his restaurants, located elsewhere, where he did not. Katz added: "I don't know what the future will bring. Things are changing." In late June 1960, the students joined CORE in the struggle to open the White Coffee Pot restaurants.

The chain had first come under attack by a small group calling itself the "United Citizens for Better Human Relations,"

---

[129] *Slack v. Atlantic White Tower System, Inc.*, 181 F. Supp. 124; 1960 U.S. Dist. LEXIS 3058
[130] Watson, p. 447.

or, more often, just the "Mondawmin Movement." The target restaurant was one of a local chain of inexpensive restaurants located at Mondawmin Mall in Northwest Baltimore, a shopping center newer than that a Northwood. Most of Mondawmin's fifty stores were integrated, but the White Coffee Pot was not. In 1957 or '58, CORE lent its support to the group, and unsuccessfully tried to negotiate with the manager. For some time, demonstrations occurred on a bi-weekly basis, drawing as many as sixty people at a time. But despite the fact that the owner's segregation policy was especially galling, the protestors could get little press coverage, and sustaining the demonstrations became impossible.

Horn explains in his thesis why their policy was especially irksome:

> They had landed a contract from the city to feed city employees, who received vouchers good only in White Coffee Pots. [Their] policy was to sell food to the City's African-American employees, but not to let them eat inside. As a result, black city workers had to eat outside, sitting on curbs, park benches, or whatever was available, summer and winter. The practice was unfair, humiliating and probably unhealthy.[131]

Nicholas Schloeder, the Gilman coach, told of the time in 1955 when a New York visitor to Baltimore had gone with an old army friend, Sam, to a ballgame, to be followed afterwards by dinner. They'd just left one place that refused to seat them, when the New Yorker noticed the White Coffee Pot across the street. "Why not eat there?" he'd asked, "it looks like a nice place." Sam must have smiled as he retorted, "You haven't gotten any smarter since I last knew ya. When they say the White Coffee Pot, they *mean* the *White* Coffee Pot."[132]

By the time CIG joined CORE in demonstrations at the Mondawmin restaurant in June 1960, it was the only restaurant in that area that was still segregated. Nonetheless,

---

[131] Horn p. 87. CIG involvement noted by Palumbos, p. 467

[132] From Goldstein's interview with Schloeder on 2/8/96. In the same interview Schloder explains that blacks and whites could sit together in "the rickety bleacher seats way up in the grandstand of Memorial Stadium.

it was not until January 10, 1961 after a meeting between the owners and students called by the President of the Mondawmin Corporation, that the *Afro* was able to report that the White Coffee Pot had agreed to a ten-day truce; its purpose "to permit the owners time to decide if they are going to drop the segregated service policy at their restaurant in Mondawmin." The Corporation was concerned that the demonstrations were hurting the other businesses, none of whom refused service to blacks. The meeting had included two of CIG's most active leaders, Clarence Logan and Doug Sands, as well as David Glenn and their attorney, Bob Watts.

The cooling off apparently ended without integration because on March 28, 1961, the *Afro* reported that leading ministers had joined the students, which now included those from high schools, Hopkins and Goucher, at the White Coffee Pot at Mondawmin, and at another White Coffee Pot at Baltimore and St. Paul Streets. The White Coffee Pot at Mondawmin began serving blacks in June but there must still have been at least one holdout. It was near the end of the school year later, in 1962, when four students from Park School went downtown to a White Coffee Pot for lunch. Billie Garner Brown, black, told of their experience.[133]

Billie had been reluctant to go to that restaurant, but had been persuaded to do so by her friends who concocted a story that Billie was to be a visitor from Argentina. As they walked in, they noted the manager, perhaps the owner, at the far end of the restaurant "dressed in a greasy apron." When he approached their table, he asked: "Where you from honey. You from Puerto Rico?" Not knowing any Spanish, Billie reverted to her school-French and answered "Oui." Fortunately, he did not know the difference. "Between his remaining teeth, the man nodded and said, "OK, I guess that is alright then." The students felt rather pleased with themselves for having fooled the restaurant into serving them. When they finished their meal and went up to the cash register to pay, one of them asked, "Do you serve Negroes in here?" and received the anticipated answer, "Absolutely not." "Oh, really? they laughed. "Well, you just did!" Billie concludes her account of

---

[133] From the interview of Billie by Goldstein on 12/30/95.

the experience:

> Screaming in a mixture of fear and pure delight, the girls ran from the White Coffee Pot, piled into the car and collapsed in laughter. The look on the gaping, toothless man's face had been indescribable. Not only had they pulled off their stunt successfully, they had increased their glory with a confession. Their adrenaline increased when they realized that in the confusion of the moment, they had fled the cash register without paying for lunch. Driving at high speed back to Park School, the girls kept turning to look behind them, fearful, though strangely exhilarated, that at any moment they would hear the wail of police sirens chasing them.

The girls "adventure," done as a lark, perhaps makes too light of the seriousness of the demonstrators trying to integrate the place, but perhaps a little levity along the way is appropriate.

Rev. Vernon Dobson also had memories to share of the White Coffee Pot located in his own neighborhood:[134]

> My Mother in the 40s would come home from her job of washing and ironing and demonstrate on Pennsylvania Avenue. There were merchants around there where we couldn't go. We couldn't sit at the counter of the white establishment, the beautiful White Coffee Pot, just about four blocks from us. You could go in and order a cup of coffee, but you couldn't sit down, you had to stand outside to drink it. And the place was beautiful, I mean it was immaculate and for a boy, for a child, it was just a dream world. So, I saw my Mother and other church women fighting that issue at an early age, and I think they were my heroines.[135]

Rev. Dobson went on to make an incisive observation as to why it was generally only the black women who were involved in early demonstrations.

---

[134] Interviewed in December 1999 by two Hopkins students; also interviewed by this writer.

[135] Rev. Dobson would undoubtedly be referring to the demonstrations in the 30s and early 40s that we discussed earlier, instigated by young people in the City-Wide Youth Forum, supported by the adults.

My father couldn't do it because the history of America is that Black men responding to our conflict were endangered of being treated as malcontents. A Black woman could be in the Movement at a time when Black men dared not. Black men did not join the Civil Rights Movement until it had been set up by Black women. Black women have always been intuitive about where the races ought to be. My Mother would tell me a person who misspoke her, "I'll slap your face." I'd say, "Mama don't." You know, she was a full family arsenal—and at no danger of getting hurt.

In May 1960, the *Afro* announced that twelve downtown restaurants were integrating as a result of student protests (they are not named).[136] Then, in July, the White Tower and Little Tavern, both having been picketed and having initiated arrests, were added. They named Howard Johnson's as the last to integrate. [137] By 1962, most of Maryland's seventeen Howard Johnsons had integrated but the one in Millington, in Kent county on the Eastern Shore, was a hold-out. However, after hearing of national CORE's plans for nation-wide simultaneous demonstrations at Howard Johnsons in October 1962, it notified local CORE that it was integrating. Maryland thus joined Florida as the first two states to achieve 100% integration of their Howard Johnsons.

•••

Most of the arrests for trespassing and obstructing free passage that occurred at the various restaurants the spring and summer of 1960 were settled in police court. However, this was not the case with those arrested at Hooper's on Charles and Baltimore Streets on June 17, 1960 (Hoopers later moved to Greenmount and 31st Street). The arrest of twelve there that day as they sat-in would eventually end up in the Supreme Court as *Bell v. Maryland*[138]— ironically named after Robert Mack Bell (because appellants are listed alphabetically and he came first) who has said he never again actively took part in a demonstration and eventually became a judge on Maryland's highest court. Bell, then sixteen, was a

---

[136] See Palumbos, p. 467.
[137] *Afro*, July 23, 1960
[138] *Bell v. Maryland* 204 A2d 54 and 84 SCT 1814, 378 US 226

Junior at Dunbar High School, had just been elected student government president, and had been asked by members of CIG to recruit students willing to sit-in.

It was the first day of their summer vacation when twelve black students from Dunbar High and a number of other schools entered Hooper's restaurant on June 17 and proceeded to seat themselves after the hostess, Ella Mae Dunlop, refused to do so.[139] They had "paid 10 cents to ride a bus downtown, sit down at a restaurant and wait for the police" to arrest them after they refused to leave following the reading of the trespass act.[140]

As their case wend its way through the system, demonstrations continued at Hooper's, and more arrests occurred.

In his questioning at the trial of the twelve demonstrators arrested on June 17, Bob Watts, their attorney, made clear that Hooper's had denied them admission purely on the basis of skin color. After the manager, Albert Warfel, read them Maryland's trespass act and they still refused to leave, he had called the police who forcibly removed them. Meanwhile, the owner, Carroll Hooper, had tried to convince the students that he had to remove them purely for economic reasons because his white customers would not tolerate their presence. Judge Byrnes, who heard the case in Baltimore's Criminal Court, rejected the defense attorneys' argument that "state support of private segregation through enforcement of trespass laws violated the Fourteenth Amendment guarantee of equal protection of the laws." He found the students guilty, fined them $10 each, and then suspended the fines, saying he did not believe they were "law-breaking people," but had been acting on principle.

---

[139] This account is based on "The Castle of One's Skin: Blacks recall protest they staged in 1960 in city restaurant," Denis O'Brien, *Sun*, 11/13/1994 and two books by Peter Irons and Bernard Schwartz. The books contain detailed accounts of the Supreme Court case and of the wrangling amongst the justices caused by this and other sit-in cases. This writer had a copy of case itself.

[140] "The Castle of One's Skin: Blacks recall protest they staged in 1960 in city restaurant," Denis O'Brien, *Sun*, 11/13/1994.

Without further involvement or consultation with the students, a legal team that included Juanita Jackson Mitchell and Thurgood Marshall appealed the case first to the Maryland's highest court, which upheld the conviction, and then to the Supreme Court, where it was accepted along with a number of other sit-in cases from around the country.

Throughout the entire 1962 term, the justices heatedly argued over these cases—some agreeing that their arrests violated the fourteenth amendment, others insisting it was a matter of property rights, some wanting the case decided on much narrower grounds. Earl Warren was the chief justice arguing that to regard a restaurant simply as "private property" was to ignore the fact that its policy of exclusion could not survive without the help of the state. Unable to reach any kind of agreement, the justices held the cases over to the 1963 term, by which time Maryland had passed a public accommodations law that forbade discrimination in public places.

The Supreme Court never did tackle the larger issue presented to it, and returned the *Bell v. Maryland* case to the state for a re-hearing, believing it moot after the passage of the above-mentioned act, which lawyers generally assumed would be applied retroactively to cases still in litigation.

To everyone's surprise, however, the Court of Appeals on October 22, 1964 upheld the convictions, declaring that they did not believe either the city or the state had intended, in passing the public accommodation laws, to repeal the trespass laws. "A month later, Mrs. [Juanita] Mitchell filed a petition asking the court to reconsider its decision."[141]

> Quietly and with no written opinion, the court agreed, and then reversed the students' convictions on April 9, 1965, clearing the students almost five years after the arrests.

Looking back, one of the defendants stated:

> We had some powerful forces on our side; to this day, I

---

[141] "The Castle of One's Skin: Blacks recall protest they staged in 1960 in city restaurant," Denis O'Brien, *Sun*, 11/13/1994. This seems a strange decision by the court in light of the fact that the General Assembly had passed a law in 1963 that exempted Baltimore from the State's trespass law. Perhaps realizing this was the Appelate Court's reason for changing its decision in this case.

don't know why it took so long to get justice.

•••

On June 30, 1960, less than two weeks after the sit-in that led to the Supreme Court case, new arrests were made at Hooper's. One of those arrested was a sixteen year old high school student, Mary Sue Welcome, daughter of a prominent black family, Dr. and Mrs. Henry Welcome.[142] On July 9, 1960, the *Afro* printed her account of the experience, in her own words. We learn how alone she felt while sitting at Hooper's, waiting to be arrested and taken to the Pine Street jail.

> I noticed a young colored boy working behind the counter. I wonder why he is allowed to handle the food the patrons ear, and yet, rather than serve us the owner would prefer young people like my friends and myself, as well as adult colored people, be arrested and subjected to indignities. It confuses my thinking!

She shares her feelings about the jail— the cell was clean, but "old, dilapidated and ugly," the walls, painted a "pale green and dirty grey," marked up with "names and pictures"— the humiliation she felt when patted down in the presence of male officers; followed by a matron jerking two combs out of her hair, only to have them returned when another said, "Give them back. Anyone stupid enough to get arrested is too stupid to use them."

She feels the "massive confusion" of the place when she finds herself amongst common criminals—"on one side a girl swearing about the policeman; on another side a woman moaning with cuts on her head; in another, a woman lamenting that her neighbors would suffer for 'squealing' on her, that God was the only judge; and then further down the corridor an inmate trying to find the way out."

But in letting Mary Welcome tell of her experience in her own words, the *Afro* also allowed us a close-up look at just what inspired these young people at this time in our history.

---

[142] She had attended Park School as a 7th grader, the first black admitted to this private school, for 1954 to 1958 when her mother removed her to send to a boarding school (See Education section).This must have been the summer between her junior and senior years in high school.

She describes the purpose of CIG, obviously why she felt a part of it, even though still in high school.

> Our organization is to dramatize our belief that human dignity is a God-given bequest and should be respected by everyone. We are trying to do our bit to help release our country from the ugliness resulting from segregation and discrimination which ignore one's dignity. Personally, I am willing to do anything to accomplish this goal, even if it means being arrested.

After her experience, she says that "what I saw and heard [behind bars] will always remain with me."

> There I was thrown with persons who really had broken laws, or committed misdemeanors, but I had only done what others around me were doing—asking to be served food. Yet, because I happened to have pigmentation in my skin, I was also breaking the law.
> This I cannot understand. God saw fit to make people with various colors, the same as he did plants and animals. Yet, I am penalized for what God did.
> Until I am supplied with better answers to my numerous questions, I shall continue to believe I am within my rights to expect equal treatment in public places for me and all human beings.

Many young blacks today fail to understand what these young people stood for, and what they achieved, even though racism, regrettably, is still with us.

•••

On November 22, 1961 five others were arrested at Hooper's: President of Manning-Shaw Realty, Warren Shaw, and the Reverends Mathew Silver, Herbert Edwards, George Crawley, and Logan Kearse, the latter coordinating many of the sit-ins. The paper reported them to be quite jovial while being booked, Dr. Kearse saying: "I decided to invite some friends to dinner because I hear they have good lobster at Hooper's." They were released after each posted a $103 bond.[143]

On January 4, 1962, Dr. Kearse and Warren Shaw were

---

[143] *Sun*, 11/23/61

again arrested at Hooper's (this was the third time) where they'd gone directly after an arraignment hearing on earlier trespass charges. They sat, along with thirty others arrested that day, for forty-five minutes before the police took them to jail. Dr. Kearse is quoted as saying:

> I didn't have time to get breakfast this morning because I had to attend court at 10 a.m. since Mr. Hooper was responsible for me being in court, I thought the least he could do would be to let a hungry man eat."

After his release this time Dr. Kearse sent a telegram to Mayor J. Harold Grady:

> We are deeply disappointed [that] moral suasion had no effect on [Carroll Hooper]. We have no alternative but to call upon you, our mayor…to enact immediately an effective public accommodation ordinance….
>
> Within a stone's throw of our courthouse and City Hall, in the heart of the seventh largest city in America, ministers and businessmen cannot seek a meal in a public restaurant without facing arrest and jailing solely because of their race.
>
> Regardless of what the state legislature may or may not do, our city officials have a primary obligation to protect us, their citizens, from the indignities we have suffered.

At the arraignment before Chief Judge Emory Niles, on this new charge they were represented by Juanita Mitchell and Archie Williams. Granted a jury trial, they were again released on $103 bail.[144]

One curious thing (little commented on and apparently one that did not occur to them at the time), happened when an integrated group of protesters were taken to jail for trying to force integration on segregated facilities. Suddenly it became alright for blacks and whites to be housed together, to eat together, to sleep together, to recreate together. The jailers' only concern was to keep the protesters separate from the other inmates so they wouldn't be indoctrinated with their "radical" ideas. One of the frequently jailed white demonstrators also stated he was glad not to be put with other white prisoners, because he feared they might have attacked him for consorting

---

[144] *Afro*, 1/6/1962

with blacks.

•••

While the demonstrations at Hooper's and other restaurants around Baltimore continued, the students also became involved in other issues, stating "We know now that demonstrations alone will not do it," but "use of the ballot" is also needed. Tony Adona, a member of CIG, told the *Afro* on July 6, 1960 that the students planned, in addition to continuing their sit-ins, "to canvass all the colored neighborhoods and precincts and urge all persons who have not registered to do so in order to vote in the coming presidential election." Working with the NAACP, their goal was to add 20,000 more registered voters.

They also took "time out" from their picketing and canvassing in August to participate in the first-ever sit-in at the Nation's Capitol. Walter Dean, Jr. gave an account of the event to the *Afro* on August 20, 1960. On a hazy bright, not too hot, sunny Sunday morning, twenty six CIG members, headed by Clarence Logan, Tony Adona and Douglas Sands, started their forty mile "walk for freedom" from Baltimore to DC.

> Everyone was in good spirits. We walked down the highway, over hard asphalt, through grassy lanes, on round pebbles. We walked with all the gusto, with all the enthusiasm, with all the hoopla that energetic youngsters can muster....
>
> The worst incident was when soldiers [of the U.S. Army passing by in a truck] threw peaches at us. While walking in the Laurel, MD area, we heard the word "n—" frequently by pedestrians and drivers....In contrast...the encouragement from drivers far outweighed the discouraging elements. Many drivers wave, wishing us success....
>
> The last three miles were the hardest....We all agreed with Cornell Morton: "the prettiest sight in the world was the sign that said WELCOME TO WASHINGTON." ...The last word comes from Pamela [Jones]: "When I think of what I did and what I did it for, I am not tired anymore, If it came up tomorrow, I would be more than willing to walk again."
>
> [The purpose of the journey was] to participate in a mass demonstration that was scheduled for the next day, Monday. After a good night's rest, a fine breakfast, and several hours of chatting and meeting many new faces, we decided to demonstrate in the Capitol Building. The time: 3 p.m.

They were at the building an hour, sitting-in, singing patriotic songs, "without commotion....They were the first to successfully penetrate the Capitol Building and to carry on a successful demonstration." Dean wrote that after their return (presumably by bus though he does not say), he went home to sleep, but the younger CIG members, still full of energy, resumed their work with the NAACP in registering new voters. Horn writes:

> In the hot dog days of August 1960 the lines of blacks signing up to vote grew so long that volunteers had to bring them water in buckets to prevent hear stroke. Newly registered voters, full of optimism, discussed the relative merits of John Kennedy and Richard Nixon as they looked forward to the 1960 presidential election.[145]

•••

Morgan was not the only place where student activists had become interested in voter registration. It had been a topic of discussion when Clarence Mitchell III, representing CIG, had attended a Student Nonviolent Coordinating Committee (SNCC) conference in August 1960.

It remained a concern when CIG (Clarence Logan its Chairman) joined the local SNCC unit (Reginald Robinson its Chairman) as hosts of a national SNCC meeting in Baltimore nearly a year later, between July 14 and July 16, 1961. Held at the Prince Hall Masonic Temple on Eutaw Street, delegates from sixteen Southern States and the District of Columbia were present. The intent was to lay out a program for the fall.

But especially notable was the fact that this conference brought together at the same time and place both Martin Luther King, Jr. (in what would be a rare appearance in Baltimore) and James Farmer. King, head of the Southern Christian Leadership Council (SCLC) and a national adviser for the student group, spoke to the group on Saturday morning, July 15; Farmer, head of CORE, a group which started the freedom rides into the South, spoke that evening.[146]

---

[145] Horn, p. 100

[146] This and the following account of the conference as reported in the *Afro* 7/16/1961. Perhaps as a portent of the future, this writer can't help but note that in two accounts the King appearance is in

Dr. King stirred the integrated audience of about 400 to singing and clapping as he recounted the success of the Freedom Riders in getting the "Negro" and "white only" signs removed from the bus station's waiting room and lunch counter in Montgomery, Alabama. "The people of Montgomery decided to lift the laws from thin paper to thick actions...They preferred walking in dignity (boycotting the buses) to the ignominy of sitting at the rear....They decided to substitute tired feet for tired souls....To those who say cool off, we must say we cannot cool off in our determination to obtain our constitutional rights." He told the group that lunchrooms had been integrated in 148 Southern cities and towns, adding, "It would have taken fifteen years to integrate lunch counters through court action."

Alluding to five recent incidents along Route 40 in Maryland where African Ambassadors had been refused service, King stressed the need for federal legislation that prohibited discrimination in all restaurants and hotels. He ended with an upbeat note, telling these mostly-young people that "this is a great time to be alive because we have the privilege of observing a drama on the stage of history which is bringing an end to the old order of colonialism and imperialism."

In his talk that evening, Farmer, who had been jailed in Jackson, Mississippi as a Freedom Rider, reiterated King's determination not to have a cooling off period. Rather, he said bus loads of Riders were already scheduled for Texas and other Southern states, proclaiming that CORE planned freedom rides in all of the Southern states by the end of the summer to test racial policies. Pointing to the fact that jailings in Mississippi were costing the state more than a quarter of a million dollars, Farmer said that segregation must be made too expensive to keep; tourism must be discouraged, pledges of full integration should be sought from industries moving to the South.

Farmer expressed especial pleasure that so many southerners themselves were supporting the freedom riders, noting that 34 of the last 40 persons jailed in Jackson,

---

large headlines, accompanied by a photo; Farmer's appearance in a less prominent placement and without a photo.

Mississippi were locals. He called those trying to uphold segregation analogous to "trying to stick your finger into the dike." "We must win," he proclaimed. "America cannot forget the burning bus, or the face of Jim Zweg in Montgomery, Alabama. Beaten and covered with blood....This is war. It continues to be a war of non-violence." Rev. Marion Bascom, a black local minister, concluded the evening summing up: "What Farmer is saying is simply, segregation is dead." The *Afro* reported:

> He called on civil rights groups to stop bickering among themselves and get on with the job at hand, that of obtaining equality for all. Taking a jab at colored Baltimoreans who spend "Too much money for boat rides and liquor," he charged them to "stop majoring in minors and minoring in majors."

•••

On Monday, June 4, 1962, the Baltimore City Council finally passed a public accommodation bill; on Friday, June 8, Mayor Grady signed it into law. It prohibited discrimination in restaurants and hotels but exempted "establishments whose average daily receipts from alcoholic beverages exceed their average daily receipts from food"— which meant taverns, night clubs, cocktail lounges in hotels and many restaurants with Class B liquor licenses could continue to discriminate. Councilman William Bonnett claimed the bill had been "railroaded" through. Councilman Jacob Edelman retorted that "the Civil War was over in 1865" and he should "stop fighting it." In general there was concern that the rest of the state was unaffected by their action and so urged the General Assembly to pass a State bill as soon as possible.

Walter Carter described his reaction to being served the next day at a downtown lunch counter.

> It's the kind of emotion you just can't describe. I sat there and the waitress served me eggs and bacon. I've been siting at that counter for five years without being served.

Leo Burroughs, Jr., speaking for the Civic Interest Group (CIG), told of his visit on Friday night with a friend to one of Baltimore's finest restaurants.

> I never ate so well. We ate the best they had. We spent

$12 and left a $2 tip.

By June 13 Karson's Inn, a restaurant on Holabird Avenue, was contesting the legality of the new ordinance through Robert Skutch, Jr. and William Cahill of the law firm of Weinberg and Green. In their petition for declaratory judgement filed at Superior Court, they called the law "arbitrary and unreasonable because it is discriminatory in its application to corporations or persons engaged in similar business" (referring to the exemptions). They also claimed it conflicted with the ordinance dealing with trespassing, and, was "vague, indefinite and obscure in its wording and phraseology and fail[ed] to set up definite standards or conduct." Finally, they claimed that because the receipts for liquor and food at Karson's varied from day to day, it was impossible to determine whether the Inn was covered or not.

CORE and the other activists might well have agreed with most of the points raised, but were pleased, nonetheless, to finally have a law that at least took one small step in the right direction toward equal rights. Neither they nor the restaurants that had meanwhile integrated were prepared for the judgement handed down in the Karson case on January 31, 1963.[147] In a seventeen page opinion Judge Edwin Harlan had upheld the Baltimore equal accommodation ordinance in most respects, but, unbelievably, ruled it "null and void" because it "is in direct conflict" with the State-wide trespass law. With a State law then under consideration in Annapolis, the decision was turned over to Attorney General Thomas Finan for his legal opinion on how it might be affected.

One black State Delegate said she was "stunned" by the decision; David Glenn, executive secretary of the Equal Opportunity Commission said it put his organization out of business; a number of restaurant owners said they had integrated and intended to stay that way; and John Roemer, vice-chairman of CORE called it "a slap in the face to every citizen and tourist in Baltimore." John added that it was CORE's belief that the trespass act itself was unconstitutional when used to enforce segregation.

---

[147] Composite from several clippings from unnamed paper/s; longest account in the *Afro*, 2/2/63.

It is time for the state leadership to come out of hiding and actively assert itself in favor of a real public accommodations bill, one that covers the entire state and all places of public accommodation.

If a strong bill goes through the legislature, this will abolish all legal loopholes for segregation.

For CORE non-violent direct action is the last defense of freedom when the executive, legislative and judicial leaders of the state fail their obligation to insure that this is a truly free state.

A "distressed" Mayor Philip Goodman in a phone call to Annapolis learned that amendments to the trespass law that would validate the city's ordinance were being prepared, and on March 23, 1963, the General Assembly passed a law that specifically exempted the city from the state law. Meanwhile, the state public accommodations bill (exempting twelve of Maryland's counties) had worked its way through the legislative process and was finally signed on March 14, 1963.

•••

Whatever limitations Baltimore's public accommodation bill might have had, it obviously was preferable to "no bill," which, in December 1962, was still the case in most parts of the state. One amusing incident happened about this very time in Pikesville, just over the Baltimore city line in Baltimore County. Four students from the private Park School went to the Field's department store in Pikesville, where Billie, who was black, had never been before. She saw other customers staring at her as she waited for her friends to find what they were looking for. Then, one woman approached and asked her: "Honey, where did you get that gorgeous tan? What did you use, coconut oil or something?" Billie, slightly taken-aback, responded: "Uh, no, I was born with it."[148]

A more serious incident also occurred in December 1962, in the all-white community of Ruxton, also just over the city line in Baltimore County. An Indian graduate student at Johns Hopkins University was embarrassed at Len-Dee's soda and lunch shop. Mr. Subramanian, 25, had gone there with

---

[148] From interview of Billie Garner Brown by Goldstein on 12/30/1995.

his 11-year old daughter and her friend to get some hamburgers. They had just sat down at one of the tables when the chef came over and told him: "You're not supposed to be served here." The two girls piped up to tell the waitresses who were standing there shaking their heads in disgust, "He's not a colored person, he's from India." They left the restaurant in tears when forced to accept their hamburgers in paper bags to be eaten elsewhere.

Mr. Subramanian was one of four winners of an Indian national Government scholarship for study abroad; in his case, to study chemical engineering. Later, the owner, Leonard DeMoss, claimed he didn't know anything about the incident, said another Indian was served later the same day—but admitted he was "lighter skinned." DeMoss pointed out that the county had no public accommodations law—the county having turned down one that fall. The county executive, then Spiro Agnew, said another was on the legislative calendar for the following week. On December 29, 1962 a *Sun* editorial commented on the incident:

> All the talk of Maryland hospitality must sound rather hollow to the Indian visitor...We can only hope that he will forgive this exhibition of short sight and bad manners and that his other experiences here will offer compensation. Yet this incident, rightly, will rebound to Maryland's discredit...
>
> The best way Baltimore county could apologize is to pass a public accommodations law similar to that in the city. The county, however, has decided that it cannot deal with the matter on a local level (though it is hard to see why) but must seek legislation in Annapolis.

•••

Students and faculty at Goucher College, located in Baltimore County, had earlier and more actively opposed discrimination than Hopkins' students and faculty. Sixty-eight of their seventy-five faculty members sent letters to one hundred businesses, including restaurants, bowling alleys and beauty shops, asking about their present policies. Though the letters were sent as "individuals," the President's, Dr. Otto Kraushaar's, signature was amongst those signing their names. The letter stated that segregation was against their "beliefs and principles" and went on to say that in the coming school year Goucher expected to again have Negro students at the college, "including several from Africa, under a special plan endorsed by the United States State Department."

Segregated facilities in the community that surrounds the college will continue to cause embarrassment not only to these students but also to the community and perhaps to the nation as well.

They asked the businesses to voluntarily desegregate and added that "we shall particularly support those establishments that are desegregated." About twenty of the businesses responded to their questionnaire; fifteen saying they were desegregated and two more expressing willingness to do so. One reply, sent anonymously, quoted the Bible to support segregation.[149]

---

[149] From an unnamed, undated newspaper clipping.

Route 40 & Beyond[150]

On April 23, 1961, three African diplomats dressed in full diplomatic attire walked into Miller Brothers restaurant in downtown Baltimore and nobody stopped them. They ate, lingered, paid the check and left. But these "diplomats" were not diplomats—they were locals George Collins, Herbert Mangrum and Rufus Welles. They took their story to *The Sun*, which broke it the next day. *The Sun* asked an embarrassed community why it would serve foreign blacks but not local blacks. Resistance continued vigorously.[151]

The same July 1961 issue of the *Afro* that had reported on the speeches by Dr. King and James Farmer at the SNCC meeting in Baltimore ran a parallel article describing the refusal of service to an ambassador from Chad, Africa at a Route 40 restaurant near Edgewood, Maryland. Cited as the fifth such occurrence, the article went on to criticize then-Governor Millard Tawes both for depending on "moral persuasion" to prevent such embarrassments instead of supporting a state public accommodations law, and, for being concerned about insults to foreign dignitaries, but not those to the state's own blacks.[152]

On August 31, Katharine Gorsuch wrote an apropos letter to the editor (paper unnamed) regarding the above-cited incident:

> The recent masquerade of young Negroes posing as foreign diplomats is admittedly distasteful to some. But it seems to me to point a much-needed lesson to those who would kowtow to foreign diplomats, whether on Route 40 or elsewhere, while ignoring the human rights of our own citizens. A light touch in a every somber situation may be just what some of us need. And who can fail to see the point?

On September 6, 1961, Wallace and Juanita Nelson and

---

[150] This was before the existence of Rt. 95, and was the main highway between DC and NY. In the accounts that follow, in addition to newspapers named and dated, this writer also had access to John Roemer's personal files which included a large number of news clippings which lacked either the name of the paper, the date, or both.

[151] According to an unnamed, undated article by Gilbert Sandler provided this writer by him.

[152] *Afro*, July 15, 1961.

their friend Mrs. Rose Robinson, all blacks from Philadelphia, were arrested after refusing to leave a restaurant in the town of North East, Maryland when ordered to do so.[153] What happened next was unusual amongst local demonstrators, and generated a lot of publicity: The three refused to co-operate, went on a hunger strike, wouldn't tell the officials anything about themselves, even went limp and had to be held up to be finger printed. "At their first hearing September 7, the three refused to walk to the courthouse and were carried by the sheriff's deputies." After twelve days without eating, the judge ordered that they be transferred to Crownsville, the state's mental institution. Deputies again had to carry them to effect their transfer. However, the doctors there declared them "perfectly sane."

> We're drafting a letter for the judge, telling him that these people are perfectly capable of taking care of themselves.
> They weren't cooperative with us, either. But it was a passive type of resistance. They wouldn't, for instance, tell us their medical history. But they're sane all right.

Transferred back to the jail, they were interviewed by Bishop Edgar Love, who declared afterwards, "They will fast till they die," telling him they will not cooperate in any way unless they are released. On September 21st they were tried separately before three separate juries; Chief Judge of the Circuit Court DeWeese Carter, in Elkton, Cecil County, presiding. All three were found guilty but there is no record of the sentence they received.

During that same September month, a team that included a representative from the foreign services office of protocol, a delegate from the White House, and a representative of the Maryland Commission on Inter-Racial Affairs made calls on restaurant owners along Route 40 in Maryland trying to persuade them to halt their discrimination against blacks— with little success. This followed two months during which time six African diplomats, including four ambassadors, had been refused service. One, the ambassador from Chad, was en route to present his credentials to President Kennedy.

---

[153] Incident pieced together from four clippings in personal files of John Roemer, dated September 1961, but newspaper not noted.

Under Secretary of State, Chester Bowles, made public
some of the comments appearing in foreign presses: A paper
in Sierra Leone called the color bar an "incurable disease" that
threatened President Kennedy's efforts to stand by Africa in its
fight for freedom from foreign rule. After a secretary of the
Nigerian Embassy was given some food in a paper bag and
told to eat outside, the Nigerian press said a personal apology
was inadequate, his treatment was an insult to the country as
a whole. (This had been in Hagerstown in 1959 and the town's
Mayor had apologized; the proprietors later informing the
Commission they would serve people of all color.)

Bowles emphasized that the situation was "well suited to
Communist propaganda purposes." He urged Marylanders, "to
demonstrate to all foreign visitors that our democratic ideals
are by no means hypocrisy." Both president Kennedy and
Governor Tawes urged immediate, voluntary desegregation of
these restaurants. Threats were made on a television program
that African and Asian nations might ask for a vote to move
the United Nations out of this country if they continued to be
embarrassed by Maryland's restaurants.

About this same time, John White, President of the
mostly black, 800-member Baltimore branch of the National
Alliance of Postal Employees called on the Governor to
consider the feelings of "native-born [black] Americans" as well
as foreign diplomats when considering the racial problem in
Maryland. He pointed to his own refusal of service at a Silver
Spring restaurant and the failure, three times, in the State
Legislature, of a public accommodation bill. The newspapers
were flooded with letters-to-the-editor, most upholding the
business men's right to decide who could and could not
frequent their establishments. But others, such as one form
Lynn Parson and Alan Smith on October 12 (probably in the
Sun) attacked Governor Tawes, quoted in part:

> It is evident to any literate observer of State and
> international politics that J. Millard Tawes has disqualified
> himself from further participation on the American political
> scene. By his inane, foolish, fatuous and bigoted suggestion
> that accredited diplomats from African nations avoid eating
> facilities in our state where there would be a chance of their
> being denied common hospitality, the genial Eastern
> Shoreman has demonstrated his true colors. He should

admit that he sees nothing wrong with such discrimination and be willing to go before the voters on such a platform...

The people of Maryland should realize that the major reason for the State's decline in political influence in national affairs is the ludicrous quality of its leadership ...The refusal of the State's public leaders to come to grips with the really important questions of civil rights, reapportionment and education (to name only three) is disgusting.

All this publicity determined members of both CIG and local CORE to extend their activism beyond Baltimore, even though they were both still demonstrating at various Baltimore restaurants, at Gwynn Oak, and at the Northwood theater.

About this same time, at Howard University's Graduate School of Social Work, Walter Carter, recently active with CORE, met a fellow-student, the much younger Stokely Carmichael, a member of SNCC. Stokely's descriptions of his recent experiences during Freedom Rides in Jackson, Mississippi stirred Walter anew. Walter had already been deeply affected by a newspaper picture of James Peck, a white minister on one of these Rides, his face covered in blood, left for dead after a bad beating. He later said, "When I saw that newspaper, I immediately joined CORE, grabbed a picket sign and haven't stopped walking since."

Now, listening to Stokely and the other students talk of their experiences and their disappointment in black adults as far as fighting for freedom was concerned, Walter was determined to do something. In no time at all, he and Carmichael became part of organizing a twin-city network of students from Washington and Baltimore, determined to end the proliferation of "Whites Only" signs in front of hotels, motels and cafes along Route 40, and on routes leading to Maryland's Eastern Shore. In the hectic months that followed, Walter found himself balancing study, family, a full-time job and activism, often alternating between writing school papers and trying to get some sleep as he, Carmichael and a car-load of students rode from place to place.

•••

According to Meier and Rudwick, as early as 1946 CORE had sponsored rides "known as the Journey of Reconciliation that were precursors of the Freedom Rides in the South and those initiated by CORE on Route 40 in 1961. The interracial teams who participated in the earlier Journey rides were testing compliance with the *Morgan v. Virginia* decision, obtained by NAACP that year, in which the Supreme Court had held that state laws requiring segregation on interstate transportation were an undue burden on interstate commerce. The Journey, limited to the Upper South, demonstrated that the bus and train companies still practiced segregation. It also precipitated some instances of mob violence from angry whites, and resulted in three of the testers (including Bayard Rustin) spending twenty-two days on a North Carolina road gang."[154] In contrast, the Freedom Rides in 1961-62 were to protest the refusal of service to blacks, whether born in Africa or America.

During the summer of 1961 and into the fall, students from Howard, American and George Washington Universities in Washington, DC, and Morgan, Hopkins and Goucher in Baltimore, many of them recruited by CIG, joined with adult members of CORE in demonstrations on Route 40. As publicity grew, students from Philadelphia and New York joined them. National CORE sent representatives into Maryland to evaluate the situation and rally support for more extensive Freedom Rides.

During this time, negotiations were going on behind the scenes between the restaurant owners, representatives of CORE, and of the State Commission on Interracial Problems and Relations (Doug Sands, head of CIG from 1953-1956, was then Executive Director of the Commission). The *Sun* reported on November 4, 1961 that an agreement had been reached the day before at a closed door session. CORE representatives had agreed that if at least 25 to 30 of the 65 facilities on Route 40, not to include ten of the largest restaurants which already served all customers, desegregated by November 11, the massive ride along the length of Route 40, scheduled for that day, would be postponed. They did *not* agree to postpone all demonstrations until March, until after the State Legislature met in February 1962. They were not impressed by the Commissioners' warning

---

[154] Meier & Rudwick, *Black Protest...*, Intro. p. 5.

that further demonstrations would make the legislators less likely to pass a Public Accommodations bill during that session.

Present at the meeting, in addition to two commissioners and two members of the Governor's staff, were Julius Hobson, CORE's eastern representative from D.C.; Joseph Sheehan, then Baltimore CORE's Chairman; Gordon Carey, from New York, a national CORE field director; Juanita Jackson Mitchell, secretary of the Baltimore chapter of the NAACP; and Dr. Logan Kearse, pastor of the Cornerstone Baptist Church.[155]

The agreement was finalized a few days later when the commission chairman told CORE "that thirty-five owners had accepted the offer, but set November 22, 1961 instead of the 11th as a target date." He added that "all remaining restaurants would drop color bars by December 15."

The front page of the Afro, November 11, 1961, sported a bold headline in one-inch letters: WHEW! NO RIDE. Reported reactions varied: James Farmer, national director of CORE, said he felt "that the decision of 35 Maryland and 12 Delaware restaurant operators to provide equal service for all was a Thanksgiving present for the American people." He added that if all the restaurants hadn't opened by December 15, "we will hit them with everything we have." Gov. Tawes called it "heart-warming news."

According to an undated report in the *Evening Sun*, Tony Konstant, resident of Bel Air, owner of a restaurant in Aberdeen, had taken the lead in obtaining the agreement to integrate from a sufficient number of restaurants along Rt. 40 to persuade CORE, at least temporarily, to end its Freedom Rides. Calling him "an inspiring example of courage and conscience in the desegregation of public accommodations," he received an Honorable Mention when awards were being given by the Sidney Hollander Foundation for 1961.[156] At that time, Konstant was quoted as saying he felt "happily unburdened" after he made the decision to end segregation in his restaurant: "I hadn't had any sleep in the last three nights...It's not an easy thing to go up to a Negro and tell him you won't serve him. It is morally wrong and Christianly wrong. There is a new Negro

---

[155] *Baltimore Sun*, November 4, 1961. [As indicated previously, Joseph Sheehan is not related to Cardinal Shehan.]
[156] Moorland Spingarn, Box 50-4, folder 143.

emerging, and we have got to recognize him." The newspaper account goes on to report that—

> [Konstant] began losing sleep on October 9 [1961] when he and seven of his fellow proprietors reluctantly agreed to study the growing crisis along the highway at the behest of Federal and State Officials....When the Congress on Racial Equality announced its freedom ride the majority of the eight committee members resented it and decided to dissolve the group.

Konstant himself is then quoted:

> When [our committee] disbanded, the freedom riders picked it up and said that if we weren't willing to do something about the problem, they were. That's when I began on my own....I'm not bitter about CORE's role in this thing. Let's face it, we never would have done it if they had not applied pressure. They were fighting for a principle.
> If I had it to do all over again I would have quietly desegregated and that would have been that. It's the only sensible thing to do.

The students, who had comprised the largest contingent of riders, weren't so happy about the ending of the Rides. They felt they had been sold out; supporting them, the NAACP called the victory "a skimpy one." They pledged "every resource to assist the CIG and other students who are willing to sit in for freedom now!" The *Afro* in another article praised the Commission and Doug Sands for having achieved this agreement, but concluded its longer report with this statement:

> It's apparent that the Route 40 truce is merely a lull in an uneasy peace threatening to explode anew unless it is recognized for what it is—the beginning of true equality for all Maryland citizens, and not the final solution to a problem which should have been solved a century ago. [157]

There is no indication of how the students felt about the involvement of one of their own (Doug Sands) in reaching the November 3rd agreement, but the fact that it was reached the same day nine students were on trial for earlier arrests in August (at two different sites on Route 40) must have made it

---

[157] This and the reaction quotes are from the *Afro*, November 11, 1961. The Evening Sun article was found in the Moorland Spingarn collection of Sidney Hollander, Box 50-4, folder 141.

especially hard to take.[158]

It was August 11, 1961 when two Negro males, Donnie Flemming and Elijah Gwynn, had been arrested after they entered the Double T Diner on Route 40 at Rolling Road in Catonsville, despite the reading of the trespass act and the manager telling them not to. On August 21, these same two, plus Clarence Logan, Douglas Curtiss, Clifton Henry, David Gould and Emily Shiling were arrested after being identified as among a "milling" crowd outside the locked doors of the diner. Most in the crowd had left when the owner asked them to leave.

At the other site, Douglas Curtiss was again arrested, along with William Holmes, and Dorothy Feldman. They had sat down at tables at the Route 40 Varsity Drive-In near Ingleside Avenue in Catonsville and "refused to leave, even though a policeman was there when the trespass law was read." The Judge ruled in this case "that the defendants had clearly flouted the law."

At their trial in December, the student's lawyers, Archie Williams, Tucker Dearing and Juanita Mitchell (who was also at the concession meeting), argued "that Maryland's trespass law specifically excluded from prosecution persons who trespass 'under a bonafide claim of right or ownership.'" They also argued "that Supreme Court decisions forbid intercession by State authorities to enforce discrimination."

Judge Albert Menchine, hearing the cases, rejected both these arguments, and, after lecturing the defendants about continuing to test laws that had already been upheld in the courts, he referred them to two trespass convictions that had been upheld by the State's Court of Appeals and were now before the U.S. Supreme Court. Before sentencing, he asked each of the students if they were aware of these cases that had resulted from arrests at Glen Echo Amusement Park on June 30, 1959, and at Hooper's Restaurant a year later.[159] When Logan and Holmes said they were aware of them, they were fined $100 each and costs. When Curtis and Feldman said they were not, they were fined $5 each and costs. The other

---

[158] Quotes and information on this trial from the *Baltimore Sun*, 11/4/1961.

[159] Both these cases recounted earlier.

five were acquitted; "three because Judge Menchine said the State failed to prove they had violated the trespass law and two because he ruled they were illegally arrested." As for the illegal arrests, the Judge said "that a police officer's action, in bringing the men to the diner's foyer where the manager asked that they be arrested, constituted an illegal arrest since the officer had seen no misdemeanor committed and had no warrant."

•••

On the planned day of the now-cancelled November 11, 1961 Freedom Ride along Route 40, hundreds of students gathered at Rev. Logan Kearse's Cornerstone Church at the corner of Bolton and Wilson streets, their original kick-off spot. Full of exuberance, they decided to picket and sit-in at restaurants all over Baltimore and Anne Arundel County. The demonstrators, mostly-students, left in "car-load lots, picketing at designated restaurants, and then moving on to others. Except for a team known as the 'special jail group,' the students left each restaurant when asked."

Little Italy was the only site where they encountered hostile crowds, were shoved, and heard such shouts as "We gave them too much freedom," "They push themselves down our throats and we'll push ourselves down their throats." "A car passed with youths waving Confederate flags. White letters on the side of the car said: 'Restaurant owners protect State's rights.' The crowd shouted approval."[160]

> The special jail group, led by Dr. Kearse, planned tactics in a closed session for several hours, then drove to Hooper's in three cars. Dr. Kearse led the way in a cream-colored Cadillac convertible.
>
> Seven of them shoved their way into Hooper's as the manager and hostess wedged against the revolving door. [Stokely Carmichael managed to get by even after it was barricaded]. Two others slipped in through a back door and all [10] were charged with trespassing after refusing to leave....

Six others were charged with disorderly conduct outside.

---

[160] Quotes and account of this series of demonstrations from *Baltimore Sun*, November 12, 1961

Interestingly, they included Dorothy Feldman who was amongst those on trial just a few days before. Obviously Judge Menchine's lecture on not "testing" settled law, and his specific reference to Hooper, had not deterred Ms. Feldman. In addition to those arrested at Hooper's, five were arrested at Dickman's, and one at the White Coffee at Baltimore and St. Paul. All the men were held at Central Station lockup awaiting a hearing, and the women at the Pine Street Station. None posted bonds.

In Glen Burnie, one man was charged with trespassing in Greco's Steak House, paid $54 collateral and was released pending a hearing. Ten were arrested in Annapolis for trespassing, nine of them from a Philadelphia college and the tenth a reporter for a Negro newspaper. Only the latter paid the bond set at $24. Thirty-three in total were arrested that day.

A very small article running beside the much longer account described above, suggests just how ridiculous discrimination based on skin color is. In this instance, several male Negroes entered the Snow White Grill on West Baltimore Street, along with a girl. After she'd been served and eaten, she announced that their "policy certainly seemed strange, because the other Negroes were not served. 'I'm a Negro,' she said. The flustered, angry waitress replied: 'You came in here under false pretenses.'"

On November 16, the *Sun* reported that Governor Tawes called on the Interracial Commission to once again try to reach some sort of resolution. He still refused to call a special session of the legislature to consider a Public Accommodations bill and sought to persuade Dr. Logan Kearse and Clarence Logan, then head of CIG, to call off further demonstrations until March, after the legislature met. Others asking a halt in demonstrations until the legislature met were the Baltimore Jewish Council, Council of Churches, Catholic Interracial Council, AFL-CIO, Urban League, NAACP, Americans for Democratic Action, and the Civil Liberties Committee. But the reply to them all was that the protests would continue.

On Saturday, November 18, four hundred people, mostly students, again gathered at Rev. Kearse's church for their second demonstration at Baltimore area restaurants in as many weeks. Clarence Logan, who was the chief organizer, had successfully attracted students not only from his own school, Morgan, but from Johns Hopkins, Goucher, Forest Park High School, Baltimore Institute, City College, Baltimore Junior College, Howard and George Washington in Washington DC, Wellesley College in Massachusetts, Harvard Divinity School, Yale and New York University. There was a social worker from Newark, N.J., and others from New Jersey and Philadelphia. These demonstrations and those on Route 40 represent the first, and one of the few times, that students from all over the middle Atlantic and northeastern states were attracted to Baltimore demonstrations.[161]

Ada Jenkins, one of CORE's original founders, said later how impressed she was with the student participants. "A lot of them were well-heeled and they had a lot of other things to do besides that. They were beginning to see through the hypocrisy."[162]

Before this group left from the rally at the church, Bayard Rustin spoke to them, reminding them they should not strike back no matter how they were harmed or abused.

> You are going into battle and I won't be surprised if some of you are hurt, but not one person who opposes us is to be harmed.

This time, as the students spread out to their designated restaurants, they were surprised when a number of their "targets" served them. On the other hand, at Hooper's and at Dickman's, officials blocked the doors so no one could get in. It was amusing when a waitress at the Snow White Grill tried to read the Trespass Act and couldn't. Stokely Carmichael helped her out. At Grace's restaurant on Eastern Avenue another waitress blamed her inability to read the Act on the fact she hadn't brought her glasses. Bayard Rustin, leading this group told her: "We don't want to harm your eyes. If you want us to leave, we will. At the House of Welch, a light-skinned Negro was served along with two whites, only informing the owner she was a Negro after she'd finished eating.

In "Annapolis, police had to carry twelve of thirteen

---

[161] Quotes and report on this series of demonstrations are from the *Sun*, 11/19/1961.

[162] James D. Dilts, *Sun*, "The Warning Trumpet", 12/1/1968

demonstrators from Antoinette's, for they refused to walk out. Three lay on the floor with their arms locked and had to be dragged out. A waitress said, 'I'm going to step over trash like that.'" All thirteen were arrested and charged with trespassing; the eleven of those who had to be carried or dragged out were also charged with disorderly conduct. Fifteen in all were arrested that day, and demonstrations were held before the jails in both Baltimore and Annapolis. The day's demonstrations concluded in front of the Governor's steps with Dr. Kearse saying a prayer:

> After such a great day it is appropriate to end it here at the Governor's Mansion...All we want is freedom. We don't want it in February or March, we want it now.

Two weeks later, 400 more gathered to again protest, including students and CORE members from Connecticut, New York and New Jersey, as well as from Baltimore. Twenty-one were arrested—four more at Hooper's, three at the Old Five Mile House on Reisterstown Road, and fourteen in three Annapolis restaurants (seven of them juveniles). [163]

For this demonstration, the student leaders, Clarence Logan, Stokely Carmichael, Reginald Robinson and Mr. Diamond, had rejected Rev. Kearse's continued participation. They said they wanted to keep the protests out of politics and he was the 4th District's Democratic nominee for the House of Representatives.[164] Mr. Diamond, a field secretary with SNCC who had seen Freedom Riders beaten in McComb, Mississippi while there registering Negroes to vote, reminded the gathering of an appropriate quote from Charles Dickens *Tale of Two Cities*: "It was the best of times, it was the worst of times, it was the age of wisdom, it was the age of foolishness."

At the close of the demonstration, there was enthusiastic approval when Walter Carter, then co-chair of Baltimore CORE, told the protestors he was recommending to national

---

[163] The account of this demonstration from the *Sun*, 12/3/1961.

[164] Rev. Kearse may not have participated in this demonstration, but he did not stop sitting-in. On January 3, after emerging from Criminal Court where he, along with Warren Shaw, real estate dealer and 30 others were arraigned on trespassing charges, he was arrested at Hooper's for the third time and again jailed. *Afro*, 1/6/1962

CORE that the Freedom Rides on Route 40 be resumed on December 16. Later he told the press he believed this Freedom Ride would be more effective than the one originally scheduled on November 11 since the demonstrators would be able to concentrate on about 30 restaurants still refusing to serve blacks rather than all 75 along the route. An eastern representative for national CORE, Edward Blankenheim, who had been on the freedom bus that was burned by segregationists in Anniston, Alabama, said we should all be ashamed that restaurants only an hour from President Kennedy's door were segregated. "Some say this isn't the time. That's right; the time was a longtime ago."[165]

•••

Typically it was Walter Carter and John Roemer, co-chairs of CORE for along period during these demonstrations, who spent many evenings together planning these demonstrations along Route 40, but it was students who made up the largest number of protestors. And so it was that on December 16, 1961, the majority of the 600 to 800 Freedom Riders (accounts vary), were students. They rode the length of Route 40, some starting in Baltimore and heading north, others starting from the north and heading south. Despite the earlier agreement by restaurant owners, they were denied service at most of the restaurants. "State Police said they put almost twice as many troopers on Route 40 as they normally use." The *Sun* explained the ride this way:

> The Congress of Racial Equality organized the ride, fulfilling its November pledge to "hit" every restart on Route 40 between Baltimore and Delaware that refused to serve Negroes by December 15. Delaware eating places are integrated....Edward Blankenheim, field secretary for [national] CORE, directed the ride from Enon Baptist Church....Walter Carter and Solomon Baylor, [briefly] co-chairman of the Baltimore chapter of CORE assisted, as did Clarence Logan, head of the Baltimore Civic Interest Group. The three Baltimoreans are Negroes. ...Several Negro ministers from Baltimore took part in the sitting-in, but no white

---

[165] Clipping from John Roemer's personal files does not identify newspaper nor date.

clergymen from the city.[166]

Only fourteen riders remained in restaurants to be arrested (one a juvenile) after the Trespass Act was read. (This brought the total number of arrests on Route 40 since November 11 to ninety-two.) One of those fourteen arrested was James Peck whose bloody photo, taken after a beating during a Freedom Ride in the South, had earlier so upset Walter Carter. The only violence that occurred on this Freedom Ride was between two Harford County newspaper editors when one punched the other "for photographing him arguing with a freedom rider." Those not arrested often picketed outside the restaurant carrying signs "denouncing racism and un-Americanism."

Julius Hobson, head of Washington DC's CORE chapter, went home after being refused service at four restaurants. He said he had nothing to do with the planning and thought the day ineffective, explaining that he felt that in order for it to amount to anything "the jails would have to be loaded, causing great inconvenience."

CORE had been warned earlier that continued demonstrations would prevent passage of a public accommodations bill in the February session of the legislature, and this indeed was given as an excuse. On February 1, 1962, the *Evening Sun* quotes Delegate Edward McNeal this way:

> In principle, I favor legislation permitting all citizens to eat and sleep in public places. I will vote for it. If it ever had a chance Statewide, that chance has been destroyed (by recent freedom rides on the Eastern Shore). I don't know if those of us who favor the bill can ever forgive them.

McNeal had been part of a group of six Delegates and Senators who had "braved icy weather to put an ear to the ground in their district." They visited five homes where they met with 125 persons who urged them to vote for the bill. "They were so busy talking they hardly had any chance to sample the coffee and cookies offered them." Among the homes visited was that of Dave and Billie Bramhall. Billie, as is discussed in the education and housing sections, was a forceful advocate of both

---

[166] Quotes and account from the *Sun*, December 17, 1961.

school desegregation and "open" housing.

As for the restaurants on Route 40, on February 12, 1962 the *Sun* reported Walter Carter informing a group of protestors that a test showed that a number of those restaurants on Route 40 who had refused to serve blacks were now doing so, indicating progress, but still not total compliance.

During this time, demonstrators who'd been arrested appeared at numerous court hearings, mostly arraignments where they entered not guilty pleas and asked for jury trials. Walter Carter, John Roemer, and a few others from CORE appeared at one such hearing in Prince George county when the charges had been *nolle prosed* (the prosecutor had formally declared he would no longer prosecute).

They were on their way back to Baltimore when they heard that later that day Governor Tawes and Mayor Grady were meeting at Hooper's. Knowing there would be press coverage, the group headed for the restaurant and while a few picketed in front, where the doors were locked, Walter and John went through the alley to an open back entrance, sat down and asked for lunch. When refused service, several business men plunked down their silverware and left in disgust. Then, just as the police arrived to escort them out, the State police arrived escorting the Governor and Mayor in. Just as they'd hoped the TV cameras caught the whole thing which made the evening news. Anything to keep the pressure on both city and state to pass public accommodation bills.[167]

•••

A month later, as a reaction to the defeat of an Equal Rights Bill, CORE called for a protest demonstration to be held on Saturday, March 17, 1962. About seventy-five CORE members gathered at Enon Baptist Church at 10 a.m. before proceeding to peacefully picket several restaurants around Baltimore. At a follow-up rally at the church, they agreed to postpone until later a "massive march" that had been suggested for the Easter weekend to give them time for more thorough planning.

---

[167] Interview with John Roemer.

Rev. Frank Williams, then-president of the Inter-denominational Ministers Alliance, warned the group about the "fragmenting of leadership," and urged them to form a coordinating committee. Perhaps he had in mind that the numbers had been limited at that day's action because so many students were in Washington picketing the White House "on behalf of leaders of SNCC who ha[d] been arrested in Louisiana and charged with criminal anarchy.... They asked Robert Kennedy, Attorney General, to intervene in what they consider illegal arrests." One group of thirty-five students had left the prior evening to walk from Baltimore to Washington to attend; two Swarthmore students were arrested during the walk for "obstructing traffic."[168]

The next large-scale demonstration along Route 40 did not take place until June 9, 1962 when about 120 students participated: eighty students from New York colleges and universities moved south along the highway, while forty from Baltimore moved north. Almost thirty restaurants were visited; six were arrested, only one of whom was from Baltimore.[169]

According to Leo Burroughs, Jr., then with CIG, later a member of CORE, they had not intended for there to be arrests because "the organization d[idn't] have enough money in their treasury to pay collateral [their bonds]." The *Sun* quotes Walter Carter as saying that the demonstrations were resumed amidst reports that African diplomats were still being denied service. Though refused service at all the restaurants entered by the integrated groups of four or five each, they encountered the roughest treatment at those in Aberdeen where, at one, the owner sprinkled them with a hose, and at another, when the owner produced a smoke screen "by injecting oil into the exhaust system of a pick-up truck parked next to the place." In Havre de Grace, a loiterer outside the Chesapeake Hotel and Restaurant struck one of the

---

[168] *Sun*, March 18, 1962.

[169] It is interesting to note that Stuart Wechsler, then from New York, was one of those arrested. More will be said of him when he is again in Baltimore in 1966 as one of National CORE's designates for its Target City project. Now an administrator at Maryland Housing and Community Development, Wechsler makes his home in Baltimore.

demonstrators from New York as he exited.[170]

Another Ride, probably the last held along Route 40, was planned for December 8, 1961, in co-operation with CORE members from D.C. and Brooklyn, NY. Walter Carter told the press, "The last time the group picketed was June 9. We try to give them time to make up their minds about the problem up there and we think we've given them ample time."

They planned to make two "runs" along the route between the Baltimore city line and the Delaware State line. "The first will be to determine the restaurants that have shifted, the ones that weren't serving last year and are now. We'll ignore those. The second run will be to carry our sustained protest against racial segregation in those facilities that have not integrated. On December 7th they called off demonstrations against restaurants in Aberdeen because an agreement had been reached between members of the Harford County Human Relations Committee and a group of Aberdeen restaurateurs. The agreement, which included five specific points regarding integration and demonstrations, had been approved by Walter Carter. It would seem that this meant the entire demonstration that had been planned for the next day was called off.

•••

During this time a few demonstrators had picketed in Montgomery County but their County Council quickly responded and enacted an anti-discrimination law. In recognition of this, in May 1962, Jack Levin, former chairman of the Maryland Civil Liberties Union, presented that year's Civil Liberties Award to the Montgomery County Commission on Human Relations for their success in "proposing and obtaining" Maryland's first "equal accommodations law."

At the same time, on May 10, 1962, the *Sun* wrote an editorial criticizing the American Association of University Professors for rejecting an invitation to hold its 1964 convention in Baltimore because of the failure of the General Assembly and City Council to pass equal accommodations laws. Over 50,00 professors were members of AAUP, many of

---

[170] *Sun*, June 10, 1962.

them black; usually 500 or so attended its annual convention each year. The *Sun* said:

> ...No city likes to be disowned...As a city in transition, Baltimore cannot guarantee that every place of public accommodation will be ready to receive every member of a racially integrated organization. Few if any cities could give such an assurance, even with public accommodation laws....By shunning Baltimore, the professors fail to support the portion of the business community that has risen to the association's standard and thus, in effect, take away the economic motivation for change....demonstration by personal example seems more likely to help foster an acceptance of further change than the stand-off attitude of the American Association of University Professors.

•••

By this time, a number of Baltimore CORE and CIG protestors began to divert their efforts away from Baltimore to the still segregated facilities along Route 50, which connected Washington and Annapolis to the Eastern Shore all the way to Ocean City. They persevered in these more southern-oriented areas despite encountering, in many places, a more vicious kind of racism than they'd ever confronted in Baltimore. One man expressed his belief that the Eastern Shore's racial attitudes were "more hostile than in Mississippi." A Hopkins Graduate, Cliff Durand, termed the area "a little Georgia," and Robert Bell called it "a different world."[171]

It was a demonstration as late as February 25, 1964 in Princess Anne (on Route 13, running south off Route 50 at Salisbury), that would best qualify for these assessments. That day 28 black students from Maryland State College, located there, were arrested, charged with disorderly conduct and disobeying police officers, as they attempted to march through town on their way to two segregated restaurants. The trouble seemed to have started when the students sat down on a street that was also Route 13 and refused to move. David Brashear, for the *Sun* next day, described the police reaction this way:

---

[171] See Palumbos, p. 472.

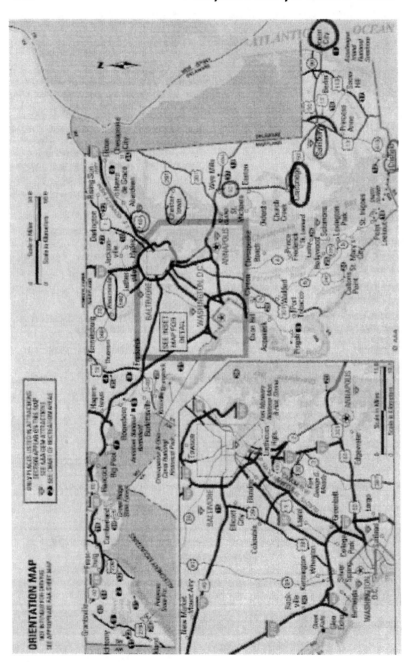

Police used clubs, dogs and fire hoses to drive the students back to the campus. Two were hospitalized at nearby Salisbury with head injuries and the college infirmary treated 57 for various injuries as a result of the demonstration....Joined by Gloria Richardson, of Cambridge [some distance away], and two other leaders of the national civil rights movement, the crowd of more than 300 Negro youth began demonstrating about 2:45 p.m. Bricks and broken bottles were thrown, police clubs were swung, and one trooper was splashed on the leg with sulfuric acid.

After the arrests, a near-riot almost took place as the students massed in front of the jail, K-9 dogs and fire hose were used to force them back to their campus. At the urging of Richardson, the students did retreat, but within a half-hour they had returned to meet the blast of the hoses head on, the pressure turned to its peak. At one point a doctor tried to get through to the students and he too was hosed; in the evening he was admitted to the jail to treat the wounded students there.

The demonstration had followed a break-down of negotiations with the restaurant owners. The head of the bi-racial commission formed the prior June criticized both sides, pointing out that since their formation a local school had desegregated, the churches had opened their doors and employment for Negroes had improved.

The day following this almost-riot, four black ministers from the Baltimore Interdenominational Ministers Alliance—the Reverends Herbert Edwards, George Crowley, Frank Williams, and Marion Bascom—met with Governor Tawes for over an hour. They were told he'd been informed by Major George Davidson, in command of the State Police in Princess Anne, that use of the dogs had been "absolutely essential and were completely under police control at all times." Rev. Bascom, unsatisfied, wondered aloud why they were never used except on blacks.

The ministers charged that (1) dogs were set on coeds watching from the sidelines, (2) State Policemen clubbed women, and (3) Police force was misused. After the meeting, speaking for the group, Rev. Bascom said they'd be back "if this does not resolve itself," adding, "We'll come back until the last vestige of racial discrimination has gone." He also took time to denounce the concurrent upheavals in Cambridge which we'll soon hear more about.

Like most places in the country, the situation was not "resolved" until legislation forced a resolution—and even then it was mostly on the surface; institutional changes are still being sought today.

•••

On January 31, 1962, the *Sun* paper weighed in with an editorial criticizing the student-run Civic Interest Group's (CIG's) persistent campaigns on the Eastern shore:

> The Shore has long been a community unto itself, resentful of outside interference. It has slowly been coming round to a more enlightened attitude toward Negroes...before CIG moved in with its policy of unilateral action. Now backs are up, attitudes have hardened, racial antipathies have been inflamed, and it takes a large segment of the State Police force to prevent bloodshed on a Saturday....If leaders of CIG are too insensitive to the delicacies of racial relations to know when to ease off, it is time that they are set straight by those who have worked longer and just as hard at the same cause.

This was not unlike the general refrain heard at the beginning of demonstrations everywhere. "Give us time; change will come." But a young generation of blacks saw no results coming from patience. The most frequent chant was "Freedom Now!", and who could blame them.

•••

Doug Sands, the former head of CIG, "regularly packed his car full of students and drove down to eastern shore communities such as Cambridge, Easton, Salisbury, Denton, Centreville, Ridgely and Crisfield."

> He would drop them off at the outskirts of town, give them time to begin protesting, and then come along in his official capacity [as Executive Secretary of the Governor's Commission on Interracial Problems and Relations] to commence the negotiations. Joining

the Baltimore area students on these protests were many white and black students from the northeastern United States. On some occasions several hundred northern students would join them.[172]

A first target of the students was Crisfield, a town of 2500, about one-fourth black, where Governor Tawes had his home. On Christmas Eve, December 1961, a group of twelve sat-in at the town's City Restaurant, the only one open, and all but two of them spent Christmas (and several days afterwards) in the Somerset County Jail.

The following Friday, December 29, a bus load of twenty-eight veteran student demonstrators from Baltimore, having gotten lost en route, arrived six hours late at their rallying point, the Shiloh Methodist Church. Even though all but two of the town's eating establishments were closed by then, at 8 p.m., observed by a crowd of at least 300 whites and blacks, some just curious, some hostile, they led as many as 120 marchers, at least eighty of whom were local blacks, through town singing freedom songs never before heard in this "tiny seafood center." [173] The youngsters were "whopping and hollering, and someone in the Crisfield Hotel threw eggs at the demonstrators as they passed but none were hit.

> Two spectators were arrested for trying to annoy the marchers. George Todd, police chief, said his entire thirteen-man force was patrolling the streets and State Police were on the alert nearby.
>
> Two groups entered lunch counters and were served. One place had stand-up service only [Gordon's Snack bar], the other [Peytons Drug store] indicated that it was serving Negroes tonight only, rather than changing its segregation policy.

At the end of a concluding thirty minute march through town, they returned to Rev. Samuel Saunders' church. President of the Crisfield branch of the NAACP, he promised "amidst cheers and 'Amens' that Crisfield's colored populace

---

[172] From Horn, p. 101; based on interviews he had with Douglas Sands, Clarence Logan and a number of others.

[173] Quotes and account of events in Crisfield are from *Afro-American*, 1/2/1962 and a Rehert account in the *Sun*, 12/29/62.

would carry on the anti-segregation activity started by the students." Phillip Savage, Philadelphia's NAACP field secretary [who had joined the demonstration after the students arrival in Crisfield], promised that "we will return" if the restaurants did not continue to serve colored patrons. If they think they can serve us and close the door to the rest of the people, they're mistaken. We'll be back if that happens.

Walter Carter, then-Chairman of Baltimore CORE, was also present. He promised his group would "sponsor demonstrations similar to the Route 40 protest of December 16, along Route 50 all the way to Ocean City. Less emphasis," he said, "will be placed on Salisbury since some voluntary desegregation has already been accomplished there"— perhaps a surprise since it had been the place of an infamous lynching in the 1930s.

In fact, the 1961 Hollander Foundation award had gone to the Salisbury/Wicomico Commission on Interracial problems for "judicious and effective leadership in desegregating public accommodations and in planning for further integration of education and employment." In his acceptance speech, John Webb credited Mayor McLemon "who had the courage and vision to create the commission," and his community as a whole. "I am awed," Webb said "by the magnitude of what is still undone." He also recognized the confidence expressed by the award that they would be able "to surmount the hurdles that lie in the future as we have those of the past."[174]

Meanwhile, in Crisfield they had managed to collect $103 to pay for the student's bus, and they left town on a high note, escorted by a state police car. But their return trip was no less uneventful than their trip out had been. The bus had a flat tire about a mile from the Bay Bridge and they had to wait over an hour in below 20 degree weather for the policeman to return with a tow truck. They then had to wait another three hours for the repair man to arrive and fix it. It was 7:30 Saturday morning before "a haggard, cold busload of riders" finally arrived back at Grace Presbyterian Church in Baltimore from which they had departed the day before.

•••

[174] Moorland Spingarn, Box 50-4, folder 145.

By February 1962, CIG's and CORE's actions on the Eastern Shore had prompted accusations that the demonstrators were subversives and the Attorney General, Thomas Finan, had agreed to investigate. On hearing of this, Clarence Logan, head of CIG, sent Finan this telegram:

> As a fifth-generation native Marylander born in Baltimore and educated in the public schools, and having served my country for four years in the United States Air Force, I welcome an investigation of my efforts and those of the students who seek with me to experience in our home state the democracy for which we fought abroad.
>
> We respectfully request an investigation of the real subversives of democracy—those owners of places of public accommodation who deny to the American citizen equal treatment solely because of race.[175]

If this was the first time that Logan had found the Freedom Riders accused of subversion; it would not be the last. Years later, according to Robert Kaufman, an avowed Socialist/Trotskyist, Clarence Logan, a leader of CIG told his that the negative treatment he'd received from their group was caused by the FBI's constant hounding of him. "They were telling me [Logan] to get rid of Kaufman and Communists and we won't bother you too much. So that's what I did, to satisfy the FBI and J. Edgar Hoover."

In an interview with Bob, he described one specific event that had provoked the above admission. It revolved around Augie Meier, the Morgan professor who was an adult adviser for CIG.[176] Bob began his story by asking, "Did you know I am the only person who was ever thrown off a Freedom Bus?"

> We were congregating at Rev. Bascom's church when a carload of white kids arrived from NYC. They were standing around, being ignored by everyone. So I went over and started talking to them, told them about the nearby Harley's when they asked where they could get something to eat. As they left, noting Augie Meier and some others in a huddle, I asked what was going on. They said Augie was afraid I was bringing down all these people from the Young Socialist

---

175 *Sun,* 2/3/1962.
176 See "Resources" for books authored or co-authored by Meier. This incident is not recounted in any of them.

Alliance. I didn't even know these kids. But I didn't see any
cause for concern even if that was where they were from?

When the bus pulled up, I got on like everyone else, all
ready to go, when Clarence Logan, one of those in charge,
asked me to get off, "So I can say something to you," he said.
So, as always obedient to the leaders, I got off, only to be
informed, "I'm really sorry, but Augie says you can't come
with us."

"Okay," I said, "but I have to go back for my books and
things." But instead, I sat back down and refused to move.
Then another of the leaders, a big, tall, muscular guy, I forget
his name, and a couple of others started leaning on me in a
very threatening fashion.

Bob said that at that point he felt they were being overtly
intimidating. Their message: "Get off or we're going to hit you,
hurt you." But he just continued to sit there, passively, for an
hour, until they called the police "to read him off." [An irony
for sure]

At that point I got up and said, "I will not dishonor the
civil rights movement by being the first civil rights activist to
be read off a freedom bus." And I left; several others left with
me, in protest. But I told them, "Go on back." I didn't want to
sabotage the movement because of their stupidity or
whatever it was.

Bob said that at first, while this was going on, Rev.
Bascom was supportive, but then he stopped talking. And
afterwards, when Kaufman went to Juanita and Lillie Jackson
(at the NAACP), he was surprised that their only response was,
"Well, Bob, you are a Socialist."

Like that's a reason. Like you are black is a reason. They
hadn't seemed to object when I ran a picket line for them in
'48.

Bob called his treatment then and on other occasions
"red-baiting"; destructive of the civil rights movement; just
playing into the hands of the FBI. "Red-baiting," in fact,
haunted the civil rights movement throughout the '60s, largely
because of the obsession of J. Edgar Hoover, then director of
the FBI, who believed the country was inundated with
communists seeking to overthrow the government. Ironically,
as a result, civil rights and civil liberties often butted heads

with one another.[177] There'd even been an implied accusation of communists-at-work during the Gwynn Oak's demonstrations when one of the owners, Jim Price, had said in a letter to the editor:

> I would like to believe that most whites who are helping the Negro are sincere in their efforts and not motivated by external influences designed to keep the internal affairs of the United States in an uproar.

Bob believed that the view of him as a "disruptive element" started back in the mid-1950s when the "red scare" was at its peak.

> I had gone to my first CORE meeting after my return from Goddard College in '54 or '55. It hadn't yet started and members were talking about some foreign policy incident that I'd just read about in the periodical, American Socialist. As I started passing out the few copies I had with me to anyone who wanted one, somebody who hadn't previously known me before claimed I was a dupe of the Communists and should be expelled. He based his accusation on the fact that the magazine also had an article by W.E.B. DuBois, by then labeled a Communist.

In September 1963, right after the church bombing in Birmingham, Alabama that had killed four little girls, Bob again felt a victim of the movement's fear of being labeled communist.

> Again, I was at a CORE meeting; perhaps 30 or 40 people were there. Everyone was very angry. Lloyd Taylor was walking up and down ranting and raving, "We need a revolution!" "We need a revolution!" The general consensus was that we needed to do something dramatic in response to the bombing. But the final decision was to form a puny little picket line someplace.
>
> At that, I got up and said, "If you're really so angry, why don't you have a real response? Go down to the Post Office and sit in in the damned post office. Climb up on the counters and stop them from doing business. The whole country would come to a standstill if they couldn't do business."
>
> I then sat down and the meeting continued as though I

---

[177] See quotes at beginning of book for Fred Weisgal's explanation of the difference between these two, found in his biography by Mill's *"...And Justice for All."* (p. 180)

hadn't even spoken.

A few days later someone in CORE got a court order banning me from participation with them. The order was based on the claim that my suggestion had frightened some people. I thought this really odd, given the anger they'd expressed, including Taylor's call for revolution.

On this occasion, Bob called the CORE attorney, Fred Weisgal, whom he knew personally, and told him he was going to the next meeting anyway, and if they tried to throw him out he'd respond non-violently and they'd have to carry him out. Fred's reaction: "They can't do that!"

Fred then called the CORE office and talked to two or three of the leaders (Walter Carter amongst them). Their reaction was non-committal, so Bob went ahead with his plans to attend the next meeting.

I raised my hand when I wanted to speak, just like everyone else. Jim Griffin, chairing the meeting, would simply give me a sort of grin, which meant I could talk. After I said my piece and sat down, I was ignored as usual.

•••

To return to 1962. In early February, despite the supposed investigation of possible subversion, CIG announced it was sending, for the first time, a bus load of demonstrators to Chestertown, site of Washington College. At noon other students from Yale, two New York colleges and Philadelphia would join them in testing the town's eating facilities.

The same day more demonstrations were planned at Easton where city officials had not yet followed through on a promise to appoint a bi-racial committee to deal with segregation issues. One owner said the mayor had attempted to organize such a committee but no businessmen could be found willing to serve. The Tidewater Inn in Easton was a curious exception to the resistance by other restaurants there. As long ago as 1956 the Sidney Hollander Foundation had awarded this restaurant an Honorable Mention for its "demonstration of hospitality extended without discrimination."[178]

---

[178] Moorland Spingarn, Box 50-3, folder 97.

By February 10th, forays, organized by CIG, had been made into Crisfield, Easton, Chestertown and Cambridge (site of a long struggle detailed in the following section) for eight consecutive weekends. An article in the *Sun* on Monday, February 12, 1962 had this to say:

> In Saturday's protest in the Kent county community [Chestertown], 150 persons, most of them students, picketed, marched through the streets, sang hymns and prayed without serious incident. Last, week, a crowd of local residents chased the demonstrators through the streets.
>
> In Easton, Saturday, one Negro [Leo Burroughs, Jr.] was arrested when he entered a bowling alley and refused to leave.

To encourage students to continue their efforts to end discrimination in all public accommodations, in and out of Baltimore, a "Freedom Month" was planned to begin with a showing of the film made of the first freedom ride from Washington through the Deep South to Jackson, Mississippi. Their bus had been set afire by local mobs. Later that week, James Farmer was scheduled to speak to an assembly at Morgan State College.[179]

Easton was again the target on the February 24, 1962 when students from thirteen colleges took part: Radcliffe, MIT, Boston University, Washington College, Beaver College, Swarthmore, Wellesley College, Simmons College, Yale, Wesleyan University, Connecticut College for Women and Andover Newton Theological Seminary. About 150 picketed restaurants and the movie theater; seven were arrested, including a juvenile from Easton.

Some of the students went to Denton, a town of about 1800 and the seat of Caroline county. Though two white youths there had barged into the group carrying a sign reading "Freedom Riders Go Home," the only violence encountered was when some of Denton's hecklers threw rocks and bottles as the group was marching back to the Bethel Church after being turned away at the theater. Groups of about twenty each went to Federalsburg and Ridgely, sitting in at a number of restaurants, but none stayed to be arrested. Yet another group of 100 or so, many of them locals,

---

[179] *Sun*, 2/12/1962.

peacefully picketed at a number of restaurants in Chestertown, which had been the site of racial violence for several weeks.

A final group of demonstrators went to nine restaurants on Route 40.[180]

> Police said that at least four carloads of integrationists, in automobiles bearing New York license tags, stopped at various restaurants but left quietly when the trespass was read to them.

Solomon Baylor, co-chairman of Baltimore CORE along with Walter Carter, said:

> Some twenty-three persons checked fifteen places along the highway. Eleven restaurants refused them service while the others, which had not previously served Negroes, did so last night.

•••

Toward Equality reported that in 1959 a Chinese Professor at Catholic University and his family were denied admission on July 4th to two beaches on the Chesapeake Bay. They are not named and there is not indication that they ever became the target for demonstrations, but Ocean City did.

Ocean City, with a permanent population of about 5,000 that included a very a small black community, depended heavily on summer tourism for its financial health. Perhaps frightened by what happened in Cambridge when negotiations broke down or were never undertaken in good faith (of which we'll hear more later), it integrated with minimal effort.

Years later, in 1968, Ada Jenkins, a founding member of CORE, in talking to a reporter, credited the intervention of a storm and the consequent need for federal money to recover, as at least a partial explanation for their "easy" success at Ocean City. Then a music teacher in the Baltimore schools, she had gone with Marshall Dinowitz, a CORE member, to "survey" Ocean City pursuant to Walter Carter's method of testing, followed by demonstrations. She said:

> We went to all those hotels, a young Jewish fellow and I. We were welcomed by the rocking chair group. You should

---

[180] Account and quotes from the *Sunday Sun*, February 25, 1962.

have seen the looks they gave us. But we found out a lot. There's always a key you can turn or a button you can push. Sometimes you have to push all the buttons to find the right one. After the Ocean City storm [in 1962], the government was providing money to rebuild. If they took a stand not to give money to those who wouldn't open their places to everyone—well, there was the key.[181]

Clarence Logan, then-head of CIG, in March 1962, had sent a telegram to Governor Tawes offering assistance to storm victims. Though he received an acknowledgement of his telegram, there is no indication there was any follow-up on the offer by either party.

Two months later, in May, John Quarles, CIG Negotiating Chairman, sent Mayor Hugh Cropper, Jr. a letter asking for an end to discrimination in Ocean City. The *Evening Sun* on May 8, 1962 quoted his letter in part:

> It has long been depressing to citizens of Maryland and liberal neighboring states that your city practices racial exclusion. At present, Negroes are permitted in Ocean City only in the capacity of laborers and servants. With knowledge of this social injustice, the Civic Interest Group appeals to the moral conscience of your City Council and the citizens to rectify this policy of racial discrimination. We're hopeful that this year's opening [usually on Memorial Day, May 30] will be on a nonsegregated basis.

The letter also reminded the Mayor that Salisbury had integrated over a year ago, and that other places along the Atlantic coast that had integrated had not suffered a loss of business. This was not the first letter Mayor Cropper had received. CORE also had written a number of times seeking a meeting, but had been put off, pleading they could not be held until the fall, after elections.

But persistence paid off and Mayor Cropper, a hotel owner himself, agreed to a meeting with civil rights leaders to discuss integration, and on May 16 met with a delegation that included Quarles and Caroline Goode from CIG, Walter Black, Executive Secretary of the Maryland NAACP Conference, Ruth Fegley, head of Baltimore Fellowship House, Rev. Frank Williams, from the Interdenominational Ministerial Alliance,

---

[181] James D. Dilts, *Sun*, "The Warning Trumpet", 12/1/1968

Walter Carter, Chairman of CORE, and Richard Thomas, from the Governor's Commission on Interracial Problems and Relations. The Mayor was not encouraging about the opening of facilities that season.

> I've been living here for 50 years and as far back as I can remember Ocean City has been segregated and you just can't come in here overnight and expect to change my way of living or anyone else's.
>
> I feel that everybody has a constitutional right. He pays taxes. He owns his properties. And I feel it is entirely up to the property owner who he takes in. It is definitely not up to the mayor and city council to try and force the issue on anybody.[182]

He warned the group that demonstrations while the city was trying to recover from the devastation of the March storm would be counterproductive. He did, however, following the meeting, form a twelve-man bi-racial commission to combat racial problems at the resort.

Perhaps in deference to the Mayor's concerns, the first "Freedom Tests" undertaken by Walter Carter, head of Baltimore CORE, after the opening of the tourist season at Ocean City, were intended to be low-key. He wished to determine whether or not blacks would be served at the city's restaurants as well as allowed use of the beach. The test days were not announced in advance so owners could not plan to serve the integrated group only on that day and then resume their segregated business-as-usual. Neither Walter nor the city were quite sure what to expect as the season opened. John Roemer recalled those early days:

> Walter was so concerned about violence on the shore that we went to Ocean City in two cars—one for whites, one for blacks—fearing that snipers might shoot at integrated cars. When we went in the ocean, a mob gathered on the boardwalk and roared at us. They were restrained from attacking only by the presence of a large contingent of state police officers.

As the summer progressed things must have improved. The *Washington Post* reported on August 6 that CORE had

---

[182] *Sun*, May 17, 1962.

been testing facilities for a month. It quoted Walter this way:

> Ocean City was open along the boardwalk. We went into the water. We used the beaches and we ate at several of the restaurants. I might say they were a cross section from the higher to the lower grades. ...All of this was done without incident. In fact, we weren't turned down anyplace. We stopped testing after we ran out of money.

A year later, on May 30, 1963, the *Evening Sun* reported that by the time the city opened for the season in 1963, its beaches, boardwalk, bath-houses and nearly all of its restaurants had integrated, as had a number of the leading hotels and motels. There was speculation that blacks who had previously used only beaches at the less desirable south end of the city, would now make use of more of the beach. John Roemer remembered one of their first visits after the beach was opened to blacks:

> A number of white CORE members were playing ball on the beach with a half-dozen young black men and women. Vacationers, merchants and police, who had never before seen black people on their white beach, seemed astonished and outraged as they watched.

The Mayor, who once had warned that it might take years to integrate his city, awarded Walter Carter a plaque, noting his "characteristic ability to inspire activism from allies and respect from those who opposed humane ideals." The award gives credence to Jim Griffin's (CORE's Chairman in the '70s) assessment of CORE's role in Ocean City. In June 1982, he told a large gathering of former civil rights activists:

> I was fortunate at the time to witness Walter P. Carter almost single-handedly eliminate the discrimination in Ocean City. When I was a child, I would always hear about Ocean City, and never have even the notion of thinking about going there for a weekend or week with my family. But Walter, through intensive negotiating, through letters, through personal appearances and press releases, was able to desegregate Ocean City.
> And he went, personally, after he had gone through a phase in negotiating where he felt that discrimination was lessening, to the point of taking his family—his two young children and his wife—down to the Shore, enrolling in a

hotel, and going onto the beaches and testing their facilities in and around the boardwalk, and, finally, to his surprise, and I'm sure he was surprised, he found the discrimination was lifted.

Now it was not as simple as I'm telling you. I'm trying to go through it and point out to you that it did not take—in some of these efforts—a number of people.[183]

•••

Having eased off in their initial plans for massive demonstrations in Ocean City during the summer of 1962, CORE turned to Westminster, the Carroll County seat. There had already been a long period of fruitless negotiations, a request to the Quakers to move the site of their annual meeting from Westminster, consultations with Westminster's Human Relations Committee, and testing. The latter included one incident when a restaurant owner's son had threatened CORE's vice chairman, John Roemer, with a knife, saying he was going to cut his throat. Roemer's memory of the incident is still vivid:

> "Go ahead," I said. "In fact, let's go outside of town somewhere, so you can get away with it. But you can't eliminate civil rights by eliminating one person. I'll be replaced."
> At that point a discussion of non-violence ensued, and the restaurant owner's son walked away, never threatening a demonstrator again.

On August 11, 1962, after Mayor Joseph Mathias refused to appoint a commission to solve the segregation problem, Walter Carter announced plans for a major demonstration in Westminster. He called Westminster "a town of contrasts." During spring training it played host to Baltimore's integrated football team, the Colts, and the rest of the year it "flagrantly abused the rights of Negroes."

John Roemer said this planned demonstration would mark "the opening of CORE's drive for freedom in Western Maryland." In addition to testing restaurants, it also would be testing a city ordinance that restricted the number of pickets, the size of signs and requirement they have a permit. CORE's

---

[183] *Evening Sun,* June 8, 1982.

application had been rejected on grounds it was "incomplete." At the end of the August 11 demonstration, participants planned to go door to door in the black neighborhood urging local blacks to register and vote.[184]

Eighteen persons, led by John Roemer and Lloyd Taylor, showed up on the 11th, and, in groups of six, tested sixteen restaurants, being served in five; no one was arrested either for trespassing or for picketing. After one group left, the waitress said, "I was so nervous I could hardly breathe."

The "integrationists" were greatly outnumbered by police, some with Canine Corps dogs, assigned to keep an eye on them, and by as many as 150 local residents who crowded the streets to watch—one of whom complained, "Our Negroes aren't like that;" another, "There are two streets here where Negroes live and they are happy the way they are." To the integrationists it felt like they were being stared at by "a thousand hostile spectators" as they walked down Main Street, especially with presence amongst them of counter-picketers.

Wearing red, white and blue armbands, members of a new youth group, "The Fighting American Nationalists," were present, led by Robert Luthardt from Glen Burnie, who said they had a permit. This group paraded in front of restaurants while CORE members were inside, passing out pamphlets stating their aim: "the application of radical tactics and aggressive battling for the conservative and traditional ideals of our American constitutional republic and our white race." They carried signs that read: "Red Agitators would destroy our Christian racial structure," "Destroy the savage Negro rapist," "Reds push intermarriage," and "Down with NAACP and CORE." The two "C's in the latter were painted to resemble the communist hammer and sickle.[185] The group did uphold the blacks' right to vote but advocated their return to Africa. (Luthardt was heard from again and again at demonstrations.)

---

[184] The account and quotes of these events are based on clippings from John Roemer's personal files that begin in August 1962 and extend to August 1964. Most are either not dated or hand-dated; and most do not state the name of the paper. Identified are at least one each from the *Sun*, the *Evening Sun*, the *Gazette & Daily* of York, Pennsylvania and the *Baltimore Afro-American*.

[185] *Catholic Review*, 8/19/62.

While this demonstration was taking place, fifteen to twenty blacks were picketing the Airpax Electronics Company, the Eastern Shore Public Service Company, the Chesapeake and Potomac Telephone Company, and the Colonial Market in Cambridge.

It was late fall before demonstrations were resumed in Westminster. In the meantime, CORE wrote letters to Don Kellett, the Baltimore Colt Football team's Executive Vice President, and to Carroll Rosenbloom, its owner, asking that they sit down and talk with them about the racism encountered by their black players while training in Westminster. The letter reminded them that their presence allowed the racists to say if their practices were good enough for the famous Colts, it should be "good enough for the little colored person."

A later letter suggested the Colts might even be losing out in recruiting the most talented players. After this letter, Kellett said he'd talked to town officials during the summer but had seen no action on their part; he agreed to try again. The Colts had been training at the Western Maryland College campus since the National Football League franchise returned to Baltimore in 1953. CORE continued by letter and in meetings to urge Kellett and Rosenbloom to relocate the Colts unless Westminster integrated.

•••

It had not been too many years that Baltimore had had a professional team, and fewer still that blacks had been on the team. There had been none as recently as the fall of 1947, and few could be found amongst any of the teams. When Fred Weisgal, the passionate civil liberties attorney, attended a game in October 1947, he may have been, like others present, seeing blacks on the field for the first time. In any case, he was so upset by their reception that he fired off an angry letter to the editor of the *Evening Sun*, printed on October 21st. Fred wrote:

> I was quite disgusted with the unsportsmanlike attitude of some of the Baltimore fans toward the Negro ball players at last Sunday's game between the Colts and the Los Angeles Dons. Every time a Negro player would run with the ball, these spectators would start to shout, "Kill that damn Nigger—murder that jig—bash in his black skull." These

people are there to watch a football game and are not there to display their ignorant racial prejudice. Remarks of this type not only discredit the Colts, but the entire city of Baltimore.

Until the advent of television, professional football was not an especially popular sport—both baseball and college football had much greater followings. It was in 1947 that the Seahawks' franchise was reborn as the Baltimore Colts.[186] It was the second season for the Los Angeles Dons—and it was almost certainly their team, rather than Baltimore's, which had the black players.

None of the few blacks that were on football teams up until 1947 had come from historically black colleges—but that year the Dons had added Ezzret Anderson, an end from Kentucky State, and John Brown, a center from North Carolina College (the same year Elmore Harris of Morgan State, Baltimore, joined the Brooklyn Dodgers in the National Football League). It was no doubt Anderson and Brown, playing for the Dons, who had provoked the racist remarks that so angered Fred.

Baltimore was still a very segregated city at that time, and clearly not ready for blacks to be part of its sports,[187] so Fred must have been especially pleased when, four days after his letter appeared, another appeared that praised his stand against racial prejudice and then went on to say:

---

[186] In the 1946 debut year of the All-American Football Conference's (AAFC's), the Miami Seahawks had had a disastrous season, both financially and professionally. Historical information about the Colts and Dons is from Peterson, *Pigskin*.... Apparently there really was an NFL's Dodgers' and an AFL's Yankees' team. *Pigskin* gives no indication that there was any connection between these and the better-known baseball teams. Nonetheless, it makes one wonder.

[187] But it did change over time. Historian Bob Carroll reports in Peterson, *Pigskin*....that when Claude (Buddy) Young was with the New York Yankees of the older American Football League and first played in Baltimore, "racists came to the stadium in blackface. Yet, when he played for Baltimore in 1953, fans voted him the most popular Colt." By then part of the N F L, the Colts added Lenny Moore, black running back and split end in 1956, and Jim Parker, guard and linebacker in 1957. Along with the growth of television, professional football was becoming a popular national sport and black players had become acceptable.

Having witnessed the game, I wish to state I have never been so utterly disgusted with the human (?) race as I was that day. If we, the criticizers of communism, fascism and all hate groups, cannot show racial tolerance at a sporting event, then I see little hope for future world peace. (signed, Syl Sherman)

•••

Almost a year after their last demonstration, on December 8, 1962 CORE again sponsored a demonstration at Westminster. Over seventy-five demonstrators from Westminster, Annapolis, Prince George County, New York and New Jersey tested all the city's restaurants, and the Carroll movie theater. John Roemer who led this group stated later that only those restaurants previously desegregated had served them, and the manager of the theater had refused to sell them tickets, but had "let 75 demonstrators in free to watch the end of the feature."[188] No one was arrested and John regarded the demonstration a success, but when he soon-after wrote "An Anatomy of Westminster" for Baltimore CORE's newsletter, the Liberator, he lamented that no local people had participated.

John assessed they were "paralyzed by fear of economic reprisals", since after their participation in a small CORE-sponsored local demonstration the year before, their jobs had been threatened. He also contrasted the attitude of students from Western Maryland, none of whom showed up, with those from more northern states who'd traveled a considerable distance to participate: he called them either "bigots" or apathetic "moderates" who wanted to "go slowly" and disapproved of CORE "radicalism."

Trying to assess what CORE should do, he concluded that leaving it to the local Human Relations Committee would get them nowhere, yet felt that CORE had neither the people nor the funds needed to hold "more and bigger demonstrations." Finally, John concluded that CORE had to "continue the difficult task of putting some backbone into the young and relatively independent local Negroes and the enlightened few at Western Maryland College. We have gotten promises and pious praises from some of these people, but

---

[188] Clipping hand-dated 12/9/62 but name of paper not noted; probably the *Sun*.

hopes and good wishes are not enough."

In March 1963 the General Assembly finally passed a weak public accommodations bill but counties could exempt themselves and Carroll County was one of twelve which had done so.[189] They had successfully argued that the legislature could not usurp their individual rights, including the right to discriminate. Not all in Carroll County were pleased by their exemption, believing this would simply make them the prime target for further demonstrations.

Eugene Nuss, Chairman of Westminster's Human Relations Committee, wrote a letter to the editor (paper not named) on March 20th decrying the committee's minimal success after fifteen month of trying to achieve "an integrated society in our county." He ended by saying: "It is discouraging to observe that in a county of over 100 churches the concept of the brotherhood of man remains a controversy."

On April 6, 1963, CORE resumed demonstrations in Westminster. John Roemer, then Vice-Chair, said they expected to adopt passive resistance "to capture the spirit of the original sit-in demonstrations. We expect to be treated as free American citizens or we will refuse to leave segregated places of public accommodation."[190] CORE recruited as many as 200 people, many from New York and Washington, to sit in at a number of sites in Carroll County that day in April. Four, including CORE chairman, Walter Carter, and publicity chair, Lloyd Taylor, were arrested at the American Restaurant in Westminster; all were released on their own recognizance to await trial.

John Roemer and Walter Carter in their next meeting with Rosenbloom and Kellett assured them that the next demonstrations would not be in Westminster but at the Memorial Stadium in Baltimore at all their football games if they did not move from Westminster. This threat no doubt provoked the closed door meeting with the Colts in April, attended by representatives from CORE, the NAACP, Urban League, Civil Liberties Union, Fellowship House, the Postal

---

[189] Baltimore City and Montgomery County had passed anti-discrimination laws in 1962; the General Assembly a weaker version in early 1963.

[190] The *Evening Sun*, April 6, 1963

Alliance, the Interdenominational Ministerial Alliance, Civic Interest Group, and the Human Relations Commission of Carroll County. It was there that the Colts owner, Carroll Rosenbloom, agreed to move the team to a new site unless all racial restrictions were removed from the area by 1964. The announcement, which had been written for them by Walter Carter and John Roemer, was made public "between the shrimp salad and the rock-and-roll trio and the champagne...at [the] annual Colt press-radio-TV backslapping party at a local hotel."

The Chamber of Commerce quickly responded that they would talk to the restaurant and movie house owners and "get this straightened out." When John Roemer attempted to eat at one of the restaurants next day, he faced a big sign on the door that read: "We'll serve niggers but not John Roemer." Because John was living in Westminster at this time, teaching in their schools, he was particularly loathed.

In June, the Chamber of Commerce asked the mayor to appoint a "board or commission to work with and among our businessmen for the purpose of accomplishing integration...in a harmonious, peaceful and orderly manner. [The same request CORE had made over a year earlier.] In July the Mayor announced that all but a tavern and part-time restaurant had agreed to voluntarily integrate. Ed Chance, by then Chairman of Baltimore CORE, said demonstrations once planned for Westminster would be held in other areas of the county if they failed to follow Westminster's lead and move toward desegregation.

Sometime during his sojourns in Carroll county, sugar had been poured into the gasoline tank of Walter Carter's car, costing him $160 to repair, no small amount in those days, especially on Walter's income, and with a family to support. In general, he was finding it hard to continue the pace he'd been keeping the last three years as either Chairman or Co-Chairman of CORE, and so when his latest term ended in June 1963, he turned the reigns over to Edward Chance, pleading a financial drain that had left him deeply in debt. He added that CORE, too, was in its worst shape yet financially; he'd had to take out a loan to keep things going, and his car was collapsing with its continuous use, driving all over the state. Walter praised the successes they'd achieved through nonviolent demonstrations—but also noted they were expensive, something too few appreciated.

•••

One final report of Westminster's resistance to integration can be found in the report of a hearing in August 1964. George Bucher John, owner of Lee's Motel in Westminster, admitted that in April he had refused to admit a black couple on their honeymoon after they'd made the reservation by phone. He declared, however, he was not breaking the law because Carroll County was not covered by the 1963 law and the 1964 law did not come into effect until two day after this event. The State Interracial Commission ruled that a violation had occurred and that a cease and desist order against future violations would be issued in the case.

•••

That same month, on August 24, 1964, with a trial in the last Westminster, Maryland trespass case still pending, Walter Carter wrote CORE's attorney, Fred Weisgal, asking about this and giving him a sort of update on those involved. He wrote:

> We are sending along this little picture [copy not available]...as a reminder that we have not been informed about the charges of trespassing resulting during this "read out" from the American restaurant in Westminster. I think you have a brief with the correct spelling of the names. Barry Lubinsky is supposed to be in California, Joel Freedman and Walter South are in New York City. Lloyd Taylor and myself, of course, are here on the Maryland scene.
>
> Virtually all the restaurants in Carroll county, especially those in Westminster, including the American, have since desegregated. You will recall that Carroll was supposed to go on a special county referendum in November, but I understand that a ruling given to the State Commission on Interracial Problems and Relations declared that the referendum...was not legal, and would not be on the November ballot. Mr. Parren Mitchell of the State Commission ...is the man who could give some details.
>
> As far as I know, Fred, the five persons arrested during this April 1963 sit-in, are the only demonstrators arrested in Carroll county, and perhaps are the only pending civil rights

cases in that area. After the first city (and I think state) public accommodations act became law, charges against many demonstrators were thrown out, I think by the proper authority in Annapolis. I'm raising these rough points for your specialized consideration in determining as soon as possible.

Fred didn't immediately have an answer to the points Walter raised. In July, Maryland's attorney general, Thomas Finan, had ordered the police throughout the State and the Maryland National Guard to stop making arrests for trespassing "even if it appears that the place involved falls outside the law, such as taverns (which had been excluded in the state act)." He was responding to the newly passed public accommodations section of the federal Civil Rights Act.[191] Congress had depended on the 14th Amendment and the Commerce Clause of the U.S. Constitution, to justify its enactment of the Act.

> The court held that the power of Congress over interstate commerce extended to those activities intrastate which so affected interstate commerce [and] the power of Congress to promote interstate commerce also includes the power to regulate the local incidents thereof...which might have a substantial and harmful effect upon that commerce.
>
> [In a case testing this reasoning the court claimed] Congress was within its power to prohibit racial discrimination by motels serving travelers, however local their operations appeared.[192]

Fred had a better answer for Walter regarding the effect this new Civil Rights Act would have on pending trespass cases after December 14th. That day the Supreme Court upheld the public accommodation section of the 1964 Civil Rights Act,[193] and ruled that Congress intended its provisions to be retroactive. Accordingly, it ordered that all charges made against demonstrators before the act was passed had to be dismissed.[194] Fred declared that their decision had "given substance to the Fourteenth Amendment. I would hope the

---

[191] *Sun* article by Nordlinger, hand-dated July 64.

[192] *Heart of Atlanta Motel, Inc. v. U.S.* et al, 379 U.S. 241; 1964 U.S. LEXIS 2187

[193] footnote, *Heart of Atlanta Motel*, 1964 U.S. LEXIS 2187

[194] *Hamm v. City of Rock Hill*, 379 U.S. 306; 1964 U.S. LEXIS 4

Attorney General would also drop the disorderly conduct and assault charges that arose solely out of racial demonstrations. That would clear the air and we could get on with everything else we have to do."

In fact, Robert Murphy, speaking for the State Law Department, declared that "most, if not all, of the about 160 cases not final will be cleared from the dockets." (Juanita Mitchell, from the NAACP, estimated the number of cases pending at about 300.) It did not please Fred when Murphy went on to say, "Convictions other than trespass, such as disorderly conduct during a street demonstration, would not be vitiated." And he also put in question his willingness to vitiate convictions arising from trespass on property not covered in the federal civil rights law, which banned discrimination "at hotels serving more than five people, restaurants, gas stations, movie theaters, arenas or other places of exhibition or entertainment." It is believed that eventually all these cases were in fact dropped.

Cambridge Explodes

For some time students had been making forays into Cambridge along with those into other Eastern Shore towns, but the fight in Cambridge is recounted separately to give continuity to its especially intense, prolonged and eventually grassroots struggle, led by Gloria Richardson, who could trace her family history in the town back to the days of slavery. It should be remembered, however, that often the previously reported events in Baltimore, especially at Gwynn Oak Amusement Park and those at the Northwood theater, were being reported in parallel columns in Baltimore's newspapers.

Cambridge, the county seat of Dorchester County, was in 1960 a very conservative, very racist Eastern Shore farming and fishing town, located on the banks of the Choptank River. With a population of 12,239, 35% black (the same percentage as in Baltimore), it was also a canning center for sea food and vegetables. Race Street was the hub of the city's downtown shopping district, and the dividing line between its segregated black and white wards.

As early as 1912, the town's blacks had elected Herbert Maynadier St. Clair, Sr., a member of one of Maryland's free black families, to the City Council, and kept him there until 1946. It was his son, Gloria Richardson's uncle, Herbert St. Clair, Jr. and *his* son, her cousin, Frederick St. Clair, who encouraged the freedom riders and provided much of the bail money for those who were arrested. That's how the St. Clairs met the two SNCC (Student Nonviolent Coordinating Committee) field representatives, William "Bill" Hansen and Reginald Robinson, and how these two came to be staying in Herbert St. Clair's home during the first few weeks of the Cambridge demonstrations.

The first exploration of Cambridge's public accommodations was made in December 1961 by Clarence Logan (black), then-head of Morgan's Civic Interest Group (CIG), along with Bill Hansen (white) and Reginald Robinson (black) from SNCC—a prelude to the first demonstration at the Choptank Inn a month later, on January 13, 1962. Picketers encountered extensive heckling and threats of violence from white bystanders and twenty were arrested—fifteen charged with trespassing, two of those also with resisting arrest; five were charged with disorderly conduct. Magistrate Baird refused their lawyers' (Archibald Williams and Juanita Jackson Mitchell) requests for dismissal. They had argued what became a common, usually unsuccessful, claim that the arrests were illegal under the Constitution's 14th Amendment. The students posted bonds of $100 each and were released awaiting trial.[195]

As CIG and SNCC were planning a second freedom ride for the next Saturday, January 20, 1962, black teen-agers from Cambridge's Mace's Lane High School were picketing the town's restaurants and drug stores. The local newspaper reported these unprecedented events as "the No. 1 topic of conversation and the people, including the moderates, are resentful." The Dorchester County Ministerial Association, which included ten whites and four blacks, requested that the planned Freedom Ride be cancelled—unlike other places, few of Cambridge's ministers were ever supportive of the movement there. They sent Clarence Logan a telegram asking for "calmness and Christian tolerance of the viewpoints of others." In a biting reply, CIG stated:

> Although some of the clergy of Cambridge have voiced vehement opposition to Saturday's Freedom Ride, they have not voiced similar public opposition to the un-Christian and immoral practice of continued racial discrimination. The ride will be held as planned.[196]

Urging Cambridge's citizens to remain calm, the State Police made their own plans for the expected 100 to 300 demonstrators, setting up headquarters in the Cambridge National Guard Armory and arranging for mass feeding of the troopers. As a consequence, there were approximately 250 troopers present and things remained peaceful at most of the

---

[195] The 14th Amendment forbids a state from denying any citizen equal protection of the laws. The attorneys argued that "private" discrimination became state action (and hence a constitutional issue) when the state was used to enforce private discrimination. For account see the *Sun*, 1/16/1962.

[196] *Baltimore News Post*, 1/19/1962

demonstration sites. However, at the Choptank Inn on Route 50, just outside Cambridge, demonstrators encountered bottle-throwing, fist-swinging whites who caused a near riot.

Bill Hansen, the white field secretary with SNCC, had to be rescued by helmeted State Police and taken to the hospital as a result of the pummeling he received at the hands of several customers while others temporarily blocked the door to prevent the police immediately from entering. *He* was the only one arrested, charged with trespassing; none of the men who had shoved him to the floor, kicked and stomped him, and struck him with beer bottles.

The burly owner claimed he hadn't needed to read him his rights because he'd told him the week before not to return; it was also claimed that the "reading" was a police practice, not a legal requirement. After Hansen's release on bail, he was cheered by a gathering at the Bethel AME Church in Cambridge. A third Freedom Ride to Cambridge was planned for the next Saturday (January 27, 1962).[197]

Told of the Hansen-incident at a nearby meeting of the NAACP, The Rt. Rev. Stephen Gill Spotswood, area Bishop of the AME Zion Church, praised the Freedom Riders and reminded a gathering of about two hundred at the St. James AME Church that "Negroes were already sitting-in fifty years ago for the right to ride Pullman cars. They also sat-in thirty years ago at dime-store lunch counters, although I don't know why—the food is so bad."[198]

Businessmen and the Dorchester County superintendent of schools claimed that as a result of the demonstrations they were canceling previous plans to integrate, and the Volunteer Fire Department decided that in retaliation they would no longer provide ambulance service to black residents. Leo Burroughs, speaking for CIG, declared that such regressive steps would only lead to more demonstrations by "those trying to bring about an end to racial inequality." He continued:

---

[197] A composite from several clippings; the only named paper, the *Sun*, 1/21/1962. A parallel column in the *Sun* tells of the Maryland Interracial Commission plan to introduce in the February session of the legislature a public accommodations bill reject by Governor Tawes. He claimed to have a better one to submit.
[198] Quoted in hand-dated clipping, 1/22/62, from unnamed paper.

Comments by civic leaders that there's a fine relationship
between the races in Cambridge is simply a 'waste of words.'
Nothing has ever gone along fine for Negroes, especially in
areas like Cambridge. The relationship is only fine as long as
the Negro is subservient.

[I'm] aware of the facts that Cambridge has had a Negro
council member for the past 40 years and that Negroes also
are members of the board of education, the hospital and
library boards and also that a Negro physician is a full staff
member of the Cambridge Maryland Hospital. But that's only
token integration. Civil rights are ignored. Those few board
memberships remind me of the master-slave relationship with
the master throwing a few crumbs to the slave.[199]

•••

In these early demonstrations, Gloria Richardson, who
would soon become a leader of Cambridge's struggle for civil
rights, was uninvolved, then working full-time managing a
drugstore. She was a graduate of Howard University with a
major in social psychology; a divorcee raising two girls, ten
and seventeen. However, the older daughter, Donna, was
involved right from the beginning; a leader in getting local
young people to participate. When the adult demonstrators of
the town gave in to repeated pressure to stop demonstrating
and give arbitration a chance, the young people, like Donna,
were upset; increasingly so as the weeks dragged on without
any results.

It was at this point in 1962 (perhaps February or March)
that the Cambridge protesters established a formal relationship
with SNCC and formed the Cambridge Non-Violent Action
Committee (CNAC) — Frederick St. Clair and Mrs. Enez Grubb
were designated co-chairs, but soon after Frederick resigned,
feeling it a conflict of interest to hold the position while also
providing bail for the demonstrators who were arrested
(perhaps viewing the committee's head as needing to be
accepted by the city as a "neutral negotiator").

Only then did Gloria, a tall, slim, light-skinned black,
with deep dark eyes, allow herself to be persuaded by the town

---

[199] *Baltimore News-Post*, 1/23/1962

to take Frederick's place—persuaded, she thought, both because the town's blacks trusted her and because they knew her family was sufficiently well off to support her and not subject to threats of job loss by whites as were so many activists. Described as "slight and graceful," yet with a "permanent scowl, and stiff jaw," she "conveyed the utter seriousness and intellect she brought to the leadership of the Cambridge struggle." It was a fortunate choice because she proved to be a talented organizer who quickly earned the title, "Glorious Gloria."[200]

For about a year, Gloria shared the chairmanship with Grubb; until such time as Grubb got ill and resigned, and Gloria assumed the chairmanship. By then Cambridge's home-grown movement had proved unique in its ability to include Cambridge's poor, and had quickly taken over from what had been started under the leadership of "outsiders."[201]

When Gloria later was asked about help from other civil rights groups during those formative years of the CNAC, she talked at length about their early-on decision to invite Dr. Martin Luther King to Cambridge, knowing his presence would bring them more press coverage and highlight their visibility.

Initially, they were quite angry when King informed them he was too busy presently, but if they still wanted him in a few years, his fee was $3,000,[202] a ridiculous amount to ask of a small, poor community just to come for one day. When they learned through the press, a year later, that King intended to come "look them over" Gloria told the press

to go back and tell him that I said when he hit the Emerson

---

[200] Description in Szabo, pp. 348-349

[201] This account comes from Szabo, "An Interview with Gloria Richardson Dandridge," from *Notable Black American Women* (Jesse C. Smith, Ed.), and from newspaper clippings in Fred Weisgal's files (paper often unnamed, mostly from the *Sun* and *Evening Sun*, but including *New York Times*, 10/4/63, *Washington Post*, 5/14/64), and subsequent articles in the *Evening Sun*, 2/25/84, 1/10/87, *Afro-*, 3/2/82, and the *Sun* 1/11/87. Also a number of clippings were received from Clarence Logan; some of these duplicates.

[202] Gloria didn't say if the message was delivered by letter, or by one of King's lieutenants.

Harrington Bridge [now the Frederick C. Malkus Sr. Bridge, which carries Route 50 over the Choptank River near Cambridge], we would be there to turn him back. So he [King] announced he had the flu and he did not come.

By then the blacks in Cambridge realized that King's early-spurning of their "cry for help" had done them a favor. He'd forced them to proceed without benefit of his charisma, SNCC members had joined them in going to jail, CORE and CIG had been there, and their own local leadership had developed and become emboldened.[203]

For the most part, CNAC depended on local people for the little money they needed—they held dances in the Elks hall, the women had suppers, and some kept people in their homes. Until they became more militant, they got some contributions from the Meat Packers and International Ladies Garment Workers unions.

Gloria also talked about the role of the NAACP. She said that originally they had supported them, had even given her mother, Mable Hayes, and her daughter, Donna, an award. But in the fall of 1961 or 1962, on the very morning when a number of black kids were to enter the white high schools, the NAACP informed the locals that national had told them not to file a suit in the federal court as they'd agreed to do. After that, Gloria told an interviewer, they had gone to Baltimore and convinced Baltimore ACLU's lawyer, Fred Weisgal, to represent them, hence severing their dependence on NAACP lawyers.[204]

NAACP lawyers did still on occasion participate in cases, and certainly the NAACP provided bail money, but it was Fred who most often represented them in court, met regularly with CNAC members, consulted with them in preparing their defenses, and offered his advice as they planned future actions. No local attorney ever dared become so involved.

•••

Soon after Gloria assumed the chairmanship of CNAC, she sought to involve the black community in a voter registration and education campaign. She wanted to show

---

[203] Szabo, p. 352, for information and quote.
[204] See Szabo, p. 353.

them that even though they might elect blacks to the city council it would not give them equality. She called her grandfather, "a gradualist," and pointed out that during his long tenure as a city councilman all he could do for blacks were things like getting parking tickets voided, getting some streets paved, and seeing that those employed in the packing company got food in winter when they weren't working. She emphasized that even though there was one black student in an otherwise white school, it didn't mean the schools were desegregated.

During the months that Cambridge was without demonstrations, Gloria also prepared a survey that high school students took door to door to determine what the people considered their real needs—e.g., health, jobs, housing, schools and public accommodations. The final analysis of data, done by Swarthmore College students and their professors, indicated that the issues were so intertwined that they needed to be tackled all at once, as a whole.[205]

Consequently, CNAC felt it impossible to prioritize the needs and thus put together a list of demands for immediate changes that would end the entire system of segregation in Cambridge: an end to the segregation polices in the police department, hospitals, schools, housing, employment, and working conditions. They presented their demands to Mayor Calvin Mowbray and the City Council for their consideration in the Spring 1963 session.[206]

Simultaneously, CNAC began to organize demonstrators who would be able quickly to respond if their demands went unheeded. And of course they were not met, and so demonstrations resumed in Cambridge on March 30, 1963, a hot, 80° Saturday. Now under Gloria's leadership, but still aided by Morgan's CIG students, fewer demonstrators than anticipated appeared for this first demonstration. White

---

[205] See Szabo, p. 350. The connection to Swarthmore was made through Stanley Branch, head of the Chester, Pennsylvania chapter of the NAACP, who was often in Cambridge supporting CNAC.

[206] Their demands were later prioritized through a house-to-house survey done with the help of Swarthmore students, the connection made through the head of NAACP in Chester, Pennsylvania.

hecklers outnumbered them. Police only appeared later, in time to arrest two black youths trying to enter the Dorset theater with tickets purchased earlier by whites.

They also arrested fifteen others, including Gloria, at a roller rink--swimming pool facility. Speaking for this group, Gloria insisted the site was not private property since it had been purchased by the city and donated to the Volunteer Fire Department which operated it. All but Gloria stayed in jail to await a hearing. She posted the $100 bail and left in time to attend an evening rally at Mount Sinai Church, "a shabby concrete-block building surrounded by trash and building materials with a rough concrete floor and lighted by five bare bulbs."[207]

On Saturday, April 6, 1963, to protest the seventeen earlier arrests, the number of demonstrators had markedly increased. They had come from Philadelphia, Maryland State College in Princess Anne county, and the CIG to join those from Cambridge in picketing at "nine Cambridge business places and offices, including the office of State Senator Frederick Malkus (D., Dorchester)," an outspoken opponent of the public accommodations bill.

They marched "six abreast and fifty strong" to the county jail, frustrating the police who unsuccessfully attempted to hold them back. This time thirty-seven, including Inez Grubb, were arrested, charged with disorderly conduct and assault on policemen.[On the same day, already noted, that Walter Carter and four others were arrested in Westminster, northwest of Baltimore.] In Cambridge, Mayor Calvin Mowbray had called on the State Police for help in taking the singing and chanting group to jail. During the booking twenty troopers continued to patrol the now-crowded jail (three 14 and 15 year olds were released to the custody of their parents) and the area was closed to traffic. After the booking, fifteen women and ten men were bused to the Talbot county jail in Easton. By then, those remaining in the Cambridge jail had been joined by an additional five who had been arrested that evening. This brought the total number arrested that day to fifty nine.

That evening, prior to the final arrests, about ninety

---

[207] Sunday *Sun*, March 31, 1963.

demonstrators had gathered at the small park near the jail for a prayer meeting. Father Joseph Stephen Burns, an ethics teacher at La Salle College in Philadelphia, who was one of those later arrested, spoke to the group. He told them:

> The only way this can work is if we believe in our own hearts that these people of Cambridge are good people who can be made to see that segregation is evil. What we did today is not allowed in many places. We're far better off than the people of Mississippi.[208]

The final five had been arrested when the leader of about forty marchers, along with a few others, refused a police order to keep single file as they returned to the Mount Sinai Baptist Church. The next day, all those arrested were released on bonds of $100 each.[209]

On April 9, the *Afro* reported that this demonstration had "served to clarify and to deepen the issues between those who want change and those who do not." It stated:

> Sharp battle lines are being drawn not only between integrationists and segregationists, but also within the colored community.
>
> Despite meetings and promises, Mrs. Gloria Richardson, co-chairman of the Cambridge Non-violent Action Committee, reports that segregation is still the rule in education, housing, employment and public accommodation. CNAC had ordered a total economic boycott of downtown stores.

Gloria also criticized the ministers who said they wanted change but refused to support CNAC. She added "wistfully": "If we had the white leadership, we could go the path of Salisbury." Only thirty miles from Cambridge, Salisbury had peacefully integrated without the need for demonstrations.

•••

---

[208] The quote and this account from the *Sun*, April 7, 1963
[209] $100 may seem minimal, but if the arrest figures are correct, excluding the three minors who had been released to their parents, that means that the 56 arrested would collectively have had to pay $5,600, a rather staggering amount. Who paid is not stated, but we know the St. Clair's often helped with bail, funds for such purposes were regularly raised by the CNAC, and some of the demonstrators may have been able to pay their own bail.

It was a month later, on May 7, 1963, that the first of many Cambridge trials started before Judge W. Laird Henry, Jr. at the Dorchester County Circuit Court. The fifty-four charged with disorderly conduct were represented by their new attorney, Fred Weisgal, who had just finished successfully arguing a death-penalty case before the Supreme Court (resulting in a new trial). Two other attorneys, Tucker Dearing of the Baltimore NAACP, and Louis Redding of Wilmington, Delaware, were there to represent those who had charges of inciting a riot and assaulting or hindering a police officer, added after their arrest, but these were not pursued.

Judge Henry earlier had agreed to try them in two groups. Gloria was among the first fifteen. (She also had been charged with attempting to incite a riot, the charge that was later dropped.) All of those in this first group testified that when they'd tried to enter the skating rink and dance hall, known as the Firemen's Arena, and were told it was private property, they'd backed off and begun to picket in an orderly manner. But witnesses testified that when they arrived the defendants were "jammed across the steps." Firemen and police testified that the pickets had been trying to push their way inside. In contradiction, a *Sun* reporter, in response to a question by Weisgal, said he'd observed no disorderly conduct.

Whatever actually happened, the judge, in a trial that lasted four hours, found them all guilty, but added that he regarded the incident as "a great deal of to do about nothing. It could have resulted in a riot, but it didn't." He also said he was astounded at the distance from which some of the demonstrators (black and white) had come. He lectured the students telling them they were duped, being led: "Your time would be more profitably spent in your books than in traveling around to strange communities and making nuisances of yourselves." He then denied Weisgal's motion to set aside the verdict and give the defendants probation before verdict.

That afternoon, the trials of the other group must have gone more swiftly because one of the news clippings from Weisgal's files stated that fifty-four in all were found guilty of disorderly conduct and fined one penny for each conviction— the trials consequently becoming known as the "Penny Trials."

In the course of these trials, the judge, obviously annoyed, had accused Gloria of being behind an article that appeared in the *Sun* April 22, "A Stalemate in Race Relations." Though Gloria denied it, the judge asked, perhaps rhetorically, "Is it fair to criticize race relations here when Cambridge is trying so hard to do what is good *for you and your people?*" [Writer's emphasis]

It would not be until 1966 that a test case would be heard that affirmed Gloria's contention, after her first arrest at the roller rink--swimming pool facility, that this facility, operated by the Volunteer Fire Department, was not a private club. By then, the federal Civil Rights Act of 1964 had passed and the U.S. District Court of Maryland granted an injunction that prevented the Fire Department from continuing to segregate the recreation facilities it operated.[210]

•••

Meanwhile, only a week after the above two-part trial, on May 14, 1963, Gloria, along with her mother and one of her daughters, was arrested at the Dizzyland Restaurant for trespassing, precipitating demonstrations that evening that resulted in the arrest of sixty-two persons. The state police and K-9 dogs were called on to assist local police.

After that, Judge Henry appointed a committee that agreed that five of CNAC's demands should be met:

(1) Complete desegregation of public places;
(2) Desegregation of the first four grades of Dorchester County's public schools by September; Negroes assigned to the school nearest their home without regard to race;
(3) Equal opportunities established in industries and stores, beginning with a ten percent hiring goal;
(4) Public housing to be built for Negroes (at a later meeting with Robert Weaver, federal housing administrator, they were assured their application would be "expeditiously processed"); sewer and sidewalk needs studied; and
(5) Police brutality ended; a Negro deputy sheriff appointed. They insisted that CNAC was ignoring the amount of integration that already existed in Cambridge, noting that 40% of the city's employees were Negro; not noting that most of their jobs were menial.

Little progress had been made in negotiations between

---

[210] *Williams v. Rescue Fire Company, Inc.* 254 F. Supp. 556 (1966)

the white leaders and integrationists on implementation of the agreed-upon demands of CIG when, on May 15, twelve juveniles were arrested while picketing the office of the Board of Education. With tensions rising once more, on May 31, Gloria wrote U. S. Attorney General Robert F. Kennedy asking him to investigate the violation of constitutional rights in Cambridge.

Gloria still had had no reply from Kennedy, when things exploded on June 10, following the sentencing by Circuit Judge E. McMaster Duer of Dinez White, 15, and a 15-year old boy (two of the juveniles who'd been arrested on April 6) to indeterminate terms in the training school. Feeling they had been "double crossed", one hundred blacks demonstrated that night. There were shootings [apparently by blacks as well as whites], brick-throwing and fires started with Molotov cocktails; one at the black owned Camper Sisters bakery, started by a gasoline-soaked mop whites stuck in the edge of its window. Twenty persons were arrested. This led, on June 11, to more rioting and clashes between whites and Negroes, two white men were injured by shotgun blasts.

Gloria again wrote Kennedy, asking him "to provide protection for all, especially the Negro community." She called the State troopers and local police that had been called in the quell the violence, "intolerable and prejudiced,...no longer neutral arms of the law." Later that evening at a meeting of 350 people who packed the Bethel AME church, Gloria urged the group to control their emotions:

> Retaliation is no good. This is not for one or two nights. I ask you not to attempt retaliation for any of the things that come from the white community or will come from the white community.

Reginald Robinson, formerly from Baltimore but at that time a field secretary with SNCC in Atlanta, told the marchers to expect a busload from New York CORE and 25 from Baltimore CORE to join them on Saturday. He urged them to bring their mothers, fathers, sisters, all your families; we should have up to 500 marchers that day.

The second march the next evening was peaceful as about 30 young people left the church, rocking and singing, "We'll walk hand in hand, black and white together." Before they reached the jail, their destination, they were joined by an increasing number of adults. Police held off white youths trying to intercede and start trouble. Inside the jail, the imprisoned boy who had given his name only as "Mr. Freedom," answered the demonstrators freedom songs with chants: "We want mattresses. We want blankets. We want food."

Mayor Mowbray sounded genuinely frustrated when he told the press:

> I don't know what we're gong to do. I personally have no solution. Things have disintegrated to the point where we can't talk and we've got to reach a point of calm before we can negotiate again.

The white leaders broke off their negotiations with the integrationist leaders; accused them of bad faith. Gloria retorted that she felt the white leaders were "plotting like Judases" and demonstrated a "lack of faith in reaching a real solution to the problems faced by the total community."

On June 14, at the request of the Mayor and City Council, Governor Tawes ordered the entire Eastern Shore Battalion of five hundred Maryland National Guard troops, and over two hundred State Police, to Cambridge "to create a climate for a peaceful settlement." They imposed a strict 10 p.m. curfew, ordered all businesses to close at 9 p.m., and ordered all establishments selling alcoholic beverages to close until further notice. With bayonets fixed they formed a cordon around the black 12th Ward of Cambridge; no whites were permitted in the area (and, presumably, no blacks allowed out).

That night about 150 blacks met in the Bethel AME Church in the second ward to discuss their future plans to end segregation, while their leaders, Gloria Richardson, Phillip Savage, secretary of the NAACP in New Jersey, Pennsylvania and Delaware, Reginal Robinson, and the Rev. Charles Bourne of Bethel AME church, met with Governor Tawes in his office in Annapolis.

The next morning, Saturday, June 15, the leaders met in Gloria Richardson's home to discuss strategy. After the meeting, Gloria, Reginald Robinson and Mrs. Betty Jews went to D.C. and conferred with Burke Marshall, Deputy Attorney General, in charge of the civil rights division of the Justice Department. They were assured that the whole Cambridge situation would be investigated.

Later, before a packed meeting in the Bethel AME church, the leaders announced their "flat ultimatum" to city officials and to Governor Tawes—if negotiations were not immediately renewed, demonstrations would resume— "if they're not talking, then we move." There was a lot of clapping and yelling in response. In the weeks that followed, the negotiations, called by the press "like walking on eggshells," were on again, off again.

Meanwhile the guardsmen continued to patrol the streets. They remained in Cambridge for 25 days, from June 14 to July 8, 1963, when it was announced they would be leaving even though nothing had really changed. Cost was the most likely reason behind the decision to withdraw the National Guardsmen: the comptroller said the cost to Maryland taxpayers for their stay had totaled nearly $100,00—Guard pay, $83,199.83; food about $14,700; and gasoline, $1,858.89.

Meanwhile, on July 1, the City Council refused to pass a public accommodations ordinance and instead adopted an amendment to the city charter which would lower racial bars in restaurants and motels as of August 20—but this was subject to a referendum, and therefore not acceptable to the Cambridge Nonviolent Action Committee (CNAC). CORE announced that a demonstration was being planned for July 3 that would bring from New York a caravan of freedom riders. Hearing that, General Gelston declared that demonstrations by outsiders were barred.[211]

On Sunday, July 7, 1963, the evening before the guard was to leave, the executive committee of CNAC met and scheduled a mass meeting at the Bethel AME. Church for the evening of their departure. This was to be followed by a mass march through town to protest continued segregation of public accommodations and the continued imprisonment at the Maryland Training School of the two 15-year old Negro youths. [Other minors who'd been arrested at sit-ins were released to their parents' custody and sent home, but expelled from school.]

As planned, the same day the guardsmen left, a group

---

[211] Crawford et al (Eds.), pp. 132-133.

of white and black young people tried to enter the Dizzyland Restaurant, provoking a confrontation. While the group prayed and sang freedom songs, the owner, in full view of police and newsmen, beat, kicked, smashed an egg on one demonstrator's head, and drenched another with water. One of those was so provoked he told the press that it was only for the sake of the movement that he hadn't reacted violently, but added that he didn't know how long he, or any of the blacks, could remain non-violent under such violent assaults. Not long as it turned out.

•••

The following Thursday night, July 11, 1963, two carloads of white men ripped down Pine Street, the main black thoroughfare, at seventy miles an hour, wildly spewing gunfire in all directions.[212]

Some of Gloria's people were standing guard in the attic of the St. Clair Funeral Home (the usual site of refuge for both CNAC members and reporters, black and white, who were covering the story) when they spotted the car, lights off, starting down Pine Street. They signaled others on the street who ran for cover as the car sped by, "flashes of fire and thunderous roars pouring out of its windows....Assuming the outriders were not through for the night, defenders of Pine Street created an impromptu symphony of steel rattling against steel as they slammed ammunition into the chambers of pistols, rifles and shotguns." [213] ...As another car came roaring past, gunshots were exchanged. The Baltimore *Afro-American* reporter, George Collins, who was present, later wrote:

> I had taken refuge behind a brick pillar against which a parking meter was standing. I will forever remember the sinking feeling that seized my entire being when I noticed the top section of the meter had been blown apart. Better the meter than my head, I thought...The next day, it became apparent why the car did not return. It was located at the

---

[212] Retrospective account by a reporter who was present, *Afro*, 7/13/63

[213] This account appeared in the *Afro-American* on 3/2/82, and he credits it with happening in August. But clipping of the time indicated Gelston was there in July, so I assume this event happened sometime in July.

National Guard building and had more bullet holes in it than a sieve. It was reported that off-duty guardsmen, who had taken their shirts off, had been hit by gunfire while riding in the car. The miracle of miracles is the fact no one was killed.

The account in the *Afro* on the Friday, July 12, as gunfire continued, gave an unofficial count of twelve injured, including three National Guardsmen and a 12-year-old boy, all but three of the injured white. George Collins wrote:

> Only the hand of God could have stayed the hand of death during the long night when bullets literally rained on the county seat of Dorchester County. Despite the presence of National Guardsmen and state policemen who bolstered the local police force, all the guns that had been accumulated in the Second Ward over the last year and a half appeared to have gone off in one mighty blast that echoes endlessly through the chilly night.
>
> For what seemed an eternity the Second Ward was a replica of the Old West as men and boys of all ages roamed the streets, stood in the shadows, and leaned out of windows with their weapons in full view. At the height of the Pine Street gun battle not a Guardsman, state trooper or city policeman was in sight.

Perhaps there were none present since it would appear, from the above account, that it was Guardsmen, out of uniform, who had started the rampage. However, the next day, Friday, July 12th, Brig. Gen. George M. Gelston, took charge and ordered the first battalion of the 110th Field Artillery of the Maryland National Guard, four hundred in all (eventually there were 900 on call), to return to Cambridge

On Thursday, before the gunfighting broke out that evening, Gelston and Col. M. D. Tawes, a third cousin of the Governor and deputy guardsmen field commander, were conferring with Gloria and other leaders at the home of her uncle, Herbert St. Clair. When they heard of the shooting, the conference ended and Gelston "sped back to the Armory carrying Mrs. Richardson and Mr. Robinson with him."

It was something of a relief when "the easy-going Gelston with his persuasive manner" took charge, even though semi-martial law was again imposed—a nine o'clock curfew was imposed, stores had to close at 7 p.m. and no alcoholic beverages could be sold. Gelston also ordered that all cars were to be searched for weapons, seized and their owners arrested. Prior to Gelston's taking charges, blacks were never sure who the Guard were guarding. However, they still did not believe that Mayor Calvin Mowbray and other city officials were doing all they could to eradicate the cause behind all this violence.

Gloria told Gelston that the demonstrations would not stop whether or not violence erupted. "We will demonstrate until the city fathers and the white power structure recognizes our just demands," Reginald Robinson, another of the Cambridge leaders, declared.

On July 15, 1963 another explosion was narrowly avoided. It started mid-afternoon when would-be demonstrators, in defiance of a ban on picketing, began leaving the CNAC headquarters in twos and threes intending to infiltrate the stores in the downtown shopping district on Race Street. "Guardsmen patrolling the area in jeeps soon spotted them and kept them on the move for almost an hour."[214] Finally, Colonel Tawes confronted Gloria and Stanley Branch, the field representative for the NAACP, and loaded them, along with twelve others, into two Army trucks and took them 16 miles north to the Easton National Guard Armory.

When those attending a previously scheduled 7 p.m. meeting at the Bethel AME Church learned of the arrests, they "seethed with anger." Several hundred, some of them inside the church, some milling about outside, pledged to march that evening unless the fourteen were released by 8:30 p.m. As Reginald Robinson, SNCC field representative, addressed the crowd, they responded with such loud stomping, clapping, and outbursts of freedom songs that it could be heard for blocks. Robinson and Phillip Savage, executive director for the area's NAACP, fired them up even more, when responding to the city's claim that their demonstrations were just "stirring up trouble."

> Why trouble's been our lot for 300 years and now we want it off our backs. We've got to let the white man downtown know that we're tired of ...living in slavery. If they

---

[214] Quotes and account from *Sun*, 7/16/63

want to stop the marching, the picketing and the sit-downs all they have to do is give us our freedom. [The weeks of turmoil] could have been settled long ago if we had had a Governor with a backbone.

Col. Tawes entered the church while "more than 100 troops had sealed off a large area of Pine Street. ...The soldiers in the front ranks wore gas masks." It was only then he learned of the group's 8:30 p. m. ultimatum, but soon after was able to announce that all fourteen of those arrested earlier in the day would be released and back at their homes by midnight.

•••

Side-by-side articles in the *Baltimore Sun* reported the need for armed National Guardsmen to continue their "occupation" of Cambridge for an estimated additional 90 days, and the fact that the Price brothers were finally agreeing to desegregate Gwynn Oak Park. An editorial reflected on the difference between the two. It asked:

> ...Why were the Gwynn Oak demonstrations, though massive in scale, so peaceful and orderly and yet fruitful, while the affair at Cambridge continues in an atmosphere of fear and bitterness?...

It concluded that—

> In addition to the two advantages of a disciplined, better led group and a limited [more clearly defined] objective, the Gwynn Oak demonstrations enjoyed the sympathetic interest of the local authorities. ...[T]he local authorities in Cambridge seemed to be in charge of the resistance to desegregation; they did not play the role of sympathetic mediators as did the Baltimore county executive and the committee he appointed...Add the circumstance that the owners of Gwynn Oak never took the diehard stand some of the restaurant owners in Cambridge took, and the reasons for the peaceable adjustment in the Baltimore county resort become clear. [215]

•••

---

[215] See comments about Spiro Agnew, then the county executive, near the end of Part I, "All Men are Created Equal." More will also be said of him in the Housing section, "CORE Ripped Apart.".

On July 19th Governor Millard Tawes appealed to all citizens in a statewide TV address to "appreciate the magnitude of the social revolution now under way." He warned that "we will face not weeks, not months of racial strife, but years," unless "all the citizens of this state" act to satisfy the legitimate pleas of Negroes for equality.[216]

Two days before this, Gloria had finally heard from Robert Kennedy, but obviously not in response to her letters of appeal for his help. In a speech he blamed *her* for the violence in Cambridge. In her letter of protest, Gloria warned that "President Kennedy himself might have to visit Cambridge to avert a civil war."[217] In a later interview, Gloria said Robert Kennedy made an about face after seeing the tabulated results, done at Swarthmore by "noted sociologists," based on the community survey CNAC had done (noted earlier). It had gone beyond census information to reveal the "abject poverty" of the town's blacks.[218]

On July 22, 1963, a conference was convened in Washington D.C. by Robert Kennedy. Negotiations lasted from three p.m. until midnight in the offices of Burke Marshall, Assistant Attorney General in charge of the Civil Rights Division. Kennedy, himself, and Marshall, sat in at times as the state officials negotiated with Gloria Richardson, Clarence Logan, head of CIG, Phillip Savage, John Lewis, chairman of SNCC, Stanley Branch and Reginald Robinson, field secretaries of SNCC.

The final five-point agreement was signed at noon on July 23 by Kennedy and Marshall; Maryland Attorney General, Thomas Finan and Edmund Mestor, Executive Assistant to Governor Tawes; Mayor Mowbray, Audry Thompson, city attorney, and Arthur Parker, President, Commissioners, all from Cambridge; and, the six civil rights representatives. Called the "Treaty of Cambridge," it lacked the activists' demand that the two Negro youths be released from the Training School, but replicated, for the most part, the recommendations that had been made by Judge Laird Henry's

---

[216] Paragraph from Sobel, p. 197.
[217] Smith (Ed.), p. 939.
[218] See Szabo, p. 351.

appointed committee back in mid-May.

However, the commitment to desegregation of public accommodations was to be implemented by the Charter Amendment, mentioned earlier as subject to referendum if wanted by 25% of the citizens, rather than by a city ordinance, which was not so subject. And, just as was feared, the opponents of integration succeeded in getting the signatures of 740, the required 25%, thus bringing it to referendum, scheduled for October. The *Afro* was wise in urging caution before believing that the almost two years of strife in Cambridge was over. Though demonstrations were suspended for now, there were no promises as to what might happen if the public accommodations amendment was defeated in October.

There was hope, however, since CNAC did now have on paper, for the first time, commitments by city officials to integration. But Gloria and others, after the signing, declared they did not regard this agreement as a "victory," but only as an initial step toward better racial relations. Attorney General Kennedy agreed, emphasizing that implementation of the agreement depended on continued good faith on both sides.

> Whether it will be implemented, whether it will mean something for that city, its citizens and the country is going to depend on the effort, good judgement, confidence and faith of Negroes and whites alike.
>
> The bitterness, the dislike and almost hatred between groups of citizens toward their fellow citizens —if this is continued—if we should concentrate on the past instead of the future, the community will suffer, the State of Maryland will suffer, and the United States will suffer.[219]

General Gelston announced that five hundred of the nine hundred guardsmen would be withdrawn; curfew would be extended to midnight; liquor stores could stay open only until eight p.m., all others until eleven p.m. Throughout the summer negotiations continued regarding the withdrawal of the final contingent of National Guardsmen, who had been in Cambridge most of the time since June 14, 1963. Gelston, as their commander, sounded hopeful: "I'm always encouraged when people are talking."

---

[219] *Sun*, July 24, 1963.

Before their eventual withdrawal, Fred Weisgal and Gloria had met with Gelston so many times that Fred and Gelston developed a kind of friendship that proved useful later during the Horizon House negotiations in Baltimore, and later still, during the riots following Martin Luther King's assassination.[220]

Meanwhile, Mayor Mowbray acted to declare county-wide desegregation of the school system (at least four grades were still not integrated after the "stair-step" plan adopted in 1955, and any requests for moves from all-black to white schools had regularly been discouraged)[221]; desegregation of the buses, library and hospitals; urban renewal to be permitted for the first time; a black woman was hired at the local Maryland employment office; a black policeman was promoted; and steps were taken to hire black postal carriers. It seemed that things might really improve for the blacks in Cambridge. They were even more hopeful when, on October 8, 1963, they learned that the NAACP had succeeded in the Maryland Court of Appeals which had unanimously reversed the sentences of the two youths who'd been sent to training school.

But all was not well. The public accommodations referendum was defeated by 274 votes (all the white wards opposing) and the NAACP blamed Gloria who had opposed the vote. She had discouraged blacks voting, stating, "Public Accommodations are a constitutional right that cannot be given or taken away by vote." Following its defeat, discussions resumed between restaurant owners and more liberal white citizens of Cambridge in an effort to persuade them to open

---

[220] See Housing sections: "Break the Noose" and "Inner City's Challenge.

[221] Meetings that included Fred had been held with the school superintendent since the earlier agreement in May, but in the fall, as school was about to open again, he still had not agreed to change the school policy to one based on geography, not race. In a retrospective article in the Sunday *Sun*, 2/23/97, it stated that "by the autumn of 1963, black children were entering previously all-white schools," but clearly this was only some grades because in an article dated May 28, 1964, Gloria cites as one of CNAC's short-range goals, "the reassignment of Negro pupils to schools based on residence." (This in an unnamed paper, probably the *Evening Sun*.)

their places voluntarily. The restaurateurs said they resented being ordered around by "the do-gooders in Washington."

Later that October, Gloria Richardson and Reginald Robinson, the field representative of SNCC, whose organization had regularly been assisting CNAC, went to Baltimore to consult with their attorney, Fred Weisgal. Fred prepared to file a suit to throw out the exemption of numerous counties, including Dorchester, from Maryland's newly-passed public accommodations law. He alleged that the exemptions contravened the Fourteenth Amendment's guarantee of equal protection under the law. The law, as passed, applied only to Baltimore city and eleven of the twenty-three counties, exempting, amongst others, Dorchester (of which Cambridge was the county seat).

On November 8, 1963, after an all-white jury acquitted a white man of molesting an eight-year old Negro girl, Gloria called for a Negro boycott of Cambridge merchants, declaring, "The bigotry of the white citizens of Cambridge has now infected our judicial system. The conclusion is now inescapable that our last vestige of hope, trial by jury, has been removed from our protection whether we be prosecuting witness or defendant."[222]

In January 1964, the U.S. Civil Rights Commission released a 49-page report criticizing the governor, private industry, economic conditions, and the state personnel commissioner for contributing to the problems of blacks in Cambridge.[223]

In February 1964, tensions again were running high, when an arraignment hearing was held on February 27 before Judge John E. Raine, Jr. in the Circuit Court for Baltimore county. Eighteen demonstrators had been taken into custody two days earlier as they picketed the Welfare and Employment Security offices in Cambridge. General Gelston testified they were not charged with breaking the law, but had been taken to the National Guard Armory in Pikesville, Maryland (a suburban community just northwest of Baltimore), and were being held there as a "precautionary rather than punitive

---

[222] The *Baltimore Sun*, November 8, 1963
[223] The *Baltimore Sun*, November 8, 1963.

measure." He said Cambridge was in "an explosive situation
that could go up at any moment." In response to their
attorney, Fred Weisgal's questions, Gelston agreed the signs
they'd used at the demonstration were not inflammatory in
themselves, but insisted their presence might precipitate
violence.

Fred argued there was no martial law in Cambridge and,
therefore, the Guards had no right to arrest the pickets.

The judge ruled that he had to release the demonstrators,
but said he knew doing so placed the Guard in an "untenable"
position in trying to maintain peace. He went on to urge the
State to appeal his ruling to the Maryland Court of Appeals for
a final ruling on the constitutional questions involved, and
Robert Murphy, on behalf of the State, immediately did so.
Afterwards, Gelston said he didn't think the judge's ruling
entirely ruled out further arrests; he felt he was entitled to
keep taking persons into custody where violence threatened.
He also said he had no plans to increase the number of
Guardsmen then in Cambridge.

•••

Things must have quieted down after this, because the
newspaper accounts of Governor George Wallace's planned
May 1964 visit to Cambridge included the statement that the
town had been relatively quiet for some months. However, a
contingent of the National Guard was still present, and racial
tensions remained high. So anticipating that a new explosion
might be precipitated by Wallace's visit, Gelston called out an
additional four hundred Guardsmen and fifty State troopers.[224]

When May 11, 1964 arrived, fifteen hundred supporter of
Wallace turned out at the Fireman's Arena, the site of so many
past Negro demonstrations, to hear him. They cheered and
applauded lustily as he "dished up his artfully distorted
version of the civil rights bill," and ranted on about the
"liberal, incompetent press," "social engineers in Washington,"
and "pinkos," and made his usual vow of "segregation forever."
It lasted about forty-five minutes, was orderly if spirited, and

---

[224] As before the account that follows is pieced together from
several different news articles; in most cases the paper unnamed
and the date determined from content.

at the end Wallace, hedged in by State troopers, was whisked out of Cambridge. There was no disturbance—*at least not there!*

Across town was another story entirely. CNAC was holding its own rally at the Negro Elks Hall. After about an hour and a half of speeches on the theme of "Freedom Now," one Howard student began to urge participants to march on the Wallace rally. Within a few minutes, at about 8:15, three hundred marchers began to spill out the door—led by Gloria Richardson, John Lewis, chairman of SNCC, several white seminarians from Catholic University in Washington D.C., and Stanley Branch, chairman of the Committee for Freedom Now of Chester, Pennsylvania.[225]

As the marchers turned onto the main business street leading downtown, Gen. Gelston's jeep pulled across, and three lines of Guardsmen spread out, blocking their way. An empty whisky bottle shattered beside the jeep, followed by a hail of stones and bottles, one of which struck a Baltimore newsman, leaving him with a big bruise on his back. Gelston stood up on the jeep seat and addressed the marchers through a megaphone, asking to speak to their leaders. Ignoring him, they all sat down in the street and began singing "Ain't Gonna Let Nobody Turn Me 'Round." Finally, after a 2½ ton truck started pushing its way through them from behind, and Gelston ordered his men to don their gas masks, Gloria stepped forward and asked her followers to return to the Elks Hall where they would talk. "The marchers then got up from

---

[225] Stanley Branch had regularly been present at CNAC demonstrations, but by this time it is hard to see how he had time. Chester, Pennsylvania was itself described as "a southern-style town," and was in the midst of escalating massive demonstrations and multiple arrests that started with demonstrators at City Hall, led by Stanley Branch. They were demanding more jobs for blacks in public employment. They wanted to get Fred Weisgal involved there because Gloria had confidence in him and the Chester people had confidence in Gloria.[Based on conversations by this writer with Tony Amsterdam, then an attorney at the U. of Penn Law school who'd become involved in Chester at the request of two local Chester lawyers; and on several current news articles in the group's attorney's, Fred Weisgal's, personal files on loan to this writer—newspaper unnamed, approximate date based on content.]

the street and slowly started back, singing, "We Shall
Overcome." Before they left Gelston told them Wallace had left
so there was no longer any reason to march.

It might have been over, but it wasn't.

At about 10:15 p.m. there was another "spontaneous"
march. About one hundred eighty demonstrators, black and
white, again left Elks Hall, arms locked, and again headed for
the white area. This time they were met by Col. Tawes, the
Governor's cousin, and Guardsmen in gas masks and
helmets. The marchers promptly sat down in the street.

Photo appeared in *Pictorial History of American Negro*, co-published by
Hammond & Co. & Year, Inc., 1965.
Used with permission of AP-WW Photos who hold the ©.

One news account stated:

[Col. Tawes] marched up to Mrs. Richardson who was
seated in the middle of the front row, pulled her to her feet
and took her some 20 feet toward the jeep. He asked her to
tell her followers to go home. She refused. Then he said she

and other leaders would be arrested. The crowd did not disperse.

Angered at his threats, they formed a wedge.

> About twenty of them lay on the ground, some on top of others, all holding on to each other, with one man at the apex of a human triangle. Col. Tawes ordered soldiers to make arrests. They had to literally tear the mass of humanity apart under a shower of brickbats and bottles.
>
> After about ten were arrested, he again urged the crowd to disperse and go home, but a hard core of about eighty remained seated.
>
> Col. Tawes waved his swagger stick and the company of soldiers, bayonets drawn, swept up the street, elbow to elbow. The man with the converted flame thrower sprayed the air several feet over the crowd and a thick white cloud descended on the mob sending it scurrying up the street with the others. The cloud was so thick you could not see through it....The tear gas was sprayed wherever knots of shouting Negroes congregated. Soon the entire area was filled with the nauseating, blinding spray.

It was all over in thirty minutes, as hacking, sneezing Negroes fled the blinding fumes. Two demonstrators ended up in the hospital, one for apparent gas inhalation, the other for a cut on his leg inflicted by a bayonet. Dozens of newsmen and onlookers were nearly overcome by tear gas. The thirteen who were arrested were hauled away to the National Guard Armory in Pikesville, "being held under military detention while the State's attorney general considered formal civil charges against them ranging from disorderly conduct to inciting to riot."

The next day, May 12, 1964, Robert Murphy, the deputy attorney general, charged them with disorderly conduct under a Cambridge ordinance that had been enacted the previous summer. It was rather stiffer than other laws on disorderly conduct, providing for a maximum penalty of six months in jail and a $100 fine. Their bail was set at $500 each.

As those at the armory were being charged, others at CNAC declared they would continue to demonstrate daily until "every grievance of the Negro community has been satisfied." In response, two 55-gallon drums of tear gas powder were flown into Cambridge by helicopter. Four hundred Guardsmen and fifty State troopers remained on the ready. Early that afternoon Robert Murphy and Gen. Gelston met at Herbert Sinclair's with the SNCC members who were in Cambridge, Stanley Branch, John Lewis, and Reginald Robinson. (Gloria was still being held at the Pikesville armory.) Later, Gen. Gelston told the press that during the ninety-minute meeting, he'd asked them for some specific demands and had offered to try "to get the proper people to sit down and negotiate with them."[226]

That evening at 7:55, after an hour long rally, about two hundred demonstrators poured out of the Methodist Church in the Negro Second ward, led by John Lewis, Gloria still held at the Pikesville armory. He urged them to leave their rocks and knives at home and to remain nonviolent. They marched the five blocks toward the main business district, singing freedom songs, and then headed back toward the church.

As they approached the church, they saw about twenty-five Guardsmen, carrying rifles with bayonets, fixed and unsheathed, forming a line across the street that blocked their way; thirty more were arrayed behind them. As they got closer, the guardsmen advanced, raising their bayonets throat high. One thrust his bayonet into a television man's light and broke it. Negroes screamed taunts. Then, when General Gelston walked in front of his men, all became quiet, and the hundred demonstrators still there sat down in the wet street.

Over his microphone Gelston announced: "Don't forget Thursday and Friday are the days you come to the armory for the donable [donated?] foods." He urged them to disperse, but

---

[226] It was in response to this offer that Gloria, at a later date, indicated the CNAC's short-term goal regarding school assignments (mentioned earlier), as well as implementation of a new city housing ordinance, and the establishment of integrated recreation areas. She also urged that a team of investigators be sent to make this a target area for President Johnson's war on poverty. She also demanded elimination of discrimination in local hiring practices and the incorporation of more Negroes in Federally sponsored job training programs. There is no indication that Gelston ever acted to involve white leaders in acting on any of these. [Based on several current news articles in the group's attorney's, Fred Weisgal's, personal files on loan to this writer—newspaper unnamed, approximate date based on content.]

asked, first, that John Lewis lead them in prayer. Lewis didn't do that, but he did urge them to "make this an orderly demonstration....This is just the beginning and not the end." The group then sang "We Shall Overcome," and slowly drifted away.

The next day, May 13, 1964, at a hearing before substitute Magistrate Betty Nelson, after Fred demanded jury trials for all those arrested, she set them down for the Dorchester Circuit Court's October term. But Fred told the press he didn't know when the trial would actually be held. They promptly posted bonds after it was reduced from the original $500 (which had kept them in jail since their arrests) to $100 for Cambridge residents, and $200 for out-of-towners. All during the hearing, about fifty demonstrators had remained outside singing freedom songs and marching. They let out loud cheers as the defendants filed out and then dispersed without incident.[227]

The *Washington Post* reported that that evening "some two hundred Negroes and about one hundred fifty whites traded insults and [tossed] about a dozen rocks and pop bottles in a tense pre-curfew confrontation on Race Street, the hub of the downtown shopping district, and the dividing line between the city's segregated wards."

> No injuries were reported in the 15-minute stand-off. It broke up shortly before 11 p.m. when National Guard officers in a conference in a mid-block "no man's land" persuaded leaders of Negro demonstrators to depart on the assurance that white hecklers also would be moved back.
>
> Later Brig. Gen. George M. Gelston walked into the Negro Second Ward and told leaders that the whites had been moved back from the ward line.

Demonstrations continued for at least two more weeks, many erupting into violence. Fred again asked for jury trials for Stanley Wise, of Washington, and for eight others arrested on a Friday night when Gloria Richardson was in

---

[227] On the same day, Fred also represented Leonard Kerpelman (who had represented Madalyn Murray in the Prayer case, at the Supreme Court), on a charge of "disorderly conduct in attempting to enter the grand jury room at the Court House." A busy day, Cambridge being a good 77 miles from Baltimore.

New York at a meeting of another civil rights group, A.C.T. Governor Tawes was meeting with all manner of state and federal officials; even explored the possibility of calling in federal troops. Gen. Gelston banned all mass meetings and rallies in the Negro section "for a ten-day cooling off period," because, he said, "unruly activity had always followed these meetings. According to an undated, unnamed news account, his ban "followed perhaps the nastiest night of demonstrations Monday night in which four guardsmen were slightly wounded and tear gas was sprayed on an unruly crowd of Negroes."

On May 27 Fred used his friendship with Dick Gregory, the black comedian, to have him fly in from New York and join him in conferring with the CNAC executive committee. Afterwards, Gregory said he would stage a show that evening and charge a penny admission to raise money for the group's bail fund. "We're going to tell the National Guard, and if they bring a penny, they can come too. They said we can't hold mass meetings but nobody said anything about entertainment." However, it was canceled after Gen. Gelston refused permission. The news account reports that by next day Gelston changed his mind, but Gregory could not stay to perform that evening because of a prior club date in New York. He did, however, promise to return later (Gloria said on Sunday), but this writer has not found any account indicating he ever did return.

•••

As noted earlier, on the following day, May 28, 1964, Gloria Richardson, Stanley Branch and Fred Weisgal, as well as Dick Gregory, all took part in a demonstration at the Social Security complex in Baltimore. Gregory had stopped off en route to the airport for a return to New York, but, judging by an account of the protest that appeared in the *Sun*, the other three were in town because they had "scheduled to meet, later that day, with Burke Marshall, Assistant Attorney General, to discuss civil rights problems in Mississippi and Cambridge. None of them would say specifically what they were going to talk about." And the writer has found no information about the meeting.

Subsequent events, however, suggest there might have been such a meeting, and that it might have helped. In any case, things quieted down in Cambridge about this time, and in July 1964 the National Guard finally withdrew—the same month President Johnson signed into law the Civil Rights Act—perhaps not a coincidence.

Those in CNAC believed this law and the War on Poverty would make a real difference in their lives. In August Gloria Richardson married her second husband, Frank Dandridge, a black free-lance photographer, whom she'd met during the Cambridge movement, and moved with him and her two daughters to New York City. At first she worked part-time for SNCC and later for HarYouAct, a Harlem-based organization that worked with youth and poverty. In the early 1980s, she began working for the New York City government and was still an employee with the Department of Aging when this writer spoke briefly with her in 1997.

Gloria had left and things were relatively quiet in Cambridge, but the CNAC continued to act on behalf of the black community at least for a period of time. In 1964, the press reported that Fred Weisgal, Stanley Wise, CNAC's acting leader, John Battiste and William Hall, (the latter three were field secretaries with SNCC who had been active with CNAC for some time) met with the State superintendent of schools the week prior to the school's opening, pleading for their integration. A few blacks had attended the white schools the year before and a few others had requested transfers for the Fall, but there wad no real integration; no blacks attended the white high school and there was no integration of the teachers. The group was asking that all students be assigned on a geographic basis. To the superintendent, James Sensenbaug's statement that he was studying the situation, Weisgal responded: "You don't have to wait when the Supreme Court ruled on it ten years ago!"

It was as late as 1966 that the case against Cambridge's Volunteer Fire Department was held, cited earlier, that forced them to stop segregating the recreation facilities they operated.[228] Things may have quieted down in Cambridge, but, like most of the rest of the nation, it still had a ways to go.

In an interview for the *Sun* in February 1997, Gloria

---

[228] *Williams v. Rescue Fire Company, Inc.* 254 F. Supp. 556 (1966)

Richardson Dandridge, then 74, is quoted as saying of her time with the CNAC: "Those were certainly troubled times, but the unity that came out of that was magnificent. People were ready and willing to fight City Hall." She also recalled "threats that my house would be bombed, and I later found out that I was No. 2 on the Klan's list after Martin Luther King." She concluded: "It was a pivotal moment in my life, and I don't think there has been anything quite like it for me since, because it involved life and death situations. The bonds to those days and people are still there and still strong."

•••

Actually, it's not quite clear that Cambridge had ever entirely quieted down; or maybe it's just that smoldering unrest was reignited when riots broke out in Newark, Detroit, Atlanta and other cities the summer of 1967. In any case, there was a heavy presence of police the day that H. Rap Brown[229], having replaced Stokely Carmichael as Chairman of SNCC, accepted an invitation to speak in Cambridge. During a forty-five minute speech on July 25, he ranted against white-owned property and declared that "when you tear down his store, you hit his religion." He also urged blacks to arm themselves and be ready to die; ready to meet violence with violence.

Scattered violence broke out an hour later, and Brown himself, as he was escorting one of the women home, was slightly wounded. In his book, *Die, Nigger Die!*, he tells how he "dove to the ground [and] rolled into a ditch" when a policeman's shotgun fire came at them from behind a bush. The shooting set off a rampage, people "tearing everything up," starting fires.

After seventeen buildings were damaged by fire during the night, Governor Agnew sent in the National Guard and

---

[229] Brown had been given the nickname, Rap, while still a student at Howard University, because of his ability to converse equally well with college students and uneducated blacks. Brown's Chairmanship of SNCC evidenced the fact that the organizaation was becoming ever more militant. Carmichael had replaced John Lewis on May 16, 1966, and Brown replaced Carmichael on May 12, 1967.

declared that Brown was personally responsible for the violence. A federal warrant was issued for his arrest. The FBI became involved but by then Brown had already left the state. Later, a Maryland judge dismissed arson charges against Brown because he felt they had been fabricated by the state in order to bring in the FBI. Ironically, later, Brown became the first person prosecuted under the Civil Rights Act of 1968, which, when passed, was intended to make stronger the laws prohibiting violence against blacks.[230]

Gloria told an interviewer how she became involved in this event even though she had left Cambridge in 1964.[231] She said that her daughter, Donna, had called her and "told me I'd better get somebody down there quick." As a consequence she had asked Brown to go to Cambridge and talk about black power to their group, now renamed Cambridge Black Action Federation. Gelston had also called her, requesting her to arrange a meeting with Brown before he spoke.

However, Rap refused to speak to any white man even at Gloria's urging, and she couldn't locate Gelston to call him back. She ended up calling his home and talking to his wife who thought everything was under control. Gloria had to advise her that her daughter, Donna, was in Cambridge and had called her to say that "firemen didn't come in, the coals are flying all over."

After it was all over, Gloria blamed Governor Agnew for stopping a number of government projects to build new

---

[230] For many years after this event, Brown's life was entangled with the law—gun charges, shootings, arrests, five years in prison, the writing of *Die, Nigger, Die!*. In 1971, while in prison, Brown had what is believed to have been a sincere conversion to the Sunni Muslim faith and adopted the name Jamil Abdullah Al-Amin. Despite testimony regarding his spirituality and exemplary life after that, his violent past was never forgotten by law enforcement, and in March 2002, Brown received a life sentence for the shooting of a Deputy sheriff. Many believed him when he said he was the victim of a government frame-up, but not the jury, apparently. See excellent article by Thelwell for more details about Brown.

[231] See Szabo, pp. 357-358.

housing for Cambridge's blacks because he hated Rap Brown
and Stokely Carmichael, called them "thugs."

> That's after Brown and others had been up all night long
> trying to put out the fires. I think it was finally some people
> way down, what we consider the really racist part of the
> county, that let them have a fire truck. Because the city
> wouldn't.

In March 1968, in a two-page letter to Governor Agnew,
Robert Moore, field director of the Baltimore SNCC office, and
Walter Lively, then director of the Urban Coalition and head of
U-JOIN, urged Agnew to stop Maryland's attempt to bring Rap
Brown back for a "legal lynching." They asked the governor to
"take the lead in pointing out your own unfortunate mistakes
in dealing with the situation in Cambridge....The question of
the day becomes, *Are you truly prepared and willing to insure
justice to the Cambridge black community?*"

Moore and Lively noted the governor's reference to Brown
as a "categorical jerk" and a "mad dog" and reminded Agnew
that a report on the riots exonerated Brown as the riot's cause.
The letter concluded that "Brown was more a catalyst of white
fears than of colored antagonisms, the disturbance more a
product of white expectations than of colored initiative."[232]

Fred Weisgal had considered becoming involved with the
accusations against Brown. After all, this was clearly a First
Amendment free speech issue. At least two versions exist as to
why, in the end, he did not. Fred simply said he was out of
town at the time. His wife, Jeanne, more recently, said:
"Brown was a terrible person. Very anti-Semitic. To tell you
the truth, I'm not sure he even wanted Fred to represent him."

In an interview in 1968, Dr. Irving Cushner, a friend of
Weisgal"s, offered a more colorful explanation:[233]

> Fred at first *asked* to defend Rap Brown. He felt that
> Brown was acting out of rage against white injustice—that he
> was entitled to a strong defense. Most of Fred's friends made
> it a special point to get in touch with him and ask him not to

[232] *Afro*, 3/16/68.
[233] From "In Pursuit of the Moral Justice" by John Dempsey, *Sun*
Magazine, Sunday, 11/17/68, p. 14.

take the case. Their reasons were the typical ones: "Burn, baby, burn" is a destructive concept; Brown is hated in Maryland, etc. None of them had any effect on Fred. But a day or two later the black militants, including Brown, came out with their statement calling the Israelis the aggressors in the Six-Day War. Because of these anti-Semitic statements, Fred told Brown he could just go shove it.

Some of his friends dispute the assessment that the Jewish community's objections played any role in ending his representation of Rap Brown, but his friend, Sig Shapiro, didn't seem to have any doubts:

> Fred got himself in trouble with the Jewish community when he started to represent Rap Brown. He stopped at their insistence. They would have railroaded him, run him out of town. Today Fred would have gotten into a dialogue with Farrakhan. He thought he could convince anyone of anything.

Whatever Fred's reasons for not wanting to represent Brown in this particular case, there's no doubt he increasingly felt unneeded, obsolete in the civil rights movement; a fact that must at least have contributed to his decision in 1969 to move with his family to Israel. We'll hear more of the rejection of this stalwart Baltimore pioneer in civil rights litigation when discussing CORE's Target City project in the section on Housing.

•••

Looking back at the whole movement in Cambridge, one might reasonably ask, as one former CORE member did:

> Why was this the most violent of the Maryland civil rights battles? White intransigence? Irresponsible leadership on one or both sides? Radicalized black militancy? [Gloria herself, in interviews, acknowledged that she had joined the militants by the time she left Cambridge] Isn't it true that nowhere else in Maryland, in the Movement, was rioting or violence used?

Gloria and others in Cambridge may have gradually given up on non-violence as a viable tool after they learned, first, that Guardsmen, out of uniform, rode through the black community, guns blazing, and, again, had pursued those attending the Brown rally with guns blazing. There's no indication they were ever arrested for these acts, even reprimanded, rather they were the same people arresting the demonstrators for peaceful actions.

Even the moderate Gelston had attempted to hold demonstrators for an indeterminate period, in a military facility, whom he thought *might* cause violence. Perhaps these actions contributed to the takeover of SNCC (an active participant in Cambridge from the beginning) and CORE by black power. Until then these groups had been totally committed to non-violence.

By the time of the takeover in the late 60s, James Farmer had already left as head of CORE, and, as we've noted, John Lewis, Chairman of SNCC, had left that organization following Carmichael's call for black power; himself soon-after replaced by the even more violence-prone Rap Brown.

Not Just Eating Places

Douglas Sands, newly appointed as Executive Secretary of the Maryland Commission on Interracial Problems & Relations, in 1961 told an interviewer for the *Southern School News*:[234]

> We are spending too much time worrying where to eat. If we spent as much time on schools as on restaurants, we would have integration by now. [Seven years after the Supreme Court decision in 1954] we find that at most one third of Maryland counties are striving for real compliance with the Court's decree and the rest are moving at a token pace or not at all.

Was he right? Sands did add that restaurant demonstrations "would have indirect value in stimulating protests against more important aspects of segregation."

> The idea of standing up and fussing is catching on. Negroes are less worried about the feelings of white people than they used to be. If they have an urge to crusade, they will.

•••

I doubt Sands was thinking about "marriage" as an alternative issue to consider, but it was one that was viewed, by both integrationists and segregationists, as a crucial symbol in the struggle for equality; one that was brought to the court's attention in 1957 and again in 1961. On both occasions, charges were brought under Maryland's ancient miscegenation law that made black-white marriages illegal.[235]

In March 1957, under that 1664 law, twenty year old Shirley Howard, white, was accused of bearing a child fathered by John Moses Billy, Negro (who was married with two other children). Her counsel, John J. O'Connor, Jr., not only traced the history of the law for the court, but pointed out that it had never been tested in modern times as far as anyone could remember. Therefore, the Maryland Court of Appeals had

---

[234] 1961 Supplement to *Toward Equality*.
[235] See earlier review of the law in Part I: "Free Blacks and Slaves."

never ruled on the law's validity.[236]

After Shirley revealed to workers at the domestic relations department that the father was a Negro, they brought the case to the public's attention and the grand jury entered the charge. After that she may have wished she'd never asked their help, but maybe they were responsible for Billy sending her $7 a week to support the baby.

At a hearing on March 27th before Judge Emory H. Niles in Youth Court, O'Connor sought dismissal of the charge before trial, contending that the law was obsolete, illegal, and based on unconstitutional racial questions. The State contended that "age DID not make a statute inoperative" and that "illegitimacy was a matter to which public policy must remain opposed." The judge ruled that "the indictment charging violation of Article 27, Section 513 should stay on the Criminal Court Docket for trial." Both Francis Murnaghan, Jr. and Fred Weisgal had been granted permission to file a "friend of the court" brief on behalf of the Maryland Branch of the American Civil Liberties Union.

On April 16, after oral arguments, Judge Niles filed a four-page opinion that granted dismissal of the indictment without trial. He said:

> In the opinion of the Court, the statute is unconstitutional and void, since it violates the principle of equal protection of the law under the Fourteenth Amendment of the Constitution of the United States.
>
> This statute applies unequally to the conduct which it prohibits in that it penalizes one class of guilty persons on the grounds of race. [It] penalizes conduct resulting in the procreation of children of mixed races, but imposes penalty only upon a white woman who participates in such conduct. No penalty is imposed upon the Negro man involved. Furthermore, if a Negro woman should become pregnant by a white man no penalty is imposed upon either the man or the woman.
>
> Although it is perfectly clear, as stated in argument, that no one has a constitutional right to beget or bear an illegitimate child, this case is not concerned with that question

---

[236] All information on the case from three clippings in Weisgal's personal files, paper unnamed but probably from the *Evening Sun*.

but with the question of discrimination by reason of imposing different penalties upon persons of different race or sex for the same conduct.

Because the judge found it to be unconstitutional, he said he felt it unnecessary to express an opinion as to counsel's objections based on obsolescence; or its vagueness in defining such words as "white woman," "Negro" and "mulatto." He also felt no need to respond to the claim that it was void under the decisions in the school-desegregation cases.[237]

Judge Robert B. Watts (who was black[238]) reminded the writer of the second occasion early in 1961 when miscegenation laws, or maybe just customs, again came into play. For years he'd been counsel to the NAACP, so it was not unusual for Lillie Jackson, President of the NAACP, to call him.

"Go right away to the courthouse," she'd urged, "there's a complaint that a white man wants to marry his black girlfriend."

I had to remind her I was now a Municipal Court Judge and could no longer practice law. "But I did call Fred," he told the writer, "and he went." The next morning there was a picture in the paper of Fred with the interracial couple. Judge Manley had ordered the clerk to issue them a license.

•••

To return to a public accommodations issue. The fact that the courts had forced public swimming pools to integrate in 1956, as noted earlier, did not mean they all did so peaceably. Further, the court orders did not affect swimming pools, roller skating rinks and other recreation facilities that claimed exemption because private, a claim that was often questionable. Neither did opposition to integration end with Baltimore's passage of a public accommodations bill in June 1962 that covered restaurants, motels and hotels; then a civil rights act in 1964 with much greater coverage. The State's 1964 law was riddled with exemptions, the federal Civil Rights Act, passed that same year, was amazingly vague. Some of the problems these flawed acts left quickly became apparent as

---

[237] In a Virginia case in 1967, the Supreme Court struck down its anti-miscegenation law, along with that of fifteen other states.
[238] He died on 10/8/98, not long after this writer interviewed him.

they were applied in Baltimore.

The city's public swimming pools had been integrated since 1956 after the decision of 4th Circuit Court of Appeals that ended "separate-but-equal" was upheld by the U.S. Supreme Court. However, as late as 1962, integration was still being actively resisted, especially in South Baltimore where the Riverside Pool was located.

There was no pool at the City-sponsored Recreation Center at Sharp and Hamburg streets, so its director, James Smith, on August 15th, took a group of about 25 black youngsters, aged seven to fifteen, to the supposedly public Riverside pool for a swim.[239] As they tried to swim, they were taunted and jeered, mud from near-by puddles was splashed on them, and they were threatened with mayhem if they dared use the diving board. Things only got worse as they left. Hundreds of adults and children who had gathered outside the gate shouted epithets and threw stones. The police escorted the black children most of the way back to the center.

After three such episodes, Mayor Philip Goodman appealed for an end to the racial tension at the pool; asked "the good people of South Baltimore" to comply with the law. He had just come from a closed-door meeting with Juanita Jackson Mitchell, representing the NAACP; Douglas Sands, executive secretary of the Maryland Commission on Interracial Problems and Relations; The Rev. Thompson from a South Baltimore church; Ruth Fegley of Baltimore Fellowship House; and two representatives from the National Alliance of Postal Employees. Also present were Edgar Myerly, city superintendent of parks, and his assistant.

It was August 23rd, only hours after the Mayor had made his appeal, when Mr. Smith and his youngsters made their fourth visit to the pool. A near-riot started as they were leaving at 3 p.m., barely prevented by the numerous policemen and two dogs assembled to help. An unruly crowd of agitators who'd been at the fence heckling the youth, had moved to the pool's door awaiting their emergence. The *Afro* in its August

---

[239] The longest account on which the following is based was in the *Afro*, 8/28/62. This is supplemented by several short undated clippings from unnamed papers.

28th edition, described the encounter:[240]

> Capt. Elmer Bowen, commander of the Southern District and Inspector Leo Kelly manned cars to lead and follow the formation out of the park. A third car followed a short distance behind. On either side were a ring of foot patrolmen.
>
> The yelling, screaming, jeering crowd still moved in. The cars could barely move as women with babies in arms, men holding small children by the hand, leisurely strolled in front of the vehicles.
>
> That's when young Felder [one of the black children] was struck by a rock thrown by someone in the crowd, which Captain Bowen said was made up of 125 or 150 children and sightseers....The youngster was taken to South Baltimore General Hospital after they arrived at the Sharp Street center. It required one stitch to close the laceration in his face.

The demonstrators included several from the segregationist Fighting American Nationalists (FAN), led by Charles Luthardt, who seemed to be at every demonstration where he thought he could add some fuel to an already heated situation. His followers were wearing red, white and blue armbands and carrying signs that read: "Wake Up White Man," "Swim With Your Own Race," White People Have Rights Too." They also sent the Mayor a letter protesting his meeting with the integrationists.

This group, linked to the American Nazi Party, didn't stop at such demonstrations either. In November that same year, they were at Dundalk High School, by invitation, speaking to the students, spouting their racist propaganda; the county school superintendent ignored the Civic Interest Group's protests. He justified his position by claiming that such groups would not go away by ignoring them.

Then, again, in April 1963, four Sudbrook Junior High School students were found distributing the group's racist hate literature described as "basically anti-Negro with anti-Semitic overtones." In this case, the students were sent home

---

[240] It ran parallel to an article about the Gwynn Oak demonstration, occurring simultaneously , and another article about a black family who faced a "nightmare" the same day. They were forced to move from Carswell Street in Northwest Baltimore after their windows were broken, paint smeared on their floors, and signs left warning them to "get out before you get hurt."

and told not to return without their parents; they received a warning that if caught again doing such they would be severely disciplined.[241]

The park superintendent had been warned in advance that on August 28, 1962, members of the NAACP would bring a group of thirty or so blacks youngsters to the pool. Ten white boys and girls were then in the pool. Three NAACP officials, about sixty-five policemen, two with dogs, and three hundred heckling spectators (which, again, included members of the Fighting American Nationalists) were present while the black youngsters swam. The FAN carried signs reading: "Washington, D.C. is a black jungle. Ocean City next?". A spokesperson for the group, Bernard Cook, said they were "against race mixing, Communism and the NAACP, which is Communist dominated."

Three men were arrested in the pool area; two, aged 17 and 20, charged with disorderly conduct and the third, 18, with assault for pushing one of the blacks The woman was arrested as the group of blacks were leaving for refusing to move back when ordered to do so by the police. After the arrests, friends took up a collection for them, presumably to pay for any fine or bond imposed by the judge at Southern Municipal Court.

On August 30th the pool had to be closed after bright green dye was tossed in the water overnight. Racial tensions increased as police arrested several black and white boys on streets near the pool for rock-throwing and threats made with a hammer.[242]

The pool, however, was again open on September 3rd , Labor Day, its last day for the season. As blacks used the pool that day, agitators wandered through the crowd of 1,000 gathered along the pool's fence enclosure, urging them to "get the niggers." Over 100 policemen were present, keeping the agitators out of the pool area itself and a few were arrested for disorderly conduct, but, as on all the previous occasions, no effort was made to disperse the crowd. A few from CORE had come hoping to use non-violent techniques to quell any

---

[241] Unnamed newspaper clippings, hand-dated by John Roemer, 11/9/62 & 4/63
[242] This account is as reported in the *Afro* on 9/4/62.

disturbance, but things got out of control so swiftly that this was impossible—all they could do was watch and hope no one was killed. John Roemer has said he was there wearing a blue suit and tie, "making me look like an undercover cop, I guess, so no one bothered me."

One reporter remarked that the scene was reminiscent of an ancient public hanging, where people brought their families and picnic lunches "to watch the fun."

Even veteran newsmen were appalled at the blood thirsty mood of the mob, and one remarked that it was worse than anything he had seen, even in Mississippi.

The racial remarks were directed not only at the swimmers, but at the AFRO reporters on the scene. The mildest remark described the reporters as "dark apes."

When the blacks were ready to leave, the police insisted that rather than walking the blacks should leave by patrol wagon to avoid the obviously angry mob. Even then, one boy of nine had his head bloodied by a thrown rock. As the police wagons pulled away, the crowd began to disperse. The police assumed everything was under control—until they heard that "blood mad hoodlums had invaded a colored neighborhood looking for someone to hurt. With sirens blasting and lights flashing, the police sped out of the park to the area."

But they were not in time to stop what the *Afro* described as "a race riot"— "South Baltimore literally blew apart."

A howling crowd of [five or six hundred] whites descended upon a heavily populated colored area in the vicinity of Leadenhall and Cross Sts., hurling rocks and bottles, and shouting abusive curses at the colored people in the street.

The attack was so sudden that it took the neighborhood completely by surprise. Many people were seated on the steps of their homes when the mob invaded the area....It was sheer luck that someone was not seriously injured. As it was, nine persons, one of them colored [when the blacks, in self-defense had counterattacked], were arrested and charged with disorderly conduct....

After the invaders had been repulsed, a swarm of policemen, who had been assigned to Riverside Pool, reached the area and restored order.

The blacks were angered by the hostile manner of the

police, did not feel they were even-handed—instead of ordering the whites to move on, they ordered the blacks to go inside their homes. And they did nothing to stop the carloads of whites who continued to drive through the area even after the police arrived.

A year later, in August 1963, CORE representatives, Edward Chance, then Chairman, Walter Carter, Joe Wase and Walter South, met with Baltimore County Executive, Spiro Agnew, in "a new attempt to mediate the discrimination dispute at metropolitan area swimming pools and quarries—the county still did not have a public accommodations law. Agnew was trying to head off demonstrations that had been scheduled for the following day after talks had collapsed between Baltimore county's Human Relations Commission, CORE and a number of the pool owners. Five owners had agreed to "try integration" but seven others maintained they were not public pools, using the guise of "private clubs" by "charging nominal membership fees and admitting all white customers."[243]

In January of 1964, the press reports that the Baltimore County Human Relations Commission once again urged passage of legislation that would desegregate the county's pools.

A month later, on February 25, 1964, the Baltimore City Council was congratulated for passing *its* first civil rights law. There was disappointment that even limited application to housing was dropped, but pleasure that it went well beyond the earlier public accommodations law that covered little except hotels, motels and eating places—even then with many exemptions.

The new law covered not only these but also inns, roadhouses, bath houses, swimming pools, all retail stores and establishments, theaters, motion picture houses, roof gardens, music halls, race courses, skating rinks, amusement and recreation parks, fairs and carnivals, bowling alleys, shooting galleries, billiard and pool parlors, garages and all public conveyances operated on land or water or in the air, stations, terminals and airports, ambulances, nursing homes, (guidance services and day care centers operated by religious

---

[243] The exact day of this account and the paper are not noted on this clipping, nor the final outcome.

groups or fraternities were exempt), public and private educational institutions, including business schools (though not parochial), health and welfare facilities, and vocational training, in union and in employment.

The mayor lauded the act's passage as "an important gain in the advancement of the cause of human dignity and equal opportunities for all." Henry Parks, a black councilman, said he resented having "my colleagues parceling out freedom bit by bit" but "I've learned to take a loss when I don't like it [fretting over the loss of the housing section]. I had to vote to get passed what I could." Another black councilman, Walter Dixon, also expressed his unhappiness at the defeat of a housing section, but added "It was the best we could get, a step in the right direction. I have lived [in the council] with the theory of half a loaf for over ten years."

The most striking thing about the extensive list of places covered by the new law may be a realization of just how much discrimination blacks had consistently been subjected to and how many different fronts civil rights organizations had to fight on to achieve equality.

•••

Another public facility with discriminatory policies, though not generally thought of as a public accommodation, is prison. It's hard to determine just when the situation at the Maryland Penitentiary came to the attention of the State Commission on Interracial Problems and Relations and to the Civic Interest Group (CIG), but an undated clipping notes that an inmate brought it to the former's attention. In a letter to them, he claimed that the Pen was "jim crowed from the top to the bottom." He noted that there was discrimination in assignment of cells, seating in the auditorium (blacks in the rear), employment and recreation—even the coffee pots in the dining room were segregated—one with a white ring marked around the base for whites, one with a black ring for blacks.

The situation probably first made the newspaper on November 17, 1962 when the comedian Dick Gregory refused to start his performance at the Pen until the 1,100 black and white prisoners were allowed to mix and sit wherever they wished in the auditorium. Warden Vernon L. Pepersack explained that the seating arrangement dated back many years before he came in 1932 and was one of the few remaining instances of segregation."

Soon after that, the CIG wrote the warden protesting the situation and taking exception to his claims. They charged:

1. There is segregation in the mess hall.
2. White prisoners sit in the front of the prison chapel, while Negro prisoners are relegated to the rear.
3. Negroes and whites are not permitted to occupy the same cell.
4. In the west and south wings of the institution white prisoners are placed in cells on the street side or the penitentiary, while the Negro inmates are placed in cells so that they are able to look only into the prison yard.[244]

In asking for an end to these practices, they asked: "How is it possible for your rehabilitation program and racial discrimination to be compatible? ...continuance of such practices can only serve to hinder the rehabilitation of the entire prison population.

The Warden "ducked" and told them they should go to the Commissioner of Corrections, James Curran, for their answer.

In December 1962, the Assistant Warden, Franklin Brough, gave a group from CIG a three hour tour that supposedly covered every aspect of the prison—at a time when the warden was away on vacation. If the tour was intended to quell their complaints, it did not succeed. Instead, speaking for the group afterwards, Leo Burroughs, Jr. said he was amazed by the segregated dining facilities which were worse than he'd expected—blacks and whites lined up and sat on opposite sides of the dining hall.

Despite the fact that 1,000 (65%) of the 1,538 prisoners were black,[245] there were only a token number of blacks in the bakery, printing shop, metal and wood shops, or even in the recreation room. Twenty-five of the 185 guards were black. Burroughs conceded that change would take time, but there should be a "blueprint." He charged there was no plan to desegregate the prisons.

---

[244] Hand-dated article, paper not named: 11/28/62
[245] These numbers compare quite favorably with the figures for April 2001—18,347 blacks (78%) out of a total prison population of 23,571!

On March 2, 1963, members of CORE met with members of the Correction's Board and complained that the prison system still was not integrated. Leo Burroughs, who now represented CORE, when asked, said, "Yes, he'd advocate force, if that was necessary." The board, perhaps rightly, pointed out that this might cause a riot and hurt the cause.

Leo Burroughs, who had toured the Pen as a member of CIG, had become CORE's project chairman, in charge of a CORE demonstration scheduled for April 1963. One day, nine members of CORE walked into the State Commissioner, James Curran's office on West Preston Street and held a ten-minute prayer service, led by the Rev. Sidney Daniels of the Emmanuel Christian Community Church. "Kneeling, the group prayed for completely integrated penal facilities throughout the state." They then went outside the State Office Building and demonstrated, carrying signs that stated: "Segregation in Jail Will Fail" and "End Prison Injustice." Later, they went to the House of Correction in Jessup and picketed.

Commissioner Curran later said that in light of the steps the State had taken (which he outlined for the press in detail) in the various penal institutions, he was "quite bewildered" at the prayer service and the demonstrations. He claimed that both the Pen and the Jessup prison were completely integrated in housing, work, play, hospital, church "and the like," and that it wouldn't be long before the entire system was desegregated

The "pray-in" prompted at least one letter-to-the-editor. On April 17, 1963 Mildred Robertson wrote:

> It was with a great deal of interest that I read about Rev. Sidney Daniels and members of CORE going to Mr. James Curran's office on Easter Monday to pray for complete integration in the penal institutions of Maryland.
>
> My sympathy for their cause would have been aroused had I also read that he, the members of CORE, the NAACP and the hundreds of pickets they use in their determination for integration, had put their time to more constructive use, and had assembled on the grounds of Druid Hill Park on Easter Monday and offered prayers that the members of their race would behave more like civilized human beings and not natives from Africa.

It's interesting to contemplate just how the crowd of

whites who gather for Easter Services in the park would have reacted if "hundreds of blacks" had shown up as the writer suggested. It is also interesting to contemplate how Africans such as Nelson Mandela would have reacted to the suggestion that they were not "civilized."

It's not clear just how or when this issue was resolved, but it is certain that over a year later, Parren Mitchell, executive secretary of the Maryland Interracial Commission, was dealing with charges of discrimination in employment at the prison filed by the Correctional Officers Association of Maryland, a predominantly black group. The *Sun* article on December 16, 1964 reported on the association's claims and the denial by Vernon Pepersack, State Commissioner of Corrections, and G.C.A. Anderson, chairman of the State Advisory Board of Corrections, at a meeting with Mitchell.

To the Association's charge that Negroes were rejected without cause after being on probation, Pepersack asserted that eight Negroes and seven white men on probation were rejected for employment. To the Association's charge that Negroes were not promoted according to merit, Pepersack admitted that only one Negro held the rank of correctional officer 2, (i.e., corporal) and none higher, but said no other Negroes had qualified on promotional lists. To the Association's charge that Negroes were assigned to the least desirable 4 p.m. to midnight shift, Pepersack said there were five Negroes on that shift, twenty-one on the 8 a.m. to 4 p.m. shift and seven on the midnight to 8 a.m. shift.

Pepersack added that of the 106 men hired since they started employing Negroes in 1955, thirty-nine had been Negroes. Despite Pepersack's denials of discrimination, Parren Mitchell took the position that an investigation was needed "to clear things up....Someone should meet with these people to hear their grievances." What, if any, actions were taken has not been determined.

•••

Meanwhile, in March 1963, Rev. Marion Bascom was denied an appointment to the Maryland Commission on Interracial Problems and Relations by the legislators in Annapolis after they were made aware of Bascom's involvement in the fight to integrate the prisons. Leo

Burroughs in a letter to the Governor from CORE commented:

> It is a sad commentary on a state legislative system that would deny a highly qualified nominee a position in a state agency merely because he happens to be vocal in his opposition to racial injustice. We are proud of Reverend Bascom's militancy...

Burroughs also reminded the Governor that both Douglas Sands, the Commission's former executive secretary, and Furman Templeton, executive secretary of the Baltimore Urban League, had resigned from the Commission because of its general ineffectiveness and lack of support. He claimed it had become a "front organization designed to fool the public into thinking that official Maryland is interested in bettering race relations when in fact it is not."[246]

James Williams expressed these same sentiments in even stronger language in an *Afro* editorial on March 23:

> A militant colored man is an object of intense dislike, an anathema in their eyesight. He disturbs the defenders of "The System" for he has the effrontery to challenge its omnipotence.
>
> The type of colored person around whom they are comfortable is one who doesn't raise his voice too loud, who doesn't ask embarrassing questions, who doesn't want too much, and who doesn't raise an outcry when he doesn't get even that. These things the Rev. Mr. Bascom is not...

•••

Earlier that year, in January of 1963, when the struggle was still going on to get a state public accommodations bill passed, CORE began to plan, with the blessings of the national office, to picket Maryland's restaurant exhibit at the 1964 World's Fair. CORE promised to make the scene at the restaurants realistic; to carry the tradition of the sit-in demonstrations then going on in Baltimore to the World's Fair. It was to take place from April 22 to October 18, 1964 and from April 21 to October 17, 1965 at Flushing Meadows, Queens, New York. With funds appropriated by the state

---

[246] *Afro*, 3/26/63

legislature, a $1.5 million building was being planned for the state's exhibit.

In April 1964, on behalf of CORE, John Roemer issued a news release declaring that CORE would demonstrate "until the Free State [Maryland] has equal public accommodation from Ocean City to Oakland." He called the present law (which exempted a number counties and a variety of public accommodations) "a sop to the integrationists" that leaves Maryland a "half-free state." Roemer added that "CORE intended to show the world that not everyone in Maryland and the United States acquiesces in segregation. Non-violent direct action at the Maryland exhibit will carry the message that the state, and the nation, cannot remain half segregated and half free."

The plans were only called off after the General Assembly finally passed a state public accommodations bill on March 14, 1964, just before the Fair's opening. Perhaps not coincidentally, with the eyes of the world focused on the World's Fair, in July a federal public accommodations bill was also passed.

•••

As we've seen before, passage of a law did not necessarily mean picketing immediately ended (the 1964 federal act was frustratingly vague and the local acts always had so many exemptions) or that compliance would swiftly follow—in this case, it wasn't really clear that the county's new law would even go into effect since signatures were being collected to bring it to referendum.

As late as January 9, 1965, three blacks who were arrested at the Conowingo Inn, a tavern, in Cecil County when they tried to purchase food and a drink. The arresting Sheriff said he did not know what was in the Federal Civil Rights Act. "I work under State law." The Magistrate in fining them $50 said the Maryland law gives "any man the right to permit any one to enter or keep anyone out."

Joe Wase, now a practicing attorney, told this writer in an interview of a violent episode he had encountered in the Fall of 1964, after passage of the public accommodation acts. It followed a rare appearance by Martin Luther King in Baltimore, on October 31, 1964, to campaign for Lyndon Johnson.

Wase was at the rally with an integrated group of CORE members, and, since they were all together, "figured they might as well do something." So, after exploring various options, they decided to picket at Glen Burnie's annual carnival, then in progress. They called the county and state police in advance to notify them of their intent, and then fourteen or fifteen of them went down [Glen Burnie is just south of Baltimore]. They tried to get in to the carnival grounds, but when they were refused admission, they set up a picket line.

"Came damn near being killed," Wase said. "We were quickly surrounded by a mob of angry whites, first a few, then a dozen, then hundreds, even thousands. They were throwing rocks. I got hit in the head. The police were right there but did nothing at all. Then, when the mob started to rush at us, the state police seemed to appear from everywhere. They had been hiding out of sight. Luckily there were no arrests and the injuries fortunately were not serious. The carnival closed early that night and did not re-open the rest of that season. When it re-opened the following year, it was integrated."

•••

Before passage of the public accommodations acts in 1964, Joe Wase had also taken part in demonstrations at the Vernon Roller Rink in Baltimore County that started in the Fall of 1963.[247]

> The rink was located in the heart of Oella, a black section of Baltimore County. The whites on their way there had to pass right by the black folks sitting on their porches and their children playing in the yard. It wasn't right they could only watch—and I joined the pickets. Fred represented the seven of us who were arrested on trespassing charges on Sunday, October 20th.

Wase went on to say that at the preliminary hearing for five of them (two for unstated reasons were scheduled for hearings the following month) at the Catonsville People's Court

---

[247] This account is pieced together from the writer's interview with Joe Wase, and articles that appeared in the *Evening Star*, Washington, D.C., the *Baltimore New-Post*, the *Evening Sun* and the *Sun*—almost daily from 10/22/63 until 11/1/63. John Roemer, with CORE, also commented on the event.

on Monday night, Magistrate Howard Muhl, Jr. told them:

> Anybody who'd demonstrate on a picket line and get arrested in that fashion is either a criminal or crazy. And if they appear before me a second time I send them to Spring Grove.

After all asked for jury trials, three of them were released on their own recognizance, including Wase. But, unfortunately, two of them, David Alexander Smith, 18, a Negro, (charged with disorderly conduct in addition to trespassing because police had to carry him from the patrol wagon) and Keith Kern, 27, white, had also been arrested the week before at the rink. So, true to his word, Magistrate Muhl ordered them sent to Spring Grove for a "report and evaluation on their mental condition." Fred violently objected:

> You must have a reason, and you have not. How can you deprive these men of their liberties when they don't even want to be tried by you? This might happen in Alabama. I can't understand how these men can be asked to do this.

The NAACP, CORE, the Interdenominational Ministerial Alliance, and the National Alliance of Postal Employees immediately sent off telegrams of protest to Governor Tawes, County Executive Spiro Agnew and to the Magistrate. Next day Fred was in Baltimore County Circuit Court before Judge John Raine, Jr. seeking Smith's and Kern's release. Fred told Raine that Judge Muhl had told the men that "second offenders and people who deliberately violate the law are insane." Bitterly denouncing Muhl's action, Judge Raine called it an "interesting legal theory" that is "untenable from any point of view—legal, medical or social." His action "was completely unwarranted" and constituted "a gross abuse, a gross perversion of legal processes...."

The conclusion is inescapable that "the magistrate acted out of rancor and with express malice....Mr. Muhl has demonstrated that he lacks judgment, knowledge of the law and judicial temperament...His precipitant sophomoric course of conduct makes it desirable that he not continue to hold such a sensitive position."

The two were released on bonds of $103 each. And Judge Raine ordered a copy of the court proceedings be sent to the

Governor and the State Senator from Baltimore county, "since they have the power to appoint these magistrates."

Muhl, who never wavered from his story, declared it was "blatantly untrue" that his decision had been based on the fact that Kern and Smith were repeat offenders, but rather it was based on their behavior as described in police reports. [248] Muhl went on to say that the police had informed him that Smith had acted "very abnormal, making numerous comical faces at no one in particular" and had made "mock speeches." The other was "very upset looking."

Insisting he based it on this and this only, Muhl told reporters, "I felt they needed help." Trouble was, Fred and a Sun reporter who were present, both categorically denied either seeing or hearing any mention of police reports, as the Magistrate claimed. After an internal investigation, Police Chief Robert Lally said that one of the four arresting officers said he'd given the magistrate a "written memorandum" that night (a statement he later rescinded), but no other reports had been prepared until the following day. Further, the chief said he'd found nothing whatsoever in any of the memorandum or reports about any unusual behavior. The State Police were expected to investigate the contradictory evidence.

For his part, County Executive Agnew "blasted the magistrate" and asked the governor to remove him from office at once to avoid further embarrassment to Baltimore County. After Muhl began to lambaste Chief Lally for "intimidating the officers to change their story," Agnew really began to blast him:

> The purpose of a hearing is to listen to the evidence. Magistrate Muhl heard no evidence, allowed no cross-examination, nor any arguments. He sat as a monarch—not as a judge, hearing only what he wished to hear and, in my

---

[248] As a footnote: Joe Wase called Smith a sort of protégé of his. They'd become good friends while picketing together. Joe described him as a big strong, strapping man of very good natural intelligence. When they met, he'd never been more than a few blocks from the home where he was born; couldn't read or write, but with Wase's encouragement had learned; had even taken a few courses at Johns Hopkins. He married a Jewish girl, but, as Wase put it, it all was moving too fast for him. He divorced, got involved with drugs, and died of an overdose.

opinion, probably following a predetermined course of action....Again, I most respectfully urge that he be removed form office immediately to avoid further embarrassment to Baltimore county.[249]

The State Interracial Commission had already joined the growing chorus of requests for the removal of Muhl—on the grounds that "it will seriously undermine public confidence in the administration of justice, and if he continues in office will inevitably create the tensions which can disrupt a healthy community." Governor Tawes said he would not rule in the controversial case until he had had time to study the circuit court transcript and all other reports.

•••

Muhl's actions prompted Baltimore county CORE to stage an even larger demonstration at the roller rink the following weekend. And so a week after the arrests that set off a state-wide controversy, eleven other CORE demonstrators again faced Magistrate Muhl, Fred again represented them. On October 29, 1963 the *Afro-American* reported that when the group stepped up to the magistrate's bench, "a hush fell over the tiny courtroom."

> The hearing went along strict legal lines....Muhl heard the lawyer's plea for each of the CORE members before him. He saw that all defendants were properly lined up and that he heard each name. Then he read the charge against each of the eleven. Weisgal entered a plea of jury trial for each. The cases began at 5:40 and ended at 6:03 p.m. for a total time of twenty-three minutes.
>
> There was no conversation other than legal formalities. Magistrate Muhl's voice was barely audible. He concluded the hearing saying, "It is agreeable to this court that jury trials were requested...and all paper will be transferred to Circuit Court for jury trials.

All defendants were released on a $103 bail. Wase was again amongst them.

A few days later, on October 31, Muhl met for 1½ hours with Governor Tawes and a number of others "to tell his side

---

[249] The *Sun*, October 28, 1963.

of the story." There is no indication of the result, but one can guess that the whole controversy just withered away. Tawes already had accused the Republican Agnew of "playing politics with a very serious matter."

The next demonstration at the Vernon's Roller Skating Rink occurred between 6:30 and 8:30 p.m. on Sunday, March 15, 1964, following a three-hour Freedom Rally earlier in the afternoon at the Unitarian Church in Baltimore. The dynamic, charismatic James Farmer, CORE's national director, had been the main speaker before a devoted crowd of 500. Delivering one of his usually inspiring, fiery messages, he warned that the nation will "face the flames of frustration to the point of no return" if it did not grant its promises of freedom.

Farmer called 1963 a good year when the civil rights movement had come of age and when blacks had overcome their fears and "stood ten feet tall"— "Uncle Tomism" and "Nervous Nelly" had their worst year. He noted it was also a year "when white allies became a part of the movement through church and labor groups and when America confronted herself in the North as well as the South." [250]

He warned that things might get tougher in 1964 as opponents got more organized—all racists are not "know-nothings," many are "skilled operators." He said things did look brighter for 1964 with Maryland's passage of a state public accommodation bill just the day before—but warned that it had far too many exemptions.

At the conclusion of the rally, which raised $500 for CORE, about 150 blacks and whites, including Farmer, headed for the skating rink where they faced a crowd of "egg-throwing hecklers." Farmer stayed for about an hour, but had left by the time the arrests began. The owner, Vernon Bush, arrested demonstrators as they left the picket line along the narrow road in front of the roller rink and attempted to enter the front door of the rink. Most "went limp" and were dragged by county police to waiting patrol wagons. John Roemer told this writer how he had been threatened with more than

---

[250] The accounts of the rally and demonstration are both from assorted clippings (paper unnamed), from a flyer and program, a Western Union telegram, and court summons.

trespassing when he'd lay down in front of the police van, under their tires, so it couldn't move. But the police had simply picked him up and thrown him in the back, and apparently forgot their threats by the time they got to the jail.

After the arrests, Walter Carter sent John's wife a telegram:

> If John does not come home tonight he will be spending the night in Jail. He will get in touch with you tomorrow. Bless the children. Everything is alright.

John Roemer, having, to his surprise, escaped additional charges, was one of the twenty-two who'd been arrested who were released on $103 bail, but the bail for two, with an additional charge of disorderly conduct, was set at $206. The bail for David Alexander Smith, a black 19-year-old, according to the paper, was set at a staggering $3,100. [*Could this possibly be a misprint in the paper? Maybe $310?*] This time, he was charged with assaulting three police officers in addition to trespassing. Both police and judge may well have remembered that it was Smith who had caused a stir when sent to Spring Grove State Hospital for psychiatric evaluation after a previous arrest at the rink. Of course, as usual, none of the egg-throwers were arrested nor even the man who'd grabbed a *Sun* photographer's camera and run.

Accusations seemed to fly following these arrests: the Baltimore County Human Relations Commission accused the county executive, Spiro Agnew, of pre-judging events after hearing only one side, undermining their efforts to investigate what happened. Agnew had accused Eugene King, black, and the only member of the Commission who was at the rink during the demonstration, of advising the picketers to lie down in the street and to go limp when arrested. CORE accused the police of brutality. Everyone accused denied the charges; the charge that King had conspired with the picketers and should be fired from the Commission were later dismissed as "unsubstantiated."

In August 1964, King's actions were again being protested. Joseph D'Anna, of the Old Mill Tavern complained that Eugene King entered his place with three friends, and then, when he'd been refused service, filed a formal complaint with the State Interracial Commission. D'Anna claimed they were a private club that was exempt from the new state law on this count, as well as the fact that more than 50% of their revenue came from liquor: this claim despite a listing in the Yellow Pages, "specializing in Italian food." King asserted he had told no one at the Tavern that he was a member of the Commission but had acted solely as an individual. A month later the Commission ruled that its members should not test facilities [*which seems ironic, given their mission*].

As for the county council's passing a civil right's bill in August 1964, as hoped, they again postponed acting, despite fact the bill was designed only to "complement the State and Federal actions." An undated editorial from an unnamed paper concludes:

> That is not much to ask of a county legislative body in the interests of simple justice and racial harmony, and it is more than time for county lawmakers to forego the delaying tactics and give the county executive some deserved help.

In October 1964, the County Council finally passed a public accommodations and job discrimination act. As a result, Frank Newell 3rd, the county State's Attorney, dropped the "approximately 730 pending criminal cases which stemmed from local civil rights demonstrations during the last sixteen months." Newell said that the enactment of the county bill just days earlier made any further court action "a moot point of justice."

These charges included arrests made at Gwynn Oak Amusement Park in Woodlawn (already discussed); the Beaver Springs Swimming Club in Cockeysville (site of negotiations between CORE and Agnew); and Vernon's Roller Rink, in Catonsville (also discussed). The charges being dropped were "against white and Negro persons from all over the United States" including Michael Schwerner, later slain in rural Mississippi. "Among the defendants were students, professional people and clergymen of various faiths." Court aides had admitted that trying each of these individual cases would have been virtually impossible.

•••

Four decades later, in 1994, a number of those involved in

the *Bell v. Maryland* case were asked by a *Sun* reporter to look
back. Robert Bell, after whom the suit inadvertently was
named, had gone on to graduate from Harvard Law School, had
practiced law, and was appointed to the Baltimore Circuit
Court, then the Court of Special Appeals, and, in 1991, to the
state's highest court, the Court of Appeals. He had this to
say:[251]

> In many respects, society is just as segregated now as it
> was in the 1950s. The courthouses, the offices, the workplaces
> are largely integrated, but when you go home, when you go to
> the schools, you don't find it much different than it was in
> 1954. The courts are not as receptive as they once were to
> racial discrimination claims and there seems to be an overall
> reluctance to enforce affirmative action programs. We've come
> a long way, but we have a long way to go. A lot of people think
> it's OK to hate an entire group of people.

Others commented on seeing—

> Ku Klux Klan rallies, court rulings restricting minority
> scholarships and blacks suing Denny's restaurants over
> preferential service, and they wonder how far race relations
> have come in the 30 years since their case...was decided.

> We did change things, but now it seems as if we're going
> backward. It's more subtle than not getting in a restaurant, or
> a seat in a [segregated] theater. But it's there and it saddens
> you to see it happening.

---

[251] Account and quotes from "The Castle of One's Skin: Blacks
recall protest they staged in 1960 in city restaurant," Denis
O'Brien, *Sun*, 11/13/1994

Part IV
Education

Striving to Learn

"If you give a nigger an inch, he will take a mile. He should know nothing but the will of his master, and learn to obey it. If you teach that nigger how to read, there'll be no keeping him; it would forever unfit him for the duties of a slave. If you learn him how to read, he'll want to know how to write, and this accomplished, he'll be running away with himself."[1]

We are fortunate to have an excellent overview of the "early education of colored youth in Baltimore," written for the *Baltimore American* newspaper on September 16, 1894. The sub-heading reads: "Mr. W. Ashbie Hawkins Writes of the System of Mental Training Prior to the Inauguration of Public Schools—Men and Women Who Devoted Their Lives to the Advancement of Their Fellows and Whose Good Works Still Follow Them." We first heard of Mr. Hawkins as a delegate at the founding of the Niagara Movement, and will later hear more of him in his roles as a teacher and principal in Maryland for ten years. Further, in 1892 he became the first black admitted to the Maryland Bar by examination.

Early in this article on black education Hawkins says:

> Maryland was a slave state with many harsh and inhuman laws on her statute books, but, as we have seen, she never made it a crime to teach the slaves or the free negroes within her borders. To this singular liberality may be attributed the many private schools which flourished here in the darkest days of slavery and which served in many ways to make the negro's burdens less hard to bear. While the state made no provision for the education of her colored population, it did not hesitate to tax the free blacks who had property, for the support of the common schools for the whites.[2]

---

[1] Douglass is quoting his master, Captain Auld, who stopped his wife from continuing to teach Douglass. P. 114, his autobiography, *My Bondage...*; slightly different version, p.25, *Life and Times*.

[2] Free blacks were legally barred only from private colleges, professional schools and fine arts schools, but they were implicitly excluded from public elementary and secondary schools and from state subsidized academies. In 1839, 1844 and 1850, free blacks had unsuccessfully tried to get city officials either to stop taxing them or to establish schools for their children. Paul, p. 25.

Although Hawkins credits Rev. Daniel Coker, in the 1800s as the first teacher of black children in the city, he probably was not. The minutes of Quaker meetings suggest that for many years prior to that Quakers had favored education for blacks, but had not always acted on it. There was a small club started about 1795 by the Quakers, William Thompson and Walter Pierpont, who taught both free blacks and slaves for several years; sometimes slave masters even contributed financially.

But in the 1800s when the Quakers began to build schools for their own children, they did not consider integrating them (right up until 1964 and the Supreme Court decision in Brown); they did, however, believe in the "separate but equal" doctrine; continued to tutor blacks in their homes as they had for decades, and in 1856 erected a building for use of blacks, and even provided three teachers.[3]

As for Coker, he opened a day school for blacks about 1811 in a building and lot purchased by the Sharp Street Methodist Church that year. He taught there for about ten years, until he decided to take a position in Liberia with the American Colonization society; the school he'd founded lasted only a few more years after his departure. Coker died in Africa several years later.[4]

In his article Hawkins names a substantial number of blacks, mostly ministers, who taught blacks prior to the Civil War: amongst them was Rev. William Watkins, "recognized as one of the best teachers of his day (1835), regardless of race." A number of his pupils went on to set up schools themselves. Another named by Hawkins, Rev Daniel A. Payne, "became afterward a bishop in his church, and the founder of the principal seat of learning—Wilberforce."[5]

Soon after Payne came to Baltimore in 1845 as pastor of Bethel Church, he was "besieged by his parishioners" to set up a school in which he "embraced all the English studies now taught in the best graded schools, [adding also] Greek and Latin classes." A number of other schools are noted, among them ones at Sharp Street ME Church, Ebenezer AME

---

[3] See Gregory, pp. 58-63 & 97-98.

[4] See Gregory, p. 66 & 75

[5] A still-existing black University in Wilberforce, Ohio.

Church, and John Wesley ME Church.

Hawkins refers to census figures that note "1,355 free black children attending school in the state."[6] Hawkins also points out that since it was not forbidden in Maryland to teach them, "Many slaves learned to read and write, much to the discomfiture of their owners."[7]

However, Gregory in his doctoral dissertation points out three factors, all with an underlying economic base, that mitigated against free blacks seeking education: (1) the menial jobs open to them barely paid enough to cover their necessities, and most schools charged at least a nominal fee; (2) with only menial jobs available to most, there was little incentive to become well-educated; and, (3) hostility toward black education by the white community threatened their losing such jobs as they had.[8] Given these conditions, it's surprising how many blacks did seek an education.

Hawkins goes on to say that "slavery agitation and the approach of the war had their effect in making the laws on this subject a little more stringent, as by the code of 1860 it was declared unnecessary in the case of orphaned free blacks for the court to require their employers to teach them." Paul writes in his history of Baltimore's blacks that in 1818, to prevent paupers and criminals among the general population[9]

> the Maryland Legislature provided that all orphans, and all children improperly cared for or not usefully employed by their parents, should be bound out as apprentices by orphans courts or local trustees of the poor. In addition to learning a trade, these children were to be taught to read and

---

[6] Hawkins gives no date but presumably before the Civil War (1861-1865); probably the 1860 census; or he could be referring to the 1850 census quoted by Gregory, p. 101 which notes a slightly larger number: 1,616 free blacks attending school. These figures could be compared with 12,679 white pupils then enrolled in Baltimore's public schools. (figure in same time-frame from Paul, p. 25).

[7] Paul notes on p. 28 that at the beginning of the Civil War Baltimore had six private schools for blacks, taught by blacks, each with an enrollment of from 50 to 100 students (both children and adults).

[8] See Gregory, p. 102

[9] Paul, p. 28

write. This program resulted in blacks skilled in a wide range
of occupations.

The final section of Hawkins' article deals with "after the
war was over."

> With the close of the war, the emancipation of the slave
> and the coming from New England of many true-hearted
> men and women with the spelling books in their hands,
> sanctified intelligence in their heads, and the love of
> humanity in their heart, the negroes' jubilee had come....The
> schools were crowded, old and young flocked to the fountains
> of knowledge. No school day too long, no night too dark for
> these searchers of the light....The American Missionary
> Association, the Freedmen's' Bureau, the Quakers, the New
> England Association and other humanitarian organizations
> took up this work and prosecuted it with vigor until they
> were assured that the state would educate the recently
> emancipated children....[10]
> The Howard Normal School, corner Saratoga and
> Courtland streets, was organized in 1867, and for a number
> of years was the only institution in the state which made any
> effort to give the negro the advantage of higher training....
> Many of those who are teaching in the various parts of the
> state today, some of our lawyers, doctors, teachers and
> business men, received their training at this institution. It
> was the high school of that day.
> The teachers were mainly white men of culture and
> education, but who, by reason of their love for drink, had lost
> their places in the white schools. Despite their downfall, our
> people were glad to obtain their services. The universal
> testimony of those who profited by their instruction is that
> they did their work well, and in every way showed their
> gratitude to their employers.

Educating blacks was turned over to the state in 1868. In
the conclusion of his 1894 article, Hawkins writes of the black
experience under the state, beginning by crediting "our white
friends" as being "solicitous about our welfare educationally"

---

[10] Paul notes on pp. 59-60 that by 1865, there were 16 schools in
Baltimore for blacks with sixteen teachers, three of them black.
The demand by blacks was so great that by July 1867 there were 22
schools in the city teaching over 2,500 students; in the counties, by
December 1867, 73 schools with 5,000 students enrolled.

in having had only white teachers in our schools "until a few years ago." These rather laudatory statements, however, seem, actually, to be setting the stage for attacking them. Hawkins thus ends his article:

> Now a vast majority [of teachers] still belongs to that race [white], so great is their interest in us, and their fear that the work will fall into the hands of improper persons, if they should give it up. We are coming, however. Many of our teachers are worthily earning the mantles [of the earlier teachers he named] and they are striving nobly to wipe out the disgrace of slavery and the wrongs of freedom.
>
> It is a sad commentary upon Baltimore's system of public instruction that it took the white teachers of our colored public schools twenty-five years, with all the best appliances of modern times, to produce a score of teachers, when [our earlier black teachers] with the crudest appliances, produced nearly every prominent minister and layman in the city for the fifty years preceding the freedom and enfranchisement of the race. They were, however, men who knew our wants, sympathized with us in our efforts, ate at our tables, worshipped in our churches, mingled with us in our social gatherings, and colored Baltimoreans will be laggards in the race till we return to our first love, till our children are taught by teachers whose souls are in their work, and who believe in the fatherhood of God and the brotherhood of man.

•••

The stage was set for the state to assume the education of blacks when the legislature, in March 1865, passed a resolution that declared that taxes paid by blacks should be used solely to pay for black schools, this amount to be supplemented by donations from private citizens or charities. It took two more years, however, before Baltimore established such free public schools (and until 1872 before the rural areas did so).

In the fall of 1867 they finally assumed full control of all the black schools (which did not go beyond elementary) and the Superintendent of Public Schools, J.N. M'Jilton, supervised their incorporation into the city system subject to the same rules, pay scale, curriculum and length of school term as white schools—but in a strictly segregated system. He also consolidated twenty-two scattered black schools into fifteen, but retained all their white and black teachers.[11]

The City Council did not approve of M'Jilton's approach to black education and in 1868 reduced his budget request of $55,000 to $15,000, fortunately not making the amount entirely dependent on taxes paid by blacks (which was even less), but nonetheless making the school superintendent's recommendation of adding two black grammar schools impossible.[12]

The school board acted to remove M'Jilton from office,[13] then acted to consolidate the number of black elementary schools to *two* (leaving the more northerly section of northwest Baltimore, where the better-off blacks had moved, without a nearby school). They also summarily dismissed all the black teachers. For different reasons both whites and blacks protested this action. They urged the school board to reconsider; called their action "the denial of rights which the Negro deserved as an American citizen and as an affront to a people striving for self-improvement and recognition."[14]

Isaac Myers (the political activist, met previously, who fought for more job opportunities for blacks), in February 1869 at a mass meeting argued, among other things, that blacks had for decades "added honor, character and wealth to the city of Baltimore....Militants and conservatives alike endorsed the petition" he circulated at the close of his speech, urging the city council to fund additional black grammar schools and to hire black teachers.

After six months, the Council finally gave in to one of the on-going demands: first ordering principals to provide grammar school classes, and then, in 1873 opening a separate grammar school for advanced black students. Additionally, in

---

[11] See Paul, pp. 64 & 109.

[12] Generally the term "primary school" refers to the first three grades of an "elementary school" that encompasses grades one to eight. A "grammar school" generally refers to one that is intermediate between primary school and high school.

[13] He was succeeded by William Creery who remained until his death in 1875. Henry E. Sheperd followed, resigning in 1882; succeeded by Henry A. Wise, Jr. until 1900; then, James H. Van Sickle, the fifth superintendent.

[14] Paul, p. 112

1871, the Council established the first of several night schools for blacks, responding to the need of children who were required to be at home during the day to tend younger children while their parents worked.

However, the School Board still refused to hire black teachers, claiming them unqualified, but also refused the request to establish high schools where they could acquire the needed qualifications. Under pressure from both blacks and whites, in 1879 the board finally agreed to again appoint black teachers, but only *"when there was a sufficient number qualified to staff an entire school."* There would be no integrated faculties. A year later, in 1880, the School Board "agreed to establish two new Negro primary schools in Northwest Baltimore and to staff these schools with a Negro faculty"—but then reneged on their promise, alleging insufficient funds.[15]

Despite all these set-backs and the inferior treatment of blacks by the School Board in so many respects, they did, for the most part, offer blacks at the elementary school level the same length of term and the same curriculum as whites. This being true, it is probably also true that Baltimore offered its blacks a better public school education than that provided by any other former slave state; a fact that can be attributed, at least partly, to the outstanding leadership provided by Baltimore's black militants. Their protests of inequalities had taken organized form as early as 1870 with the formation of the Colored Advisory Committee which became the Colored Equal Rights League in 1880.[16]

In general, Baltimore's public schools were not able to keep up with the city's growth— from 267,354 in 1860 to 508,957 in 1900—and as a consequence lost the position of educational leadership in the country it had held in the 1860s. By 1900, it had 64,720 students and 1,676 teachers, 150 of them men. There was a shortage of classrooms for both blacks and whites, and school facilities were so bad they were considered health hazards.[17]

---

[15] Paul; p. 232-233

[16] See Gregory, p. 224

[17] www.bcps.k12.md.us; Baltimore Public School System, 1866-1900

•••

After the School Board reneged on its promise to build two new primary schools for blacks, the more militant black leaders—Joseph E. Briscoe and the Reverends Harvey Johnson, William Alexander, and P.H.A. Braxton—began to speak out with more urgency on the inequality of educational opportunities provided for blacks, at protest meetings and in personal confrontations with School Board members. As a small concession the Board reopened four night schools they'd closed in 1881, and established a two year high school in space appropriated from the already overcrowded building that housed the Grammar School and a primary school.

Real progress was not made, however, until after the founding of the Brotherhood of Liberty by the Reverend Harvey Johnson in 1885 (its story already told) and, two years later, the forming of the Maryland Educational Union. Brotherhood officials encouraged the black pastors to hold regular day classes as well as the more common Sabbath Schools, and by 1885 there were thirty-two such serving several thousand black children, taught by black teachers who'd been denied appointments in the public schools.

Some black teachers, especially in Northwest Baltimore, held classes in their own homes. Another resource for black education were the long existing debating and lecture societies which offered adults instruction and discussion in subjects ranging from their African heritage to the merits of union organizing to more abstract subjects such as Philosophy. In 1890, there were approximately twenty-five of these still functioning.[18]

Since the School Board was adamant about not allowing an integrated staff, some in the black community worried that the demand for employing only black teachers in black schools would result in segregated schools staffed with too many poorly training teachers. In contrast, other blacks began to oppose white teachers teaching their children and demanded totally separate schools for blacks. They felt compelled to this position after the city refused to allow an

---

[18] See Paul, pp. 229-230 & 234.

integrated teaching staff.[19]

The finding of the Flexner Report, conducted in 1916 by Abraham Flexner and Frank Buchman, two national experts on public schools, should have laid to rest one of the arguments against all-black schools. It found that black teachers were just as well-trained as white teachers, "in fact, the percentage of college trained black teachers was exactly double that of the white."[20]

Despite these two points of view in the black community, in 1889 when a new facility to house the High School and Grammar School finally opened in the Northwest, twelve black teachers were appointed—and black enrollment increased. Then in 1896, the black City Councilman, Dr. John Marcus Cargill, proposed legislation, passed by the City Council, that provided separate buildings and faculty for the two schools, and created a more advanced curriculum for the "Colored High School."

The same year Cargill introduced an ordinance that called for the replacing of all the white teachers in the black schools with black teachers. The ordinance was weakened with a number of conditions before passage, but, in effect, it "meant that eventually black schools would have black teachers and that black professionals would be hired in large numbers." [21]

As this dual system moved forward, the need for a reliable teacher training institution increased.[22] The city's response in 1900 was the opening of the first public school for the higher education of blacks: the Colored High and Training School, with a room set aside in the high school for "colored teachers." In 1926 the two were separated and one became the Fannie Jackson Coppin Normal School; in 1931 it finally offered a three-year teacher training program; and in 1938 extended this to four years.

The city approved a name change to Coppin Teachers College in 1939, making it the first public four-year college for blacks in the state. Then, in 1952, the state having taken over the college, it moved it to its own site in West Baltimore, in the

---

[19] See Paul, p. 304-305
[20] See Gregory, p. 279
[21] Greene, *Black Republicans...*p. 208.
[22] Coppin's complete story can be found in Gregory, pp. 419-436

midst of a large black community; completely separate from any other institution for the first time. It gradually extended its original mission, and, in 1963, as Coppin State College, awarded its first Bachelor of Arts degree.

Paul, in his assessment that follows, seems to believe that it was blacks who sought a separate, segregated school system, but it was the white establishment that imposed this as a condition for hiring black teachers. So rather than contradicting their opposition to growing segregation in other areas, this was just one more example of the trend. Clearly it was better to have a segregated system with black teachers than to have no black teachers at all. Paul wrote:

> In the 1890s and 1900s black leaders objected to the overall trend among whites to implement greater racial separatism within the general and broad context of community life—in theaters, hotels, public parks, political functions, public transportation, etc. Yet, by seeking to take advantage of this trend in demanding absolute racial separatism in the public schools, black leaders ironically followed a course that functionally would serve as an accommodation to the broad, community-wide movement for racial segregation.[23]

• • •

Thus having succeeded in staffing the black schools with black teachers, black leaders began to demand instruction in manual training, wanting it to include carpentry, engineering, printing, mechanical drawing, soldering and related areas. They had adopted the then-pervasive Booker T. Washington philosophy that held that manual training would allow blacks to effectively compete with whites for skilled jobs even when excluded from trade union apprenticeships (which didn't prove to be the case).

Harry Cummings, the black City Councilman who had both preceded and followed Dr. Cargill in that office, introduced an ordinance in February 1892, eventually enacted, that led to the creation of a Manual Training School for Colored Youth.

Dr. Cargill, in turn, in 1896 succeeded in getting its name changed to the Colored Polytechnic Institute, believing this

---

[23] Paul, pp. 305-306

would give it a standing comparable to the white Polytechnic school.

However, as Sherry Olson points out in her history of Baltimore, "the school board stepped cautiously between the demand of the black community for marketable skills and the demands of white elements to keep blacks in their place. ...Consequently, no construction skills were taught except carpentry, no new crafts like radio and automotive work were taught, and the only subjects for girls were trade cookery and cafeteria services."[24]

In 1902 the city merged the Colored Polytechnic Institute with the Colored High School, and emphasized manual training. John Murphy at the *Afro America Ledger* was not pleased with this de-emphasis on "stimulating the mind," and certainly would have vigorously objected to the statement made by Richard Biggs, the school commissioner, in 1913. Reflecting still the sentiments of Douglass's slave master—"*Learning will spoil the best nigger in the world*"—Biggs warned against higher education for blacks as making them desirous of things beyond their reach and unfit for the lives they will lead.[25]

That year the school narrowly missed becoming exclusively a trade school, thanks primarily to Harry S. Cummings, the black City Councilman, by then serving his third term. He warned that the black community would be aroused in opposition to such a move.[26] The advanced subjects at the high school were retained after passage of his resolution requiring the School Board to reconsider measures it had announced that would have eliminated its "higher branches of learning."[27]

Despite this success, blacks continued to receive decidedly inferior schooling to that provided whites, except, perhaps, at the elementary school level. Between 1898 and 1915, the city built no new schools for blacks; instead they assigned black children to hand-me-down white schools that already had been labeled "unfit for use." Further, in the years from 1900 on into the 1930s, all the black schools were so

---

[24] Olson, pp. 326-327.
[25] See Fee, p. 63
[26] See Paul 327-328
[27] See Greene, *Black Republicans*...p. 209

overcrowded that most had to resort to half-day sessions.[28]

After the Strayer Report, authorized by Mayor Broening, came out in 1921, pointing to curriculum deficiencies and harshly criticizing, among other things, the physical plant of both white and black schools, the city built its first school for blacks above the elementary level: Frederick Douglass Senior-Junior High. When it opened in September 1925, with its two gymnasiums, a sizable library, serviceable shop areas and a room for new business-related courses, it quickly became a source of great pride in the black community. It replaced the Douglass Institute which had been located in a building purchased earlier by forty blacks for "the intellectual advancement of the colored portion of the community."

Blacks, proud of their new school, were pleased to find that city and school department officials, parents, community leaders, ministers and students had all turned out to celebrate its opening. Fee in her history of Baltimore notes that the future jazz musician, Cab Callaway, then a sophomore at the school, was among the students present for the big inauguration ceremony.

Fee goes on to say that during the first decades after its founding, a third of Douglass's graduates went on to college or normal school (teacher training schools); thousands of black Baltimoreans became teachers, salespeople, business owners, clerical workers, industrial employees, and governmental officials. In addition to Cab Callaway, Fee lists, among others, such prominent graduates as Thurgood Marshall (Supreme Court Justice), Parren J. Mitchell (U.S. House of Representatives), Lillie Mae Carroll Jackson(NAACP) and Carl Murphy (*Afro-American* newspaper). [29]

One of Douglass' more recent graduates, Janice Woolridge, recalled in an interview with a Hopkins student how strictly disciplined it was when she was there:

> We couldn't chew gum or anything like that. And we couldn't talk in line, and the boys used to make eyes at me. That was my main problem, I think. I remember one boy

[28] See Olson, p. 277.
[29] See Fee, pp. 63-65

touched my arm in line: he was put out of school for that.
That's the way it worked. It ended up a very exclusive school.
We did all the operettas; one teacher taught us social graces;
like a finishing school. The teachers were from the big
colleges so we also had French, Spanish and Latin.

A special word needs to be added about one of Douglass'
teachers, Herbert M Frisby, who retired as head of the school's
Science Department in 1961. After a fifteen year effort, he was
responsible for the "first State-sponsored memorial raised to a
Negro in Maryland, the first ever placed in the State
House....The bronze plaque is dedicated to [the Maryland-
born] Matthew Alexander Henson, co-discoverer of the North
Pole with Robert Edwin Peary and the first man to actually set
foot on that gelid spot."

Frisby had been interested in Henson since sixth grade,
had become his friend and biographer, had made seventeen
trips north of the Arctic Circle "and in 1957 was the only
English-speaking person on an International Geophysical Year
Arctic expedition to Spitsbergen, off the coast of Norway."
Becoming only the second black ever to go to the pole, he had
accumulated in his cellar a "museum containing furs, Eskimo
artifacts and souvenirs of his travels in the Arctic region."[30]

•••

Accepting another of the 1921 Strayer Report's
recommendations, the city appointed its first black
administrator with city-wide responsibilities, Dr. Francis M.
Wood; a first-time recognition that blacks could be capable
administrators. Additional appointments of blacks to
administrative positions came only slowly and "grudgingly";
required constant agitation by blacks along with that of a few
influential whites. In 1928, a black counterpoint to the white
Public School Teachers Association was formed: The Baltimore
City Association of Teachers in Colored Schools. Then, in 1945
when Elmer Henderson succeeded Dr. Wood, the position he'd
held was elevated to that of Assistant Superintendent, in
"charge of the general administration and supervision of the
division of colored schools." This gave black public schools, for

---

[30] The *Evening Sun*, 12/6/1961.

the first time, the same structure as the white system, making them partners, if not equals.[31]

Another small but progressive steps can be discerned in the 1947 awards given by the Sidney Hollander Foundation.[32] That year the award was given to the City Department of Education, received on its behalf by Dr. William Lemmel, elected school superintendent in 1946, "for integrating teaching staff."[33] After assuming office, Lemmel had immediately set out to organize integrated committees and meetings of teachers and principals, and had selected an integrated administrative staff. He constantly sought out ways to create good will and cooperation between the black and white school systems.

Dr. Harry Bard, curriculum specialist, also received the Hollander award that year "for programs of intramural activity for culturally deprived (colored) children." This hardly seems adequate to reflect all he did to encourage integration. He oversaw an "interracial program called the Baltimore Community Study Program conducted through the City Department of Education. It was designed to bring black and white teachers together, as well as city institutions and community groups. It sponsored debating contests between students in blacks and white high schools as well as a number of other cultural programs.

---

[31] Gregory, pp. 305, 316-317. Gregory had access to the School Board Minutes of 1943 & 1946.

[32] For more information on this foundation, refer to footnote in Employment section: "Gradualism."

[33] From an article by George Collins in Moorland Springarn, Box 50-5, folder 179. Also see the article in *Journal of Negro Education* by George Grant, Dean at Morgan State College (1955) and Banks' thesis, p. 34.

Blacks Demand Higher Education

What became Morgan College[34] was founded in 1867 as The Centenary Bible Institute, located in the Sharp Street Methodist Church in downtown Baltimore. There were just nine boys enrolled when it held its first class in October 1872; its purpose, to train "pious young men, especially colored, for the ministry in the Methodist Episcopal Church."

In 1874, the Institute became co-ed (there were then twenty-five students enrolled), but a regulation stated: "There shall be no communication between the sexes by gesture, by glance, by notes or otherwise." Needless to say, this was a rule not easily enforced. On a more positive note, from the beginning the Institute enrolled a number of "pious young white men" as well as "colored."

The Institute did not offer college level courses, but did require its students to have achieved success in basic arithmetic and geography, composition, grammar, spelling, reading and the church's catechism. Students not able to meet these qualifications for admission were referred to black teacher-training school at the corner of Courtland and Saratoga Streets, administered by the "Baltimore Association for the Moral and Educational Improvement of the Colored People." [35]

Early in 1872 the Institute purchased the house and lot at 44 E. Saratoga Street for $7,500. But by 1881, having outgrown this space, the college moved to a new, more spacious building at the corner of Edmondson and Fulton. The Institute had accepted a challenge by Dr. John Goucher (a prominent minister and soon to become a member of the Board of Trustees), who purchased the lot and promised another $5,000 if the Institute could contribute $6,500—which it was able to do with the help of students, the black churches and a legacy from the estate of Thomas Kelso. Soon after the new building's dedication the number of students increased to 136 and the faculty to four (including its first

---

[34] The account that follows is based on Wilson's book, a comprehensive account in Gregory's dissertation, and shorter works by McConnell and Horn.

[35] Wilson, pp. 159-160 & 23 and Gregory, p. 190.

black teacher, Thomas B. Snowden, a graduate of Howard University and Boston Theological Seminary).

The Institute then divided into three departments: Theological, Normal and Preparatory. The attrition rate was high, largely due to economic reasons, but nonetheless by 1890 there were 223 students enrolled. Under the leadership of the Reverends Lyttleton F. Morgan, a benefactor and Board Chairman (after whom the college was named), and John Goucher, by then Board Vice-Chairman, an effort to gain college status for the Institute was undertaken.

On February 21, 1890, after the State Legislature acceded to the change in status, the Institute changed its name to Morgan College and a substantial number of new courses were added to the curriculum. Eventually this move toward collegiate status would result in well-trained professionals in a number of fields.

Meanwhile the college was again outgrowing its space. And when the Carnegie Foundation in 1907 offered the Institute a $50,000 matching grant, the college was again able to meet the challenge. However, it took until 1917 before Morgan's Board of Trustees felt they had found the site they'd been looking for, one that would accommodate not only their present needs but also allow for future growth. That year the Ivy Mill property came on the market, located in what was then Lauraville, Baltimore County.[36]

The sixty-seven acre tract of land at what is now Hillen Road and Cold Spring Lane was in a choice location near Montebello Park, near the holdings of some of Baltimore's most prominent families. The history of the Ivy Mill property dated back to the Revolutionary War when there had been a grist mill on the site. Later, in the 1870s, a rich granite stone quarry was discovered and worked primarily by blacks. McConnell, in his history of Morgan Park, writes:

> [These black workers], with their families, lived in a row of little stone houses near what is now Cold Spring Lane and in a small settlement nearby. Most of them hailed from around Ashland, Virginia, and had come to Baltimore to help dig and construct the Lake Montebello water works....When Morgan

---

[36]The site was annexed by the City of Baltimore a few years after the Morgan purchase.

acquired the site, some ten Black families lived on the tract. The old mill was partly occupied by a Black family and partly used as a county school for Black children. [*He does not say what became of these families and the school as the site was developed.*][37]

The existing Hotel-Road House on the property at the corner of Hilton Road and Grindon was converted into classrooms and a library. Three existing stone houses were also repaired.[38] They were being prepared for the college's use when word came that a Morgan-affiliated preparatory school, the Virginia Collegiate and Industrial Institute, in Lynchburg, Virginia had burned down on December 17, 1917. As a result, its principal, Lee Marcus McCoy, and his family, its teachers and students were invited to move into these houses.

This was in keeping with the college's intent to not only locate the college on the purchased property, but also to create a healthy community next to the college that would house about 300 families.[39] These plans so upset the whites in the adjoining community that they first protested, then took legal action. In 1918, having finally succeeded in fighting off the opposition (that story detailed in the housing section, "Early Legislation"), Morgan continued its growth and development, successfully achieving accreditation by the Middle States Association of Colleges in 1925 and again in 1935.

Herbert O'Connor was mayor in 1935 when the federal courts ordered the state either to admit blacks into white colleges or provide the separate, generally equivalent opportunities. Rather than admit them, O'Connor undertook

---

[37] McConnell, pp. 1-2. It seems strange on several counts that blacks were, and had been, living at the Ivy Mill site at the time of Morgan College's purchase: the insistence on confinement of blacks to a more restricted area; the lack of their mention in the history of Morgan by Wilson; and the fact that white neighbors were both so opposed to the introduction of blacks to the area and their apparent surprise, noted later, when President Spencer testified that blacks had been living there (not the blacks referred to by McConnell).

[38] Does this mean the black families had by then left, or were they asked to leave? As for the prep school in Virginia, nothing else is said of its history and how it became connected with the Baltimore school.

[39] See Olson, p. 278.

raising the money necessary to purchase Morgan College from the Methodist church.[40] Near the end of 1939, the Maryland legislature passed a bill authorizing the transfer of Morgan College from private ownership to the state. $225,000 was appropriated to compensate the Board of Trustees; $125,00 to be used for improvements in the college's physical plant. Maryland was the last of seventeen states with separate systems of education for blacks and whites to provide for their higher education within the state.[41]

When it became clear in 1937 that Morgan would become a state college, Dr. Spencer stepped down as Morgan's President after fifteen years. Dr. Dwight Oliver Wendell Holmes, then-Dean of the School of Education at Howard University, succeeded him as Morgan's sixth President, *its first black President.* His formal installation took place on November 19, 1937 "in the Douglass High School auditorium where Holmes had served as Chairman of the Science Department during 1902-1917. Presiding over the ceremonies was Judge Morris Soper, Chairman of the Board of Trustees."[42]

> The years 1943-46 witnessed substantial increases in enrollment, faculty doctorates, and operational budget....Salaries rose substantially....by 1945, professional and graduate schools accepted Morgan graduates without question....In 1947-48, there were twenty-one full professors, sixteen associate professors, twenty-one assistant professors and twenty instructors." During Dr. Holmes tenure which ended in 1948, full-time enrollment of students had increased from 302 in 1937 to 1,305. Dr. Martin D. Jenkins, a Howard University graduate, then became Morgan's second black president.

Dr. Jenkins was still President during the 1960s Civil Rights Movement.

•••

W. Ashbie Hawkins, who wrote the article already quoted extensively, was born near Lynchburg, Virginia in 1862,

---

40 Callcott, George, p. 56.
41 Wilson, p. 85 & 95-96.
42 Gregory pp. 399 & 403-404

during the civil war.[43] He came to Baltimore in 1881 to attend Morgan College and after graduating taught for three years; then was a school principal for seven more. In 1889, while still principal of a Towson school, he entered the Maryland Law School along with another black, John L. Dozier. However, despite the fact that it had, just the year before, graduated two blacks with honors, Harry Sythe Cummings and Charles W. Johnson, at the end of Hawkins' first year at the Law School, he and Dozier were notified by its Dean, John Prentiss Poe, on behalf of the Regents, that they were not to return.

The *New York Times* reported on September 15, 1890 that nearly all of the ninety-nine white students in the Law, Medical and Dental departments of the university had "sent a petition to the Faculty protesting against the admission of any colored students to the Law School." The regents held a number of meetings discussing the issue.

> [They] finally resolved that it would be unwise to endanger the school or jeopardize its interests in any way by any longer allowing colored students to attend the school in the face of such manifest opposition. A number of students had left the school and others had refused to enter because of the presence of the two colored men, and the school was continually liable to those losses so long as that state of affairs lasted.

Cummings and Johnson were the first and last blacks to graduate from the law school, and Hawkins and Dozier the last blacks to attend, until 1936 when a successful law suit forced the law school to integrate. They both later obtained their law degrees from Howard University and were admitted to practice on May 29, 1893. Hawkins became associated with the lawyer, George W. McMechen, who caused a stir that led to passage of housing segregation laws after he moved his family to the previously all-white McCulloh Street (which will be elaborated on later). Together, Hawkins and McMechen "erected the first office building in Baltimore for Negro professional men which they named the Bannecker building

---

[43] The information about Hawkins and the law school come from the *Baltimore News Post*, 4/7/1941, *Daily Record*, 4/5/1941, *Evening Sun*, 4/3/11941, and the *New York Times*, 9/15/1890. Also can be found in Bogen.

for the famous Negro scientist from Maryland." In addition to becoming quite a prominent lawyer, Hawkins at one time edited *The Lancet*, a Baltimore publication that "engaged in furthering the cause of the Negro."

W. Ashbie Hawkins died at Provident Hospital on April 2, 1941, aged 78, after an illness of seven months. His obituary in the *Baltimore News* described him as "a quiet, courteous, kindly man, active in the councils of the African Methodist Church." [His father, Robert Hawkins, was pastor of a Negro Methodist church where Ashbie was born.] The obituary added that "at one time he ran for the United States Senate against the late John Walter Smith and polled a large vote."

•••

There had been a brief period late in the 19th Century when the University of Maryland Law School had allowed the two blacks, Harry S. Cummings and Charles W. Johnson, to graduate before again adopting segregation. Also, the Maryland Institute of Arts and Design had admitted a few blacks in the years from 1826, when it was founded, until 1895, but then it too changed its policy to whites-only admissions. In fact, a case they won in 1898 helped Maryland's other white-only private institutions to continue their segregation policies while still receiving public funds.

Clark v. Maryland Institute[44] had turned on whether the Institute was a public or private institution, and the decision that they were private and hence not in violation of the 14th Amendment, even though they received public monies, allowed them as well as other private segregated institutions in Maryland to do the same. The case was not appealed to the U.S. Supreme Court. So it was that Johns Hopkins, the Women's College of Baltimore[45] and the two Normal Schools—Towson State, established in 1866, and Frostburg State, established in 1902—continued to discriminate and to receive public funds.

In June 1915, Carl Murphy, owner of the *Afro-American*

---

[44] *Clark v. Maryland Institute*, 87 Md. 643, 41 A. 126 (1898). See Levin pp. 495-496 & Gregory, pp. 338-339.

[45] Later named Goucher College after John Goucher who had been a loyal Morgan College trustee.

newspaper and a graduate of Harvard, was refused admission to Hopkins' Summer School, being told that colored weren't provided for. He complained to the Legal Committee of the national NAACP but they did not act on it, presumably feeling it would not make a good court case. Howard University and Catholic University in Washington, D.C. were the only near-by colleges available to blacks well into the 20th Century.

As Maryland continued to resist establishing higher education facilities for blacks, and grossly underfunded the few that did exist (Princess Anne the only state funded black college in Maryland), pressure for admission to white-only colleges continued to grow. Between 1922 to 1932, black college enrollment increased from 5,231 to 22,609,[46] most having to go out-of-state. One man above all others, Charles Hamilton Houston, was determined to force integration of the superior all-white schools, not just in Maryland but country-wide.

Houston was special counsel for the NAACP from 1935-1940, a member of its national legal committee from 1940-1948, and its chairman from 1948-1950. Before that, from 1929 to 1935, he was Associate Professor and Vice Dean of the Howard University Law School, committed to turning it into a first-class law school that graduated black lawyers capable of undertaking a legal battle against segregation. Soon after Thurgood Marshall enrolled in 1930, he became Houston's favorite pupil. Marshall later called Houston his teacher, mentor, colleague and friend, the father of civil rights.

After he became "the first full-time salaried lawyer for the NAACP," Houston continued his mission to find black lawyers able to fight against legal segregation. Having given up on making significant inroads toward equality through the ballot, Houston was ready to turn to the courts to fight for blacks' social, educational and political rights.[47] For this purpose, he'd nourished a coterie of black lawyers that included Raymond Pace Alexander, William H. Hastie, Thurgood Marshall, Leon A. Ransom, and James M. Nabrit.

Houston's long-term strategy was to begin with gaining the admission of blacks to graduate and professional schools,

---

[46] Figures from Watson, p. 94
[47] See Darlene Clark Hine in Franklin & McNeil (eds.), pp. 39 & 48

believing that this offered the best chance for destroying the
legal fiction of "separate but equal," knowing that providing
truly equal facilities at that level would be untenably
expensive. Further, since the number of blacks affected would
be small and the best educated, their cause would be the least
likely to arouse heated opposition by whites. This achieved,
the NAACP would move to desegregate undergraduate
colleges, then high schools, and finally grade schools.[48]

There was another reason for Houston's strategy. He
believed that without access to good professional and graduate
study, blacks could not develop the kinds of leaders the race
needed to overcome their inferior status.[49]

The NAACP chose Baltimore as a "natural starting place"
for their plan, for the wealth of its graduate schools, the
strength of its NAACP chapter, the prestige of its black
newspaper, the *Afro-American.*, and the emphasis blacks had
placed on education since the 1840s. These could be counted
on to develop the "mass interest" in each case that Houston
felt important for success. Recognizing Baltimore's unique
position as part Northern, part Southern, Houston personally
wrote a number of articles for the NAACP publication, *Crisis*,
intended to "stir up the black communities."[50]

One of the first, perhaps the first, case undertaken by the
NAACP was *University of Maryland v. Donald G. Murray*,[51] a
case brought to national's attention by Thurgood Marshall in
1935. Hearing that the twenty-two year old Murray (who'd
graduated from Amherst College the year before) had been
rejected by the University President and its Board of Regents
because of his race, Marshall felt it was time for his own
"sweet revenge." Marshall gone to Howard University Law
School and become a protégé of Houston's (then Dean of the
Law School) only after his own rejection by the University of
Maryland Law School in 1930. Marshall had begun actively
looking for a suitable candidate that would allow him to file a

---

[48] See Olson, pp. 367-368. Also see Darlene Clark Hine in Franklin
& McNeil (eds.)
[49] See Darlene Clark Hine in Franklin & McNeil (eds.), pp. 40-41
[50] See Darlene Clark Hine in Franklin & McNeil (eds.), p. 49 &
Olson, pp. 367-368.
[51] 169 Md. 478, 182 A. 590, 103 A.L.R. 706; 1936 Md. *LEXIS* 51 (1935)

case against the school immediately after he had passed the Maryland Bar in 1933, opened a practice in Baltimore, and become counsel for the Maryland branch of the NAACP. When the discrimination case went to trial before Judge Eugene O'Dunne in Baltimore City Court on June 18, 1935, Marshall introduced it and then Houston took over the argument.

The case took only one day, but one that extended from early morning until after 5 p.m. The state was not able to persuade the judge either that the University was not a state institution and hence not subject to the equal protection clause of the 14th Amendment to the US Constitution, nor that the state's provision of a number of $200 scholarships to go elsewhere was an adequate alternative for blacks seeking admission to the Maryland Law School.

Houston attacked the scholarship argument on three grounds: First, they were so limited in number that no single student could count on receiving one; second, even if obtained, they wouldn't pay for the entire tuition cost in most places, and certainly not for the added costs of transportation and housing required to go to law school out of state; and, finally, a graduate from a law school in another state would lack the courses (and contacts) particular to the practice of law in Maryland.

Since the state had no provision for establishing another law school equal to that of the University of Maryland, the university was ordered to admit Murray. Judge O'Dunne's decision was upheld by the Court of Appeals of Maryland on January 15, 1936. It was a landmark decision of sorts, giving teeth to the equal protection clause of the 14th Amendment to the US Constitution, asserting that equal meant equal, but the case did not establish that segregation itself was illegal. Judge C.J. Bond speaking for the appelate court stated:

> Equality of treatment does not require that privileges be provided members of the two races in the same place. The State may choose the method by which equality is maintained. Separation of the races must nevertheless furnish equal treatment.

Judge Bond also stated that the "equal treatment" must be available "now", and that the number affected did not matter; "it is the individual who is entitled to the equal protection of the laws."

Since there was no need to do so, the judge did *not* rule in this case on the question of whether the state could meet its equal treatment by providing the full costs for any black student going out of state to study law. Despite the limitations of their victory, Murray was admitted to the University of Maryland Law School. Since the Board of Regents had not appealed their case to the U.S. Supreme Court, it took another similar case in 1938, *State of Missouri ex rei Gaines v. Canada, Registrar,* before the doctrine established by the Maryland court would apply to all the states. In this even stronger case than *Murray,* "the Supreme Court rejected a pretended equality of opportunity." [52] These two cases at least opened the door to professional education for Maryland's blacks.

Perhaps it was the *Murray* case that led the Maryland Sate Commission on Higher Education of Negroes in 1937 to investigate conditions in the black schools—an investigation that found "dramatic funding disparities and drastically inferior facilities, as well as inferior course offerings in every field. The only conclusion that could be drawn was that the state had failed to make anything like equal provisions for its blacks.[53]

•••

In 1947 a case was brought against the Maryland Institute for the Promotion of Mechanic Arts that provoked reference to an earlier 1898 case,[54] *Clark v. Maryland Institute,* already discussed. This new case started on a Spring day in 1947 when the American Civil Liberties Union (ACLU) referred Leon Norris to Fred Weisgal, a Baltimore attorney, then barely out of law school. This thirty-two year old black veteran had walked into Weisgal's office incensed that he'd been denied the right even to see the registrar at the Maryland Institute: "Just because I'm black."

---

[52] *State of Missouri ex rei Gaines v. Canada, Registrar,* 337, 59 S.Ct. 232, 83 L.ED. 208 (1938). See Levin, p. 494

[53] *Poderesky v. Kirwin, President of Univ. of Md.* 838 F. Supp. 1075; 1993 U.S. Dist. LEXIS 19493

[54] *Clark v. Maryland Institute,* 87 Md. 643, 41 A. 126 (1898)

My skin color didn't prevent me from fighting for my country with a combat engineer unit in the South Pacific. And I was good at art while at Douglas High before I left to join the Army. Now I want to study and teach art, not continue to work in my father's tailor shop, and the Maryland Institute is the only place I can get what I need.

I want to sue! Will you take my case?[55]

Early in March Weisgal filed a complaint in the District Court of the United States, *Leon A. Norris v. Mayor & City Council of Baltimore & the Maryland Institute...*, requesting the following relief:

(a) a declaratory judgment that Norris be received as a student at the Institute on the same terms as other residents of Baltimore City without regard to race or color;

(b) that the Institute be enjoined from excluding him solely based on race or color;

(c) in the alternative, if the Institute is a private corporation not under the restraints of the Federal Constitution, the Mayor and City Council be enjoined from appropriating any public money or allocating any public property or other resource to the Institute.

The suit asked for damages in the amount of $20,000.

Weisgal, aware of his inexperience, must have felt a little overwhelmed by the potential importance of this case—so he turned for advice to the person whose work had impressed him most while he was still in law school. He went to Washington, D.C. to seek out Dr. Charles Hamilton Houston who had left his staff position with the NAACP in 1940 to return to private practice with his father. Weisgal still remembered how excited he'd become when reading Houston's arguments in *University of Maryland v. Donald G. Murray* (1935) and by the more recent case, *Kerr v. the Enoch Pratt Free Library (1945)*. Both had resulted in favorable decisions. Fred believed that the *Norris* case shared similarities with

---

[55] This case was first written up by this author in her biography of Fred Weisgal: *"...And Justice for All": The Double Life of Fred Weisgal, Attorney-Musician*. It was based, primarily, on clippings and notes in his personal files.

these and therefore would be of interest to Dr. Houston.[56]

When Weisgal entered Dr. Houston's office for the first time, he was impressed by the handsome, imposing six-foot, 200-pound figure before him, with his piercing gray eyes and thinning gray hair. Later Weisgal called him "a brilliant man with a slow, deliberate manner of speaking; his choice of words magnificent. He had the unique ability to reach the very heart of a problem, quickly and efficiently. He was strong and honest and his love for mankind amazed me. I owe to him more than to any man, my love for the law."[57]

That's how Houston became one of the attorneys of record[58]—and probably also why they received $2,000 towards costs from a fund that had been given to the NAACP by the *Afro-American* newspapers for the purpose of instigating legal action against color barriers affecting Baltimore citizens. As we'll see later, the NAACP apparently had no fondness for Fred.

Weisgal and Houston became close friends as they spent long hours together during the next three months preparing Norris's case. And as the wee hours of the morning often crept around on these occasions, Fred surely would have assumed his favorite pose—jacket off, shirt sleeves rolled up, tie dangling, shoes kicked across the room, sock feet on his desk, coffee cup in his hand, and a Pall Mall hanging from his mouth. And as typical, he most certainly would have been serious, inquisitive, demanding, one moment; the next, cracking a joke to lighten the mood and relieve tension.

Early in June 1947, the case went to trial—apparently not experiencing the long delays between filing and hearing that most cases encounter today.[59] Arguments ensued about initial

---

[56] *Kerr* was reviewed by this writer in Employment section: "The Great Depression", as inspired by the City-Wide Young People's Forum.

[57] From news article by Ray Abrams, "Law Day and Houston," May, 1963.

[58] W.A.C. Hughes, Jr. and Harry Levin are also named on the record, but there is no other mention of them. Perhaps they helped with the research and writing of briefs.

[59] Ironically, victories such as those Fred won over the years are responsible, at least in part, for today's delays. Courts now recognize more rights of defendants, resulting in more cases—and more procedural rights result in cases taking longer. This so,

contracts with the city after the Maryland Institute was incorporated on January 10, 1826 as a private corporation—how it was largely destroyed in the big Baltimore fire of 1904. It was argued that since the Institute, on its present site, had been funded by insurance money and a gift from Carnegie, it was not now clear on what authority the city continued to give the Institute money.

The point was also made that between 1826, when it was founded, and 1895 when there was a change in its guidelines, three or four blacks had been selected for scholarships by city councilmen (the form of city contribution to the Institute), and had attended the Institute without any apparent "upheaval." However, in 1895 (ironically, the year Dr. Houston was born), "the school's heads adopted a resolution to admit only white students, 'because the appointment of colored students was believed to have decreased the number of white pupils in attendance.'"[60] This had been the prevailing policy since.[61]

Congress has never appropriated enough money to enable an increase in the number of judges needed to keep up.

[60] Probably from *Afro-American*—neither paper nor date are included with clipping. The point made in this 1898 case, *Clark v. Maryland Institute*, was that this was a private educational institution which receives public aid, but is not a part of the public school system, and therefore could lawfully apply a racial exclusion policy.

[61] Simultaneously with his arguing the *Norris* case, Weisgal also represented Fellowship House's Art Center, integrated, and the only facility available to blacks wishing to study art. Fellowship House had been started by Ada Jenkins (black) just as WWII was ending as a place where blacks and whites and Christians and Jews could meet and interact together as equals. In addition to the arts program, it had a choir, did theater, held an annual Seder Service and sponsored various other activities. Ironically, the art center not only received little-to-no funding from the city, but was also taxed.

Fred wrote the Board of Estimates requesting both that the Center be granted the same exemption from taxes as other educational institutions, and that he (Fred) be given "an opportunity to come before the Board to request that the Art Center receive an annual appropriation of $5,000 from the city." [The Maryland Institute Norris was seeking to gain admission to received annually, $26,000 to $30,00 from the city, in the form of scholarships for students, and $16,500 from the state. The Art Center at Fellowship House received $2,900.]

It's unclear how long this initial *Norris* trial lasted, but Judge W. Calvin Chesnut did not render his decision until June of 1948, a year after the trial's start.[62] Unfortunately it was not favorable. The judge declared, essentially, that the courts had held that discrimination by *private* educational institutions was legal, and that, unlike in the *Enoch Pratt Library* case, the Institute was not *primarily* supported with city and state funds. Allocation of "citizens' moneys" to private schools (in this case scholarships) was a tax issue, more properly heard in city or state court. It was not a constitutional issue appropriate for the federal courts. Weisgal and Dr. Houston discussed an appeal but Houston was against it. "The time is not right," he'd said. Houston was looking for the right time and the right case to appeal all the way up to the Supreme Court—and win. A favorable ruling there would apply to *all* the states—their ultimate goal. Weisgal shared Houston's belief that this was not the case—a loss at the Supreme Court level would have been devastating to their ultimate goal.

•••

Sometime later Weisgal recalled their walking out of the courtroom together at the end of the *Norris* trial, already despondent over their loss. "We were looking for a place to have lunch, ending up at the railroad station where eating

---

At the hearing they granted, which had wide support from prominent citizens supporting the Art Center's position, Fred was called a "radical" by one of the Board members, his past editorship of *People* (a small leftist publication) was questioned, and there were implications, denied, that the Communists had an interest in the case. A decision was postponed at the time of the hearing, and this writer found no additional information as to whether or not either the tax exemption or the increased funding requests were granted. That they were seems unlikely since the City Council, on the whole, was not a liberal-minded body and didn't give more moneys easily even in the best of circumstances.

[62] Perhaps Judge Chesnut was distracted by the case Alger Hiss filed in Baltimore that year charging Wittaker Chambers with libel. This case, which Chesnut was in charge of, was aborted after discovery of the "pumpkin papers" and Hiss subsequently was convicted of perjury for denying accusations that he was a Soviet spy (the statute of limitations made a charge of espionage impossible).

together in Baltimore was about the only place that was legal. The white restaurants would not serve Houston. It just burned me up. Here was a man who was an outstanding constitutional lawyer, a man who had been first in his class at Amherst, who had led his class at Harvard Law School, who had been dean of the Howard University School of Law—and he could not be served because of the color of his skin. I remember him telling me that the reason he fought in court so hard and so long was because he did not want his son subjected to the indignities which he was forced to suffer."

It was a painful loss, especially for Weisgal, who was not yet as used to losing these kinds of cases as was Houston. But Houston assured him it was not a total loss. It was one more in a series of cases before the lower courts that supported his belief in an incremental approach to desegregation.[63] Houston felt these cases served to raise the political consciousness of "grassroots" black people who historically had been afraid to cross the white man for fear of losing their jobs or worse. At the same time, the lower court cases provided an opportunity to test arguments and gain insights into judges' thinking so that effective strategies could be developed for a "big" case later.

This approach was also in keeping with Houston's belief that, initially, more success could be achieved by attacking the lack of "equality" in education, mandated by the "separate but equal" doctrine of *Plessy (1896)*, than by attacking segregation head-on. [*Looking back one might ask if he was right. If "quality" had remained the issue, would we have so many inferior, neglected, and, in any case, re-segregated schools in our inner cities as we now have?*]

Weisgal later declared his work with Houston on the *Norris* case as the beginning of a "fruitful friendship" and "of a rich and productive association." Regrettably it was cut short by Houston's untimely death in April 1950 following a massive heart attack—only two years after *Norris*. Houston was just fifty-four.

---

[63] *Norris* is not cited in reviews of the history of *Brown v. Board of Education*, but it was in fact one of many that laid the groundwork for this historic case that finally ended segregation in public schools—or at least declared it unconstitutional.

He had lived long enough to hear the U.S. District Court's decision upholding the University of Maryland's right to bar a "colored girl" from attending its Nursing School—but not long enough to hear the U.S. Circuit Court of Appeals overrule this decision—Houston's last of many victories. If he'd lived, Charles Hamilton Houston most likely would have argued *"Brown v. Board of Education of Topeka" (1954)*, the fruition of all his work on this issue, rather than Thurgood Marshall.

It was fitting that at Dr. Houston's memorial service held in Baltimore, Donald Gaines Murray was called on to review Houston's achievements that started even before he graduated from Harvard University Law School in 1922, LL.B., cum laude. It was, after all, Dr. Charles Hamilton Houston and Thurgood Marshall who had enabled Murray to become the University of Maryland Law School's first black graduate.

•••

It was a year after the *Norris* case, in 1948, that the Sidney Hollander Foundation (discussed earlier) selected St. John's College in Annapolis for their annual award, "for integrating its student body." However, the school declined because it feared acceptance would "cause trouble." As a consequence, no award was given that year.[64]

It was two more years, in 1950, before the Foundation selected another education-related institution for an award. That year the Reverend Arthur A. North, S. J., dean of the evening and graduate divisions of Loyola College, accepted the award on the college's behalf "for accepting colored students in all areas of college life." In accepting the award, Rev. North noted this as an important trend that was occurring throughout the country.[65] Perhaps, but not always voluntarily.

Regarding the University of Maryland, the booklet, *Toward Equality* puts it rather succinctly:

> Even after Negroes had been admitted to Johns Hopkins University,[66] Loyola and St. John's College,[67] H.C. Byrd, then

---

[64] Moorland Spingarn, Box 50-5, folder 179.
[65] Moorland Spingarn, Box 50-5, folder 179 and box 50-1, folder 38.
[66] Hopkins Hospital hired its first black, Dr. Ralph J. Young, part-time, in 1947.
[67] It admitted its first residential student, Martin A. Dyer, in 1948

president of the University of Maryland, and the Board of
Regents resorted to subterfuge and untenable legal defenses
to avoid doing what was clearly inevitable. And in the end,
the Baltimore public schools had adopted a desegregation
policy before the University opened all its door to
Marylanders without regard to skin coloration.[68]

In the years from 1935 to 1953, Harry "Curley" Byrd,
President of the University of Maryland, agreed that funding
should be equalized between the white and black colleges, but
"vehemently opposed integrating the University's graduate and
professional schools."[69] In refusing to go beyond the court's
mandate regarding admission to its law school in *University of
Maryland v. Donald G. Murray*, Byrd found himself again in
court in 1950. That April the Maryland Court of Appeals
ordered the University to admit Esther McCready to its School
of Nursing in a case that had followed her refusal to go out of
state to Tennessee for her training. The U.S. Supreme Court
refused to review the decision.

Then in October of that same year Judge John T. Tucker,
in Baltimore's Supreme Court, declared that a "special
graduate course in sociology set up for one colored student in
Baltimore was not equivalent to admitting that student to the
regular University curriculum."[70] He forced the University to
open its Graduate School of Sociology to Parren J. Mitchell
who became the first black student admitted to the College
Park Campus (the Law School was in Baltimore). Mitchell later
became the first black U.S. Congressman from Maryland.

Then, out of defenses, the University, early in 1951,
signed a "consent decree" that allowed Hiram T. Whittle to
enter the School of Engineering, and thus become the first
black undergraduate at College Park and the first to live in a
college dormitory. Finally, in April 1951, the University opened
its graduate schools in Baltimore to blacks, but it did not open
its undergraduate courses to blacks until after the Supreme
Court in 1954 declared segregated education unconstitutional.
Ironically, most of the 1950 cases were pursued by attorney

---

[68] *Toward Equality*, p. 51
[69] *Poderesky v. Kirwin, President of Univ. of Md.* 838 F. Supp.
1075; 1993 U.S. Dist. LEXIS 19493
[70] *Toward Equality*, pp. 52-53

Donald G. Murphy, the first black admitted to any part of the University (the Law School).

By 1954, Dr. Wilson H. Elkins had succeeded Byrd as President. He stated: "There will be no discrimination whatsoever." The out-of-state scholarships were ended and in the fall four blacks enrolled as undergraduates.[71] However, discrimination did not end, especially at the University's main campus in College Park (UMCP); it simply took on less blatant forms. In Poderesky v. Kirwin, President of Univ. of Md., in an attempt to justify the continuation of its Banneker Program, aimed at attracting blacks to the campus, the university itself recounts not only its earlier resistance to integration, but also its deliberate undercutting of its supposed integration plans. Some examples of UMCP's history of continued discrimination it offered the court in 1993:

> In 1963, a faculty committee refused to allow students to form an on-campus chapter of the Congress for Racial Equality. The following year the university discouraged Martin Luther King, Jr. from speaking on campus, and, that same year, the Dean of Student Life forbade campus chaplains from participating in civil rights activities. ...[However], despite its worries about the effect that Dr. King's presence on campus might have, [it] permitted George Wallace to speak a the school in 1964, ...[attracting] the largest crowd in the history of the University.
>
> As late as 1969 its Board of Trustees reported, "it is only recently that formerly white colleges [have] made more than perfunctory efforts at other race recruitment."
>
> Off-campus housing was completely segregated and when an integrated dormitory was established for a summer "citizenship" program in 1966, the Ku Klux Klan marched in protest....It is not surprising the black student enrollment stayed below 1% of the undergraduate population from 1954 until the end of the 1960s....The administration refused t establish a separate office of minority recruitment and provided only partial funding for the recently created Equal Opportunity Recruitment Program with the Admissions Office....Opposition towards minority recruitment existed at the highest levels of the University administration.

In 1968, the U S. Department of Health, Education and

---

[71] *Toward Equality*, pp. 53

Welfare's Office of Civil Rights (OCR) began pressuring the state of Maryland to integrate its institutions of higher learning. But it was not until 1985 when UMCP submitted a *fifth* compliance plan that the OCR was satisfied that the university was actually attempting to integrate its campus. It was then that the university had introduced the Benjamin Banneker Scholarship Program as their most important recruitment tool.

The law suit, *Poderesky v. Kirwin, President of Univ. of Md.*, charging that the Banneker Program, aimed exclusively at blacks, was unconstitutional, had been initiated by an Hispanic student after he had been denied a Banneker scholarship. After a *very* lengthy exploration of all the arguments on both sides, the United States District Judge, Frederick Motz, on November 18, 1993, ruled in favor of the University, allowing the Banneker Program to continue.

"Poly A" and "Brown"[72]

If the colleges and professional schools were beginning to open up, as had been suggested by Reverend North at Loyola, whether by court order or voluntarily, perhaps it was time for the NAACP to tackle the next education level as intended in their master plan to end school segregation. In any event, Baltimore was ready for that move and in 1952—two years before *Brown v. Board of Education*—presented the NAACP with a high school case that came to be referred to as "Poly A". It came at a time when Baltimore, then the sixth largest city in the nation, still had

> segregated parks, drinking fountains, restaurants and restrooms as well as schools. Interracial marriages were against the law; black and white student athletes were not allowed to mix on the playing field....The telephone company, the Fire Department and the gas company, for the first time, had agreed to hire a few black employees, but they were an exception. The Police Department had a few black patrolmen, but they all walked beats and were not assigned to patrol cars.[73]

The Polytechnic Institute, for white boys, was one of two manual training schools opened by the city in 1892, supposedly with equal offerings, but after only one year, the city dropped mechanical engineering from Colored Manual's curriculum, and eliminated its preparatory department. A change of name to Colored Polytechnic in 1898, as previously noted, did little to bring it to the level of quality education found at the white Poly, nor did it help when it was merged with the Colored High School in 1901.

In the meantime, the Polytechnic Institute became a four year high school offering a unique, widely acclaimed "A" course, triggering the "Poly A" case that was important to Baltimore, despite the fact it would be argued on the "separate and equal" doctrine, at a time when the national NAACP had

---

[72] *Brown v. Board of Education of Topeka et al,* 74 SCT 686 or 347 US 483 (5/17/1954) and 75 SCT 753 or 349 US 294 (5/31/1955)
[73] "Breaking the Color Barrier at Poly in 1952," Sandra Crockett, *Sun,* 11/27/88.

decided to abandon that doctrine in favor of litigation directed at the abolishment of segregation altogether.

The case began to take shape on June 16, 1952 when representatives from the Americans for Democratic Action, the NAACP, and the Council for Human Rights met in the offices of the Urban League's director, Furman L. Templeton. That day they formed the Coordinated Committee on Poly Admission—and agreed to keep all their negotiations from becoming public—which, rather surprisingly, they were able to do even as others became involved.

Their intention was to end segregation at the fifty year old prestigious public high school, the Polytechnic Institute, that offered *white boys*, who could meet its strict entrance requirements, a four year "A" curriculum that included specialized pre-engineering courses. Its graduates who went on to accredited colleges of engineering were usually admitted as second year students. Needless to say there was no "equal" high school for black boys.

One of the first tasks undertaken by the new Committee was to find out the law. They found that on the state level segregation was a "policy" rather than mandated by law. The City Code[74] was less specific. It obligated Baltimore's Board of School Commissioners "to organize separate schools for colored children and to establish as many schools for the education of the colored children of Baltimore city as may, in the judgment of such Board, be necessary." The Committee objected to this wording as leaving too much discretion to the School Board. Under its terms they were free to decide against establishing separate facilities as unwise and to choose instead to admit the applicants.[75]

The most difficult task faced by the Committee was identifying a number of black boys entering ninth grade who would both qualify and be interested in breaking the color barrier and attending Polytech. After teachers and counselors helped locate sixteen potential candidates, meetings were held with them and their parents. Their names were then sent to the Superintendent of Schools who worked with the committee

[74] *City Code*, 1950, Article 32, Sec. 22, p. 1074.
[75] See Templeton, p28.

in assuring that the prospective students fulfilled all the application requirements. By July 10 when the School Board held its last meeting for the summer, the Poly Committee had ready for them the names of ten students who had been deemed fully qualified. Board members were divided in their response and postponed a decision until after they received an opinion from the City Solicitor.

Meanwhile, the Committee garnered the support of Governor Theodore McKeldin and Baltimore Mayor Thomas D'Alesandro, Jr. for admission of the black students to Polytech, and the School Board laid out an alternative plan to establish at Douglass High a course equal to that at Polytech.

In August, the City Solicitor referred the Board to the 1935 *Murray* v. *University of Maryland Law School* case and the subsequent Supreme Court decision, and gave an opinion that declared "equal" outweighed "separate." Templeton quotes his opinion:[76]

> It seems to me that the only real question before the School Board is whether the proposed curriculum in one of the Negro schools which has been planned and set up by the staff, will be substantially equal to the Polytechnic "A" Course. If it will be substantially equal, then under the City Code we must continue the policy of separate schools. If it will not be substantially equal to the Polytechnic "A' Course, then under the Constitution of the United States we must admit the boys to the Polytechnic "A" Course, or abolish that curriculum.

This, therefore, was the issue before the School Board when it met on September 2, 1952. For the first time on August 22, the secrecy maintained until then was broken when the newspapers published an announcement from the School Board that they were holding a special open meeting to consider the issue. As a consequence, the room was packed as the Board, as was their custom, sat around a table listening to at least ten people who spoke to the issue.

Dr. Templeton, head of the Urban League, spoke first, giving some of the history of Polytech and its admission standards, and then introduced the League's attorney,

---

[76] See Templeton, p. 25.

Marshall Levin (later a judge). Levin reviewed a number of the Supreme Court decisions regarding the education of blacks and their relevance to the proposed integration of Poly. He also questioned the School Board's ability to guarantee that the $78,000 needed as a minimum amount to establish the separate curriculum at Douglass would be forthcoming.[77]

The final speaker was Thurgood Marshall, then general counsel for the NAACP, who also stressed the legal aspects of the case, echoing arguments he would soon present to the U.S. Supreme Court in the *Brown v. Board of Education* case. He noted the psychological effects of segregation, and emphasized that it was impossible to replicate the "fifty-years of well-trained know-how" offered by Polytech.[78]

Speaking between these two, also on behalf of admission of the black boys, were Robert Roy, assistant dean of Johns Hopkins University School of Engineering, Percy Bond, Director of Admissions and Placements at Morgan State college, William Lemmel, Superintendent of Schools, Dr. Houston Jackson, the black Assistant Superintendent, head of the "Division of Colored Schools," and William Rogers, Chairman of the State Commission on Interracial Problems and Relations. There were only two rather tentative arguments made in favor of a new program at Douglass: someone read a prepared statement from the Polytech PTA and a representative of the Alumni Association of Polytech testified.

The School Board then went into executive session to vote on whether they believed the courses offered by Douglass would be equal. The vote was five to three that it would not; the Board President, Roszel Thomsen, declaring he would have voted with the majority if his vote had been needed to break a tie. Walter Sondheim, Jr., who would succeed Thomsen as President of the Board, announced the Board's decision that the Negro students who had applied would be admitted.

Long a proponent of integration, Sondheim called the decision "a fine example of the Baltimore spirit." [79] Most of the Board members had shown their liberal bent, willing to consider integration, but not in a position to overthrow the

---

[77] See Templeton, p. 26 and Thomsen, p. 237
[78] See Templeton, p. 27 and Thomsen, p. 238
[79] See Banks, p. 33

existing law and ask for across-the-board integration of the schools. However, given the close vote in the Poly case and the Board's timidity in integrating *any* other school, Glazer may be giving the board, collectively, a bit more credit than they deserved. He wrote in a recent article appearing in the *City Paper*:

> A more hidebound board, one that viewed race in a different light could have easily claimed that a Douglass High "A" course would be equal and left it at that, maintaining that the black school system was equal despite the hand-me-down books, antiquated equipment and decaying infrastructure. This was the established view...but the board took advantage of an opportunity to upend the established view, and took a significant first step toward elevating Baltimore's second class citizens to first class students.[80]

In an interview with this writer on August 20, 1997, Marshall Levin had this to say about his appearance at the hearing:

> It was a particularly significant case for me because of the ruling by the Board coming as it did before the Brown case, and the fact that Thurgood Marshall was there—even though he wasn't that great despite his greater experience than me.

In a retrospective article, Judge Roszel Thomsen had this to say of Mr. DeHuff, then principal of Polytech:

> [He] handled the matter very wisely. A day or so before classes started, he called to his office the leaders of the school, including the class presidents and captains of the athletic teams, and assigned one of them to each of the incoming boys, to see that they were integrated promptly and properly into the student body. They were, and thereby Baltimore was able to implement [without going to court] its own landmark decision a year and a half before the decision in *Brown v. Board*.[81]

Students interviewed many years later did not agree that things had gone quite so smoothly as Judge Thomsen had implied. However, they did credit the principal, Wilmer

---

[80] Aaron M. Glazer, "Course Correction," *City Paper*, 9/5/2001.
[81] Thomsen, p. 238.

DeHuff, who initially opposed the entry of blacks to Poly, for seeming "to go out of his way to make the black youngsters feel welcome." It was, undoubtedly, an easier task at Poly than it would have been at any neighborhood school, because Poly drew its students from all over the city, its student body typically representing different ethnicities, the poor, middle-class and rich.[82]

In 1988, and again in 2001, some of the students shared their memories:

> Albert Hawkins, Jr.: "It was a brain-and psyche-crushing experience. I am damn near 50 years old and getting through those four years it still the hardest goddam thing that I have ever done." After a stint in the Peace Corps, he went on to become a corporate vice president for an Arizona computer company.

> Everett Sherman: He recalls at age thirteen walking from an all black world into a sea of 2,800 white faces. But he found only a few "outwardly hostile." What puzzled him most were the ones that "treated me one way in school, but outside of school, they didn't even know me." He graduated from Morgan and worked as a network project manager in Reston, Virginia.

> Robert Young was, perhaps, the least fazed by the experience. Unlike the others, he had traveled with his parents who worked for the government and he lived in an integrated neighborhood. "I didn't understand what all the hubbub was about. My parents taught me never to worry about what people call you. Only to worry about how you react." He became an IBM executive in Bethesda.

> A number of the students recalled that Edward Savage, one of the first black students, used the boxing ring to "fight his way through four years of high school." Boxing was promoted by the school as a way for students to settle arguments. Savage became a draftsman for the city and later a successful engineering designer for a Baltimore firm. He died in 1986 of a stroke.

> Milton Cornish, Jr. recalls that it was not until reading Sandra Crockett's 1988 article that he realized he wasn't the

---

[82] Quotes by next four are from "Breaking the Color Barrier at Poly in 1952," Sandra Crockett, *Sun*, 11/27/88. Other information can be found in article by Aaron M. Glazer, "Course Correction," *City Paper*, 9/5/2001.

only black who'd found it tough going at Polytech. "I discovered I wasn't the only one who went home and cried at night. We not only had to bear the burden of trying to succeed in a white world; we also carried the hopes and aspirations of our race. That's awfully tough to do when you're fourteen." He went on to become an emergency management specialist for the Army Corps of Engineers. Three of his children became engineers, one after earning a Poly diploma in 1976 with the school's first female graduates.[83]

Carl Clark received a Ph.D. in physics from the University of South Carolina and taught for forty years, the last five at Morgan.

Bowler concluded his account of the Poly case in the *Sun* by noting that by 1997 Poly had "turned out numerous accomplished black students since its integration;" three-quarters of its students then African-American.[84] By 2001, Glazer reports that Poly's student population now numbers 1,184, 72% black, and that its "A" course is still regarded as one of the best engineering preparatory programs in the nation.[85]

•••

Perhaps encouraged by the successful integration of Polytech, the Maryland State Teachers Association removed the word "white" from its constitution in 1952, allowing the admission of black teachers to full membership for the first time. However, while Polytech was a success in itself, and perhaps helped prepare the city for the *Brown* decision that came two years later, its situation was regarded as "unique" and did not lead to desegregation of any other public school, despite efforts by the NAACP, black ministers and concerned citizens to extend its scope.

The NAACP's attorney, Juanita Jackson Mitchell, petitioned the school superintendent and the Board of School Commissioners for admission of twenty-four blacks girls to the Advanced College Preparatory Program at the all-girls, all-

---

[83] Mike Bowler, "Breaching the Race Barrier at Poly", *Sun*, 4/27/97
[84] These quotes and those following are also from the Mike Bowler article, *Sun*, 4/27/97.
[85] Aaron M. Glazer, "Course Correction," *City Paper*, 9/5/2001, p. 21.

white Western High School. This petition too was supported by a large number of "experts" and community people but it was denied. The Board contended in this case that the girls could get an advanced academic program at the all-black Douglass High School.[86]

Efforts to enroll four black students in the printing program at the all-white Mergenthaler Vocational High School were also unsuccessful. However, Superintendent John H. Fischer did respond by instructing his staff to proceed at once to establish "a substantially equal" printing program in a black vocational high school that would include equal equipment and equally qualified teachers. Also, all-black Dunbar High was the recipient of a printing program for the current semester, and a regular printing program was added to the projected Carver Vocational-Technical High School. But Mergenthaler remained all-white.

The School Board, all white except for one black physician, Dr. Bernard Harris, clearly was not ready, so soon after Polytech, to again breach the wall of segregation in Baltimore.

•••

Despite this reticence on the part of the Baltimore School Board to extend its decision to admit blacks to other schools than Polytech, the fact integration had been accomplished there with so little fanfare, and the fact that the School Superintendent, William Lemmel, had already taken a number of steps toward integration with teachers and administrators, negates any surprise one might have felt to learn of the city's School Board's quick and positive response to the Supreme Court ruling in *Brown v. Board of Education* that school segregation was unconstitutional. On Monday, May 17, 1954, the court had unequivocally ruled that in the field of public education the doctrine of "separate by equal" had no place and that separate educational facilities were inherently unequal.[87]

Two key board members, Walter Sondheim, Jr. and Eli Frank, heard of the ruling while they were at a luncheon at the Sheraton Belvedere. A reporter tapped Sondheim on the

---

[86] See Banks, pp. 35-37 for information regarding this case and that of the black vocational high school

[87] *Brown v. Board of Education*, 347 U.S. 483.

shoulder and handed him a slip of paper with a scrawled message informing him of the Supreme Court's decision. Three days later, on May 20, he became President of the Baltimore City School Board; on May 26 he was sworn in; and on June 10 "we desegregated the schools," Sondheim recalled during an interview.[88] As reported by the U.S. Civil Rights Commission in 1961, Baltimore had become the only southern city to have complied with Brown.[89]

In contrast, the separate State School Board accepted the "wait and see" opinion of the State Attorney General, Edward B. Rollins. His opinion was the exact opposite to that of the City Solicitor, who had earlier advised the Baltimore School Board that no state law required segregation of the schools; rather segregation was a matter of local custom. Rollins advised the State School Board that state law *required* segregation, and therefore they could not move forward with integration until the decision of the Supreme Court became final "or an effective date is set by the Supreme Court."[90]

The year's delay by the court in making that ruling, and its ambiguous mandates that school systems make "a prompt and reasonable start toward ending separate schools" and then proceed "with all deliberate speed" have been severely criticized in recent years as the cause of much of the turmoil that surrounded school desegregation in the years that followed. Like many other jurisdictions throughout the country, Maryland's counties were relieved that the final decree of the Supreme Court on May 31, 1955 did not demand immediate compliance. All of Maryland's public schools still were not integrated as late as 1959.

As suggested, Baltimore City did not wait. Unlike the State's Attorney General, Baltimore's City Solicitor advised its School Board that in light of the Supreme Court's decision that separate schools were inherently unequal, the present City Code deprived blacks of equal protection under the 14th Amendment, and, therefore, the city had to desegregate its

---

[88] The incident recounted by Goldstein, who interviewed Sondheim on 3/11/96.

[89] See Bowler, p. 7

[90] See Grant, p. 278.

schools. Hence, at the School Board's June 1, 1954 meeting, with little debate, it was agreed that the city's schools should open on September 7, 1954 on a non-segregated basis. Baltimore had become not only the only Southern city to desegregate its schools but the first segregated school system in the country to approve a plan to integrate.[91]

The school superintendent had immediately drawn up policies in regard to teacher assignments, pupil admission and transfers and school districting.[92] On July 14, Dr. John H. Fischer met with Baltimore's teachers and told them of the plans for integration. (Fischer had replaced Lemmel as Superintendent of Schools in February 1953 after Lemmel was fatally stricken by a heart attack while addressing a state senate committee urging a more generous salary schedule for teachers.)

In the fall of 1954, Baltimore had 143,690 pupils, 55,878 of them black (almost 39%)— only about 1,800 black children took advantage of the "free choice" policy adopted by the city and entered formerly all-white schools.

Students Walk Out at Southern High, September 31, 1954
Courtesy of Mike Waller, publisher, *Baltimore Sun*

---

[91] See Orser, p. 71.
[92] See Grant, p. 280

It took about four weeks for white parents opposed to the integration to organize and start trouble: orchestrating a "Three Day Strike" at Southern High, to begin on Thursday, September 30, 1954.[93]

Mothers Picket School #34, Carey & Washingon, September 30, 1954
Courtesy of Mike Waller, Publisher, *Baltimore Sun*

There were, at the start of the protests, thirty-nine black children at Southern out of a total of 1,788. Black parents kept their children at home; white students spread across the city urging other students to join their strike. About eight hundred whites gathered outside Southern carrying signs such as "Negroes Not Allowed," "Keep Southern White." Gregory wrote:[94]

> The disorders culminated in a mass march on City Hall from Southern High School by about two thousand whites on October 4. The crowd was made up largely of those of about high school age. The police, under the firm guidance of mayor Thomas D'Alesandro and Police Commissioner Beverly

---

[93] See Banks, pp. 47-49 and Gregory, pp. 367-369
[94] Gregory, p. 369

Ober, had little trouble containing and dispersing the crowds.

Mayor D'Alesandro, Jr. urged citizens to keep "cool heads and calm consideration." The School Board, Superintendent Fischer, his staff, the press, civic groups, ministers and other community groups all came out in opposition to this open resistance to desegregation; the picketing and strike, the last major incident, ended in a matter of days.

The Hollander Foundation gave its 1954 award to Superintendent Fischer that year for his "outstanding contribution toward the enforcement of equal rights and opportunities for Negroes in Maryland." In his acceptance speech, Fisher credited the smooth road to integration to "the common consent of the overwhelming majority of the people of Baltimore that all of our children should be educated free of any barriers based on race."

Honorable mention went to John H. Schwatka, Principal of Southern High School, for his "resolution, determination, and positive action during the 'disturbances last fall' when the schools were undergoing integration in accord with the Supreme Court's decision." In his acceptance, Schwatka thanked the clergy, police department, press, radio and television stations.

Fischer turned over his $250 award money to the William H. Lemmel Memorial Scholarship Fund, which had been established after his sudden death, dedicated to "bringing more good teachers to our classrooms."[95]

•••

Things would not, however, continue to go as smoothly as anticipated by all those praising Baltimore's success in having quickly and peaceably integrated its schools. The policy of "free choice" resulted in the first year in only about three percent of the black children going to formerly all-white schools; about twenty white children in formerly all Negro elementary schools, none at the higher levels. The distribution of teachers wasn't much better; "during the 1955-56 school year, there were eighty-one Negroes teaching in formerly all-

---

[95] Moorland Spingarn, Box 50-3, folder 79 (A staff newsletter published by the Baltimore Public Schools, 6/3/1955)

white secondary schools,...twenty-six in formerly white elementary schools."

There was one white teacher in a formerly black secondary school, none in the formerly black elementary schools.[96] In 1963, fifty three of the city's 189 schools still had all white faculties, and sixty-seven schools had faculties that were all-black.[97]

As Sherry Olson wrote in her history of Baltimore:

> [The School Board's "freedom of choice" plan] left to principals the authority to permit or refuse transfers between schools. It located new high schools in the outer fringes of the city. Families who could afford it moved in response. From 1954 to 1970, white children withdrew from the city schools at the rate of ten thousand a year to enter schools in the suburban counties....By 1958, half the children in the city schools were black; in 1978, two-thirds.[98]

One white teacher, Eunice Clemens, stated that in one year, from 1959 to 1960, her elementary school's class changed from one with two blacks to one that was almost all-black. The Supreme Court had ended legal segregation, but "residential segregation, the reluctance to leave friends and relatives in neighborhood schools, and the cost of transportation," as well as the "out migration of whites" all "contributed to the continuing widespread segregation."[99]

In 1959, after twenty-nine years in various positions in the Baltimore school system, six as Superintendent, Dr. John H. Fischer left Baltimore to become Dean of the Teacher's College at Columbia University in New York. He told Samuel Banks in a personal interview on September 12, 1975, while Banks was writing his Ph.D. thesis, that his major regret was the city's inability to achieve a truly integrated community.[100] Clearly he had perceived the failure of Baltimore's policies,

---

[96] These figures are found in article by Fleming, Associate Professor of Political Science, Morgan State College.
[97] See Bowler, p. 7.
[98] Olson, pp. 369-370
[99] Reported in Orser, p. 153.
[100] See Banks, pp. 50-52.

however well-intentioned they may have been.

•••

There was a certain irony in Fischer's decision to accept a position at Columbia's Teacher's College at this critical juncture in Baltimore's efforts to integrate its schools. That's where many of Baltimore's black teachers had obtained their degrees when Maryland's teacher-training colleges had refused them admission. And, perhaps as a consequence, explains why the study of education in Baltimore for the *Community Self-Survey of Inter-Group Relations* found that *in the years between 1950 and 1952, more black teachers than white teachers had academic degrees as well as more teaching experience.*[101]

Ironically, it was Maryland's determination to keep its schools segregated that made this possible. Beginning in the early 1930s, the state began to provide "Out-of-State Scholarships" for blacks rather than integrate its professional schools, ending the program only after *Brown* mandated their integration. The scholarship program continued until 1955, despite a court's rejection of the University of Maryland Law School's argument, as early as 1935, that the scholarships satisfied the law's mandate to provide "separate and equal" education for those seeking a law degree.[102]

Apparently their use as a substitute for state-provided teacher education was not contested. In an interview years later, one of the recipients, Rebecca Carroll, called the program "silly" and "stupid," adding, "We were pained and angered that we couldn't go to school in our own state, but we also knew this was something we could take advantage of." And hundreds of Maryland's black teachers did.

At Maryland tax-payer's expense, they obtained Masters and Doctorates not only from Columbia in New York, but also from such notable institutions as the University of Chicago,

---

[101] As previously noted, this was not the first time that this finding had surprised those looking at teacher qualifications. The Flexner Report in 1916 had also found black teacher qualifications at least equal, often better, than those of whites.

[102] The *Murray v. Univ. of MD* case.

New York University, Oberlin in Ohio, Howard University in Washington, D.C., the University of Pennsylvania, the University of California, Boston University, and Temple University in Philadelphia.[103]

Columbia and New York University, however, were the colleges of choice for the majority, because of their proximity. Scholarships, which varied in amount from year to year, were never enough to allow teachers pursing a degree to quit their jobs and study full-time; not even enough to cover the cost of hotel stays and restaurant meals. So on weekends and during the summer, teachers drove or took an early-morning train to New York, attended classes, and returned late at night. Most had relatives or friends with whom they could stay if overnight was essential.

The list of Baltimoreans who took advantage of these Out-of-State Scholarships is impressive. To name a few: Samuel H. Wilson Jr., founder of Arena Players; Lena K. Lee, a longtime principal who became a lawyer and state delegate; Rebecca Carroll, who retired as a deputy city superintendent in 1981; Alice Rusk, long the chief librarian for city schools; and Wilbur G. Valentine, who served, ironically, on the University of Maryland Board of Regents from 1977 to 1982.

> To win a scholarship, students had to possess the 'qualities of health, character, ability and preparatory education required for admission to the University of Maryland' By law, the state reimbursed scholarship winners the tuition and expenses they would have paid at College Park....By 1949, the scholarship pool had grown to $100,000, supporting 400 students.

This program collapsed with the U.S. Supreme Court's *Brown* decision in 1954, but another ruling four decades later adds a touch of irony to the whole issue of black-white education experiences. The U.S. Court of Appeals for the 4th Circuit ruled that the Banneker Scholarship program at the University of Maryland, designed to help attract black students to its main College Park campus, discriminated

---

[103] Information and quotes about "Out of State Scholarships" are from article by Mike Bowler, "Gifted, Black—They were Paid to Study Elsewhere," *Baltimore Sun*, 8/14/95.

unlawfully against those who failed to qualify because they were not black. In refusing to hear the case, the U.S. Supreme Court, in essence, upheld the decision.[104]

The two studies, one in 1916 and one in 1955, that found black teachers at least as qualified as the white teachers, often better, should have put to rest the still commonly held perception that black students suffered by being taught by black teachers. More likely black students suffered in comparison to their white counterparts because of factors the white power structure preferred to ignore—the poverty environment from which the majority came, the decrepit school buildings they were forced to attend, the absence of equipment and supplies their teachers needed, and on and on.

•••

Only public schools were affected by the *Brown* decision, but it wasn't always clear whether that included such as Maryland's four training schools for delinquent boys and girls. However, in 1961, the Maryland Court of Appeals ruled that they were educational institutions and hence subject to the Supreme Court ruling, and so were integrated.[105] Juanita Mitchell (attorney with local NAACP) and Jack Greenberg (attorney from national NAACP), among others, were counsel for appellees in this case. Such sharing in cases, beginning in 1949, led Greenberg to note after Mitchell died in 1993:

> Going to court with Juanita was an intimidating task for me but more so for our opponents and the judge. She argued with a passion that was hard to deny. It was rumored that some judges ruled in her favor simply because they preferred not to respond to the power of her arguments and personality.[106]

Following soon after the courts' decision regarding the

---

[104] *Podberesky v. Kirwin* (U of MD president) 956 Fed. 2d. 52 (1992) and *Kirwin v. Podberesky*, 514 U.S. 1128 (1995)

[105] *State Board of Public Welfare et al. V. Myers, Minor, etc.* 224 Md. 246; 167 /a. 2d 765; 1961 Md. LEXIS 484. Although this case applied, directly, only to the Boys Training School, clearly it affected them all; the state would hardly have wanted to litigate each one separately.

[106] Greenberg, "In Memoriam"

state training schools, the Order of the Sisters of the House of Good Shepherd integrated their two institutions for delinquent girls in Baltimore.[107]

Even though the Supreme Court decision did not directly affect city's private schools, most in fact responded. The Catholic schools, some of which had always been integrated, took steps along with the city to make sure they were all integrated. Park School, which had already decided to integrate, immediately stated that all its grades would be open to blacks. McDonogh and Friends Schools stated they would integrate theirs one grade a year—which, of course, meant it would take twelve years for them to be fully integrated. Gilman did not admit its first student until the fall of 1965. We can thank Ruth Goldstein, a Park School student, for an account of the experience of two of these private schools, Park and Gilman, when they integrated.[108]

•••

By the time the *Brown* decision came down in May 1954, Park had already decided to integrate, but did not admit its first student until the Fall of 1954, and then only one—Mary Sue Welcome, daughter of Dr. and Mrs. Henry Welcome, a bright youngster from a well-off family living in Liberty Heights, within walking distance of the school. The twelve-year-old was not even made aware of the fact that she was to be the first black at Park School.

Park School had been established in 1912 at a time when no other private school would admit Jews. Reflecting the views of its wealthy and liberal Jewish founders, from the beginning, Park welcomed both Jews and non-Jews as students, and was dedicated to "progressive education and freedom from all political influence."[109] It did not even consider the admission of blacks. However, as early as 1945, Park students were

---

[107] 1961 Supplement to *Toward Equality*.

[108] From Goldstein, Ruth, a research paper done for her Advance Placement "C" course at Park School Curiously, Park School denied her access to their archives.

[109] Goldstein, from *Park School: A seventy-five Year History*, Jean Sharpless 6/62

ready to break with tradition. That year two Park School seniors participated in a two-day integrated conference held by the Baltimore Inter-racial Fellowship.

Further, even before 1950, Park, unlike Baltimore's other private schools, had participated in interscholastic sports, including basketball, with Dunbar, the black public high school—and members of the two teams even ate together in their respective cafeterias after games. This was such an affront to "acceptable" behavior that Park came near to being expelled from the private school athletic league.[110]

In 1953, the student council petitioned the Board of Trustees and Headmaster, Hans Froelicher, for desegregation of the school. Despite the coldness of the administration's response, they learned that the Board and Headmaster, had already begun working on a plan for desegregation but did not want "interference" by the students, nor did they want "news of their decision to leak out until they were prepared to announce it, backed by their gathered reasoning." The odd denial by Park of access to the school's archives makes it impossible to know more of what that reasoning.

In any case, it was the following Fall that Mary Sue Welcome entered seventh grade at Park School. In an interview with Goldstein in 1995, she stated her chief problem while there "developed from the change in environment: the difference between her all-black public school and an all-white private school....She describes how some students arrived at school in chauffeured cars, while she arrived on foot. Many of the girls wore designer clothes, while her father would never dream of spending that much money on a blouse or skirt." Goldstein quotes Mary Sue:

> My classmates' parents owned the Hecht Company, Stewart's, Gutman's, Weiss Cadillac and their whole culture was entirely different. I had parents who...my father was a doctor, but he was not one who showered material things. He did not believe in that. I went into an environment where materialism was...was everything.

---

[110] Goldstein does not offer an explanation as to why they were not. Perhaps that would have been revealed had she been allowed access to the school's archives.

Mary Sue spent four years at Park, but left at the end of her Sophomore year. Goldstein writes:

> She never felt comfortable in the all-white environment even though she had found a life-long friend while playing field hockey and even though no one ever said or acted cruel or rude to her. Many factors contributed to her departure, among them, the Park Schools' relocation to its Brooklandville campus.
>
> The commute would have been an effort and unlike the other students she did not have a car. She had also become "brattish," a habit she believes she picked up from Park. Her mother was deeply into politics while her father traveled a great deal. In the end, her parents resolved to send her to a boarding school where she would find a more regulated environment.

Park School, which had taken its name from its location near Druid Hill Park, had been within walking distance of the Liberty Heights area where the Welcome's lived, but in the year following Mary Sue's departure, would open at its more exclusive Brooklandville campus in Baltimore County, north of the city. Also in 1958, the same year Mary Sue left Park, her mother, Verda Welcome, was elected to the state legislature. In 1963, she was elected to the state Senate.

Two years before Mary Sue Welcome left Park, the school had finally in 1956 enrolled another black student, Billie Garner Brown. She became the first black to *graduate* from Park. Billie had started the academic year at Pimlico Junior High School, but was removed by her mother after she was convinced that it's all-white faculty was discriminating against her intelligent, hardworking daughter. Billlie was consistently receiving "D"s or "F"s on papers "her mother, who held a Master's degree in English from Columbia University," had scrupulously proof-read. As Goldstein explains:[111]

> One day the two decided to try an experiment. Her mother wrote the book report. Sure enough, the report came back with a large, looping red "D" scrawled on the front page. Mrs. Garner marched into the school and demanded to speak with the English teacher. She unleashed her disgust at

---

[111] Based on interview by Goldstein of Billie on 12/30/95

the teacher whose actions she considered to be disrespectful, disgusting, and altogether absurd. Within the next several day Mrs. Garner had enrolled her daughter at Park.

The shock of Park for Billie was not her race, but the behavior of the other students—their lack of discipline, their feet up on desks, chairs, and out the window, and "they could run a substitute teacher out of the classroom in seconds." Billie called her first year at Park, "God awful." She felt surrounded by students who didn't know how to act or behave around her. On the rare occasion she was invited to one of their homes she was embarrassed to be served by a black employee.

It all seemed to get better after she met and became friends with an Israeli exchange student—also an outsider. She was Jewish, but unlike most of Park's students, orthodox. Shared Billie's reaction to the other students "liberal behavior."

Today, about 15% of Park's students are minority, the majority of those black, one or more in each of its grades from first through high school.

•••

It was over a decade after the *Brown* decision before Gilman School enrolled its first black student. Stuart Simms entered the tenth grade at Gilman in 1965 and graduated in 1968, along with three other black students.

The Simms family had never heard of Gilman when they began their search for a high school that offered a small student-to-teacher ratio and rigorous academic demands. A friend had suggested Gilman. To reach the school, Simms had to take a bus from his home in Govans, up York Road, and then walk the remainder of the way. And perhaps even more so than the black students at Park, Simms felt in his first year like he had entered a different world, all too conscious of the existing deep socio-economic differences between himself and the other students. It helped that his particular class happened to have those other blacks and also an Arab-American.

Stuart told Goldstein[112] he thought most of the people at the school, the faculty and others, were ready for the change. The school had always had a very high sports profile which

---

[112] Goldstein interviewed Simms on 12/26/95

brought them into contact with other schools, other neighborhoods, through wrestling, football, basketball and cross country.

> I was playing football and basketball. ...When we first went up to St. Paul's, it was ugly. The fans weren't pleasant. The other team initially was not pleasant either and I was surprised at that....St. Paul did not have any [blacks] at the time....I guess these situations were more significant for the school and the coaches and the team than for me...and probably for those that followed after me.
>
> [On the positive side], there was always support for me inside and outside the school, from classmates and family. ...The kinds of things that I bumped into were not isolated to Baltimore. They were the kinds of things the whole nation was being tested with at that time, issues that had similarities in the fight for public accommodations to fair housing. So, yes, I would run out on the field at St. Paul's in front of people who seemed like they were adults, but just did not act like they were.

A not uncommon phenomenon that still exists today: "At the same time that Stuart was feeling pressure from all white private schools, he also felt it from a predominantly black high school During a football game at Edmondson High, fans hollered and yelled at him. It was almost as though they felt by going to Gilman, he was a traitor."

Not all the teachers at Gilman were supportive. When discussing with one his plans for college, she told him he'd be lucky to graduate from Gilman. It would be great to know her reaction when he showed her acceptance letters from Brown, Yale and Dartmouth.

The school did initially lose several donors and several students, but most donors came back after a short time. Some had been concerned that by seeking out black applicants, Gilman would be increasing the pool of applicants without increasing the available slots, hence raising the level of competition. To allay this concern, the school increased the size of its upper school from approximately two hundred students to four hundred.

In an interview with the school's coach, Nicholas Schloeder, he seemed please to note that even though Gilman had been slow to integrate, when it did it acted "swiftly and sincerely to respond to race-inspired incidents, such as racial epithets written on school grounds.[113]

1968, the year Stuart Simms graduated from Gilman, was marked by the death of Martin Luther King on Thursday April 4 and the riots that followed. "The man who had so passionately advocated the way to equality through peace was now dead, [and] his message of nonviolence was [at least temporarily] suspended." Gilman held its usual morning chapel the next day, Friday. "The Headmaster, Ludlow Baldwin, gave a touching speech on the assassinated man who had become a martyr. As students filed their way into chapel, they were greeted by a white spray-painted sign: 'White America, Wake Up.' Whether written by a white or a black student, no one knows. But the sentiment appears to have been expressed correctly."[114]

---

[113] Interviewed by Goldstein, 1/8/96
[114] From Goldstein's interview with Nicholas Schloeder, 2/8/96

Fighting Against Resegregation

Regrettably, by 1961 it was clear that resegregation of the city's schools by race and income was fast occurring: school budgets had been cut, teachers were paid less than their county counterparts and many of those who now taught in the city schools were "provisional." [115] Over the decade after *Brown*, Baltimore had constructed fifty-two new schools, but thirty-two of them were in white neighborhoods. Approximately one thousand white students had left the Baltimore City Schools.[116] The city's free choice policy, selective districting[117] and busing were of especial concern to those in the city trying to maintain an integrated community. They had reason to doubt that the city sincerely wanted an integrated school system.

CORE and other groups did not sit idly by as they saw this happening. In September 1958, a march on Washington in support of integrated schools had attracted 12,000 black and white youth from all over the country, representing "schools, colleges, churches, labor unions, social clubs and settlement houses. Adult leaders and advisers for the youth march also came from all races, religions and professions." The *Sun,* on April 18, 1959, in noting the above, reported a second "Youth March for Integrated Schools:

> According to a spokesman for CORE, the march is intended to "protest the shameful roadblocks placed in the way of peaceful integration in so many sections of the South." The marchers also will urge the President and Congress to take prompt action for integrated schools.

---

[115] Olson, p. 370

[116] Found in Goldstein who credited *Maryland, A Middle Temperament,* p. 581, as source.

[117] In theory, schools were only "districted" when they became overcrowded, meaning that no one from outside the districted school area could choose to attend it (despite "free choice" policy), except for "health" or "public interest" reasons. However, children within the districted school area, were free to transfer to any non-districted school. This policy left a lot of lee-way to the decision makers, who were accused of manipulating their "districting" decisions to favor white neighborhood schools to the detriment of poor, mostly black neighborhoods.

Influencing school policies, however, proved far more difficult than had the fight for equal access to public accommodations.

A year later, in the fall of 1960, George B. Brain became Baltimore's 12th School superintendent, replacing Dr. Fischer who left to become Dean of Columbia University's Teacher's College. By then, Baltimore's school system had gone from 60% white in 1954 when it integrated to majority black— 87,634 black students and 82,588 white, a reflection of the exodus of whites to the suburbs. It was also an exodus, for the most part, of Baltimore's upper and middle classes, a fact that would deplete the city's schools of "interested parents" and the city of a substantial part of its tax-base. Superintendent Brain predicted, shortly after is arrival in Baltimore, that "by 1970, half of Baltimore's children would be 'socially deprived.' He was on the money...and money was leaving Baltimore."[118]

In 1961, a year after Brain's arrival in Baltimore from Washington state, Billie Bramhall, white, wife of a Johns Hopkins professor, was one of those whose community was still integrated, but whose neighborhood school had become virtually all-black. Billie led a group of parents down to the Superintendent's office to protest the fact their policy of bussing in black students to their community from more crowded schools elsewhere had simply accelerated the rate at which the community's white parents were transporting their children out.

Nothing had changed when, a year later, another white mother, Dorothy Sykes, complained to Superintendent George Brain (who had succeeded Dr. Fischer) after she was notified that her child's school was going on shifts. She contacted Edward Holmgren at Baltimore Neighborhoods, Inc. (BNI) seeking a lawyer to pursue a case against the Department of Education. He put the two women in touch with each other and with the attorney, Melvin Sykes (no relation), who agreed to counsel the informal group of black and white parents which Billie Bramhall and Dorothy Sykes had quickly put together.

These two intelligent and insightful women realized that their

---

[118] Bowler, p. 6. Also found at www.bcps.k12.md.us, "The Old Order to the New Order, 1957-1997" (Bowler reproduced verbatim without acknowledgement).

problem was part of "a general city-wide issue and decided to attack the general question of segregation and overcrowding in the whole school system."[119] They early-on interviewed Superintendent Brain at some length and gained his permission to access a huge amount of information from the school system data. They also were able to review the minutes of School Board meetings from 1954 to 1961, and the handbooks of administrative policy and procedure of the Department of Education. They talked to principals and teachers in the public school system, and to personnel of the U.S. Commission on Civil Rights (after reviewing its publications), the U.S. Office of Education (after studying publications of the National Education Association), and officials from the national and local branches of the NAACP, among others.

During the next several months, as they accumulated and assessed all this information, they exchanged a number of letters with Brain both to alert him to their findings and to make sure they had their facts right as pertained to the Baltimore Department of Education.

In February 1963 the parents' group felt ready to share their report, "Seven Years of Desegregation in the Baltimore Public Schools" with Superintendent Brain and the School Board President, Eli Frank, who had succeeded Walter Sondheim after the latter resigned to head the Baltimore Urban Renewal Commission. At a private meeting with them, Holmgren, from BNI, and Melvin Sykes, representing the parents, agreed to prepare copies of the report for all the Board members, and granted Brain and Frank until April to study the report and reply. In harsh words, the report accused the school system of "intentionally segregating schools and overcrowding Negro schools by

> (a) not building enough schools in the inner city. A look at the parents' group's working document on school building, riddled as it is with follow-up notations, is proof positive of their thoroughness. After each conclusion, there are notes, such as: "Billie: I'm going to try to document this with information I have been getting from Mort Hoppenfeld of Rouse & Co.," "Billie: depending on what we find," and "I also want another paragraph comparing our school construction program with several other cities showing similar school

---

[119] Crain, p. 73

populations and total patterns for the past twenty years";

(b) 'districting' white schools to keep Negroes out; and

(c) refusing to issue transfers to Negroes to permit them to attend predominantly white schools."[120]

Frank appointed an ad hoc committee of the School Board to respond to the report, and during the months of April and May, its members met several times with representatives of the school administration, as well as with representatives from BNI and the parents' group.

Quibbling over words and definitions, the board's ad hoc committee at first claimed "the report was not clear enough to comment on, that it showed no valid evidence of discrimination, and that its recommendation that the school system adopt a policy of 'forcing' integration would be of questionable legality."[121] Eventually they prepared a report for the School Board's June 6th meeting that accepted one of the parents group's demands—that they drop districting—but, in general, contended that all the parents' charges were unfounded.

The parents group, in order to respond to many of the ad hoc committee's complaints, worked day and night to complete a revision of their initial report. The finished product, titled "Eight Years of Desegregation in the Baltimore Public Schools: Fact and Law," was ready for the Board's June 6, 1963 meeting. Signed by twenty couples and/or individuals, in something over forty pages of statistical analysis and legal citations, it sought to delineate areas of agreement and to sharpen issues which were still in dispute, hoping to assist the Board in exercising its constitutional duties. Nonetheless, the Board unanimously adopted its ad hoc committee's report.

The parents' group was prepared to go to court, and the NAACP, which supported the group, was ready to begin demonstrations if the parents' negotiating tactic failed. Neither of these steps proved necessary. Further private meetings between board members, Superintendent Brain, Melvin Sykes, Billie Bramhall and a few others eventually led to a consensus

---

[120] Crain, p. 74 This first report by the Parents Committee is no longer available, replaced by the second, final report, "8 Years of Desegregation..." which was provided this writer along with some of the working documents.

[121] Crain, p. 74

in favor of the school administration taking actions that would meet the parent group's demands.

> By the end of the summer [of 1963], the school system had purchased enough school buses to transfer five thousand students and... the transfer policies were liberalized and all districting was eliminated, which also introduced Negroes into several previously all-white schools. Then, the board ...committed [itself] to drop "color-blindedness" and to establish a policy of integration....The sudden integration of previously all-white schools met with short-lived opposition.[122]

There is little doubt that the parent group's success was helped by the fact it included both black and white parents, by the thoroughness of its reports, by the group's willingness to keep negotiations private and not attempt to embarrass the School Board, by the elitist and fairly liberal composition of the School Board (many also were part of the Greater Baltimore Committee which sponsored BNI, which, in turn, supported the parents), and by the fact that a personal relationship already existed between the group's lawyer, Melvin Sykes, and the School Board President, Eli Frank, also a lawyer.

•••

On November 5, 1964, after a two-year study that involved an estimated 1,500 people, a Citizens School Advisory Committee that had been appointed by Supt. Brain in October 1962, presented him with a three volume, 530-page report, with 303 recommendations.

They were intended as a guide for the city's schools through 1975.[123] What is more than a little curious, is the fact that this on-going study by the Citizens Committee is *nowhere* referred to, by either side, during the time that the parent group was, simultaneously, examining school records, preparing their

---

[122] Crain, p. 76. In this statement Crain also asserted that all double-shifts were completely eliminated, but other accounts do not support this claim. (See Bowler) From personal experience, the writer knows that five full years later her son was on double shifts at Roland Park Jr. high school, not even an inner city school.

[123] Information and quotes regarding the Citizen Committee's report are from the *Sun*, 11/6/64, and four articles by George Rogers that appeared on consecutive days in the *Evening Sun*, 11/10 to 11/13/1964.

report, meeting with the Superintendent and School Board, and, finally, having its recommendations acted upon.

As might be expected in a list of 303 recommendations, there are many fine ones that, if acted on then, might have left a school system less in disarray than the one now found in Baltimore.

The report had looked squarely at the challenge faced in educating the disadvantaged youngsters of the inner city, and offered more than 50 recommendations directly aimed at overcoming their learning and environmental handicaps; they offered 34 others dealing with this in part; and 43 that touched it "lightly" on the problem. They saw these youngsters as "innocent victims of circumstance that trace back to generations of progenitors whose opportunities for economic and social development were minimal or non-existent."

Just a few observations and recommendations contained in the report::

(1) A course in "family life" that would help shape and nurture the total individual in all aspects—values and abilities. Perhaps naively, but interestingly, the report linked improved classroom behavior to a decline in street crime; an improvement in marriage education with a decline in illegitimacy and divorce; improved personal hygiene with a decrease in hospital and health costs.

(2) It surmised that "money alone would not solve the school's problems, but insufficient funds would prevent any solution. They went on to state that the city would need more money that the State legislatures would be willing to appropriate. Observing that democracy's future rests with education, the report concludes that "How we resolve this great social problem [need v. resources] may well prove American democracy's most crucial test. Education holds the promise of "prevention and possible cure of many of our critically urgent social problems—reducing relief and welfare roles, problems of the aged, crime and juvenile delinquency, and others."

(3) It pointed out that between 1954 and 1964 the number of classroom teachers rose from 4,550 to 6,349. But the number of provisional teachers—not fully qualified—had nearly tripled in the same period. It is interesting that in 2001, a Baltimore grassroots organization, ACORN, was responsible for a well-documented report that showed a correlation between poor school performance in today's

Baltimore schools with those that had a disproportionate
number of provisional teachers—and that it was the schools
with the neediest students who were staffed with the largest
numbers of provisional teachers.[124]

(4) It suggested allowing teachers to specialize, and,
instead of emphasizing smaller classrooms, do more re-
grouping of students for different purposes, and introduce
"independent study." They also stressed the need for greater
emphasis on English, written communication, and in depth
science courses.

It also pointed out the importance of school libraries to
supplement the public libraries. Those responsible for this
report almost certainly would have been shocked by the
recent closure of five branches of the Enoch Pratt Public
Library in the very neighborhoods that need them most. This
contrasts sharply with the practice in city's such as Chicago
which is building new libraries as a means of stabilizing and
renewing run-down neighborhoods. One can hardly help
thinking that a commitment by the powerful Greater
Baltimore Committee could have saved these branch libraries
when opposition to their closure by the *Sun* and by ACORN
could not.[125]

Before any of the recommendations could be acted on, Dr.
Brain left to head an education school at Washington State
University.[126] After a short interim tenure by Edwin Stein,
Laurence G. Paquin was appointed as Baltimore's next School
Superintendent in 1965. Why he ignored such a comprehensive
study of the school system is a mystery. No less so, the fact that
no one in any of the numerous departments of today's
Department of Education, contacted by this writer, had ever
heard of the report, or had the slightest interest in it—despite
the fact that "someone" made a brief reference to *a* report, as
Brain's "legacy," on their web site.

•••

Less than a month after Superintendent Paquin started
his job in 1965, he proclaimed that the school system was in a

---

[124] An overview of the study appeared in *City Paper*, May 2 and
May 16, 2001 and the *Sun*, May 3, 2001.
[125] See *Daily Record*, 7/19/2001, *Sun*, 4/3/2001 and a *Sun* Editorial
7/22/2001
[126] Bowler, p. 8

financial crisis, bemoaned the lack of an adequate tax base in the city, and expressed the need for more help from the federal and state governments. Dr. Paquin inherited the seventh largest school system in the nation with 190,000 students, 17,000 of them on "double shifts." Thirty percent of its schools dated from the 1880s.

That same year, the parents group prepared an eleven-page follow-up report to their original study, again making no reference to the Citizens School Advisory Committee's 3-volume report; nor is it mentioned when they subsequently met with Superintendent Paquin on December 15th. The follow-up report concluded

> that although segregation was rapidly abolished on June 10, 1954, a two-school system in practice continued in Baltimore City....following desegregation there continued the same pattern of initial choice of school, funneling into junior high schools and senior high schools, school construction designed to discourage integration and teacher assignment intended to conform to racial patterns....As a result, much of the present school system with some noteworthy exceptions is the old segregated system.

All hopes of creating/sustaining an integrated school system had become virtually impossible in light of the city's de facto segregated neighborhoods.

> [In March 1966], the Community Relations Commission reported that 75% of the city's elementary pupils and more than half of secondary students were in "virtually segregated" schools, while 90% of black teachers were in schools that were 90 to 95 percent black.[127]

•••

Billie Bramhall, who had headed the parent's group, was among the "group of influential citizens" invited by Mayor McKeldin to meet with him on June 3, 1966 to discuss "unfinished business to which we must address ourselves." The Task Force included an Education Committee, headed by Hans Froelicher (Headmaster at Park School and President of the Citizens Planning and Association) and Martin Jenkins (President

---

[127] Bowler, p. 9

of Morgan State College); and an Education sub-committee to deal with the public school system, headed by Billie.

A year later, in June 1967, the Education Committee submitted to the School Board a 12-page paper with a "Series of Recommendations on Integration and Quality Education in the Inner City." It's surprising that once again no reference is made to the 303 recommendations made in the Citizens School Advisory Committee's 3-volume report that had appeared less than three years earlier. The transmittal letter which accompanied the Mayor's copy of the report from Billie Bramhall's sub-committee, advised him that she would leave Baltimore that summer "because her husband's professional duties will be, from now on, in Pittsburgh." The letter continued:

> Her departure is viewed with great regret because the work which she accomplished with her Committee has been of inestimable value....Her Committee has been able uniformly to offer documented closely reasoned criticisms, appreciations, and suggestions, which are already having a constructive effect on public education in the city. Her capacity for accomplishment is notable.
>
> Her impulse to do our work comes from a generous and statesman-like insistence that the search for equal rights fundamentally involves all stages of education. Her skill as Chairman is evidenced by the fact that her own contribution always emerges as part of the findings of a strong committee structure. We are sure you will want to join us in this word of gratitude to a citizen who has made a signal contribution to our city.

All this and they didn't even know that as chairman of CORE's, then the Activists', Urban Renewal Committee, Billie was simultaneously demonstrating equal skill and resourcefulness in researching and writing an even longer report, *Recommendations and Analysis: Baltimore Urban Renewal and Housing Agency (BURHA) and Department of Housing and Urban Development (HUD)* (more later).

After Billie moved, the letters she received from her friend and fellow-committee member, Una Corbett, uphold the earlier assessment of her contribution to the Education Committee. In a letter dated August 25, 1967, Una exclaims: "We miss you terribly." She goes on to say that Eli Frank is leaving the School Board, McElroy will become president, and D'Alesandro is expected to become mayor.

Una also tells of a meeting with Frank held to object to the proposed selection of the next appointment as School Superintendent. Una had been present along with Homer Favor, Joseph Howard, Walter Carter, Vernon Dobson and Parren Mitchell. They proclaimed there was no one at 25th Street (location of Department of Education) who had any interest in education or the inner-city children. "He [Frank] was stunned by our opposition....We felt we had triumphed."

All was not going quite so smoothly, however. For example, that same year (1967), "Hyman Pressman [City Comptroller] led a group of parents in throwing miniature school buses in the harbor as defiance against school busing.[128]

•••

While the parent group was reaching an agreement with the School Board in 1963, which they hoped would both help end white flight from the city and sustain an integrated school system, another battle was already brewing. It grew to fruition when Paquin proposed to create thirteen comprehensive high schools; each with a "fully integrated campus offering everything from vocational training to college preparatory courses."[129]

> The "Paquin Plan" ran into a wall of resistance at City College which would have lost its identity as an exclusive college preparatory school. City College parents and alumni, who were (and still are) politically influential, took their gripes to a City Council hearing called by Councilman (and City alumnus) Schaefer [who would later become one of the city's longest reigning mayor].

In September 1829, Baltimore opened its first public school—for whites—exactly one hundred years after the city's founding— "public" referring to open access rather than to funding. In 1839 Baltimore opened its first high school—for whites—Male Central which was intended both to turn out teachers, on the one hand, and to prepare students for college, on the other.

At some point its name was changed to City College:

---

128 *Afro-American,* 4/9/1988
129 Bowler, p. 10

"college" then meaning only that it was a school beyond the grammar school level. As the third oldest public high school in the country, City is a rarity in having retained the word college as part of its name. Perhaps it did so to reflect the pride its graduates feel in City's having become recognized for its pre-collegiate training—especially its rigorous "A" course, consisting of English, history, foreign languages, literature, social studies, and the theoretical sciences, that allowed students to graduate in three years rather than the standard four. No such "A" curriculum was available in the black high schools, Douglass and Dunbar.

Two opposing views of City's history and future were reflected in two letters-to-the-editor, printed side by side in the *Sun*, on November 10, 1963 [while Brain was still Superintendent]:

One, from Charles Cherubin, claimed that City had a 126 year history of preparing students for "the highest positions in the arts, in government, in business, and in the professions." [70% of its graduates are estimated to have gone on to college.] Cherubin suggests that a comprehensive high school could not achieve the same results.

> To destroy City College in the interests of the catch-all slogan "quality education for all" would be an unbearable irony....Baltimore is one of the few cities in the country that can offer to the sons of its citizens of modest means the benefits of a prep school education that is at least the equal of the kind the rich can buy for their children....In the best sense it is City College that has been able to offer quality education for all who could benefit from it....Can it be wrong or selfish to want to preserve the integrity of a living institution?

The second letter, by Marcia Kallen, then Chairman of CORE's Education committee, accused City College's principal of announcing "he does not want his school to be open to all students, but only to those who are going to college." Her view of City College is quite different from that of Cherubin:

> For the first 60 years of its existence college preparatory courses were unknown. Not until the colleges set up entrance requirements in the 1890s were such courses inaugurated. After 1900 City College, like other local and national high schools, provided academic courses for the college bound, commercial courses for students going into business, and general vocational courses for those seeking skills for immediate

jobs...Dr. Julius Hlub now would make it exclusive....

Is not race the real issue here, since City College has always had a comprehensive curricula offering but never before so many Negro students? [blacks were primarily enrolled in the business and vocational courses and hence would have been eliminated along with those courses]...No school should be permitted to choose the type of students it is willing to teach....continue our public school tradition of democratically embracing a wide variety of students in all our schools so that all will profit educationally and add inimitably to the culture and cohesiveness of our community.

It was not until December 1965 that a 45-page report was completed and circulated, signed by twenty distinguished Baltimoreans (both black and white). Called "City Forever," the report, at great length, lauds the uniqueness of City College amongst Baltimore's high schools, lays out all the achievements of its graduates, and describes the many honors and awards the school has received. It also suggests that City is not very good at teaching the non-academic subjects. It asserts that

while the delay in deciding the fundamental question of City College's future has necessarily had some adverse effect on the school, City still has intact its two major assets—its superb faculty and its large number of high quality college preparatory students [which the report claims elsewhere as having dropped from 75% of the total to 55%]. An end to the uncertainty, and a restoration of the school to a standard day of instruction concentrating on the humanities, will keep City College as attractive and valuable as it has traditionally been to qualified college-bound students drawn from throughout the city, and as important as it has always been to the general community.

The fight over the future status of City College represented a shift of emphasis away from integration per se to more complicated issues regarding school locations, curriculums and such. Melvin Sykes, who was a white attorney and a graduate of City, was the prime mover behind the report, resulting in its often being referred to as the Sykes Report.

In sharp contrast with Paquin's view, Sykes believed the admitted overcrowding at City should be resolved by eliminating all the vocational and business courses then taught there (and hence the students taking them) and make it a selective admission school offering only pre-college academic courses. On the other side were such as Jim Griffin, a black member of CORE, who believed the school should remain a comprehensive high school like all the others, retaining its vocational and business courses.

"City Forever" supports Sykes' position by arguing that a special academic school, as the proposed, is neither "elite' nor undemocratic, as claimed by those wanting it to become a comprehensive high school. Further, the report's supporters argue that their position definitely is not anti-black, claiming that approximately a third of its 2,108 college prep students are black.

A critique of the report[130] points out that, in fact, the tables provided in "City Forever" indicate that in 1960-61 only 2.5 % of blacks enrolled in college prep are in the Advanced and Special Curricula (the "A" course) while 17.5 % of the whites are; five years later the percentages are 3.5% blacks and 21.6% whites. They assert that these numbers would only become worse if the school becomes exclusively academic.

They qualify their criticism of the "City Forever" report as not being so valid "if the Baltimore City Public School System were doing as good a job in providing quality education to students stigmatized by the nefarious overtones of race and class as it is doing for the privileged." They suggest strengthening the entire public school system rather than singling out City for special treatment.

> After all, City College distinguished itself while serving the community as a comprehensive school. There is little reason to believe that it cannot continue in this vein by utilizing enough imagination to deploy the incidence of overcrowding equitably.

At a meeting of the "Sykes Report" group with Dr. Laurence Paquin, the school superintendent, and others in January, it was rejected after critiques by both the School Board and teachers found its data skewed and flawed.

However, when Dr. Paquin presented his own plan in the Spring of 1966, the "fight" seemed only to become more heated than ever; Sykes produced another huge report in response to

---

[130] The copy furnished this writer by Melvin Sykes is unsigned, but presumably was done by the Dept. of Education.

their critique, emphasizing especially that Paquin's plan did nothing to relieve City's overcrowding. The eventual "compromise" seemed an odd one: City could remain specialized (along with Polytechnic and the two girl's high schools, Eastern and Western). It was not required to offer business and vocational courses, but could not have over 75% of its students in a college-prep program.

•••

At the same time the fight over City College was taking place, another was occurring at the all-black high school, Dunbar. Dunbar was the second comprehensive high school (Douglass the first) Baltimore had provided for blacks; their response to increased enrollment by blacks. Dunbar was initially a Junior High School, on Baltimore's east side, and had gradually added a tenth, then eleventh and finally a twelfth grade, graduating its first high school class in 1940.

The community, once proud of their school, by 1965 found Dunbar's physical plant in a state of decay, Dunbar's equipment outmoded, and more than a third of its 2,000 students had been labeled "slow learners" and thrust into a dead-end "basic curriculum." Charles E. Brown, a recent graduate and former student body president, commented: "If we can't learn at school where can we learn? We want better education now, not five years from now." He blamed his schooling plus lack of money as reasons he was now working at Sparrows Point, Bethlehem Steel, rather than having gone to college.[131]

Part of the decline in academically oriented students might be explained by recent comments by a teacher who was in the school system when it was officially integrated. She said:

> [Anticipating the integration], the principals of the middle schools skimmed off the top the best students and sent them to Poly, Western and Easter. So Douglass and Dunbar were left with only one or two good classes. But by and large they not longer had the same caliber as before integration; after that, the very good students went other places....The same thing happened at the black colleges, like Morgan—not everybody, now, but you got more mediocre people there.

---

[131] *Sun* paper, April 9, 1965.

In March 1965, CORE took Dunbar on as a project. Along with its student off-shoot, SCORE (Student Committee on Racial Equality), CORE claimed that many graduates of Dunbar couldn't read and that instruction, in general, was poor. This was at the very same time that Sykes' group was advocating shifting City's vocational and business classes to this school as better equipped to teach them.[132] And it was also at a time when building of a new Polytechnic-Western High School was starting at a cost of $15,000,000, the most expensive school in the city's history.

For four days about one hundred students marched outside the school's entrance from 2:30 when classes ended, until 3:10 p.m. Some carried signs reading, "Economic Suicide". They knew they were being short-changed by the system in a way that would permanently affect them; prevent their getting decent jobs. They planned to block entrances to the school on Friday morning, and to ask students to stay out of classes for a half-hour, then, for the rest of the day, to attend classes but do nothing. They wanted the co-operation of the teachers, but the teachers were under order from the Principal to conduct their classes as usual.

Then, on Thursday evening, Dennis Crosby, president of CORE's Education Committee and a department head at Dunbar, told CORE's executive board, meeting at Knox Presbyterian Church, that he'd received word the PTA had finally agreed to support the students. "We've tried to involve the PTA in protests for two years," he added, "but in the past the organization was controlled by the Dunbar school administration." With this promise from the PTA, CORE canceled its planned protest "for now"—and Crosby met with their attorney, Fred Weisgal, to "discuss possible court action if CORE's demands were not met."

The half-dozen policemen who'd been sent to the school Friday morning, just in case, found everything calm and peaceful

---

[132] From clippings in the *News-American*, Friday, March 5, 1965, and two unnamed papers for same date. Also, from *Sun*, 3/10/65, and April 9, 1965. Part of this account first appeared in the writer's self-published book, *"...And Justice for All."* She is also in possession of a hand-written account of CORE's plans sent her by its author, James Griffin, then CORE Chairman.

as students quickly entered the building to escape a driving downpour. There had been rumors that some SCORE students planned to strike on their own but this never happened. All day the students passed quietly from class to class without any visible disturbances in classrooms or corridors.

That morning, Weisgal and CORE chairman, Jim Griffin, met with Principal Robert Diggs and Gordon Woelper, a Department of Education supervisor for the Dunbar school district. They discussed the claimed school deficiencies and the charges that school officials were intimidating students who'd demonstrated earlier in the week. After the hour-long, closed meeting, all Weisgal would say was, "The meeting was interesting and we cleared the air on some of the issues involved in the protest. We are looking forward to the 8 p.m. meeting at Dunbar on Tuesday and hope many PTA members will attend." The plan was, at that meeting, to draft a formal protest to be submitted to the school board at their next meeting on March 18.

SCORE and CORE threatened larger, more militant demonstrations and court action if the following demands, contained in a 6,000-signature petition were not met:

1. Construction of a new Dunbar High School on or near the present site at Caroline and McElderry streets.

2. Replacement of the school's basic curriculum for slow learners with a "crash program" of remedial reading, writing, arithmetic and better job training.

Even though they were eventually shown a copy of the Middle States' creditation report that claimed the school was well maintained and in good condition, CORE officials disagreed, contending that the existing Dunbar building was in such poor condition that needed programs could never be implemented there.

At the Tuesday, March 9 meeting, a sixteen-member committee was formed "to iron out differences in a push for school improvements." Four members were selected from each of four groups: CORE, SCORE, the Dunbar PTA and the school alumni association. CORE agreed that after-school picketing would not be resumed until the committee had had time to take action.

Mrs. Hattie Harrison, president of the PTA, announced she would be meeting soon with Edwin Stein, the acting superintendent of schools, at his invitation. She also indicated she didn't subscribe to all CORE's demands and did not approve of picketing. She added: "I don't think this is CORE's baby. We moved in because we thought we could help. We're here to build up rather than tear down." About forty people

Photo Courtesy of Mike Waller, publisher,
Baltimore *Sun*, 4/10/1965

attended the meeting, including Milton Goldberg, president of the Baltimore Teachers Union. But in the end no real decisions were made and nothing changed, as had happened so often before. Disgusted by this lack of action, demonstrations by students and CORE resumed. Then, on April 9, 1965, after presenting their demands to the School Board, Jim Griffin, Rev. Robert Clark, a pastor of East Baltimore Methodist Church, and 21 students and CORE members led a 26-hour sit-in and sleep-in at the 25th Street School Board head-quarters. They hoped to pressure the administration into building a new Dunbar High School. They were finally ejected after 26 hours (the building closing for spring vacation), several having to be carried out.

Three years later, in 1968, Mayor D'Alesandro appointed Jim Griffin to the school board (an appointment that must have surprised many). There he made full use of this new venue to continue his fight for improvements in black schools., and quickly gained a reputation as a trouble-maker. Nonetheless, coincidence or not, it was also in 1968 that the decision was finally made to build a new Dunbar. To this day the "new" Dunbar serves as "a center of educational, political and social activity in its East Baltimore community."[133]

Before agreement was reached on a new Dunbar, Laurence Paquin had died of cancer (1967); Thomas Goedeke had become acting Superintendent for a brief time (1967-1968), and Thomas D. Sheldon had become the next Baltimore School Superintendent (1968-1971).

•••

In a letter on November 24, 1968 to her friend and fellow education-activist, Billie Bramhall, Una Corbett described Dr. Paquin as a strong superintendent who'd won strong community support against an "entrenched group" in the fight over City College. She sounded disheartened that there no longer seemed to be much interest in integration.

Perhaps that lay at the heart of her June 1969 letter that informed Billie, still interested in Baltimore despite having left the city in 1967, that she'd resigned from the Mayor's Task Force Committee on Equal Rights in Education, a role she'd once shared with Billie. Una lamented that while, previously, the Mayor's appointments to this committee were all people with experience either in education or civil rights, those recently appointed hadn't a clue why they were there or what to do. "I have simply lost faith in the ability of the Committee to achieve anything for equality in education for the children of Baltimore....I see no evidence that the Task Force as constituted at the moment has either the skill to develop a fruitful community involvement, or the spirit to make it humanly creative."

Accompanying a letter dated July 3, 1969 from Una to Billie is a copy of her resignation letter, and you can almost hear a plaintive sadness as Una writes: "The situation has changed so there is little place for some of us. But we did achieve something once, long ago....

Since you left there has been no one to carry on....I have often longed for you, with your skill in handling people, and

---

[133] Bowler, p. 29

with your ideas of how to try to make changes and improvements....I think our new superintendent Sheldon expects this community group to provide outlet for protests and take the heat off the administration."[134] Of the present school board, Una writes: "Mrs. Farring is the only bigot left, but Sweeney and Tingle vote with her. [Phil] Macht goes with the four Negro members, and there are hot times at Board meetings with Jim Griffin the most forceful and adamant."

When Mayor D'Alesandro swore in Jim Griffin in 1968, he was breaking with the tradition of having a representative from Johns Hopkins and the University of Maryland, and in selecting primarily well-off, elitist white men. At the time he said he wanted people "more representative of the community" and more "in tune with the times."

Jim Griffin had grown up in Baltimore, his father was a laborer at Sparrows Point. Griffin had been on the football and track teams at Dunbar High (class of 1950); had become a physical therapist when few blacks were. He was deeply committed to the black community, and served as Chairman of Baltimore CORE for many years. An article in the *Evening Sun*, January 22, 1971, didn't mince words in stating that on the board Griffin was "blunt and rude, to the point of shocking, at times." The article also pointed out that Griffin and the other black board member, Elizabeth Murphy Moss, "campaigned for more black principalships in white as well as black schools. They scrutinized vocational education, charging inadequacy."

In another undated and unnamed newspaper article, the reporter asked Griffin if he felt his three roles—School Board member, State employee (at the time in its personnel office) and CORE activist—represented a conflict of interest. His reply: "How could they? They're all for equal opportunity."

The appointment in December 1968 of Larry Gibson, then a 26-year-old attorney, and Samuel Daniels, former teacher and head of the Council for Equal Business Opportunity, brought to four the number of blacks on the Board. Liberals

---

[134] Thomas Sheldon replaced Laurence Paquin as Baltimore School Superintendent in 1968 after the latter died of cancer on Columbus Day, 1967, after only two years on the job.

became pitted against conservatives and what had, in the "old days," been polite exchanges, became bitter exchanges that reflected both racial differences and the very different backgrounds of its members. The Mayor's attempts to tone things down with new appointments met with little success.

The member's biggest disagreement seemed to be over the stewardship of Dr. Thomas Sheldon as superintendent, leading to his resignation in January 1971. His opposition to community control of the schools "angered the Congress of Racial Equality and others who were advocating community control over budgets and the hiring and firing of staffs." However, the action that seems to have precipitated his resignation was the school board's rejection of all eleven of his nominations for school principals and their demand he put together a new list—which he refused to do.[135]

Edgar Jones, in an article in the *Sun* dated February 7, 1971, suggests that Sheldon should not have been criticized for the job he did during his thirty-one months as superintendent, in trying to fulfill the mandate given him on his arrival in Baltimore from Long Island. The board chairman, Murnaghan, had asked him to "move the schools into an integrated society."

Jones credited Sheldon, among other things, with having streamlined the administration, assigned the most-ever blacks as school principals, and greatly expedited school construction. He also had warned book publishers that none would be purchased for Baltimore schools "that were not racially sound and equitable in their presentation," and had instituted a testing program that would hold schools accountable. Sheldon was not against teaching black history and culture, as some had accused him, but rather had objected to the idea that black children had to be taught differently than white ones.

---

[135] Bowler, p. 12

Education Turmoil Continues

Once upon a time, from 1925 to 1946, David Weglein served as Baltimore City's school superintendent. The system was totally segregated, several of the schools single-sex, the atmosphere described as "placid." Never again. Henceforth, education, seemingly, was destined to be forever in turmoil. It did not end with the death of Laurence Paquin, nor the resignation of Thomas Sheldon who'd succeeded him. Nor would it end with the appointment of Roland Patterson who found controversy spinning around him throughout his four years on the job.

When Dr. Patterson came to Baltimore from Seattle in 1971, the same year Donald Schaefer was elected Mayor, to become Baltimore's first black Superintendent of Schools, the city was in process of losing 13% of its population, and the majority of its population was by then black. By the time he was fired, 70% of its public school students were black.[136]

In February 1970, more than a year before Patterson's arrival (while Sheldon was still Superintendent), Eastern High School, an all-girl's school, which by then had gone from all-white to four-fifths black, erupted in violence after a white teacher used a racial epithet in speaking to one of the students. The police were called and arrested eleven girls for disorderly conduct. This triggered even more disturbances, spreading first to near-by City College High School, and then to other high schools, even junior highs.

Sit-ins and demonstrations at City Hall and at school headquarters followed, quickly becoming a black revolt against the white power structure that prevailed in the school board, the superintendent's office, the teachers, the police, and most of the city's institutions. The student's revolt led to an even greater decline in white enrollment in the public schools.

Patterson had been given two mandates when he was hired: "reshape the system and get rid of the 'deadwood' at 25th

---

[136] The interim *acting* superintendent, Sterling Ss. Keyes, was also black and perhaps could claim he was the first. Information about the crises preceding Patterson and in 1974 from Berkowitz. Also see Bowler.

Street school headquarters." Kalman Hettleman, then on the school board, later said, "We were looking for somebody to shake up the system, not a pea of the same pod."[137] It was not a mandate that would endear Patterson to either administrators or teachers; his poor relationship with them later becoming one of the charges against him. But things seemed reasonably calm during the early years of Patterson's reign, until 1974. That year a teacher's strike and a confrontation with the Office of Civil Rights in the Department of Health, Education, and Welfare (HEW) over desegregation occurred, almost simultaneously, having catastrophic repercussions.

In February 1974, the teacher's union ignored an injunction by the circuit court against a teacher's strike, and, by the strikes third day, only 16% of the students were in school and less than a quarter of the staff. While the mayor declared the teacher's salary and benefit demands beyond the city's financial possibility, the strikers continued to emphasize their low pay compared to that paid in the neighboring counties, their poor working conditions and the crowded classrooms.

It was the winter of the Watergate hearings and growing gas shortages. Both the public and Patterson sympathized with the teachers, Patterson stating he'd been complaining for years that the school system was underfinanced.

As the strike continued, Mayor Schaefer began a campaign to woo public opinion away from the strikers by emphasizing the relationship between teacher's pay and city tax rates, already high; and also appealed to the teachers to understand that "the city contained about a fifth of the state's population but nearly two-thirds of its welfare caseload."[138] The mayor realized that to give in to the teachers would not only open Pandora's box for other unions to demand increased pay for their members, but also that an increase in taxes to meet their demands would precipitate further flight from the city of middle class whites, decreasing still further his tax base. "What am I going to do"? he lamented.

The schools were technically still open, but virtually empty by March 4, 1974 when a tentative agreement was reached between the city and teacher's union that featured a

[137] Bowler, p. 13.
[138] Berkowitz, p. 422

six percent wage increase. Teachers and students returned the next day, but the teachers felt betrayed by their union which had won for them so little while they lost four weeks pay on strike.

Anger increased on all sides after John Gallagher, a delegate to the state legislature from Baltimore, introduced a measure that would abolish the school board and put the city school's management in the hands of the mayor and city council. James Griffin and Larry Gibson, both black members of the school board, called the proposal a racist conspiracy.

The measure never passed, but the black community, in general, felt that the white political structure had prevailed in the strike. They had achieved a settlement that avoided a tax increase, but in so doing continued to deprive the increasingly black school population of the funds needed for their education.

A second crisis was almost simultaneously brewing. By 1970, as a result of Title VI of the 1964 Civil Rights Act, the city was receiving about 11% of its funding from the federal government. This was a badly needed infusion of money, but there were penalties attached for failure to desegregate. In April 1973, HEW put Superintendent Patterson on notice that he needed to rebut charges that there was "substantial dis-proportion" in Baltimore's schools. Patterson realistically blamed racial segregation of the schools on demography, declaring, "shifting population trends...thwart [the city's] best efforts."

There was no decision by HEW until the winter of 1974, right in the middle of the teacher's strike. Patterson then was told that based on the data they had, more desegregation was needed. HEW declared the city's open enrollment policy ineffective as regards pupils and teachers. Patterson was given only thirty days to come up with a plan to increase integration, but, in light of the strike, extended it until the end of April. The city was in a bind; they couldn't afford to lose the federal funds, nor could they afford to lose their already tenuous tax-base by forcing further desegregation on the whites still remaining in the city.

As anticipated, whites felt threatened by the proposed busing plan and became decidedly vocal in their opposition. The plan the school board unveiled in late May included pairing schools at the elementary level and magnet schools at the high school level. Student-led marches and protests followed.

The school board reacted by cutting the number of elementary schools to be paired, provoking Larry Gibson to call the plan a farce. It was a foregone conclusion that more trouble lay ahead. The city was in a catch-twenty-two. The more they "tinkered with mechanisms to produce racial integration—a concept that could only mean racially proportionate schools in a school system that was 70% black—the more it risked losing its white, middle-class residents. If those residents left the city or withdrew their children from the schools, the situation could only worsen....The *Brown* decision had provided the impetus for the city to take steps that many people already favored, but the court decisions of the 1970s forced the city to take steps with which many people disagreed."[139]

On Labor Day 1974, Mayor Schaefer returned from a vacation in Ocean City to meet with Superintendent Patterson at City Hall.

> Outside, marchers were protesting the junior high 'feeder' plan, which, in effect, had put an end to the concept that city junior and senior high students could attend the school of their choice. Inside, Patterson was using charts and graphs to explain the plan to Schaefer. The two men, both with strong personalities and both on edge, began shouting at each other. Their relationship was never mended.[140]

After the School Board voted on June 10, 1975 to fire Patterson unless he resigned by June 24, State Delegate Walter Dean, Jr. said, "Roland Patterson's days were numbered from the day he came here. The system can't deal with aggressive black leadership." Jim Griffin, who'd left the School Board a year earlier, was arrested that day, along with Benjamin Phillips, an *Afro-American* photographer, for disorderly conduct. Griffin had approached the table where Board members were seated, complaining that the meeting was "out of order" because not held in a public place. The Board room in the 25th Street administrative building held only seventy; many who'd come could not get in—e.g., only three of the fifty ministers were admitted.

---

[139] Berkowitz, pp. 429-430.
[140] Bowler, p. 14

Phillips' and Griffin's trial was postponed twice at the request of Griffin's attorney, Milton B. Allen, who had been the city's first black state's attorney. He felt a constitutional issue was involved: "We're dealing with a situation where a citizen exercised his right under the 1st Amendment at an alleged public meeting and was arrested for doing what the constitution says he has a right to do."

Griffin, who had served on the board for twelve years, was upset that the Board had been meeting in secret sessions since January in an attempt to prevent community input in the Dr. Patterson issue.[141] The *Afro* photographer had been arrested when he refused to heed an order to desist his photographing and leave, and instead continued to follow Griffin and the arresting officers into the side room where they were taking him.[142]

On July 29th, after nearly three hours of testimony, Judge Robert Gerstung in Western District Court denied an acquittal motion by Griffin's attorney and scheduled September 22nd for final arguments. That day he was found guilty of disturbing the peace and fined $50. In doing so, Judge Gerstung informed Griffin that the right to freedom on speech was limited, using the old Oliver Wendell Holmes' example of not being able to yell "fire" in a theater. He rejected the argument that the board meeting had been illegal.[143] This writer found no report of the disposition of the photographer's case; it quite likely was dismissed.

Meanwhile, following the Board action on June 10, 1975, Patterson declared he would fight the School Board all the way. In his evaluation, the Board had proclaimed Patterson "deficient in several crucial areas of performance," but his supporters at a meeting at the New Shiloh Baptist Church (one paper reported 300 present, another 900) were convinced his firing was motivated by racism, as they combined prayer and politics in "a two-hour vignette of the 1960s civil rights struggle." After a rousing rendition of "We Shall Overcome" and "We Shall Not Be Moved, Patterson told them: "Blacks can no longer wait for 'some day' to overcome," and the crowd gave

---

[141] Letter to the Editor by Griffin in the *Afro- American*, 6/14/75.
[142] He tells his story in the *Afro-American*, 6/14/75
[143] *Sun*, 9/24/75

him a standing ovation. Parren Mitchell, then a member of the U.S. House of Representatives, went further, stating "that 'black people are considered an impotent entity to be shoved around' and that the white power structure of the city is trying to erode the power of the black community by 'picking us off, one by one.'"[144]

After Patterson exerted his right to a public hearing, one was scheduled for 10 a.m. on Friday, June 20th at the War Memorial Building (across from City Hall downtown) which held 315. His supporters objected to this, too, because it was scheduled for a time when most of Patterson's supporters would be at work. However, there was no lack of attendance that day—about forty girls from Eastern High were part of the mix supporting Patterson; they'd marched from 25th Street to the War Memorial Building.

However, the hearing was delayed until July 2, by a series of injunctions, ending with a 24 hour delay, signed by Supreme Court Justice, Thurgood Marshall, that temporarily stopped "an order from the state Court of Appeals dissolving a 10-day injunction issued by Judge Joseph C. Howard of the Baltimore Supreme Court." The deadline of June 24th set by the Board for Patterson's firing had passed during all the delays. [145]

On July 2nd and each of the six days of hearings that followed, the War Memorial was filled to capacity—this writer, then a librarian in the school system and a Patterson supporter, amongst the numerous supporters outside who were picketing in protest of the board's and Mayor Schaefer's actions. Inside various board members were testifying to the specifics in the 18 of 52 criteria in which the board had found Patterson lacking—most revolving around his relationship with the board, staff and personnel.

The city auditor and director of city finances raised questions about his fiscal responsibility even though the Board had earlier given him a satisfactory rating on this point. They were probably especially provoked by the fact he'd used, they claimed illegally, the education office to print and mail to teachers and others a 65-page report of Patterson's defense of

---

[144] *Evening Sun*, 6/12/75 and *Sun*, 6/12/75
[145] An account of hearings & aftermath in the *Sun*, June 6, 14, 19, 30, July 2, 3, 9, 13, 18 and August 8, 19, 1975.

the board's charges against him, and other pro-Patterson materials. Lacking from both sides was any discussion of Patterson's accountability to the city's school children.

The hearings that had spanned two weeks and involved sixty hours of testimony from school administrators, city officials and board members, ended as one might have expected—after all, the board members were at once acting as judge, jury and witnesses. On July 17, 1975, the School Board voted 7 to 2 to fire Roland Patterson.

Within hours, Larry Gibson filed a request with the U.S. District Court for an immediate stay of the board's action, but it was rejected by Judge Frank Kaufman at an afternoon hearing; and an August date was set for a preliminary injunction hearing against the firing. But Patterson left his office at the Board of Education that day, remarking, "I left a big bottle of aspirin for my successor." And, on August 7th, Larry Gibson withdrew his request for the injunction.

But on September 4, Gibson filed a suit in U.S. District Court of Maryland against the School Board claiming it had violated Patterson's freedom of speech when its members asserted some of Patterson's statements, critical of the city government, were reasons for his dismissal. The suit asked that Patterson be reinstated in his $50,000 a year job, and for one million dollars in damages (an earlier charge of racial discrimination was dropped as too difficult to prove).

In October, a controversial fund-raising letter sent to school employees asked their help in paying legal expenses. The letter claimed that Patterson had been fired because he refused to "bow to the Mayor (Schaefer) and other political interests and to play Uncle Tom."[146]

Patterson, of course, was not reinstated nor did he receive a million dollars from the city, but his supporters were still stewing when the Mayor appointed Mark Joseph, who had been advisor to the Mayor for two years, to head the School Board. Jim Griffin declared: "The appointment will signify the official takeover of the city schools by City Hall, giving the Mayor complete control of the schools and the education of its students." Patterson moved on to become a district superinten-

---

[146] *News-American*, 10/8/75

dent in the Bronx, New York, in a decentralized system where he did a much-appreciated excellent job. After he died of cancer on August 9, 1983, a Bronx school was named after him.[147]

•••

In 1976, soon after John L. Crew had been appointed as the next Superintendent, Gregory assessed the state of education in Baltimore, as in most large cities. He wrote:

> In the nation's cities, Baltimore included, under the present patterns of living in urban areas, there is no longer an adequate number of whites to balance the large racially ethnic minorities. In this absence, education that is qualitatively no different from that in the affluent suburbs [needs] to become a reality. The tendency to underfund education or to decrease the number and quality of educational programs when blacks become a majority has to be overcome.
>
> The need is for a school system adequately funded, adequately staffed, and dedicated to the production of quality education for the students attending. The expertise to do this already exists, we have not developed the will. A nation that can marshal its vast wealth to put men on the moon in a single decade should be capable of solving the problem of producing quality schools for *all* of its citizens.[148]

In Baltimore, funding remained a major problem, suggesting that an all-out commitment to quality education remained lacking. The "blame administration" mentality that did Patterson in remained, resulting in numerous reorganizations of the school system, decentralizing, recentralizing, and so on. Simultaneously any number of "programs" were introduced in various of the city's schools, usually ended, successful or not, for lack of funds.

•••

Soon after Crews' appointment in 1975, he declared, "I'm going to show the world that black kids can learn as well as whites. I'm going to do it in five years." [149] And that is what he

---

[147] *Afro-American*, 11/8/75. Patterson had received only $26,119 in salary and vacation pay after his firing; nothing in severance pay.
[148] Gregory, pp. 459 & 482
[149] Bowler, p. 16

set out to do. This seems to be the beginning of a 25-year fixation in Baltimore on test scores. But Crew in his tenure that lasted until 1982 also "got money for refurbishing City College, and opened it as a city-wide, coeducational liberal arts school in 1977. He also developed a successful School for the Arts, and improved the special education program, especially important after the 1975 federal Education for All Handicapped Children Act was passed, requiring that each handicapped student have an individual education plan.

In 1977 the school board mandated an end to "social promotion," a practice that found many junior high school students not even able to read. The 1980 census found that "2,000 adult Baltimoreans had less than a fourth-grade reading ability. In the schools these statistics were reflected in high dropout rates, 14,000 daily absentees and thousands of poor underachieving youngsters."[150]

In 1982 Alice G. Pinderhughes became school superintendent, the first woman to hold the position.

> She was an insider who had worked her way through nearly every job in the system. She had better political connections than her predecessors—and better relations in the business community. It was during her tenure that the Greater Baltimore Committee (GBC), Baltimore's Chamber of Commerce, and BUILD, a church-based community group, joined the school system in the Commonwealth Plan, a major effort to help students graduate and provide them with college and job opportunities.[151]

Her "connections" undoubtedly explain why she held the position until 1988 when Mayor Schmoke "ushered her" into retirement. During Pinderhughes relatively long tenure, she oversaw the recentralizing of the school system, and the move of its headquarters from 25th Street to North Avenue. Patterson's decentralization, and along with it his reasoning, were now completely dead.

---

150 Bowler, p. 18
151 This quote and in following paragraph are from Bowler, pp. 18-20. A College Bound program still exists that both GBC and BUILD still support, but is now run as a separate, not-for-profit Foundation.

> [Patterson] wanted to move decision-making closer to the schools, which would "make it possible to hold the individual accountable for his decisions. This should result in an improvement of the individual's performance." But it was too much too fast.

Despite her connections, Pinderhughes was frustrated like all those before her, and all those to follow, by lack of adequate funds. "Baltimore was becoming increasingly a ward of the state...local sources had declined from nearly 50% in 1980 to 36% in 1987. She was proud of the "comprehensive, well-worked out" plan, "Focus on Individual Success," developed under her guidance, which she handed over to Richard Hunter, ready for implementation, after Mayor Schmoke hand-selected him as her replacement. "Forced" by the Mayor "to retire at the end of the school year," Pinderhughes was undoubtedly still bitter, when she later remarked, "I don't know what happened to it."[152]

Superintendent Hunter, the seventh superintendent since 1960, was appointed by Mayor Schmoke in 1988 as a "unifier," stating, "We need someone to bring all the elements together."[153] This was probably an impossible task in the best of circumstances, but especially so as Hunter set out to "redo our whole curriculum," saying it would be "multi-cultural and multi-ethnic" and "put more focus on" the city's special education, and compensatory and vocational education programs," "geared to the "expectations" of the city's employers.

It sounded like a return to the Booker T. Washington philosophy that focused on vocational training as a way for blacks to succeed while appeasing whites. Hunter said this shift in emphasis was made necessary by the "Maryland School Performance Plan," which had been based on the 1989 report of the Governor's Commission on School Performance, known as the "Sondheim Commission," after Walter Sondheim, its chairman and former president of the school board.

What Hunter quickly learned was that Baltimore was a conglomerate of very different neighborhoods with very different ideas of what was best for their community; their ideas often worlds apart. He left as Superintendent in 1991, bitter even six

---

[152] Bowler, p. 19; www.bcps.k12.md.us.
[153] Bowler supplement, p. H-14

years later, saying his career had been wiped out. Walter G. Amprey followed.

•••

The schools first legal suit regarding state funding dates back to 1983, another was filed in 1987, and yet another in 1990. A consent decree was issued in 1996, but because the city still is no where near parity with other systems in funding, the ACLU is considering returning to court. One suit that questioned the city's handling of special education dates back over thirteen years. In this case, Bowler states that Amprey the 'visionary' has been reduced to

> paying daily fines for contempt of court, seeing millions of dollars withheld by the General Assembly because of his alleged management failures and seeing some of his administrative appointments rejected by the oversight team established to compensate for his managerial deficiencies in special education.[154]

Meanwhile the city has seen a number of programs come and go. Among them: the Barclay-Calvert program; a plan for "enterprise schools" that would give each of 20 schools considerable latitude in their operations; "Tesseract," marketed by a profit-making firm, experimented with private control of a number of city schools, Education Alternative, Inc. (EAI) was given management of nine schools with the promise that, with the same amount of funds allotted other schools, they'd improve test scores; a similar arrangement with Edison to take over three schools; Sylvan Leaning Systems, a Columbia-based tutoring program, provided educational services to families, schools and industry; "Efficacy Institute" aimed to train teachers who would change the "culture" of the schools; and "Success for All" combined techniques in the teaching of reading with individual student attention and parental involvement. This program was a success in Baltimore, and is a success in 475 schools in 31 states, but was abandoned in Baltimore when the schools using it changed principals.

Despite all the experimenting, there was little improvement

---

[154] Bowler supplement, p. H-19

in student performance. In 1997, the Maryland General Assembly established a City-State Partnership designed to carry out authentic educational reforms in the Baltimore City Public School System. A new school board was appointed and a Master Plan developed that was to make all Baltimore's schools of equal quality and equal to all those throughout Maryland.

In a national standardized test given that year to 8th graders in 32 states, 9% of Baltimore's students passed the math test, 12% passed the science test, and 28% passed reading, the third lowest in the nation.[155] Excluding the special high schools and looking only at the neighborhood high schools, entering freshmen numbered about 1,000; the number graduating between 190 and 200.

State Superintendent, Nancy Grasmick, placed fifty of the city's 179 schools on the "reconstitution list" because of their poor showing on the "Maryland School Performance Assessment Program" (MSPAP).—that is, they're under orders from the state to reform. Bowler notes a whole list of deficiencies in the city's schools.

> Almost everything from basic classroom instruction, to computers, to special education, to art and music instruction, to field trips, to physical education, to vocational education, to class size, on and on, show signs of the skimpy operation forced on Baltimore schools by a budget that doesn't stretch far enough.

It's impossible to answer the question Bowler asks: "How mush of this is due to poor management, and how much is threadbare budgeting? The state hasn't even come close to equalizing funding for the Baltimore system as mandated in the Partnership agreement. Every Maryland governor since Marvin Mandel in the early 1970s has emphasized poor management as the source of Baltimore's failures, while every superintendent since Roland Patterson, of the same era as Mandel, has emphasized state funding."[156]

It's not clear that Bowler's is even the right question. Perhaps that asked by Kalman Hettleman, long involved with

---

[155] www.bcps.k12.md.us; "The Master Plan" & "A New Era of School Reform."
[156] Bowler supplement, p. H-22

the schools, in an article for the *Baltimore Sun* on August 26, 2000, is more to the point:

> Who in the state power structure will take over and lead the struggle to ensure that all disadvantaged children have adequate opportunity to meet state academic standards?

Could one look to the powerful Greater Baltimore Committee's 42 member board of directors for the answer? They certainly have the economic clout. Their own web site declares: "The GBC's Board of Directors is a diverse group of the area's foremost businesses leaders. Together, they are perhaps the most influential group of Baltimore's corporate citizens." Does the Board's make-up tell us anything? Seven are black, all but six have their place of business in Baltimore, but only eight live in the city.[157]

One might also ask, "How much real power do blacks have to force changes in Baltimore, which has the fourth largest school system in Maryland?" Looking at the number of blacks on the school board (six black, three white) and employed in the school system, one would think considerable.

> Baltimore's public school system is the city's third-largest employer, with more than 11,400 people [12,126 full-time in 2000], a number surpassed only by Johns Hopkins University and Helix Health. About 60% of those employees are African-American, and many are among the so-called middle class. The school district plays a vital social and economic role in the African-American community, and when considering reform ideas and proposals, this economic connection could not be dismissed.[158]

In the year 2000, there were 103,077 students enrolled in Baltimore's 184 schools, 87.2% black. 73,000 students were eligible for free or reduced price meals, suggesting that real school progress may depend on a simultaneous attack on poverty. However, test scores in 2000 do offer a ray of hope; progress has been made since the abysmal results in 1997. In 2000, the math and reading test scores for students in grades 1 to 5 exceeded the national average.

---

[157] See www.gbc.org, "Board."
[158] Quote and statistics in www.bcps.k12.md.us; "The Master Plan" & "A New Era of School Reform."

Part V
Housing

Legislation & the Courts

*All citizens of the United States shall have the same
right, in every State and Territory
as is enjoyed by white citizens thereof
to inherit, purchase, lease, sell, hold, and convey real
and personal property.*
Civil Rights Act passed by the U.S. Congress in 1866,
re-enacted in 1870.

Most of the blacks who arrived in Baltimore before 1880 seeking a better life were from rural areas further south, had little money and few jobs open to them. Consequently, they were forced to rent "shanties," and to double up in the cheapest housing they could find. Baltimore's first slum soon followed—in the Southwest part of the city that became known as "Pigtown." An 1892 account described Pigtown as a place with "foul streets, foul people, foul tenements, foul air"; filthy water, open drains, lots full of high weeds, ashes and garbage; people who seldom washed, "who loiter and sleep around the street corners and never work; vile and vicious women...lounging in the doorways or squatting upon the steps, hurling foul epithets at every passerby...".[1]

There is no doubt that the conditions in this section of Baltimore were appalling, but that all the occupants were as described, very unlikely. One can only assume that rural life, and life further South, was even worse, since blacks continued to arrive. By 1900, they numbered 79,258 out of a total population of 508,957.[2]

Legal segregation had not yet taken firm root and those few blacks who could afford to, perhaps as many as 250, moved away from the cheap slum housing to the northwestern part of the city, purchasing hand-me-downs houses around St. Mary's Orchard and Biddle Streets from whites, who began to move beyond the city's boundaries after the development

---

[1] Found both in Power, *Apartheid*, p. 290 and Olson, p. 233, quoting *Baltimore News*, 9/20/1892. Historical information and quotes that follow, unless otherwise noted, come from Power, *Apartheid*, pp. 289-328.

[2] Figures from 13th Census in the Abstract published by the Bureau of Census.

and extension of cable and electric railway service.

These were the "respectable" up-and-coming blacks, the black community's business and professional people. They held notable social events such as that of Mrs. L.W. Lee, who had "a swell colored reception" on New Year's Day 1886 serving celery and winter delicacies.[3] By 1910, though some whites still continued to live in the area, the number of blacks had grown to 8,392—still a miniscule number compared to the 84,749 blacks then in Baltimore (an increase of over 5,000 in just ten years).[4]

The houses purchased by these few blacks on Druid Hill Avenue, even though hand-me-downs, were once described by W.E.B. DuBois as "stately three-story town houses" on "one of the best colored streets in America."[5] Their black owners did all they could to disassociate themselves from the white-perceived image of blacks as lazy and worthless.

Despite this effort, the increasing presence of blacks aroused the prejudices of many whites and gradually ended the fluidity of relations between blacks and whites that had prevailed for many years. In fact, as late as 1908, no attempt had been made, legally, to restrict blacks to any particular section of the city and no single ward was yet exclusively black. Nonetheless, black wards were rapidly developing, especially in the Northwest, as blacks moved in and an increasing number of whites moved out. For example, the once prosperous area bounded by Biddle, Preston, Druid Hill, and Pennsylvania Avenue was beginning to deteriorate as 12,738 blacks crowded together. Over 200 houses, crammed into alleys and the minor adjacent streets, had been converted into almost 300 apartments, many just a single room, causing major overcrowding.[6]

As early as 1881, the then-president of Johns Hopkins University, Daniel Coit Gilman, had founded the Charity

---

[3] See Olson, p.233.

[4] Figures from 14th Census in the Abstract published by the Bureau of Census. Baltimore was ranked 72nd in home ownership by blacks out of 73 southern cities with black populations of 5,000 or over. (Power, *Apartheid*, p. 308).

[5] Quote found in Watson, p. 63.

[6] See Power, *Apartheid*, p. 295, Olson, p. 235.

Organization Society to provide the poor (both blacks and whites) with needed food and clothing, and, later, sponsored playgrounds and public baths. Doctors, concerned that black mortality was nearly double the white average, tried to help. Dr. William Osler at Johns Hopkins Hospital, Dr. William Henry Welch and Dr. John S. Fulton, founded the Maryland Public Health Association.

But since the major resources for treatment of these diseases were designated for whites, and nothing allocated to prevent the creation of the slums responsible for the high rates of cholera, typhoid and tuberculosis in these areas, their best efforts had little impact. Reflecting as always their second class status, there were recommendations that a new City Hospital be built for whites, and the old ones turned over to the blacks. At the few existing hospitals that received both races, the accommodations and treatment were inferior. For example,

> [Mercy] had a 'poorly ventilated' railroad ward, an 'absolutely unventilated' ward for immigrants, and for colored patients an old building 'inferior' to those. At the homeopathic hospital the colored patients were housed in 'a slightly remodeled stable.' 'Only at Johns Hopkins Hospital and Bay View are the two races treated equally well or badly, as the case may be.[7]

Besides the lack of needed medical care, the city did nothing to improve either the sanitary conditions nor the water supply in black areas, nor did it do anything to increase the number of jobs and housing open to blacks. Instead, "blame the victim" became commonplace. The inevitable slums and the ensuing epidemics, vice, crime, pauperism and anarchy they fostered were all blamed on the blacks.[8]

Established in 1906, the Baltimore Colored Law and Order League, along with several white Progressives, made efforts to prevent the Liquor Board from issuing licenses for saloons in the Druid Hill Avenue district, and urged them to enforce ordinances against liquor sale to minors. However,

---

[7] Olson, p. 270
[8] Power, *Apartheid*, pp. 192-294.

they were regularly rebuffed.[9] Instead the police rounded up rowdies, the adults fined or taken to jail, and the juveniles to the Cheltenham Negro Reformatory for Boy or the Industrial Home for Colored Girls.[10]

In the ensuing years, as neighborhoods one by one deteriorated, those blacks who could afford to moved further out did so, expanding the black district westward into the 15th and 16th Wards, and then the 17th; Druid Hill Avenue initially serving as an invisible western boundary. Rarely was the expansion into formerly all-white wards entirely peaceful. Black families moving into these areas often faced rock-throwers and threats of race riots. In one house in Arlington where windows were broken, the occupants became so frightened "they waved a white tablecloth from a window as a truce signal," and then moved out.

> Windows were broken and black tar was smeared on white marble steps. And when a black family moved into a house on Stricker Street they were attacked and the house was stoned. But white terrorism was no match for the combined purchasing power of housing-hungry blacks.[11]

By the time the Colored Law and Order League was established, half the black population of the city was living in the northwest, the highest share still professionals, literate and youthful. Between 1900 and 1910, just one ward, the 17th, had become 60% black. Despite the absence of segregation laws, both black dealers and whites wanting to build housing for blacks were stymied in their efforts to purchase land. With blacks thus limited to second-hand homes left by whites to meet their increasing demand for housing, realtors were able to charge above market prices for

---

[9] See Paul, p. 397. This writer recalls meeting with the Liquor Board and other officials in the 1970s in a like attempt, for the same reason, to persuade them to limit licensing in inner city neighborhoods, and meeting with the same lack of response. The fact that saloons regularly followed the move of blacks into an area, seemed, almost, like a deliberate effort to "prove" that the black lifestyle was inherently inferior.

[10] See Paul, p. 397

[11] Olson, p. 279. See also Power, *Apartheid* t, pp. 297-298.

sales and rentals, impoverishing some blacks desperate to move to escape the literally deadly slums.

In the summer of 1910, George W.F. McMechen, a Yale law graduate and practicing attorney, was the first black to break the invisible boundary of Druid Hill Avenue and move his family to a house on McCulloh Street in the formerly all white Eutaw Place neighborhood. This caused such an uproar that it was necessary to call the police to protect the family. In a recent interview with Hopkins students, Janice Woolridge, a black whose family lived one block over from Eutaw Place on Madison Avenue, told her interviewers:

> We weren't even supposed to go over there [to the white Eutaw Place neighborhood] unless you were going to work. That's how close we lived but how far apart. The wealthy folks lived there. It was society hill. They had mansions. Now, of course, they are mostly apartments...still gorgeous homes. Madison Avenue where I lived had been like that when we first moved there as a group. And those homes are still very well maintained because most of them were homeowners.

Soon after McMechen's move, on July 5, 1910, a group of whites petitioned the Mayor and City Council to pass legislation that would stop blacks from moving into their communities and would designate specific boundaries beyond which blacks could not move. After much controversy, in December 1910, the Council, on a strict party vote—all Democrats in favor—passed a very restrictive housing bill. After the City Solicitor declared it constitutional, on December 20, 1910, Mayor J. Barry Mahool signed it into law.

Garrett Power in his article, "Apartheid Baltimore Style", calls this "experiment in apartheid at best a sell-out of Baltimore plutocracy, and at worst an invidious denial of housing to Baltimore's blacks. Yet Mayor Mahool, who is remembered as a champion of social justice, eagerly signed the ordinance without apology."[12]

Soon after, in the first criminal case brought under the ordinance, "Judges Harland and Duffy of the Supreme Bench of Baltimore, declared the ordinance ineffective and void

---

[12] This and followed quote: Power, *Apartheid*, p. 300 & 303. He gives an extensive account of the history of these ordinances.

because it was 'inaccurately drawn.'" There is no published written opinion in this case so the actual reasoning is unknown. However, the judges may have referred to its faulty title which lacked a reference to racial segregation of housing. The court's adverse opinion merely prompted the City Council to try again, and Mayor Mahool signed a revised version on April 7, 1911.

Less than six weeks later, on May 15, as his last official act, Mahool signed into law a third version of the segregation ordinance that the City Council had enacted to correct a technical flaw in the second. Mahool had been defeated in the primary by the Democrat, James H. Preston, who became the new mayor on April 16.

That Mahool, with his otherwise strong progressive stances, should sign these Ordinances, serves to emphasize just how deep white sentiments were regarding housing segregation—something that became all too clear again when the issue was tackled during the 1960s Civil Rights Movement. Power writes:

> Baltimore Mayor J. Barry Mahool, who was known as an earnest advocate of good government, women's suffrage, and social justice, signed into law "an ordinance for preserving peace, preventing conflict and ill feeling between the white and colored races in Baltimore city, and promoting the general welfare of the city by providing, so far as practicable, for the use of separate blocks by white and colored people for residences, churches and schools.[13]

Power added that *Baltimore had become the first city in the United States to pass a segregation law [presumably referring to housing segregation specifically], aimed at blacks* [writer's italics]. The city's ordinances became known as "the Baltimore idea" and served as models for similar laws passed, soon after, by Southern cities in North Carolina, Virginia, Georgia, Kentucky, South Carolina, Alabama and Missouri.[14]

Power concludes by warning us to be cautious even of proposals made in the name of social reform for within such "righteous rhetoric" may lie "the racist propensities of

---

[13] Power quoting from Baltimore, Md. Ordinance 692, May 15, 1911.
[14] Power, *Apartheid*, p. 310.

democratic rule." The title of the ordinance claimed its purpose as "preserving peace, preventing conflict and ill-feeling between the white and colored races, and promoting the general welfare of the city...."[15] Mahool may not have so intended, but, Power writes, Baltimore Ordinance 692 "set the stage for understanding the development of a covert [*pretty up-front this writer would maintain*] conspiracy to enforce housing segregation, the vestiges of which persist in Baltimore yet today."[16]

•••

It was not until two years after passage of this third Ordinance (#692) that it was challenged by John E. Gurry, "a colored person," after he was charged with unlawfully moving into an all-white block. At trial, Judge Ireland Elliott dismissed the charge against Gurry, finding the ordinance contradictory in its provisions—in one part excluding whites from blocks "in whole or in part" black, and in another excluding blacks from blocks "in whole or in part" white; thus in precluding either whites or blacks from moving there, it would result in depopulating a block.[17]

The state, of course, appealed the lower court's dismissal of the indictment against Gurry, and eight appellate judges heard the case, *State v. Gurry*.[18] The state was represented by William L. Marbury; Gurry by the black attorney, W. Ashbie Hawkins,[19] who vigorously attacked these segregation ordinances at every level. On August 5, 1913 the Court of Appeals of Maryland affirmed the lower court's dismissal of the indictment.

It was October 7th before they issued a lengthy opinion that embodied their reasoning. They had differed with the lower court in its interpretation of the ordinance, believing it did permit either blacks or whites to move onto mixed blocks, hence not differing in its treatment of blacks and whites and hence not discriminating "as prohibited by the Constitution or

---

[15] *State v. Gurry*, p. 546.
[16] Power, *Apartheid*, p. 289.
[17] Power, *Apartheid*, p. 305
[18] *State v. Gurry*, 3 Baltimore City Court at 263.
[19] Hawkins fight to become a lawyer recounted in Education section: "Blacks Demand Higher Education."

statutes securing civil rights, [so] it is not necessary to discuss that question further."[20] However, what they went on to say on this subject is so revealing of the thinking about blacks at that time (perhaps still), that a lengthy passage is quoted— and it leads one to wonder why they did not uphold the ordinance.

> No intelligent observer in communities where there are many colored people can fail to notice that there are sometimes exhibitions of feelings between members of the two races which are likely to, and occasionally do, result in outbreaks of violence and disorder.
>
> It is not for us to say what this is attributable to; but the fact remains—however much it is to be regretted—and if a segregation of the races to such extent as may be permissible under the Constitution and laws of the land will have a tendency, not only to avoid disorder and violence, but to make a better feeling between the races, every one having the interests of the colored people as well as of the white people at heart ought to encourage rather than oppose it....

The appellate judges go on to quote Justice Brown in *Plessy v. Ferguson* as having declared that even though the object of 14th Amendment was meant to enforce the absolute equality of the two races before the law, it could not have meant to abolish distinctions based on color or social standing; nor to enforce "a commingling of the two races upon terms unsatisfactory to either."

They continued:

> If the welfare of the city, in the minds of the council, demanded that the two races should be thus, to this extent, separated, and thereby a cause of conflict removed, the court cannot declare their action unreasonable.
>
> It was acknowledged by the counsel for the appellee, both in the brief and in verbal argument, that for years there had been more or less friction resulting from the occupancy by colored people of houses in blocks theretofore occupied wholly by white people. With this acknowledgement, how can it be contended that the city council, charged with looking to the welfare of the city, is seeking to make an unreasonable use of the police power, when it enacts a law which, in their opinion, will tend to prevent the conflict?

---

[20] *State v. Gurry*, p. 551.

The appellate judges then go on to discuss laws that have been upheld which required separate railroad coaches for blacks and whites, separate schools, and that have prohibited marriage between whites and blacks. They do not deny the power of police to enforce violations of these or any criminal laws. They therefore conclude in this section of their opinion: "It only remains for us to determine whether the ordinance as drawn should be sustained."[21]

In the end, the primary grounds on which the Appeals Court invalidated the ordinance and declared it unconstitutional was the fact that it wholly ignored "all vested rights which existed at the time of the passage of the ordinance." It lacked any provision "for some sufficient public notice of what blocks are affected—which are to be white, and which colored." And in some instances, in denying an owner the right to live in, rent or sell property legally purchased prior to the ordinance's enactment "would be a practical confiscation of his property."[22]

Again, the Baltimore City Council was not deterred from its segregationist stance. Even before the Appeal's Court wrote its full opinion, the Council acted on the rationale of their per curium judgement and for the fourth time revised the city's housing segregation law. On September 25, 1913 they passed the fourth version, Ordinance 339, that provided "that nothing herein contained shall be construed or operate to prevent any person, who at the date of the passage of this ordinance, shall have acquired a legal right to occupy, as a residence any building or portion thereof...from exercising such legal rights."[23]

At first blacks appeared to be well served by this segregation law, for, as whites fled "mixed" blocks, blacks were able to buy their houses at below market value. However, with blacks still, for the most part, confined to a small, compact area of the city, this meant that the housing available to them would not grow even as their numbers did; and this meant that housing prices for blacks would increase even as their quality inevitably declined.

---

[21] The lengthy quotes are from *State v. Gurry*, pp. 551-552.

[22] *State v. Gurry*, pp. 552-553

[23] Power, *Apartheid*, p. 306, quoting Baltimore, MD Ordinance 339 (September 25, 1913).

Once again, the middle-class blacks in the northwest wards turned to the Baltimore Colored Law and Order League in an effort to fight off speculators, but it became futile as speculators gradually "outbid homeowners for the houses and converted them into tenements for three or more families." As the "lower classes" spilled into the area, entrepreneurs soon followed, filling their streets and alleys with the same saloons and gambling dens the better-off blacks had tried to escape, as well as numerous billiard halls, dance halls and several brothels. As we've already noted, the self-help League proved helpless in its efforts to persuade the city to stop issuing liquor licenses and to stop protecting these "vice districts.[24]

There were those in Baltimore's white community who were concerned that the restrictive housing segregation ordinances were causing a spill-over of crime and contagion into the white areas, but they were no more successful than the blacks' self-help League in pressuring city officials to take note and do something. About this time, H.L. Mencken is quoted as saying:

> The persons who govern us have never thought to look to this matter. When the darky tries to move out of his sty and into human habitation a policeman now stops him. The law practically insists that he keep on incubating typhoid and tuberculosis—that he keep these infections alive...for the delight and benefit of the whole town.[25]

Mayor James H. Preston, who had succeed Mayor Mahool, supported the segregation ordinances, despite admitting their deleterious affect on the health of whites. He is quoted as saying:

> [W]e call upon these people to serve us in our households, prepare our food, tend our children and perform countless other services wherein personal contact is a matter of course. Regardless of our efforts to maintain [a] sanitary and healthful environment for ourselves and families the insidious influence of slum conditions is carried into our very midst to defile and destroy.

---

[24] Power, *Apartheid*, pp. 306-309 & Olson, p. 278
[25] Mencken quote and the following by Preston are found in Power, *Apartheid*, p. 307

He did not seem sufficiently concerned to rescind the ordinance and completely unconcerned that black deaths from tuberculosis 260 times that of whites, and from diseases generally 96 times higher than that of whites.[26] In fact, Mayor Preston wrote to the President of the New York Title and Mortgage Company in 1917 to brag about the effectiveness of the city's segregation ordinance and its positive effect on property values and "on the condition of both races."[27] This, apparently, was the opinion of the majority of whites.

•••

In 1915, after Thomas S. Jackson was convicted under the city's fourth segregation ordinance, Ashbie Hawkins appealed, asserting that this law was no more constitutional than the three that preceded it. However, the Court of Appeal postponed hearing it until February 1918, until after the U.S. Supreme Court had rendered its decision in a similar case, *Buchanan v. Warley* (1917), that was then before them.

The national office of the NAACP had shepherded this case to the highest court, challenging the constitutionality of a Louisville, Kentucky ordinance that forbid blacks to live on a block that was more than 50% white and vice versa. It was first argued in April 1916 before seven justices; but then, again, before a full bench; Baltimore's City Solicitor was among the twelve who submitted amicus briefs [friend of the court] supporting the ordinance. The court ruled unanimously that the Louisville housing segregation ordinance was unconstitutional.[28]

Hence the same arguments were made in *Jackson v. State* (1918):[29]

> The 14th Amendment and the statutes enacted in furtherance of its purpose operate to qualify ad entitle a colored man to acquire property without state legislation discriminating against him solely because of color.

Both the U. S. Supreme Court and Maryland's Court of

---

[26] Power, *Apartheid*, p. 307

[27] Power, *Apartheid*, p. 310.

[28] Power, *Apartheid*, pp. 312-313

[29] *Jackson v. State*, pp. 910-911.

Appeal distinguished between housing segregation laws and other Jim Crow laws they had sustained, based on the "separate and equal" doctrine, finding this was not possible in the case of property rights. The court continued its argument:

> [*Buchanan v. Warley*] does not deal with an attempt to prohibit the amalgamation of the races. The right which the [Louisville] ordinance annulled was the civil right of a white man to dispose of his property if he saw fit to do so to a person of color and of a colored person to make such disposition to a white person....We think this attempt to prevent the alienation of the property in question to a person of color was not a legitimate exercise of the police power of the state, and is in direct violation of the fundamental law enacted in the Fourteenth Amendment of the Constitution preventing state interference with property rights except by due process of law.

The State Appeal Court concluded:

> The Baltimore segregation ordinance is clearly opposed to the principle declared and enforced by the Supreme Court in holding the Louisville ordinance to be invalid, and we can therefore have no hesitation in deciding that the present ordinance is likewise unconstitutional.

After the failure of the fourth attempt by the Baltimore City Council to pass a housing segregation ordinance that would pass constitutional muster, they did not try again—but this did not mean that the city ended its fight to maintain segregation. It did not even end the City's attempt to use the criminal law to enforce housing segregation.

•••

No longer able to depend on legislation, "containment" and "slum clearance" became the new weapons of choice to continue the desired segregation of blacks.[30] To begin with, the Mayor published articles, used rumor as a tool to manipulate people, and used existing white neighborhood associations to denigrate blacks and stir up racial fears.[31] The

[30] Power, *Apartheid...*, info and quotes (unless otherwise noted), pp. 315-319
[31] Olson, p. 278.

media, as now, was instrumental in creating and perpetuating a negative image of blacks. The influential *Sun* took a stand against lynchings and riots but seemed to find lesser attacks on blacks amusing. They regularly depicted blacks as "brutes" and gave rave reviews to the racist books as *The Clansmen* and *The Leopard's Spots* and the film *Birth of a Nation* (the book on which it was based was by Thomas Dixon, formerly a student at Johns Hopkins University).[32]

But even more insidious than the rumors and stereotyping, Mayor Preston conspired with representatives of the Real Estate Board of Baltimore, City Health Department, City Building Office and neighborhood associations to discourage whites from selling or renting to blacks in any white area. When harassment, peer pressure and suasion did not work, and a real estate agent or home owner sought to contravene the city's containment policy, they were threatened with code violations and property condemnation.

All too soon, this conspiracy to prevent blacks from moving to new areas became institutionalized: banks "redlined" districts where they would not extend mortgage financing, and the Federal Housing Administration denied support in neighborhoods with "inharmonious racial groups." As late as 1950, the National Association of Real Estate Brokers, Baltimore a member, provided this in its code of ethics:

> The realtor should not be instrumental in introducing into a neighborhood a character of property or occupancy, members of any race or nationality or any individual whose presence will clearly be detrimental to property values in the neighborhood.

Along with these actions, the Mayor used "health" as the rationale for removing blacks from areas where they were not wanted, but in fact simply moved them from one slum to another, irrespective of health considerations. The city withheld services: garbage and refuse wasn't collected, rats proliferated, inspectors took bribes, and houses were not connected to the sewer system, which had been completed in 1914.

---

[32] Olson, p. 279

In addition, Sherry Olson refers to the results of studies made between 1913 and 1917 that confirmed that blacks were charged more for rent than whites for the same accommodations, forcing blacks to economize on food, and to take in relatives and boarders in order to pay. This, while poor blacks were being forced to spend a full third of their income for housing, white property owners were accumulating capital, which, in many cases, was the beginning of "slumlord dynasties" in Baltimore that lasted into the 1940s, even the 1970s.[33]

Introduced in 1920, zoning became another political tool used to discriminate on the basis of wealth, race, and national origin. Power writes:

> In Baltimore, zoning opened a political marketplace. Brokers and builders used zoning to manipulate real estate transactions. Small businessmen obtained advantageous locations. Large retailers created the "right atmosphere" in the central business district. Heavy industry stifled neighborhood objection to smoke and stench.
>
> The rich slowed the rate at which their emptying downtown houses were being converted to flats and boarding houses, and buffered their new neighborhoods from the hurly-burly of the city. The middle class kept their cottage-suburbs exclusive of blue-collar rowhouses. The working class fought commercial incursion and the "negro invasion." Local politicians managed the market, but not the use of land.

Power concludes that "nothing has changed. Localities continue to prefer the majority's prejudice to the minority's need."[34]

•••

In sharp contrast with the city's governmental and civic institutions, the courts, even though never specifically outlawing segregation, had proved helpful in protecting the legal rights of blacks. They had refused to uphold all four legislative attempts to enforce housing segregation. The courts would again prove helpful when Morgan College attempted, in 1917, to escape the invisible boundaries that were holding

---

[33] See Olson, pp. 276-277. "Alley housing" was described at the beginning of this section.
[34] Power, *Unwisdom*, p. 669-673

blacks in a contained area of Baltimore, and sought to move Morgan to its newly purchased property on Hillen Road and Cold Spring Lane just north of Baltimore city.[35]

Protests to the college's buying and occupying the property began immediately after the transfer of ownership was recorded in Towson. Whites in the surrounding neighborhoods publicized the names of realtors, brokers, and attorneys who were involved; started a hate mail and telephone campaign; and, once, a committee of over fifty citizens, headed by the Assistant Superintendent of Schools in Maryland, visited Morgan officials trying to persuade them against the move. Leaving both disappointed and disgusted, "the president of the local community association declared his preference to live near a community of 'ignorant and tractable negroes' rather than one of 'educated negroes.'"[36]

These tactics having failed to stop the Morgan purchase from going forward, four white families, represented by the well-connected attorney, Edgar Allan Poe[37] filed a complaint in the Circuit Court of Baltimore County on August 6, 1917. In their case, *Russell I. Diggs et al v. Morgan College, a Corporation, etc.*, their main complaint was the college's intent to build residential housing on a part of the site for "persons of the colored race only and not necessarily connected with the college," which would introduce Negroes "into the midst of the already well developed and flourishing white residential section surrounding and adjacent to said proposed Negro colony" resulting "in irreparable injury to your orators and their property in said neighborhood."[38]

In response, the court pointed out that Morgan's actions

---

[35] The account that follows is based on Wilson's book and shorter works by McConnell and Horn. It is a continuation of Morgan's history begun in the Education section: "Blacks Demand Higher Education."

[36] Power, *Apartheid*, p. 308.

[37] He was the son of the Maryland Law School dean, John Prentiss Poe, who'd notified Hawkins that he could not return to his school. This writer has not ascertained the exact relationship of this family to the famous poet, Edgar Allan Poe (1809-1849), but they are both descendents of the Poe family that came from Ireland to the U.S. in the 18th Century. (*Baltimore: It's History & Its People*)

[38] *Diggs v. Morgan,*.133 Md. 264 (1918)

were within the rights accorded them in their Charter, Chapter 357 of the Acts of 1900. It pointed out that the charter put no limits on the kind of school Morgan could establish and allowed the acquisition of property that would help support the school. The court, accordingly, on March 9, 1918, ruled in favor of Morgan.[39]

Represented by Edgar Allan Poe, the white community appealed, and their case was heard on March 12, 1918 (decided October 30). Making the same arguments as in the lower court, they asked for an injunction that would bar Morgan from building residential housing for blacks. The Court of Appeals of Maryland not only upheld the lower court's decision but added that it was only natural for a college to look to the future possibility of growth and so to purchase more land than immediately needed.

The court further pointed out that real estate was typically a favorable form of investment. It must have been particularly upsetting to the whites pursuing this case when the court referred to the decisions in *Buchanan v. Warley* and *Jackson v. State* which had advised that the mere fact of blacks living in a neighborhood was not sufficient to deem it a public nuisance.[40]

Having failed in the courts, the white community, Poe still representing them, sought to have Morgan's Charter nullified through legislative action. President John Spencer himself (who was white) successfully argued against this, claiming that such an action would mean that no charter in the state could be depended on.

When Poe argued that public sentiment was against this move by Negroes into a formerly all-white area, President Spencer not only pointed out that such sentiment had never been tested, but additionally referred to a test that *had* been made. The so-called Poe Amendment which proposed to deprive blacks and other ethnic groups of voting rights had been soundly defeated at the polls in 1905.

When the opponents claimed the presence of Negroes would lead to conflict, President Spencer surprised at least some of them by declaring that between eighty and one

---

[39] Suit initiated at the Circuit Court for Baltimore County in Equity.
[40] *Diggs v. Morgan College,* 133 MD. 264; 1918 Md. LEXIS 125.

hundred blacks had been residing there for some time [those from the burned-out school in Lynchburg, Virginia]. An occurrence reported by Wilson in his history of Morgan suggests that at least some in the community were already aware of the Lynchburg groups' presence on campus. Wilson reports that on January 8, 1918, three months prior to the legislative hearing, "a tragic incident was averted by diplomacy and common sense." [41]

> Principal McCoy was sitting in his office on the first floor of Young Hall [the name given one of the houses] one night when the doorbell rang. He turned the porch lights on and saw a white woman standing there. He did not open the door, but she let him know that she had trouble with her car on Hillen Road and that she wished to use the telephone. Principal McCoy requested her to wait for just a minute; he returned to his office and called the police. In a few minutes the police arrived. They said to Principal McCoy: "Professor, you used your head tonight. This woman wanted you to let her in; then she was going to scream 'rape'! The men in the car planned to come to her rescue and take care of you."

At the conclusion of the arguments before the Judiciary Committee, it refused the community's request that they rescind Morgan's Charter.

Having once more failed, the whites now were able to get two different bills introduced in the General Assembly; the first preventing the school from locating where now proposed; the second forcing the sale of the property in contention, referred to as the Ivy Mill Property. Both failed. A third bill that also failed would have prohibited black residences in the area that encompassed the Morgan property.

Finally, Morgan could move forward, as planned, which included the creation and development of a residential area to be called Morgan Park. President Spencer and Morgan's Trustees made an agreement with the George R. Morris Company to build approximately 130 houses on the site, laying out very specific requirements as to frontage, lot size, etc, but to include a "variety of housing styles ranging from one story cottage types to more spacious structures."[42] A

---

[41] Wilson, p. 163
[42] McConnell, pp. 10 & 23.

number of covenants were also developed that were to last in perpetuity, including restrictions forbidding "factories, saloons, stables, along with swine or cattle of any kind"...

> also any nuisance noxious or dangerous to the health. The erection or maintenance of business houses of any kind, hospitals, asylums, or institutions of kindred nature were not permitted unless approved by the committee [formed for enforcement]. Domestic fowl such as chickens and pigeons were not to run at large. Chicken houses, garages, or other outhouses were to be erected in keeping with the design of the dwelling erected.[43]

A preliminary sales promotion was begun in August 1918, described by the *Afro* as "an epoch in the history of the colored people of Baltimore."[44] So was born Morgan Park which would, within the next several years, become a thriving community with "City Sewer, Electricity, Concrete Footways, City Water, City Gas, Macadamized Streets and Annex Taxes."[45] The first home actually ready for occupancy was in 1921; others soon to follow; the original occupants came from "various walks of life."

Over the years, the community has had such notable residents as Dr. W.E.B. DuBois who lived there from 1939 to 1949; Dr. Regina Goff, who became the first black to head the Office of Education under the Department of Health, Education and Welfare; and Dr. Carl Murphy, President and Chairman of the Board of Directors of the *Afro-American Newspaper* chain, and a prominent supporter of civil rights activism.[46]

Tensions remained as Morgan Park developed, as the surrounding white community grew in numbers, and as the college expanded and achieved accreditation by the Middle States Association of Colleges (in 1925 and again in 1935). However, for the most part, the two communities simply

---

[43] McConnell, pp. 11-12.

[44] McConnell, p. 12

[45] McConnell, p. 13.

[46] See McConnell, pp. 22-23, 57-59 & 61-62. McConnell's history includes quite lengthy profiles of many of Morgan Park's residents.

ignored each other.[47]

•••

Few blacks were as fortunate as Morgan in being able to build new housing in the areas outside the city ghettos where most were confined in ever deteriorating housing. The supply of housing available to blacks did begin to expand somewhat following Baltimore's annexations in 1918 that tripled its area. These annexations allowed the city to incorporate the West Arlington and Mount Washington neighborhoods with their fine frame residences; Roland Park with its mansions; Govans with its small country cottages; Hamilton and Lauraville with their modest bungalows (and the site of Morgan College's property); Gardenville; and Highlandtown, Canton, and Brooklyn, with their rowhouses for the working class.

The Mayor hoped that the homes in Baltimore's New Annex would not include rowhouses, so that it would attract a wealthier population that would provide more tax income for the city.[48] This approach was incorporated in an Act passed by the Maryland General Assembly in 1912.

However, in 1916, the Court of Appeals ruled that "aesthetic purposes" was not sufficient to "invade the property rights" guaranteed by the constitution. It declared the 1912 Act "prohibiting the building of dwelling houses within certain limits of Baltimore City...unless of brick, semi-detached and at least ten feet apart, or if of frame, twenty feet apart," unconstitutional.[49]

Something has already been said of the New Deal employment policies initiated by the federal government during the Great Depression of the 30s as they affected blacks, but there were also policies initiated in the area of housing. And just as the anti-New Deal Mayor (Jackson) had thwarted efforts in the field of employment, so did he conspire with real estate interests to do the same with housing programs.

---

[47] The Education section ceded to "Housing" the telling of the conflicts encountered by Morgan in its move to the Ivy Mill property, but the Education section again took up Morgan's story after 1935.

[48] Power, *Unwisdom...*, pp. 652-653.

[49] *Byrne v. Maryland Realty Company*, 129 Md. 202 (1916).

They prevented altogether the building of two public housing projects that had been planned by the Housing Division of the Public Works Administration (one for whites and one for blacks in the most blighted areas). Mayor Jackson, as ever, disapproved of any incursions by the federal government and insisted that they would have to pay a "service charge" for any land they used for public housing. Any other arrangement, he asserted, would amount to unfair competition with private developers in the city, a position, not surprisingly, endorsed by the Real Estate Board.[50]

Other groups in the city, including labor unions, Carl Murphy at the *Afro-American*, and religious leaders were not so enamored of the Mayor's position. They all appealed with him to change his position, but he remained firm, killing the public housing project.

Prospects for public housing emerged again after passage in 1937 of the Wagner-Steagall Act that created the United States Housing Authority. True to their former positions, the Mayor and Realtors not only opposed building public housing, but also the creation of either state or local housing agencies. In this instance, however, thirty-two black and white fraternal groups, religious and civic societies, and organizations of the unemployed joined to form the Baltimore Citizens Housing Committee. They held well-publicized meetings, sent petitions to the mayor and city council, and generally sought public support in opposition to the mayor. The extent of the need for better housing had been revealed in a 1936 survey made by Frances Morton while still a graduate student of Social Work. By 1940, Baltimore

> had the dubious distinction of having the highest percentage of dilapidated housing, the greatest number of outside toilets and the highest TB death rate of any of the ten largest cities in the country. When its first housing code was enacted in 1942, an estimated 50,000 houses were in flagrant violation.[51]

---

[50] Argersinger, p. 94-95

[51] From reprint of an article by Hans Froelicher, Jr. , Pres. of CPHA, that appeared in now defunct publication, *Marriage & Family Living*, Vol. XVII, #2, May 1955.

The Citizens Housing Committee was sufficiently successful in its demands for a public agency to deal with housing that the mayor and council later that year acted to create the Baltimore Housing Authority. From this eventually flowed the Citizens' Housing Council, and eventually the Citizen's Planning and Housing Association (CPHA) in 1941—an organization headed for years by Frances Morton and one that is still in existence. Once thought radical, by 1941 the citizen's group had turned from tenant support to working with the city's social agencies and planning commission.[52]

Meanwhile, in 1939, Baltimore's first public housing had been approved and the razing of 250 dwellings had begun, displacing 3,000 residents. The Edgar Allen Poe apartments would house 298. This writer thought the choice of names ironic—hopefully intended to recognize Baltimore's famous poet and short story writer, rather than the very racist attorney, a distant relative by the same name, who had tried time after time, amongst other things, to disenfranchise black voters.

These activities, noble as they perhaps were, did little to ease the housing situation for the majority of blacks. Amy Bentley writes that by 1940 blacks had, for the most part, been limited to an area no more than three square miles; an estimated 78,000 per square mile forced into the oldest, worst part of the city. Housing for blacks remained one of the city's most explosive issues even in wartime.[53]

> In July 1943 eight hundred whites—three-fourths of them women—[the leaders white clergy] marched on the office of Mayor Theodore R. McKeldin to protest a proposal to build homes for twelve hundred black war workers in an undeveloped site along side Herring Run Park.

Mayor McKeldin did not take kindly to their rudeness, telling them an interracial commission had selected the site. Soon after, a survey of housing available to blacks stirred still

---

[52] Information regarding the building of this first public housing found in Argersinger's, Chapter 4, which gives a complete history of the groups mentioned. More will be said later about CORE's opposition in the 60s to the kind of razing that took place.

[53] Bentley, pp. 428-429 includes quote in paragraph following.

more controversy when its chairman, white, asserted that available black housing wasn't as bad as had been claimed. However, the blacks on the commission found otherwise. "Housing continued to be a problem even as the war ended and the numbers migrating to the city slowed."

By the end of the war, the percentage of blacks in the "old city" had grown from 15% to 30% while the white population had decreased by half. Baltimore had become a city with a black core, surrounded by a white ring—a phenomenon that would remain even as blacks gradually penetrated former white barriers and spread out the city's main corridors; whites simply moving still deeper into the suburbs. George Callcott calls it "a replacement of wealth by poverty, power by powerlessness." The rich and middle-class had "left behind their old houses for the people who could afford no better."[54]

During the 1960s, when the civil rights organization, CORE, started its drive to end housing segregation, it adopted the mantra, "Break the Noose," the words circled with a rope, giving it a double-edged meaning. More will be said later of this, and of the "containment" and "slum clearance" policies that endured into the 1960s and beyond.

---

[54] George Callcott, p. 83-84.

Restrictive Covenants

When whites were stymied legislatively in their efforts to keep blacks out of *their* neighborhoods (the Supreme Court having held in 1917 that racial zoning was unconstitutional), they took the policy of containment into their own hands and began to attach restrictive covenants to any sales of housing in white areas. These prevented a buyer, in perpetuity, from selling or renting same to blacks or Jews.

Douglas Connah, Jr. writes that "this became so popular that it, more than anything else, molded today's widespread neighborhood segregation." As we've indicated before, the federal government aided and abetted this segregation, since the FHA (Federal Housing Administration), "whose creation sparked the post-depression building boom, insisted on the restrictive covenant (and even wrote a model covenant) as a condition to insuring mortgages." [55]

•••

In *Meade v. Dennistone et al*, the Court of Appeals of Maryland on January 11, 1938 upheld the use of these restrictive covenants, as long as the buyer was made aware of it.[56] It would be another ten years before that opinion was reversed.

It began at a meeting on November 14, 1927 of property owners in an area of twenty-four square blocks bounded on the north and south by 25th Street and North Avenue and on the east and west by Barclay and Charles Streets, where a covenant was agreed upon. The grounds for this court case were laid when the former owners of 2227 Barclay Street, Anne, Francis, and Mary Tighe, and Anna Gugerty, who had all signed the covenant, deeded the property to Frank Berman on November 4, 1935, who, in turn, on October 22, 1936 had contracted to sell it to Edward Meade.

A bill of complaint, intended to stop Meade from occupying the house, was filed by two other residents on Barclay Street, Mary Dennistone & Mary Becker. Nonetheless, on November 24, 1936, Meade and his family did move in;

---

[55] Connah, *Congressional Record*, E2431.
[56] *Meade v. Dennistone*, No. 26, 196 Atlantic Reporter, 330-336 (1938)

soon after, the bill for injunction against Meade and Berman was filed.

At trial, the defense pointed out that by this time there was already one negro family in residence near-by his address, and also a negro business that catered only to whites. Further, they pointed out that only one block away, the area was predominately black. Their counsel argued further that any enforcement of the area's covenant would contravene the 14th Amendment to the Constitution. Nonetheless, the lower court in Baltimore enjoined "Edward Meade, a negro, and his family from using or occupying the house and premises known as No. 2227 Barclay street,...

> enjoining him 'from procuring, authorizing or permitting any Negro or Negroes, or person or persons, either in whole or in part of Negro or African descent to use or occupy said premises,' and enjoining Frank Berman, Edward Meade's vendor or assignor, from permitting Edward Meade and his family, or any negroes or persons of African descent, from occupying the premises.

In the appeals court, William Marbury, Jr. again represented the white appellees, and, this time, William A.C. Hughes, Jr. represented the black appellant. That court found that even though the housing segregation laws had been found unconstitutional, the court had not decided the question of segregation per se. It held that neither the 13th, 14th, nor 15th Amendments prohibited private individuals from entering into contracts respecting the control and disposition of their own property." It added, however, that the distinctions made by the courts as to what is allowable segregation and what is not is difficult to explain, and has left cities, where housing is a problem, with no satisfactory solution. The court makes an interesting observation on its way to assuring the continuance of the problem.

> The large, almost sudden, emigration of negroes from the country to the cities, with the consequent congestion in colored centers, has created a situation about which all agree something ought to be done. In Baltimore city, with a population of about 850,000, one-seventh is negro, occupying a relatively small portion of the city's territory, though the colored area has been, in the last several years, rapidly expanding. Since the decision under the 14th

Amendment, supra, no public action can be taken to solve what has become a problem, and property owners have undertaken to regulate it by contract.

In the end, the court had this to say:

> It may be an anomalous situation when a colored man may own property which he cannot occupy, but, if he buys on notice of such a restriction, the consequences are the same to him as to any other buyer with notice. There is no law which forbids the property owners to agree that any given territory shall be all white or all colored....
>
> It has been settled by a long line of decisions in this state that our statute, requiring deeds conveying an estate of inheritance or freehold, or any declaration or limitation of use, or any estate above seven years, to be executed, acknowledged, and recorded as therein provided, is applicable to grants of or covenants for easements on land....
>
> It is our opinion, therefore, that this agreement is lawful and enforceable, not opposed to the public policy of this state, of which the defendants had constructive notice, and the decree should be affirmed.

•••

Nine years later, Fred Weisgal, then barely out of law school, became the attorney for Ethel Marks in another covenant case in Baltimore. It came at a time when the national office of the NAACP was accumulating cases that might be brought before the Supreme Court in hopes of abolishing the legality of restrictive covenants. Mrs. Marks' case came to the public's attention when the September 20, 1947 edition of the *Afro-American* carried the bold headline: **Court Upholds 'Hate' Covenant; GI's Wife, Children Homeless; Mother Fails to Fight Suit**.[57]

Mrs. Ethel M. Marks hadn't appeared in court on September 16 1947 when the Northeast Baltimore Improvement Association asked Judge John T. Tucker for a judgement

---

[57] Fred's having undertaken such a case so early in his career presaged the fact that he would soon become famous in Baltimore as a civil rights/civil liberty's litigator. Information on this case, including newspaper articles, are from the personal files of Fred Weisgal, which were available to the writer while working on his biography, *"...And Justice for All."*

against her. She hadn't even consulted a lawyer when she'd received a notice to appear. Consequently, Judge Tucker had upheld, by default,[58] the Association's covenant that barred blacks from occupying the property at 1539 N. Caroline Street (not far removed from the earlier Barclay Street case). When she received his order to vacate, she told the *Afro*:

> I was confused and bewildered on learning of the ruling. I really didn't understand the implications of the restrictions on the house when I moved in.

With its nine rooms and bath, it had just seemed perfect for her and her six children, who ranged in age from five to sixteen. She hoped, too, her husband, who'd been in the Army for two years and was now stationed in Japan, would soon be joining them. She was insulted when she later read the testimony given by Mr. Kennedy, the President of The Northeast Baltimore Improvement Association.

> Colored people do not take care of their homes and they allow them to deteriorate. Once they move in, the neighborhood goes downhill fast. I am too old to start buying another home today.

The real estate broker who testified was just as bad:

> As a general rule, colored people do not take care of the property they occupy. The social situation between white and colored, being what it is in Baltimore, the white occupants would be obliged to move. Anyone forced to move would have great difficulty finding a new home.

Before she'd moved into the house, Mrs. Marks had never heard of this supposed 2,000-member group of owners, and of their commitment to keep blacks out of the 65 block area they represented. And just as in the earlier case, testimony that other blacks were already living nearby the controversial Marks' place hadn't seemed to make any difference. [In a number of these restrictive covenant cases, the argument had been made that the presence of blacks in an area, in and of itself, invalidated a covenant since the area was no longer white.]

Mrs. Marks, not surprisingly, was chagrined and upset by

---

[58] A party not showing up at a court appointed time loses their right to plead their case, and thus automatically loses.

the eviction notice issued by Judge Tucker on September 16, 1947 and belatedly sought an attorney's help—Fred Weisgal's. He immediately sought a record of the case and attempted to have the default decree set aside. He wanted a rehearing on the merits, because then, even if he lost, there would at least be a basis for appeal, difficult as that would be.

Since the Supreme Court's 1926 decision in *Corrigan v. Buckley* that neither the 5th, 13th nor 14th Amendments "prohibited private individuals from entering into contracts respecting the control and disposition of their own property," the prevailing view had been that racial covenants were private actions that had the court's tacit approval.

As we've seen, this view had been affirmed in 1938 by the Maryland Court of Appeal in *Meade v. Dennistone.* Arguments that judicial enforcement made the covenants "state action," and hence subject to the 14th Amendment had simply been brushed aside.[59] But Fred lost even his first motion to have the default decree set aside.

•••

After Mrs. Marks had come to his office, Fred had immediately contacted Charles Hamilton Houston, who, assisted by Phineas Indritz (on leave from his job at the Solicitor's Office of the Department of Interior), was preparing oral arguments for the Supreme Court covenant cases, *Shelley v. Kraemer* and *Hurd v. Hodge*, a companion Washington, D.C. case. He had not heard from them until after the denial of his motion to have the default decree set aside. It was September 28th when Fred received a letter from Indritz. Referring to her case, it read:

> *The fact that the majority of the property owners in the block whose property is covered by covenants have now agreed to remove the covenant, is an unusual factor in your case. [It raises the question of whether or not the covenant is still valid as a "volunteer" private agreement.] I think I can make use of this point in the Supreme Court argument on the pending cases.*

The testimony in the original trial that blacks were

59 See Vose, pp. 18-19.

already in the area had resulted in an undercurrent of feeling amongst those whites who were present that a "complete infiltration" of blacks into the area was inevitable. From Mrs. Marks' point of view, this reaction had prompted a favorable action. These whites began to collect signatures of owners in the area willing to revoke the covenant. This was "a new twist" that had not existed previously in restrictive covenant cases.

Indritz requested a summary of the case to date and a copy of the motion regarding the fact that a majority of neighboring property owners had agreed to remove the covenant. He suggests a press release pointing this out—which he'd then like a copy of. [*There is nothing in Fred's files to indicate whether any or all of this was ever done.*] Indritz' letter continued:

> *May I suggest that you not only argue, in your case, that it would be an abuse of discretion for the judge not to delay action in view of the impending decisions by the Supreme Court, but also that, just as a covenant frequently is refused enforcement on the grounds of change of neighborhood caused by the actual moving in of many restricted persons, so in your case, the agreement to release the covenant amounted, in law, to a change of neighborhood and therefore brings your case within the changed neighborhood doctrine.*

Then, in a letter dated December 12, 1947, Houston requested from Weisgal a copy of the complaint in the *Marks* case which had been filed in the Baltimore City Court by the Improvement Association's President.

Only four days later, in a long letter dated December 16th, Houston wrote to Lillie Jackson at the Baltimore Branch of the NAACP (sending Fred a carbon copy). After explaining to her the circumstances of the case, Houston goes on to say that he'd received notice of the case only after Mrs. Marks had a notice of eviction from the sheriff and the time for appeal had passed, "so there was nothing more we could do in the Maryland courts." He continued:

> *Mr. Weisgal and I worked out a draft of a complaint for injunction in the Federal courts, including a temporary restraining order, on the ground that the enforcement of a restrictive covenant by a State court violated the 14th Amendment to the Constitution.* [The same argument, as mentioned previously, that, so far, in other cases, had been

dismissed by the courts.]

I asked Mr. Weisgal about the cost and he replied that Mrs. Marks had no money whatsoever; that her husband was with the occupation forces in Japan and that she was left alone with a house full of children. Mr. Weisgal told me that he had applied to you, but that the Baltimore Branch would not enter the case unless he would agree to step out as counsel.

I then called Mr. Carl Murphy [owner of the Afro-newspaper], explaining to him that in my opinion this case tied right in with the cases filed before the United States Supreme Court, and that it might be possible to get a preview of the argument before the Supreme Court in this case. Mr. Murphy said that he could probably find about $50 or $60 for costs. Mr. Weisgal got an appointment with Judge Chesnut for 4:00 the next afternoon and an agreement with counsel for the white property owners that they would hold the sheriff off until after a hearing before Judge Chesnut.

I decided that the case was so important that I went over to Baltimore myself, at my own expense, to appear with Mr. Weisgal. I notified Mr. Murphy and he sent a reporter to cover the case....It soon developed that argument was going to be more extensive than anticipated, whereupon [the judge] set the case down for argument December 22, at 10:00 a.m. Meanwhile Mrs. Marks remains in her property.

I am writing this letter to find out whether the Branch wants me to continue personally in the case. I think it is important and brings up several important questions....

If the Branch wants me to continue in the case, I shall be glad to do so on the usual terms. Will you please check with the Legal Committee as soon as possible and advise me, because if I am to be in Baltimore next Monday, December 22. I wish to know about it as far in advance as possible.

There is no record of Mrs. Jackson's response. It is most likely that her "condition" that Fred "step out as counsel" had to do not only with the local NAACP's desire to dominate the civil rights' agenda, but also with the dissension that had been going on for some time within both the local branches and the national NAACP.[60] There was a growing resentment of "liberal

---

[60] At least at a later date, August Meier confirms Baltimore NAACP's "aggressive and militant leadership [that] seemed to want to dominate the civil rights agenda in Baltimore. More than one meeting in Carl Murphy's office was required to set things straight and even yet, as late as 1962, the NAACP-Branch-President, Lillie Jackson, would

Jews" fighting for black rights, and a growing sentiment that black attorneys should take over. But in this case, Houston's commitment must have mollified Mrs. Jackson's objection to Fred's involvement since he remained as counsel.

•••

The last information available about this case is an incomplete article from the *Afro* reporting that Judge Calvin Chesnut declined to issue an order staying Mrs. Marks eviction from the covenant-covered property because she had *failed to exhaust her remedies with the State courts*. In so ruling, he was upholding Judge Tucker's refusal to set aside the default decree, and was, in essence, denying them the right to have the case tried on the merits—because Judge Tucker's decision had not been appealed in a timely manner.[61] The article continued:

> Following dismissal of the petition, Fred E. Weisgal, the attorney who argued in Federal Court with Charles Houston, said there still may be a possibility of staying the eviction until after the Supreme Court decision in the covenant cases slated for a hearing in January. This stay of eviction would have to be effected through an agreement between the white property owners who brought the covenant proceeding and Mrs. Marks.

We do not know if this happened, but can hope that Mrs. Marks' eviction was delayed until after the Supreme Court's favorable decision in the other covenant cases.[62] It would seem especially appropriate that her case be dismissed in light of the fact that the *voluntary* nature of the Northeast Baltimore

---

come to a CIG [student activist group] meeting and rise to say, 'You still belong to us!'" Meier also tells us why Murphy was so powerful: he not only headed the *Afro-American* newspaper chain, but also was on Morgan State College's trustee board, and was influential on the boards of the Urban League and NAACP., August Meier, *A White Scholar...* (pp. 22 & 26) It seems safe to say that this was as much the problem at the time of the covenant case as it was later.

[61] Legally, if a deadline is missed, no further action can be taken in a case, thus it becomes impossible to "exhaust" the remedies that otherwise would have been available.

[62] Information on *Shelley v. Kramer* & *Hurd v. Hodge* follows.

Improvement Association's covenant agreement was brought into question when a substantial number of its members signed a petition expressing their willingness to revoke it.

•••

The first Supreme Court case alluded to, *Shelley v. Kraemer* (which combined restrictive covenant cases from Detroit, Michigan and from Missouri), was argued in 1948 by Thurgood Marshall and Loren Miller (Charles Houston and William Hastie, among others were named on the brief). Among the sixteen organizations that prepared amicus briefs asking the court to strike down restrictive covenants were the American Jewish Congress, American Civil Liberties Union, National Lawyers Guild, CIO, A.F. of L., American Veterans Committee (signed by Phineas Indritz), Congregational Christian Church, and the American Association for the United Nations (signed by Alger Hiss). At the behest of President Truman, Attorney General Tom Clark also prepared a supportive brief. Solicitor General Philip B. Perlman argued for the United States that the restrictive covenants should not be enforced.

Perlman was a native of Baltimore who had entered politics in 1923 when the newly-elected Mayor Jackson appointed him as City Solicitor and designated him to head a committee to promote *de facto* racial segregation. Later Perlman supported the use of zoning to keep blacks segregated. President Truman had appointed him as Solicitor General at the urging of Maryland Governor William Preston Lane. After Perlman argued against the use of state powers to enforce private covenants in the *Shelley* case, "national civil rights leaders called to express their profound gratitude, and Perlman became committed to the struggle for African-American rights....By 1960 he was writing a strong civil rights plank for the Democratic National Committee."[63]

Chief Justice Fred Vinson, whom Truman had appointed to the court, wrote the opinion in the *Shelley* case. The court reversed the opinion in the lower courts and ruled that while

---

[63] Power, *Public Service*...pp. 62-63, 65, 67-68. Perlman maintain his home in Baltimore, but while Solicitor General, he resided, during the week, at the Shoreham Hotel in D.C. He died of a heart attack in his room there in the summer of 1960.

"private agreements to exclude persons of designated race or color from the use or occupancy of real estate for residential purposes d[id] not violate the 14th Amendment," to use state courts to enforce private contracts did violate the equal protection clause of the 14th Amendment.

Vinson's concluding paragraph read:

> The historical context in which the 14th Amendment became a part of the Constitution should not be forgotten. Whatever else the framers sought to achieve, it is clear that the matter of primary concern was the establishment of equality in the enjoyment of basic civil and political rights and the preservation of those rights from discriminatory action on the part of the State based on considerations of race or color. Seventy-five years ago this Court announced that the provisions of the Amendment are to be construed with this fundamental purpose in mind. Upon full consideration, we have concluded that in these cases the States have acted to deny petitioners the equal protection of the laws guaranteed by the 14th Amendment. Having so decided, we find it unnecessary to consider whether petitioners have also been deprived of property without due process of law or denied privileges and immunities of citizens of the United States.
>
> The judgment of the Supreme Court of Missouri and the judgment of the Supreme Court of Michigan must be reversed.

In Charles Houston's complementary case, *Hurd v. Hodge (1948)*, this ruling was extended, making crystal clear that judicial enforcement of restrictive covenants was unconstitutional. However, neither of these cases actually rendered invalid private agreements achieved by the parties through *voluntary adherence* to the terms. Nonetheless, following these decisions, most of the pending cases around the country were summarily dismissed. It was perfectly clear that without state enforcement blacks could purchase any home and ignore the covenants, whoever had written and signed them.

The court's decisions raised hopes among many blacks that they would indeed now be able to live "anywhere they wanted." But others warned:

> No one need either hope or fear that the Supreme Court's action will change the situation quickly. The Ghetto wall is

merely breached, not demolished.[64]

Almost immediately after the *Shelley* decision, property owners sought to circumvent the decision by *assessing damages* from white owners who broke restrictive covenants by selling to blacks. It was not until another Supreme Court decision in *Barrows v. Jackson* (1953) that states were also precluded from acting to collect these assessed damages on the same grounds as the two restrictive covenant cases.[65]

Some claimed that *Shelley*, "marked a new sophistication in comprehending the power of the state, and particularly of courts as an arm of government, in enforcing rules of social conduct."[66] However, in reviewing the history of blacks' fight for equality, it would seem that at least as early as the 1800s, they had often turned to the courts, often successfully, both to protect their rights and to extend them. Vose, in his study of covenant cases, gives primary credit for these successes to the preparedness of the lawyers in presenting arguments against them. He wrote:

> Analysis of the Negro victory in the *Restrictive Covenant Cases* forces the conclusion that this result was an outgrowth of the complex group activity which preceded it. Groups with antagonistic interests appeared before the Supreme Court, just as they do before Congress or other institutions that mold public policy. Because of organization the lawyers for the Negroes were better prepared to do battle through the courts. Without this continuity, money, and talent they would not have freed themselves from the limiting effects of racial residential covenants, notwithstanding the presence of favorable social theories, political circumstances, and Supreme Court justices.

Despite these major victories, as some blacks had warned, they did not free blacks of housing restrictions. As we will soon see, the courts consistently rejected 14th Amendment arguments in housing-related cases during the 1960s civil rights drive for open housing.

---

[64] *Washington Post*, May 6, 1948, p. 16.

[65] See Vose, pp. 233-234.

[66] Vose, p. 248; longer quote following, Vose, p. 252.

Blockbusting

During the years 1930-1960, when Baltimore's black population increased from 142,000 to 326,000, racism was sufficiently entrenched to sustain the conspiracy between white homeowners, the real estate industry, financiers, and the Federal Housing Administration that successfully "contained" most blacks within the "blighted districts" of Baltimore's old city. There was even controversy over providing any housing at all for the growing number of blacks. Such reputed liberals as Senator Millard Tydings was quoted in a newspaper article as saying, on July 21 1943:[67]

> [The Senator] today joined those opposing the erection in or near Baltimore of a federally financed public housing project for "immigrant" Negroes, asserting there is "no justification" for continued importation of Negro workers but on the contrary there is a "surplus" of Negro labor in the area."

The FHA, which had been established in 1934 during the Depression, maintained that a healthy neighborhood needed to be "homogenous," thus ensuring that racially integrated neighborhoods had no chance. With the FHA, for the most part, denying insurance to blacks, other insurance companies and banks followed suit. Ironically, the blockbusters who bought up the properties of fleeing whites at depressed prices, borrowed money for their investments from the same banks that denied making loans directly to black buyers. In an unpublished report written in 1983, the local organization, St. Ambrose Housing, assessed the role of FHA this way:

> Neither white nor black families, in effect, could qualify for FHA insured loans in racially integrating communities. Black families, for that matter, could not obtain FHA insured loans anywhere! Between 1934 and 1963, [before] FHA reversed its policy, over ten million white families bought FHA houses, mostly in the suburbs, and virtually no black families. This policy explains more than anything else, with the possible exception of the automobile, why Americans live where they live and why our communities look the way they do.

Despite the outlawing of restrictive covenants, first by the

---

[67] Clipping did not name the paper.

state in 1866, and then by the federal government in 1968, second-hand housing within already blighted areas remained the only option open to the vast majority of blacks. "The 1950 Census revealed that Negroes, constituting 23.8% of the population in Baltimore, occupied only 19% of the total dwelling units." This 19% accounted for 47% of the city's units that were "dilapidated or without a bath and toilet, 63% of all city units considered dilapidated or without running water and 40% of all over-crowded city units. The median income of nonwhites was 62% of the white median income."[68] For the most part, the public seemed oblivious to these conditions, and the costs created by the policy of racial containment.

Two housing markets—one white, one black—became firmly entrenched during this period. A rare breach of the policy by a real estate operative occurred in 1945 when Daniel W. Spaulding,[69] a light-skinned black, sold a house on Bentalou Street in an all-white West Baltimore neighborhood to a black person. Spaulding had moved with his wife, Hazel Washington, from Ellicott City to Baltimore in 1943, and because he was often mistaken for white, especially by whites, had been able to complete the real estate courses given at the segregated University of Maryland, while working downtown as a waiter at the Belvedere Hotel to support his family.

After he became a real estate broker, barred from joining the real estate organizations that would have given him access to the information, Spaulding made a habit of surveying white neighborhoods during evening hours to note house for sale signs. Using the North Carolina Mutual Bank owned and founded by his cousin, he would then secure financing for selected black families. He was thus responsible for the first black family to buy a house in a formerly all-white neighborhood in Baltimore.[70]

As funny or sad as Spaulding's methods might seem, he was an exception that had little impact on the housing situation

---

[68] Baltimore Urban League *Annual Report* for 1952.

[69] He was another of those blacks who graduated from Lincoln University in Pennsylvania with a commitment to work for "justice for blacks."

[70] See Mark, p. iii, and "Daniel W. Spaulding, 89, real estate broker cracked color barrier," Gary Dorsey, *Sun*, 7/22/1999 (an obituary).

faced by most blacks. In fact, their situation worsened during World War II when all new housing construction stopped, and worsened again later when school building, slum clearance, urban renewal and expressway construction displaced large numbers of blacks from their homes—even those within the limited areas where they had been confined.

Replacement housing was often promised, but rarely forthcoming; the few units of public housing that were built were a far-cry from meeting the need. Louis Azrael noted in a March 8, 1946 article in the *News-Post* that "even if [housing construction] should return to peace-time levels, [it] would still be worse than in any other of the nation's biggest cities."

•••

Over the next two decades, defacto segregation continued unabated. Within the old city of Baltimore, rowhouses, an effective way to house large numbers of people in a small area, were the most common type dwelling, and the reason why, early-on, Baltimore rated so highly in home ownership by whites. The larger of these rowhouses, built mostly of brick, often extended back as far as forty to fifty feet, some without windows in the inner rooms.

The Mayor may not have wanted these row houses to be built in the New Annex, but thousands followed the trolley lines out from the city center, the old style for blue-collar workers, a popular new kind of "daylight" row house with at least one outside window in every room, for the white collar workers and skilled craftsmen. The first mansions, which were more what the Mayor had in mind, appeared in the North-Northwest suburbs of Roland Park and Guilford, inhabited by the city's prominent merchants and professionals—excluding not only blacks but also Jews from the area.[71]

Sherry Olson gave an example of Guilford's exclusivity, stating that in the 1930s, "Julius Levy was the only Jew with a house in Guilford, and the newspaperman, the breadman, and the milkman wouldn't deliver to him."[72]

---

[71] See Power, *Unwisdom*, p. 649-650.
[72] Olson, p. 325.

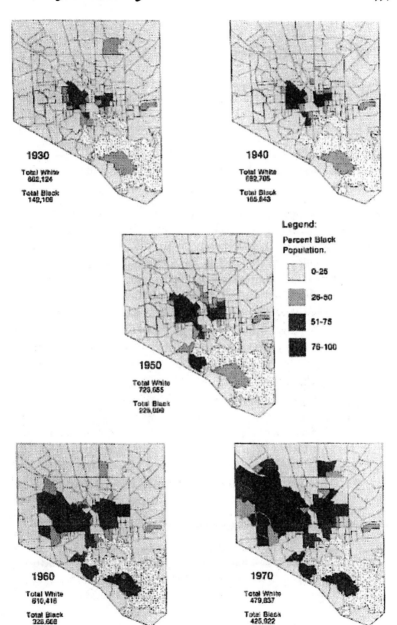

Maps from page 2 of W. Edward Orser's, *Blockbusting in Baltimore: The Edmondson Village Story.* ©1994. Reprinted with permission of author.

Other areas were just as resistant and did not take it lightly when the occasional black was able to find a house in an otherwise all-white neighborhood. The *Afro*, in an article, titled "Baltimore...Not Mississippi," told how a black longshoreman, Roland White, was forced to move his family from Montpelier Street because "my wife can't take it any longer. She's scared to death." Shots had been fired through the kitchen window and lodged in the opposite wall of the kitchen. He told the reporter they had moved to Montpelier after the cellar of their house on Holbrook had filled with two feet of water.[73]

As late as 1962, a Cherokee Indian family was forced to abandon their attempt to move into a house on North Chapel Street in Hampden (just north of the city) after confronting a jeering crowd and being threatened with a bomb. Although offered protection by the police, no arrests were made, and an editorial in an unnamed paper asks, "Why?" "Free speech does not extend to threats of bodily harm, and the right to peaceable assembly does not include the type of behavior that leads to riots and bloodshed." The *Afro* article points out:

> Our edition of the pocket digest of the laws which all policemen carry says that it is a misdemeanor willfully to disturb any neighborhood by loud or unseemly noises. It also says that when one person threatens another with bodily harm and appears about to carry out the threat, it constitutes assault. It is time for the Baltimore police to stop looking upon race mobs as peaceable citizens and start asserting themselves against those who shout threats or refuse to clear the area.

The editorial might also have asked why it was that when blacks were the ones making threatening noises, the police were only too ready to make arrests.

Still meeting opposition, on March 5, 1965 an unnamed paper reported that the family of Mrs. Elnora Walker was driven from her home on Malden Avenue in the white Woodbury section of the city (just to the Northwest of downtown) by a "jeering crowd of whites, some brandishing anti-Negro signs, a

---

[73] These incidents are from clippings in John Roemer's personal files loaned to this writer; many undated, others without name of newspaper.

few throwing rocks....The crowd, estimated at 75 persons, most of them teen-agers, sang 'Bye, Bye, Blackbird,' and chanted segregationist songs." One carried a sign, "Out Nigger." The families front door window was smashed.

Mrs. Walker told the reporter "the white policemen were standing there but they weren't doing anything about protecting me. They did not even try to find out who was throwing the rocks. I'm not afraid for myself but I am for the children" (who ranged in age from eight to fourteen). She said she wanted to live in a place where her four school-age children could attend the same school and a place that would be easier to heat. When she moved, the landlord, Raymond Weinberg, had agreed to pay for the utilities. Mrs. Walker insisted she hadn't realized she was moving into a white neighborhood, adding she had "no intention of block-busting for anybody."

•••

With such a shortage of housing, and with blacks still confined to such a small area of the city, blockbusting was bound to follow.

Blockbusting is defined as "the intentional action of a real estate operative to settle an African-American household in an all-white neighborhood for the purpose of provoking white flight in order to make excessive profits by buying low from those who fled and selling high to those who sought access to new housing opportunities."[74] At first it had referred to any sale to blacks in a white neighborhood, and for some time white realtors refused to make such sales, fearing the repercussions of breaking the taboo. This did not always mean, however, their hands were clean.

During the 1950s, blockbusting became rampant in Baltimore. For instance, "Mal Sherman, a well-regarded member of the Baltimore Real Estate Board, testified to the U.S. Civil Right Commission about his company's activities on the northwest side of the city in the early 1950s." He declared that rather than making a sale directly to a black in a white neighborhood, they would refer it to a black real estate broker for a "third referral fee." Sherman, in effect chastising himself, stated "We did not have the guts to participate in making

---

[74] Found in Orser, p. 4

black sales;" rather than be labeled a blockbuster, "we worked through black brokers."[75]

About this same time the city undertook the comprehensive self-survey of Baltimore, mentioned in earlier sections, that included a survey of real estate practices (reproduced here).[76]

SUMMARY OF RESPONSES BY FIRMS AS TO SALES, FINANCING
AND RENTAL POLICIES FOR NEGRO, JEWISH AND OTHER CLIENTS

Type of Service and Qualification	Percentage of Responses		
Sales	Negroes	Jews	Other
Will sell to the group in any section of the city, if they are the same economic and social class as the neighbors	17.8	54.3	63.0
Will sell only in areas occupied by some of the group	57.8	28.3	24.0
Will not sell to them at all	24.4	17.4	13.0
Financing			
Will finance the group in any section if they are same economic and social class as the neighbors	60.9	68.6	72.6
Will finance only in areas occupied by some of group	30.4	19.6	17.6
Will not finance them at all	8.7	11.8	9.8
Rentals			
Will rent to them in any section of the city	16.1	47.0	58.3
Will rent only in certain sections	58.1	32.4	22.3
Will not do rentals at all with the group	25.8	20.6	19.4

---

[75] Orser, p. 86. Michael Marks writes in his history of Baltimore Neighborhoods Inc. (BNI) that Sherman was, at one point, forced to close his business as a result of his attempts to integrate both residual neighborhoods and the real-estate industry. He had persuaded a Pikesville realtor to sell a house in its Scott's Hill development to John Mackey, a black player for the Baltimore Colts football team. "Fortunately, James Rouse, the visionary developer of an integrated community at Columbia, Maryland, mid-way between Baltimore and Washington D.C., shared Sherman's values and as his sales manager encouraged him to put his ideals into practice. Eventually, he again established his own his real estate firm, and, ironically was elected president of the Greater Baltimore Board of Realtors that had early-on repudiated him. pp. vi & 17.

[76] "Baltimore Community...", p. 58.

Orser found that in the early days of blockbusting at the end of World War II, operators stuck to areas near the ghetto borders that were shunned by most agents and lending institutions. Later, as mortgages became available in "changing" neighborhoods, they took full advantage of the opportunities this offered, often with big financial pay-offs.[77]

The "blockbusters" clearly had no qualms about violating the "conspiracy of containment" and would sell a formerly white-owned house to a black at a premium price. They would then capitalize on this as an initial sale roused panic amongst the whites, enabling them to buy up whole blocks of houses at well below market value and resell them at premium prices to blacks desperate for decent housing.

Giddy with the success of such an easy money-making scheme, they added a new wrinkle. They would then borrow from financial institutions in order to sell to high-risk blacks on "buy-like-rent contracts." Then, with the first missed payment, they would foreclose, leaving the desperate black without a home and the worse off for his investment.

With this technique, the same house could be sold over and over to any number of buyers, thus enabling the blockbuster to make money both from sales to the poor and to better-off blacks. Before blockbusting was made illegal, tens of thousands of houses had changed from white to black ownership.[78]

•••

Two white neighborhoods that have been extensively studied reacted quite differently to the blockbusting tactics that forced them to confront blacks moving in: **Edmondson Village**, a neighborhood of mostly row houses, populated by middle-class white-and blue-collar workers, was located just outside the city's borders to its west; and **Windsor Hills-Ashburton**, a neighborhood of mostly detached houses on sizeable lots, populated largely by college-educated professionals, was located nearer the inner city, to its west.

Edmondson Village

Soon after Edmondson Village Shopping Center opened

---

[77] See Orser, p. 4
[78] See Power, *Apartheid*, pp. 320-321

on May 7, 1947, it became the focal point of a grateful community for shopping, or just "hanging out," and they quickly adopted its name for themselves. Attracted by the new row-houses, by the mid-fifties the Village had become a stable, settled community of mostly blue-collar white workers; the area's "golden years." [79] But also in the mid-fifties the city began to see racial changes in its neighborhoods, none more so than in its western and northwestern suburbs that included Edmondson Village where it was "systematic and extensive." Real estate speculators quickly moved in to take advantage of the panic and confusion, often inducing it themselves by their actions.[80] The process went like this:[81]

(1) After a house "for sale" was located in an all-white block, the potential for racial change and lower property values comes into play. The speculative agent begins telephone calls, even door-to-door contacts, claiming that blacks are moving in, offering market value or higher as an inducement for whites to sell to him.

(2) The agent continues showing the house to blacks even if at first he's turned down by a number of blacks either unable to afford it or not wanting to be first. Undeterred, the agent often deliberately moves in a large, ill-behaved black family, charging only a minimal rent. As the formerly quiet neighborhood is suddenly disrupted by the loud carryings-on of children and adults, and their numerous black visitors, the agent is ready for his next step.

(3) He now goes down the block warning the residents that their neighborhood is changing and offering to buy their houses. The first ones are sold at a profit. Those who wait awhile take a loss. Within a year or two, the block becomes predominantly black. By that time, the disorderly family has moved away.

(4) The white residents have all left by the time market prices rebound from the deflated prices realtors paid fleeing whites, and the blacks desperate for housing are then charged grossly inflated prices.

Studies have indicated that, contrary to what many have assumed, the vast majority of blacks who moved to Edmondson

---

[79] Orser, pp. 48-49.
[80] See Orser, p. 95.
[81] See Orser, p. 102 and "Latest Problem...", p. 84.

Village at the height of the blockbusting were roughly of the same socioeconomic status as the whites who were departing; their reasons for the move were the same as that of the whites—improved housing and access to services. Blacks interviewed by Orser thought things might have been different if the whites had stayed long enough to get to know their new neighbors, but instead they'd immediately panicked and moved.[82]

Regrettably, the neighborhood institutions, especially the churches which had a great influence in the community, did nothing to halt the exodus. Instead of seeking to welcome the new arrivals and trying to integrate them into the community, the clergy preached against moving only as a necessity for maintaining the community as white.[83] They even turned away blacks who tried to attend their churches. The only church that did not simply depart as the whites departed was St. Bernardine's, and it made the transition from a white to a black church as the result of a decision by the Baltimore Archdiocese to deliberately develop a new black constituency. To accomplish this they assigned one black and one white pastor to the church who initiated a new style of service. One parishioner described the change as different from the old as "night and day; dead and alive."[84]

Thus it was, with next to no forces to stop it and many working to propel it, between 1955 and 1965 Edmondson Village experienced an almost 100% turnover, approximately 40,000 people having changing places. Orser concludes that "community stability in general and the character of neighborhoods relative to race and racial integration, have always depended to a great extent on institutional factors." He goes on to say that prejudices and fears make whites vulnerable to manipulation, but this is not the only ingredient required. Also needed are

> the systematic application of blockbusting tactics and speculative real estate practices, the formal and informal mechanisms of a dual housing market, and the absence of either commitment or will to prohibit and regulate such practices from both the public governmental and private

---

[82] See Orser, p. 152
[83] Orser, p. 110
[84] See Orser, pp. 152-153.

business sectors combined with residents' proclivities to light the fuse and produce the explosion.[85]

Windsor Hills-Ashburton[86]

U.S. News & World Report in 1958 related one incident on Grantley Road, on the edge of the Ashburton community that resulted in a complaint being filed with the Maryland Real Estate Commission seeking their help. The white homeowner, a widow who lived on Grantley Road, complained that a salesman, without identifying himself or his intent, had persuaded her to sell her house. When she learned that the realtors intended to resell it to blacks, she tried to get out of the deal, but they'd refused unless she paid their commission. The firm, of course, denied any misrepresentation to the widow, and claimed they were only attempting to act in a nondiscriminatory and democratic manner. No action was taken by the Commission.

At the time there were about twenty real estate firms in Baltimore, referred to as "blockbusters," that specialized in such purchases from whites and re-sales to blacks. They advertised lavishly in the *Afro-American* newspaper, proclaiming "luxury homes in newly breaking neighborhoods"; promising down payments of $500—or none. Even more insidiously, after a neighborhood had "changed" to one housing middle-class blacks, black realty firms were sometimes responsible for turning it over again—intentionally or not, they would sell to low-income families, re-creating the very conditions that the original middle-class black purchasers were attempting to escape.

Melvin Sykes, a white attorney who then lived in Ashburton and was a leader in fighting blockbusting, had this to say:

> Lots of people in these neighborhoods are living on pensions or some other fixed income. Often their house is a lifetime investment. They don't want to sell at a loss and

---

85 Orser, p. 168.

86 See the article, "Latest Problem...", p. 84; called to this writer's attention by Melvin Sykes, who lived in the neighbor of Ashburton that organized in an attempt to fight back.

move to a strange neighborhood. But it's a pretty frightening thing when you look down your street and all you see are those flaming signs that say, "Sold—Sold—Sold."

As blockbusting was reaching epidemic proportions in 1958, the Ashburton and Windsor Hills neighborhoods began an all-out attempt to counteract it by creating an atmosphere for "peaceful coexistence" with the new black arrivals. Aided by the blacks themselves, a group of white residents banded together not only to encourage the remaining white owners to stay, but also actively to seek out other whites willing to buy houses in the area when they were put on the market. The goal was not to stop integration, but to maintain the quality of their homes and neighborhood so it would stay integrated. The white Edmondson Village residents never even considered such an approach.

•••

Ashburton was a suburban-type neighborhood of mostly single-family, detached houses, twenty to twenty-five years old. Though the area was no longer regarded as "fashionable," both the houses and surrounding lawns and gardens were well maintained; the streets were tree-lined; it took only fifteen minutes to drive downtown; its schools were uncrowned, and shopping was just five minutes away. Ashburton had seen a large influx of well-to-do Jewish families after World War II, but by the mid-fifties, its families, mostly professionals and business people, included all faiths and ages. All this was available for a third less than the cost of an equivalent-sized new home in the further-out suburbs.[87]

The first blacks, a high school principal and his family, moved into the area in 1956; during the next twelve months, another twenty professional black families moved in; in 1957, another forty to fifty. Even if you included the black homeowners in an expanded Ashburton area, early in 1959 there were still only 110 black families, about 5% of the total

---

[87] Much of the information about Ashburton-Windsor Hills comes from an article by Ellsworth Rosen who, as we'll see, was himself a main player in the neighborhood's efforts to end blockbusting and maintain an integrated neighborhood. Sykes, also an involved resident, referred the writer to this article.

number of families in the area. Yet, already, the real-estate newspaper ads were stating, "Ashburton—Colored."

The usual process of the blockbusters was in full swing: house-to-house and telephone campaigns—"they're coming, they're coming"—proliferating for sale signs, some not even for sale; actual refusals to sell to whites and the showing of houses to blacks mainly at night; rentals to poor blacks knowing they would be disruptive and unable to keep up payments; and so on...

Most of the whites figured that "change" was inevitable "because you can't change people. You can't make them live where they don't want to."

Though agreeing with the latter sentiment, there was a group of whites who began to ask, "Why, if we want to live here, should we be pushed out?"

At the instigation of the wives, one evening in 1958, Lenore and Ellsworth Rosen (Ellsworth, in public relations) got together with Judy and Melvin Sykes[88] in their living room to discuss this question. The Sykes had moved to Ashburton in 1954; the Rosens, who moved to Baltimore from Hartford, Connecticut, bought their home in Ashburton late in 1957— despite warnings that it was turning "colored." The couples' first act was to gather together twenty of their neighbors who formed the Ashburton Area Association, the first such association open to blacks and whites alike.

They must have gotten a reputation as a changing neighborhood as early as 1955, because it was in March that year that the *Sun* reported a broker, Edwin Pitcher, had told the police he received a frightening phone call:

> I just came from a meeting. If you sell that house [a three-story frame apartment building] on Talbot Road [in Windsor

---

[88] At least partially accounting for his interest in City College, already discussed, Sykes was said to have had the highest grade point average ever recorded when he graduated from City College (a high school) in 1940. He next graduated from Johns Hopkins University with honors, and after two-years in the military, graduated from Harvard Law School, magna cum laude, in 1948. In a later awards ceremony, it was noted that his law practice consisted largely of appellate cases for well-known law firms, requiring a degree of scholarship that others are not equipped to provide.

Hills] to a colored person, I am going to have you killed by a professional killer, and I mean it.

The meeting referred to had been attended by about 75 members of the Mount Holly Improvement Association; held in a recreation center at Gwynns Falls Parkway and Clifton. Mr. Pitcher had recently advised the owner that if he wanted to sell his building he would probably have to sell to a Negro, and had, accordingly, advertised it three times in the *Afro*. Prior to this action, the house had been on the market for six months "without a nibble," and the owners needed to sell for financial reasons." Such a sale would have been blockbusting of a sort since the nearest blacks at the time were five to six blocks away. However, in this case, blockbusting does not seem to have been a factor if Mr. Pitcher's account is to be believed.[89]

Perhaps because this wasn't really an effort at blockbusting it did not seem to stir to life the long dormant Windsor Hills Improvement Association, headed by Sidney Hollander, Jr. This happened only after members of the Ashburton group approached him in 1958. Windsor Hills, just north of Ashburton, was an older area with a greater variety of homes and a few apartments, "built on winding lanes on a hillside, only minutes from the Hillsdale Golf Course." After agreeing to ally their Association with the Ashburton Association, Hollander "recommended block meetings and active solicitation of white families to buy homes."[90]

> You can't afford ideology in your program. The most ardent liberal will find that your association must discriminate, not against Negroes, but in favor of white buyers. There is no other choice under the pressures that exist.

The Ashburton group mailed out 1100 letters, stating:

> We welcome all good neighbors regardless of race, creed or color. But we understand, as we trust everyone will, that experience shows that the key to keeping up the quality of this or any neighborhood is to attract a sufficient number of new white homeowner families.[91]

---

[89] *Sun*, March 17, 1955
[90] Ironically, this would probably be found to be unconstitutional under current Supreme Court thinking.
[91] Two quotes, Rosen, p. 140

In response, they acquired 400 members; enough to begin holding small group meetings block by block. Rosen, in his article, "When a Negro Moves Next Door," describes one such early, typical gathering of about twenty in a block leaders living room. Those present included two doctors, a lawyer, a business man reputed to be a millionaire, and Otho P. Pinkett, a black who managed an 825-unit public housing project in another part of the city. The whites were somewhat surprised by the presence of a black who advised them that the simple solution to "protecting their home and way of life" was not to move. In his soft-spoken and articulate way, Pinkett told the group:

> Don't think you can escape the problem simply by putting your house up for sale and running away. Times are changing faster than most of us realize. Even if you move far out in the suburbs, I can virtually guarantee that by the time you finish paying off your next mortgage—and it will be a lot higher than the one you have now—you'll face the same situation. There will be Negroes living near you. [Smiling, he concluded] As a matter of fact, if this area turns all Negro, I plan to move out to the suburbs with you.

Rosen concludes:

> It is shock treatment, as a rule, when a Negro walks into a supposedly all-white meeting—and the shock, in turn, heightens the subsequent realization that Mr. Pinkett's intelligence, sense of values, desires and plans for the community are no different from those of others in the room.[92]

After this meeting, at least two of those who'd planned to move changed their minds. In meeting after meeting, the Association's members were kept busy calming neighbors, steering whites to decent, reliable real-estate agents, and seeking ways to stop the shady blockbusting practices. One white resident on Talbot Road in Windsor Hills not only determined to stay but changed occupations from dietician to realtor and sold 30 homes in the area to whites. One such, William A. Martin proclaimed: [93]

> "We wanted a good, big house at a price we could afford, and there it was"—roses, lilacs and fat trees, close to downtown. "We

---

[92] Two quotes from Rosen, p. 139
[93] *Baltimore News Post*, April 14, 1961.

don't have to go 10 miles and spend $10,000 more."

Grantley Road, mentioned earlier, again became a focus of attention when Alan Kleiman and others who lived across the street from 3800 Grantley Road complained that the brokers, Manuel M. Bernstein and Warren S. Shaw, with the Manning-Shaw Realty firm, were still showing the house to potential buyers two months after a Sold sign had been displayed. Rosen notes in his article:

> The Sold notice—usually a luminous, orange-red sticker pasted over For Sale signs—was as effective as a quarantine poster in spreading panic through a block....

On a number of grounds, the Commission found the two brokers guilty of violating the "statute prohibiting continued and flagrant course of misrepresentation, misleading or untruthful advertising and improper dealings as result of posting of a sold sign on property which was not in fact sold," as well as a finding, on a more technical point, that "broker and his associate had violated statute requiring listing contract to specify a definite termination date without notice from either party." [94]

As a result, the Commission suspended their license for three months. Bernstein and Shaw then appealed the decision to the Baltimore City Court, and after they upheld the Commission's finding, to the Court of Appeals of Maryland. Melvin Sykes represented the families on Grantley Road when the appelate court heard the case on December 18, 1959. They too upheld the Commission.

After this victory, the Associations sought to ban For Sale and Sold signs all together and especially from areas where "changing" was taking place.

> Working with Windsor Hills and other areas, [the Ashburton Association] called on the city to enforce that part of its zoning ordinance which prohibits advertising signs in residential neighborhoods. The city solicitor ruled the Sold By signs illegal, and as complaints poured into the Bureau of Building Inspection, notices of violations went out and the

---

[94] *Bernstein v. Real Estate Commission of Maryland*

signs disappeared. [95]

Soon after the ban went into effect, the number of Sold and For Sale signs in one notable block went from twenty-three to just six. In early 1959, in Windsor Hills, between fifty and sixty of its 600 homes were occupied by blacks. And as proof, if such is needed, that black ownership does not in itself run down a neighborhood, one home that had been converted into three units by its white owners was promptly reconverted into a single home when purchased by a black.

Rosen, in his article "When a Negro Moves Next Door," recounting his own experience, concurs with this. He notes that the lesson learned in Ashburton and Windsor Hills was that neighborhoods do not deteriorate when blacks move in—*if* whites do not panic. He adds:

> But if blockbusters succeed, speculators sooner or later convert houses to multifamily rental units or open the door to downgrading by placing properties in eager but ill-equipped hands. The garbage collections that were sufficient for a single-family area become inadequate for the greatly increased number of families. The neighborhood ceases to oppose zoning changes that bring service stations, machine shops and other commercial establishments. Change and violations alike go unchecked under the city's loosely written and poorly enforced zoning laws.[96]

Another point Rosen makes, recently restated to this writer by his then-neighbor, Melvin Sykes, is that neighborhoods do not have the power or resources to fight blockbusting on their own. Hence their appeal to the Greater Baltimore Committee (GBC) which was composed of approximately one hundred of Baltimore's most prominent business men. Melvin made clear that the appeal to them was not ideological, which they probably would have rejected, but one based on their self interest. The neighborhood associations needed the support of these power brokers if the

---

[95] Rosen, p. 141. As gratifying as this was, it was many years before the City Council passed an ordinance outlawing the practice; and some years after that ,they again began to proliferate as the result of the US Supreme Court declaring such laws unconstitutional on "free speech" grounds.

[96] Rosen, p. 141.

policy of containment—the root cause of the blockbusting—was ever to end.

Observing the city's formerly "blockbusted" areas today, all virtually 100% black, it must take more than an alliance with the GBC to keep a neighborhood integrated—or at least a great deal more than the members of this prestigious organization were willing to do. At the root of the problem is racism.

•••

The Greater Baltimore Committee (GBC) had been organized in 1955 as part of the Citizens Planning and Housing Association (CPHA), itself organized in 1941 to fight the growth of slums in Baltimore (referred to previously). By 1958, GBC was an independent organization that focused its energies on rebuilding Baltimore's downtown. Rosen suggests their organization was able to get GBC's help by focusing on

> the economic effect of neighborhood change on the city's cultural, educational and social life but also the need for higher income families to support downtown rehabilitation and renewal. We asked GBC to consider the opening of additional areas of new and old housing to the Negro residents; a stimulation of public awareness of the practices that cause disorderly change, and to seek ways and means to enlist the cooperation of real-estate brokers in preserving the city.[97]

James W. Rouse, an influential member of GBC, was quite influential in garnering the organization's support for creating a new organization, Baltimore Neighborhoods, Inc. (BNI) to work with changing neighborhoods. He was a mortgage banker, urban renewal expert, and a strong proponent of integrated neighborhoods (as we indicated previously).

At a conference titled "Changing Neighborhoods," sponsored by GBC on November 25, 1958, Rouse convincingly expressed his belief that the exodus from the city of medium and upper income families to the suburbs, replaced by lower income families of either race, posed a serious economic threat to the whole metropolitan region. He recommended creation of a city-wide organization composed of representatives from civic

---

[97] Rosen, pp. 32 & 142

and labor organizations, improvement associations, the Real Estate Board of Greater Baltimore, the Greater Baltimore Committee, the city and state governments and building and commercial associations. GBC was to provide clerical and professional staff assistance during the new organizations formative period. [98]

With blockbusting rapidly spreading to all parts of the city, the need for a city-wide organization to counter it was apparent. And so less than four months after the conference, on March 20, 1959, BNI's bylaws and Articles of Incorporation ware ratified with James W. Rouse representing GBC, Sidney Hollander Jr., President of the Windsor Hills Association, and Ellsworth Rosen, President of the Ashburton Association, as incorporators. The three above-named plus Frank Gray, Lawrence Larsen, Henry Muller and Furman Templeton, then head of the Urban League, composed the original Board of Directors (later it included Melvin Sykes). With the leaders of the Ashburton and Windsor Hills Associations included as founding members of BNI, their continued involvement in seeking changes in real estate practices in their areas was assured; however, their efforts were now supported by a city-wide group.

BNI's original charter laid out an overly-ambitious nine-part set of goals, but by March 23, 1961, in order to gain the IRS non-profit status needed to attract foundation grants, its mission was restated in a single sentence that qualified it as charitable and educational— "to lessen neighborhood tensions, eliminate prejudice and discrimination, to enforce, promote and defend human and civil rights secured by law, and to combat community deterioration and juvenile delinquency."[99]

Soon after this, Andrew Bristow, a member of the Board of Directors of Citizens Planning and Housing Association (CPHA), became BNI's first (interim) Executive Director. On December 21, 1961, the *Afro* reported a meeting of Bristow with 38 citizens in the offices of the NAACP. Also present was the BNI board member, Sidney Hollander, Jr. He advocated that "colored citizens" be encouraged to act as "pilot families"

---

[98] Information found on pp. 2-3, of Mark's draft copy provided this writer.

[99] Mark's draft copy, p. 5.

and go into the all-white county areas to purchase homes, and that whites in those areas be encouraged to stay. He had proposed this as the only way to prevent an all-black city, adding, "I as a white citizen have no influence with the Real Estate Board or the county commissioners."

Juanita Mitchell, on behalf of the NAACP disagreed, saying the Real Estate Board had to be tackled head-on, and Warren Shaw of the Manning-Shaw Realty Co. (the subject of the suit discussed earlier) posed a number of questions for the group to think about: "Would an all-colored city be objectionable?" "What has BNI done to protect colored renters from shabby homes with high rents, or to portray the true living standards of bonafide colored homeowners?" Perhaps her most challenging question was: "Why has the sinister term 'blockbusting' been applied to the sale of homes to colored in areas formerly all-white when these sales are part of the refusal of colored to accept the former type housing available to them?"

Juanita might have urged "strawbuying" as an alternative term, and better method of achieving the same end. Unlike "blockbusting," when a white sympathizer with the black need for housing "strawbuys" a home in a formerly all-white neighborhood expressly for a black, there is no deliberate play on a neighborhood's racial fears, for the purpose of making a quick profit.

As reported by the *Afro*, no decisions were made at this meeting.

Later in 1961, Edward Holmgren was chosen as BNI's permanent director. He had excellent credentials for his work in the area of housing in Chicago, the city to which he returned in 1966. An early campaign undertaken by BNI (successful, no doubt, because of the support of the Board of Realtors), was to end the newspapers' practices of separate listings for blacks and whites in their real estate ads. At the same time, BNI published, without much success, its own list of "Best Home Buys" in established neighborhoods, hoping to stop "steering" of whites away from these areas.

BNI also consistently opposed "redlining" by mortgage lenders, and worked to build support for open housing legislation. However, nothing it did ever stopped the flight of whites as blacks gradually moved out the city's corridors, first to its old boundaries and then to its new boundaries after the annexation.[100]

Oddly, residents of those areas being overtaken by blacks were amongst the strongest opponents of open housing legislation, not recognizing that open housing legislation would provide blacks with the alternative housing markets that were needed to end the lucrative, destructive blockbusting tactics they were then confronted with.

•••

As for the two areas discussed in some detail, neither Edmondson Village, which had worked to keep its community all white, nor Ashburton-Windsor Hills, which tried to achieve an integrated community, were successful; nor was BNI in stopping white flight and achieving integrated communities. Windsor Hills perhaps came the closest to success, managing to keep a few whites, including Sidney Hollander, Jr. who only moved years later, but even he would not have called the community truly integrated.

Early in 1960, Ellsworth Rosen, who had played a leadership role in fighting blockbusting in Ashburton, left Baltimore to accept a more lucrative public relations job with a Jewish Charity in Boston; and in 1965, Melvin Sykes' family, orthodox Jews, followed their synagogue, Beth Tfiloh, to the upper Park Heights area.[101]

George Laurent, who replaced Ed Holmgren as Executive Director of BNI in 1966, was left to feel his way between the structure and mandate that defined BNI, and his instinctive support for the direct action of the civil rights organization, CORE, which, in 1965, made ending housing segregation its top priority.

---

[100] The movement out the corridors from the Baltimore's center can be seen on the map reproduced earlier. An early move was along the Northwest Corridor (Liberty Road-Reisterstown Road-Park Heights Avenue); then, along the Northwood Corridor (York Road-Loch Raven Blvd.-Hillen Road); and, finally, along the Northeast Corridor (Hillen Road-Harford Road-Belair Road-Sinclair Lane). From a paper given this writer by St. Ambrose Housing Aid Center; an organization that came to Baltimore in 1968.

[101] This synagogue has joined with the Jewish community in this area in developing and maintaining facilities for both the blacks and whites. So far, they have succeeded in keeping it integrated.

CORE: "Break the Noose"[102]

Prior to 1965, CORE had been too involved with attacking job discrimination and segregated public accommodations to devote time to housing discrimination. In any case, housing discrimination was such a complex issue that it was hard even to determine where to start in tackling it. This may account for the fact that in all the years the Sidney Hollander Foundation gave awards,[103] only twice did they single out housing-related issues for the award.

In 1955, the Baltimore Urban Renewal and Housing Agency (BURHA) received the award "for its voluntary and effective removal of racial barriers in public housing occupancy"—an especially ironic choice given the controversy engendered ten years later by the CORE report on BURHA policies, and its supervision of *very* segregated public housing developments, as well as a suit by ACLU as recently as 1995.[104] In 1956 another housing-related award went to the interracial organization, Northeast Baltimore Inter-group Council, "for outstanding promotion of community relations...[for] promoting better understanding and increased relations between the races in this area." Its efforts were especially notable, taking place as they did at a time of changing neighborhoods.

By 1964, state and federal legislation had passed in the areas of employment and public accommodations, forcing the public to get used to integration. And so it was felt by those at the first conference on equal opportunity in housing held in

---

[102] Much of what follows comes directly from two unpublished books by the writer: her autobiography, *Bloody Breathitt 'n Beyond*, and the biography of CORE's lawyer, *"...And Justice for All."* In writing these sections of the books, she depended not only on her memory but also on her scrapbook of news clippings, letters and flyers, accumulated at the time. She also had access to additional clippings from Fred Weisgal's files and from a local CORE official, John Roemer.

[103] For more information on these awards, see footnote in Employment section, "Gradualism/Tokenism." Sidney Hollander, Jr., who played a significant role in the previous section on "Blockbusting", was co-founder, along with his brother, of the Foundation, esablished in honor of their father.

[104] Both discussed later.

Washington D.C. in November 1964 that opposition to integrated housing was also weakening. W.H.C. Wilson, past president of the Real Estate Board of Greater Baltimore, said at the time:

> Baltimore City and the surrounding counties will not be truly stabilized communities until ALL of their respective residential areas accept integration. As one who until recent years tried to evade this subject, it is now my firm conclusion that we can and we must change our community attitudes toward equality of opportunity in housing if we expect to support both the economic and moral fiber of metropolitan Baltimore....I have changed my attitude that open housing can be accomplished on a voluntary basis. I now feel legislation is the answer. It is a case where moral right supercedes property rights.[105]

If only the optimism expressed at this conference had been the reality for a larger body of Marylanders, CORE's subsequent struggle might not have been so difficult—and Baltimore and environs might look differently than they do even today.

•••

The writers' involvement with CORE, to be recounted in the first person, began with a hearing on an open housing bill, followed by the formation of CORE's Housing Committee and her subsequent deep involvement in CORE actions.

June 1, 1965 started like many others when I drove my husband to work (an Economics Professor at Johns Hopkins University) so I could have the car for the day, then stopped in the Hopkins cafeteria for coffee before returning home. Dr. Wickwire was there, too, and we started talking, as we had on so many other occasions. He suggested I might be interested in going down to City Hall that evening to hear the discussion on the Fair Housing Bills that would be voted on that evening. "Walter Carter will be there. I think you'd like to meet him," he'd said.

I'd read about racial hatred before, and about demonstrations, but this was my first time seeing it close-up. As I approached City Hall, I saw demonstrators carrying both neatly stenciled and homemade placards calling for "Open Housing." They walked quietly in a circle in front of the steps leading to the entrance, ignoring the jeering, spitting, name-calling crowds who passed them. By the time I entered, the City Council Chamber was already overflowing, even the small balcony that overlooked the chamber was crowded. I rather forcefully squeezed myself between two women sitting on one of the benches that formed a semi-circle facing the councilmen— whose big cushioned chairs formed their own semi-circle.

The Chairman, Tommy D'Alesandro, sat in a chair in middle, behind the raised podium where he would preside. The room was hot, the sweaty bodies crammed together were causing a smell as unpleasant as the words that were soon pounding against my eardrums. I had never before heard such vile language, seen such hate and intolerance manifest on the faces of people surrounding me. I felt sick to my stomach. I felt embarrassed to be white.

The "testimony" these ordinary-looking neighborhood folks were presenting to the city councilmen with such venom could be boiled down to that of one woman: "You can have those kinky-haired, dirty black apes living next to you if you want, but you ain't ever going to make me live next to one." And one man: "Our home is our castle. We don't want no Niggers near it." The contrasting well-documented evidence for open housing that was presented by those in favor could barely be heard above the chorus of boos, the name-calling, "Nigger!" or "Nigger Lover!" Worse.

The two Fair Housing ordinances that would have outlawed racial discrimination in the sale of much of Baltimore's housing were defeated by a twelve to eight vote.

Afterwards, outside City Hall, I joined the group of CORE members talking to Walter Carter. He seemed close to tears as they talked about the scene that had just unfolded and the need to start an all-out drive for fair housing in Baltimore. I introduced myself. Dr. Wickwire had told him I was coming.

A few days later Walter had a Letter-to-the-Editor printed in the *Sun* that pretty much summed up how we all felt that night: "This is a brutal revelation that they [the city councilmen] remain hundreds of years behind the beautiful documents which could give rise to a truly democratic society.... Together the good-thinking people must join the nonviolent civil rights movement in its effort to achieve an open and high-level metropolitan housing market, now"—but even the experienced—or maybe especially the experienced CORE activists—knew this would not be easy.

They were not even heartened by the report that Mayor McKeldin was "disappointed by the vote," as he told the press, but instead were asking, "How deep and vigorous was his support really? How come he was able to get the Council to do his bidding on all sorts of other issues but not this one?"

For me, I believe the hate I felt in the City Council chambers that June night, the enthusiasm to "create justice" that I felt in the room at my first CORE housing committee meeting which soon followed, and the sheer magnetic power of Walter's charisma were more than enough to release all those pent-up feelings "to do something" I'd harbored for so long. They were more than enough to trigger the passionate commitment to activism that followed.

•••

As for CORE's taking on housing segregation as its top priority in 1965, neither the city's zoning policies nor those that allowed blockbusting and covenants were directly responsible. Rather, the decision grew out of CORE's frustrated efforts to force Baltimore to provide equality of education for black children in the public school system. CORE members had come to feel that integrated housing was a necessary prerequisite to achieving their education goal.

As a consequence, in 1964, while some CORE members continued to persevere in their efforts to effect meaningful changes at the black Dunbar High School, others began to focus on housing issues; beginning by spinning off a less-activist group called Contemporary Trends in Housing, a group not unlike BNI in purpose, but not beholden to the Baltimore establishment as was BNI. This new group would "test" housing as a means of heightening awareness within in the black community of the linkage between schools and housing, and also of the relevance of segregated housing generally.

By June 1965, Walter Carter estimated that approximately twenty-five "all-white" apartment projects had either rented to blacks or had expressed a willingness to do so. Through its "shopping days," Contemporary Trends Housing Committee had fulfilled its mission; it had successfully acquainted better-off Negroes in the community with suburban housing, had established the presence of discrimination in much of Baltimore's housing market, and had quietly penetrated that market in a few places using FHA financing.

CORE now felt it was time to take a more activist stance, formed a Housing Committee, and selected Walter Carter as its first Chairman. Even though frustration with the City's public education practices had led to this new focus on housing, it was obvious from the start that CORE was also well aware of the negative impact the city's "containment" policy had on black housing. Walter explained the role of his new Housing Committee this way:

> We're not pushing for integration, but desegregation, a choice to stay in the city, or to move out. For too long, we've been locked into an urban colony with a choice between one evil—slum housing, or a lesser evil—sneaking into a hostile community.

Walter, too, was well aware of the "big picture" and frequently referred to his view of Baltimore as a microcosm of urban America. Neither North nor South, but, in close proximity to the nation's Capital, he felt that Baltimore reflected problems common to both. He felt that if positive changes could be made in Baltimore, it would demonstrate what was possible nationally. This vision inspired him as he struggled to find strategies that would achieve CORE's goals.

Of course, CORE's new campaign was not the first time housing discrimination had been attacked in Maryland, just the first time CORE had given it top priority.[106] As we've recounted elsewhere, way back in the forties, Fred Weisgal, at the request of ACLU, had attacked housing covenants when he represented Ethel Marks. Then, in August 1963, as CORE's attorney, Weisgal represented the pickets of a fast-growing housing project in Belair, near Bowie, Maryland.

For a month pickets marched there each weekend, singing,

---

[106] Unless otherwise noted, this account is from the *Washington Post*, the *Evening Star* (Wash. D.C.) and unnamed newspapers, for the dates noted in the text.

chanting, standing in, sitting in, protesting the whites-only occupancy policy. Then, a group of nineteen whites and Negroes, mostly students, conducted a "sleep-in" at the Levitt & Co. builder's office. They were arrested for trespassing, and on August 16, 1963 the Levitt corporation filed a $100,000 damage suit in circuit court, and Judge Ralph Powers signed an ex parte injunction prohibiting any further actions on the streets in front of the sales office. The local CORE leader, Alfred Ochs, "with a deep sense of moral indignation," urged all those banned by the injunction to halt demonstrations within the bounds of the order. So they moved to the nearby public roads, but did not stop their protests.

Fred Weisgal was representing them when, on August 27, 1963, Judge Powers renewed the injunction for another ten days, until September 5. On behalf of CORE, Fred filed a motion to move the case to Federal Court for trial. The papers he filed stated that Levitt's agents had refused to sell homes in the community to Negroes, and had an admitted policy not to show or sell any house to Negroes.

William Levitt said the policy was based on the fact that other builders in the Washington area do not have an open occupancy policy. Weisgal contended that pressing trespass charges in the magistrate courts, and their issuance of an injunction, amounted to State action in violation of the 14th Amendment that forbid *State enforcement* of discrimination (an interpretation propounded by the Supreme Court in the landmark covenant case, *Shelley v. Kramer*, in 1948).

On August 30, Weisgal went before the U.S. District Court of Maryland to argue his case for their assuming jurisdiction. He called Levitt's suit an attempt "to invoke the assistance of the judicial arm of the government to deny to the pickets their right to meet in public and to protest against oppression, economic and otherwise." He also asked that they vacate the restraining order on picketing. "It is a restraint of the right to publicly assemble to protest against social and economic discrimination on the basis of race."

After Levitt sought to have their case returned to the Prince George's County Circuit Court, declaring the Federal Court had no jurisdiction, Chief Federal Judge Roszel Thomsen scheduled a hearing for September 12 to hear Weisgal's arguments concerning the federal court's right to deal with the picketing injunction.

During the two days of hearings, the Judge said the law did "tend toward Mr. Weisgal's argument if he can show a fair trial could not be had in the county court or if he shows the State Constitution denies a man equal civil rights." On the other hand, he expressed concern that if CORE won this case, State courts might lose their right to try any trespass case, alluding to the Gwynn Oak Park arrests as an example. He took the case "under advisement" rather than render an immediate decision.

Meanwhile, while awaiting this hearing, twenty more pickets were arrested for trespassing after they entered the company sales office. The second injunction had expired on September 5.

On September 17, Judge Thomsen handed down a seven-page opinion which sent the dispute back to the State court, refusing to go into the merits of the CORE protest. "The State courts, as well as the Federal courts, are bound to protect rights guaranteed by the Constitution of the U.S. However, the defendants have not referred to any Maryland law or municipal ordinance which denies them any civil right relevant to this case....

Referring to Mr. Weisgal's argument, that the issuance of the restraining order amounts to State action, Judge Thomsen stated that this assertion cannot justify removal....The petition also cannot be removed on grounds that the parties involved lived in different jurisdictions and are entitled to have a Federal Court forum." Following this decision Judge Powers again enjoined picketing or trespassing on the Levitt property until further hearings.[107]

That hearing, which sought a permanent injunction against CORE picketing, took place on October 7 before Judge Powers in the Prince George's County Circuit Court. Levitt's attorneys said the issue was where to draw the line between the firm's right to sell to anyone it chooses and CORE's right of assembly and free speech. He submitted that Levitt's sales were being adversely affected by the picketing (which, of course, was an intention of the demonstrators—to make it economically

---

[107] Account of Judge Thomsen's decision from the *Sun*, 9/18/1963.

more beneficial for builders and apartment owners to have a non-discrimination policy than to discriminate).

In his two-page written opinion, Judge Powers quoted two decisions by the Maryland Court of Appeals that upheld the right to discriminate and to use the police to arrest trespassers in the restaurant sit-in (*Bell v. State*) and at Glen Echo amusement park (*Griffin v. State*). He also acknowledged that a number of cases, including these, were then before the Supreme Court. But, in the end, he ruled that until such time as the Supreme Court overruled the Maryland Court, Levitt had the right to a permanent injunction.[108]

•••

In another early housing-related action, in January 1965, Jim Griffin, CORE's Chairman, wrote a media-distributed letter to Mayor McKeldin that attacked his appointment of Morton Macht as Chairman of the Community Action Program of the War on Poverty because of Macht's connection with segregated housing. Walter Carter and John Roemer, then Housing Co-Chairs, continued the attack in August with another letter; repeating the statement made in the earlier one: "It is not possible that key persons of the Poverty Program can identify with the people of the dark ghetto if they are connected with discriminatory housing developments, which keep the people of the ghetto walled in."

In this second letter, CORE points to the Action Plan of the agency which admitted that housing was one factor in blacks not getting a job even when they had received the necessary education. They conclude: "If Mr. Macht's housing and apartments have not been available or are not immediately made available on an equal opportunity basis, he will be guilty of promoting the unhealthy condition that you appointed him to correct." The appointment remained.

Whether or not Macht worked with the Mayor behind the scenes in an effort to get an Open Housing Ordinance passed cannot be determined. But, on April 5, 1965, City Council President, Thomas D'Alesandro III, at the request of Mayor McKeldin, had introduced Ordinance 1083, an open housing

---

[108] Opinion published in *Daily Record*, October 29, 1963.

amendment to the City Code.

•••

On June 2nd, 1965, the evening after the Fair Housing bills had been defeated, I went to my first strategy meeting with CORE's Housing Committee in their small, dingy office at 2316 W. North Avenue, in the basement of Philathea Hall's home (Walter's sister)—used also by an elderly man who prepared income taxes for poor blacks for 50¢ each.

People were sitting on desks, atop file cabinets, in rickety wooden chairs, in the cramped office, all angry over the City Council action, all ready to start picketing the Council Chambers and Councilmen's homes. But Walter adamantly rejected specific people's homes as targets: "This is not about people, this is about issues, what is morally right." He convinced us that we did not have enough militants, community support, or funds to start picketing apartments immediately. "We need first to let people *see* that we are trying to resolve the issue with negotiation, education and mediation—*without* the use of demonstrations."

I experienced that night for the first time the charisma that drew people to Walter, a power I never ceased to admire—an ability speak with such confidence and resonance that both new and timid and experienced and aggressive demonstrators were willing to continue peacefully on picket lines despite threats, boos and the vilest of epithets thrown at them, and even in the presence of white-hooded Klansmen, holding the leashes of vicious-looking dogs by their side.

Walter could speak with such eloquence and empathy to white church and civic groups whose members opposed equal rights for blacks that he successfully nudged them in his direction—even inspiring a few to join us—they'd most always invite him to return. When questioned why he bothered with such groups, he'd simply say, "You can't expect people to change radically, suddenly. Next time I'll nudge them a little farther." He firmly believed you got nowhere by censoring others for not thinking as we do. Walter once wrote of the "dynamics":

> People must not be censored for not thinking as others do. Keep the issue alive. Speak to the Issue.... They could

give money. They could march. They could picket. They could go to jail. They determined the extent of their participation....And when groups would not come to us, we went to them.

The strongest dynamic is this: Do you really want Freedom? Do you really want to tear down all the segregation that you can identify? Do you want to rid yourself and others of the effects of the accumulation of segregated existence? If so, this is the essential thing to work like hell on.. to keep people involved—involved in all phases, especially trying to bring out the leadership potential in them, by allowing them to even stumble against the foe.

Lloyd Taylor, one of his friends and fellow CORE members, described Walter's ability to connect with people this way:

Walter, to me and many others, appeared to see beyond human misery and oppression to the good in men. He could hate in an irate manner that wrong-doing and discriminatory act of an oppressor, but, nonetheless, could converse with the person in smiles. He could describe vividly the many faces of fascism, but, nevertheless, he held the warm friendship and deep admiration of many whites. The essence of his life appeared to be that he projected whatever hatred he felt upon the acts of wrong-doing , and never on the wrong-doer.

One reporter called his use of words "pure poetry." She wrote, "He sang a song of fellowship and good will to all...He had the awe inspiring capacity to turn others on—to a quest for social freedom and a belief in a better world."[109] One of Walter's writings preserved by this writer in her files reads:

In this age of rapid transit and technological 'advance,' we've had to absorb everything from the sprawl of megalopolis-Americanus to landing a couple of blue-eyed cats on the Moon. In contrast, the Movement for human rights and dignity has only stirred-up a wispy breeze...and no profound winds of freedom have swept through the scum of the slums, nor even through the pallid asbestos havens of the cold outer city.

The extent that black babies downtown remain painfully deprived is only a small indication of how much the

---

[109] Christine Hall, *Baltimore Sun*, 8/8/1976.

overwhelming majority of Americans remain deprived of
reality...of sensual reality about life as it is, and as it will
have to be, if we are going to save this hypocritical nation
from human starvation. No longer can we expect the
liberation of the black man in America to become realized
until white folks sober up...and cease being so intoxicated by
their physical assets that they lose their humanity and rob
others of their dignity.

At that first strategy meeting on June 2, 1965, Walter
gave everyone a chance to blow off steam and offer
suggestions. Finally, it was agreed that we'd write a letter, to
be signed by Walter, as Committee Chairman, to the Home
Builders Association which was meeting at the Tail of the Fox
Restaurant in Timonium on Thursday, June 17th as well as to
the Maryland Association of Real Estate Boards. Walter wrote
this of CORE's approach.

> Since Baltimore does not have many militants, we felt the
> best way to get real interest worked up on this issue was to
> try to involve all types of persons around this issue on which
> we had strong convictions. We were putting in a great deal of
> work on the problem but we felt it of the greatest significance
> that others see that we were trying to resolve the issue with
> the initial process of negotiation, education, and mediation—
> without the use of demonstrations.

The letter CORE wrote, signed by Walter Carter and
Barbara Mills and released to the media, asked that officials of
the organization use the occasion to "let Maryland take the
lead in ending the disgrace of discrimination without having to
be coerced by unnecessary pressure or the federal
government." It continued, in part:

> Housing remains as one of the most important areas of
> discrimination. And this barrier will be swept away. It will go
> because it is wrong. Fair-minded whites know it is
> wrong....The question is 'How will it go? Will it require the
> familiar sequence of protest, strife and the resulting
> disruption of all citizens?....Colored citizens have too long
> suffered from this wrong....No organization is better placed
> than yours to take the lead....
> No bolder step could be found than a bold declaration at
> your June 17 meeting to oppose discrimination by financiers,
> builders, brokers, owners and managers of apartments both

in and around the inner city and in the suburbs....It is too late to continue to advocate the policy of providing adequate and good housing for Negroes in proper areas. Equal access to all housing is essential....We hope you will accept this appeal as being consistent with the highest principles of democracy and brotherhood.

After the letter was ignored by both groups, I personally hand-carried a list of CORE's demands to Samuel Gorn, President of the Apartment House Owners Association of Maryland (AHOA) in his office not far from my home in Mt. Washington. It asked that Gorn arrange for representatives of CORE to meet with builders, owners, managers and financiers who were involved in apartment development in order to discuss with them the following proposals:

1. A public declaration of support for integrated housing in the arranging for financing and building of all apartments in the entire Baltimore metropolitan area.

2. A further declaration of a policy of "open occupancy" in the selling and rental of all apartment units.

3. In accordance with this policy of open occupancy, all apartment houses advertising will state, as part of the advertisement, "Rentals on an Open Occupancy Basis."

4. All advertisements for apartments will appear in both Negro and white news media so that members of both groups will be fully informed of the new policy.

5. Negroes, as well as whites, will be employed to "show" model apartments to the public. They will also be employed as apartment managers and in the Real Estate Management offices.

6. Both as an association and as individuals connected in any way with apartment development, positive steps will be taken in a community education campaign to prepare them for acceptance of city and state "Open Occupancy" laws. Similar educational steps will be taken within your own organizations to prepare yourselves and your employees.

7. Public support will be given to new efforts to pass a City and State "Open Occupancy" bill.

These became CORE's goals for the rest of its campaign to open housing in Baltimore to people of all races.

It was several weeks before Gorn replied, but he did arrange for a 7:30 p.m. meeting on Thursday, July 29, in the Hospitality Room of the Sheraton Inn in downtown Baltimore.

In addition to Walter and me, five other CORE members and six representatives of other groups were designated to meet with them. On the night prior to the meeting, CORE scheduled a public meeting at Baltimore's YWCA to explain to all those interested *why* we were meeting with representatives from the Apartment House Owners Association, and what we were asking of them. Our press release made all the papers for the first time—The *Sun, Evening Sun, News-American* and *Afro-American.* All our proposals were included.

In preparing for the scheduled meeting with the Apartment House Owners Association (AHOA), I met with Melvin Sykes, a friend and the attorney who'd been so involved in trying to end blockbusting in the Ashburton area. I wanted to discuss our proposals, and the legal aspects of ownership, loans and taxes. He referred me to a then just-published article in *Playboy* magazine on all aspects of the on-going boom in apartment house building.

"I thought that was just a girlie magazine with a great centerfold for men."

"Ah, yes, but they also have some well-researched, factual articles in each issue to add respectability."

So off I went to buy it, feeling very embarrassed, but just as Melvin had said, the article was excellent and the information it contained proved invaluable during our meeting with the AHOA. I had an answer every time one of its members started to tell me how much money they'd lose if they started renting to blacks.

I'd learned that IRS rules permitted double depreciation at the beginning, allowing the builder to have his equity returned in only a few years. In addition, after three years, the builder could sell and have his profits taxed under the more liberal capital gains law at a maximum of 25%. Further, depreciation was allowed on the entire investment even though the owner's or builder's equity was often as low as 3%. I suggested that the builders were well aware that if rentals were slow after completion, the IRS permitted a five year extension of the depreciation allowance against future income. In other words, an apartment owner's depreciation was picked up and carried forward as a loss. I had countered with these various points as the apartment owners offered us "financial loss" as the rationale for their not integrating their apartments.

"How do you know all that?" they asked, almost incredulously.

I just smiled.

The AHOA representatives were ready to deal with activists who made outrageous demands, but had not expected activists steeped with information about the real estate industry, loans, investments, and tax laws. I think too few confirmed activists understand the importance of a factual underpinning to the position they take in their demands for change. I believe that being able to empathize with your opponents—understanding where they're coming from—is crucial to being able to present your demand in a way they cannot simply dismiss. My educational background enable me to do this for CORE and Walter was perceptive enough immediately to realize its value. Facts may not *change* anyone, but they do, generally, elevate a discussion of issues above the level of name-calling.

Over a week later, the AHOA issued a statement endorsing state or city open occupancy laws, but they refused to recommend voluntary racial integration of their members' properties—about two hundred of the then-existing 757 apartment complexes in the metropolitan area. AHOA representatives told the press, "Experience compels us to conclude that voluntary action will not work. There is a vacancy problem now, particularly in the high rises. We can't afford to lose any more from the city and experience shows you try to integrate and it turns completely black. The whites run."

They, of course, could not tell us when, or even if, such legislation would ever be passed and even their agreement to "support a public education campaign to create sympathy for and acceptance of open occupancy" did not suggest that they would initiate such, with the public or with their colleagues, as our proposals had asked. They rejected as "ridiculous" the proposal that blacks be hired. "That's asking us to fire people we have now just because they are white."

Even though CORE regarded their response after our first meeting as "a delaying action," we did agree to another negotiating meeting on Tuesday, August 10, 1965, with the intent of again pressing "voluntary integration now." Walter pointed out that previous experience in the case of motels and restaurants had shown that voluntary desegregation was needed *before* the City Council would pass legislation.

Various members of the AHOA delegation admitted that they probably *could* influence their owner-members voluntarily to desegregate if approached personally, but that they "didn't have the time" and "it wouldn't work anyway." They expressed a wish to continue talking at future meetings, but CORE rejected this unless they could produce an agenda with new ideas that were worth discussing. They left saying they would do so but never contacted CORE again.

When AHOA held firm in their position that they would take no steps to open apartments until legislation was passed, CORE's Housing Committee felt it had no alternative but to move ahead in its efforts to "break the noose" around the inner city.

•••

I began to spend many, many hours in the two cluttered, dingy, roach-infested basement rooms that were CORE's office. More often than not I didn't even stop to go out for lunch but bought one of the nice juicy hamburgers from a little carry-out place down the block. I quickly learned, however, that keeping it *in* my hand as I worked was a good idea.

That first time I made the mistake of putting it down on my desk as I turned around to get something out of a file. I actually screamed out loud when I turned back to see that in those brief seconds a whole herd of roaches had discovered an unusually appetizing treat. I never really got used to the roaches and we carried on a regular battle after that, me spraying the office regularly, almost every evening before I left the office—but in row houses, it is hard to eliminate roaches in just one place. I was always worried about taking them home in my purse or briefcase, but it seems I never did.

CORE's offices were not in a very pleasant part of Baltimore and the black CORE members worried about me when I was in the office alone — which was a lot of the time— so I always kept the door locked. However, actually, I always felt safe in that musty little place. I only felt threatened later, not by blacks, but by the Ku Klux Klan and John Birch Society.

As our housing demonstrations attracted more and more attention, I frequently received obnoxious, threatening letters from both hate groups. Some were real works of art—little pictures and words, cut from magazines, pasted all over the envelopes, creating one big hate-filled montage. Sometimes I'd find a Klan leaflet (like that reproduced here) tucked under the windshield wiper of my car, parked in front of the office. On more than one occasion, Walter had sugar poured in his car's gas tank.

WAKE UP AMERICA

Some years ago the Knights of the Ku Klux Klan distributed millions of hand-bills like this!

Communism Will Not Be Tolerated

COMMUNISM

Destroys Free Government and All Its Institutions

THE KNIGHTS OF THE KU KLUX KLAN IS AWAKE!

The KNIGHTS OF THE KU KLUX KLAN has never stopped its fight on COMMUNISM.

The CONGRESS of the U. S. laughed — They investigated — reported that there was no COMMUNISM in America.

Today the government itself has awakened to the real danger facing us. The conviction of spies has been so numerous that we hear no more about "Red Herring."

COMMUNISM is being taught in our PUBLIC SCHOOLS.
(Ask your children)

COMMUNISM is being taught openly in OUR COLLEGES.

COMMUNISTS are in key positions in many of our Unions.

COMMUNISTIC ideas are being fed to you and your children through the Motion Pictures.

Even some of our Preachers have COMMUNISTIC ideas and are including them in their SERMONS.

The KNIGHTS OF THE KU KLUX KLAN is fighting against Negro Domination to protect our WHITE WOMANHOOD — to uphold the kind of DEMOCRACY given to us by our FOREFATHERS.

PRO COMMUNIST The Anti-Defamation League of the B-nai B'rith calls Gentiles "Goyin," (which means cattle) and seeks by block negro voting, smear tactics to build Jewish Communist Dictatorship in the United States. THIS WE MUST PREVENT.

The KNIGHTS OF THE KU KLAN KLAN is fighting COMMUNISM and all other ISMS except PURE AMERICANISM.

If interested in our crusade write

United Klans of America, Inc.

National Office: Suite 401, Alston Bldg., Tuscaloosa, Alabama

— or —

For Information In Maryland Write To National Office

P.O. Box 7887 Baltimore MD 21221

FOR WHITE MEN AND WOMEN

Having met Walter through his trusted friend, Dr. Wickwire, it had been easy for me quickly to become a trusted and valued new member of CORE, and especially so when it was learned that I could give important day-time hours to the movement that had been lacking until then since all the other active members had full-time jobs.

Soon my days were filled with doing background research on issues we were dealing with, writing letters, addressing and stuffing envelopes [*How I wish the term "Ms." had been acceptable at that time. It would have saved me much time and fretting, trying to decide whether or not to address the undesignated females on our mailing list as "Mrs." or "Miss."*].

My children still remember evenings at home in front of the fireplace when we'd collate letters and circulars; stuff and stamp envelopes together. I bought supplies, ran errands, answered the phone. With my faulty typing, and with the help of the light box my son Alan made for me in Cub Scouts, I made countless stencils for the thousands of mimeographed flyers we mailed and handed out. Under Walter's direction, I made phone calls—and increasingly, spoke to all kinds of civic and church groups—explaining and urging their participation—begging ministers, leaders of interfaith groups, heads of black sororities and fraternities, and anyone else we could think of, to either give us their membership lists for mailings and contacts, or to write them themselves and encourage their participation in our rallies and demonstrations. Sometimes, when requested, I attempted to polish Walter's "poetry." Evenings I went to CORE strategy meetings, committee and membership meetings.

Walter taught me how to do press releases—"Never give them expected turn-out numbers for meetings or demonstrations," he'd say. "Then they can't flout a smaller number as a failure if the turnout is less than hoped for." Sometimes I ran all over the city, hand-delivering a press release to each of the city's newspaper offices and radio and TV stations. Walter taught me to shorten my rambling sentences, add punch. "Ministers, especially, won't read past the first few sentences. Use lots of alliteration. Go to black Sunday services. You'll catch on to the power of their rhythms! It's important in appeals to black people."

Later, when the term "black" began to come into use, we sort of had to learn together when to use "Black", "Negro," "Colored." It was touchy—some still deeply resented being referred to as black, others just as vociferously resented being called Negroes, a few still preferred Colored. Walter was good at sort of instinctively knowing which group would prefer which, and it didn't happen too often that some disgruntled listener would come up afterwards to chew us out for having called them "Negro" or "Black."

Walter also told me, "You need to understand that many blacks are very conservative, resistant to change, fearful of demonstrating, and fearful that a speaker trying to rouse them to action might be a Communist—they fear being exploited again, as many felt they had been in the 30s."

Then Walter explained the need to understand that the black community in Baltimore is divided into two factions— the East Side blacks (predominately lower income) and the West Side blacks (predominately higher income with more professionals). "They don't like each other very much; West Siders feeling they are 'better'"—an attitude that I found to be pervasive all the way from the richest blacks to its street criminals and prisoners.

Walter seemed to be the only person in Baltimore who was trusted by both factions; who could get everyone behind him. He did "the walk and the talk," as they say, with politicians, academics, church people, non-believers, the rich, and the poor—but remained his own person, always self-effacing, always aware that whatever "power" he had belonged to his troops and not to himself (a trait also common to his hero, the head of national CORE, James Farmer)

Everyone recognized and respected the fact that Walter could not be co-opted, nor corrupted, by anyone. Walter himself laughed at the idea, but most all who knew him thought that one day Walter would be Mayor of a united Baltimore.

In a later piece he wrote, Walter said of this time:

> We did what a good CORE chapter is supposed to do, we kept developing the issue, allowing for group differences, allowing for participation by different persons in whatever way made them feel most comfortable. Soon the housing committee had as many members attending housing meetings as the chapter itself had attending membership

meetings. We were able to publicize meetings in the AFRO, time and place. The Dailies were not too hot carrying our stuff, but some interest was gradually developing.

Our mailing list reached into the twelve to fifteen hundred size as we included the people who were in Neighborhood Associations, those attending the Presidents conference on Equal Opportunity in Housing sponsored by Baltimore Neighborhoods, those who helped in the voter registration, clubs, etc. Most significant of all we had a capable person [this writer] who was able to put in more hours on this project than most people do on regular jobs. Combined with her book knowledge of the subject and physical labor needed to make it tick, was the invaluable CORE know-how and soul contributed by the person in the chapter who had been consistently more active since the Rt. 40 days [himself].

Walter knew just about every demonstrator in the area and had the ability to speak effectively to all types of persons in a way that would stimulate them and help them relate to the issue in a way that was meaningful for them.

•••

It was during this time of outreach and information gathering that the writer met Fred Weisgal for the first time. Even though he lived only two blocks from me, and both of our children went to Mt. Washington elementary school, I had not met him until that evening when I joined Walter and John Roemer in his living room for one of the many strategy sessions Fred was a part of. At first the talk was about Walter and John's still-pending public accommodation trespass cases. Fred told them, with the new laws in place, he didn't expect them ever to come to trial, but, he added, "the housing sit-in cases you're going to start accumulating will be something else again."

Fred planned to use, over and over, the same arguments he'd used at Bowie a few years back, and earlier in the restrictive covenant cases. He knew he was right; the state was illegally enforcing discrimination in numerous ways. He hoped, eventually, a judge would be brave enough to agree.

Somehow, perhaps in discussing what our "housing demands" should be, quotas also came up for discussion. I still remember that Fred's friend, Gene Feinblatt, who was also present, vehemently opposed our even considering them.

He pointed out how, in the past, they'd been used effectively to limit, even exclude, qualified Jews from colleges and such—a dangerous concept that could too easily backfire.

As we talked and strategized, there was no evidence of the convalescing heart patient that Fred then was, and nothing in our conversation that would have clued me in. [I knew nothing of it until after his second heart attack some years later.] Fred had sounded gung-ho, not like someone with plans to cut back, to limit his involvement with CORE. In fact, it had been only four months, more-or-less, since his April attack.

• • •

On July 4th, 1965, one month after the city council had defeated the two open housing bills, the *Baltimore Sun* reported that the Council's President, Thomas D'Alesandro III, had appointed a 48-member Housing Education Commission. The resolution read: "This city needs the work and efforts of a vigorous and effective commission to study problems of open housing and to supply, where needed, the education and the reason to persuade the community."

It was divided into three sub-committees to study "property values in integrated areas, community attitudes about integration, and property maintenance in integrated neighborhoods. The fact that these subjects had been studied the year before and could be found in the November 1964 *Report of the Baltimore City Housing Study Advisory Commission*, headed by Albert Berney, seemed to make no difference.

When asked in September to appear before D'Alesandro's Housing Education Commission, CORE's Housing Committee agreed that they should refuse. Walter summed it up for us this way: "No intelligent person would be fooled by these stalling tactics....A drive from suburbia to the inner city anytime during the day is sufficient study of this problem...." CORE again urged the housing industry to "issue a strong statement that they have taken the leadership" in a move to get quick solutions to the problem. Of course, no such statement was issued.

• • •

At CORE's final meeting with the Apartment House Owners Association of Maryland, AHOA refused to take any steps to open housing until legislation was passed. The next day, Wednesday, August 11, 1965, CORE's Housing Committee met to discuss its next step. There were forty to fifty blacks and whites present, including representatives from the National Alliance of Postal Employees, the Catholic Interracial Council and many local churches.

As usual, the discussion was heated at times and many were ready to start demonstrating the next day. But once again, after letting everyone vent their feelings, Walter moved in with his *fiery coolness*—I don't know any other way to describe it— convincing us that we didn't yet have the numbers and backing to prevail in demonstrations. "First we have to use the opening that the Apartment House Owners Association (AHOA) gave us and start a big education campaign."

It was agreed that we would have a "kick off meeting" at 2: p.m. on Sunday, August 15 (the second anniversary of the March on Washington), at the Mount Zion Methodist Church at Liberty Heights and Wabash Avenues. We talked about how we had to "Break the Noose" that the suburbs had drawn around the inner city and this soon became our logo. We used it on letterheads, flyers, and buttons; a powerful symbol with a double-edged meaning at a time when lynchings were still taking place. I still have two of those buttons: one gold, one white.

The first flyer announcing the start of CORE's drive was mimeographed (there were no copying machines, no computers and no scanners; all materials either went to the printer, or had to be drawn and typed on stencils and then mimeographed, a difficult and messy processes). This flyer described the results of discrimination in housing as "second-class, over-priced housing, tricky and exorbitant financing, overcrowding, defacto school and recreational segregation, excessive weekly rentals for inferior housing." It asked that we remember: "If you are white you can take flight, if you are black you must stay back in a deteriorating housing pocket." It promised that participation would be a "blow to housing Jim Crow."

Walter and I then went to work developing two educational flyers to be printed. One of these, headed, **"Speak Out For Freedom,"** listed ideas for doing so, and ended with, **"Tell Your Landlord You Believe in Democracy."** The second handbill, titled **"*Racial Discrimination in Housing is Bad Business!*,** enumerated reasons, again listed "Things You Can Do," and, ended with, "**Good Business and Human Dignity Go Together.**"

The Sunday morning of our scheduled kick-off meeting, the *Sun* paper carried an article stating that cattle prods had been issued to some of the city policemen. Troy Brailey, Vice President of the National Chapter and President of the Baltimore Chapter of the *Negro-American Labor Council*, had sent telegrams to Governor Tawes and Mayor McKeldin protesting. "As a concerned citizen of the now peaceful Negro community I am concerned and disturbed about the motive underlying the acquiring of this device by our city's Police Department."

When Police Commissioner Schmidt was interviewed by an *Afro-American* reporter later in the week, he admitted that several months earlier, the FBI had conducted a special course for the Baltimore police to train them in crowd and riot control, and that "certain equipment was recommended." He denied having anything *called* cattle prods, but finally admitted that they had "electrified persuaders."

An editorial in the *Afro-American* contended that the issuance of cattle prods only added to the police department's poor image in the black community. With a forty-percent colored population, there were few black police, no colored captains, and the department had admitted in court to 300 raids on colored homes without search warrants. The editorial concluded: "If the police department is going to use cattle prods, it is asking for trouble."

Walter was sure that it was FBI agents who had caused all the fears and hype about our activities in the first place. He was well aware of well-dressed strangers, most likely FBI, who attended our meetings from time to time. However, no one really cared, because all we did was open anyway. It was our own activists who distributed circulars inviting anyone interested to attend our meetings. It was CORE who made a point of sending press releases in advance of any actions we planned.

Needless to say, the threat of cattle prods did give a special tone to our Sunday "kick-off." Fear of what might happen was reflected on the faces of the fifty or so people who gathered to begin our education drive. We were all well aware of how cattle prods had been used against peaceful demonstrators in the "deep south." We broke into groups of six to ten, each group going to a different apartment development in the Baltimore area to distribute leaflets inside and outside the Model Apartments and Rental Offices.

Everyone was a little nervous as we drove along the Jones Falls Expressway to our destination in the suburbs, some of us, including me, undertaking such activism for the first time. But even for the old hands (and we made sure there was at least one "old-hand" in each group), cattle prods and the housing issue were new. We wondered if it was a bad omen when we suddenly realized, as our car zipped along the Jones Falls Expressway, that we were almost out of gas. But when we found an open gas station without too much trouble, we laughed at ourselves and decided to concentrate on our good luck. Fortunately, the whole day went smoothly after that, for us, and for all the other groups.

Shortly after our second "educational" outing, I wrote a newsletter for CORE that we sent to all members and to any others we thought might be interested, outlining the work of the Housing Committee to date and its rationale. The heading stated:

Let's ALL JOIN HANDS and Announce to the World with Proud Heart and
Clear Conscience that America Really Stands for FREEDOM and EQUALITY—
FOR EVERYONE—NOW!

It pointed out that after President Johnson signed the Voting Rights Bill on August 6th, housing was the one remaining field that had barely been touched by federal, state or local legislation, and that it would almost certainly be the most difficult field in which to establish equal opportunity without legislation. It continued: "It is far more complex in structure than most of the others—involving financial institutions, builders, owner syndicates, realtors, real estate managers, politicians and other vested interests." It went on:

Housing touches all of our personal lives more closely than the other areas—it literally brings the problem 'home' and forces each of us to examine deeply his own values and beliefs....But it is also for this very reason that when one group is excluded from an area, there is the clear implication that they are considered not fit to live there....

I could put it no more aptly than my son did at four years old when he asked, 'Why do Negroes live all bunched up together? It's just like they were all caught in a lasso.'....

If we don't want to discover that Watts is not 3000 miles away in Los Angeles but right outside our door in Baltimore, we must start to disentangle that lasso—NOW. The future health and vitality of our cities depend on effective desegregation.[110]

We can never really solve the problems of segregated schools, recreational facilities, public accommodations, etc., or resolve the differential treatment in the supply of innumerable community services until large-scale progress is made in the field of an open housing market.

The newsletter concluded that our drive to help "educate the public," had been endorsed by the NAACP, National Alliance of Postal Employees, Baltimore County League for Human Rights, American Labor Council, and the Anti-Poverty Action Commission.

CORE now proceeds with its own methods of 'active education' and 'creative tension.' Following two Sundays of planning and minor skirmishes, the real kick-off in this new phase will begin at 1 p.m., Saturday, August 28, from Lafayette Square at Carrollton and Lanvale Street. From there we will proceed to our pre-designated target. Keep in touch with our housing committee if you wish to be kept abreast of this campaign. We can use your encouragement and active support now more than ever before.

The newsletter was signed by Walter, and, at his insistence, by me: "After all, it was your idea, you researched and wrote it."

Well aware of the recent riots in Los Angeles, as the time for CORE's announced demonstrations approached, rumors of a riot in Baltimore spread. Mayor McKeldin issued a warning that the Governor had agreed to state reinforcements of the city police in the event that street violence occurred over the weekend. "Nor will we hesitate to invoke federal power if we must." He added that there was no "firm basis" for the rumors but had taken these steps "as a matter of ordinary prudence"

---

[110] A reference to the major riot that had occurred in Los Angeles from August 11-16, just weeks before this.

to assure that no Watts-type occurrence would happen here.

On Wednesday, August 25, 1965, preceding the scheduled August 28th date for more activist-type CORE demonstrations to begin, Cardinal Shehan, who had previously supported open housing legislation, received a letter from Walter urging him to use his influence in getting prominent Catholic builders and realtors to voluntarily open their housing. In his telegraphed reply the next day, the Cardinal rejected the singling out of individuals of one faith as a piecemeal and inappropriate solution.

> It would seem to me that the matter of open occupancy deserves the attention of the full building and real estate community, and not merely a segment. Recalling the experience in connection with the commercial banks, you will remember that my approach was to all the banks, and there was sufficient time available to devote to the matter to bring about a satisfactory understanding among the parties.

The Cardinal stated his concern that CORE had not come to him earlier, adding that he was leaving for the Vatican the following week. But, he assured Walter, he shared his "desire to see adequate housing made available to all persons regardless of race".... and, that on his return from the Vatican Council, he would "be happy to render whatever assistance I can in striving for a solution."

On Friday, August 27, representatives of the Human Relations Commissions of Baltimore City, Baltimore County and Anne Arundel County met with representatives from the Home Builders Association of Maryland and the Real Estate Board of Greater Baltimore to discuss the possibility of voluntary desegregation of housing. No decisions were made other than to meet again and to include representatives from BNI (which now, among its other efforts, trained volunteers to "test" for housing discrimination), the Apartment House Owners Association, and various activist organizations engaged in civil rights activities in that meeting.

CORE did a lot of hard work in preparing for our kick-off: many letters sent and phone calls made, speeches, appearances at church services, leafleting neighborhoods and parking lots, trips to the printer for signs, news releases, and much more—much of it done by Walter and me. Saturday afternoon, August 28, the day for our first activist demonstration, finally arrived. About one hundred demonstrators gathered at Lafayette Square for a pep talk by Walter, our Housing Chairman, and by Jim Griffin, who had become Baltimore CORE's Chairman after Walter had resigned. Walter seemed as nervous as if this had been his first demonstration, worried, I think, that any violence would kill forever our efforts to achieve voluntary integration, or to get a Fair Housing bill passed. He had asked Herb Callender, a national CORE field secretary, to join us and to give us a thorough grounding on nonviolent picket line conduct before we went on our first real demonstration.

It was emphasized over and over that no one should carry anything that even looked like it could be used as a weapon, including sticks and pocket knives. Only assigned monitors, wearing arm bands, were to speak to any press who might be present, and, indeed, questions from anyone should be referred to them. Heckling should be ignored—no stooping to their level.

It was also explained that any apartment "testing" would be planned in advance and "testers" would be pre-designated. As one CORE spokesperson later explained to the press: "After a small delegation goes in to test, what we normally get is a polite, 'No, we do not cater to the Negro trade.'"

Unless sit-ins had been planned, the small delegation would then leave and resume picketing with the others. If there were to be "sit-ins," who they would be and whether or not they would stay to be arrested, would also be planned in advance. With few exceptions, these rules were carefully adhered to in this and every demonstration that followed.

Half the group then went to Wellington Gate Apartments at 1400 East Northern Parkway, a suburban development, and half to Belvedere Towers, a new high-rise at 1190 West Belvedere Avenue. For two hours we walked back and forth in front of the developments, singing Freedom Songs and carrying our neatly printed signs calling for "Fair Housing for Negroes Now!" "A Choice in Housing Now!" "Speak Out for FREEDOM" and "FREEDOM NOW."

> *I woke up this morning with my mind set on Freedom*
> *I woke up this morning with my mind set on Freedom*
> *Hallelu, Hallelu, Hallelujah.*

I'm walking and talking with my mind set on Freedom...
Folks in Baltimore got their minds set on Freedom....
All God's children got their minds set on Freedom....

When Walter heard one of our demonstrators call the black doorman at the Belvedere an "oreo," he got uncharacteristically angry.

"Never say that of any Negro, and, especially an older Negro! He's doing what he has to do; what many before him have had to do—to feed and house himself and his family. He doesn't need to be humiliated by you, too—you, who say you are fighting for *all* Negroes. Remember that! Remember it always!"

Before we disbanded for the day, we sang *We Shall Overcome*, as we did at the end of nearly every demonstration thereafter. But this was my first time, and it's hard to explain to those who have never been part of a group picketing for something they believe in with all their hearts, just how those words drew us together, bonded us forever. In this age of "political correctness," it's hard to convey what we felt together, blacks and whites—a belief that, in time, we would have equality; that both blacks and whites would be changed, changed for the better, for a better world. "Integration" was not a bad word, and it did not mean, for us, that we would end up an homogenous blend of color.

Oh, Deep in my heart, I do believe We shall overcome someday....
We are not afraid....
God is on our side....
Black and white together....
We shall integrate....

Thirty years later, it still moves me to tears when I hear it, remembering those times together, what hopes we had, realizing now how much work is still left to be done.

The *Sun* paper next day reported that "with city policemen standing by in case of trouble, the marchers drew the attention of passing motorists but few spectators gathered to watch and *hardly anyone* [my italics] bothered to heckle." The reporter was unsuccessful in his efforts to learn the name of our target for picketing the following day.

On that day, Sunday, August 29th, there were about sixty-five picketers at Joseph Meyerhoff's Lockwood Apartments at Loch Raven Blvd. and Belvedere Avenue. In addition to CORE members, picketers included state legislative Delegate Clarence Mitchell 3rd, two officers of the Baltimore Teachers Union, Cleveland Chandler, a Morgan State College Economics Professor with his two small children, representatives of the National Alliance of Postal Employees, and a Sparticist member. ("Sparticist" was a Communist group whose two or three members sometimes gave us trouble, because they carried different signs and cared not for our rules of behavior, but who were impossible to exclude.)

Simultaneously, there were also about twenty-five picketers at Essexshire Gate and at Carrollwood East in Baltimore County, both medium-priced housing that "Negroes can afford," according to William Ross, president of the Baltimore County League for Human Rights, who had spearheaded these demonstrations.

But also, on the same day, our first apartment sit-in and arrest was taking place at yet another site—Edward Myerberg's new Chartley II Apartments in Reisterstown, just north of Baltimore. Week after week Walter had been out in front leading our picket lines, or walking amongst us, encouraging us, inspiring us, planning strategy. And today he would take the lead again in a new phase of our demonstrations.

The sit-in had started after the rental office offered an apartment to a white "tester," Fred Nass, sent in by CORE, and then refused to rent to Walter when he requested a same-size three-bedroom apartment. Not realizing, at first, that they knew each other, the rental agent informed Walter that Fred had rented the last apartment. Walter said later, "I was genuinely interested in renting one for my growing family."

The rest of that day and through the night, those sitting-in were ignored. Outside, picketers had maintained an all-night vigil, carrying signs and singing our Freedom Songs, one especially appropriate.

> We shall not, We shall not be moved
> We shall not, We shall not be moved
> Just like a tree That's planted by the water
> We shall not be moved..

Jim Griffin, Fred Nass, Dave Eberhardt, Walter Carter Sit-in. From author's scrapbook, dated 8/31/1965. Probably from *AfroAmerican* but paper's archivist could not locate; possibly from *News American*, now defunct.

The verses continue.

> *Fighting segregation, We shall not be moved....Marching for fair housing, We shall not be moved....Fighting for our Freedom, We shall not be moved....Black and white together, We shall not be moved....*

Dave Eberhardt, one of those sitting in, has since written an account of the events, quoted with his permission.[111]

We waited through the next morning, groggy from a night's rest on the floor. Some of the tired picketers came in and stretched out on the floor to get some rest. At about noon a representative of the Maryland Interracial Committee

---

[111] It is part of Dave's unpublished memoir given to this writer with permission to use. Eberhardt later became director of Offenders Aid and Restoration (OAR), a group matching prisoners with volunteers for support while in Baltimore City jail; still at City Jail, he is now responsible for prisoner's group activities.

came out to mediate. Myerberg's attorney was also on hand offering various ploys to get us out of the sample apartment. We were beginning to draw unwelcome publicity for his boss. First he offered to meet us on a Wednesday, then a Monday, then immediately...anywhere but in the model apartment. He still refused to give any policy statement. So, it's obviously segregated, we "happily" concluded..

Then the hammering began! Burly men were covering the back of the apartment with sheets of plywood. They came in and tore out our only toilet. They attached a hose to the only water tank. We got a little nervous. "Maybe they're gonna flood us out," Walter speculated as they brought the hose in. But for some reason they drained the tank. Did they thing we were drinking it?

The crowd of picketers and onlookers was growing. A lumber truck pulled up in front of the apartment and a carpenter made measurements as if to block up the front window. We had stocked up with food for the long haul: jugs of water, gallons of peanut butter, loads of crackers, grapes, bananas, candy, even bags as replacement for the toilet. But the end was near.

After twenty-five hours of sitting-in in the empty Chartley model apartment, a warrant was obtained, and Walter Carter, 42, Negro, David Eberhardt, 24, white, and Raymond Ford, 19, Negro [missing from the picture], were arrested for "unlawfully and wantonly" trespassing. Earlier, before nightfall, Jim Griffin, Negro, and Fred Nass, white, shown in the picture, had left.

Dave continued his account of the sit-in following their arrest:

They led us out to a paddy wagon and took us to the nearest station where we waited for processing. We chatted with the agent who'd sworn out the warrants....We signed a prisoner's meal ticket and the jailer took our belts (so we wouldn't hang ourselves I suppose) and then took us into the lockup. Walter regaled us with imitations of civil rights leaders; we chatted with a Mr. Smallwood who was awaiting trial for assault and battery and listened to the jailer kidding our friend, Ray [Ford] as he took his fingerprints. Soon they transferred us to a magistrate.

At this arraignment hearing, the word "wanton" was stricken, at Dave's request, and their request for a jury trial was accepted. They were released on $105 bail each. No trial date was set. Later, Walter said, "There was nothing wanton about what we did. It was a "considered and compassionate" act. Dave concluded his later account by stating:

> Some persons with baseball bats at the exit alarmed us [as we were leaving the court house], but it turned out they were softball players who had disturbed the peace.

When the press asked Myerberg about the boarding up and turning-off of the water in the apartment, he denied knowing anything about it. For his part, Walter told them: "I was willing to sit-in for as long as the Gemini 5 astronauts, Conrad and Cooper, flew in space [eight days]."

• • •

On Saturday, September 4th, a chartered bus[112] brought about fifty demonstrators to Edward Myerberg's Reisterstown housing development, where they again "paraded," as the *Sun* reporter called it, with their Fair Housing signs, and then walked the six blocks to Chartley II, singing as they continued marching:

> *O' Freedom, O' Freedom, O Freedom over me*
> *and before I be a slave*
> *I'll be buried in my grave and go home to my Lord & be free.*
>
> *No segregation, No segregation, No segregation over me....*
> *No Jim Crow, No Jim Crow, No Jim Crow over me....*
> *Fair Housing, Fair Housing, Fair Housing over me....*

Four pre-selected demonstrators[113] then entered the rental

---

[112] It was rare for us to make any special arrangements for transportation. Typically we congregated at some inner-city, black church before departing for the day's target. There never seemed to be a problem with finding space in those with cars for those arriving by bus—sometimes eight or more in each. I do not recall why a bus had been chartered on this occasion: Perhaps because it was our first demonstration in the county, no regular bus route yet established.

[113] There was no fancy way of selecting those to sit-in. As we congregated to go on a demonstration, Walter usually discussed the procedure for the sake of those unfamiliar with it and asked for volunteers. It was rare that anyone who offered was known by Walter beforehand, their situation and circumstances. It also was rare to turn anyone down who wanted to sit in.

office to talk to Vincent Zito, the sales manager, about the date that his housing would be available. When he told them, "Next summer," they said they'd wait until they received from Mr. Myerberg a statement regarding his policy on sales and rental to Negroes. "Okay," said Mr. Zito, "You may stay until the office closes." However, he called the police and soon afterwards told them the office was closing. Two of the "testers" then left, but two others remained until the police arrived and dragged them out. Surprisingly, they were not arrested.[114]

On Saturday, September 11, 1965, 25 demonstrators arrived at the Colmar Apartments, a small new development tucked away on a little dead-end street, overlooking Northern Parkway, not far from my house on Crest Road. My son, Alan, then nine, joined me for the first time at a demonstration that day and was fascinated by the whole experience. It was not unusual to have whole families participate in these demon-strations——babies in carriages, toddlers riding piggy-back on Dads' shoulders; oldsters, including one on crutches, there week after week; professionals; blue collar workers; students; teachers; people of all sorts—male and female, black and white. It was a heartening sight to watch as they all marched, chanted and sang together. We were certain We *Would* Overcome.

As planned, Margarita Patterson, 32, a Negro housewife, went into the rental office to seek an apartment and was told by the manager, Edward Dentry, that they were not integrated and did not rent to Negroes. She then went to one of the empty apartments and started to sit-in, promptly joined by Tom Lewis, 25, a white artist, Fred Nass, 34, a white social security employee, and Jim Griffin, 33, a Negro vocational counselor and Chairman of Baltimore CORE. They were arrested by Northern district police at 9:30 p.m. for trespassing, after Mr. Dentry swore out warrants. The next morning, after asking for a jury trial, Judge Joseph Broccolino, Jr. released them on $104 bonds each.

---

[114] In April, the following year, 1966, the Baltimore FHA office did, for a short period, impose sanctions on the Myerberg company, the developer of Chartley II, and said no company that Mr. Myerberg was associated with would be eligible for FHA mortgage insurance. Exactly why the sanctions were removed after a short time is not clear since he did not open his developments to Negroes.

Afterwards they said they'd been threatened with an insecticide, but Mr. Dentry, when asked about this by the press, said, "Every Saturday night we fumigate our sample apartment. Out of deference to them, we did not tonight. The picketing we have no objection to, but the lying around like a bunch of animals we did."

The next day, on Sunday afternoon, a group of twenty-five or so were again back at Colmar, marching and singing—in the pouring rain:

> Paul and Silas bound in Jail
> Had no money to go that bail
> Keep your eyes on that prize
> Hold on, Hold on, Hold on, Hold on,
> Keep your eyes on that prize, Hold on, Hold on.
>
> Jack and Jill Went up the hill
> Jack came back with the Civil Rights Bills
> Keep your eyes on that prize....
>
> Fight all day Fight all night
> Just to gain my civil rights
> Keep your eyes on that prize....
>
> Got my hands On the Freedom plow
> Wouldn't give nothing for my journey now
> Keep your eyes on that prize....
>
> The only chain That man can stand
> That's the chain of hand in hand
> Keep your eyes on that prize....

Five more people were arrested for sitting-in: Walter Carter, 42, Negro, Marion Lummis, 24, white, Nelson Gilbert, 19, white, Harold Smith, 31, white, Ricardo Turner, 18, Negro. After they pled for a jury trial, Judge Howard Aaron set bail at $100 each and ordered the cases sent to the grand jury in a brief hearing in Northern Municipal Court.

Because we knew that Victor Frenkil was the owner of the Colmar Apartments, the week following these arrests, CORE sent a telegram to the Mayor complaining about the city's awarding his company contracts to build the new Polytechnic and Western High Schools. "We believe that [this contract award] is a violation of the non-discrimination clause in city contracts," a subject that CORE had previously written the Mayor about and regarding which we were meeting with Sam

Daniels, then head of the Community Relations Commission, in drafting a new provision.

In the Mayor's reply, he said that we knew he was sympathetic with our concerns and repeated that he had asked that the present anti-discrimination clause which covers only maintenance and construction contracts be extended to cover all firms which dealt with the city in services or supplies. However, he concluded that we cannot "legally penalize one corporation which is operating in conformity with the law because the owner is a stockholder in another corporation which might have a policy that does not meet all moral requirements but, nevertheless, is not in conflict with, or covered by, existing legislation."

Walter also sent a telegram to Victor Frenkil, informing him that we would again be at the Colmar Apartments on Saturday, September 18, to again test the racial policies there. He invited Mr. Frenkil to meet with CORE either that day at Colmar or any time before that. We received no reply, and when I checked on the apartment on Friday, I learned that the office had been closed since mid-week. Therefore, on Saturday, a few of the thirty or so demonstrators stayed at Colmar, but the others split into five teams, going to Belvedere Towers on West Belvedere Avenue; St. Agnes Apartments, on St. Agnes Lane (another apartment development where Alan, my son, joined me in picketing, this time with Susie, my daughter, as well); Westgate; Parkside Gardens on Moravia Road; Pleasant Heights on McClean Blvd.; and the Purdue Garden Apartments on Purdue Avenue—asking at each site for applications for an apartment. Parkside and Belvedere refused to give them applications and St. Agnes told them there had been a death in the manager's family and that they were not giving out applications.

The next day, on Sunday, we ran into some different tactics than those we'd encountered at the other apartments. To quote from the *Afro*: "At the Americana Landmark Apartments on Greenspring Avenue, a white applicant was quoted a price of $170 or $180 (with balcony) for a two-bedroom apartment...but a colored applicant to the same place was quoted a price of $250 for a two-bedroom apartment and informed he would have to wait for the opening of a new unit."

The *Afro* article continued: "At the Blue Fountain Apartments...white applicants were given a simple, one-page sheet termed 'general information sheet.'...Colored applicants were presented with a detailed, two-page termed 'application Blue Fountain Apartment Club.'....They received application blanks from ten others....The civil rights group conducted sixteen separate tests Saturday and Sunday following an announced policy of intensified demonstrations at Baltimore apartment houses."

On September 27th, one of our new white demonstrators at Colmar, Beverly Sokal, had a Letter to the Editor published in the *Evening Sun*. She stated, in part:

> For the last few weekends I have walked with others on the demonstration line sponsored by the Congress of Racial Equality before apartment houses that do not accept Negro tenants. This has opened my eyes wide in admiration for the confident and dignified method of non-violent expression that CORE has developed....The Congress of Racial Equality emulates democracy by a non-extremist, well thought out, non-violent program that should draw more of the freedom loving people of our city to swell its demonstration ranks.

On October 5th, our attorney, Fred Weisgal, took the court by surprise with his arguments for dismissal of the trespassing charges against the nine arrested at Colmar. He claimed that the defendants rights of equal protection under the Fourteenth Amendment were violated by the state, whose governmental agencies "have been substantially involved in every stage of planning, construction, regulation, and maintenance of the Colmar Apartment development." He stated, according to the *Evening Sun*:

> [The defendants] went to the development with the intention of renting homes. Public advertisements and solicitation without limitation to color were made by the owners, but the defendants were informed that apartments would not be rented to Negroes....The ensuing demonstrations protesting the alleged discrimination were an exercise of the right of free speech....Municipal Court action in issuing warrants for the arrest of defendants constituted state enforcement of the alleged policy of racial segregation at the development...
>
> The judge did not have probable cause to issue the

warrants...It was explained that tax money provides police protection, fire protection, garbage collection and other services to all houses in the city, and that public employees could not be used to support segregation. Any prosecution of the defendants puts the state in the position of perpetuating unlawful racial discrimination in housing.

The charges, of course, were not dismissed, but it would be some time before any of the housing-related trespass cases would come to trial.

On Sunday, October 10, CORE demonstrators went, first, to Kensington Gate Apartments at Woodbourne Avenue and Loch Raven Blvd. where about twenty-five of us marched peaceably with no intent to sit-in. Then, we went on to the Dutch Village Apartments at McClean Blvd. and Northern Parkway. There, at first, we also just marched back and forth carrying our signs and shouting, "Freedom, Freedom Now!—and singing:

> *If I had a hammer/I'd hammer in the morning*
> *I'd hammer in the evening/all over this land*
> *I'd hammer out Justice/I'd hammer out Freedom/I'd*
> *hammer out the Love*
> *between my brother and my sister/all over this land.......*

But we had other plans for Dutch Village. At the designated moment, Walter and Jim Griffin went in to inquire about renting two-bedroom apartments. "We don't rent to niggers", they were told.

After Walter and Jim were so rudely dismissed, I entered the rental office with four others, as planned, to sit-in.[115] We made ourselves comfortable on the plush sofas and chairs, watching as others came in to ask about renting apartments, leaving no space, of course, for them to sit down. We just ignored the frustrated rental agent as she kept demanding that we leave.

"I'll give you one last warning," she finally said, her voice taking on an almost beseeching note, "or I'll have to call the police." It seemed forever that we'd been sitting there before

---

[115] The newspaper reported it as: "Barbara Mills, 37, white, wife of a Hopkins University professor; Fred Nass, 34, white, Social Security employee; Raymond Ford, 19, Negro, machinist; Anthony Thompson, 18, white, a student; and Ricardo Turner, 18, Negro, YMCA employee."

John Riehl, one of the owners of Dutch Village, appeared, followed by two burly police officers. It was already beginning to get dark, almost eight o'clock I think, when Mr. Riehl read us the Trespass Act and swore out the warrants for our arrest. Again, the police asked us to leave voluntarily, but we ignored them too, still just sitting there, waiting for the next step.

Looking totally exasperated, the two officers then took each of us in turn to the paddy wagon, not easily. As our bodies stiffened, they had to bear our full weight, more or less dragging us out the office door to the wagons, and then lifting us in. As he stood watching, I asked Hal Smith, a friend and regular demonstrator, to call my husband and tell him that I had been sitting in, had been arrested and didn't know when I would get home.

At the police station, the men were locked up. Ordinarily, any women would be taken to the Pine Street jail for women, a notoriously outdated and disgusting facility, but because they knew we would all shortly be out on bail, they chose to leave me at the station, sitting in the room with the police officers. Actually, the officers were unexpectedly considerate of all of us—sent out for hamburgers and cokes. Fred had been called and within a few hours the bondsman was there to post the $104 bail for the three of us who were then released. Fred and Ricardo chose to stay in jail overnight.

On Monday morning, October 11, when we all appeared in court, we pleaded "Not Guilty" and asked for a jury trial. Our bail was then continued for those released the night before, and Fred's and Ricardo's was set for $104. An arraignment date was set for November 15th for "indictment # 4960, Raymond Ford, et al."

Undeterred, the following Sunday, October 17, about thirty demonstrators went to the luxury high-rise Carlyle Apartments on West University Parkway where about thirty demonstrators sat-in in the lobby for three hours without being arrested. Then, on October 24, about twenty-five returned. This time, after they were refused rental applications, eleven of the demonstrators started a sit-in and refused to leave when asked. All were arrested after Bud Martin, the manager, sought warrants. Each received bail of $104.[116]

It was about the same time as these latest demonstrations were taking place that the Housing Study Advisory Committee of the Baltimore County Human Relations Committee issued a report recommending:

(1)   that the Commission propose enactment of open occupancy legislation for Baltimore County,

(2)   that it explore the possibility of joint action with the city in securing metropolitan or state-wide open occupancy legislation, and

(3)   that members use their influence in urging federal legislation. Spiro Agnew, then Baltimore County executive, who at times was called upon as a "sympathic mediator," opposed all but federal legislation and said efforts at voluntary compliance should continue.

When a reporter asked Walter Carter his opinion, he stated, "We ask that the Human Relations Commission of Baltimore County immediately demand that the Real Estate Commission of Maryland take the licenses of all real estate brokers and agents who have so flagrantly misrepresented the real estate codes of the state."

---

[116] Alberta Scott, 53, Thomas Scott, 41, Ricardo Turner, 18, Douglass Dyson Jr., 17, Robert Jennifer, 17, John Gee, 20, James Griffin, 33, Donald Huck, 24, David Eberhardt, 24, Richard Green, 17, and David Cohen, 28. At this point, newspaper articles had stopped stating whether or not those arrested were Negro or white as they always had in the past.

Rallying the Troops

Realizing that sit-ins were not getting the type of attention needed to provoke change, CORE decided to rally its troops for a march that all Baltimore would have to pay attention to. On October 14, 1965, about fifty people from eighteen organizations met at Fellowship House on North Hilton Street, under the Chairmanship of Dr. Furman Templeton, then head of the Urban League. We felt excited and relieved when they unanimously endorsed CORE's drive for open occupancy. We agreed to "make every effort to assure mass attendance at a Rally and March against segregated housing that was planned for Saturday, November 6th." It was also agreed that the Federation of Civil Rights Organizations and CORE would jointly sponsor the event. James Griffin and Walter Carter were named as Co-Chairmen.

Less than two weeks later, on October 25, a supper meeting was held at the Prince Hall Grand Lodge, Eutaw and Lanvale Streets, attended by about 106 members of clubs and organizations throughout Baltimore. After a delicious meal cooked by church women, the group discussed the rally to be held in the Lodge, followed immediately by the march to be led by James Farmer, CORE's national director, who had accepted our invitation. Various persons were selected to share the platform and say a few words before Sam Daniels, Grand Master of the Lodge and director of the Community Relations Commission, introduced Farmer, who would be the main speaker. Herb Callender, CORE's national field director, was again to be on hand to organize the marshals and assure a peaceful march.

When questioned by the press about the planned rally and march, Walter called it "the beginning of a national attack on Northern slums and Southern swamps, both of which are creations of segregated housing....This is a demonstration to show that we are tired of being forced to live in housing where rats and roaches eat better than the people and at times even eat the people." He stated three immediate policy goals:

1) to awaken the City Council to pass an open occupancy law for Baltimore;

2) to get the city to study, and, if needed, pass rent

controls and to foster a "rent withholding" plan whereby
slum residents could hold back rents from landlords who
refused to improve properties;

    3) to get the Mayor to appoint a Negro to the "lily-white"
city zoning board.

    Hundreds of mimeographed letters dated October 26th
and signed by Walter Carter and Barbara Mills were sent "To
All Freedom Lovers." It asked for help in determining if blacks
would "win full citizenship in America in our lifetime." After
reviewing the past several years of struggle in public
accommodations, the Freedom Rides, voting rights and so on,
the letter urged the participation of old hands and new: "We
believe your participation now can help bring the importance
of the housing issue to national attention.

    On the back of a copy of the letter in John Roemer's file,
is a personal note from Walter urging John to help turn out
Friends (Quakers). The note ended this way: "We need a good
audience for Farmer. I fear the KKK will out draw us. Wouldn't
that be a hell of a mess! Knowing that you will do your best, I
remain Your friend in the Fight. Walter."

    On November 2nd, the *Afro* reported that James Farmer
had sent telegrams to several of Baltimore's prominent
clergymen, thanking them for their endorsement of the drive
to end segregated housing and said he was looking forward to
seeing them, *with their congregations*, at the rally [something
that rarely happened at our demonstrations, even when the
ministers were present]

    It was one time when many clergymen, black and white,
did urge their congregations to join them at the march, and a
time when prominent black churches allowed Walter and me
time during regular Sunday services to discuss the issues and
"explain" the march—which at least some blacks looked upon
with suspicion.

    I still remember the occasion when Rev. Vernon Dobson
had arranged for me to speak to a large gathering of black
Baptist ministers. More than one expressed his suspicion that
we were fronts for the Communists— "we're not going to be
used by them again as we have been in the past." Fortunately
Rev. Dobson spoke up to complement my assurances that this
was not the case in our present fight for Negro rights. It was at
Rev. Dobson's church on Druid Hill Avenue where our

demonstrators most often gathered about noon on Sundays before going to our selected targets. Often, services ended about the same time and the congregation would wish us luck, but rarely did a church member join us.

Bishop Austin Murphy gave Roman Catholic priests and seminarians permission to take part. Nuns got permission from their superior to attend our planning meetings and the march—a time when they could not do so without their Mother Superior's blessing. Cardinal Shehan sent regrets that he would be in Rome at the time of the march.

Thousands of letters went out, not only from CORE but from the large number of supporting organizations, including one from my husband, Ed, and from Morgan College Professor, Cleveland Chandler. They sent personal appeals to all public school educators and college faculties urging them to attend and support the new sophisticated drive for fair housing. Leaflets (some hand-drawn and mimeographed by this writer in the CORE office, some printed) were distributed in neighborhoods and parking lots, the city was canvassed to find shops willing to display posters announcing the march, motorcades went throughout the city, their bullhorns announcing the march and urging all to join in. Full-page ads advertising the march were donated by the *Afro-American*, and smaller ads were run, without cost, in the *Sun, Evening Sun* and *News American*.

On November 6th, the big day, the Prince Hall auditorium, was overflowing, far beyond its rated capacity of 2,500. An article had appeared in the *Afro* earlier, accompanied by a photo of Mr. Farmer talking to a young person in Bogalusa, Louisiana, stating he would be "flying in to our march" and would no doubt give us a "first-hand account of his drives in this KKK stronghold."[117] I don't recall his doing so, but he did rouse the audience when he proclaimed that if it weren't for the non-violent movement that

---

[117] I therefore assume that he was once again in Bogalusa—although in his book, *Lay Bare the Heart*, he tells only of an encounter with the Klan there in 1964—a place, he says, where the KKK had its largest per-capita membership. The threats by the Klan against his life at that time were taken sufficiently seriously that even the Governor was roused to send officers to protect him.

was "awakening a sleeping giant, the nation would have been subjected to a sizable blood bath."

James Farmer, Courtesy of Mike Waller, Publisher, *Baltimore Sun*

Farmer called slum housing, un-employment and discrimination in housing "the seeds of violence," and continued, as re-ported in the *Afro*, "the only way to kill the seeds is to get rid of slums, rats, leaky roofs and cockroaches and give freedom of choice in housing...." He called for rebuild-ing today's slums and making them places that people could look on with joy and want to live in. He con-cluded, in his impress-ively deep voice, with a quotation from a poem: "America has never been America for me. But by this oath I swear, it will be."

The crowd then poured into the street to begin its twenty-block march to Horizon House, the new high-rise apart-ments, at the corner of Calvert and Chase Streets. Since I was buried amidst the thousands, marching, singing and chanting, I turn to the *Sun*'s report for an overview of the impressive event. They wrote:

> Integrationists, fired by the presence of a national civil rights leader, sang and marched through Baltimore in a four-block long column demanding an end to segregated housing and the Negro ghetto. Led by James Farmer, the marchers, lined up three abreast and carrying signs, paraded peacefully under sunny skies, accompanied by a score of city policemen [on foot and motorcycles and a cordon of ten mounted policemen on horse back].
>
> Divided about equally between Negro and white,...the marchers, from elderly to the toddlers, from those dressed in business suits to the young CORE members in starched

denim uniforms, paraded through the [Mount Vernon and Mount Royal sections] in a manner more lighthearted than grim.

Marchers circle Francis Scott Key Memorial at Eutaw and Lanvale Streets.
Courtesy of Mike Waller, *Baltimore Sun.* © 11/7/1965

Their progress watched by people gathering on street corners and hanging out of upper windows, the demonstrators sang over and over in an optimistic mode the civil rights movement's anthem, "We Shall Overcome."....Along the way they were saluted by a little elderly Negress, sitting on the front steps of a house [on West Biddle]. Her sweater and shoes had holes in them and her soft voice hardly carried as she repeated over and over, 'Amen, Lordy. Amen.'

We stopped our march on the blocked-off Chase Street side of Horizon House while two black families, Mr. And Mrs. Raymond Haysbert (the business manager of Park's Sausage) and Mr. and Mrs. John Staten (Director of Baltimore's Head Start program), went around the corner to the front entrance, intending to try to rent an apartment. The *Sun* continued:

> The entrance was surrounded by city policemen and the plate glass doors were locked. Inside the entrance stood a special policeman and a man who identified himself as Samuel Gorn, who owned the property." He told them they were closed for the day.
>
> Meantime, Mr. Farmer was urging the crowd 'not to go home and forget about this. If you keep up the pressure you will get some action from you City Council. Let this be heard by the powers that be: we will not be turned back and we will not stop.' The marchers then reformed their ranks and paraded back to the starting point.

On the same day, the *Sun* reported on a nationally organized Klan rally of about 2,000 persons who had gathered in a cow pasture in Rising Sun, Maryland—the very evening of our march—race-baiting and cross-burning. "The Klansmen spoke from a platform of boards mounted on a truck frame, which was decorated with two black paper wreaths....A sign between the wreaths proclaimed, 'Never. Today-Tomorrow-Forever!'...Most of the Klansman's speeches dealt with the standard themes of the anti-Negro 'invisible empire'—jokes about Negroes, tirades against President Johnson, sermons on crime in the streets and the evil of race mixing."

After our rally, I offered to drive Farmer to Washington D.C. where he had yet another meeting to attend that evening, and yet another speaking engagement the next day. He already looked exhausted. I felt honored just to have in my car beside me this notable man I admired so much. I know we talked some as we drove along the Baltimore-Washington Expressway, but I have no idea what about. I felt pleased when I looked over at him and saw that his eyes were closed, that he was resting peacefully—a rare opportunity, I suspected. I felt enriched just to be sharing a space with him.

On November 14th, the week after the march, there were demonstrations at the Marylander Apartments on St. Paul Street, at University One Apartments on East University Parkway, and at the Carlyle Apartments on West University Parkway. All were within walking distance of Johns Hopkins University.

At the Carlyle, white testers were told that they could move in immediately when they inquired about renting, while four Negroes who inquired immediately afterwards were told that it would take thirty days to process their applications. Seventeen persons then sat down in the lobby and refused to leave even after Thomas Keane, the rental agent, read them the Maryland Trespass Act. They were charged with trespassing and arrested by the police about 8:15 that evening. Bail was again set at $104 each, but only four paid, the rest electing to stay in jail. They were not named in the paper as they always had been up until then.

On November 15th, Fred Weisgal was again in court arguing for dismissal of all the trespassing indictments on the same First and Fourteenth Amendment grounds—the state was perpetuating a policy of racial segregation. He told the court those arrested were only responding to an ad that stated apartments were available. It didn't mention color. They sat-in only after the rental agent said they didn't rent to Negroes.

That brought to thirty the number who'd now been charged with trespass and who'd requested a jury trial. All these would, collectively, be brought to court for trial in May 1966.

The small group of CORE activists who had given so much to building the housing issue and organizing the hugely successful November March for Fair Housing were exhausted. The immediate burst of energy that had followed the march and the inspiring speech by Mr. Farmer was clearly on the wane. We simply didn't feel up to sustaining the momentum we'd worked so hard to build during the five months since the housing bills had been defeated in June. The thunderbolt that was soon to hit us didn't help.

•••

On Christmas Day that thunderbolt hit—hard! After the excitement of my kids opening their presents and a late breakfast, I sat down to look at the paper—only to see in big headlines across the front page of the *New York Times*, **Farmer to Quit as CORE Director**; next day in the *Baltimore Sun*, **C.O.R.E. Head to Step Down**. The articles explained that James Farmer was resigning as head of national CORE, effective March 1965, to head up a new national literacy program (never funded, torpedoed by politics before it even started). What a Christmas present! I was stunned, unbelieving.

I don't think any of us in Baltimore CORE who met and talked so often were even aware of the black/white internecine warfare that was tearing national CORE apart, certainly not how serious it was. That was something we learned about later—much to our horror—when the "new" CORE invaded Baltimore. At the time, in answer to media inquiries, Jim Griffin, our Chairman, blamed Farmer's resignation on lack of financial support for CORE. That was something we were feeling ourselves, not internal conflict between the roles of blacks and whites in the organization—nor about what CORE's role should be.

Oh, the purpose of CORE and the proper role of blacks and whites in the movement was discussed from time to time, none more passionate on the subject than Walter himself, but it was not a divisive issue, perhaps because of Walter's magnetic charisma that held us all together—the unwavering focus on equality for blacks.

Walter, even more than the rest of us, seemed shaken by the announcement. He seemed to take it personally—like a near-mortal blow. To say that he admired Farmer would be a gross understatement—to say he was his hero is still inadequate. To say he worshipped him would be only a slight exaggeration. In any case, he clearly felt abandoned by his hero; by the person he admired most in all the world. For a time, the very heart seemed to go out of him.

The first time I saw Walter after the holidays, he seemed a changed man. Instead of bursting enthusiastically into the office to discuss strategies for the future, he came dragging in, looking dreary and forlorn, and slumped down in the chair opposite my desk.

"Do my lips look purple to you"? he asked. "I think I'm going to have a heart attack." (Ironically that's how he would eventually, unexpectedly die.)

Walter often worried about being sick and again having to spend time in a hospital as he'd had to do in the 50s when he got tuberculosis—a time that seemed to embarrass him as much as anything. He said of it: "I really thought that was the end of the line. It took eight months in the hospital to get well."

Soon after that depressing conversation in the office, Walter came in looking even more despondent and told me: "I have to resign from CORE. Please, understand. PLEASE, don't ask me to stay." He knew how persuasive I could be; he was *my* hero and everything he felt about Farmer, I felt about *him*. *How could he do this? I needed him; we all did.*

Walter, of course, knew all that and it weighed heavily on him—but he felt he had to quit as Chairman of the Housing Committee. It wasn't the first time he'd "resigned" nor would it be the last. Walter seemed born to lead, he knew it, and he was so profoundly committed to equal rights for his people that quitting proved impossible for him—even when he was exhausted, even when one part of him wanted to, even when he knew he should.

•••

Early in January of 1966, after Walter's resignation as Chairman of CORE's Housing Committee, Sampson Green, one of CORE's most stalwart members, and I were appointed as Co-Chairs. We neither felt adequate to fill Walter's shoes, but our co-chairmanship was at his request and had the members' endorsement, so we felt we had to try to carry on and give Walter the time he asked for to recoup. It was not a time when CORE could rest on its past achievements. We had once again to fight for passage of a Fair Housing bill. Fortunately for us, Walter could not sustain his desire for complete withdrawal and took on the newly-created title of "Chairman of Special Projects."

When the Baltimore City Council had started its winter session, back in November of 1965, about the same time as we had started organizing our November rally and march, it still had before it a Fair Housing bill that had been introduced by Councilman Walter Dixon—one that I had written for him and that Melvin Sykes had checked over to be sure it was legislatively sound before passing it on to a receptive Mr. Dixon. However, no one expected that the Council would give it serious consideration—and, of course, they didn't.

But then, less than two weeks *after* our rally and march, Thomas D'Alesandro III, the City Council President, introduced his own broad open housing bill, which was immediately supported by Mayor McKeldin. The mayor stated: "I'm delighted that he's introducing it. I shall do everything in my power, as I have done before, to see that there are no second-class citizens in Baltimore, and no discrimination because of race or religion." Many of the City Councilmen whose votes would be needed for it to pass were less enthusiastic.

On November 12 an Open Letter (copies to all the media) was sent to Mayor Theodore McKeldin, City Council President Thomas D'Alesandro, III, and all other political leaders professing a desire for fair housing for Baltimore City. Signed by James Griffin, Walter Carter and Reginald Lewis for CORE; Eugene Chase, Chairman of the Anti-Poverty Action Committee; Lawrence Hawkins, Chairman of the Civil Rights Committee of the National Alliance of Postal & Federal Employees; Troy Brailey, President, Negro American Labor Council; and Thomas Juliano, Vice Chairman, Contemporary Trends Housing Committee,[118] it read, in part:

> Thousands of citizens actively stood up against residential segregation on November 6th in Baltimore's congested ghetto. While this massive demonstration was primarily aimed at breaking the "segregated housing noose," the participants were even more concerned about the evils perpetuated by the existence of that rigid noose— dilapidation, deterioration, rat infestation, and exploitation. And the greatest concern of the marchers was the brutal way thousands of citizens are being dehumanized as a

---

[118] These were groups with their own mandate, not activist civil rights organizations, but groups that could be counted on to support the activists: lend their name to publicity, giving the activist organizations greater credibility, give them access to their mailing lists, include information on demonstrations in their newsletters and mailings, offer their facilities f or meetings or their equipment for copying, sometimes contribute money, on occasion appear at demonstrations, etc.

consequence of being trapped in this "choking noose." Like all fair-minded citizens, CORE is greatly moved by the strong participation of our local residents, and we are beginning anew to re-shape our program to achieve a desegregated housing market.

It then reviews past defeats in passing fair housing legislation, and chides the "education studies" that followed. It then recalls that Mr. D'Alesandro complained that the Mayor did not involve the council before he presented his ordinance. "Now we are alarmed that Mr. D'Alesandro has not involved the Mayor in formulating his proposals. We ask that you take civil rights off the political merry-go-round and get to the urgent business of passing this legislation now, right now." It continues:

> This open letter is to urge you at City Hall to take your talking and studying away from your fictional ties, away from your personal interests, and to join together with cohesiveness and determination to get a strong and meaningful fair housing bill passed. If the citizens of Baltimore are to believe in this goal, and are to accept the rightness and necessity of freedom or choice in housing, they must know first that their leader really are committed to it, and area honestly fighting for it....thousands of citizens have spoken. Now is the time for the leaders to speak. Now is the time for the leaders at City hall to act loud and clear.

A December 1st *Sun* editorial stated: "The passage of a fair housing ordinance in Baltimore is as inevitable as three and one making four." On the other hand, a December 4th *Afro* article was titled: "Getting Housing Bill Not Easy." CORE agreed and felt that a great deal of work would be required if it was to pass. Did CORE have the energy to go another round? On December 9th, opponents held a rally in the Hamilton area of the city to organize "an educate-your-councilman" campaign against the bill. They predicted defeat.

On December 11th, The Greater Baltimore Committee, the prestigious businessmen's organization that had sponsored the forming of the Baltimore Neighborhoods, Inc. (BNI), announced its support, declaring:

> [The group] recognizes the need to make available the benefits of full citizenship to all citizens of this city...The continuation of a policy of discrimination in housing is morally and economically wrong...In supporting this

legislation, the Greater Baltimore Committee specifically rejected the proposal that such legislation must first be enacted on a state or metropolitan basis.

Just as the religious, labor and business leadership of this city must take the initiative on matters which are intrinsically right, so must the city of Baltimore exercise a high degree of leadership in its metropolitan area..... The Greater Baltimore Committee, chaired by James Rouse, announced its support, recognizing "the need to make available the benefits of full citizenship to all citizens of this city." Meetings for and against the bill were being held by neighborhood organizations throughout the city.

Oddly, as reported in the *Sun*, on January 8, 1966, the Baltimore grand jury also urged enactment, stating:

> There is an extremely large percentage of Negroes at most health facilities, and at least 75% Negro population in correctional institutions, a large percentage of which are repeaters...It must be recognized that the environment, overcrowding and other deplorable conditions which exist in the Negro areas breed crime and lawlessness and are detrimental to health and must affect all residents in those areas, regardless of their status in the community. As this situation is detrimental to the welfare of the entire city, this grand jury, after careful consideration, believes enactment of a fair housing ordinance would be helpful in improving such conditions.

Mayor McKeldin, Hyman Pressman, the city comptroller, and Dr. Matthew Tayback, the deputy commissioner of health, amongst others came out in favor of passage. Representatives of seventy-four Presbyterian churches adopted a resolution favoring the open occupancy housing bill. Walter met on the Hopkins campus with students from six different campuses in the area to discuss ways they could help—and decisions were made to write letters urging their college's administrations to come out publicly for the bill; to be followed by demonstrations, if necessary.

(None of the colleges did, as an entity, declare their support for the bill, though many faculty members and students did, as individuals—and the Hopkins President, Milton Eisenhower, strengthened the policy he had announced in December when he'd said that the university would ask all persons listing rooms and apartments with the university housing bureau to stop discriminating against Negro and foreign students in renting their properties, saying he was afraid of losing needed housing for students if he should make it mandatory. In January, he stated that beginning in the fall the university would list no housing for students, faculty or employees with any landlord who had not signed a nondiscrimination pledge.)

A public hearing on the new Fair Housing ordinance was scheduled for Thursday, January 13, 1966 at the War Memorial near City Hall in downtown Baltimore.

Lawrence Cardinal Shehan agreed to be the star speaker. This was said to be the first time in American history that an archbishop had participated directly in the deliberations of any city council—and he followed through despite threats on his life after the announcement was made. Perhaps, as a native Baltimorean, he felt a special obligation to speak out.

It was an amazing experience sitting in that jam packed auditorium that evening. The papers next day reported an audi-ence of over 2,000— two-thirds estimated to be supporters. I had to catch my breath in disbelief as the boos and catcalls spewed out when the Cardinal appeared to open the hearing—and no one could have been more startled than he must have been when several tomatoes splattered on the stage, but he remained cool as a fresh summer's breeze—

Cardinal Shehan speaks to rowdy crowd.
Courtesy of Mike Waller, Publisher, *Baltimore Sun*

which would have been most welcome in that hot, stuffy room—as he continued to speak of the "overwhelming per-suasive moral argument" in support of fair housing legislation and warned against "the explosive potentialities of the ghetto." The mixed boos and applause for the Cardinal set the stage for three hours of a rowdy and boisterous affair which didn't adjourn until almost eleven that night.

In addition to Cardinal Shehan, advocates for the bill included Episcopal Bishop Doll, Methodist Bishop Lord, the president of the Council of Churches, the president of the Baltimore Jewish Council and Rabbi Shusterman of the Baltimore Board of Rabbis. Also, Arthur Stinchcombe, chairman of Hopkins' Sociology Department and Dominic Fornaro, president of the Baltimore Council of AFL-CIO, amongst others.

Opponents included Harry Berman of the Apartment House Owners Association of Maryland [*where were the association's members who had told CORE the year before that they would work to garner support for the bill?*], representatives from the Maryland Petition Committee, a known segregationist group, the Taxpayers Interest League and various neighborhood associations.

There was one speaker for and one against the bill from the Real Estate Board of Greater Baltimore, an odd contradiction in arguments. As the *Afro* described it, the arguments by all these groups, pro and con, were "practically a carbon copy" of those heard at the previous hearing—maybe not with quite the vulgarity that had made me nauseous last time round, but pretty sickening nonetheless.

As the time for the hearing had approached, political wisdom had it that the bill would be defeated by a 13 to 8 vote. D'Alesandro told the press that he "was swimming against the current." Less than a week later, on January 17, the council refused to delay a vote on the bill, as D'Alesandro had hoped—time to permit a buildup of church pressure on several key Catholic councilmen. Clearly fearing exactly what D'Alesandro hoped for, the council called it out of committee for a vote that evening, and killed it 13-8 as had been predicted. Next day the *Sun* reported:

> Mr. D'Alesandro, looking dejected as he walked from the Council chambers, said he felt a city fair housing bill has 'no chance at all' in the life of this Council. He added that he intends to introduce a metropolitan area fair housing bill at the next meeting of the Metropolitan Council. Some Councilmen who voted against the city bill last night have indicated they would favor a metropolitan bill.

Later in January, speaking at an all-day housing conference sponsored by the Methodist Church, D'Alesandro praised the religious leaders who spoke in favor of the open housing bill at the War Memorial but added, "We've had too much opposition from the lay leaders of white parishes who aren't listening to their pastors...Unless the Church gets in at the community level, with dialogue and discussion, we won't get the kind of change we're talking about."

Civil rights leaders in and out of CORE felt dazed and incensed by yet another defeat—actually the third rejection of an open housing bill, the second one I'd actively been witness to. Walter, again speaking for CORE, said:

> Our problem is how to keep a quarter of a million black people channeled in creative activities despite their sharp resentment at this indignity at the hands of the City Council....You tell me how to keep thousands of Negroes quiet while they are suffering in slum housing because of racial discrimination... The City Council is allowing the city to die and this will destroy the metropolitan area...like snatching out the heart of a person.

Walter agreed with other doomsayers who felt that open-occupancy legislation could never be achieved through the fledgling Metropolitan Area Council, as D'Alesandro had suggested, and added that "only a major crisis would force Governor Tawes to support a state bill....We need demonstrations that will attract national attention."

CORE tried to keep up the momentum that had been created city-wide in support of the bill by asking that they fill the City Council chambers at their next three sessions in "silent" protest of their action in defeating the bill.

On January 25, 1966, the day after the first of those three sessions, Alan Lupo wrote a long article in *The Evening Sun* (with a picture of me at work), which I quote, almost in its entirety, because it captures so well our work at CORE. Appropriately he titled it, "Mechanics of a Demonstration.":

> Mrs. Barbara Mills, 37, slim and blond, had spent the afternoon cranking out 4,000 pink handbills in the low-ceilinged real estate office that the Congress of Racial Equality uses for a headquarters....

Coutesy Mike Waller, Publisher, *Baltimore Sun*

She would take a sheaf of 50 to 100 sheets of pink paper and place them under an inked roller, and she would press the button, and out would come the printed story of how the Negro is trying to become a political force in this city.

"...the heartless gall to vote down your rights...You are here to acquaint yourself with the thirteen ...councilmen who have turned the City Council into a White Citizens Council ... fixed the tightening noose around the necks of all colored citizens...."

It was not the kind of intellectual effort that normally satisfies the educated wife of a Johns Hopkins University economics professor. It is the kind of work that costs Mrs. Mills about $50 a week to pay for a woman to care for her two children.

At 9 A.M., Barbara Mills left her home...to begin a very long day. She cashed a check, bought some stamps and pens and paper for CORE, picked up some circulars [from the printers], delivered a package of 1,000 envelopes and got a sandwich to eat at CORE headquarters about 1 P.M.

Then she began stenciling and answering phones ("No, we can't provide transportation, but perhaps you know someone in your neighborhood...") and mimeographing. ...The mimeograph machine crunched and jolted to a stop, and she took out another sheaf of paper.... Some call this drudgery, and some call this commitment. Whatever you call it, it is one way to begin a demonstration.

...When the Council bell rang at 5 P.M., only a few Negroes and white sympathizers were on hand....Some from CORE began straggling inside and started passing out handbills ("Know your councilmen. Visit, write, phone"). Outside, some Negroes and whites began picketing ("...We'll remember in November.")

Inside, [one councilman] was making a long speech criticizing Mayor McKeldin for "mere lip service" to the cause of open occupancy.

Barbara Mills sat in the first row of the gallery next to Walter Carter, who had been CORE housing committee chairman. The edges of his nose were red from a bad cold. "I'm worn out," he said. "The doctor told me to rest up."

The gallery was packed now with about 100 persons. The pickets had left their signs outside and had joined others inside. But altogether, the protesters numbered only about 125 to 150. ..."I thought we were going to blow the whole thing," said Mr. Carter. "We made a mistake on the first notices and said 5:30, instead of 5: P.M. And we didn't work the churches Sunday because of the snow. And it's cold today. We hope to triple this number next week." [But we didn't. Both money and people were too exhausted to pursue the issue further.]

...[One] councilman was yawning, [another] appeared to be sleeping. His face was propped up on his left hand; his eyelids closed.

"There's something in the air," Mr. Dixon was insisting...this matter of rebellion..."

Robert Kaufman, Baltimore's own "Trotskyist," prepared to journey downstairs to the foyer, where he would hawk his publication and that of others, "'Sparticist' on sale for a dime; 'Negro on the March' for 50 cents. Ten cents for 'Sparticist'."

Mr. Dixon had finished, and Mrs. Mills and Walter Carter and an old man with gray hair and a whole gallery full of demonstrators were on their feet.

"Bravo," they were yelling. They applauded loudly, and Council President Thomas J. D'Alesandro 3rd asked for order, and Charlie Panuska opened his eyes.

Early in February, Walter Carter wrote an inspiring and fiery piece, "A Cry From the Heart," in which he reviewed all CORE's actions and named many of those who'd participated, actively and behind the scenes; people he never forgot, and never missed an opportunity to praise. Only a few paragraphs are quoted.

As the issue of open occupancy developed, we all gained a deeper meaning for the necessity of removing the tightening noose from the captive black housing market as being essential to freeing the black man from the evils of overcrowding, exploitation, segregated schools, and all the concomitant problems such as dilapidation, deterioration and rat infestation that infect the lives of the inhabitants of the ghetto. However, the City Council, for the third time, ...sadistically ignored the basic human needs of the black people.

...Since we were unable to pool sufficient resources to develop a crisis of sufficient proportions to destroy the segregated housing market, it was not surprising when George Collins of the *Afro-American* and others warned that the housing law would not pass. The real estate forces are powerfully unjust, as we all know, and their financial resources match their injustices. We are right, but we cannot have sufficient might to move that power without substantial sums of money—$20,000 at least! CORE, as a chapter, has never attracted half that much yearly for all its work and all its successes.

...An all-out mobilization of our limited resources are now more urgently needed than ever before to stem the tide of the counter-revolution, which is much worse than the huge KKK rallies, and the blatant defamation of our spiritual leaders. ...A deathly threat to the colored folk of this area is under way in projects that consist of "nigger removal."...without affording the slum-dwellers any means of escape from its oozing swamps!

...Without a renewed intensity of our efforts to sustain aggressive freedom drives with the best of all our effort working in concert, it is questionable that even the rugged of us will ever become free, because they are clearly distorting and twisting every document of brotherhood, from the Bible to the Bill of Rights. ..."NEVER, NEVER, NEVER BLACK MAN WILL YOU BE FREE!!" Not here in the Free State of Maryland!—and if not in Maryland, brother, where?

We are all bound together in this war [for freedom].... We are bound together, and love him or hate him, we are bound together with the white man in America. The white man, who is good but spineless, is too damn busy seeking his own safety, his own pocket-full of green backs, to ever come to grips with his fellow dollar-driven, doom-driven white brother. He is too obsessed to realize that our democracy, our very salvation is at stake and his very obsession, his fanaticism may squelch the value of the almighty green-back dollar he is now so pre-occupied with.

•••

CORE's attention turned to arranging a benefit performance to feature Dick Gregory, who had agreed to come at the invitation of our attorney, Fred Weisgal, who'd remained friends with him since the Cambridge days. We were hoping his name would help replenish our meager treasury. One paper reminded its readers of early appearances by Gregory in Baltimore:

> Baltimoreans remember Mr. Gregory's leadership in protest demonstrations at the Social Security complex and his instant integration of the Maryland State Penitentiary during a personal appearance (both discussed in a previous section).
>
> When colored and white inmates at the prison were segregated in an audience awaiting Mr. Gregory's performance, the comic refused to go on until the prisoners were mixed and allowed to sit where they wished.
>
> The most prolific of the comedians using black humor has added to his national prominence by using his personal funds and talents in the civil rights movement.
>
> Mr. Gregory received a gunshot wound while in a march in Chicago protesting de-facto seg-regation in the schools and barely missed being arrested while cam-paigning for New York's mayor John Lindsay during an impromptu street rally in front of Harlem's Hotel Theresa.

The event was planned for Sunday after-noon, February 13, 1966 at the Prince Hall Grand Lodge auditorium. With most other CORE members at work all day, responsibility for most of the "arranging" fell on me—but that didn't prove to be easy.

In early February, Baltimore had one of its biggest snowfalls ever—and another, and another. I found myself skidding and slipping and sliding around the city, by car and by foot, visiting our printer for posters, visiting stores to get them displayed, visiting all the newspapers, asking for free space for ads—mostly granted—and again, to all the media—radio, TV and newspapers—pressing on them news releases. Then, when the time finally arrived and 2,000 or more people were once again crowded into the Grand Lodge, reminding me of our November housing march crowd, we all had to wait two hours for Mr. Gregory's arrival. He had been delayed by the bad weather.

Gregory quickly made us all feel he had been worth waiting for. The applause was thunderous when he called Baltimore "one of the most corrupt cities in America." We all laughed and agreed when he compared the recent rioting in Watts, California to George Washington's patriots and the Boston Tea Party. "The Watts explosion happened just as would any bunch of forgotten greasy rags in a closed room. They both became combustible and caught fire." Gregory had said. Of the courts, he said, "Injustice wouldn't exist if the courts weren't corrupt."

Gregory continued, "Our problem is not a fight of white against black or we would have lost by now. It is a fight of right against wrong and never in the history of the world has wrong triumphed for very long. They're going to have to assign one cop per colored person if America wants us to observe law and order without justice."

At another point he said, "In the south, the colored man is trying to outlive the violence of the Klan. In the north, the colored man is trying to outlive that rat in his bedroom." He predicted violence in Baltimore. It's going "to hit this town if the white folks don't do something and the colored folks stop being scared."

Gregory had been a huge success in raising our spirits and making us laugh in the process, but his appearance did little to boost our treasury. Admission was free and when Mr. Gregory paused for the proverbial hat to be passed for donations, he did surprisingly little to hype the crowd into digging deeply into their pockets. Still we were grateful to have had the opportunity to hear him.

•••

Less than a month after Mr. Gregory visited Baltimore, another speaker, Bayard Rustin, arrived at the invitation of

Dr. Chester Wickwire. On March 25, 1966, the Johns Hopkins University newsletter reported the event this way:

> Vociferous right wing elements marred civil rights leader Bayard Rustin's speech at Levering Hall last Sunday. The interruptions by members of the Ku Klux Klan and the National States Rights Party (NSRP) culminated several days' activities aimed against Rustin.
>
> According to an article in the Baltimore *Sun*, four youths were arrested late Saturday night for distributing "obscene" material alleging Rustin's arrest for perversion [and draft dodging] several years ago.... A cross was purportedly burned on the Hopkins campus several days prior to the Rustin appearance. The speech Sunday was preceded by a picket line in front of Levering composed of some twenty-five NSRP members attending the speech.
>
> Representatives of the KKK were inside Levering distributing copies of The Fiery Cross, a [KKK] newspaper printed in Alabama. The KKK contingent coughed, conversed, and cracked jokes during the first part of Rustin's speech. A security officer removed one particularly vocal member...and the rest of the Klan...then filed out....
>
> ...The gray-haired rights leader called for a coalition of Negroes, churches, and unions to press for job training and guaranteed wages in a peaceful social revolution that would better the economic situation for the Negro population....
>
> In a question and answer period after the speech, Rustin replied to a query about the war in VietNam by stating that "President Johnson is now trying to bludgeon Congress into putting more money into VietNam and cutting funds for the Great Society."

Dr. Wickwire said afterwards that it was a good thing for people on campus to be exposed to the ultra-rightists who picketed, heckled and jeered at Bayard Rustin. "Now the members of the university community would know what these people are really like." Perhaps if the larger community had also seen the Klan in action on this occasion they wouldn't have been so surprised to see it in downtown Baltimore less than two months later.

Meanwhile, in April, James Farmer was again in Baltimore, speaking at the annual luncheon of the Lafayette Square Community Center. He praised its cultural and educational programs—at a time when he was still awaiting Congressional

approval for the national literacy and job training program that
Sargent Shriver, then head of the Office of Economic
Opportunity, had assured him, before he'd left CORE in March,
was "all set". [It was never approved.]

During his speech he praised CORE for having saved the
nation from a bloodbath with its Ghandian-type of non-violent
actions, and deplored the lack of communica-tion between the
Negro middle class and the Negro lower, class—"the forgotten
man, the dispossessed, the drop-out, the unemployable."

In appreciation of his leadership, Tom Lewis, one of CORE's
most active demonstrators, presented James Farmer with a large
painting he'd done for him for the occasion.

Tom Lewis and James Farmer hold painting as Ricardo Turner,
another CORE member, looks on. Picture is from author's
scrapbook, dated 4/23/66. Possibly from *AfroAmerican*, but paper's
archivist could not locate it. Possibly from *News American*, now
defunct.

CORE Ripped Apart

Early in April, 1966, Lincoln Lynch, the Associate Director of national CORE, together with James Griffin and Walter Carter, announced that Baltimore had been chosen as the target city for an all-out attack on discrimination in every area because it still remained one of the most segregated of urban centers in the country.

Photo by Carl X Harden; provided by David Eberhardt

A background paper they prepared for our members stated, amongst other things:

> A concerted and major thrust will be made in the area of housing with all its concomitant evils because housing holds the key to a lasting solution of the problems in many other areas.... The first of a series of Demonstrations started this drive on April 17th and they will continue until the job is done. A free market must be made available as a necessary concomitant to our work with the inner-city community in organizing them into an effective protest group against the evils of exploitation, dilapidation, overcharging, poor municipal facilities, etc. from which they have suffered for too long.
> [Another prong of attack] which is closely related will be in the direction of Urban Renewal which has so far operated

essentially as Negro removal. The Negro has not only been excluded from the outer city but is now being removed from the inner city and more and more compacted into a donut circling the city where he has fewer and fewer houses to choose from and is consequently more and more at the mercy of slumlords who can overcharge, overcrowd and neglect him....

In every area CORE is determined to open all doors so that Negroes can come in with the same human dignity and full rights as those now taken for granted by all other American citizens. CORE will seek the support and work extensively with many other organizations. Such co-operation is both desirable and necessary to the attainment of the goals for which we are all striving.

Calling their national project, "Target City," they set up their office at the corner of Gay and Eden Streets in a poor section of Baltimore's East Side, under the direction of Walter Brooks. Ignoring Baltimore CORE, they announced a breath-taking agenda for the summer; designated a New York staff person to be in charge of each. Ominously, any

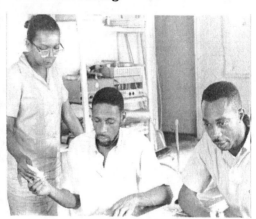

Baltimorean, Margaraeat Patterson, volunteer in Target City offices; with Walter Brroks and Tony Perot from National CORE. Photo by Carl X Harden; Provided by David Eberhardt

mention of desegregating housing was missing from their agenda:

1. The organization of welfare recipients to fight the abuses of the welfare system. Mr. Danny Gant.

2. Action in advisory capacity on community efforts to upgrade and integrate Baltimore schools. Mr. Tony Perrault.

3. An extensive voter registration drive in low-income black neighborhoods to put on the voting rolls tens of thousands of politically underrepresented people. Mr. Howard Quander.

4. Action in advisory capacity on improvement of housing in the center city. Mr. Stu Wechsler.

5. Co-operation in the unionization campaign of the Maryland Freedom Union in the Baltimore retail area. Mr. Mike Flug.

6. The development of community organizations to fight for improved living conditions in low-income areas. Community people, Staff, Volunteers.

There will be extensive non-violent direct action—demonstrations, street corner rallies, canvassing—to crystallize issues and mobilize the people of the Negro community to act for changes that will bring power over their community into its proper repository—into their own hands.

On April 26, 1966, there was a banner-headline across the front page of the *Afro-American*, declaring: "COMMUNITY SUPPORTS CORE." It had long quotes from ten prominent black leaders in Baltimore, stating "why action is needed." Dr. Martin Luther King even sent his endorsement of CORE's plans and the Interdenominational Ministerial Alliance stated that they would back the Target City program 100%.

The state Interracial Council met secretly to discuss CORE's plans and decided they'd act as sort of referees between CORE and Baltimore's political leaders for the coming summer. The United States Community Relations Service stationed staff members in Baltimore for an indefinite period. Maj. Gen. Gelston, a veteran of the Cambridge riots and now Baltimore's acting police chief, became concerned about the possibility of riots.

Walter Brooks and Stu Wechsler often stopped in CORE's office on North Avenue while I was there working. It wasn't long before they began to question me about my motives for being involved with CORE. Soon, they were asking why I didn't stop my work with CORE and go back to the Kentucky Appalachia area where I lived as a child and work with "my own people" who were poor and uneducated. The activist members of Housing Committee who were seeing the most of these newly-arrived national CORE members, were beginning to feel a dark foreboding that changes were a-brewing that we did not like.

•••

The week *before* national CORE announced its selection

of Baltimore as their "Target City" to eliminate all discrimination once and for all, local CORE had launched an all-out campaign to open apartment houses in the entire Baltimore area, legislation or no legislation. After careful consideration of possible choices, it had decided to make Horizon House the regular site for a sustained attack on housing discrimination.

A number of factors had led to this choice. To begin with, this new down-city, eighteen-story, hi-rise apartment building was owned by Samuel Gorn, the President of the Apartment House Owners Association, with whom we'd negotiated early-on. Further, due to the November "March and Rally", it was already known to the thousands who'd participated. Also it was easily accessible for demonstrators to come by car or bus.

And finally, its high visibility down-city would attract the wide-spread publicity needed to effect real change in the apartment house owners' segregation policies.

Baltimore CORE's purpose was to make Horizon House a *symbol*; the site where CORE would continue to demonstrate until *all* of the Baltimore area's apartments were open to all. This was important, since by now we were well aware of the importance of obtaining "freedom of choice" as a prerequisite to successfully tackling the inner city's slum conditions. The influx of people from national CORE that soon descended on Baltimore never understood our Horizon House project, and thus regarded the local campaign only as an effort to open one luxury apartment. This lack of understanding would all too soon destroy the support CORE had worked so long and hard to garner over so many months.

The first demonstration at Horizon House took place on April 17, 1966, more than a week prior to national's announcement regarding their choice of Baltimore as "Target City." That day, passing traffic stopped to gawk as one hundred demonstrators marched back and forth in the front of Horizon House for three hours, carrying signs that read: "Freedom of Choice in Housing," "Freedom to Escape the Ghetto," "Break the Noose from the Housing Ghetto," "Down with the Captive Market," and "Housing Segregation Causes Slums."

The apartment's manager immediately locked the doors, necessitating his standing just inside the whole time, unlocking and re-locking the door each time a resident wanted to leave or enter. Before our departure we formed our usual circle and crossed arms to sing "We Shall Overcome." Sampson told us as we hummed, what a wonderful job we'd done... "Either they desegregate it or they can keep it closed...We'll come back four times a week, five times..."

"No comment," yelled an official through the glass of the locked outer door.

The papers reported that about twenty-five police were on hand in case of trouble, and that, at one point, there were a half-dozen counter-marchers. One counter-marcher was Charles Luthardt, leader of a group called Fighting American Nationalists, carrying a sign announcing: "CORE's Three Rs—Robbery, Racism and Rape." He was running for governor. Identified standing across the street were Vernon Naimaster,

Grand Titan and Layton Brown, King Kleagle of the Klan, who said they were "just observing."

On April 28 the Baltimore *Sun* announced: "City Seen Chosen For Rights Drive Because Negro Riot Not Likely." It quoted Herbert O. Edwards, the executive secretary of the Interracial Commission, as having said:

> The Congress of Racial Equality [referring to the New York Target City group] may believe since Negroes are less restless in Baltimore than they are in other large American cities, chances for violence are minimal... and this may be one reason [they] chose the city for an anti-segregation drive....Negroes have been living in Baltimore for long periods of time and have become apathetic... there is probably more apathy among the Negro leadership and it goes down to the Negro masses...the masses don't expect very much and don't get very much.

National CORE took issue with Edward's statements, declaring that Baltimore was chosen, among other reasons, because the "proportionate Negro population is extremely high and class differences extremely strongly drawn" and because its proximity to other urban areas make it "easier to gather forces for demonstrations."

By May first, there were over two dozen KKK members counter-demonstrating with us at Horizon House—most wearing white hooded robes with red and blue trim—said to have been a Maryland first. Most Marylanders by then would have forgotten or been unaware of a resurgence of Klan activity in Baltimore in the 20s soon after the end of WW I.

Vernon Naimaster wore a red and green robe that identified him as "the Great Titan of the Maryland Klan," and Layton Brown, as "King Kleagle", wore a bright red cape and led the Klan marchers, carrying an American and a Confederate flag. There were three "security guards," gray-clad, wearing heavy boots and helmets, tough-looking German police dogs on short leashes by their sides. Naimaster told the press, "We're going to be out frequently now."

I thought they looked like a bunch of buffoons, but I remembered their deadliness in Birth of a Nation, and I'd heard enough horror stories about their treatment of blacks, that I, and everyone else took them dead seriously.

Even the police were worried, perhaps for once with real

cause. About twenty of the police formed a line between our demonstrators and those of the Klan, separating the two groups from any physical contact with each other. As usual, we clapped and sang our freedom songs and ignored the Klan's signs, "God Segregates Man," "McKeldin Lives in All-White Area," "Support Our Police Join KKK," and others—and their steady stream of vile taunts and racial epithets.

Photo from *Afro-American* newspaper:
a gift to this writer from their newsman, George Collins, May 1966.

The whole thing took on something of a circus atmosphere—or perhaps more accurately, one of a horror side show. Residents of the high-rise were hanging out the windows watching, passing cars were holding up traffic as they paused to watch, and a crowd, estimated to be as high as two hundred, gathered. Amazingly, there were no incidents, but we shared the concern of the police commissioner, Maj. Gen. George Gelston, that blacks, not bound by CORE's non-violence tradition, would, in the weeks to come, be drawn to the site by the Klan's presence and cause trouble.

Next day, both the State Attorney General and Maj. Gen. Gelston questioned the use of police dogs at demonstrations, clearly meant to intimidate the CORE demonstrators—but concluded they did not have the authority to forbid use of the dogs unless the dogs actually disrupted the picketing.

On May 3rd, George Collins began his report in the *Afro*: "I never dreamed that I would live to see the day when the Ku Klux Klan would be parading in the heart of Baltimore. You can bet your life this will be a long, hot and maybe violent summer." Fortunately, it never did produce violence, and all this commotion had a definite up-side for our Housing Committee: the media loved it and we got publicity we would not otherwise have had. Many readers were shocked at the Klan's appearance at Horizon House and vowed to join us in the weeks following.

But all this commotion also had a down-side: On Tuesday, May 4 Samuel and Morton Gorn, owners of Horizon House, filed in the Circuit Court a nineteen-page bill of complaint requesting an injunction restraining the named defendants from "conducting, participating in, or inviting or encouraging others to conduct or participate in any demonstrations" at Horizon House.

Named in the complaint were CORE, Walter Carter, Sampson Green and me; the Klan and its leaders, and Charles Luthardt. The Gorns attached exhibits asserting that CORE not only sought open occupancy but also wanted advertising in both Negro and white news media and wanted members of both races to be employed to show model apartments to the public (all of which had been on our list of demands when we had met with the Apartment House Owners Association the year before).

On Friday, May 6, after a hearing that lasted from 10 A.M. to 8:30 P.M., Judge Charles Harris issued an injunction limiting CORE to ten pickets and counter-picketers to an equal number—the two groups to remain at least ten feet apart. It allowed picketing only between 2 P.M. and 5 P.M. on Sundays and forbade parking at curbside during demonstrations, any blocking of the entrance, and any "shouting or raucous singing."

The order banned the use of dogs or other animals and the carrying of any weapons, meaning clubs, large flashlights, knives, firearms and large handles on signs. (The Klan had

had their signs mounted on quite heavy poles and also had carried long flashlights and sticks attached to their waist.)

Walter Carter, Sampson Green and I—represented by attorneys Marvin Braiterman, Carl Rachlin, Mrs. Elsbeth Levy Bothe, John King and Marvin Polikoff (Fred Weisgal was out of town at the time), all giving their services pro bono—testified on behalf of CORE. We contended that there was no evidence to justify an injunction, that the police had testified to our cooperativeness, and that the Klan wanted the injunction because it would affirm their intent of "driving CORE off the street."

Though the judge's remarks at times indicated sympathy with CORE's goals, he stated, "It works an injustice to and violates the rights of innocent parties to restrict their use of the sidewalk and to make them feel embarrassed by having to pass through the picket line of one group of demonstrators or the other."

Suddenly, Walter Brooks, the Target City project coordinator, was speaking to the press on our behalf. Interviewed by the *Afro,* before the hearing on the injunction, he was reported on May 7 as saying, "We are ignoring the injunction threat and are going full speed ahead. Any injunction would be a clear violation of our constitutional rights." We of local CORE who had developed and spearheaded this whole housing drive for over a year were concerned. We knew he, in fact, opposed our demonstrating at a "luxury" apartment, and had no understanding whatsoever of the "what" or "why" of what we were doing, and the work that had gone into acquiring the growing support for our efforts that we now had.

After two meetings of the local Housing Committee on Saturday, May 7, to decide whether or not we'd honor the injunction, Walter Carter told the press that CORE could not discourage members or supporters from demonstrating if they wished to do so, and that we would continue to mobilize the community. He also stated that we would seek to have Judge Harris's ruling rescinded.

The same day, the press reported that the chairman of the civic committee of the Interdenominational Ministerial Alliance, Rev. Marion Bascom, had asked for a meeting with the Mayor. He wanted to discuss steps that could be taken that would improve housing, job opportunities and schools for Baltimore's 400,000 Negroes in order to head off future massive demonstrations.

In the May 8th edition of the *Sunday Sun*, it was reported that Lincoln Lynch, associate national director of CORE, had said, "This particular injunction is of crucial importance to us. It would take away our only weapon, would cripple us...Public protest is our only course—we don't intend to let the courts be use as a vehicle for preventing this expression." He also told the Sun that he had come to Baltimore the day before "at the urgent request" of local civil rights groups.

On the same day, Sunday, May 8, instead of defying the injunction by demonstrating in front of Horizon House, about 150 of us met at the church across the street and heard a series of fiery speeches from Walter and a number of others.

Courtesy of Mike Waller, Publisher, *Baltimore Sun*, 5/8/1966

A police motorcycle escort, the state's attorney general and the police commissioner, Maj. Gelston, were on hand as we left the church to march the ten blocks from in front of the apartment to the court house. It was a powerful statement as we sang "We Shall Overcome" and "We Shall Not Be Moved," carrying red, white and blue placards, reading, "March for Baltimore Together Today for Human Dignity." Those in front carried a huge banner that read, "The Issue Is Justice and Dignity." Luthardt was there with a sign saying "Luthardt for Governor," and a Klansman had one saying, "Black Razor

Slashers to Africa."

The Chairman of the Baltimore Federation of Civil Rights Organizations told the press, "Though we might be crippled, we're still here."

The marchers gather around the courthouse steps as Walter Carter gives one of his inspiring speeches. Courtesy of Mike Waller, Publisher, *Baltimore Sun*

In addition to Walter Carter, Walter Lively, a leader of the Union for Jobs & Income Now (U-JOIN), and Lincoln Lynch from National CORE also spoke before we left for home—all denouncing the injuction and declaring the intent to keep demonstrating.

That evening Hal Smith, one of our most faithful CORE supporters and a close friend of Walter's, came back to the office with Sampson Green and me. We were all fired up after our march and still furious about the Judge's restrictive orders on our picketing. "What could we do about it?" was the topic of discussion.

Talk began to center around our earlier research on possible targets for demonstrations; one in particular, Baltimore's new Civic Center. It had been built downtown with urban renewal funds, on a site that had previously held housing for blacks—and it had been built by Joseph Meyerhoff, President of the Home Builders Association—with whom we'd also unsuccessfully negotiated the year previous, along with

Samuel Gorn and the Apartment House Owners Association. Meyerhoff was a prominent Baltimorean known for his contributions to cultural, civic and charitable organizations. We had ruled this target out only because we thought it would be harder to make the connection between the Civic Center and our goal of "freedom of choice in housing" than it would be using Horizon House as a target.

But as we talked that afternoon, getting increasingly hot and angry, we thought, "Why not raise the issue of this as a potential target?" Hence we drew up the telegram to Mayor McKeldin and the City Council that the press later called "the most blistering letters the group has yet sent." Of course, in addition to the telegram, I had to type it on stencil and run copies off on the mimeograph. It was late in the evening by the time we'd done this—and then run all over the city to hand-deliver them to all the media.

On Monday, May 9, Mayor McKeldin and the City Council received copies of the CORE telegram, signed by Sampson Green and me, as Co-Chairs of the Housing Committee, and by H. Wharton Smith (Hal), CORE's public accommodation chairman. It read, in part:

> Now Baltimore courts not only have added to an already explosive situation by joining the City Council in saying to the colored citizens 'never,' but have gone further by equating and treating alike non-violent protests and KKK intimidation.
>
> They have joined forces with Klan efforts to put CORE out of business. They have told CORE non-violence does not pay....They have removed the only means of releasing pent-up emotions and hate created by a bigoted human society....By depriving us of our constitutional rights in such a flagrant manner, the courts may be responsible for putting more strain upon human endurance than can be tolerated without an explosion.

The telegram warned of direct action against all events at the Civic Center—including asking black performers not to appear there—if "positive action" was not immediately taken.

> We do not want to move against all Civic Center events and conventions in Baltimore because of the indignities and humiliation Negroes face coming unknowingly to a segregated, backwater city, but your injunction will leave us with no other choice.

We asked the Mayor to intervene with the courts. On May 11, Mayor McKeldin told the press that he was rejecting our appeal for action in response to the court injunction and he wrote a letter to me that said, amongst other things:

> Apparently I must again remind you that early in my Administration I introduced the comprehensive civil rights bill now in effect; and that on that occasion I called into my office a number of groups and individuals, representing all segments of this community and secured their support for this important bill.

On the same day, he told them he had invited Rev. Frank Williams, President of the Interdenominational Ministerial Alliance, to his office for a conference on race relations and that he had expressed the hope he could count on their organization for assistance during the coming weeks and months. The Mayor also said he hoped the meeting with Rev. Williams and meetings with others he had been holding in recent weeks would culminate soon in an announcement of "possibilities that exist for continuing the positive atmosphere out of which productive and meaningful action might flow."

• • •

On May 12, the courtroom was jammed with CORE members, sympathetic clergymen, lawyers and even representatives of the Ku Klux Klan, when Fred Weisgal and a group of five lawyers appeared before Judge Harris to ask that his injunction severely limiting picketing at Horizon House be vacated. The Judge opened the hearing by saying that "this court is not going to be bulldozed by any of your clients." Then, he startled Sampson Green and me when he asked us to take the stand to explain a telegram we'd sent the week before to Mayor McKeldin (with copies to the press), warning of violence unless the temporary injunction was vacated.

The judge refused Fred's motion for a private hearing on this, exclaiming that "nothing in Maryland law provides for a private, off-the-record conference in the judge's chambers in a matter such as is before the court." When Sampson and I refused to testify, the judge declared that later we would be ordered to show why we should not be held in contempt "for issuing public statements critical of his injunction." I must admit we felt rather frightened, but Fred seemed unperturbed, and rightly so as it turned out, because he never did follow through.

As for the main issue, Weisgal began reading from a lengthy section on injunctions contained in one of the many law books that were piled up on the Judge's bench. Others attacked the right of Gorn and Horizon House to maintain a segregated facility, and argued that freedom of speech and assembly was "not subject to being quelled" because of its effect on the public.[120]

When another of CORE's attorneys questioned whether he was qualified to hear the case, Judge Harris replied that he had no prejudice and that the case "was not going to be tried in the press or on public street corners." In the end, Judge Harris said there is a "contemptuous way to act which will not be tolerated in this case"—and the injunction remained.

During the noon recess, a number of local and national CORE members went to Horizon House and started marching with their signs, "Make Baltimore a Free City," and "March for Baltimore Together Today for Human Dignity." On the Judge's orders, three from local and two from national were arrested. They were taken directly to Judge Harris's courtroom and ordered to remain there until he finished dealing with CORE's petition to rescind his injunction.

And so, in concluding the hearing on the injunction, the judge said he personally opposed segregation and supported Fair Housing legislation, but he was not a legislator, and whether he liked it or not, the owners of Horizon House had a right to pursue a policy of segregation until an open-occupancy law was passed. He did *modify* his order, "on a trial basis," to allow CORE *twenty* pickets at a time—ten on the Calvert Street side and ten on the Chase Street side. *[Big deal, we thought.]* "I do it mainly because of the explosive situation we have and the fact some members of CORE have apparently shown they can act within the bounds of the law." He did not increase the number for the counter-demonstrators.

---

[120] There is a letter in Fred Weisgal's files that suggests he'd consulted his friend, Tony Amsterdam, on the issue of injunctions, and that Amsterdam had had his students at the University of Pennsylvania Law School research it. Most of this information is from the *News-American*, 5/12/66

Judge Harris then turned to the five who'd just been arrested. After the three local CORE members promised the Judge they would not again picket at Horizon House except under the terms of his restraining order, they were released pending further contempt charges. The two from national, Lincoln Lynch and Stu Wechsler, refused such a promise, declaring they were not bound by his order since they were not from Baltimore. The judge ordered them jailed "until you have purged yourselves of this contempt."

As they were led away, about fifteen local and national CORE members followed them to the jail, singing "Ain't gonna let no injunction turn me 'round." They declared they would continue to hold a vigil outside the jail until the two were released. During the night as many as fifty persons were there; five stalwarts were still there at daybreak. All night they had continued to hold aloft signs saying, "Free Baltimore Now," "We Want Justice," "Freedom to Picket Now," "Free Lincoln and Stu."

As local CORE members opened the newspaper on Friday the 13th (an appropriately ominous date), they learned that Fred had told the reporter of his intent to go to Federal Court to seek the release of the two still jailed, stating they were being illegally held for violating an unconstitutional court order.[121] Further, the paper noted that Fred planned to challenge the whole injunction, and especially the condition that limited picketing to Sunday afternoons—the condition that had been violated, leading to the arrest of the five the day before. Fred contended that the police, not the courts, should decide whether or not there were too many pickets. "You just don't do this on the basis of the apartment owner coming in, unless the police say they can't control the situation."

Then, the same day, local CORE's leaders again learned, via the press, that Floyd McKissick (national CORE's Director who'd replaced Farmer) had alerted all two hundred CORE chapters throughout the country to be prepared for a possible mass convergence on Baltimore to protest the court injunction. He'd said, "It could affect all future demonstrations if it is

---

[121] Just a year before Fred's friend, Tony Amsterdam, had published a 119-page article in the Penn Law Review on the "removal of civil rights cases from state to federal courts." He was regarded as a leading scholar on such techniques (*Time* magazine, 12/10/65)

allowed to stand."

Needless to say, local CORE members were upset to learn about these actions via the press. The general consensus at their next meeting was that they were losing control of their campaign—intended as a vehicle for opening housing to blacks throughout the city. They were at a loss to explain why Fred was no longer meeting with them in developing strategy—why he wasn't even keeping them informed of developments.

Fortunately the earlier threats Judge Harris had directed at Sampson and me did serve to prevent us from joining the four local CORE members who again defied the injunction and were arrested. They were jailed for contempt of court along with the two already there. Judge Harris said he'd looked further into the law on contempt and felt he had broad authority and wide discretion in this field. As the defendants were leaving the courtroom,[122] Dave Eberhardt, reading from a paper, said "CORE hopes to speed legislation for Open Occupancy." Judge Harris remarked that he hoped for such legislation soon, too, in order to resolve the "unhappy situation we find ourselves in." He added that he had arranged with the Chief Judge of the Maryland Court of Appeals to hear any appeals before their summer recess.

After a second night's vigil outside the jail, where six from local and national CORE were now jailed, Rev. Frank Williams, with a delegation from the Ministerial Alliance, met with the Mayor. Afterwards, Joseph Allen, the city solicitor, with Mayor McKeldin's approval, submitted two petitions to Judge Harris on behalf of the City of Baltimore—one to intervene in the case and the other to modify the injunction as to permissible days and hours for demonstrating.

The press quoted the petitions as saying that the city "takes the position that the injunction as issued is excessively restricted"...and, as a consequence, "could result in a threat to the peace and order of the community." The next day, Saturday, May 14, the judge released those who had been jailed. The Sun reported the Mayor as saying, "I think all parties were agreed that this was necessary to relieve a potentially explosive situation."

---

[122] Dave Eberhardt, Jim Griffin (who had told the judge just the day before he would not do so again), Willard Dixon and Michael Flug.

Within ten minutes of their release, all six were back picketing at Horizon House, declaring that they felt their unconditional release "constitutes a revocation of the original order." Lincoln Lynch (national CORE's Associate Director), who had been amongst them, said they were not "defying the court's order," but rather just "exercising our constitutional rights." He also said, in discussing his jailing with the press, that the food had been "abominable."

He added that the only reason he could discern for the fact that Baltimore County spent $7 a day on their prisoners and Baltimore City spent only $2.35 was the fact that most of the City's prisoners were black. Judge Harris did not order them again arrested and said he would not enforce the provision in his injunction that designated specific hours for the demonstrations. But he did add that the six men were released on their own recognizance and were still charged with contempt of court. He also said the hearing on the injunction had been changed from Thursday to Monday, May 16.

On Sunday, May 15, six weeks after the initial demonstration at Horizon House, a large number were there again, including Klan members in their full regalia and Luthardt, the candidate for governor, who was dressed this time in his construction worker attire—white overalls and an orange helmet.

About 1:30, an hour after we started marching and singing, Lincoln Lynch, from national, had a lengthy conversation with Baltimore's acting police chief, George Gelston, the City Solicitor, Joseph Allen, the sheriff and the State's attorney, all present at the demonstration. They advised Lynch that the injunction still forbade CORE's picketing on the Calvert Street side of Horizon House—reserved for the counter-picketers.

When they continued in defiance of the warning, sixteen of the CORE pickets were arrested by the *sheriff*—eleven from Baltimore, again including our chairman, James Griffin; three from national, again including Lincoln Lynch; and two from Pennsylvania. As they were taken to the paddy wagon, Mr. Lynch said, "We are amazed that the city now finds itself in a position of having the full force of law enforcement—the police and the sheriffs—being used to reserve areas for Klan activity by arresting CORE." [In court the next day Judge Harris fined them $25 each—later suspended—and released them, "since there had been no violence," he'd said.]

There were no further arrests, even though CORE defied another of the injunction's conditions—the limit to twenty pickets at a time in front of the apartment. And by order of Gelston, the nine CORE pickets who sat for an hour in the middle of the street at the intersection of Calvert and Chase streets—the location of Horizon House—also were not arrested, as expected, but rather were protected by a line of police barricading access to the street which had already been closed to traffic.

At about 3:15 there was a bomb scare and five fire engines arrived and searched the public areas for about a half hour, then left. Finally, about 4 p.m., after singing, "We Shall Overcome," the Reverends Bascom and Williams led about 175 demonstrators to the jail to protest the arrest of the sixteen pickets. We had been there marching and singing for well over three hours.

> We're going to walk, walk.
> We're going to talk, talk.
> We're going to walk, walk,
> To the land of freedom.

At the height of the demonstration there had been a phalanx of seventy-five policemen; and the spectators, both pro and con, were estimated to number approximately three hundred.

On May 18, the *News American* carried a large photo of Layton Braun, the Klan Kleagle, holding a note he'd found tacked on his front door on Sunday. It read, "Mrs. Layton Braun, Sr. get out of this house. You're in danger." He blamed it on CORE, trying to intimidate him by threatening his pregnant wife. He said that the Klan was being accused of being a violent organization, when in fact they had complied with *all* the conditions of the injunction from the very beginning and still were. It was CORE that was consistently breaking the law.

He said that he opposed CORE's position on Horizon House. "We feel the demonstrations are no more than a threat to disenfranchise the white working people. He said they were trying to usurp the rights of "white citizens." He went on to announce the Klan was holding a big rally on Saturday, May 21, in Rising Sun, Maryland—their usual place—when a fifty-foot cross would be burned.

•••

On Monday, Tuesday, and Wednesday, May 16, 17, and 18, there were long closed door meetings with the police, the sheriff, city officials and the attorneys for CORE and Horizon House, discussing further modifications of the May 7th injunction—already modified twice.

In court on Monday, Judge Harris said he was willing to make changes by "a trial-and-error process that arises out of our experience on the sidewalk."—*which was a strange decision since there had never been any problem "on the sidewalk" prior to his issuing the injunction in the first place.* He also said the Court of Appeals judges had said they would act only when someone tested his *final* decision—which seemed like was never to be. Fred told the judge that Lincoln Lynch had authorized him to say that pickets would march properly and abide by reasonable restrictions—but that they intended to take to Federal Court the question of the validity of the whole injunction order.

Regrettably it had become crystal clear to the most active members of local CORE that Walter Brooks, national's Target City project coordinator in Baltimore, and Lincoln Lynch, national CORE's Associate Director, had taken over as the decision-makers and spokespersons for our project. Every report now was of some directive or input that had been given by national. Knowing that from the start national had neither understood nor approved of local's campaign, this obviously did not portend well for achieving the goals established when the Horizon House project was launched in the spring.

Stu Wechsler, a member of Target City, recently admitted in a conversation with this writer, that when they came to Baltimore, most of them had already faced rigid opposition in the South and expected to find the same in Baltimore. "We were young, brash and unprepared for Baltimore's complexity and subtleties. We were not willing to listen and learn before plunging forward with our 'romanticism of poverty' and belief that both the black and white middle-class was irrelevant to what the movement should be about."

This was certainly the feeling they left us with even then, so it was of especial concern to all of local CORE's Housing Committee that our long-time and trusted attorney, Fred Weisgal, was participating in closed-door meetings with the police, the sheriff, city officials, and the attorney for Horizon House, and with national CORE people, to the exclusion of the local leaders. This both hurt and angered us as we tried to understand why this was happening. Was Fred just so absorbed by the legal issues involved that he felt it unnecessary to make time for consultation with local? Or did Fred, possibly, think that by working with the more widely known national leaders, he had an unparalleled opportunity to enhance his own reputation, hence prestige? Our speculations was, of course, an attempt to make sense of what was going on.

The Mayor, who'd always been concerned with black-white relations in the city, had also begun to meet with blacks and whites to consider various steps he might take to ease housing-related issues—CORE claimed this was caused by national CORE's presence, and his concern that Baltimore might become "hot" this summer if some action wasn't taken now.

On May 18 the press reported that after two meetings in his office, Mayor McKeldin had announced that "an informal understanding" had halted demonstrations at Horizon House pending meetings of city officials and civil rights leaders, and later the same day *members of Target City CORE* affirmed that Sunday demonstrations at Horizon House had been called off until the attorneys completed their negotiations.

On May 19, Mayor McKeldin admitted to the press that he had met with Samuel Gorn, a co-owner of Horizon House and nine other owners of downtown apartments to try to get an agreement from them to open their apartments to blacks. He emphasized that he was *not* trying to get a city-wide agreement—*the whole point of our committee's plans when we started the campaign at Horizon House.*

As the Mayor continued his negotiations daily, national CORE worked with Clifton Henry of the Baltimore Federation of Civil Rights Organizations in arranging a mass meeting for Sunday, May 22, 1966 at Prince Hall Masonic Temple, where Lincoln Lynch would discuss Target City plans for the summer.

About 250 were present when James Griffin announced that Samuel Gorn, along with seven other apartment house owners had signed a conditional agreement not to discriminate on the basis of color. There was wild applause at the Temple when Jim made the announcement.

Whatever Fred's reasons were for ignoring local CORE, members of the Housing Committee were not pleased to learn next day, via the press, that the Mayor had reached an agreement with Samuel Gorn and eight other apartment owners that they would stop discriminating on the basis of color after an additional number of downtown high rises did likewise. Another condition of the agreement had been that CORE end its demonstrations in front of Horizon House.

[*Members of local CORE's Housing Committee felt it really bizarre that this agreement had been reached in their project without any prior consultation; without even a prior notice of the impending agreement before its announcement to the press.*]

Barbara Mills & Sampson Green, local CORE Housing Co-Chiars; Lincoln Lynch, national CORE; Jim Griffin, local CORE Chaair; and Fred Weisgal, our attorney, who holds agreement with Horizon House. Photo by Sterling Paige. © *AfroAmerican.*, 5/24/1966

Having had no input in formulating the agreement, not even agreeing with it, Sam and this writer, as Co-Chairs of local CORE's Housing Committee, found it hard to participate in the photo-op that had been arranged at Horizon House to affirm CORE's acceptance of the Mayor's agreement.

But we were there, feeling it was impossible to avoid without making obvious our growing conflict with national CORE. The *Afro* published this photo of us taken in the lobby of Horizon House: Fred holding the conditional agreement with Jim Griffin, local CORE's Chairman; Lincoln Lynch, national CORE's Associate Director; Sampson Green and me looking on. Fred and Jim are the only ones who seem to have managed a smile.[123]

Immediately afterwards, the press reported Walter Brooks as having said that "the campaign against the luxury apartments did not focus accurately on the major problems of Negro residents of the inner city....We expect few Negroes to apply at the desegregated high-priced dwellings since few can afford them. National CORE found itself committed to the program against the luxury homes when it arrived because the local chapter had focused on Horizon House for some time. With that target now out of the way, CORE leaders hope to move on to what they call more pressing issues. Slum housing, rather than luxury living, is a top-priority item in the CORE program."

As we had known all along, Target City CORE hadn't a clue what our local movement had been about.

Had Target City immediately begun to tackle the tough issue of slum housing as promised, perhaps national's usurping of local CORE's project would have been easier to take. Instead, while we were still trying to make sense of why Fred had abandoned local CORE leaders, we read in the May

---

[123] Though indicating progress of a sort, two articles appearing in the newspaper (not named) about a year later indicate just how incomplete the struggle for open housing still was. On 4/8/69, the Marylander, a large apartment in the vicinity of Hopkins we'd once picketed, paid a black $500 in damages after being charged with "subjecting him to discriminatory rental policy." Then, on 8/69, Judge Alexander Harvey 2nd, the same judge formalizing the prior agreement, "enjoined the Village of Purnell," an apartment and townhouse complex on Forest Park Avenue from renting any two-bedroom apartment until a complaint of bias against Negroes was heard. This complex was owned by the same Gorn who owned Horizon House. The agreement he'd reached with the Mayor had had little impact on his practices in general!

23rd edition of the *Afro* that the Mayor's apartment house agreement was CORE's first major victory—and that their second had come within an hour when they'd succeeded in desegregating a tavern on The Block (Baltimore's Red Light District).

The *Evening Sun* reported that moments after Walter Brooks announced Target City's "assault on public accommodations," Mr. Lynch and seventeen others were in the Florida Bar on East Baltimore street, waiting for service...the owner calmly told the sit-ins: 'We don't serve colored here.'

The continued refusals produced sidewalk pickets, who marched in a tight circle outside the bar as a crowd gathered and additional police were called in. Six more men, holding CORE signs, sat in the middle of the street [in front of its "famous" bars and strip joints, known locally as "The Block"] as the pickets marched on the sidewalk and the eighteen would-be patrons sang freedom songs within the dim tavern."

Shortly after, the police chief, Gelston, had those in the street arrested for "obstructing traffic." He then went into the bar and after a long conversation with the owner, the other CORE demonstrators were served.

On May 23, after a two-hour meeting with the twenty-two bar and "night club" owners on the Block, Mayor McKeldin declared that the Block had agreed to serve persons without regard to race, color or creed. The press quoted him as saying, "This is another example of businessmen acting together in behalf of the general welfare of our community. It is my hope that others will follow their splendid example." He attributed much of the success to Lincoln Lynch, stating, "It is my impression that CORE is a responsible organization that has always carried on its programs in a responsible manner."

Was this how they intended to further their goal of helping the poor? Is this what they thought sounder than our housing drive? We didn't know whether to laugh or cry as we saw what was happening to our movement. Already, a week earlier, the Target City Office had been accused, in their fund-raising letters to the City's most prominent businessmen, of making threats of "summer riots" if they were not forthcoming with contributions to support their summer program. Of course, they'd denied it, but copies of letters we saw came close, if not quite that blatant.

CORE asks home builders to act on discrimination

PICKETS MARCH FOR OPEN HOUSING

4 ARRESTED DURING SIT-IN

CORE's big push for housing on

Pickets Sit Through Night Protesting Racial Housing

FREEDOM NOW

11 jailed in housing protests

6 MORE PICKETS ARE ARRESTED

17 ARRESTED FOR SIT-INS

5 CORE protesters freed on $104 bail

Housing rally

Interest grows

Farmer To Lead March Here,

Opening Housing Drive

2,000 Integrationists March Here

D'ALESANDRO URGES BROAD OPEN HOUSING

FOES OF BILL ON HOUSING

FAIR HOUSING

BILL KILLED IN 13-8 VOTE

Klansmen Picket In Robes

BOO CARDINAL

BREAK THE POLITICAL NOOSE.

Rights Leaders Embittered On Open Housing Defeat

Two Housing Bills Killed; Blockbusting Curb Gains

C.O.R.E. OPPOSES LIMIT ON PICKETS

Horizon House first target of CORE unit

Break the Noose

INTEGRATION PLEDGED BY 9 APARTMENTS

Mayor Seeks Accord By Apartments On Open Occupancy

A Montage of Headlines Tell the Story of Our Efforts to Open the Real Estate Market to All. *How could we not be bitter that national CORE had moved in to thwart our efforts right at the peak of our campaign.*

On May 24, 1966, in the midst of all the turmoil over the Klan and injunctions, the pending cases of those charged with trespassing during the fall of 1965 were scheduled for trial. On that day, all forty of us were summoned to court, pretty well filling the court room, but the nine charged at Colmar were scheduled to be tried first—a jury trial that lasted three days.

Victor Frenkil, owner of Colmar, and a prominent Baltimorean was not called to testify. The prosecutor's chief witness was Edward Dentry, the manager, reviewed how he had obtained warrants for the arrests on advice from police; how one group appeared on Saturday and stayed in a sample apartment for several hours, one stretched out on the floor; how the next day, a group "rushed into my office and sat around reading the comics from the Sunday paper so that I couldn't work."

When questioned about the racial policies of the apartment complex, he said that Negroes "were welcome to look," but they were not integrated—the "objectionable" were kept out. On further questioning by our attorney, Fred Weisgal, Mr. Dentry stated, "First I size them up as to appearance. I wouldn't want to put someone in who looks morally and financially wrong....Based on looks and my eighteen years experience, I can tell."[124]

In his cross examination, Fred also emphasized that the apartments' advertisements invited the public to look at the apartments. It did not say all but colored citizens.

One of the defendants, a secretary at Johns Hopkins University, testified she had received a Colmar rental flyer in the mail. In his testimony, Walter Carter said, "I just wanted a nice apartment for my family." Others of the defendants testified to CORE's methods of selecting those who sit-in at demonstrations and their motivations.

A police officer's testimony contradicted the claim that Mr. Dentry had made that the demonstrators had been disorderly. And Fred had a surprise witness, the State's Attorney Charles Moylan Jr., who testified that the city's trespass act had been

---

[124] The judge had in his hand the recent conviction of a married man on charges of embezzlement, larceny and bad checks, who had maintained a girlfriend in one of the Colmar Apartments—not so moral.

invoked *only* in civil rights cases. After the closing arguments, Walter and I went for lunch with Fred in one of the tiny little coffee shops on one of the near-by side streets.

We had hardly gotten back in the court room when the jury filed back with an acquittal. The prosecutor was livid, raging, unbelieving, and as he passed us leaving, unwilling to start any other of the cases that day, he muttered, "You'll not get away with this. You'll be tried again and convicted!" But *none* of the cases were ever again called for trial.

A few days later, another Municipal Court Judge questioned the use of the state trespass law as the basis for arrests, calling the statute "misleading or poorly drawn." I don't know if this was a factor or if they just felt that if they couldn't win Colmar, which clearly they'd thought was their strongest case, then why waste time and money on retrying it—or trying any of the others.

So what had CORE really won with their acquittal? Other than not going to jail, not much, judging from an article that appeared in the newspaper two full years later.[125]

In September 1968, a Negro couple "testing" the Colmar Apartments' rental policy were told none were available, but within two hours, two different white couples were shown available apartments; the owner, Victor Frenkil, telling the press there were actually 27 vacancies. Confirming the discrimination, Baltimore Neighborhoods, Inc. said it had received a number of complaints in the last several months, making it hard to believe Frenkil when he claimed three Negro families lived there. However, immediately after a city official made inquiries at the development, one Negro couple who had waited for months for action on their application to rent, suddenly were told it had been "found".

•••

Returning to 1966, on June 18 that year, less than a month after the Colmar trespass trial ended, the *Sun* carried a story, titled, "CORE CHIEF HERE TO HEAL RIGHTS RIFT." It started:

---

[125] The hand-dated clipping is in John Roemer's files but the paper, probably the *Sun*, is not noted.

Floyd McKissick, national director of the Congress of Racial Equality, flew into Baltimore yesterday for a meeting designed to placate non-CORE civil rights leaders and to receive reaffirmations of support for the CORE summer project.

The article continued:

...The Baltimore Target City project has been slowed down and somewhat threatened by some recent family quarrels and wounds and some mistakes which the national leaders are patching up.

...Yesterday's meeting with local civil rights leaders (thirty in all) was mostly, although not fully, successful, according to some persons who attended.

Jim Griffin, Baltimore CORE Chairman, with Lincoln Lynch and Floyd McKissick from Ntional CORE. Photo by Carl X Harden; provided by David Eberhardt.

...CORE's difficulties arose early. Some of the factors:

1. The national organization "researched" the city, then selected it as a target, but did not coordinate its plans with local civil rights groups.

2. It came into Baltimore with wholesale attacks on the city...

3. [They] personally angered many local civil rights leaders by what has been considered an "arrogant" or "abrasive" attitude.

Rev. Bascom accused national of making "generalizations," such as "that nothing significant in the area of civil rights has gone on in Baltimore."

Mrs. Juanita Jackson Mitchell accused the national CORE officials of "an arrogant nonviolence...and said they were "dishonest" in saying that Baltimore's civil rights record was the worst in the nation. She spoke of the local NAACP's record (most of which has been reviewed by this writer earlier)—of a successful fight to integrate the University of Maryland law school in 1935; of a legal attack on racial covenants in real estate contracts in 1939; a march of 2,000 people to Annapolis in 1942 to protest police brutality; and successful integration of swimming pools, Sandy Point Beach and Fort Smallwood in 1955 and 1956. Continuing, Mrs. Mitchell said emphasized the community's long history of militancy even during a time when it was most unpopular. And she pointedly referred to the legal aid and bail money the NAACP had provided during CORE's 1961 Route 40 Freedom Rides.

Walter Carter, who represented the very heart of the original CORE headed by James Farmer, was the subject of another lengthy article in the *Sun*, also on Saturday, June 18, titled, "Carter Leaving Post in CORE." Though denying to the press that it was related to the growing dissension between members of local CORE and those involved with Target City— something the press was beginning to get wind of—we knew it did. The article read, in part:

> ...Yesterday, [Walter Carter] announced that he was stepping out of any active policy-making role in the organization for "an indefinite" time. "Truthfully, I am exhausted," said Mr. Carter. I have not had a vacation from CORE for six years....In the nonviolent war, the general must also be the foot soldier....It is an exhausting task."

[The article then reviewed his many actions, adding, "His victories were sweet to him and he did not deny it."]

> When he was served for the first time in a White Coffee Pot in 1962, he exultantly told a reporter, "It's the kind of emotion you just can't describe. I sat there and the waitress served me eggs and bacon. I'd been sitting at that counter for five years without being served."

[The article then says something of his background and his disappointment in not finding more people willing to work for social change after he came to Baltimore. It went on—]

> Mr. Carter, whose conversation is articulate, colorful and flavored with good humor, speaks of the civil rights movement in both racial and social terms, drawing on his experiences as a Negro and his education and training as a social worker.

He sees the city as being dominated by a city council which is dominated by "Citizens Council elements. The City Council is allowing the city to die and this will destroy the metropolitan area—like snatching out the heart of a person."

Mr. Carter sees CORE today as "the cutting edge of the civil rights movement. People are never happy with surgery," he said, "but we have a congenital defect in the American Society."

About this same time, in July 1966, Walter took a letter to the *Afro* that gave his version of black power—and expressed his dream—something Baltimoreans would do well to recall even as they repeat each year that of Martin Luther King.[126]

It is my dream to see the day when we colored citizens, we civil rights leaders and catalysts, we who operate under different banners [and he names sixteen] CAN GET TOGETHER , AND BEGIN A UNIFIED, AND DIVERSIFIED new effort to resolve our common problem.

We should direct our aggressiveness against our common foe, 'CHUCK, THE OPPRESSOR,' and liberate ourselves from this web of confusion, that gives comfort to our oppressors....While the masses of panic-driven whites continue to look for refuge in suburbia, in the hi-rises, way up above us, we should want 'ACTIVATED BLACK POWER' to deal both with ourselves, and with our white oppressors who have systematically rendered us with powerlessness.

I am not advocating that we adopt one plan of action in dealing with the complex economic, political, psychological, physiological and what other realities that have kept us in subjugation...It seems to me, that the least we could do is to appreciate the beautiful promise that 'creative diversity' can produce. Consider the artistry of Duke Ellington's great band, that blends freely the improvisational uniqueness of a variety of instrumentalists, while hearing the same drummer.

Perhaps it is asking too much for us civil rights advocates, with our collective minds set on freedom and liberation, to also hear the unceasing beat from far away Rhodesia all the way up to Max Roach.

•••

---

[126] *Afro-American*, aptly quoted this letter in its entirety on August 7, 1971, after Walter's death, since it so represents his belief in unity as the only way to successfully fight oppression.

When Target City arrived in Baltimore, the city had gotten a first-hand taste of what would soon be a *new* CORE, but after it was chosen as the site for its 23rd annual convention, to start July 1, 1966, the city would see the birth of a far more radicalized CORE than ever envisaged by its founders. At the time national CORE chose the site, the intent was to give more exposure to their Target City Project, but, as it turned out, it would also give more exposure to the aborning Black Power Movement.

In addition to reporters from various big national papers, a six-man field crew from England's BBC radio network flew in to cover the convention. The city had mixed reactions to all this attention—and what happened at the convention didn't make them feel any better.

On July 2nd a long article in the *Baltimore Evening Sun* headlined its report: "KING DERIDED AT C.O.R.E.'S CONVENTION." It reported that Mrs. Fannie Lou Hamer was wildly applauded when she'd said in her keynote address,

Carmichael with unidentified man.
Photo by Carl X Harden; provided by David Eberhardt.

"While he's having a dream, I'm having a nightmare." Mrs. Hamer also chided the press: "[They] will pick up one thing, 'black power,' and go to hell with it.... The white people have had it for 400 years and nobody said anything." She added that integration was something fostered by whites to keep the black people from real power.

That evening, Rev. King canceled his speech scheduled for the next day, claiming "a prior commitment."

Stokely Carmichael was quickly invited as his replacement, and followed the same theme as Mrs. Hamer. Stokely urged CORE to adopt a policy of "black power" instead of integration. He attacked "white liberals who live in lily white suburbs" and added that anyone who objected to the term "black power" was a "racist." He also appealed for more self-respect in the black community. Meier and Rudwick quote Carmichael:

> The only way we gonna stop them white men from whuppin' us is to take over. We been saying freedom for six years and we ain't got nothin'. What we gonna start saying now is black power....Ain't nothin' wrong with anything all black 'cause I'm all black and I'm all good. Now don't you be afraid. And from now on when they ask you what you want, you know what to tell them.[127]

The crowds he electrified shouted back, "Black Power! Black Power!" This writer had previously heard Stokely speak at Morgan, and can attest to the thrill he generated in his audience with his enormous eyes and passionately fiery speech. Howard Zinn said of him:[128] "He gave the impression he would stride cool and smiling through hell, philosophizing all the way." I was not surprised that it was he who first raised his clenched fist and shouted, "Black Power."

When Baltimore's Mayor McKeldin arrived, just as Carmichael was completing his speech to the convention, he was approached by the national director of CORE's board and specifically asked not to speak, as scheduled. The Mayor replied, "I want to do whatever I can do to help you and the cause," then turned and left. He was not rescheduled for next day as he had been advised he would be.

On July 4, the *Sun* reported that at a mass rally that drew fewer than 300, James Farmer had criticized the Federal anti-poverty program as a failure—a mere palliative," insensitive to the needs of the poor—and announced he had withdraw a request for Federal funds for the national literacy program he had left CORE to head. [Mr. Farmer was, rightly, very bitter over the lack of support he'd encountered in Washington, and all the broken promises he encountered. Two days after this talk in Baltimore, the paper announced that he had been hired as an $80-a-day consultant in New Jersey's War on Poverty. It was expected to last for thirty-five days, for a total payment to him of $2,800.] This event could well be seen as a

---

[127] Meier & Rudwick (eds.), *Black Protest*...Intro, p. 19.
[128] Zinn, *You Can't Be Neutral on a Moving Train*, p. 53

presage of the treatment history would accord this early civil rights leader in contrast to the accolades showered on Martin Luther King.

On July 5, the *Afro-American* had a big headline across the whole of its front page: **"CORE OKAYS 'SELF DEFENSE' McKissick Suggests King Resign; VietNam War Hit."** Below were four separate articles, headlined:

"Mayor Says Target City Could Be Summer's Safest"—

The Mayor, "With the help of CORE we'll achieve some of the goals we've been working toward. We are ashamed of ourselves, we need you here to help us do what we have not been able to do. We've got to have open housing." Commissioner Gelston, who has given the city police a brighter image since taking command, agreed that "with some luck" Baltimore could get through the summer in better shape than a number of other large cities.

"'We'll meet violence with violence'—CORE"—

(The story is of a scene created by forty convention delegates at an East Side bar over the price of drinks.)

"Non-violence stand stirs controversy"—

When CORE unanimously resolved on Monday to put an end to non-violence as a philosophy, a drastic new image had been given the activists of the movement and the predictions range from 'it's the only way to stop the brutal beatings of rights workers' to fears rights workers are heading for a bloodbath. In Chicago, Dr. Martin Luther King called for a meeting of top movement leaders. And in Baltimore, civil rights leaders immediately called for a meeting with CORE leaders to determine exactly where CORE stands. At stake could be the support given to CORE's Target City Project plus the financial backing promised. Across the nation, fear of what could happen was the first reaction of many.

"A Suggestion for Dr. King"—

CORE director Floyd McKissick suggests Dr. Martin Luther King resign before the Nobel Peace Prize winner is humiliated by having the masses desert him over the non-violence issue. Mr. McKissick said, "Non-violence as a philosophy is dying. Colored people are buying guns all over this country and they don't have the temperament they had in 1960, to accept beatings...King is a great leader, the foremost figure in the civil rights movement. He should resign while he is on top."

On July 9, an *Afro* editorial stated, in part:

> If the summer heat made Baltimoreans inclined to nap, the CORE annual convention awakened them.... We are not alarmed by CORE's promise to protect itself from attacks, violent bullets, bombs and night fires.... What gives us concern is that this step can lead to an underground movement and violence without restraint. This is the kind of open warfare we have seen in VietNam, Ireland and in the former African colonies of the big powers. The risk is calculated and from this point on, no holds will be barred. These are our young people and we can disagree with their plans and their methods. Our sorrow is that we could not pass on to them the first class citizenship they desire and hope for without excuses and without delays.

The *New York Times* reported that the "attacks on the Negro bourgeoisie...white liberals and the U.S. 'establishment', reflected, according to experienced observers, the emergence of class conflict within black communities, as well as antipathy toward the white middle-class." The other dominating theme that was increasingly manifest, in speeches and in the workshops, was that calls for housing integration were part of a white conspiracy to break up concentrations of blacks so they couldn't vote as a block and elect persons of their own color to represent them.

One evening during the convention, Fannie Lou Hamer spoke at a small Baptist church on the East Side of Baltimore to a grassroots audience that could not be at the convention. She was short, stocky and had a slight limp, but her blazing eyes and her skin, weathered from years as a sharecropper, drew you to her at once—and even more so when you knew all she'd been through in the South when she'd spoken out and helped register blacks. And we all admired her for the fight she'd put up in Atlantic City at the 1964 Democratic Party Convention when she'd led the fight to have the Mississippi Freedom Party delegation seated as the true representatives of the people of the state—and for having then run for Congress.

It was a typically hot and sweaty mid-summer Baltimore night—no air conditioning, of course, but fans, advertising the local undertaker, were whipping away throughout the room, trying to stir up a breeze. The church was filled to the rafters, even people outside were piled up on each other by the windows, hanging over the sills, trying to see and hear this woman. I think I may have been the only white person present that night, and I remember little of what she said, but I do remember well that she was very fiery and impressive, "telling it like it is in white America," as they say. I'm sure she repeated what she'd told the Democrats in Atlantic City, "I'm sick and tired of being sick and tired"—and added some of what she'd said in her speech to the convention. And before the evening was over, there was some real swaying and shout-inducing Baptist hymn-singing too.

Activists Break Away

On June 30, 1966, the day before national CORE's convention had started, members of local CORE's Housing Committee made a press release announcing that they were disbanding and forming a new group, "Activists for Fair Housing" (soon shortened simply to the Activists). Even though we did not disapprove of Target City's stated goals—nor the fact they'd announced that theirs was no longer just a "summer program"—we definitely knew we couldn't work with them—nor as subordinate to them—the role they saw us in. The release included the names of officers for nine committees, plus an office manager. Walter agreed to act as a Consultant, Sampson Green and Fred Jones were appointed as Co-Chairs and me as Secretary-Treasurer.

Earlier in the month we had written an open letter addressed to all the individuals, ministers, churches, groups and organizations which had befriended us in OUR STRUGGLE FOR A FREE HOUSING MARKET." It was signed (directly on the stencil) by Walter Carter, Sampson Green, me and fourteen other of our most active members.

Attached was a list of over fifty apartments, along with their builders and or managers, the rental price range, whether there were any Negroes living there, and any information we had about their rental policy. The nine that had just signed the Open Rental Policy were specified, as well as the two who supposedly were open but had refused to make a public announcement. As usual it was typed on stencils and enough copies mimeographed to send to all the media and everyone on our mailing list. The letter started:

> Without your support we could never have had the inspiring March and Rally last November...nor have been able to win our first victory which saw the owners and manager of nine apartment houses agreeing to voluntarily open their apartments...Such an achievement on a voluntary basis may be a first in the country!

It went on to say:

> Much work remains to be done....until all racial discrimination in housing is obliterated, Negroes will continue to be limited in the choice of housing available to

them and so continue to be subject to overcharging,
overcrowding and exploitation....Ghetto conditions which
force poorer Negroes to live in dilapidated, deteriorated, rat-
infested left behind housing...will always exist...until we have
a genuinely free housing market.

It asked for help in continuing our work of opening all the
apartments on the attached list. Urging them to write and call
managers and owners, to organize "shopping days," to become
active with us, concluding, "Please let us hear from
you....Yours for Freedom and Dignity, "Committee for the Free
Housing Market." This letter had been a precursor to our
break with CORE to form the new, independent organization,
"The Activists for Fair Housing."

Our "purpose and creed" read:

Dedicated to promoting a more just and equitable society
for all people through such community organizations and
action as necessary to remove all vestiges of racial
discrimination: Exploitation, enforced segregation,
ghettoization of mind or body, and the alienation and despair
created by deprivation of the incentives and opportunities to
succeed. We believe that if the USA is to be a united, free and
democratic society, every right, privilege, opportunity and law
now extended to its white citizens must immediately be
extended to its black citizens, without further equivocation.

As we continued to meet and try to define ourselves, there
was some talk of moving in a "black power" direction, but
mostly the discussion was about what kinds of actions we
should undertake. The agenda we finally adopted and mailed
to the press and our old membership list was very ambitious.
It included organizing tenants, beginning with those renting
properties owned by Edward A. Myerberg, our old antagonist.
We were also considering direct action against Joseph
Meyerhoff, via the Civic Center, as Sam and I had suggested
earlier in our letter to the mayor—and the possibility of
demonstrations at nearby Fort Meade.

•••

In the Fall of 1966, the Activists were distracted from any
further consideration of the ambitious agenda they'd outlined
by the need to become involved in Spiro Agnew's campaign to
become Governor. Though a Republican, he had been fairly

liberal during his years as Baltimore County Executive. In contrast, his opponent was the Democrat, George Mahoney, who was making the centerpiece of his campaign, "Your Home is Your Castle, Protect It." The blazing slogan could be found on the sides of buses and on highway billboards.

It was a frightening, blatant attempt to cater to the emotions of all those opposed to open housing. I doubt many realized it, but it mimicked an election campaign by the Democrat, Edwin Warfield, in 1903 who exclaimed, "This election is a contest for the supremacy of the white race in Maryland...the white man is the highest type of the human family; the Negro is the lowest."[129] I guess we can take heart from the fact that while Warfield won, Mahoney did not.

Members of the Activists, perhaps others, spent hours at Rev. Bascom's church in the heart of the black community running off leaflets that supported Agnew and attempted to expose the vile racism Mahoney represented. We spent many more hours distributing the leaflets throughout the black neighborhoods, urging people to register and to vote. We hired loud speakers, installed them on our cars and toured these neighborhoods, proclaiming the same message—and had to go to court to fight city councilmen's efforts to stop us, claiming we were violating the "noise ordinance"—though, of course, we were doing nothing different than innumerable others who used such loud speakers for innumerable other reasons.

On Sundays we spread out to deliver our message to as many as possible during Sunday services in the black churches. It was like our massive organizing for our rally and march all over again—and again it worked. The papers later reported that Republican Agnew, who ran on a surprisingly liberal platform, got 50% of the vote, Democrat Mahoney 40%—in a state where Democrats outnumbered Republicans three to one. The number who supported Mahoney is frightening, but even more so the fact that Democrats in the primary had nominated this man, who openly favored "keeping niggers down," to represent them.

Initially the Activists had no reason to regret their efforts on behalf of Agnew. During his first year as Governor, his

---

[129] Paul quoting Warfield, p. 274.

budget included an increase in aid to anti-poverty programs; he pushed through an open housing bill; brought the state's public accommodations bill in line with the federal act; repealed the law banning interracial marriage; and opposed most capital punishment. An action in April 1968 is representative of his change during his second year in office. When 227 black students had come from Bowie State College to Annapolis to voice their grievance, and then had refuse to leave the statehouse when it closed for the day, Agnew had them arrested.[130] By the time he was chosen by Nixon as his Vice President, whatever credentials he'd had as a liberal had long since dissipated.

The Activists were later faced with the fact that their efforts to get Agnew elected as Governor were responsible, in large part,[131] for bringing him to the attention of Nixon, who chose him as his running mate in the subsequent presidential election—a disastrous choice for all who cherished equal rights. He was to become famous (before leaving in disgrace) for such phrases as those quoted earlier: "nattering nabobos of negativism," "hopeless, hysterical, hypochondriacs of history," and "effete corps of impudent snobs" (referring to Vietnam protesters). He also had this to say of protesters: "We an afford to separate [protesters] from our society with no more regret than we should feel over discarding rotten apples from a barrel."

•••

Meanwhile, with the Governor's election behind us, the Activists started a campaign at Fort Meade using a rather elaborate two-sided flyer. It was a tricky theme to develop without seeming to criticize the many black soldiers serving in VietNam and offending their families. However, we wanted to try. An article, hand-dated October 1966, probably from the *Evening Sun*, reported that Leo Burroughs, Jr., on behalf of the Activists, had told reporters we'd been "rebuffed" at a meeting with Fort Meade officers when we'd asked them to

---

130 See *Current Biography* 1968 p. 10
131 Also his treatment of prominent blacks at a subsequent meeting with them in 1968 made him a darling of conservative Republicans. See section on Housing," Inner City's Challenge."

"declare segregated housing adjacent to the base off-limits to Army personnel." The Army's spokesperson told the press they couldn't do this because "the Army has no authority to tell apartment owners that their buildings are off-limits because they are segregated."

As we continued to leaflet and speak to officers and enlisted men in their rec halls and lounges, the chief officers of the base served us notice that we were no longer welcome on the base. Then, suddenly, the roads leading to the base that had previously been open to all were manned and we could no longer gain access.

As a consequence, enthusiasm for this undertaking waned. In the end, however, our campaign may not have been as ineffective as we thought at the time. Less than a year later, on June 30, 1967, the *Sun* reported that the Secretary of Defense, Robert McNamara, had "declared off-limits any racially segregated apartment or trailer court within seven miles of Fort Meade." It quoted him:

> The decision to take vigorous action in eliminating gross discrimination against military families in the Fort Meade area is another step in our accelerating program to assure fair treatment for all armed forces members.

The article went on to say:

> The Defense Department reported that there are 13,042 servicemen posted at Fort Meade; of these, 1,809 are Negroes....that 38.4 % of white families lives within seven miles, 2.7% from eight to fifteen miles and 58.9% more than fifteen miles from the post; for Negro families, the comparable figure are 4.6%, none, and 95.4%. The Secretary said only four of thirty-three rental complexes within seven miles of the post are "equally available to all military families....It is clearly evident that the morale and welfare of Negro families assigned to Fort George Meade, and the operational efficiency of this installation, are being adversely affected by the existence of racial discrimination."

•••

Joseph Meyerhoff had been our target before on a number of occasions but now we decided to make him our main focus. He was not only the largest builder and financier of middle-income housing in the metropolitan Baltimore area, but also had offices in Chicago, Cincinnati, San Francisco, Miami, Memphis, Atlanta, York, and Harrisburg. He had received the Yeshiva University Heritage award which honors "outstanding individuals who have perpetuated noble ideas of justice, learning and philanthropy basic to the Jewish heritage," yet ignored the efforts of influential Jews who had urged him to integrate the housing he built and financed.

Meyerhoff was on the Board of Trustees of Provident Hospital and President of the Board of Directors of the Baltimore Symphony Orchestra. He was a major contributor to the new downtown Meyerhoff Symphony Hall that had been built on recently flattened urban renewal land—displacing many poor blacks, as well as the old German restaurant, Deutschus Haus, where we had often gone after demonstrations to eat, relax, and feel re-energized by the lively polkas it played.

We began this campaign with a letter to Governor Agnew signed by Eugene King, Chairman of the Baltimore County League for Human Rights, James Griffin, still Chairman of Baltimore CORE, and Cleveland Chandler, Chairman of the Activists.

The letter informed him of our plans for an "educational demonstration" to be held at the Inaugural Ball on January 27th, chosen because the Baltimore Symphony Orchestra would be playing. It went on to say that "so long as segregationists, unwilling to recognize the rights of all our citizens, continue to be given positions of civic responsibility and leadership, such demonstrations as this must occur with ever greater frequency." The letter urged Governor Agnew to remove him from Presidency of the Orchestra, and if he remained, to withdraw state funds from the symphony.

> It is time the State, the City and the citizens of Maryland began to recognize the part they are playing in subsidizing and upholding entrenched patterns of discrimination to use now the powers they already have at hand to alter this situation.

In February we held another "educational demonstration" at the SUN LIFE Building, Meyerhoff's office building, further advising demonstrators that there was ample parking in the DownUnder Garage also owned by Meyerhoff. The leaflets handed out at these demonstrations included all the information about Meyerhoff, his connections, his holdings and his segregation policies.

As Spring approached, Meyerhoff had still not responded either to our members or to Jewish community leaders who had urged him to sit down with us to discuss voluntarily integrating his developments. He had even refused to participate in the Metropolitan Baltimore Conference on Equal Opportunity in Housing, sponsored by the President's Committee on Equal Opportunity in Housing. We began to write to blacks who would be performing at the new Symphony Hall, explained our campaign and asked them not to appear until Meyerhoff opened his housing to all.

The Hall was in a convenient location for a renewed housing drive, and the tie to Meyerhoff seemed clear enough. We were also encouraged by the fact that a year earlier, in May, the Interdenominational Ministerial Alliance, under the leadership of Rev. Marion Bascom, had lodged a complaint with Meyerhoff when he scheduled the orchestra to play at the segregated housing development, Joppa Town, near the eastern end of Route 40. They had asked the one full-time black member, Wilmer Wise, associate first trumpet player, not to perform, as well as Cleophus Lyons, a part-time member. The Mayor sympathized, said he objected to segregation anywhere, but added, in effect, the show must go on because they have a contract.[132]

Beginning late in the Spring of 1967, for several consecutive weeks, a dedicated group of Activists and their supporters appeared every Fridays and Saturday, handing out leaflets to passersby and attendees at the Symphony Hall. But, just as had been the case at Fort Meade, the linkage to housing discrimination seemed hard to put across; again it proved hard to arouse enough people to participate to enable us to "make a statement." [133]

Everyone seemed demoralized—and the growing call for "black power" was definitely eroding the coalition that had always been so important— "Black and White Together," which we'd sung so often together, was increasingly coming into question. Be that as it may, future events proved that we had been right in assessing the significance of both Ft. Meade and Meyerhoff when choosing them as targets. In August 1968, shortly after the Defense Department issued its aforementioned decree, Joseph Meyerhoff "opened" the 5,000 apartments he owned in the Baltimore area and, soon after that, most of the smaller builders in the area followed suit.

---

[132] *Afro-American* newspaper, May 21, 1966.

[133] One night en route to the demonstration with a black co-worker, I was stopped by the police who cited me for a turn from the wrong lane—dozens of blocks back. He had been tailing me since and had stopped me, we were sure, because he was a black man with a white woman. The case was dismissed in court.

•••

It was near the end of that summer that I received a letter from Fr. Phil Berrigan resigning from the Activists' Advisory Board, a pretty moot issue by then anyway since we had no further actions planned. Civil Rights, as we'd known it, was being overwhelmed by Black Power and the Peace Movement.

Fr. Philip Berrigan was a good case in point. He had not only been one of our most faithful housing demonstrators, but had immediately accepted our request that he be on our new Advisory Board after the formation of the Activists. Now, however, he was increasingly spending his time in Baltimore and in various other parts of the country, speaking against the war in VietNam and participating in picketing and public vigils designed to promote peace. He'd even been asked to Washington by Dean Rusk, Secretary of State, to discuss his views at a meeting that lasted two hours. The church had unsuccessfully tried to dampen-down these activities.

On October 27, 1967, Fr. Berrigan was joined by two other of our faithful demonstrators, Tom Lewis, the activist-artist who had painted the civil rights montage for Farmer, and David Eberhardt (as well as the Rev. James Mengel), in what was probably the first really dramatic protest against the VietNam War— pour-ing blood on draft records in downtown Baltimore.

On November 9th, they were arraigned after Judge Northrup appointed the civil rights attorney, Fred Weisgal, as their counsel.

Fr. Phil Berrigan with Fred Weisgal, the groups appointed attorney, outside the courthouse during a break in their trial. Courtesy of Mike Waller, Publisher, *Baltimore Sun*, 4/2/1968

In the months following, prior to the beginning of their trial in April 1968, numerous motions and hearings took place; the start of the trial delayed briefly because of the riots following King's assasination (of which we'll hear more later). Meanwhile, Fr. Berrigan had written me a letter:

> I think it would be best, Barbara, if you dropped me from the Advisory Board. There is not only the on-going complication of the peace issue, but also every indication that we're going to jail following our trial. These and other factors tend to make me more useless to the Activists than before, if that's possible.... At any rate, best wishes and regards. You deserve profound respect and commendation. [signed] Peace and freedom, Phil.

I tried to persuade Phil, as everyone in the movement called him, to stay on, but he felt the civil rights movement was irrelevant with the world endangered by the fighting in VietNam. I countered by saying, "What difference does it make if we destroy the world if we can't even solve our racial problems here at home?" We agreed to disagree and parted "directions," with mutual respect and friendship intact. [Making it hard to believe he died on December 6, 2002.]

> By the time Phil wrote me, I had virtually ended my own involvement with the all-but-defunct Activists, but never "moved on" to the VietNam Peace Movement as so many others did. The ending of the movement that had united so many seemed to have been foretold with the loss of James Farmer as director of national CORE, and then of Walter Carter as leader of the movement locally.....Or maybe, in both instances, it just seemed that way. It's always hard to know, what if...?

After the end of the Meyerhoff demonstrations, this phase of the Activists' history had pretty much ended. What turned out to be our last letter to members and supporters was signed by Co-Chairs, Sampson Green and Prof. Cleveland Chandler (soon to leave his position at Morgan State College for a position with the Equal Opportunities Commission in Washington, D.C.).

The letter read:

> During the last year we have launched numerous programs and activities designed to move ahead in bringing equality of opportunity in housing for all citizens in Baltimore and Maryland. also, we have been deeply interested in getting more decent housing for many families who now live in

horrible slum conditions.

We have realized some progress on these two broad fronts. However, prospects are dim for the kind of advancement that will substantially reduce the many housing problems that most Negro families face.

Unless there is greater dedicated effort and participation on the part of those who have contributed their time and money to this deserving cause in the past, we cannot expect to break through the barriers of discrimination and injustice in the housing market. We, therefore, call upon you to renew your involvement and membership in the Activists for Fair Housing....

There was little response. It just seemed that the peace movement had overwhelmed the civil rights movement; it just seemed that increasingly the times weren't conducive to confronting racial discrimination.

•••

On October 24, 1967 Walter Carter wrote a letter to one of the *Sun* reporters [Stephen], that both expressed his concerns about the movement, and, as was common with him, praised a number of those from diverse backgrounds whom he felt had contributed—a number of them not names most would have associated with civil rights. It read in part::

The thing that haunts me most of all is the fear that both the civil rights movement and the social welfare (with its new and awakening dimensions) will fail to grapple successfully with the accumulation of multiple ills which afflict our people. I'd like to see us in Baltimore rise to these awesome challenges, and wage a constructively winning war. ...I must admit the signs of this kind of vitality are absent from the scenes of battle at the moment....

If we could keep people alive and/or with us, such as Laurence Paquin, L.D. Reddick, Herbert Edwards, et al, we could have a bit more hope. The illnesses of Harry Mills [who died of cancer soon after this] and Fred Weisgal [at the time recovering from his second heart attack] also make this goal more difficult to realize though they still make major contributions.

Norman V.A. Reeves of the Bill Moore Center would be a giant without his muscular dystrophy, and Chester Wickwire has been and continues to be one of our most vital forces while carrying the results of polio. Walter Lively [in the worst ghetto area in East Baltimore] and Dr. Daniel Thurz [head of University of Maryland School of Social Work] are wealthy with the credentials to meet these challenges though starting from rather opposite ends of the spectrum. There are others.

Walter went on to mention Dennis Crosby for his crusade for quality education, Roscoe Herring and Fred Jones, demonstrators in "the pre-Target-City days" who had become heads of strong neighborhood associations, and Michael Schwerner who "got his baptism at Gwynn Oak Park."

Walter also was pleading his own health, his need to make a living, and the guilt he felt at neglecting his family as reasons he felt no longer able to lead. By that October of 1967, the Activists, too, seemed ready to abandon their endeavor to end housing discrimination, either inside or outside the ghetto.

Thurgood Marshall and the NAACP had put their trust in the law to end segregation and some strides had been achieved; Martin Luther King, James Farmer, Walter Carter and so many others[134] had looked beyond the law and attempted to touch Americans' hearts and souls, and they, too, had won some victories; then, "Black Power", assassinations, riots and the Vietnam War intervened to disrupt the progress of both these methods.

The unity of goal to achieve integration—black and white together—seemed at an end. "Black Power" nationally and "Target City" locally, with their attacks on white liberals and emphasis on the poor had ended "togetherness" and made "class" into a divisive issue. It was the end of an era, but it was not yet be the end of either the Activists or of Walter Carter's leadership.

•••

It is hard to say whether this decline in the civil rights movement encouraged the Ku Klux Klan in Maryland. Small

---

[134] There were dozens and dozens of activists in Baltimore and Maryland alone during the 1960s who should be remembered—young and old, professionals and blue-collar workers, black and white. Together they faced indignities, sometimes police brutality, and often arrests, many time and time again, in an effort to open Maryland's houses, schools, restaurants, stores, theaters, beaches, pools, parks and the rest to all races. Any attempt to list them all is impossible.

though their numbers night have been, they clearly still had the ability to intimidate.

> In 1968 in Cecil County, an unnamed paper reported the arrest of a 36-year old Ku Klux Klan member for attempting to bomb a civil rights leader's home.
>
> Police were staking out the Negro leader's home following a tip that another attempt to level it with a bomb would be made. A bomb had been set off there late last month.
>
> Police confiscated a 12-stick bundle of fused and capped dynamite which had been placed near the house about 2 a.m.

The police said the bundle "would have demolished the house, which is a cinder-block bungalow on Red Toad road in the Somerville area." Some white neighbors expressed shock: "He is an outstanding colored man. I don't think anybody should be bombed out." "They're real nice people."

A year later, in 1969, an unnamed paper reported on a cross-burning rally of the Ku Klux Klan on a farm hilltop in Finksburg, Maryland that drew 170 men, women and children, "some in the flowing satin robes of the Klan." It continued:

> The 30-foot cross, set afire by   eleven torch-bearing Klansmen, while a record player blared 'The Old Rugged Cross; could be seen for four miles through the dark green valleys of Carroll county.

Speeches denounced Negroes and claimed that politicians were "running this country straight down hill."

> The bullets spent on all those civil rights workers and the likes of Martin Luther King and Robert Kennedy and that brother Jack of his were well spent as far as I am concerned.

They claimed the Klan was recruiting members as fast as the NAACP.

Bill Moore & Walter Carter

After Walter Carter, in 1966, renounced any leadership role in the Activists, he turned his energies to a favorite project he'd had little time for until then—the creation of "an Educational Center devoted to the exciting history and culture of Black Americans" in the three-story row house that had been Bill Moore's home before he left for Mississippi in the spring of 1963. It seemed a fitting time for such an undertaking since it was Bill Moore's death that year that had prompted Walter's *first* resignation as Chairman of CORE.

Thoroughly disgusted when he heard of his death, Walter had said: "Bill saved his money to pay for his own death; for [the sake of] living individuals who do not have enough respect for their own rights and the rights of their fellowmen to send CORE a lousy dollar bill....you get so angry you do not know who to strike at sometimes." He was Baltimore CORE's first member to be martyred in nonviolent action.

Walter's goal now was to have a formal opening of the Bill Moore House on April 23, 1967, the 4th anniversary of his death.

●●●

Bill Moore was a tall blond, 35-year old ex-Marine, a postman, a member of CORE, who was murdered on April 23, 1963 as he was walking to Mississippi to deliver a letter to Governor Barnett. His body was found that night on a desolate stretch of highway in front of a roadside park near Attalla, Alabama. He had been shot in the head.[135]

When Bill was asked about people calling him a "rebel" and a "screwball," he would agree. And he never tried to hide the fact he'd spent time in a New York State mental institution as a schizophrenic, but rather had written his autobiography titled, *The Mind in Chains*, published in 1955.

Bill began his Freedom Walk modestly with a 27-mile trek to Annapolis on February 18, during the Northwood theater

---

[135] This account is a composite based on clippings from the *Afro* and various other newspapers (most not named); from copies of letters from both local and national CORE; from a partial diary kept by CORE and SNCC members who undertook to complete Moore's walk; and accounts of the final memorial service in Baltimore.

demonstrations, delivering a note to the Secretary of the Senate asking that "we place human rights above property rights, and abolish segregation in all forms in the state of Maryland.

Then, on Friday, March 22, he made the 41-mile trek to Washington D.C. carrying a letter to President Kennedy. It told of his planned 1,000 mile Freedom Walk from the White House to Mississippi, within the next few months, to deliver a letter to Governor Barnett— "the furthest I've ever walked to deliver a letter."

He went on to explain that two of his great grandfathers were from Mississippi; had fought in the Civil War. "I was raised for seven years in that state...The South is like my second home. I used to think as they now think...." He had spent four years in the marines, served in the Pacific during World War II, had lived in England and Spain, and had only moved from Binghampton, New York to Baltimore in November of 1962.

Announcing that a postman always rings twice, Bill made a second attempt to see the President on April 20 before he headed south for Mississippi. In this letter he told the President if he wished to write to

Picture of **Bill Moore** found on CORE brochure. Source of original unknown.

Governor Barnett, "I would be delighted to have the opportunity to deliver your letter also."

> I will be engaged in interstate travel, and, theoretically, under the protection of the 14th Amendment to the Constitution...I am not making this walk to demonstrate either federal rights or state rights, but individual rights....hopefully, to illustrate that the most basic of freedoms of peaceful protest is not altogether extinguished down there. I do not believe that such a walk has ever been undertaken before. I want to show that it can be done.

Bill was not allowed to see the president. He left from D.C. that evening by bus for Chattanooga, Tennessee where he started his walk, having refused to heed Walter Carter's urging that he wait a week before starting his walk so he, too, could go along. Bill was wearing two signs, back and front: "End Segregation in America" (sometimes another that read, "Eat at Joe's, both Black and White") and "Equal Rights for All— Mississippi or bust." His letter to Governor Barnett said, in part: "The White Man cannot be truly free himself until all men have their rights." He urged the Governor to be gracious.

> Give more than is immediately demanded of you. Make certain that when the Negro gets his rights and his vote that he does not, in the process, learn to treat the white man with the contempt and disdain that, unfortunately, some of us now treat him.

•••

Maybe Bill would have been pleased that his death had finally gotten the attention of President Kennedy. At a news conference, he called the shooting "an outrageous crime," and said the FBI would be offered to help in the case. Baltimore CORE determined to organize a mass march of major civil-rights organizations to continue the march, calling it the "Moore Trek;" they asked the Attorney General Robert Kennedy for a Federal investigation. We've already quoted Walter Carter's reaction to the murder. One letter-to-the editor expresses another Baltimoreans reaction:

> ...I am tired of being taxed to death to protect the rights of people in Laos, Germany and the rest of the world, and here in Mississippi and Alabama an American can be murdered and the Federal Government states it has no jurisdiction to do anything about it....If it is money that is needed, then I suggest that the foreign aid budget be cut a few hundred million dollars. If it is courage that is needed, then I suggest that the head of our Government ask God for it.
>
> Did the North win the Civil War to preserve the Union or did those who fought and died in that great struggle fight and die in vain?

In Alabama, state and county authorities immediately launched a massive search for the killer. Governor George Wallace, despite being a rigid segregationist, called the killing a "dastardly act" and offered a $1,000 reward for the arrest and conviction of the killer; he also warned those who sought to continue the trek that they would be arrested. Many of the residents in the community near where the shooting occurred seemed "ashamed and embarrassed;" some comments, "This wasn't a racial issue. It was just pure damned meanness," "It was a brutal, senseless and idiotic crime."

The diary found on Bill's body noted only small incidents his first three days, mostly name-calling, heckling; a few shouted supporting comments. The April 23rd entry also noted no special problems; the last entry:

> A couple of men who had talked to me before drove up and questioned my religious and political beliefs. And one was sure I'd be killed...Feet sore all over. Shoes too painful, walking without them. Adopted by hungry, thirsty road-foolish dog. Only kids adopt dogs.

Only two days after the rifle shooting that left a sprawled body with shots to his face and back of his head, blood-spattering on the signs he was carrying, two suspects had been taken into custody by the sheriffs of Dekalb and Etowah counties (questioned and later released); a third man, Floyd Simpson, was being sought. On April 28, this 40 year-old shopkeeper with six children was charged with first-degree murder. Matching tire tracks and a ballistics report on his .22 rifle had led to his arrest and charge.

Bill Moore left a wife and three children from a previous marriage. About 150 persons attended his funeral in Binghampton on April 27, 1963—about 600 others gathering outside the crowded funeral home. The services were broadcast on television. Baltimore CORE, with the sponsorship of twenty-one civic and community groups and five individuals, began to plan a memorial service in Baltimore for Sunday, May 5th, while SNCC and CORE continued with their plans for 15 to 20 "disciplined" white and black members from each group to complete Moore's walk. James Farmer, head of national CORE said:

> [This Freedom Walk will constitute] a dialogue with America, a case of pointing out that this man's murder, while an isolated act, was symptomatic of the schizophrenia in American life.

Eight blacks who were members of SNCC were arrested on May 1st when they joined walkers in Attalla, Alabama. Twenty-two of those, blacks and whites, who already had trekked through Georgia, were arrested, as they expected, when they crossed into Alabama. They'd already been pelted with eggs and one had been hit with a rock. All of the *marchers* were charged with disturbance of the peace. All refused to accept bail while awaiting the decision of a U.S. District Court hearing on an injunction filed to prevent their arrest—a hearing which would not be held before May 17. A dozen Alabama patrolmen with clubs extended had prevented newsmen from crossing the border with the marchers.

After the 55-minute Memorial Service at the Unitarian Church in Baltimore on May 5th, Bill Moore's widow told the *Afro*, "It was the most beautiful thing I have ever seen in all my life. Please tell them how happy they made me and I'll be grateful for the rest of my life." The 900 seat church was full as "glowing homage" was paid to the Freedom Walker. Morgan Singers from the State College sang "You'll Never Walk Alone," "My Lord, What a Mornin'", "Let Us Cheer the Weary Traveler," and "I'll Never Turn Back No More." A ballad, sung to the tune of "You've Got to Walk that Lonesome Valley," was written by Don West for the memorial service honoring his memory:

> Chorus: Oh, Bill Moore walked that lone-some high-way,
> He dared to walk there by him-self,
> None of us here were walk-ing with him,
> He walked that high-way by him-self.
>
> Verses:
> Yes, he walked to A-la-ba-ma,
> He walked that road for you and me,
> In his life there was the pur-pose,
> That black and white might both be free.
>
> He walked for peace, he walked for freedom,
> He walked for truth, he walked for right
> End segregation in this country
> Eat at Joe's both black and white.
>
> The lyncher's bullets know no color
> As they come whining thru the night,
> They've brought death to many a Negro
> And William Moore whose skin was white.

They shot him down in cold blood murder
Two bullet holes were in his head,
His body lay upon the road-way
Where lynchers left him cold and dead.

Each man must walk his lonesome highway
Each must decide it for himself,
No one else can do that for you,
You've got to walk there by yourself!

Some day we'll all walk there together
And we'll knock on Freedom's door
And if they ask, who was it sent you,
We'll say a man named William Moore.

He walked for peace, he walked for freedom
He walked for truth, he walked for right,
End segregation in this country
Eat at Joe's, both black and white.

•••

Afterwards, a number of Bill Moore's friends purchased the house where he had lived and established the William L. Moore Foundation. Later, Hal Smith who'd given $8,000 toward the $10,000 purchase price, said raising the money for the purchase was easy compared to the difficulty later encountered in trying to get non-profit status for the Bill Moore Foundation.

Dr. Wickwire and Walter Carter both testified to its goals at the IRS, and sought to refute arguments that it was an "activist front" for CORE. But, with Walter involved, they kept insisting, "How could it not have an activist purpose?" The opening paragraph of a letter to prospective Board members is enlightening, however, regarding CORE's view of the significance of the house.

Even though CORE is an organization that believes that direct action is now needed to bring about our goals of freedom, equality and human dignity, we are also concerned about deeper aspects of this "Freedom Generation." For this reason CORE bought the Bill Moore house in 1963 and is concerned that it be opened as a lasting Human Rights Center dedicated to the collection and preservation of records relating to the freedom movement and to an awakening and deepening of understanding of the Negro and his role in our society.

Ironically, Walter and this writer were working at the Bill Moore House on June 6, 1966 when we heard that James Meredith, another loner, had been shot on the first day of *his* walk to Mississippi. A black contractor had just been hired to renovate the place, install new electric wiring, build shelves and panel over the old, cracked plaster walls. We were in the process of deciding which kind of paneling we wanted.

I had been coming there off and on for months, working under Marva Dates' instruction (another member of CORE and a Librarian at the Enoch Pratt), sorting through and cataloging books. They were in cartons and paper sacks, scattered willy-nilly in every room—books on blacks Walter had been collecting for years—others donated by friends. My husband wrote a letter to his publisher, John Wiley and Sons, asking them to contribute any relevant books they publish. There were approximately 1,000 books by the time it opened.

On one wall of the reception room was a photo of Bill Moore, wearing the placard that read, "End Segregation in America" on one side, and "Black Or White Eat At Joe's" on the other. Beside it hung one of President Kennedy, also murdered in 1963. On the wall opposite was a painting by the Negro artist, John Fayson, Jr., then an inmate of the Maryland State Penitentiary, serving a ten-year sentence for burglary, that had been donated by his attorney, Fred Weisgal. There were other donated paintings lining the walls of an upstairs room where it was hoped lectures, drama and films would take place.

A group of sorority women, including Walter's wife, Joy, and his sister, Philathea, were also meeting there evenings, planning a fund-raising lottery—the main prize an elegant fur coat that had been donated for that purpose. Later, a breakfast at the Bill Moore House was planned for the Board of Directors, all the ministers, and civil rights leaders who had supported CORE—to "show off" the place and to gain their help in fund raising. Altogether close to $20,000 was raised before the Center's opening in April of 1967; an occasion that got excellent press coverage locally and nationally.

Folks were reminded of Bill Moore's book, *The Mind in Chains,* about his service as a Marine; and of his joining with 400 Morgan State College students in jail during their desegregation struggle at the Northwood Theater (the first white to go to jail with them). Copies of his last letter to President Kennedy and the one he'd carried to Governor Barnett were handed out.

Those attending the Center's opening spilled out into the streets where chairs were arranged for them. Music was provided by a number of jazz groups, including the Freddie Hubbard quartet, and by others including the St. Agnes College Choir.[136]

•••

During lunch breaks and before we'd part for the evening after working together readying the center for its opening, Walter and I talked a great deal about the state of the movement—locally and nationally. It troubled Walter deeply that so many blacks didn't *feel* equal—no matter what they might say. And he hoped that seeing at the Center all that blacks had achieved in their own right would increase their belief in themselves.

At times Walter talked about himself taking a different role in the movement—toyed with the idea of abandoning the fight for "integration" and starting a "black" movement focused on heightening black self-esteem. He talked of "black power" long before Stokely Carmichael created a stir shouting "Black Power" during the continuation of the "Meredith March" by civil rights activists.

Walter thought of black power as a positive force, and believed, if coupled with "black is beautiful," it would build pride and self-confidence. Blacks would then not try to be "as white as possible" by bleaching their skin and straightening their hair. He wanted "black power" to tumble down "white power" in order to create "people power." He was against its use as a vehicle for separatism, as had been preached in the past by Garvey and then by the black Muslims (to be followed in the future by Farrakhan).

Yet he admired many things about the Black Muslims,

---

[136] It is regrettable that the Center was later allowed to go into bankruptcy and sold by the bank. What happened to its wonderful collection is unknown. This demise of a place with such potential happened after this writer had left Baltimore. An attempt to stop the bank sale, occurring the very month of her return to Baltimore, was unsuccessful.

and especially appreciated Malcolm X. During the time when there was much fear amongst the general public of violence by the Black Muslims, engendered mostly by the press, Walter would explain to me how Malcolm *prevented* violence, as no one else could. "Don't you know he stopped a riot in Harlem with his very eloquence," he'd explain. "His fiery, anti-white speeches were outlets for pent-up hate and violence, not really calls for violence."

Later that year (during 1967), after Walter left his position with the school system and accepted an appointment as Assistant Director of the VISTA Training Center, he included militants in the panels of speakers brought together as part of the trainees program. He thought it important they hear not only his own point of view regarding black-white relations, but that of the Black Muslims and of Julius Hobson, who'd left CORE to found a more militant civil rights group, ACT, in D.C. I frequently went down to hear these fascinating discussions and got quite used to seeing the Muslim women dressed in their long, flowing white gowns and head scarves—no matter how hot—and men talk about the blue-eyed white devils. They did not generate fear despite their fear-provoking words, and did provoke admiration with their ability to increase membership amongst the poor and criminals and inspire them to turn their lives around.

•••

Dr. August Meier, then Morgan State College history professor and advisor to its student activist group (CIG) whom we've encountered previously, described the appeal of the Black Muslims:

> To those willing to submit to its rigid discipline, the Nation of Islam gave a sense of purpose and destiny. Its program offered them four things: an explanation of their plight (white devils); a sense of pride and self-esteem (black superiority); a vision of a glorious future (black ascendancy) and a practical program of uplift (working hard, saving money, and uniting to create Negro enterprises and prosperity)....[They] were a distinct help to the civil rights organizations, for their talk of violence and their hatred of blue-eyed devils frightened white people into becoming somewhat more amenable to the demands of the

integrationists.[137]

Meier's understanding, even appreciation, of the Muslims grew, perhaps, out of the debate he'd had on March 28, 1962 with Malcolm X, then the Muslim's most famous member. Before an audience numbering some 1,400 at Morgan State College, they had taken part in what the *Afro* described as a verbal slugfest; they stood toe to toe, quarter neither asked nor given.[138] Each talked for thirty minutes, followed by twenty minute rebuttals. Malcolm's main points as reported by the *Afro*:

> "The only way for the colored man in America to achieve equality is to ask the white man for his 300 years of wages he should have received as a slave, in the form of land, and to start a new state.... Segregation is something a superior forces on an inferior. But separation is an action between equals...." He criticized civil rights groups for trying to "force integration."...He called President John F. Kennedy a "political hypocrite."

While Meier reportedly questioned how separation was possible.

> Since the basic resources are owned by white men, it would be futile to try to support an economy without these resources." He also asked where a proposed new state would be located. He proclaimed that the issue was not integration but "how are we going to achieve the cause of human dignity in this country." He said the sit-in movement was being more successful than the Muslims in achieving this goal....The kind of doctrine the Muslims preach is the same as that which such groups as the Nazis and the fascists preached—supremacy and a deified leader. These movements have their greatest appeals in moments of crisis....The stereotype picture of the white man which the Muslims have is the same stereotype that whites have of colored people." He accused the Muslims of hiding behind their color because they were afraid to compete with whites.

The *Afro* concluded its report by stating that a question and answer period followed the talks, and after it was all over, 100 students crowded around the Muslim leader asking

---

[137] Meier & Rudwick (eds.), *Black Protest...*, Intro, pp. 13-14.
[138] *Afro*, March 31, 1962.

questions. Meier is said later to have referred to the debate as
an exhilarating experience.

•••

I suppose it was at least partly because of the debates I
heard at VISTA and my discussions with Walter that I was not
"put off" when black power seemed suddenly to take the
nation by storm, alienating many previously supportive white
liberals. Like Walter, I thought the black power advocates were
probably right—that it was a necessary part of making blacks
feel equal, a prerequisite for their taking an equal place in our
society beside whites. I had heard Walter proclaim so often,
"How can you be equal if you don't feel equal?" Walter had
prepared me for "black power," just as he had made me
understand so many things about blacks and their fight for
equality.

CORE & the Poor

A slum area is the most expensive real estate in any city. It affords little in the way of taxes, yet it consumes tax money with abandon. Some of this money is for social services to alleviate the symptoms of poverty. Much of it is for police, prisons, hospitals for alcoholics and drug addicts, and similar economic waste as well as waste of human lives. Rev. John F. Cronin, S.S., Catholic Review, 7/1/66

It wasn't "black power" that had decimated Baltimore CORE at the height of its Horizon House project in May 1966, but more a lack of appreciation of the organization as a whole by those who'd arrived from national. Clearly they never understood our Horizon House project and seemed oblivious to the projects we'd simultaneously undertaken on behalf of the inner city poor.

Ourselves recognizing the latter efforts as inadequate, Baltimore CORE, at first, welcomed the arrival of Target City, expecting that their added money, manpower and intent to focus on the inner city would supplant what we'd attempted there, and leave us to concentrate on opening up the housing market city-wide in order to relieve the growing black pressures for access to more and better housing.

It was unfortunate for all concerned that Target City did not provide the support we'd looked forward to; that it was not more open to learning what Baltimore CORE had done prior to their arrival.

•••

In 1965, at a time when Baltimore CORE was most active in seeking to make "housing choice" a reality for all, it formed an Urban Renewal Committee. Its mandate was to explore the connection between "choice" and the city's urban renewal, slum housing, and public housing policies that were based on the city's long-held "containment policy" previously discussed. Heading the committee were William Bush, a long-time active CORE member who was especially interested in slum housing issues, and Billie Bramhall, an employee of Hoffman Associates, which had been hired by the city to prepare a "Five-Year Plan" for Baltimore's future development. We've already met Billie as she tackled the issue of school integration, beginning in 1961 and continuing until 1968 when she left Baltimore. But she also added her thoroughness and insightfulness to the housing issues surrounding urban renewal.

The first task of the new committee was to become familiar with the Urban Renewal Act and how it impacted on housing in the black community. Could CORE justify a demand to cut-off urban renewal funds to Baltimore until it passed Fair Housing legislation?

It surprised and pleased CORE when Mayor McKeldin stated his support for such a policy at a September 13, 1965 meeting of Baltimore Neighborhoods, Inc.—a nonprofit organization, mentioned earlier, that sought to stabilize the city's racially mixed residential sections through education, and to broaden housing opportunities for blacks by making discrimination unpopular.

At the same time that Mayor McKeldin had made his statement, William Bush asked Robert Weaver, then the administrator of the Federal Housing and Home Finance Agency, to take a similar stand, but Weaver declined.

After the Mayor announced his support for a moratorium on Urban Renewal, the City Council President, Thomas D'Alesandro, III, asked the Mayor to rescind his statement and declare that urban renewal and fair housing were best kept as separate problems. "No sense in mustering the joint opposition into a single, formidable army," D'Alesandro said.... "This tactic will not gain councilmanic support for fair housing legislation and it could lead us to a dead-end street with no urban renewal and no fair housing legislation." After this attack, Mayor McKeldin did seek to back down from his statement supporting the withholding of federal funds, but he's already been heard by over fifty attendees at the BNI meeting.

In the Fall of 1965, President Johnson pushed through legislation that created the Department of Housing and Urban Development (HUD). Early in 1966, soon after his appointment to head this new department, the Housing Committee wrote Secretary Robert Weaver,[139] with copies to President Johnson,

---

[139] Weaver was a Harvard-educated economist, once an advisor to President Roosevelt on "black issues," and later appointed to various government positions. He was the first black to serve in a President's

Attorney General Katzenbach and a number of others—as well as to all the media (all typed on stencils and run off by me, as were all such documents prepared by CORE). Signed by James Griffin, Baltimore CORE Chairman, Walter Carter, Special Projects Chairman, and Sampson Green and myself as Housing Co-Chairs, the letter outlined CORE's position:[140]

> We are writing to you in sheer desperation after months of non-violent demonstrations and negotiations to break down the walls of the Negro housing ghetto in Baltimore. Despite the concerted efforts of civil rights groups in Baltimore, not one new home or apartment outside the ghetto is open to Negroes in all of metropolitan Baltimore. The Baltimore City Council has rejected a fair housing ordinance for the third time and the surrounding counties refuse even to consider fair housing legislation.
>
> Unless something is done now to sever the housing noose that is strangling the Negro community here, Baltimore is certain to erupt in the same destructive way that so many other large cities have erupted in past summers. The right to a free choice of decent housing cannot be ignored except at the city's peril.
>
> Negroes make up 40% of Baltimore's population, but the white people of the city pretend that we are not there at all, and exclude us from the political and economic power structure. We are the sixth largest city in the nation, located only an hour's drive from Washington, but the federal government pretends that we are not here either.
>
> Mr. Weaver, you understand the Negro housing ghetto and its causes and effects better than anyone else in the country. You have written extensively on this and related subjects; you have endorsed government efforts to achieve fair housing; and you have for years directed government housing programs. But in Baltimore your influence has not been felt.
>
> In fact, the very agencies which you direct have in Baltimore been the agents of housing segregation. Under the urban renewal programs which your agency finances,

---

Cabinet., appointed by President Johnson in 1966 after the creation of the Department of Housing and Urban Development (HUD).

[140] Why neither the letter nor the attendees at the meeting that followed were from the Urban Renewal Committee I'm now unsure, but I believe it must have been because that committee was conceived of as primarily a research committee.

Negroes are being forced out of their homes. They are being forced into already over-crowded Negro slums or into segregated public housing, also financed by your agency. Negroes are barred completely from your agency's FHA-insured housing, despite the President's Executive Order on Equal Opportunity in Housing. Thus, your agency's action or inaction is resulting in the perpetuation and extension of slums and segregation in this City.

The facts have been abundantly documented before federal, state, city, and county investigating bodies. They have been attested to by CORE officials and members who have been insulted and turned away in FHA-insured developments as in others. [Quotes from reports follow and statements of reports that HUD has in its office—and fact that despite this, FHA, public housing, and builders still receive federal funding from his office...]

In Baltimore, Federal and City complicity in slums and segregation have created a crisis so grave that it calls for immediate action. I urgently request that you meet at once with officials of CORE to plan a federal action program in Baltimore to eliminate all federal subsidy of slums and segregation.

The letter stated the specific demands CORE proposed to discuss with Weaver:

1. That you publicly acknowledge the proven fact that housing discrimination is total in Baltimore, that there is no need for further investigation, and that action is urgent.

2. That you personally visit Baltimore to make it clear to city officials and the real estate industry that they are required to take affirmative action to achieve integrated housing wherever federal funds are involved.

3. That you spell out an affirmative program for immediate integration of all government-aided housing and renewal activities with statistical checks on compliance.

4. That you cut off federal funds from all government-aided housing and renewal until there is positive evidence that desegregation has taken place.

The letter closed by urging Weaver to take prompt, vigorous, and meaningful action. "We can assure you that we intend to pursue this matter with determination. Please let us know by return mail when we can meet with you."

Weaver did reply and on Friday afternoon, March 11th we had a three-hour meeting in Washington, D.C. with him and top officials in his department. We discussed the issues raised in CORE's letter, our demands and the actions Weaver planned to undertake. On April 7 we received a letter from him asking us to document the information we had regarding discriminatory practices, as soon as possible, and "you are assured that it and all other such complaints will be promptly processed and sanctions applied as the facts warrant."

Since we felt Weaver already had all the documentation he needed—and the power to act—we wrote a letter, signed by the same four persons, to President Johnson, reviewing again the number of studies already in the hands of HUD and asking him to "instruct the Secretary to immediately institute an action program...and advise him as to the action programs he may carry out under present executive authority." Despite feeling it was not needed for HUD to act, CORE started a major study of Baltimore's urban renewal practices, which would take the better part of a year to complete.

Additionally, representatives of CORE continued to meet with FHA officials (who were the most recalcitrant in even acknowledging the problem), and with Baltimore's Urban Renewal and Housing agency (BURHA) regarding segregation in public housing—succeeding in getting a plan from them that would give priority, as vacancies occurred, to blacks willing to move into now all-white public housing projects and to whites willing to move into now all-black projects.

Bob Embry, then head of BURHA, implemented the plan and it worked for a time, but never really succeeded in achieving integrated public housing developments—few blacks were willing to face the verbal, even physical attacks, they faced, or feared facing, in a "white" building, and even fewer whites would even consider moving into a "black" building.

•••

In mid-February 1966, the Potomac Institute, a private non-profit research agency, released a report declaring that open housing legislation was unnecessary because the government already had the power to enforce fair housing under Title VI of the 1964 civil rights law. The Institute reasoned that since there is federal involvement in the building of almost all new housing—roads, water, sewers, electricity, education, etc.—the law which barred discrimination in *all* facilities using federal funds should be applied to housing.

The Institute proposed that federal money be withheld from an area or neighborhood which practices racial exclusion—that federal agencies require housing desegregation plans from communities before releasing the moneys allotted them [a proposal that members of CORE and the Activists would also soon put forward, much to the consternation of the city's power-brokers.] The Potomac Institute report said the about-three million colored citizens living in thirteen metropolitan areas across the country, including Baltimore, were denied desegregated housing because these areas had no open occupancy legislation.

•••

The study CORE's Urban Renewal Committee undertook in 1965 after its meetings with HUD Secretary, Robert Weaver, was not yet complete when the Activists parted from CORE,[141] so it ended up as an Activist project. Billie Bramhall was still its driving force, aided by this writer and Neil Curran, a friend of Billie's and an employee of Baltimore's Urban Renewal Agency. Neil surreptitiously supplied us with many of their internal agency documents, while Billie brought us copies of the housing-related materials, not in the public domain, from the Hoffman Associates where she worked in preparing the City's Five-Year Plan.

For a year, the three of us met together with some frequency to discuss what documents we needed and how best to write the report so the connection between urban renewal, housing for blacks and Fair Housing legislation would be clear to the public. We wanted, among other things, to see if we could justify a cutting-off of urban renewal funds to Baltimore until they passed Fair Housing legislation.

We titled the final twelve-page report, completed in August 1966, *"Recommendations and Analysis: Baltimore Urban Renewal and Housing Agency (BURHA) and Department of Housing and Urban Development (HUD)"*; a separate document of equal length was in the form of a talk. As usual I had typed both versions on stencils, and mimeographed dozens of

---

[141] The break-up described in section "CORE Ripped Apart."

copies—many of which we mailed to members of our new Activist organization, with a cover letter signed by Sampson Green as Chair.

In addition to the report's background analysis that reviewed all the relevant legislation, and statistics on Baltimore's urban renewal, public housing and relocation actions since the Housing Act of 1949, there was a summary of the city's future plans and a set of ten recommendations (three dealing with specific projects not reproduced). The report began—

...After discussions with HUD and BURHA officials, consideration of legislation and practices in other cities, and a careful analysis of the past, present, and future proposals for Baltimore, the Activist for Fair Housing make the following recommendations:

1. HUD should give immediate attention to strengthening and spelling out the requirements for an acceptable "Workable Program." Especial consideration should be given to Senator Robert Kennedy's proposal to amend the Workable Program requirement of Urban Renewal to make it area-wide, and to make it include a specific and affirmative plan for desegregation.

2. HUD must stop hiding behind the concept of "locally conceived, locally initiated, locally planned and locally carried out" programs as an excuse for their own inactions....[Shades of what's to come with Congress's 1995 proposals to turn already shaky federal mandates back to the states] The Housing Act and its amendments, the Executive Order of President Kennedy, and Title VI of the Civil Right Act are all tools that can be used by HUD now....The burden of proof [should be] left to the opponents that HUD is exceeding its legal mandate.

3. Fair Housing legislation is essential in the City, and, preferably, also in the surrounding counties. Relocation cannot be adequately undertaken without it. Until BURHA is able to make use of this essential tool, all further project funds should be withheld from Baltimore.

4. [All programs] intended to aid in relocation and increasing the low-cost housing supply should not be confined to urban renewal areas....All further funding for imple- mentation of these programs should be withheld until they can be use on a metropolitan-wide non-discriminatory basis.

5. Rehousing of slum families should receive priority over Urban Renewal projects that directly benefit the business

and professional community...All projects undertaken by BURHA should consider rehousing as a primary, not an auxiliary goal....first constructing the same number of new housing units that they plan to demolish...

6. A condition of eligibility for building contractors in any urban renewal project should be a pledge by the contractor that he will adhere to a policy of non-discrimination in employment, renting and selling in all his construction projects, not just in those undertaken for Urban Renewal.

7. All future Baltimore Urban Renewal project plans must be examined in light of the goal of a decent home in a decent environment with the intent of achieving, in the long run, quality, integrated environments for every American family. If plans cannot meet this criteria they should not be allowed to proceed further.

During the fall and winter months, Billie and I spoke to numerous church and civic groups about our findings and recommendations—often in a debate format with Jay Brodie from BURHA as our "opponent." Needless to say, the biggest controversy swirled around the demand that federal funds be withheld, but Billie Bramhall and this writer certainly did get the groups before whom we spoke *talking*. Our appearances ended with the request that individuals and representatives of church and civic groups write letters to HUD, BURHA, the press and others supporting our findings and recommendations. Unfortunately, funds were never cut off, and if our study had any impact on the way BURHA acted, it was not noticeable.

But we kept trying. Along with other members of the Activists, we worked with the attorneys, Fred Weisgal and Melvin Sykes, to develop a legal case to stop funding to all entities that discriminate. An eleven-page "proposal for a Comprehensive Suit Attacking Housing Discrimination" was prepared, full of legalese and citing numerous cases. The relief sought was described as "broad but realistic" and included:

A. Injunctions restraining licensing agencies from granting or renewing licenses to realtors, builders, financing institutions, title insurance companies and others who discriminate in public and private housing;...

D. Orders to zoning boards and planning commissions and related governmental activities to produce plans to "sanitize" their previous rulings and inducements which have aided the formation of the discriminatory pattern;

E. If the anti-trust approach is used, appropriate injunctions and treble damages.

Soon after Spiro Agnew's election, Activist members also put together a comprehensive letter sent to the new governor. It explained, quoting a number of legal cases and actions by other governors, why he should issue an "Executive Order" forbidding the Real Estate Commissioners (as an agent of the State whose members he appoints and whom he "supervises and regulates") from perpetuating "racial and other invidious discrimination" in purchase, sale, leasing, listings, advertising, etc. of housing.

I'm not sure now why our efforts to change HUD's policies, and why pursuit of these suits ended. Perhaps it had to do with the fact that Billie Bramhall left Baltimore for Pittsburgh in 1967, a year after our study was completed. Certainly she was missed by CORE's Urban Renewal Committee, just as she was by those on the City's Education Committee where she also played a vital role right up until the end. In Pittsburgh, Billie soon found a job with the city's Planning Office, having presented our study as part of her credentials. And after she moved again, to Denver, in 1975, she went to work for the city's Planning and Community Development office where she remained until her retirement.

It may simply have been that all thoughts of pursuing our suits stopped after the 1968 Supreme Court decision in *Jones v. Mayer* [392 US 409 1968] that found that the 1866 Civil Rights law passed pursuant to the 13th Amendment barred all housing discrimination, private as well as public."

> This decision, taken along with the 1968 Federal Housing Law [Civil Rights Act, title VIII, 42 USC 3601-3619 1976]—which prohibited discriminatory practices by real estate brokers, builders, and lenders—dismantled the dual housing market. In Baltimore and in the other urban areas that share much of this housing history, the white market and the black market merged into one housing market.
>
> Disappearance of the dual housing market does not mean that housing is desegregated, that racial discrimination has been eliminated, or that good housing is available for the poor. Residential housing in Baltimore remains in-large-part segregated... Baltimore's 15,000 public units, along with the

various federally subsidized units, fall far short of meeting the demand [of its poor and near-poor for decent housing]. And it is impossible to locate a new subsidized low-income housing project without encountering outraged community opposition. Thus most of Baltimore's poor (both black and white) continue to live under slum conditions.[142] [*Written in 1983, still true in 2001*]

The resistance to change is obvious when one notes that in 1968, Baltimore County withdrew its application for a Federal planning grant rather than comply with the requirement that they present evidence they were attempting to meet their low-income housing problems, and had plans for public facilities, land use, zoning and other relevant matters designed to meet national housing goals.[143]

•••

As the Urban Renewal report was being worked on under CORE's aegis, it took time, also, to explore complaints by the tenants on Fels Lane, a tiny black community in Ellicott City (just outside Baltimore), who were threatened with eviction. On August 30, 1966, at the invitation of one of Fels Lane's young tenants, Fred Weisgal, our attorney, and this writer met with the residents.

The city had taken over the property on Fels Lane as part of a fifty-two acre renewal area. A private developer had drawn up plans to erect garden apartments as replacements, renting for $65 to $85 a month. These would replace the houses they now lived in for $8 a week. Because it was taking the developer longer than expected to get funding, the city had become the resident's landlord.

Their houses were in dreadful condition. There was no inside plumbing and a single pump, located in a shed, the only source of water for the entire group. They wanted Fred's advice on starting a rent strike—and also help in preventing their removal until they were provided with alternate, decent housing. As we listened to them in the crowded, tiny living room, I wondered if they knew that this had been the birthplace

---

142 Power, *Apartheid...*, p. 322.
143 Hand-dated clipping from John Roemer's files; article by Gerald Fitzgerald, but no newspaper noted.

of Benjamin Banneker (in 1791)—a black astronomer, inventor, mathematician and gazetteer; an appointee of President Jefferson, credited by many of his biographers with having laid out the wagon-wheel-like street plan for Washington, D.C. I wondered, Were conditions like this when he lived here?

Their situation was similar to that of another small black group living in similar conditions in Towson, just north of Baltimore. They, too, had come to Fred. They, too, were fighting their removal by Baltimore County, in this instance to make way for new department stores and parking lots.

Regrettably there was little Fred could do for either group when the courts wouldn't allow rent to be put in escrow. And, as for CORE getting involved, there was too little money, the numbers directly affected were too small, their locations too remote, their causes too local. It was simply impossible to get the kind of publicity and widespread support needed to win fights like this; local CORE did not have the resources in people or money that a full-scale fight would have required.

•••

Unable to help these small groups of poor black tenants, CORE was, nonetheless, deeply involved in efforts to implement the War on Poverty Act passed by Congress in 1964. It began with The involvement began with a fierce struggle with Baltimore's elected officials who resisted all efforts to get more of the poor named to the boards which would implement the act.

The Poverty Act's stated intent in creating local Community Action Agencies (CAAs) was to shift the emphasis away from the national level to the poor themselves in local communities; to give them more say in identifying and solving their problems.

This was an exciting concept for all except the status quo establishment (the mayor, city hall, and the city's power brokers). Not without reason, the establishment regarded this as a federal effort to supercede local jurisdiction; an effort to bypass existing political machines in order to build patronage armies financially tied to Johnson and his allies—many of the same fears that had caused Baltimore to resist implementing programs initiated by President Roosevelt during the 1930s Depression.

CORE had immediately opposed the appointment of Morton Macht, part of the establishment, as head of the CAA created under the Act's mandate. But the inherent conflict with the elected officials was not solved when poor health forced Macht's resignation after a year. Following him were, first, Gordon Wohlman, head of the Geography Department at Johns Hopkins, and then, Parren Mitchell, a black with a history of supporting the goals represented by CAA.

It seemed the closer any grass-roots group came to gaining some power that might actually help eliminate the conditions of their poverty, the more road blocks they encountered—the City Council began to oppose all its programs claiming they were efforts toward back-door integration. It probably added to the Council's fears when Walter Carter left his position with the Department of Education to accept one as Assistant Director of the VISTA Training Center (for volunteers committed to work with the poor in implementing CAA programs). In March, Joseph Allen, City Solicitor, ruled that Baltimore's anti-poverty workers—those VISTA workers Walter Carter was training—could not participate in protests or demonstrations during their on-duty hours. By May 1967, the City Council was seeking to pass legislation that would change its relationship from an advisory role to one that would give them complete control over CAA's programs.

Some of this reaction was no doubt generated by the formation of a Rent Strike Committee that was fighting with the City Council for legislation to allow the withholding of rent as a weapon to force landlords to make needed repairs. The Committee's intent was primarily educational, but in meetings with them, Sampson Green and this writer, representing CORE's Housing Committee, urged the organizing of a rent strike. Meetings of this ad hoc group were held in the CAA office, but CAA itself remained neutral on the issue. After this meeting, a letter signed by Walter Carter, Sampson and me went to Mayor McKeldin with copies to the media. We urged the Mayor immediately to take actions within his power before "the heat of summer impregnates the mass of humans imprisoned around you in morbid squalor." Four actions were specified:

1. No more multiple dwelling licenses be granted until the house is fully inspected and brought up to full compliance

with 'standard dwelling' specifications

2. That all multiple dwelling units be frequently re-inspected and that any license now in effect or granted in the future immediately be revoked if a house is not kept up to 'standard dwelling' specifications.

3. That the numbers, salary, and qualifications of building inspectors be sufficiently high that these requirements can be fully, vigorously and immediately implemented.

4. That the Welfare Department be required to withhold welfare payments to clients for rent, to be held in escrow, until his dwelling unit meets standards. Simultaneously with this action, the landlord's license must be revoked so that he cannot evict the tenant with the prospect of renting to someone else.

During this time, CORE wrote one other biting attack on ghetto housing conditions that was distributed to all the news media. The statement began with an expression of CORE's support for the rent strike law; it urged lawmakers to "do everything within their power to eliminate the sickening slum conditions of Baltimore." The statement went on to deplore "the already crowded ghetto [which] is becoming more crowded as public policy increases the Negro demand for substandard slum property while at the same time refuses to adequately enforce health and decency standards with landlords." CORE concluded its letter:

It is our contention that 'respectable' segregationist realtors, publicly assisted housing programs, and public officials are all working together with the slumlords in allowing exploitation and dilapidation to grow to proportions that will soon become irremediable to the ultimate detriment of the Negro and to the whole community.

CORE agrees with rent strike law supporters' position that lawmakers must remove thousands of inner city residents or tenants from a feudal-like existence and relationship with their landlords 'by balancing justice toward the side of the tenant with new laws.'

As noted, VISTA workers were, in essence, banned from participating with the Rent Strike Committee and the law was defeated. Parren Mitchell complained that CAA was becoming increasingly subject to the whims of the politicians, something that was apparent after he resigned in 1968 to run for Congress.[144]

By that time in 1968, this writer was no longer active in the movement and Walter Carter had left his position at the VISTA Training Center to accept an appointment as Director of Community Organization for Model Cities. His qualifications to be the new head of CAA were obvious— especially since there had already been talk of merging the two agencies, CAA and Model Cities. I was surprised when Walter called me one evening while I was eating supper.

"I'm calling," he began, "because Mayor D'Alesandro has just asked me to be Director of the Community Action Agency." He sounded concerned at the enormity of responsibility he would be undertaking and asked me if I'd help—especially in providing the research-type materials he felt he'd need "to do the best job for his people," as he put it. As might be expected, I jumped at the opportunity he was offering to work with him again.

We arranged a lunch meeting for the next day at Jimmy Wu's Chinese restaurant on Charles Street. It felt good to be talking with Walter again, to hear him eagerly, eloquently, expound on the wonderful opportunity he felt this job offered him to help Baltimore's too-often neglected and discriminated against citizens. But, at the same time, he expressed his concern that he'd be restrained in his efforts by the bureaucracy, and simultaneously be perceived as having been bought off by becoming part of that bureaucracy. He needn't have worried; he was restrained before he even started.

Less than a month after our lunch meeting, the City Council refused to confirm Walter's appointment. The councilmen's memories were still too strong of the many times, as a leader of CORE, he had attacked them—too worried that he might actually achieve changes in Baltimore that they still opposed. When he called to express his disappointment and thank me for having been willing to help

---

[144] Parren was defeated on this first run, but elected when he ran again in 1970. Soon thereafter he initiated the still-functioning Congressional Black Caucus as a vehicle to give blacks a collective, hence stronger, voice.

him, he tried, as was his way, not to show his hurt, disappointment and bitterness but it was obvious. This was the last time I ever spoke to Walter.

Soon after, he resigned from Model Cities, saying, "When I came to this job, I asked that political influence be kept out, and nobody responded. I asked for a commitment, and it was not forth--coming." He went on to become "Special Assistant for Race and Poverty" to the Jesuit Provincial and an Associate Professor of Sociology at Loyola College. He also once more resumed the fight against housing exploitation in the black ghetto—a fight he was immersed in, literally, when he died—a fight we'll hear more of later.

Lack of adequate funding, along with these events explain in large part just why the well-intentioned Poverty Act never succeeded in conquering, even making a dent, in the pervasive inner-city poverty amongst blacks—not because government programs don't help, as is today's assessment of what happened, but because the power structure can't bear to see a success that might threaten its power. The immediate result of the Act's failure was increased frustration amongst the ghetto poor after having had their hopes raised. And so, paradoxically, it helped feed the increased and growing militancy amongst so many civil rights activists; it aided the rhetoric of the "black power" movement.

•••

This writer undertook one last project before leaving Baltimore. That project was compiling for Baltimore Neighborhoods, Inc. (BNI), for the first time, a compendium of the rights and obligations of both landlords and tenants.

In the fall of 1969 I went down to BNI's offices to talk to the director, George Laurent, about a possible job. I hoped he might have some sort of housing-related project I could work on, maybe mostly at home. He explained he had no funds to pay me, but that wasn't my concern. I wanted something challenging to *do*.

BNI's emphasis had always been to stop discrimination and block busting through testing and education. But it so happened at the time I approached him, George had been getting an increasing number of phone calls from tenants reporting lack of service by landlords and asking about their rights. There was no single resource available for answers. "How would I like to research and write a Landlord-Tenant Manual?" he asked me. It sounded like a great idea; an obvious extension of the work I'd collaborated on in the preparation of the Activist's Urban Renewal report. I eagerly said, "Yes."

I began to read, read and read; historical stuff about land laws, related articles and studies, and finally, the hodge-podge of existing laws and regulations that governed landlords and tenants in Maryland. Occasionally I called our lawyer-friend, Melvin Sykes, for guidance in ferreting out this information, and regularly I met with a BNI committee of attorneys and others involved with housing to review what I was doing. The attorneys seemed impressed by my thoroughness and accuracy, and by the recommendations I made for changes in the law. It gave my ego a much-needed boost.

By the time I left Baltimore, I had completed the first comprehensive "Manual of Landlord-Tenant Relations," as well as an accompanying "Study Paper." The Manual was published by BNI in September 1970 and has been updated annually ever since by an attorney. The study paper was used by George Laurent at legislative hearings; eventually resulting in changes that did, indeed, improve tenants' rights, including a new rent-escrow provision—at last.

Inner City's Challenge

Those in Baltimore CORE, who had already given so much of themselves to the Movement by 1966 when Target City CORE arrived on the scene, still hoped that, despite having created such havoc with our chapter, they would finally begin serious work with the poor as they'd promised.

However, we knew that even with commitment, doing so would not be an easy task. It is hard to get the poor involved since most are so occupied with just-surviving that they have little energy left for organized protest. Additionally, once fired up to demonstrate, they are more difficult to control than are the disciplined civil rights demonstrators committed to non-violence that CORE is used to dealing with. The specter raised of potential violence is what frightened many in the Baltimore community, especially when coupled with the new black power rhetoric.

A local newspaper reported in June 1966, that Target City, and what was left of the old CORE, had published a four-page pamphlet that adopted CORE's old slogan, "Break the Noose", for its title. Still grandiose in their intentions, they laid out a "master plan" that encompassed

> a campaign to get more people welfare benefits; efforts to unionize low-wage fields; an attack on urban renewal abuses and enforcement of housing codes; the establishment of 'freedom schools' to teach Negro history and culture; voter registration; and 'educating the community' for greater school improvement and racial integration.

The stated intent was to start in an area of about four blocks, bounded by Bond and Federal streets; Gay and Aisquith; Greenmount and North Schroeder; Linden and North avenues; Fremont and Washington boulevard; Pennsylvania and Lafayette. The area would later be extended to "the most densely Negro areas in the East and West Baltimore inner-city."

A *Sun* paper photo tells the story of one of their early efforts, which, perhaps surprisingly after all the recent black power rhetoric, is in keeping with such old-guard efforts as those supported by the NAACP.

Marchers on Pennsylvania Avenue, in the heart of the black community, as they
proceed across the city to remind people that voter registration closes today,
August 15, 1966. Photo courtesy of Mike Waller, Publisher, *Baltimore Sun*.

It is not known whether those from national were aware
of the long-existing organization, U-Join (Union for Jobs and
Income Now), also located in Baltimore's Eastside. It seems
likely that at least initially they were not, since they clearly
believed the poor had had no advocates until their arrival. As
its name suggests, U-JOIN was a labor-union oriented group,
headed by Walter Lively. Its stated purpose was to "give people
in the neighborhood more self-determination and more control
over their destinies."[145]Lively had formed the group in 1962,
with the help of students from Morgan, Hopkins and
Goucher,[146] soon after he moved to Baltimore from
Pennsylvania where he had helped form both NAACP and
CORE chapters.

---

[145] Unless otherwise cited, the information about Lively can be
found in "Organization Man for the Other America," James Dilts,
Sun, 6/16/68
[146] They later left the organization and it became all-black.

By 1962 he had already been jailed twenty-two times during demonstrations in the south and during the Route 40 Freedom Rides. When asked what he'd been doing at these, he said simply: "We were trying to become free."

It was in May 1966 that U-JOIN decided to tackle housing conditions in the ghetto. Their foray into this area began with an attack on the use of potbelly stoves, unvented gas heaters and manual hot water heaters, common in the ghetto, because they were responsible for an inordinate number of fires. U-JOIN circulated a petition demanding that a provision be inserted in Baltimore's new housing code outlawing them.

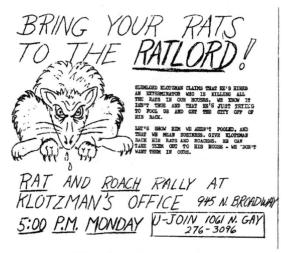

On May 24, 1966 (the very same day that CORE's housing trespass trials started), the *Sun* reported that U-JOIN was picketing in front of Jacob Klotzman's realty office with placards reading, "No Rent for Rats" and "Outlaw Pot-Bellied Stoves." After the landlords succeeded in defeating the provision, U-JOIN took on the landlords in earnest, picketing and demonstrating.

On August 16, they found themselves in People's Court (a strange name for a court that primarily rubber-stamps landlords' requests for evictions). Fred Weisgal was representing them when a very unusual event occurred—Judge Carl Bacharach upheld the rent strike of one of Klotzman's tenants after making a personal visit to the home and observing for himself the defunct light sockets, tilted floors, broken plaster, and a leak over the bathtub. Back in court, he said, "The lady of the house should be commended for the way things have been kept neat." He then appointed Weisgal to hold James Wilson's rent. "I'm going to see that the rent is not paid until repair work is done."

U-JOIN called this decision a victory. And Maryland Delegate Frank McCourt called it "a good thing, a necessary thing," adding, "It's about time the courts and the legislature took action. My rent strike bill, introduced last March was defeated. As a candidate for the senate, I will reintroduce that bill if elected." The defeated bill would have "established a special division of Peoples Court to tighten control over tenant evictions and require slum landlords to keep their properties in reasonable repair and in a habitable condition."[147] The formation of a Rent Strike Committee and its impact on the role of VISTA workers has already been discussed.

U-JOIN, immediately following the court's decision, began handing out leaflets to tenants in the area, 500 within just a few days, saying "Don't give your slumlord any rent this week if you want to get your house fixed up. Get in touch with U-JOIN. If your slumlord takes you to court, there is a good chance the judge won't give him the rent until after the house is fixed." They wanted to test Bacharach's decision which was so sharply at variance with the People Court's usual practice of enforcing a landlord's suit for rent.[148]

Klotzman wasted no time in his own test of the decision. First, the Wilsons, who had nine children, were evicted. After four years in the same house, the inspectors suddenly determined that the ceiling was too low on the two attic rooms that were used for sleeping. Then, Klotzman filed a writ of mandamus to get his $70 back, but Weisgal returned it voluntarily after the eviction, saying the case had become moot. Klotzman also appealed the right of a Rent Court judge to make such a ruling. Letting the decision stand would mean that any tenant could go on a rent strike to pressure landlords

---

[147] *Afro* 1/18/66. The earlier quotes are from *Afro*, 8/20/66.
[148] Clipping hand-dated 8/66 from John Roemer's files. Paper unstated; article by Daniel Drosdoff

into improving dwellings.[149]

With Judge Bacharach's apparent support of a tenant's

Eastsiders at Home Photo by
Carl X Harden; provided by David Eberhardt

right to withhold rent until repairs were made, it was surprising to learn a full two years later, on April 11, 1968[150] that the Judge himself was being charged "with failing to make repairs or to clean up trash and debris at #31 South Washington Street of which he is one of the owners."

The newspaper article reports that the judge was "embarrassed" at his court appearance (as he certainly should have been) and said he would take it upon himself to rehabilitate the property, something that should have been done a long time ago.

No doubt as a result of Bacharach's ruling in the Klotzman case and the continuing efforts to get a rent strike law passed, in November 1966, the inner-city landlords formed a new organization, the Metropolitan Property Owners Association, aimed at *protecting the rights of property owners*. On hearing about it, U-JOIN's attorney, Fred Weisgal, proclaimed:

This is the kind of thinking which is responsible for the deplorable conditions which exist in low-rent housing in Baltimore. Instead of concerning

---

[149] What could better demonstrate the upper hand of a landlord than the fact he could evict a tenant based on the illegal condition of his property—and still collect the rent.

[150] From John Roemer's files; newspaper not noted.

inhabitable living conditions and flagrant violations of the housing code and other innumerable wrongs which constantly afflict the poor tenant, these landlords concern themselves with only one thing—their pocketbooks.

Eastside Children's "Playground" Photo by Carl X Harden; provided by David Eberhardt

On January 30, 1967, Chief Judge Dulany Foster ruled that People's Court judges did not have the authority to hold rent money in escrow until housing violations were corrected. He expressed his sympathy with the intent, said he knew the awful conditions many were forced to live in, and declared there should be legislation enacted to remedy this. But, for now...

About this time, in a long two-part article for the *Catholic Review,* Michael Arisman wrote:[151]

If the combination of bias and economics serves to keep the bulk of the Negro population confined to the inner city, it is a combination of political indifference and undue consideration for slum landlords which keeps the city from

---

[151] The following quote and that by Judge Rogers are from a lengthy two-part article in this writer's files, dated only 6/3, but content suggests it was probably in 1967.

modernizing and enforcing housing and health codes. Whatever the views on the Negro, there is no evidence to suggest the majority of Baltimoreans oppose protection for tenants making housing complaints, defense of tenant rights in his dealings with the landlord, or the elimination of such safety and health hazards as pot-bellied stoves or horse stables in residential.

Judge Henry Rogers of People's Court is quoted as saying that "a housing court which is forbidden to consider anything but whether rent has been paid, and not whether necessary repairs have been made by the landlord, is wholly inadequate." It is hard to believe that these judges were totally powerless to make landlords comply with the city's own health and safety laws. As for Baltimoreans, in general, they may not have opposed decent housing for the poor, but neither did they stir themselves to support the tenants' demands for such nor the laws that would have helped them obtain it.

In 1967, Walter Lively, an independent, agreed to run for a City Council seat from the Second district on the Republican ticket. He "obtained two used suits from a minister, put $1 worth of leather patches on the elbows of his "65 cent sport coat, and became a candidate," his campaign costing him $30. He campaigned on "ridding the taxpayer of the cost of corruption"; was defeated by "the racist campaign conducted two of the Second district Democratic candidates."

Later Walter Lively took a position as head of the Urban Coalition, another group formed after passage of the 1964 Poverty Act. Its mandate was to "provide more business opportunities in the ghetto...; to combat racism in the city...; and to influence legislation..... But like a number of others, after the City Council refused to confirm Walter Carter to head the CAA, in October 1968, Lively resigned. The *News American* notes in a retrospective article on February 3, 1974 that at the time "some coalition members were unhappy with Lively's 'militant position on anti-poverty issues and his participation in neighborhood demonstrations.'" There is no doubt that Lively was a radical, which certainly would have upset the powers that be—"a little to the left of CORE and a little to the right of SNCC" (with whom they shared offices on North and Greenmount).

In November 1968, a month after Lively's resignation as head of the Urban Coalition, he became an international representative for the AFL-CIO American Federation of State, County and Municipal Employees.

By 1974, six years later, Lively, who, like Walter Carter, had once been thought to have the potential to be mayor of Baltimore, had seemingly dropped off the radar screen. He had left the union job, and was "devoting most of his time to a housing rehabilitation program in the Guilford area, [and] a printing shop operation."[152] He also "helped found the Baltimore Black History Museum in the old Broadway branch of the Enoch Pratt Free Library, which a community group he headed purchased at auction in 1971 for $5,000."[153] Madeline Murphy wrote of this:[154]

> His dream was to build the museum into an institution that would develop the cultural and organizational talents of neighborhood people, for he was concerned about the problems of the people who lived around the museum, who came to him for help, who needed a first aid station to patch up, temporarily, the trauma, the benign neglect and the festering cancers, brought on by a callously indifferent society.

Regrettably, by 1976, building was "vacant, unlocked, with windows broken and much of its interior ripped apart,"[155] reminiscent of the fate of the Bill Moore House, another attempt at a Black Community Museum that had failed. Things clearly had turned sour in this once promising leader's life; making news on May 22, 1976, not for his activism, but rather for shoplifting two New York strip steaks from a Giant Food Store in the Rotunda Mall that landed him in jail.

Then, only four months later, all the papers were recounting the life and achievements of this "mild mannered, vibrant personality" who had won a "multitude of friends in all segments of the community."[156] On September 10, 1976, at the remarkably youthful age of thirty-four, he had died at Johns Hopkins Hospital of an aneurysm, a cardiovascular ailment.

---

[152] *News American*, 2/3/1974
[153] *Evening Sun*, May 17, 1976.
[154] Afro, 9/18/1976
[155] *Evening Sun*, May 17, 1976.
[156] *Afro*, 12/7/68

Madeline Murphy said of him:[157]

> He had the tinge of brilliance, that forced people to re-
> think their beliefs, re-examine their biases and reshape their
> political philosophy.

•••

After the Activists, with Walter Carter's permission, took
over the old CORE office in the basement of his sister's house
on North Avenue, their Chairman, Jim Griffin, stayed with
CORE and moved with what was left of local CORE into Target
City's East Baltimore office. Jim recently told this writer that
afterwards he did a lot of door-to-door canvassing in the area,
soliciting information about the tenant's problems and seeking
their support.

Fred Weisgal also continued to represent CORE and
those at Target City rather than the Activists. Stu Wechsler,
one of those with Target City, recently recounted for this writer
one occasion that involved Weisgal—about a year after Target
City first came to Baltimore. It is indicative of both the
problems encountered in trying to organize the poor, and the
potential for violence that it can generate. The photo certainly
captures the police's readiness in case of violence.

Police on Eden Street. Photo by Carl X Harden; provided by David Eberhaardt

---

[157] *Afro*, 9/18/1976.

Stu's account follows.

> We were demonstrating in front of this segregated bar in the middle of a black area in East Baltimore. It was in response to the owner's shooting of a black kid. The demonstration was a kind of organizing tool, to get people out in the street, let them know CORE was there, and, hopefully, then reach them on other issues like housing and jobs. It got kind of dicey.
>
> I was driving a sound truck at the time and accused of running over a police officer, which I didn't do. Fred subpoenaed a television news clip of the incident and at the trial played the tape back and forth for about fifteen minutes. I was found not guilty. I thought Fred was a wonderful lawyer.

Of more importance than their integrating the bars was the organizing of Welfare mothers. Countering the growing separtist ideology of Target City, George Willey founded the National Welfare Rights Organization, an activist-oriented group that included both black and white welfare mothers as members. Its goal was to make sure all eligible mothers were enrolled in the welfare program and to improve the benefits available to them.[158]. Two photos help tell their story.

Dorothy Hutchinson, representing Welfare Mothers Committee, meets with Mayor McKeldin, complaining about school lunches and other issues.
Photo by Carl X Harden; provided by David Eberhardt.

---

[158] See Meier & Rudwick, *From Plantation to Ghetto*, p. 349

Children demonstate at Welfare Office. One sign, (the signs made by
the children) reads, "We Need More Clothes."
Photo by Carl X Harden; provided by David Eberhardt.

In addition to acting as Target City's attorney, Fred
Weisgal also helped the group obtain two manpower training
grants from the US Department of Labor that enabled them, in
co-operation with Humble Oil Corporation, to develop projects
intended to "train high school dropouts as gas station
attendants and managers."[159]

The first grant, in 1967, was for $121,475 and resulted in
59 of 101 trainees graduating, seventy employed and six
incarcerated. The second grant, a year later, was for $301,136,
the largest sum ever granted a civil rights organization. It was
intended to train 120 more gas station attendants and initiate a
new program to train sixty-four secretaries.[160]

Target City was prone to inflamatory rhetoric, but even
without it, the very fact of their working to better the lives of
poor blacks on the East Side roused whites in the area to their
own provocative rhetoric, as can be seen in Carl X's photo of
the demonstration organized by the White Citizens
Council/Birchites.

---

[159] Meier & Rudwick, *CORE*, p. 410.
[160] James D. Dilts, *Sun*, "The Warning Trumpet", 12/1/1968

Photo by Carl X Harden; provided by David Eberhardt.

Milton Holmes, a former union organizer, administered the job programs and took over as head of Target City after Danny Gant left and returned to New York. He clearly sought to tone down the violent rhetoric and proclaimed:

> We're trying to come up with more positive, democratic alternatives to violence. The potential of violence is definitely here because of the racist society we live in. The white people have not been sincere in their efforts to improve the status of black society. This one slice of bread we've received has just made us more hungry.[161]

The greatest challenge to their effectiveness on the Eastside may have come with the riots in April 1968.

•••

On Thursday, April 4, 1968, the Rev. Martin Luther King, Jr. was murdered in Memphis, Tennessee. On Friday, April 5 the worst riots Washington, D.C. had ever seen broke out.

Madeline Murphy recalled that the Baltimore "black community was in a catatonic state" At a meeting that evening of some of the black leaders, Danny Gant, chairman of CORE's Target City, called for out and out militancy, "vowed to

---

[161] James D. Dilts, *Sun*, "The Warning Trumpet", 12/1/1968

get guns and start up a revolution." But Walter Lively advocated a total work strike as the "only sane way to express our outrage." [162]

Murphy adds, "Our aim was to get all black people working as domestics, waitresses, etc. not to go to work, and we were at strategic bus stops with flyers the following morning at 6 a.m." Later they joined others at "Metropolitan Church in Lafayette Square to lay plans to diffuse the pent-up hostility by having a rally in Lafayette Square. But in the midst of the meeting on Saturday, all hell broke loose and we dispersed."

It was Saturday, April 6, 1968 that it broke out in Eastside Baltimore's inner city right near where U-JOIN and Target City had their offices. Along with these groups organizers, a number of black ministers began going into the communities where the most virulent rioting was going on; tirelessly trying to cool things down.

One of the few whites who dared join them was Dr. Chester Wickwire, Johns Hopkins Chaplain, who told this writer that he spent most of a night on the tumultuous, dangerous ghetto streets, working to prevent the spread of violence and looting to Hopkins and the suburbs. Black doctors arrived to treat those injured in the rioting.

After the curfew was declared for 4 p.m., black lawyers were recruited to defend the looters. Recently, Fred Weisgal's wife, Jeanne, told this writer that Major Gelston himself asked for Fred's help. She recounted:

> We were at a restaurant when Maj. Gelston sent a taxi for us. When we got to the Armory the fumes from spilled canisters of tear gas were horrible. Then we went to East Baltimore and brought out Danny Gant [one of those with CORE's Target City project]. He was scared.

According to Fred Weisgal's law partner, Morris Lasover, the courts were held open 24 hours a day during the riots, and for some time after, to process those arrested—and Fred, with little or no rest, spent many hours defending those charged with disorderly assault and breaking and entering. A year later one looter—typical of many others—described his

---

[162] A composite of two articles by Madeline Murphy in the *Afro*, 4/9/88 & 9/18/76.

experience for the *Sun*:

> I was on Prestman and Fremont...going over to [Pennsylvania] Avenue to hit a couple pawnshops...for a radio and maybe a good watch. A couple soldiers picked me up...I came up for trial the next week and the lawyer they gave me asked me whether I was guilty. I said, "By your standards, Yes." So he told me to plead guilty...because I was. The judge gave me probation.[163]

He went on to assess it, in retrospect, this way:

> The lawyer said it was fair, and I suppose it was...But I'd like to see the same sort of fairness applied to the Jew merchants who've been cheating us for years or the landlords. They're even worse crooks, but have you ever heard of any of them being arrested, tried and sentenced in less than three days without even having a witness appear against them. That's what I call white man's justice.

The organizers from Target City and U-JOIN also faced "white man's justice" even as they worked to stop the rioting. One such victim was Stu Wechsler, from national CORE, who recently told me how he came to get arrested and spend about a week in Jail.

> It was Palm Sunday, [April 7] during the day. There was marshal law and everyone was supposed to be off the streets. Gelston had given CORE people passes—said we could be out on the street helping until the regular army came in, but regular police didn't always agree with Gelston [whom they found too liberal, too tolerant of protesters], something we didn't know. So I went along when the police came into our office and asked me to come down to talk to some guy who refused to get off the street until he talked to me. I was about half way there when cop cars came from all over, jumped the curb in front of me, threw me in the car and drove to Eastern District. I was arrested and put in a jail cell with about fifteen people.
> This, despite having Gelston's pass in his pocket which he showed Councilman Bob Douglas when he was touring the jail. He took the pass and showed it to the Captain (a jail officer), and assumed he would then be released. But he never saw the pass nor Douglas again until the trial.

---

[163] *Sun*, April 7, 1969, "Long Way to Go..."

They kept everyone in jail for three days, without even permitting phone calls, so no one even knew where I was. Eventually, while they were out in the exercise yard, I managed to unscrew one of the call boxes dial "0," connecting to the prison switchboard.

In a ruff, gruff voice, I said, "Give me an outside line, please," and they gave it to me. I called CORE office and said, "Come get me." I'm not sure what happened next—if I got out on bail or if everyone was then released after processing. In any case, Fred was informed.

Stu had hardly been back in the CORE office before he was arrested again, because he "fit the description of somebody who'd been vandalizing property." But when no one could recognize him, because he wasn't the person involved, he was released.

I told my wife, "We're getting out of here." So we got in the car that night and drove up to New York—that was probably a week after the riots started—and stayed there till the riots were over.

Bob Douglas was the only witness Fred Weisgal called when the trial for violation of curfew started. After he told about the pass he'd given the Captain, Stu was found innocent.

I had been arrested by this real bad guy, Sgt. Francis, who was responsible for killing one of the only four people who died in the riots: two died in a fire, one was shot by a security guard, and one was shot in the back by a Baltimore City policeman. That was Sgt. Francis.

Walter Lively was another of those arrested while trying to calm the rioters. He was charged with fire bombing a store for no better reason than that he had been observed "as suspiciously present" at a number of fire scenes even before the police or firemen arrived. Lively declared he had been there "to help black people caught in the flames and to administer first aid."[164] The charge against him was later dropped. However, this was just one more occasion of the police hounding Lively because they regarded him as a "firebrand."

On the front page of the Tuesday, April 9, 1968 edition of

[164] *Sun*, 9/11/1976.

the *Baltimore Afro-American,*[165] two columns on the left are headlined, "Caisson drawn by 4 mules in final farewell," and the two columns of the right are headlined, "Five dead, 3,000 jailed, troops on duty." In between, under a photo of a "blazing inferno" are two other headlines, "Hanoi agrees to talk peace," and "Riot brings misery, suffering to innocent." The article on the right read:

"The whole block is on fire!"
"They are looting Provident Hospital!"
They are raiding Lutheran Hospital!"
"Fire bombs are falling everywhere!"
Baltimore's luck had run out.
A four-day nightmare is griping Baltimore with no signs of letting up....
These grim statistics ...
Five dead. 2,200 arrests. 3,000 hurt. Nearly 400 fires.
Property damage? No one knows. A conservative estimate by army officials put at "millions."
Human suffering and misery is also incalculable.
It is threatening to get worse.
...1,900 Federal troops—another 2,000 scheduled to be committed—General George M. Gelston concerned about still another problem—a food shortage.

The *News American* reported that on Palm Sunday morning, April 7 (the second day of Baltimore's riots): [166]

A young man in a purple suit wheeled home a shopping cart piled high with hams. Crowds grown sullen immobilized a passing automobile, a police car, and rained bottles on fire fighters. The firemen, tired and angry, crouched under their trucks and let a block burn while the National Guard tried to flush the people out of the buildings. On Sunday evening the President sent in five thousand regular soldiers. Tents bloomed again overnight like century plants in the city parks....
By Monday sleepless street people of CORE and U-JOIN were everywhere, "That's enough baby, you've taught 'em a lesson, now let's calm things down." Major Gelston's credibility and experience in Cambridge, Maryland, provided a basis for confidence. Six deaths were considered riot

---

[165] The *Afro-* was a twice weekly paper.
[166] Can be found in Olson, *Baltimore...* , pp. 382-383.

connected; rumors of sniping were never confirmed.... Twelve hundred fires had burned. Most of the thousand burnt-out stores were white owned, many Jewish owned, some owned by "soul brothers."...Some were places that had refused to serve blacks in the 1960s.

On Wednesday, twenty-two thousand Baltimoreans, black and white, trooped out to cheer the Oriole's opening day game. The mayor threw out the first ball....The fires dropped to two hundred, only a third over an average day.

There were still a few sporadic fires and lootings, but by Thursday, April 11 things had quieted down in Baltimore, and the governor lifted the midnight to 7 a.m. curfew, allowed the bars to re-open, and sales of gasoline to resume, but he kept the ban on firearm sales.

The Friday, April 12, 1968 edition of the Baltimore *Sun*, reported that some 190 food establishments had been looted, burned out or vandalized, and that lootings had numbered 1,987 and arrests 5,710 before they stopped keeping statistics. Ironically, the police announced that by the 12th no major crimes were being reported; adding that "the populace was behaving itself far better than on a normal weekday." With 4,900 regular troops and 5,700 Maryland National Guardsmen present in the city, this is hardly surprising.

It is well to note that despite the rampage and extensive destruction, it was property rather than people that was attacked. In their book, *From Plantation to Ghetto*, Meier and Rudwick conclude that the black masses by this time felt they could get away with destruction of property without facing white, retaliating mobs. These authors further contend that "when it became evident that the destruction in black neighborhoods hurt blacks as well as whites, that mostly blacks rather than whites were killed, and that violence did not bring appreciable improvement in the life of the urban slum dwellers, the civil disorders of the late 1960s ceased....the advocacy and use of violence as a deliberate program for attacking [the problems of the black poor] remained in the realm of fantasy."[167]

As the destruction abated, on April 11, Governor Spiro

---

[167] Meier & Rudwick, *From Plantation to Ghetto*, pp. 307-308

Agnew invited 100 pre-selected (by his aides), mostly black leaders, to meet with him in Annapolis. They included several ministers, and, among others, Parren Mitchell, director of the Baltimore Community Action Agency; David Glenn, director of the City Community Relations Commission; Homer Favor, director of Morgan State College's Institute for Urban Studies; Dennis Crosby, president of the Baltimore Teachers Union; and James Griffin, both chairman of Baltimore CORE and Race Relations officer for the State Department of Personnel.[168]

Governor Agnew had barely begun to read a long statement he himself had prepared when about half of the group angrily walked out, Rev. Marion Bascom in the lead. They were incensed by Agnew's accusation that the group had met secretly with the black militants he called "Hanoi-visiting, caterwauling, riot-inciting, burn-America down types."

He accused them of encouraging the rioting, and, out of "a perverted concept of race loyalty," not condemning the provocative speeches of Stokely Carmichael for fear of being called "Mr. Charlie's boy." This was particularly galling since many of them had personally spent hours on the street trying to calm things down, and, because it was they who had worked so hard to get Agnew elected.

One of those who remained, Samuel Daniels, former director of Baltimore's Human Relations Commission, told the Governor that his statement (which he continued reading) was insulting, offensive and an attempt to divide the civil rights community. Those who walked out made a statement that the *Sun*, on Friday, April 12, printed. It read, in part:

> Shocked at the tone and fervor of the Governor's remarks, a number of us decided that the meeting had no possibility for constructive action. It is not our desire to fan the flames of violence.... We have worked hard to prevent violence, senseless killings and the maiming of the innocent...We urge those voices of goodwill that are now existent in the white community to speak out urgently for justice, truth and peace. The black community cannot do the job. The people of Maryland, black and white, require leadership of the first order in bringing about those changes for which black men

---

[168] A complete report of this meeting and the Governor's text can be found in the *Sun*, Friday, April 12, 1968.

are fighting and dying in Vietnam.

Agnew must be made to know that he cannot treat black men and women like children. Agnew must be made to know that all Americans are going to share fully in the fruits of his country.

Agnew must be made to know that the old technique dividing and conquering will not work. We call upon all people of goodwill, black and white, to let the Governor know that he failed to demonstrate enlightened and concerned leadership today and that he failed to divide the black community.

Mayor D'Alesandro, who had seen a copy of the Governor's text prior to his seeing the delegation, anticipated the delegation's reaction, and accordingly had tried, unsuccessfully, to get the Governor to tone it down. At a press conference afterwards, he said the Governor's action had strained relationships between the city and State administration.

D'Alesandro sought to emphasize his own stand. "The city and the whole country was hard hit by the force of the disturbances, but I believe that it absorbed the punch with remarkable resiliency. ...The vast majority of the people, black and white alike, did not participate in the disturbances and do not approve of them. We cannot permit the disturbances to divide the community into two separate camps.

Up until this time, these black leaders had regarded themselves as moderates, but now felt they should become more militant. However, their actions, as important as they were, remained, for the most part, moderate. For example, they started the Opportunities Industrial Center (OIC), mentioned previously, that provided job training for the underemployed and unemployed in the community, as well as literacy classes and child care services. Recently Rev. Dobson had this to say to the Hopkins' students interviewing him:

We have a Head Start Program next door [to his Union Baptist Church]. Every year we're taking 200 kids, one of whose qualifications is being at or near poverty. I'll take these kids and I will test them out against any kinds coming out of any schools anywhere, and they will be ahead of them. Now, why? Because that's the power of a Negro school.

Parent and teacher have an equal expectation for the

child. We believe that the child has the capacity to learn. Where the child is incapacitated it is our responsibility to correct it. The child must have a full stomach; the child must have a clean, warm environment; not just physically clean, but spiritually warm.

The people who embrace these children when they come in must understand that they are vessels in whom God has delight. These kids are smart, I mean they are smarter than most of us. And, finally, they must see that their journey, properly empowered, is empowered not only by their family but by the community. Now that's the way we set it up and it works.

I've been able to "make it" because of the sacrifice of untold hundreds of thousands of people who have walked by, who vesseled my well being [as in "vessels of God]. And I am going to see that the only way community happens, is that we pass it along.

•••

A year after the riots, on April 7, 1969, the *Sun* published statements of a number of "leaders in the black and white community" who'd been asked if they perceived that things had either improved or worsened since then. Their responses tend to reflect, even as they still do today, the differences in perception of blacks and whites when assessing the same situation. The following are excerpts from some of their statements:

Parren Mitchell, former head of CAC, professor of Sociology at Morgan (black): the City Council has been even more opposed to anti-poverty programs, Model Cities, rent supplement, open occupancy. "Baltimore is becoming a black city, and the trend is almost irreversible. Because of this, I feel a lot of city officials are writing off efforts to improve the city.

Mayor Thomas D'Alesandro (white): "We've concentrated in two areas—jobs and education. We have one of the strongest Manpower efforts in the country, our $80 million bond issue for new schools passed, our rat-eradication program is very successful and we're working on housing."

David Glenn (black), executive director of the Community Relations Commission: "The mayor has tried to do something at the surface, and I can't complain because it's all to the good. But what we need is revamping of the entire system and until we do that little will change..."

Rabbi Abraham Shusterman (white), senior rabbi at Har Sinai: There seems to be more of a polarization than a year ago. For example, there are fewer meetings between groups of people who ought to be bound together by ties of fellowship and co-operation—minister for instance—who no long get together....The loss of the person-to-person relationship in the riot set us back a quarter century. It will take another generation to overcome.

Mrs. Frances McDonnell (black), an Eastside mother of three school-age children who went to work every day of the riot: "I don't see much difference in the community. Housing is still rotten. Stores charge the same high prices for bad food; all they've done is seal up the windows with bricks. The schools—well, the schools have been sliding backward for decades." More positive about job opportunities, she adds: "Jobs are really opening up to the poor man now, and this information is getting to the community..."

•••

By 1969, Target City, like the rest of the movement, had become sufficiently militant they wanted no more whites as part of their organization; not even "whiteys," such as Fred Weisgal and Stu Wechsler, who had devoted much of their lives to fighting for the rights of blacks. In some ways, of course, it was "safe" for the movement at this point to "cast off" pioneer attorneys such as Fred. There were now more black lawyers practicing in Baltimore, as elsewhere, who could be called upon if needed, and lawyers no longer had to be daring to undertake a civil rights case. But even more importantly, by this time there were fewer major issues left that were amenable to court action, and fewer and fewer demonstrators being arrested in that cause.

Racial tensions, internecine warfare, and inadequate funding all contributed to Target City's inability to achieve its goals. "[It] foundered completely in the spring of 1967 when the director departed amid mutual recriminations with CORE's national headquarters concerning the financing and management of the project."[169] To the local CORE members who had split with them at the very beginning, their ultimate failure had always seemed inevitable.

---

[169] Meier & Rudwick, *CORE*, p. 410

One of Baltimore CORE's founders, Ben Everinghim, had this to say of the CORE of 1968:

> I'm completely unsympathetic to the philosophy of CORE today. It's a separatist, divisive philosophy. It's an essentially negative philosophy. It's not an attempt to change people's minds and attitudes. It's an attempt to twist arms. They're saying it's better to wreck the whole Establishment than to try to change the development of the present one into something more acceptable.[170]

As for Fred Weisgal, we don't know how he reacted to his ultimate rejection by a movement he'd given so much to, but it was a well-known fact amongst his colleagues that he did not, in general, accept rejection easily. Be that as it may, in 1973 he told a reporter:[171]

> While I personally disagreed with their militancy and with certain anti-white and anti-Jewish statements made by members of CORE [and Student Non-Violent Coordinating Committee (SNCC)], I never spurned my black friends, nor did I lose my basic liberal inclinations.

In fact, Fred so identified himself with the underdog that there were times, even as the years passed, when he still reproached himself for not having taken on H. Rap Brown as a client. Perhaps his memories of the beginnings of these civil rights groups were still so powerful he couldn't just walk away and forget. He'd been in on the organizing of SNCC back in 1954, and had been present at the inaugural meeting of the Students for a Democratic Society (SDS) in 1962—when "four kids showed up and the focus then was on peace." Fred told the reporter:[172]

> My argument against the black anarchists is that they don't have the capacity or ability to think up answers to problems. It doesn't require any thought to throw a Molotov cocktail at a slum building. But it requires a great deal of thought to build up the ghetto; to change things for the better. The militants go around shouting that whitey is a

---

[170] James D. Dilts, *Sun*, "The Warning Trumpet", 12/1/1968
[171] *St. Louis Jewish Light*, 3/7/73
[172] Reprinted on a flyer announcing Fred's 1972 lecture tour; original source not given.

fink, whitey's no good, whitey this, whitey that, and they refuse to make any distinctions. There are a great many whites who are color blind. Nothing is going to be accomplished by going out and hating all whites indiscriminately.

•••

It was soon after Fred's dismissal by Target City that he decided to move with his family to Israel. They remained there from 1969 to 1981, returning to Baltimore in 1987. Already having had two prior hear attacks, Fred died of another on June 17th, 1991. He was 71 years old. It was only in 1995, while this writer was in Baltimore seeking to clarify some details regarding Fred's involvement in the civil rights movement, that she learned of his death. After returning home, I came across a note in my files I'd once written, undated, its purpose forgotten, but it now seemed a fitting eulogy. It reads:

> Dedicated to Fred Weisgal, one of the truest friends a person could have—a lawyer deeply and unswervingly committed to the pursuance of right, justice, humanity, dignity and equality for all persons.

•••

By 1969-1970, Target City like so many other civil rights groups, was having trouble financially and otherwise. Michael Davis wrote an article in the *Evening Sun* on June 24, 1970 titled, "Old-Line Rights Groups Shrink." It reported a 50% decline in NAACP membership from the 21,000 recorded in the late 1950s. The Urban League's had dropped 62%. Officials from these organizations pointed to the drop of white support after the April 1968 riots. Mr. Bright of the NAACP is quoted as saying that "When we went around to our merchant friends to solicit contributions, they told us, 'you broke our window.'

There is a lot of confusion among white Baltimoreans about civil rights organizations. All civil rights organizations aren't the same. The only thing we all ever agreed on was the March on Washington and even that took some doing."

Davis goes on to say that "Civil Rights organizations like the Southern Christian Leadership Conference [Dr. King's organization] appear to receive wide support from the black community when they stage benefits here, but do not seem to have usurped memberships from local organizations." This is not a surprising fact since they never had any other presence in Baltimore. What is more surprising, or ironic, is the fact that Dr. King is the only civil rights leader remembered and celebrated in Baltimore today.

The one group not even acknowledged in Davis's article is the Activists which revived again in 1970 and made waves with its demonstrations against slum landlords and its research, substantiating their claim that many of these landlords were getting rich on the backs of poor blacks. That this should be so, after Target City's failures and demise, was a true irony, since it was they who had self-righteously attacked the founding members of the Activists for their neglect of the poor.

•••

As for CORE today, the writer quotes Ed Chance, one of Baltimore CORE's most active members in the 1960s.

> The CORE that was saying "Fredom Now" and "Black and White Together" is not the CORE you see on television now, represented by Roy Ennis. I don't know what that is. I think they are getting paid. They would agree with the Klan, seriously they would. It is rightly crooked. We did not represent anything crooked. Only reason that we have CORE now is because they keep showing Ennis on Fox News and all that—having him speak out on things because they know that he will take a very right–wing approach.[173]

---

[173] Interview with Hopkins students in December 2000. Later also interviewed by this writer.

The Activists Reborn—Twice

"In contrast to its truly amazing record in housing construction for the upper half of America's income groups, the nation has made an inexcusably inadequate record in building or upgrading housing for the poor to provide them with decent, standard housing at rents and prices they can afford.."
Report of the National Commission on Urban Problems, Dec. 1968.

A series of anti-blockbusting acts between 1960 and 1968 should have ended this practice—and for a time it seemed to. In Baltimore, soliciting properties door-to-door, by telephone, or by distributing circulars became a misdemeanor; later, in Maryland, inducing or discouraging a sale on the basis of race became a misdemeanor; and, finally, as part of the 1968 Civil Rights Act, any attempt, for profit, to induce a real estate transaction on a racial basis became a civil offense. But the will to enforce these laws was noticeably lacking; offenders were regarded by the State's attorney's office as "businessmen," not as criminals. As a consequence, by January 1969, as noted in the *Sun*, blockbusting again had become pervasive:[174]

> Between April 1965 and July 1966, well-known Baltimore real estate speculator bought 25 row houses from white people along two blocks of the Alameda south of 33rd street and sold or rented them to Negroes. Typical among the houses was one that was bought for $6,500 and sold two months later for $11,950....
>
> Residents of some parts of Northwood have recently begun to notice speculators expressing renewed interest in their homes. This follows a decision by the state's attorney's office not to prosecute a speculator for admittedly breaking the city's anti-blocking ordinance.

Efforts were made by the churches in the Northwood area to unite and fight white flight; the Northeast Community Organization (NECO) was formed as well as a number of other neighborhood associations. Vincent Quale, a Jesuit theology student at Woodstock College, who'd had similar experience in Chicago, Boston and New York, helped, noting that investors

---

[174] Long article by Douglas Connah, Jr., "Blockbusting in Baltimore: less blatant and rapacious," *Sun*, 1/26/69.

in the area were dividing houses into two-family apartments and changing rentals from monthly to weekly at increased rates (a typical practice in housing for the poor).

A month later, Quale is reported as telling a group that two men "single-handedly changed the neighborhood" between East 33rd and East 28th Streets, and the Alameda and Hillen road. He goes on to say that whites are told that "property values decline when a Negro family moves into the neighborhood." As a consequence, they "sell their homes for less than their value, and Negroes buy them for more than they are worth."[175]

Clearly neither the 1968 Federal Housing law and the re-activated 1866 Civil Rights Act that forbid discrimination by real estate brokers, builders and lenders, nor the various anti-blockbusting laws had ended the practice of blockbusting, only forced it into a somewhat more sophisticated form than that practiced in the 1950s.

The end to the dual-housing market they had promised could be seen only in the fact that "white brokers" no longer denied "black brokers" access to listings of "white" houses for sale. CORE's picketing, demonstrations and arrests over the years may have played apart in the passage of "Open Housing" laws, but neither they nor the "testing" and educational efforts of Baltimore Neighborhoods, Inc. (BNI) had resulted in any wide-spread acceptance of integrated communities.

And so it was that in 1969 Vinnie Quale established St. Ambrose Housing Center, a non-profit organization that still exists, committed to providing a full continuum of housing-related aid to Baltimore's white and black homebuyers and home owners.[176]

---

[175] Clipping hand-dated 2/69, paper not named.

[176] Described in an internal document provided the writer: "We provide permanent rental housing for people in shelters, help people buy houses, counsel delinquent mortgagors, offer legal services as well as a homesharing program. We rehab houses for the elderly, operate an intervention buying program to preserve homeownership in five outer city neighborhoods, renovate vacant houses and buildings and assist churches and other non-profits with their housing projects. Each year with 50 full-time staff we provide housing assistance to over 3,000 families."

Connah ends his article, quoted previously, with a telling "vision":

> One is tempted to conjure up a vision of a great, never-ending game of follow the leader, with the white man out in front, running as hard as he can one step ahead of the middle-class Negro in Bermuda shorts, himself one step ahead of a slum landlord dragging a fatherless welfare family along, the whole group spreading out Liberty Road, out Reisterstown Road, out Loch Raven Boulevard, with the government man bringing up the rear, cleaning up everything with urban renewal.

By May 1969, Thomas Edsall is reporting "explanations" made by three speculators as to why their resale home prices are more than their purchase prices. Louis Singer, Anthony Piccinini, and Morris Goldseker all declare that they spend "from a minimum of $1,000 to as much as $3,000 for renovations on each home, settlement fees, property taxes, salesmen's commissions and also guarantee all repairs on newly purchased houses for one year....The real estate firm provides the financing for the purchaser,"[177] which means the purchaser can forfeit his home if for any reason he does not complete payments. Blacks subjected to the price mark-ups called it "the black tax," and the elderly people who most often were the white victims called it "the grey tax."

Another type mark-up was the creation of a ground rent (which the speculator kept title to), typically worth about $1500, a common phenomena in England but almost unique to Baltimore in this country. Another common ploy of the speculators, including the above named, was the use of "lease with option contracts." For example:

> Thomas Lewis and his wife, a Negro couple, signed a lease with option contract with Lee Realty under the impression they were buying their home. Actually they rented 1628 East 32nd street for $65.50 every two weeks. They put up an additional $350 for an option on buying the home at the end of the lease for $13,500. Lee Realty [a Goldseker company] paid $7,200 for the house. The lease states that if the tenant ever allows the rent to become overdue by more than 10 days

---

[177] "How speculators profit as neighborhoods panic", by Thomas Edsall, hand-dated 5/4/69, paper not named.

he loses the option to buy. In only one of nine cases...has the tenant actually bought the home.[178]

At about this same time, Walter Carter, now "Special Assistant for Race and Poverty" to the Jesuit Provincial and Associate Professor of Sociology at Loyola College (positions he took after the City Council refused, in 1968, to confirm him as director of the Community Action Agency) invited Vinnie Quale to speak to his class. Afterwards, Walter and Sampson Green, head of the newly revived Activists, committed to undertake the issue of speculation in racially changing neighborhoods as a project—they would spearhead the demonstrating while others did the back-up research. It seemed the right issue for the Activists with its black and white membership— a substantive city-wide issue that affected both whites and blacks. Baltimore Neighborhoods, Inc. (BNI) and the Catholic parishes were able to get most of the new neighborhood associations involved—the Catholic church had supported Fr. Vinnie Quale in creating the St. Ambrose Housing Aid Center; and John J. Martinez, a Jesuit teacher at St. Bernardine's Roman Catholic School, had agreed to Chair the Activist's Housing Committee.

On May 10, 1969, the Activists released a 300-word statement titled, "Stay of Exploitation," that demanded that Goldseker, within a week, act to reduce its rents by 37.5%; "renegotiate" all its land-installment contracts and lease options "according to fair market value;" and establish a "financial pool equivalent to 10% of its gross income to provide interest-free mortgages to the poor." Fr. Martinez is quoted as saying the Activists had chosen to concentrate their actions on the Morris Goldseker Company (operating under as many as fifty names, including Lee Reality, Fairfax Investment Corp., Best Realty, Arbor, Inc., Rainbow Realty, Woodhaven Investment Corp and D. & E.), because he was "the biggest [of the slumlord-speculators] that we know of."[179]

---

[178] "How speculators profit as neighborhoods panic", by Thomas Edsall, hand-dated 5/4/69, paper not named.

[179] Orser, p. 96. Also see Olson, p. 379 which states he alone bought 1,700 homes in Baltimore in the 60s. Also, an article by Eric Siegel for the *Sun* on 2/5/78, stated that the reason he created so many

Even though Fr. Martinez agreed that Goldseker "may have performed 'a service' by renting to Negroes at a time when other firms refused," he added that "the service came 'at a very high price.'"[180] As Samuel Gorn's Horizon House had earlier become the Activists' symbol of segregated housing, Goldseker was to become the symbol of the speculators who turned previously all-white neighborhoods black. A newspaper article quotes Sampson as saying:

> "His being the target was incidental. The protests were directed at the whole exploitative operation" of banks that redlined black areas of the city and the "political structure" that was insensitive to the problems of black families desiring to purchase homes, which made it possible for individual speculators to profit.

The Activists followed a long established strategy of research, organization, picketing, economic pressure, and court suits. Then, at what was probably the first demonstration in their new campaign, on August 9, 1969, six picketers arrived at Goldseker's downtown offices on Franklin Street, including Sampson Green and Horace Davis, president of the Edmondson Village Community Association. All six were arrested by the police for trespassing after they tried to present a letter to Goldseker.

Later, before Judge Avrum Rifman, they complained that the district cell block was indecent, unhealthy, and unfit for humans. The judge agreed, offering even harsher words: barbaric, similar to the black hole of Calcutta. He postponed a decision in their case pending the result of a civil case between the parties then in Circuit Court (presumably referring to the Goldseker injunction suit not heard until October). The young

---

companies was because "he realized that the way the tax laws were written, a number of small companies would pay less in taxes than one large one." Be that as it may, it made it much harder for the Activists to discover his holdings—and his profits.

[180] Article, "Activists, Inc. Prods Realty Firm," hand-dated 5/10/69, by Stephen Lynton, paper not named. Also see article by Eric Siegel, *Sun*, 2/5/78 that discusses how Goldseker began to accumulate his wealth during the Depression when he was managing foreclosed properties for others; "buying up these bargain houses and renting them out."

black attorney, Larry Gibson, represented them at the hearing.[181]

Every Saturday morning for something over two years, 20 to 50 people, Jesuits, poverty lawyers, veteran civil rights activists, and many of Goldseker's own customers congregated at the Union Baptist Church on Druid Hill Avenue before starting their picketing. In order to present a united front to the city, they formed a loose confederation, the Black United Front (without formal structure or officers), that included not only the Activists, but also such diverse groups as CORE, the NAACP, U-JOIN, the Soul school, black policemen, workers from Bethlehem Steel, and from the Laundry Worker's Union.

In September 1969, after some 4,000 hours of work, the Activists, along with at least nine sponsoring neighborhood associations, published "Communities Under Siege." Using the Lusk reports on metropolitan real estate transactions in the city for the years from 1960 to 1968, "some 200 volunteers carded data on the buying, price, sale price, mortgage, interest rate and other information on 60,000 housing transactions in all parts of the city....The Rouse Company key-punched the cards for the computer study."[182]

A major part of the publication documented the "differential between purchase and sale prices in Edmondson Village compared to a similar but racially stable row house area in northeast Baltimore." It also documented the difference in price between FHA houses sold in the same Edmondson Village tract with those sold by Goldseker. A final section of the report deals with "Real Estate Company Activity in the Liberty Heights and Park Heights Corridors." The conclusion is that blacks get less than whites for their dollar, and that there is a wide discrepancy between fair market house values and prices charged by Goldseker companies.[183] Charlie Oaks from the Edmondson Village area said of the report: [184]

> [It] clearly reveals that a small band of real estate exploiters in Baltimore have taken more money from black home buyers than from white home buyers, the basic cause

---

[181] Information from the *Afro*, 8/17/69.
[182] *Evening Sun*, "Housing Exploitation Charged," March 5, 1971.
[183] From the Report's Table of Contents, and from Orser, p. 134.
[184] *Afro American*, 9/26/70

of turning the city into slums.

And Horace Davis, President of the Edmondson Village Neighborhood Association, went even further:

> It should not take any psychologist to understand how stripping blacks of proportionately more of their dollars when they earn much less on the average than whites, not only runs down neighborhoods, but it upsets parents, and runs rampant in ruining black families.

Reinforcing these two themes, the study concluded:

> No statistics...can ever document the strains which the real estate and financial industries of the city created in the neighborhoods mentioned in this report. Hidden behind these statistics are parents who have to work two and three jobs together to pay the housing bills, children who must suffer from the absence of their parents and in overcrowded schools, deteriorating properties which cannot be improved because the necessary money is already sunk into the over-priced market.

In October 1969, Goldseker went to court asking the judge to end the chanting and picketing. Producing four months of reels of movies and tape recordings of their demonstrations, he told Judge James Perrott it was hurting his business. A sample from the tapes played in court was reported in the *Washington Post.*[185]

©AfroAmerican, 7/24/1971
Last demonstration of Walter Carter, second from rear., with the big Afro, then popular.

---

[185] "Black Home Buyers' Protest Hits Baltimore," Leonard Downie, Jr. *Washington Post*, October 18, 1969.

"Who is Goldseker?" a shrill female.
    "What do we want?" a voice sang out.
    "Exploiter!" a full-throated chorus chanted back.
    "Who is he exploiting?"
    "The People," they answered.
    "Stop the exploiting!"
    "When?" "Now" "When-n-n?" "NOW!"
    The recorded sound of rhythmic chanting grew shrill and loud, bouncing off the marble walls of the high-ceilinged Baltimore Courtroom.

Judge Perrott ordered "the pickets to abide by ground rules: only fifteen could march at one time, at least three feet apart; no disturbing 'screaming and shouting'; no dogs or weapons allowed (even though no testimony showed that any had been present before)." The Activists' team of lawyers, headed by Kenneth Johnson, and including John King and Larry Gibson, appealed to federal court.

In a recent conversation with Ken, a recently retired Baltimore Circuit Court judge (ironically, he had replaced Perrott on the bench), he told this writer that the case went directly to federal court because it was a First Amendment issue that involved free speech and "prior restraint." The terms of the injunction, however, would have remained effective until the extensive hearings on the issue in July 1971.[186]

On December 22, 1969, the *Evening Sun* reported that the Montebello and Edmondson Village Community Associations, and 76 black homeowners from those areas, filed their own suit in federal court: "a lengthy housing discrimination suit against Morris Goldseker and eighteen of his corporations." After months of investigation it claimed that Goldseker "participated in, advanced, supported and exploited" the city's containment policy by his "buying, selling, renting and leasing practices." His practices in 24 census tracts in the named area went from a 97% white population in 1950 to 7% white in 1967.

There were a number of charges including "violation of federal civil rights laws, illegal antitrust conspiracy ad violation of Maryland usury laws." It sought over $2 million in damages and an injunction against Mr. Goldseker's real estate companies.

---

[186] Quotes from "Black Home Buyers' Protest Hits Baltimore," Leonard Downie, Jr. October 18, 1969.

Chief Judge Roszel C. Thomsen was assigned the case; Ronald Shapiro and Larry Gibson, who had prepared the case along with Ken Johnson, represented the Activists.

In February 1970 an unnamed newspaper reported the arrest of twelve picketers, including six children. They appeared before Judge Robert J. Gerstung charged with "shouting and howling", disturbing the peace while again picketing Goldseker's Franklin Street office. Larry Gibson, again representing them, said it was part of their chant: "We are going to ride your backs until you stop the tax." He also claimed the police contention that the picketers blocked traffic because drivers stopped to see the action was not valid since this was not an intentional act on their part.

About the same time, in February, the Activists published a follow-up study to "Communities Under Siege," titled, "Baltimore Under Siege: A Conspiracy to Defraud Home-buyers."[187] Designed to bolster their housing discrimination suit against Goldseker, it documented the part played by several savings and loans which refused to make direct loans to purchasers, but instead made large loans to the speculators that enabled them to carry, under harsh terms, the mortgages in their home deals.

It also enabled speculators to create land contracts and lease options; Goldseker claiming this enabled persons to buy who otherwise couldn't afford to, the report suggesting the practice was just another way to make it easier to foreclose on buyers when they missed payments. Governor Marvin Mandel was implicated in the conspiracy as a director of the Jefferson Federal Savings and Loan Association from its formation in 1964 until 1969 when it stopped making these loans, and as President of Oldetown Savings and Loan in the early 1960s before it was taken over in 1965 by Jefferson. These were two of the worst offenders.

The Governor tried to absolve himself of any blame by saying his were not paid positions, and he made no money from the Association's transactions. This study also

---

[187] Unlike the earlier report, this writer has been unable to track down the later report, so information is entirely from newspaper articles—which gave it extensive coverage.

highlighted the roles of the FHA and VA in helping create and
sustain two housing markets.

In July 1971, the federal appeal of Judge Perrott's
restrictive conditions for picketing at the Goldseker office,
imposed in October 1969, still had not been heard. The
attorney, Ken Johnson, who was handling this appeal,
recently told this writer that the federal judge had urged him
to return to Judge Perrott in circuit court and ask for a
reconsideration of his decision, emphasizing the First
Amendment aspect.

What happened on July 10, 1971 suggests that in the
intervening year plus after the court mandate in 1969,
picketing of Goldseker's offices had continued under the court
mandated restrictions. It was on that date, at the regular
Saturday meeting of the Black United Front that Walter Carter
urged that they defy the terms of the injunction and go to jail
if necessary.

No doubt it was this project that had promoted, during
this same time, the creation of the Black United Front,
described to this writer by both Ed Chance and Rev. Dobson
as an effort to bring together all of Baltimore's anti-
discrimination groups, from the Black Panthers to the
Ministerial Alliance, under one loosely organized umbrella. For
a while, representatives from these wildly diverse groups met
every Saturday evening at the Union Baptist Church, Ed
Chance acting as Chairman.

After their meeting on July 10, 1971, Walter, Horace
Davis and a few others contacted a number of black and white
leaders, ministers, politicians, and community leaders to ask
for their support for a demonstration on July 17th. About sixty
showed up to demonstrate and the media gave it wide
coverage. Goldseker's efforts to head off another
demonstration on July 24th failed. Instead, Congressman
Parren Mitchell, two State Senators, three members of the
House of Delegates, one city councilman, and a number of
ministers appeared with the regular activist demonstrators.

Goldseker then contacted Judge Sodaro asking that he
summon the group to appear before Judge Perrott on Monday,
July 26, 1971. His right to issue such a summons was
questioned but Walter and one other (unnamed, possibly

Sampson Green, John Burleigh or Fr. Martinez) agreed to appear on Tuesday to represent the whole group in an attempt to have the injunction revoked.

John King was present to represent them and Judge Perrott, despite being annoyed that all the demonstrators were not present, finally agreed to proceed with just these two representing them all. Things were going poorly for the Activists until after Dr. Chester Wickwire and Dr. Peter Rossi appeared on the third day to testify on their behalf.

Their testimony apparently impressed the judge and after the fourth day of hearings, on Friday, July 30, he announced he was not sending anyone to jail for violating his earlier injunction. He then reprimanded them and imposed a $250 fine against the Activists, but did not enforce payment. He then lifted the restriction on the number of pickets so long as they did not block the entrance to the Goldseker office. To celebrate their victory, Walter announced that they intended "within the next several months to mobilize the whole city to end exploitation in all aspects of housing."[188]

Next day, July 31st, at the regular meeting of the Black United Front at the Union Baptist Church, Walter, after announcing their victory, urged "continued efforts to create true economic unity." He had just proclaimed, 'I **will commit the rest of my life to make this city a fit place where our kids can live...**' when suddenly he touched his chest, said, 'I have a pain,' and keeled over. He was given heart massages and mouth-to-mouth resuscitation, while and doctor and ambulance were called. He was taken to nearby Maryland General Hospital, but it was too late. At approximately five p.m., only forty-eight years old, he died of a heart attack. Baltimore suddenly had lost one its most valued civil rights leaders.

Lengthy obituaries appeared in all the Baltimore newspapers. To quote from only one: by Kiser Barnes, a 27 year old Morgan graduate and director of Community Relations with the Maryland Human Relations Commission:[189]

---

[188] Most of the information from the Walter Carter Memorial booklet. Written in the first person, it does not say who the "I" is, and writer has not been able to ascertain this (possibly Horace Davis).
[189] *Baltimore Afro-American*, 8/3/1971.

...I recognize in him the spirit of Denmark Vesey, Nat Turner, DuBois, Malcolm, King, Evers and the host of named and unnamed black men who fought relentlessly against oppression and who died the death of black warriors who fought the good fight for freedom. They told me that his heart stopped beating in Maryland General Hospital, Baltimore, on a cold, dreary and wet July 31, 1971. The implication being that his heart betrayed his soul, his body and us, who are left behind, who clung to him and leaned on him one time too many times.

We who were schooled by him know that the real betrayal began 352 years ago by whites who exchanged humanity to exploit and oppress black people... He was tired. But we didn't know it. And even if we had known, I doubt if commitment would have allowed him to step down. And I guess even those of us who are committed must share some of the blame.

Although we knew his complete commitment gave him little rest, we never really hesitated to put another problem on his shoulders. Problems, which we now have to carry ourselves and possibly could have carried while he lived. But is it not the role of a great leader to take responsibility where none want it, and to provide direction where none cannot? This is what he did. This is how we remember him.

Both sides of the 1200 block of Druid Hill Avenue were lined on Wednesday awaiting the arrival of Walter's flag-covered coffin from the funeral home for the noon service at Union Baptist Church. 550 people were crowded together inside as the processional, headed by Rev. Vernon Dobson, arrived. Lawrence Cardinal Shehan and Parren J. Mitchell were honorary pallbearers; the active pallbearers included those who'd been most active with him for so many years: John Burleigh, James Griffin, William Bush, John Roemer, Larry Ageloff and Irwin Auerbach. Norman Reeves, President of the Wm. L. Moore Foundation and always a close friend of Walter's fainted after delivering one of the eulogies. Another eulogy was given by Dr. Chester Wickwire, the friend who had been responsible for introducing this writer to Walter. A poem that expands on his eulogy is included in a memorial booklet prepared by Walter's friends.

With Dr. Wickwire's permission, parts of it are included

here.[190] Called, *Trees That Reach Farthest Upward*, it was dedicated to "our friend, who let us walk with him."

Reminder of timberline on a high mountain
>
> trees that reach farthest upward
> toward the sky and summit
> good men model life, lift time.

At timberline
>
> where storms, rain and snow fall mercilessly
> winds whip their jagged line
> trees stand weather-worn, low to the ground
> sometimes double-trunked, lonely
> high above even-topped trees in the forest below
>
> Those who came close to him know
>
> Walter Carter stood at timberline
> on the edge of change
> reached for the summit for his people
> often alone
> above men of shorter vision, less courage.

"This tree was never quiet"
>
> He saw loneliness of the city
> He heard cries of laborers
> He was angered when he could not break bread with his neighbor
> He suffered when justice was denied at the gate...
> He set a plumb line in the city and we did not measure up
> He had too much integrity, imagination, determination
> He was too...unbuyable, too...free
> Swift witness against oppression and exploitation.
>
> He was not cynical or calculating enough to wheel and deal where
> freedom and dignity were at stake.
>
> His life became a mirror in which
> injustices and hypocrisies made us ashamed and grotesque.

"No tree in the garden of God was like it in its beauty"
>
> Walter Carter was a heroic figure
> among non-heroes
> He wore himself out

---

[190] The original formatting has been altered in the quoting for "space" reasons.

for his people, for blacks, whites,
Baltimore, Maryland, America.

We are in his debt
this city, state, land
are in his debt.

"A tree growing when we were sleeping"

Walter Carter is Baltimore's Liberty Tree
our Tree of Liberty

Dying
he brought us together
he showed us what it means to be human
to love one's neighbor

Why do we require such a price from a man and his family to teach us how to live?

Francis M. O'Connor, S.J., who only met Walter after he took the position with Loyola, credited Walter with making him really understand the black struggle for equality and acceptance in the United States. He added:

Sensitivity to some of the implications of the black struggle was only one lesson I learned from Walter Carter. Another equally impressive lesson he taught me was the personal price a man pays for a cause to which he commits himself heart and soul. That the cost of commitment comes high was a message that Walter lived out.[191]

On November 14, 1974 about one hundred people attended a groundbreaking ceremony for a new elementary school to be built in Northeast Baltimore named after Walter; a school that was to include a swimming pool, library and gymnasium, according to plans. A mental health facility on Fayette Street was also named after him; Walter having been a member of the Community Health Council of Maryland. The Council had been pressing the University of Maryland's Baltimore complex to recognize its "white racist image" and be more responsive to the black community's needs. But the anniversary of Walter's birth or death is not celebrated; missing the opportunity to herald him as a role model that both blacks and whites can be proud of. Instead, Baltimore is

---

[191] *The News American,* 8/23/1976

in danger of forgetting him entirely as fewer and fewer of us who knew him are left.

•••

With the loss of Walter's dedication and leadership, the activism of the Goldseker campaign pretty much ended. However, the housing discrimination suit filed two years earlier was still pending. In late January 1972, it finally went to court before Judge Roszel C. Thomsen in a non-jury trial. Larry Gibson, Ronald Shapiro and Ken Johnson were among the attorneys representing forty-one black individuals or families who purchased homes from Goldseker (thirty-five had been dropped in pre-trial hearings) and the Montebello and Edmondson Village Community Associations in pursuit of their case against fifteen of Goldseker's corporations (three of these had been dropped). Former judge, Thomas J. Kenney, represented the Goldseker interests.

The plaintiff's attorneys asserted that Baltimore's separate housing markets created an "artificial scarcity" of housing that enabled speculators to overcharge blacks. As reported in the *Evening Sun*:[192]

> The suit asked relief under the terms of the Civil Rights Act of 1866 which guarantees black citizens the same rights to purchase and own property as are possessed by white citizens in every state of the United States.
>
> The law suit asks for a court order to prevent Goldseker and his companies from continuing the practices against which the litigation is directed and asks for triple damages under the antitrust laws.

The original demand for $25,000 punitive damages for each of the plaintiff homebuyers and the class-action component that claimed to represent all blacks who had bought or attempted to buy homes from Goldseker companies had been dropped. "Also dropped were demands that Goldseker and his companies be required to get out of the real estate business and a portion of the suit alleging violations of the common law and Maryland laws against usury and fraud."

---

[192] *Evening Sun*, 1/24/1972

After several days of testimony there was a month's break before the trial resumed at the end of February. The director of research for the Johns Hopkins Center for Urban Affairs gave statistical testimony regarding segregation and the consequent difficulty of Baltimore ever being able to desegregate. William Durr, a teacher of urban sociology at the University of Baltimore, called Baltimore's residential racial segregation "institutional racism."

Less than two weeks later, on March 9, 1972, the *Evening Sun* announced that the suit had been dismissed "with prejudice" that morning by Judge Roszel C. Thomsen, at the request of the plaintiffs' lawyers. Referring to the hearings as having been on-again, off-again since June 1970, the Judge said:

> The evidence which was presented by the plaintiffs showed the difficulties under which black people have labored in purchasing homes and the need for federal, state and local action to assist them in necessary financing.

The plaintiffs' lawyers, who had given their time *pro bono* (without charging), claimed they had been hampered from the start by lack of funds to pay duplicating costs, recorder's charges to depose witnesses, and other expenses. The final problem seemed to involve lack of funds to pay a substitute expert witness to appraise the plaintiffs homes and to "tie together [in court] the previous complex, and at time confusing, testimony... concerning the prices charged by the Goldseker companies compared to the fair market value of the houses."[193] No explanation was given as to why a last-minute substitute expert was needed.

As disappointing as this outcome was for the plaintiffs, the case had not been a total loss. The media coverage it generated contributed to the financial institutions opening up so that black homebuyers could get regular FHA and VA financing, and lease options and land contracts became rare.

The most ironic twist, however, came with the death in 1973 of Morris Goldseker. According to the terms of his will, a

---

[193] Evening Sun, 3/10/1972.

Goldseker Foundation was established (its assets ranking in the top 10% of foundations nationwide) that was, primarily, to make grants in the Baltimore area, especially aimed at projects for the disadvantaged.

> The will further stipulated that the grants could be awarded only to nonsectarian organizations that did not discriminate on the basis of race or religion [he was a non-practicing Jew]. Between 1976 and 1985 the foundation conferred grants in the amount of $7 million. In July, 1989 it combined with the Baltimore Community Foundation; during the 1989 fiscal year the enlarged philanthropy conferred $1,556,768 in grants to thirty-four nonprofit organizations for programs in categories of community affairs, education, health, human services and neighborhood development.[194]

Goldseker had never married and was said to be married to his business. And so, even in life regarded as "an enigma," the reasons given for his final generosity varied— from those who regarded it as the mark of a guilty conscience to those who believed he was only continuing what he always said was his desire, "to help the poor." Goldseker apparently was genuinely perplexed by the attacks on him.[195]

•••

A footnote on the Black United Front which, until Walter's death, had been meeting every Saturday at the Union Baptist Church. Ed Chance had this to say in interviews with Hopkins students in December 2000 and more recently with this writer.

> Support for the Black United Front had already begun to wane by the time Walter died; the meeting the night of his death was an attempt to revive it. But Walter's death proved also to be the Black United Front's death knell.
>
> I can't think of anything Black United Front really accomplished. We were very Afro-centric. You know,

---

194 Orser, p. 171-172
195 "The Riddle of Morris Goldseker's Legacy," *Sun*, 2/5/78

by that time we were all wearing Dashikis. We decided to wear long hair and the women would wear their hair au-natural. It was a culture thing....

You know, when I was a kid in North Carolina and you called me Black, those were fighting words. Then it switched. All of a sudden, Black was beautiful. ...Then all of a sudden the light-skinned Blacks began to feel that they weren't Black enough. Anyhow that all stems from the situation of slavery.

•••

It was in 1974 that the Activists underwent its third and final revival. This writer had left her husband, returned to Baltimore, and, using her newly earned Masters of Library Service degree from Rutgers University, obtained a job as librarian in the public school system at the Joseph Briscoe middle school. It was near Sampson Green's office, so we sometimes met for lunch, and, inevitably, soon started talking about reviving the Activists, whose incorporation status had been allowed to lapse after Walter's death. We contacted Legal Aid about getting it re-incorporated and Sam introduced me to a friend of his, Ralph Moore, who was excited at the prospect of some real action again in the field of housing.

Ralph was considerably younger than Sam and I. He'd been a student at Loyola High School when Walter had been an advisor and lecturer there. And later he'd picketed Goldseker with him during the years between 1969 and 1971; he'd been at Union Baptist Church when Walter had collapsed and died. At the time I met Ralph, he was *teaching* at Loyola High. Later he worked with Dr. Wickwire at Johns Hopkins, still later at St. Ambrose Housing, and now heads Baltimore's Center for Poverty Solutions.

Goldseker was no longer a creator of slums but there were still plenty of slumlords, especially on Baltimore's East Side. Using city plat maps, we identified all the landlords in that area and designed a survey questionnaire for their tenants.

For the next several weeks, after school each day, the three of us went house to house asking tenants about the condition of their homes and how they were treated by their landlords.

On the basis of our findings, we selected Harvey Berman as our target and began to recruit former, and new, activists to meet with us to strategize. This is what we were doing at Fr. Henry Offer's church, St. Francis, the evening that uninvited guests began to appear. First, state delegate Bob Douglas dropped in, friendly enough. Then, City Councilman, DuBurns, appeared. He informed us, very angrily, "I am the keeper of sheep; I give out cookies around here. Get out, or else!" And he left. I was stunned.

"I didn't know we lived in Nazi Germany!" I exclaimed, hoping the two departing backs would hear us. I was further taken aback to learn that our earlier strong civil rights supporter, Fr. Offer, whose church we were in, had bought into this "territorial attitude" and had *called* these two politicians to tell them about our meeting.

Threatened though we were, we continued with our plans to organize East Side tenants, especially Harvey Berman's, and to start picketing his office, Republic Realty. In the old CORE-Activist style, a delegation first met with him with a list of demands without any results.

Then, in July of 1975 we picketed for the first time, demanding that he rescind the second rent increase he'd made in less than a year. After he claimed that increased taxes had forced them on him, we checked and learned that on most of his properties they'd gone *down*.

Following a number of demonstrations, the area tenants decided at one of their meetings to form a separate organization from the Activists, but still under its umbrella. They voted to call it S.H.A.C.K. (Save Housing through Action and Community Knowledge) and elected Charles Hopkins, a young, outspoken black man, living in the area, as their chairman.

For some reason Sam and Ralph had reservations about Charles, so arranged a meeting with him at his house to "check him out." Sitting amidst his paintings and hearing him discuss a business he intended to start, they came away believing Charles was "nutty as a fruitcake"—as Ralph put it. They wanted to have a police check run on him but I objected, always suspicious of the police and feeling it was a violation of his civil liberties. *Big mistake* it turns out—though even if done it might not have prevented the events that followed soon after.

We woke up one morning soon after, to newspaper headlines that Charles had been arrested and taken to Perkins State Hospital (a mental hospital) after he'd gone into the temporary City Hall and shot it up. One councilman had died of a heart attack. Seems he had gone to City Hall the day before to get a business license and had been rejected. Furious, he'd tried to interrupt a City Council meeting and been escorted out by Councilwoman, Mary Pat Clark. He'd been loudly shouting he was an officer of the Activists and claimed the Activists would start picketing the place if he didn't get his license.

This event pretty much blew the Activists' credibility and led to the total collapse of our tenant organizing efforts. The only comfort we could take from the whole mess was the fact that Harvey Berman's shoddy business practices had been brought to the City's attention, and soon after he was put out of business.

•••

Unfortunately, that did not end the need for improved housing for the majority of blacks in Baltimore. Today the commitment for decent housing is still missing; its lack most certainly tied to discrimination, not as markedly different from that encountered in the 1800s as one might have hoped. It sounds like an old refrain when Ralph Moore said, in a speech in January 2001:

> We should start that process [of making life in Baltimore fairer and more just] by actively working to ensure that every citizen in Baltimore has equal access to every neighborhood in Baltimore...fair housing for all.

We will hear more from Ralph, who now heads the Center for Poverty Solutions, in the concluding section. On January 20, 2001, at a Baltimore Neighborhood Inc. Conference: "Talking about Race in Baltimore: Private Dialogue and Public Discourse," Ralph forcefully presented some pungent observations that should be heeded by us all. Clearly he was still riled up by the speakers at an earlier meeting in Northeast Baltimore. They had vigorously opposed the City's plan to acquire ten HUD foreclosed houses in this area and move into them Section 8-eligible former public housing residents. [Section 8 is a federal rental subsidy program.]

Part VI
In the End

Race, Still an Issue

Fights to end legal segregation have been won, and it would be hard to deny that life is better for blacks now than it was before the Civil Rights Movement of the 1960s. There are no more humiliating signs, "Black only" and "White only," there are more job opportunities open to a better educated black population, there is more freedom of choice in housing, even black schools are better equipped and in better repair, but there are still few, if any, integrated communities or integrated schools, and the majority of Baltimore's blacks are poor. Institutional racism is still pervasive.

In 1980, in Baltimore, blacks outnumbered whites for the first time—*to what effect?*

In 1986, after Donald Schaefer, Baltimore's long-time Mayor, was elected Governor of Maryland, the city elected its first black mayor—Clarence "Du" Burns, long-time city councilman from Baltimore's east side. This was the same councilman who once ordered Ralph Moore and this writer not to enter his community to talk to tenants, informing us, very angrily, "I am the keeper of sheep; I give out cookies around here. Get out, or else!" And he stomped out of our Activists' meeting at St. Francis church, where we were strategizing our campaign against east side landlords who deliberately let their properties deteriorate.

A year later, another black, Kurt Schmoke challenged DuBurns in the primary and won. Schmoke had been at City College during the fight there, recounted earlier; later had gone to Yale, Harvard Law School, and to Oxford University in England as a Rhodes scholar. He was Baltimore's State's Attorney before being elected mayor. He served for three terms; followed in 1999 by Martin O'Malley, a white former City Councilman.

And what happened to the city during this time? Baltimore was acclaimed a renaissance city. A number of beautiful high rise office buildings went up in its center; a number of blacks work there, but most occupants, black and white, retire to the suburbs at the end of the working day.

On the city's downtown waterfront can be found a

flourishing Inner Harbor, replete with restaurants and upscale stores, an aquarium and a replica of an 1854 topsail schooner offering day trips. It has replaced what was once derelict row, replete with flop houses and drunks. And the Harbor's nearby neighborhoods have been gentrified, attracting mostly young, white, well-paid professionals. A few new high-tech companies have set up operations in Baltimore, offering jobs to the qualified, mostly white.

And what of Baltimore's black majority? The NAACP has moved its national office to Baltimore. A few magnet schools have been added to the city's public school system, the most outstanding, a high school for the arts that has attracted a multi-cultural student body. Dunbar High, still with a black student body, has formed a partnership with its neighbor, the Johns Hopkins East Baltimore campus, offering a health-care professional program. City College now offers a prestigious International Baccalaureate. The private schools actively seek black students and faculty, as do the colleges. But what proportion of Baltimore's blacks, still mostly poor, enjoy these amenities?

Looking inland to the East and West sides of Baltimore, one finds deteriorating public housing, more houses boarded up, more dope addicts than available treatment facilities to help them.[1] The murder rate is amongst the highest in the nation, as is the rate of incarceration; the number of prisons has expanded to hold the increasing number of mostly young black men convicted of crime.

In the 1990s, the first of the high rise public housing complexes to be demolished, Lafayette Courts, was imploded, reminding this writer of the Activists' study on Urban Renewal in the 1960s. We asked then, "What of those displaced?" This time, the Maryland Branch of the American Civil Liberties Union (ACLU) asked, "What are the city's plans?" And when they found out that the plan was to "rebuild segregated public housing," they filed a civil suit against the U.S. Department of

---

[1] See the vivid account of the drug culture destroying one West side Baltimore neighborhood (where this writer once owned a house) as told in *The Corner: A Year in the Life of an Inner-City Neighborhood* by David Simon & Edward Burns (1997).

Housing and Urban Development on behalf of a number of tenants,[2] declaring their plans "both unconstitutional and illegal under civil rights statutes." Race, indeed, is still an issue.

•••

Eleven family public housing projects had been built or acquired in Baltimore since 1964. Seven of them were within four blocks of existing black segregated family housing projects; two others were in areas 98% black; and two were located on an isolated industrial piece of outer-city land that resulted in a self-contained neighborhood of public housing residents. Further, the 2800 "scattered site" units, authorized by HUD in 1967, are clustered in racially segregated areas that are amongst the most economically depressed, blighted and drug infested in the city.

The city's plan was to demolish and replace 3,000 dwellings, representing one quarter of the total units, that had been developed since 1964 as segregated housing. Their rebuilding plan would simply have replicated the existing segregated locations.

ACLU accused the city of intentionally refusing to make use of other alternatives that would disestablish segregation and provide displaced residents with desegregative housing opportunities; to rebuild in the same segregated areas, as they planned, would mean perpetuating segregation for the projected forty year life-span of any new project. ACLU asserted that "Baltimore has consistently and up to the present (1995) bowed to white community pressure to prevent the development of any family public housing in neighborhoods that were predominantly white."

Plaintiffs who have asked for a transfer to a better neighborhood have been told HABC (Housing Authority of Baltimore City) has nothing to offer them, beyond other public housing in segregated neighborhoods as blighted as their current segregated neighborhoods. Similarly, plaintiffs who have requested to escape their segregated living

---

[2] Civil Action # MJG 95-309, *Carmen Thompson, et al vs. U.S. Department of Housing & Urban Development, et al.* (January 1995). The information about Baltimore's public housing is from the briefs in this suit.

situation by using a Section 8 certificate (government pays a portion of the rent) have been denied access to that as well.

Plaintiffs will suffer concrete additional harm if defendants are allowed to proceed with their replacement housing plans; this harm includes living in isolation from the larger community in dangerous neighborhoods. For Plaintiffs' children there are, in addition, the devastating consequences of attending segregated and inadequate schools, of seeing first-hand violent crime, drug dealing and drug abuse; and of being subjected to pressures to engage in antisocial behavior.

To avoid the expense and inconvenience of litigation the plaintiffs and defendants, denying "all liability for all actions, practices or omissions raised in the plaintiffs' claims," agreed to a "partial consent decree." The decree required that as public housing was demolished, more use would be made of Section 8 certificates which allow the tenant to find housing in the private market anywhere in the city. It also required that replacement units be built in neighborhoods other than those already majority-black and majority-poor. Ironically, five years later, the decree has had the unintended consequence of halting rebuilding, and a continuing search for units that would accept Section 8, while displaced tenants of demolished public housing move into still existing overcrowded and deteriorating housing. Again, this writer is reminded, thirty years later, of the Activists' Urban Renewal study in 1966.

•••

Race, indeed, is still an issue. On January 20, 2001, Baltimore Neighborhoods, Inc. (BNI) felt the need to sponsor a conference: "Talking about Race in Baltimore: Private Dialogue and Public Discourse." One speaker, Dr. Matthew Crenson, professor of Political Science at Johns Hopkins University, quoted a comment made by Mayor Schmoke as he was leaving office:

> Baltimore is a city where issues of race continue to be important, but they are issues no one wants to talk about. It's almost as if people would like to ignore the fact that race continues to be a significant factor determining the quality of life here in the city and the metropolitan area.

But Ralph E. Moore, Jr., a former member of the Activists civil rights group, and now director of the Center for Poverty

Solutions, had no qualms at all in speaking about it. Early-on he quotes from a book by David Rusk, *Baltimore Unbound: A Strategy for Regional Renewal*, published in 1996 by the Abell Foundation:

> Almost half of city neighborhoods are "poverty neighborhoods" where 20% or more of the residents fall below the poverty line. In one-fifth of city neighborhoods, more than 40 percent of the residents are poor. Of the region's 137,000 poor Blacks, almost three quarter (72%) live in poor neighborhoods—almost 32% live in neighborhoods of extreme poverty. By contrast, of the region's 90,000 poor whites, only one in four (24%) live in poor neighborhoods.

Ralph talks about some of the silent walls he perceives as separating the races in Baltimore. First, the divide between those living in public or subsidized housing administered by the Housing Authority of Baltimore City and the rest of us. He asked whites why they were surprised that these folks wanted to live in better neighborhoods:

> For generations they have had the worst schools, the fewest jobs, the most vacant houses, the most lead paint in the occupied houses, the slowest, most decrepit buses traveling through their neighborhoods, the fewest commercial establishments, the highest crime rates, the most liquor stores [one councilman estimated 1300], the highest instances of infant mortality and morbidity for all, the most trash on their streets, [the most open air drug markets] and the fewest safe places for their children to play. Now why would anybody want to leave that?

Then, there's the partition created by the schools—

> About 90% of the students in Baltimore's public schools are Black...most of the white children from Baltimore's neighborhoods go to parochial or private schools, while the Baltimore City Public schools stumble or fall with a few exceptions.
>
> Each year, when I speak to the Greater Baltimore Committee's Leadership Program, I ask the same question, "If the Schools were populated by 90% white students instead of 90% Black students, would there be so much complacency about the very low performance of the students? If there weren't so many poor children in our

schools would we be doing more about them?" Race is definitely a factor.... Nothing short of shutting down large segments of the school system and reorganizing, retooling, rethinking and rebuilding will fix them, I'm convinced.

Mike Bowler wrote that a school system thrives on individual ingenuity, and the sad reality is this:

At a time when society requires more technical skills of its high school graduates, more knowledge of how to write and think critically, more scientific knowledge, more knowledge of how societies function and political systems operate, more knowledge of the workings of government, city schools have had to lower their standards to cope with the current generation of students.[3]

Have *had to* or just *have*? The school board just recently closed seven schools in poor neighborhoods, justifying their action by stating:

With a capacity for 131,000 students and a population of 98,000, the system maintains to much unused space.

What if the powers-that-be, the Greater Baltimore Committee, for instance, instead of supporting the closings had insisted that money be provided so these schools could offer the children smaller classes, special teachers and a creative curriculum? To no avail, the *Sun* opposed the closings, as did local residents and the activist grassroots organization, Association of Community Organizations for Reform Now (ACORN).

Ralph Moore, at that racism conference, also talked of the barrier of transportation and jobs.

The mass transportation system keeps people from exploring and getting jobs out of Baltimore City. For the poor who are moving from welfare to work we must get them to jobs that pay living wages. 35% of the entry level jobs in the Baltimore area are inaccessible by public transportation....
The buses don't go where the better paying, low skilled jobs are: Harford County, Howard County and even part of Baltimore County. The poor need access. There is an invisible wall that keeps black folks out of the suburbs. Its

---

[3] Bowler, p. 28.

presence is marked by the end of the bus lines, the last subway and light rail stops. Extend the mass transportation outward from the city...and ignore the pressure (and lies) of folks who claim public transportation is a disguised freight car for Black crime.

And so we see that despite the city's renaissance, race still makes a difference. Inequalities are still found in Baltimore's school system, in job training and employment opportunities, in housing availability, and in the justice system which arrests and incarcerates a totally disproportionate number of blacks. Just look around. *What do you think the City would look like if the following black-white percentages were reversed?*

In 1970, Baltimore City's black population constituted 46% of the total, while across the line, in Baltimore County, the comparable percentage was 3%. In 1980, the black percentage of the city population was 55%; for the county, it was 8%....

Meanwhile, the suburban fringe has pushed far to the west, across the Patapsco River into rapidly expanding sections of Howard and Carroll Counties, doubling the distance from the city center reached by the 1950s and 1960s in the Westview area [in Northwest Baltimore]. Many of these areas tend to be relatively affluent and predominantly white preserves.

Thus, in spite of some change, the traditional pattern of new suburbs as havens, older urban areas as resegregated and secondhand suburbs repeats itself in the push and pull of the contemporary metropolis.

•••

Fortunately there are still a few people and organizations struggling to make a difference. Ralph Moore at Poverty Solutions is one such. Another is the alliance of religious groups who have built BUILD into an organization active on many fronts. But perhaps the most promising is the arrival in Baltimore of ACORN, a branch of the national grassroots organization.

At first they tackled mostly housing issues, especially the practice of predatory lending that takes advantage of low-income workers who are unable to qualify for standard bank loans. But since the arrival of Mitch Kline in 1999, ACORN has been active on many fronts.

Unrestrained by an "establishment board," as are some of the older activist groups such as Baltimore Neighborhoods, Inc. (BNI) and St. Ambrose Housing, ACORN is unrestrained in its organizing and demonstrating. It now has a membership of about 2,000, composed, primarily, of Baltimore's welfare and working poor, each of whom regularly contributes from $5 to $20 monthly, the amount automatically drawn from a bank account, through a draft system, each has established. ACORN has also allied with at least one of Baltimore's most liberal unions, AFSCME Local 44.

City Paper writes almost in awe of ACORN's ability to turn out these people. The June 13, 2001 article begins:

> Workers packed Gillis Memorial Church in Park Heights on June 5 in a bid to restore jobs and services they fear will fall under the blade of Mayor Martin O'Malley's fiscal-year 2002 budget.

But the writer soon exclaims:

> What caught our attention was the grass-roots mobilization afoot—the pre-meeting plastering of neighborhoods with 2,000 posters, the mass mailing to 10,000 homes, the phone bank that dialed 6,000 people, the repeated message from the podium that hundreds of citizen Joes and Janes united shall overcome.

And all important questions are asked:

> *Could this be the sound of clergy banding together and neighborhoods coalescing into a coalition...? Could it be that a new Movement is underway?*

RESOURCES
● **Permission for quotes sought and graciously given: quotes from other sources fall under "Fair Use" or © holder could not be located.**

Published Books

● Argersinger, Jo Ann E., *Toward a New Deal in Baltimore: People and Government in the Great Depression*, University of North Carolina Press, ©1988.

Baltimore, Its History and Its People, Vol. III, NY, 1912, pp. 687-693.

● Bancroft, Frederic, *Slave Trading in the Old South*, Published by Frederick Ungar Publishing Co., 1931; New edition, University of South Carolina Press, ©1995.

Bell, Derrick, *Race, Racism & American Law*, 3rd Edition, Little, Brown & Co., ©1992.

Berlin, Ira, et al (Editors), *Free At Last: a Documentary History of Slavery, Freedom, and the Civil War*, The New Press, NY, 1992.

Berlin, Ira & Leslie S. Rowland, *Families & Freedom: A Documentary History of African-American Kinship in the Civil War Era*, The New Press, NY, ©1997

Blockson, Charles L., *The Underground Railroad: First-Person Narratives of Escapes to Freedom in the North*, Prentice Hall, 1987.

Brown, H. Rap, *Die Nigger Die!*, Dial, N.Y. ©1969.

Brugger, Robert J., *Maryland: A Middle Temperament, 1634-1980*, Johns Hopkins University Press in association with the MD Historical Society, ©1988.

● Callcott, George H., *Maryland & America: 1940-1980*, Johns Hopkins University Press, ©1985.

Callcott, Margaret Law, *The Negro in Maryland Politics, 1870-1912*, Johns Hopkins Press, ©1969.

Chapelle, Suzanne Ellery Greene, *Baltimore: An Illustrated History*, American Historical Press, ©2000

Christianson, Scott, *With Liberty for Some: 500 Years of Imprisonment in America*, Northeastern University Press, ©1998

Cooney, Patrick L, & Henry W. Powell, *The Life and Times of the Prophet Vernon Johns: Father of the Civil Rights Movement*, (no publisher given) ©1998 (e-Mail plcooney @ AOL.com)

Crain, Robert L., *The Politics of School Desegregation*, Aldine Publishing Co, Chicago, ©1968

Crawford, Vicki L., Jacqueline Anne Rouse, and Barbara Woods (Eds.), *Women in the Civil Rights Movement: Trailblazers & Torchbearers, 1941-1965*, "Gloria Richardson & the Cambridge Movement" by Annette Brock, Carlson Publishing Inc. NY ©1990.

664

Douglass, Frederick, *Life and Times of Frederick Douglass*, (edited & abridged by Genevieve S. Gray, Grosset & Dunlap, Inc., NY ©1970)

Douglass, Frederick, *My Bondage and My Freedom*, originally published 1855, reprinted by Johnson Publishing Co., Inc, Chicago, ©1970

Douglass, Frederick, *Narrative of the Life of Frederick Douglass, An American Slave*, originally published in 1845 by The Anti-Slavery Office (Penguin Books, NY ©1982).

Farrar, Hayward, *The Baltimore Afro-American, 1892-1950*, Greenwood Press, Westport, Connecticut, 1998.

Fee, Elizabeth, Linda Shopes, Linda Zeidman (Eds.), *The Baltimore Book: New Views of Local History*, Chapter 9, "Sparrows Point, Dundalk, Highlandtown, Old West Baltimore: Home of Gold Dust and the Union Card", Temple University Press, ©1991

Fields, Barbara Jeanne, *Slavery and Freedom on the Middle Ground: Maryland during the Nineteenth Century*, Yale University Press, ©1985.

Foner, Eric, *Reconstruction: America's Unfinished Revolution, 1863-1877*, Harper & Row Publishers, ©1988.

Franklin, John Hope & McNeil, Genna Rae, (eds), Chapter 4, "Youth Initiative in the African American Struggle for Racial Justice and Constitutional Rights: The City-Wide Young People's Forum of Baltimore 1931-1941", *African Americans and the Living Constitution*, Smithsonian Institution Press, Washington, ©1995.

Hill, Oliver, *The Big Bang*, Four-G Publishers, Winter Park, FL, 2000.

Irons, Peter, *The Courage of Their Convictions*, Free Press, MacMillan, NY, ©1988.

Janvier, Meredith, *Baltimore in the Eighties and Nineties* [a memoir, 1800s], Roebuck & Son, Baltimore, ©1933.

Jordan, Winthrop D., *White Over Black: American Attitudes Toward the Negro, 1550-1812*, University of North Carolina Press, ©1968.

Kellogg, Charles Flint, *NAACP: A History of the National Association for the Advancement of Colored People*, Vol. I, 1909-1920, Johns Hopkins University Press, ©1967

Koger, A. Briscoe, "The Negro Lawyer in Maryland," © 1948 [No other information given]

Lewis, David Levering, *W.E.B. DuBois: Biography of a Race, 1868-1919*, Henry Holt & Co., 1993 and *W.E.B. DuBois: The Fight for Equality & the American Century, 1919-1963*, Henry Holt & Co, ©2000.

Marks, Michael, *History of Baltimore Neighborhoods, Inc. (BNI)*— [incomplete draft copy provided this writer by the author, 1999].

Mayer, Henry, *All On Fire: William Lloyd Garrison & the Abolition of Slavery*, St. Martin's Press, ©1998.

● McConnell, Roland, C., Marva E. Belt, editor, *The History of Morgan Park: A Baltimore Neighborhood 1917-1999*, Morgan Park Improvement

Association, Inc, ©2000.

Meier, August & Elliott Rudwick (ed & intro), *Black Protest in the Sixties*, New York Times Quadrangle Books, Chicago, 1970 (a paperback edition, not used, Markus Weiner Publications, Princeton, NJ, ©1991]

Meier, August & Elliott Rudwick, *CORE: A Study in the Civil Rights Movement, 1942-1968*, Oxford University Press, New York, ©1973.

● Meier, August & Elliott Rudwick, *From Plantation to Ghetto*, 3rd Edition, Hill & Wang, division of Farrar, Straus & Giroux, Inc., NY, ©1976

● Meier, August, *A White Scholar and the Black Community, 1945-1965*, University of Massachusetts Press, ©1992

● Olson, Sherry H. *Baltimore: The Building of an American City*, Johns Hopkins University Press, ©1980

Orr, Marion, *Black Social Capital: The Politics of School Reform in Baltimore, 1986-1998*, University Press of Kansas, ©1999.

● Orser, Edward W., *Blockbusting in Baltimore: The Edmondson Village Story*, University of Kentucky Press, ©1994.

Peterson, Robert W., *Pigskin: The Early Years of Pro Football,*. Oxford Univ. Press, ©1997.

Reutter, Mark, *Sparrows Point: Making Steel-The Rise and Ruin of American Industrial Might*, Summit Books, Division of Simon & Schuster Adult Publishing Group, ©1988 by Mark Reutter.

Schwartz, Bernard, *Super Chief: Earl Warren and his Supreme Court*, NY Univ. Press, ©1983.

Scott, Emmett J., *Scott's Official History of The American Negro in the World War*, ©1919, reissued by Arno Press & the N Y Times, ©1969.

Sellin, J. Thorsten, *Slavery and the Penal System*, Elsevier Scientific Publishing Co., ©1976

Simon, David & Edward Burns, *The Corner: A Year in the Life of an Inner-City Neighborhood*, Broadway Books, Bantam Doubleday Dell Publishing Group, ©1997.

Smith, Jesse C. (Ed.), *Notable Black American Women*, Gale Research Inc. 1995.

Sobel, Lester A. (ed.) *Civil Rights 1960-1966*, Facts on File, NY 1967.

● Strohmeyer, John, *Crisis in Bethlehem: Big Steel's Struggle to Survive*, Penguin Books, [© by Adler & Adler, Chevy Chase, MD, 1986).

Vose, Clement E., *Caucasians Only: The Supreme Court, the NAACP, and the Restrictive Covenant Cases*, University. of California Press, ©1959

Wade, Richard, *Slavery in the Cities: The South 1820-1860*, Oxford University Press, ©1964.

Wagandt, Charles Lewis, *The Mighty Revolution: Negro Emancipation in Maryland, 1862-1864*, Johns Hopkins Press, ©1964

Watson, Denton L., *Lion in the Lobby: Clarence Mitchell, Jr.'s Struggle for the Passage of Civil Rights Laws*, Wm. Morrow & Co., Inc., Harper

Collings Adult Division, NY, ©1990 (© now held by University Press of America, Lanham, MD.)

Wilson, Edward N., *The History of Morgan State College: A Century of Purpose in Action 1867-1967*, Vantage Press, NY, ©1975.

Wright, James M., *The Free Negro in Maryland, 1634-1860*, Columbia University, ©1921

Zinn, Howard, *You Can't Be Neutral on a Moving Train*, Beacon, Boston, ©1994.

Articles

Alpert, Jonathan, "The Origin of Slavery in the U. S.: the Maryland Precedent," XIV, *Am.J.Legal Hist.* 189 (1969)

Arisman, J. Michael, "Civil Rights Here: A Look at the Issues", *The Catholic Review*, 6/3/1966.

● Bentley, Amy, "Wages of War: The Sifting Landscape of Race and Gender in World War II Baltimore," *Maryland Historical Magazine*, Vol. 88, Winter 1993.

Berkowitz, Edward, "Baltimore's Public Schools in a Time of Transition," *Maryland Historical Magazine*, V. 92, #4, Winter 1997.

Bogen, David Skillen, "The First Integration of the University of Maryland School of Law," *Maryland Historical Magazine*, Vol. 84, Spring 1989, pp. 39-49.

Brown, Christopher C., "Democracy's Incursion into the Eastern Shore: The 1870 Election in Chestertown," *Maryland Historical Magazine*, Vol. 89, #3, Fall 1994, pp. 338-346.

Connah, Douglas, Jr., "'Blockbusting' in Baltimore," article done for Law School, entered in the *Congressional Record* by House Rep. Samuel N. Friedel, March 26, 1969, V. 115 #52 E1430-2433. [copy provided this writer by the author]

Della, M. Ray Jr., "The Problems of Negro Labor in the 1850's", *Maryland Historical Magazine*, Vol. 66, #1, Spring 1971.

Fleming, G. James, "Racial Integration in Education in Maryland," *Journal of Negro Education*, Vol. XXV, #3, Summer 1956, pp. 273-284.

Froelicher, Hans Jr., "The School and Its Role in Community Development," *Marriage & Family Living*, Vol. XVII, No. 2, May, 1955, 162-168.

Grant, George C., "Desegregation in Maryland Since the [1964] Supreme Court Decision," *The Journal of Negro Education*, v. XXIV, # 3, 1955.

Greenberg, Jack, "In Memoriam: Juanita Jackson Mitchell" *MD Law Review, U of MD School of Law*, Spring 1993, (52 Md. L. Rev. 507)

Greene, Suzanne Ellery (now Chapelle), "Black Republicans on the Baltimore City Council, 1890-1931," *Maryland Historical Magazine*, Vol. 74, #3, September 1979.

"Latest Problem for Cities in the North: 'Blockbusting'", [no author given], *U.S. News & World Report*, December 5, 1958

Levin, Harry O., "The Legal Basis for Segregated Schools in Maryland," *The Journal of Negro Education*, v. XVI, #4, Fall, 1947.

Levy, Peter B. "Civil War on Race Street: The Black Freedom Struggle & White Resistance in Cambridge, MD, 1960-1964," *Maryland Historical Magazine*, Vol. 89, #3, Fall 1994, pp. 291-318.

Milobsky, David, "Power from the Pulpit: Baltimore's African-American Clergy, 1950-1970", *Maryland Historical Magazine*, Vol. 89, #3, Fall 1994, pp. 275-289.

Perlman, Philip B., *The Journal of Southern Legal History*, Vol. IV, #1 & 2, pp. 61-70.

● Power, Garrett, "Apartheid Baltimore Style: The Residential Segregation Ordinances of 1910-1913," *Md. Law Review*, V. 42, 1983, 706-761.

● Power, Garrett, "The Unwisdom of Allowing City Growth to Work Out Its Own Destiny," *Maryland Law Review*, V. 47, #3, 1988, 626-674.

Power, Garrett, "Public Service and Private Interests: A Chronicle of the Professional Life of Philip B. Perlman, *Journal of Southern Legal History*, Vol. IV, #1 & 2, pp. 61-69.

● Rosen, Ellsworth E., "When a Negro Moves Next Door," *Saturday Evening Post*, April 4, 1959 (Renewed, BFL & MS, Inc.).

Ryon Roderick N., "An Ambiguous Legacy: Baltimore Blacks and the CIO, 1936-1941", The *Journal of Negro History*, Vol. 65, #1, 1980, pp. 18-33.

Shoemaker, Sandy, M., "We Shall Overcome, Someday": The Equal Rights Movement in Baltimore: 1935-1942, *Maryland Historical Magazine*, Vol. 89, #3, Fall 1994, pp. 265.

Szabo, Peter S., "An Interview with Gloria Richardson Dandridge," *Maryland Historical Magazine*, V. 89, #3, Fall 1994, pp. 347-358.

Templeton, Furman L, "The Admission of Negro Boys to Baltimore Polytechnic Institute "A" Course," *The Journal of Negro Education*, v. XXIII, #1, Winter, 1954.

Thelwell, Ekwueme Michael, "H. Rap Brown Jamil Al-Amin: A Profoundly American Story," *Southland Prison News: A Prisoner-based News Service Covering Florida to New England*, Vol. 5, #3, March 2002.

Thomsen, Roszel C., "The Integration of Baltimore's Polytechnic Institute: a Reminiscence," *Maryland Historical Magazine*, MHS, Fall, 1984.

Towers, Frank, Serena Johnson & Slave Domestic Servants in Antebellum Baltimore," *Maryland Historical Magazine*, Vol. 89, #3, Fall 1994, pp. 334-337.

Dissertations and High School Research Paper

Banks, Samuel Lee, *A Descriptive Study of Baltimore City Board of School Commissioners as an Agent in School Desegregation, 1952-1964*, PhD, (Education), George Washington University, 1976 (University Microfilms International, Ann Arbor, Michigan, 1981)

Goldstein, Ruth, a research paper done for her Advance Placement "C" course at Park School in 20th Century History. A copy, with permission to use, was supplied this writer by her teacher, John Roemer. *Included are interviews of all the black students involved, a number of the teachers and several others.*

Gregory, Clarence Kenneth, *The Education of Blacks in Maryland: An Historical Survey*, dissertation, Doctor of Education in Teachers College, Columbia University, ©1976 (Xerox University Microfilms, Michigan, 1986) *[Author could not be located to ask permission.]*

Horn, Vernon Edward, "Integrating Baltimore: Protest and Accommodation, 1945-1963", Masters thesis, Dept. of History, Univ. of MD, 1991. *[Permission to quote graciously given by author on 4/26/02]*

● Palumbos, Robert M. "Student Involvement in the Baltimore Civil Rights Movement, 1953-63," a Master's thesis, Johns Hopkins University, reprinted in *Maryland Historical Magazine*, Vol. 94, Winter 1999. *[Copy provided this writer by author along with his extensive collection of newspaper articles]*

Paul, William George, *The Shadow of Equality: The Negro in Baltimore, 1864-1911*, PhD thesis, University of Wisconsin, 1972 *[Author could not be located to ask permission.]*

Reports

Activists,Inc. "*Communities Under Siege: A Computer-Based Study*," Sept. 1970.

Activists for Fair Housing Report: *"Recommendations and Analysis: Baltimore Urban Renewal and Housing Agency and Department of Housing and Urban Development*," *(prepared by Billie Bramhall & Barbara Mills)*, August 1966. Addenda by Billie Bramhall, October 13, 1966.

Baltimore City Public Schools, "The Master Plan," "A New Era of School Reform" and "The Old Order to the New Order, 1957-1997." www.bcps.k12.md.us

Baltimore Community Self-Survey of Inter-Group Relations: An American City in Transition, Maryland Commission on Interracial Problems & Relations and Baltimore Commission on Human Relations, 1955.

Baltimore Neighborhoods, Inc. (BNI) conference report: "Talking about Race in Baltimore: Private Dialogue and Public Discourse," 2001.

Baltimore CORE's Employment Committee, "Report on Discrimination in Employment by the Commercial Banks of Metropolitan Baltimore," 1965.

Baltimore Urban League *Annual Report* for 1952

Bowler, Mike, *The Lessons of Change: Baltimore Schools in the Modern Era*, report commissioned by the Fund for Educational Excellence, ©1991; Supplement, 1997. (Also on the Baltimore City School Web site without accreditation— www.bcps.k12.md.us.)

League of Women Voters of MD, report, *"Equal Opportunity in Housing"*, #101, 10/65

League of Women Voters, "School Construction Report," unpublished report furnished by Billie Bramhall, (about 1966-67)

Maryland Commission on Interracial Problems and Relation to the Governor and General Assembly, *Annual Report*, January 1962.

Mayor's Task Force for Equal Rights, "*Series of Recommendations on Integration and Quality Education in the Inner City*," to Board of School Commissioners, June 26, 1967.

Rusk, David, *Baltimore Unbound: Creating a Greater Baltimore Region for the 21st Century, a Strategy Report*, Abell Foundation, distributed by Johns Hopkins Univ., 1996.

St. Ambrose Housing, unpublished report regarding role of FHA, written in 1983

● Sidney Hollander Foundation, Inc, *Toward Equality: Baltimore's Progress Report,*. 1960 & *Supplement*, 1961. [Personal copy of Sidney Hollander loaned to this writer]

Sykes, Melvin, Billie Bramhall and parent's committee, "*Eight Years of Desegregation in the Baltimore Public Schools: Fact and Law*," June 1963.

Sykes, Melvin and others, "*City Forever? A Tradition at the Crossroads*," December 1965 (followed by a critique by the Board of Education)

Sykes, Melvin & Committee for Academic Excellence, "*The Paquin Plan: a Critique*," May 4, 1966

US Dept. of Commerce, *County and City Data Book*, 1994, US Census Bureau "Quick Tables," and Baltimore City MapStats from FedStats, found on the internet. Earlier Census data was also used.

Newspapers & Miscellany

ACLU newsletters

Bowler, Mike, "Breaching the Race Barrier at Poly," *Baltimore Sun*, 4/27/97 & "Gifted, Black—They were Paid to Study Elsewhere," *Baltimore Sun*, 8/14/95.

Carter, Walter, an unpublished he called "A Cry From the Heart."

Correspondence from Una Corbet to Billie Bramhall regarding education (1967); Miscellaneous correspondence with Fred Weisgal from Tony Amsterdam, and from Charles Hamilton Houston & his assistant attorney, Phineas Indritz; and correspondence that originated with Baltimore CORE

Crisis, NAACP Magazine, a perusal of decades of issues for information related to Baltimore.

Crockett, Sandra, "Breaking the Color Barrier at Poly in 1952," *Baltimore Sun*, 11/27/88

Dilts, James, "The Warning Trumpet", *Baltimore Sun Magazine*, 12/1/1968

Eberhardt, Dave, Unpublished memoir, used with Author's permission.

Glazer, Aaron M., "Course Correction," *City Paper*, 9/5/2001

Hawkins, W. Ashbie, "Early education of colored youth in Baltimore," *Baltimore American Sunday Morning*, September 16, 1894.

Johns Hopkins' student newsletters

O'Brien, Denis, "The Castle of One's Skin: Blacks recall protest they staged in 1960 in city restaurant," *Baltimore Sun*, 11/13/1994

People, a small, left-leaning, bi-weekly paper published in 1943-44 by Fred Weisgal.

Poem, "Trees that Reach Farthest Upward," written in Memory of Walter Carter, civil rights activist, by Chester Wickwire [permission to use by author]

● *Sidney Hollander Foundation materials*, found in Moorland Spingarn Research Center's collection, Howard University, Washington, DC, Selections from Boxes 50-1 to 50-10, folders 1-185, containing speeches and newspaper articles from 1942 to 1967. [Provided writer without charge at request of Sidney Hollander, Jr.]

Numerous newspaper clippings from all of Baltimore's newspapers, including the *City Paper* and *Daily Record*, and from the *New York Times*, *Washington Post* and miscellaneous others, many no longer in existence. These are footnoted throughout, including name and date where known (her own personal collection and that of others loaned to writer often did not note this). Several internet cites are also noted.

Writer's Publications

Mills, Barbara, *"...And Justice for All: The Double Life of Fred Weisgal, Attorney & Musician,"* American Literary Press, ©2000 [based on numerous oral interviews plus Weisgal's personal collection of correspondence, legal cases and newspaper clippings.]

Mills, Barbara, *Bloody Breathitt 'n Beyond, An Autobiography*, (unpublished) ©1998 [includes writer's own extensive involvement with Baltimore CORE and the ACTIVISTs as demonstrator and executive officer closely involved with planning and preparation of materials. Includes flyers, correspondence, reports and scrapbook of newspaper clippings and other materials compiled at the time]

In addition to copies of Weisgal, CORE and Activist correspondence in this writer's possession, several of those she talked to sent copies of related correspondence, reports and newspaper clippings in their collections. All are footnoted in text where appropriate.

Writer's Oral Interviews (listed alphabetically)

Larry Ageloff (CORE activist/Employment), Tony Amsterdam (attorney, reg. Cambridge), Mildred Atkinson, Chief Judge Robert M. Bell, Maryland Court of

Appeals (Public Accommodations and overview of writer's manuscript), David Bogen, University of Maryland Law School (reg. his writings on early housing-related issues), Judge Elsbeth Bothe (attorney in public accommodations & housing cases), Mike Bowler (Baltimore school system), Billie Bramhall (Education & Housing issues & copies of *correspondence with Una Corbet*), Ed Chance (CORE activist/Chairman), Doug Connah, jr. (reg. Housing/Blockbusting), Marva Dates (CORE activist), Rev. Vernon Dobson (personal experiences and use of his church), David Eberhardt (CORE activist), Larry Gibson (attorney reg. ACTIVISTS law suit), Jim Griffin (CORE activist/Chairman, School Board member), Sidney Hollander, Jr. (reg. Hollander Foundation awards), Kalman "Buzzy" Hettleman (Education), Robert Kaufman (activist/Socialist), Mitch Kline (ACORN projects), Judge Marshall Levin (Poly A case), Clarence Logan (regarding CIG actions), Michael Marks (regarding BNI history), Rev. John Martinez (ACTIVIST/Goldseker materials), Ralph Moore (activist/poverty issues), Robert Palumbos (reg. his thesis and loan of multiple clippings used), Garret Power, University of Maryland Law School (reg. his writings on early political and housing issues), Vinnie Quale at St. Ambrose Housing, John Roemer (early CORE activist, memory plus numerous newspaper clippings), Rev. Douglas Sands (CIG & State Interracial Commission), David Swanson (ACORN projects), Melvin Sykes (reg. Education & Blockbusting), Joe Wase (reg. Public Accommodations), Judge Robert Watts, since deceased (attorney for CIG, and sometimes CORE & NAACP), Stu Wechsler (reg. CORE's Target City), Dr. Chester Wickwire (personal experiences while Chaplain at Johns Hopkins).

Oral Interviews by Johns Hopkins Students

Rita Crooms, Rev. Vernon Dobson, Chester Wickwire, Ed Chance, Janice Woolridge.

Researched Legal Cases (listed alphabetically)

Bell v. Maryland 204 A2d 54 and 84 SCT 1814, 378 US 226

Bernstein v. Real Estate Commission of Maryland, 156 Atlantic Reporter 2d 657-664 (1959)

Boyer et al v. Garrett et al, 88 F. Supp 353; 1949 U.S. Dist. LEXIS 1889. Also 183 F. 2d 582; 1950 U.s. App. LEXIS 2983

Brown v. Board of Education of Topeka et al, 74 SCT 686 or 347 US 483 (5/17/1954)
and 75 SCT 753 or 349 US 294 (5/31/1955)

Byrne v. Maryland v. Maryland Realty Company, 129 Md. 202; 1916 Md. LEXIS 142.

Carmen Thompson, et al. v. U. S. Dept. of Housing & Urban Development, et al, Civil Action #MJG 95-309

Chance v. Lambeth et al, 186 F.2d 879 (4th C. 1951*) and Atlantic Coast Line Railroad Co. v Chance,* 198 F.2d 549 (4th C. 1952)

672

Dawson et al. v. Mayor & City Council of Baltimore et al, 220 F2d 386; 1955 U. S. App. LEXIS 4923 (also Mayor et al v. Dawson, 350 U.S. 877 S. Ct. 133; 1955 U.S. LEXIS 168).

Diggs v. Morgan College, 133 Md. 264; 1918 Md. LEXIS 125.

Durkee v, Murphy, 1942, 181 Md. 259, 29 A. 2d 253

Hamm v. City of Rock Hill, 379 U.S. 306; 1964 U.S. LEXIS 4

Hart vs. State, 60 Atlantic Reporter, pp. 457-463, (1905)

Heart of Atlanta Motel, Inc. v. U. S. et al, 379 U.S. 241; 1964 LEXIS 2187

Jackson v. State (No. 1), 103 Atlantic Reporter 910-911 (Court of Appeals MD, 2/27/1918)

Jones v. Mayer, 392 U.S. 409 (1968)

Lonesome et al. v. Maxwell et all Dawson et al v. Mayor & City Council of Baltimore et al Isaac's et al v. Mayor & City Council of Baltimore et al. 123 F. Supp. 193; 1954 U.S. dist. LEXIS 2989

Meade v. Dennistone et al (No. 26), 196 Atlantic Reporter 330-336 (1/11/1938)

New Negro Alliance v. Sanitary Grocery Co., 303 U.S. 552 (1938)

Poderesky v. Kirwin, President of Univ. of Md. 838 F. Supp. 1075; 1993 U.S. Dist. LEXIS 19493

Shelley v. Kraemer, 334 U.S. 1; 1948 U.S. LEXIS 2764

Slack v. Atlantic White Tower System, Inc., 181 F. Supp 124; 1960 U.S. Dist. LEXIS 3058

State v. Gurry, 88 Atlantic Reporter, 228-9 (Court of Appeals MD, 8/5/1913) & 546-553 Court of Appeals MD, 10/7/1913).

State Board of Public Welfare et al. v. Myers, Minor, etc. 224 Md. 246; 167 A. 2d 765; 1961 Md. LEXIS 484.

University of Maryland v. Donald G. Murray (No. 53), 182 A. 590; 1936 MD LEXIS 51.

Williams v. Rescue Fire Company, 254 F. Supp. 556 (1966)

Winkler et al. v. STATE, 194 Md. 1; 69 A. 2d 674; 1949 Md. LEXIS 378.

Acknowledgements

A special thanks to Sidney Hollander, Jr. who allowed me to make use of his only copy of *Toward Equality* and provided me with free access to his papers that were donated to the Moorland Spingarn collection at Howard University, to Jeff Korman at Baltimore's Enoch Pratt Free Library who loaned me a copy of the *Baltimore Self-Survey* for as long as needed, and, of course, along with others in the library's Maryland Room, retrieved, copied and mailed me any number of newspaper clippings. Also, thanks go to Paul McCardell, Librarian at the Baltimore Sun, who graciously retrieved photos and articles for my use. The same was done, exceedingly promptly, on several occasions by Fr. Peter Hogan, the archivist of black-related material at The Josephites House on Calvert Street.

Thanks also need to go to John Roemer who trusted me with his personal collection of civil rights clippings, and to Billie Bramhall and Melvin Sykes who sent me copies of education-related reports and letters in their possession that numerous persons at the Baltimore Department of Education proved completely unaware of.

Others who both talked to me and sent helpful materials were Judge Marshall Levin (regarding Poly A), Judge Elsbeth Bothe, Clarence Logan (regarding CIG actions), Michael Marks (regarding BNI history). Garret Powers and David Bogen from the University of Maryland Law School (early housing-related issues), Rev. John Martinez (Goldseker materials), Vinnie Quale at St. Ambrose Housing, David Eberhardt & Jim Griffin (biographical info), Marva Dates (loan of book on history of Morgan), Mitch Kline & David Swanson (regarding ACORN projects), Mike Bowler (copy of historical overview of Baltimore school system that he had prepared as well as other education-related newspaper clippings), Kalman "Buzzy" Hettleman (education-related clippings) and Robert Palumbus, who sent a copy of his Master's thesis, along with copies of news clippings he'd used. I'm also grateful to a number of others who talked to me at length: especially John Roemer, Larry Ageloff, Robert Watts, since deceased, Rev. Vernon Dobson, Dr. Chester Wickwire, Ed Chance, Mitch Kline and Robert Kaufman.

In doling out thanks, I certainly can't forget my son, Alan, an exceedingly busy "poverty lawyer," who found many of the early legal cases for me and did a great job of critiquing the whole manuscript, pointing out errors and making invaluable suggestions. I'm also grateful to Johns Hopkins Prof. Carl Christ, John Roemer and Chief Judge Robert M. Bell, Maryland Court of Appeals (after whom a Public Accommodation's suit that went to the US Supreme Court is named), who all read parts of the manuscript and offered helpful comments. John Roemer, at one time an officer and an activist with Baltimore CORE, now a teacher at Park School, also sent me, with permission to use, a helpful paper written by one of his students regarding private school integration experiences following the *Brown* decision.

A final note: parts of Baltimore's story, especially in the housing section, include long segments of the writer's personal story that also appear in her unpublished autobiography, *"Bloody Breathitt" 'n Beyond*, and the biography of Fred Weisgal, Baltimore CORE's attorney, *"...And Justice for All,"* published by his friends and colleagues. These are listed in "Resources," along with many other sources of information.

Index

Born in Daytona Beach, Florida, childhood in "Bloody Breathitt," Kentucky. Graduate of Brown University, Providence, RI; Masters from University of Birmingham, England and Rutgers University, New Brunswick, NJ. Activist and Officer with Baltimore, Maryland's CORE chapter in the 1960s. After divorce, worked as inner city school librarian, then with delinquents, mentally ill, homeless, prisoners and abused women before retiring in 1991. Two children, both attorneys: Susan servicing primarily immigrants; Alan, tenants and prisoners. Two grandchildren. Now lives in Cranston, Rhode Island.